SHAKESPEARE: THE CRITICAL HERITAGE
VOLUME 4 1753–1765

THE CRITICAL HERITAGE SERIES

GENERAL EDITOR: B. C. SOUTHAM, M.A., B. LITT. (OXON.)
Formerly Department of English, Westfield College, University of London

For a list of books in the series see the back end paper

SHAKESPEARE

THE CRITICAL HERITAGE

VOLUME 4 1753–1765

Edited by
BRIAN VICKERS
Professor of English and Renaissance Literature,
ETH, Zürich

ROUTLEDGE & KEGAN PAUL : LONDON HENLEY, AND BOSTON

First published in 1976
by Routledge & Kegan Paul Ltd
Broadway House, 76 Carter Lane,
London EC4V 5EL,
Reading Road,
Henley-on-Thames,
Oxon RG9 1EN and
9 Park Street,
Boston, Mass. 02108, USA
Set in 11 on 12 pt Bembo
and printed in Great Britain by
W & J Mackay Limited, Chatham

ISBN 0 7100 8297 5

FOR
ARTHUR SHERBO

General Editor's Preface

The reception given to a writer by his contemporaries and near-contemporaries is evidence of considerable value to the student of literature. On one side we learn a great deal about the state of criticism at large and in particular about the development of critical attitudes towards a single writer; at the same time, through private comments in letters, journals or marginalia, we gain an insight upon the tastes and literary thought of individual readers of the period. Evidence of this kind helps us to understand the writer's historical situation, the nature of his immediate reading-public, and his response to these pressures.

The separate volumes in the *Critical Heritage Series* present a record of this early criticism. Clearly, for many of the highly productive and lengthily reviewed nineteenth- and twentieth-century writers, there exists an enormous body of material; and in these cases the volume editors have made a selection of the most important views, significant for their intrinsic critical worth or for their representative quality—perhaps even registering incomprehension!

For earlier writers, notably pre-eighteenth century, the materials are much scarcer and the historical period has been extended, sometimes far beyond the writer's lifetime, in order to show the inception and growth of critical views which were initially slow to appear.

Shakespeare is, in every sense, a special case, and Professor Vickers is presenting the course of his reception and reputation extensively, over a span of three centuries, in a sequence of six volumes, each of which will document a specific period.

In each volume the documents are headed by an Introduction, discussing the material assembled and relating the early stages of the author's reception to what we have come to identify as the critical tradition. The volumes will make available much material which would otherwise be difficult of access and it is hoped that the modern reader will be thereby helped towards an informed understanding of the ways in which literature has been read and judged.

B.C.S.

Contents

Preface

This fourth instalment of *Shakespeare: The Critical Heritage* continues its reconstruction of the mainstream of Shakespeare's reception between the seventeenth and the nineteenth centuries, as it affected public discussion across this period. That is, in addition to the kind of literary criticism which one would expect to find collected in this series I have included material from Shakespearian scholarship—work on the text of his plays and his sources, for instance, poetry to or about Shakespeare, and much material from the theatre: excerpts from the adaptations of his plays, theatrical criticism, both of the adaptations and of the original plays, and discussions of acting and interpretation. With this wider scope I hope to present the major materials from which one could draw a more integrated picture of Shakespeare's reception than we yet have.

The value of such an attempt is, I hope, self-evident, and the justification for giving it this form is that in effect all these areas were interrelated. The literary criticism was produced because of the high status of Shakespeare's reputation; his general prestige is reflected in the way he dominated all other dramatists in actual stage performance. Yet the aesthetic ideas of the period determined that his plays should be changed to conform to current concepts of dramatic structure or style. These aesthetic ideas are also evident in the scholarly discussion of how he used his sources, and can be seen affecting the very text of his plays as established by editors, who complain at his offences against the critical canons and emend (or even suppress) accordingly. The interpretation of Shakespeare by the common reader and theatre-goer is much affected by the choice of repertoire and the style of performance: it is arguable that Garrick's Shakespeare had more influence than Dr Johnson's. Yet the sustained debate over his text and how it should be edited made the literary public more conscious than ever of the importance of textual accuracy, even of punctuation and meaning as transmitted (rightly or wrongly) by an actor's delivery. Literary criticism, textual criticism, scholarship, acting, adapting, book-reviewing—all these activities influenced each other and were influenced in turn. To understand the movements of Shakespeare's reputation one must take notice of them all; and if it were not impracticable, given the format of this series, I would want to present visual material in order to document theatre costumes, scenery, styles of production, and other relevant areas. Our interest in Shakespeare must necessarily be eclectic.

In collecting this material I am indebted to the following libraries, their donors, and their most helpful staff; if I single out those with whom I have had personal contact that does not lessen my gratitude to the others who are unknown: the British Library (and especially Ian Willison), the Bodleian Library (Paul Morgan, William Hodges, and his admirable staff in the Upper Reading Room, W. Andrews), Cambridge University Library (Nigel Hancock, A. J. Illes, A. G. Parker, Janice Roughton, and W. G. Rawlings), the Birmingham Shakespeare Library (W. A. Taylor), the Beinecke Library of Yale (Joan M. Friedman). I am grateful to Ian Thomson for verifying references at times when I was unable to be in England, and to Ilse Fannenböck and Christian Casparis for help with the proof-reading and index.

B.W.V.

Introduction

'With us islanders Shakespeare is a kind of
established religion in poetry'

I

That sentence by Arthur Murphy, part of a rebuke addressed to Voltaire
in the *Gray's-Inn Journal* in 1753 (No. 140b), is revealing of the increased
prestige of Shakespeare in the 1750s and 1760s. The gradual ascendance
of praise over blame which was noted in the previous volume[1] continued with enthusiasm. In Murphy's eyes 'SHAKESPEARE stands
at the head of our dramatic writers; perhaps at the head of all, who have
figured in that kind in every age and nation', a verdict which Daniel
Webb repeated in 1762 (No. 195). For John Armstrong in 1758 (No.
164), 'SHAKESPEARE perhaps possessed the greatest compass of
genius that ever man did', while the author of 'The Poetical Scale' in
that year (No. 167) gave Shakespeare the maximum marks for genius,
ahead of all other English poets (second place is shared by Spenser,
Milton, Dryden, Swift and Pope). Thomas Francklin, Professor of
Greek at Cambridge, and professional defender of Greek tragedy,
nevertheless ended his essay on the Greeks with the affirmation that all
their virtues were 'united and surpass'd in the immortal and inimitable
Shakespeare' (No. 180). In Edward Young's essay on originality Shakespeare was credited with 'adult genius', that which 'comes out of
nature's head . . . at full growth, and mature' (No. 179), and if Shakespeare is to be compared with any other writer only Homer will suffice
(Nos 139, 140b, 154a, 171, 187, 199).

The current of idolatry was so strong that writers in this period drew
attention to it as a specifically English phenomenon, peculiar to 'us
islanders', as Murphy put it. Edward Gibbon, writing in the late 1780s,
recalled the formative influence that Voltaire's theatre at Lausanne had
on him in 1757–8, with its productions of plays by Voltaire himself and
Racine: 'The habits of pleasure fortified my taste for the French theatre,
and that taste has perhaps abated my idolatry for the gigantic genius of

Shakespeare, which is inculcated from our infancy as the first duty of an Englishman.'[2] The estimate of Shakespeare's genius naturally emerged in the contrast with French 'reason' and 'rules'. Thus in his imaginary conversation between Boileau and Pope (1760, enlarged 1765: No. 181) Lord Lyttelton produced the following exchange:

Boileau. A veneration for Shakespeare seems to be a part of your national religion, and the only part in which even your men of sense are fanaticks.
Pope. He who can read Shakespeare, and be cool enough for all the accuracy of sober criticism, has more of reason than taste.

The Earl of Orrery made the same point: 'I forget the name of the French author who says, that the English are Shakespeare mad. There are some grounds for the assertion. We are methodists in regard to Shakespeare. We carry our enthusiasms so far, that we entirely suspend our senses towards his absurdities and his blunders' (No. 172). Both Lyttelton and Orrery invoke French disapproval only to defend Shakespeare. One observer who noted the trend with less than total approval was David Hume, recording in 1754 the suspicion 'that we over-rate, if possible, the greatness of his genius' (No. 145).

In its particular formulations the praise of Shakespeare was expressed in traditional modes by both poets and essayists. Absolutely typical is this stanza by Gray from *The Progress of Poesy. A Pindarick Ode* (1754), lines 83–94:

III. 1.
Far from the sun and summer-gale,
In thy green lap was Nature's* Darling laid,
What time, where lucid Avon stray'd,
To Him the mighty Mother did unveil
Her aweful face: The dauntless Child
Stretch'd forth his little arms, and smiled.
This pencil take (she said) whose colours clear
Richly paint the vernal year:
Thine too these golden keys, immortal Boy!
This can unlock the gates of Joy;
Of Horror that, and thrilling Fears,
Or ope the sacred source of sympathetic Tears.
*Shakespeare

In this tradition Shakespeare, poet of nature, was celebrated for his power to move the passions across the whole range of experience, but especially at the extremes. In Joseph Warton's classification of English poets Shakespeare is one of only three who excel in the 'sublime and pathetic' (No. 158), and in his commentary on Virgil (1753) Warton, discussing the 'sublime scene' of the death of Oedipus in Sophocles' *Oedipus Coloneus* (which, he claimed, makes the reader's hair stand on end in terror) could think of 'no piece of dramatic poetry that excites terror to so great a degree, except perhaps the *Macbeth* of Shakespeare'.[3] Bishop Hurd, in the first edition of his *Letters on Chivalry and Romance* (1762) praised the depiction of Prospero's magic as an example of Shakespeare's skill in the 'terrible sublime' (p. 50). From the time of Dryden Shakespeare's excellence at creating fairies, witches and other elements of the supernatural had been celebrated, and we find the tradition continuing through Warton's essays on *The Tempest* (No. 139) to the poetic recreation of John Gilbert Cooper (No. 147). That enjoyable *frisson* of being confronted with fear—within the manageable context of a play or a novel—so widely expressed in the eighteenth century, can be found here in the admiration for the ghost scenes in *Hamlet*, as expressed in two essays by Arthur Murphy (Nos 143, 161d), by an anonymous writer in the *British Magazine* for 1760 (No. 182: the ghost scene is 'undoubtedly the masterpiece of poetical painting in the gloomy way'), and by one 'K.L.' in the same journal some three years later (No. 197). Variations on these themes can be found in an anonymous ode which praises Shakespeare (No. 183) and in the enthusiastic writings of Edward Watkinson (No. 199).

Effusive though these panegyrics may be, they are not entirely blind to the opposing view. Shakespeare had faults, that must be admitted, but—the argument goes on in the same breath—his beauties far exceed them. The principles involved are stated trenchantly by Dr Johnson: 'In writing, as in life, faults are endured without disgust when they are associated with transcendent merit' (*Rambler* 158; 21 September 1751); and, more critical of the dominance of rules: 'Rules may obviate faults, but can never confer beauties' (*Idler* 57; 19 May 1759). The relative estimating of Shakespeare's 'Beauties and Faults', although often disvalued by modern critics as a mechanical exercise, was nevertheless one of the most persistent modes in eighteenth-century criticism. An utterly representative example of it is this poem by one Samuel Rogers, 'Rector of Chellington, in Bedfordshire':[4]

> Great Shakespeare, with genius disdaining all rules,
> Above the cold phlegm or the fripp'ry of schools,
> Appeal'd to the heart for success of his plays,
> And trusted to nature alone for the bays.

Despairing of glory but what rose from art,
Old Jonson applied to the head, not the heart.
On the niceness of rules he founded his cause,
And ravish'd from regular method applause.

May we judge from the favours each poet has shar'd,
Insipid is ART when with NATURE compar'd.

The dominant reaction is to admit his faults but to more than excuse them. So George Colman imagines Shakespeare offering all his faults (puns, bombast, incorrectness) to the bonfire, yet being nobly excused by both Aristotle and Longinus (No. 138). Hume's account of Shakespeare, although cool and critical, points to the presence of 'irregularities' and 'absurdities' as well as 'beauties', yet suggests that we 'admire the more those beauties on account of their being surrounded with such deformities' (No. 145), a view also expressed by 'K.L.' in 1763 (No. 197). This type of apologia could be taken to ridiculous extremes. Johnson had warned in *Rambler* 158 that faults 'may be sometimes recommended to weak judgments by the lustre which they obtain from their union with excellence; but it is the business of those who presume to superintend the taste or morals of mankind, to separate delusive combinations, and distinguish that which may be praised from that which can only be excused'. An example of just this type of 'weak judgment' is given by the author of 'The Poetical Scale': 'When Shakespeare is execrable, he is so exquisitely so, that he is as inimitable in his blemishes, as in his beauties' (No. 167)—but if they are blemishes who would want to imitate them? More sober statements that Shakespeare's beauties, measured by the criteria of nature, are superior to his faults, conceived of by 'the rules', can be found in nearly all the major critics represented in this volume: in Warton (Nos 139, 158), Murphy (Nos 140, 161e), Edward Young (No. 179), George Colman (No. 187), and Lord Kames (No. 193). The writers of the theatre reviews in the journals and newspapers, such valuable indicators of common opinion, concur. Arthur Murphy, the theatre critic in the *London Chronicle* for 1758, believed that an English audience will acquit Shakespeare of any faults in gratitude for the pleasure he gives them,

a pleasure which no art or correctness could give; and while the beauties of this admirable author are so brilliant and so numerous, I should be ashamed to own that I had suffered my attention to be taken off from them long enough to discover any of his defects. For who indeed but the most dull and stupid of wretches would employ his time in a quarry of diamonds with raking after dirt

4

and pebble-stones, because such things might probably be found there? (No. 170b)

The critic in the *Universal Museum* for 1762 (No. 191c) varied the metaphor, asserting that the beauties of *Cymbeline* 'far eclipse the faults that are here and there to be espied', and concluding with some distaste that 'it is a disagreeable task to look at spots in the sun'.

As the balance shifts towards stressing Shakespeare's beauties it takes on, as we see from these last two examples, an increasingly hostile and polemical tone towards those who find fault. In his essay on Pope in 1756 Joseph Warton attacked the 'nauseous cant' of the French critics and their followers, who stated 'that the English writers are generally INCORRECT. If CORRECTNESS implies an absence of petty faults, this may perhaps be granted', but it is no criterion with which to judge genius (No. 158). In his programmatic essay on taste (1759, 1764) Alexander Gerard poured scorn on 'excessive or false refinement', which praises 'trifling excellencies' and quibbles at the imperfections found in Shakespeare and Homer: for 'a noble *boldness* of genius' is to be preferred to 'that *precision* and constant attention to every trifle which produces a cold and languid mediocrity' (No. 171). This new spirit of generous acceptance and excusal of unimportant errors can be seen, too, in Edmund Burke's discussion of the sublime in 1759, describing the reactions of an enlightened reader of Shakespeare:[5]

In his favourite author he is not shocked with the continual breaches of probability, the confusion of times, the offences against manners, the trampling upon geography; for he knows nothing of geography and chronology, and he has never examined the grounds of probability. He perhaps reads of a shipwreck on the coast of Bohemia; wholly taken up with so interesting an event, and only sollicitous for the fate of his hero, he is not in the least troubled at this extravagant blunder. For why should he be shocked at a shipwreck on the coast of Bohemia, who does not know but that Bohemia may be an island in the Atlantic ocean? and after all, what reflection is this on the natural good Taste of the person here supposed?

Shakespeare, the author of an essay comparing him with Corneille concluded, was 'too great a genius to be methodical' (No. 182).

The newly generous apologias attempted to disarm the opposition by describing it as 'petty' or 'trifling', yet a small but articulate group of critics held that Shakespeare's faults exceeded his beauties. The chief exponent of this view in our period was Mrs Charlotte Lennox, who in a book with the deceptive title *Shakespeare Illustrated* (1753–4, No. 141) surveyed the sources of twenty plays and concluded that Shakespeare was not only derivative in borrowing his plots but wherever he had diverged from his source he had done so for the worse. In his criticism of *Othello* Rymer had discussed the source and concluded that '*Shakespeare* alters it from the Original in several particulars, but always, unfortunately, for the worse' (Vol. 2, p. 27): here is Mrs Lennox's guiding star, which she follows with remorseless industry. The catalogue of Shakespeare's 'absurdities' and 'improbabilities' grows wearisome by determined reiteration, for it is seldom that Mrs Lennox finds anything good to say about any of Shakespeare's greatest plays, and this refusal to admit the presence of any virtues reduces her book to the level of a one-sided *idée fixe*. Yet her literal-minded pertinacity, rather like Rymer's, does throw up some awkward questions about Shakespeare's plotting, especially in *Measure for Measure*, and, in *Much Ado about Nothing*, the odd apparent complicity of Margaret with the villains. A detailed discussion could show that many of her objections are in effect addressed rather against the conventions of Elizabethan drama, in particular plots based on Romance traditions, yet still there are cogent points. In discussing *Lear*, for instance, where Warton and Murphy give detailed but indiscriminately approving accounts of the King's passive behaviour throughout, she, by focusing on Lear's bribery to obtain flattery, highlights Shakespeare's own criticism of Lear in the opening Acts. The modern reader is likely to be offended by the brusqueness and self-confidence of her criticism, and he may be surprised to find how respectfully contemporaries greeted her work. Dr Johnson admired it, and wrote a preface to the book (albeit a curiously self-contradictory one[6]), and the reviews were impressed. The *Monthly Review* article (perhaps by the editor Ralph Griffiths) said that her 'remarks . . . are very judicious and truly critical, . . . chiefly intended to prove that *Shakespeare* has generally spoiled every story on which the above plays are founded by torturing them into low contrivances, absurd intrigue, and improbable incidents': for him it was an 'ingenious and entertaining work'.[7] An exception to the general endorsement of her work came from the novelist Richardson, writing on 8 December 1753 that the book attempted 'to rob Shakespeare of his Invention', and reacting protectively, even piously:[8]

Methinks I love my Shakespeare, since this Attack, better than I did before. Great, injured Shade, I will for ever revere Thee, for what I have read, and, many years ago, seen acted of thine; and hope to live to read the rest of Thee, the far greater Part; which has been postponed, as the Reformation of the

Roman Governor of Judea was, in hopes of a more convenient Season than yet I have found.

Most of Mrs Lennox's objections to Shakespeare can be seen as deriving from Neo-Aristotelian or Neo-classical principles. The canons of decorum, probability, and the rules (innocuously conceived as 'nature methodiz'd') were invoked by these opponents of Shakespeare. Thus Oliver Goldsmith, delivering what seems to be a justifiable complaint about the lower levels of theatrical taste in 1759, nonetheless included within his criticism Shakespeare's 'pieces of forced humour, far-fetch'd conceit, and unnatural hyperbole'[9] (No. 174). Similar criteria were appealed to in two attacks on Shakespeare by Tobias Smollett[10] (Nos 159, 194). The first attack, in the course of a review of Warton's essay on Pope, complains of Shakespeare's 'glaring improprieties' in even his 'most distinguished personages'. Hamlet's 'To be or not to be' is said to be thrust into the play without motivation, since Hamlet has no 'reason . . . to take away his own life'. (Of course, this is to ignore Hamlet's melancholy and despair, so graphically rendered in the play up to that point.) Othello is said to be given 'a puerile lamentation', and Macbeth's apostrophe to sleep is described as a series of 'conceited similes which ill describe the horror of his mind'. Here, evidently, argument from critical principles has degenerated into mere animus. In his second attack Smollett repeats the claims that Hamlet has no reason for suicide and that he fails to allow himself to be murdered by Claudius's false embassy to England, and then embarks on a blow-by-blow account of the 'To be or not to be' soliloquy, this 'heap of absurdities'. Unfortunately his method consists in postulating the need for total logical consistency while refusing to consider the unity of emotion or feeling created by Shakespeare. It is easy to cast parts of the speech into syllogistic form in order to show their failings as logic, yet Smollett seems perversely unaware that Shakespeare was not trying to write syllogisms. Nor does he attempt to understand Shakespearian metaphor. Other sections express Neo-classic concepts of the dignity of tragedy— the word 'rub' is 'a vulgarism beneath the dignity of Hamlet's character', and 'a bare bodkin' is 'but a mean metaphor'. Although Smollett goes on to defend Shakespeare against some of Kames's criticisms,[11] the general tone of his piece is one of forbidding disapproval, thinly supported by argument.

The modern historian may find himself in a double position here: while primarily concerned to investigate what the writers of this period thought about Shakespeare, and why they did so, he cannot help observing how feeble these criticisms are. As again in 'Sir' John Hill's disparaging review of *Antony and Cleopatra* (No. 178), such complaints as that against the anachronistic reference to billiards, or that Juliet seems to carry a supply of daggers around with her, betray a pedantic streak of mind which is indeed 'trifling' and 'petty'. But the canons of Neo-classicism were also expressed with more seriousness and coherence. That characters should be consistent from first to last is a demand as old, at least, as Horace's *Ars Poetica* (the relevant verses from which were frequently quoted in this period, as earlier). Joseph Warton listed as one of Shakespeare's three 'characteristical excellencies' the 'preservation of the consistency of his characters', and said of it that 'to portray characters naturally, and to preserve them uniformly, requires such an intimate knowledge of the heart of man, and is so rare a portion of felicity as to have been enjoyed, perhaps, only by two writers, Homer and Shakespeare' (No. 139), a judgment that Colman also expressed (No. 187). It was in terms of consistency of character that the orator and critic, Thomas Sheridan, made the first analysis of 'Hamlet's delay', as James Boswell reported in his London Journal for 6 April 1763 :[12]

He made it clear to us that Hamlet, notwithstanding of his seeming incongruities, is a perfectly consistent character. Shakespeare drew him as the portrait of a young man of a good heart and fine feelings who had led a studious contemplative life and so become delicate and irresolute. He shows him in very unfortunate circumstances, the author of which he knows he ought to punish, but wants strength of mind to execute what he thinks right and wishes to do. In this dilemma he makes Hamlet feign himself mad, as in that way he might put his uncle to death with less fear of the consequences of such an attempt. We therefore see Hamlet sometimes like a man really mad and sometimes like a man reasonable enough, though much hurt in mind. His timidity being once admitted, all the strange fluctuations which we perceive in him may be easily traced to that source. We see when the Ghost appears (which his companions had beheld without extreme terror)—we see Hamlet in all the agony of consternation. Yet we hear him uttering extravagant sallies of rash intrepidity, by which he endeavours to stir up his languid mind to a manly boldness, but in vain. For he still continues backward to revenge, hesitates about believing the Ghost to be the real spirit of his father, so much that the Ghost chides him for being tardy. When he has a fair opportunity of killing his uncle, he neglects it and says he will not take him off while at his devotions, but will wait till he is in the midst of some atrocious crime, that he may put him to death with his guilt upon his head. Now this, if really from the heart, would make Hamlet the most black, revengeful man. But it coincides better with his character to suppose him here endeavouring to make an excuse to himself for his delay. We see too that after all he agrees to go to England and actually embarks.

'In short', Boswell concluded with satisfaction, 'Sheridan made out his character accurately, clearly, and justly.'

That Shakespeare satisfied the criterion of character-consistency was recognised even by Neo-classicists who faulted him on every other head. In the midst of her disapproving review of *Troilus and Cressida* Mrs Lennox conceded that 'Troilus . . . is every where consistent with his Character of a brave Soldier, and a passionate and faithful Lover' while Cressida is at once recognisable in 'the Character of a compleat Jilt' (No. 141). Yet, Mrs Lennox went on,

Her not being punished is indeed an unpardonable Fault, and brings the greatest Imputation imaginable upon *Shakespeare*'s Judgment, who could introduce so vicious a Person in a Tragedy, and leave her without the due Reward of her Crimes.

'*Cressida* is false, and is not punish'd' (*Shakespeare: The Critical Heritage*, Vol. I, p. 250): those words of Dryden in 1679 show the consistency of Neo-classical principles. The demand for poetic justice is made several times by Mrs Lennox: the catastrophe in *Hamlet* is deplorable because 'the brave, the injured *Hamlet* falls with the Murderers he punishes', and 'one Fate overwhelms alike the innocent and the guilty', a judgment repeated in exactly those words about *King Lear*, in which Shakespeare has 'violated the Rules of poetical Justice'.

It would be easy to dismiss Mrs Lennox, were it not for the agreement of other less bigoted critics on some of those issues. No less a figure than Arthur Murphy declared that as *Hamlet* 'now stands, the Innocent, contrary to Tradition [i.e., the story as told in the sources], falls with the Guilty' (No. 161d), and Lord Kames objected that whereas Desdemona's death was due to 'a regular chain of causes and effects directed by the general laws of nature', through which we glimpse 'the hand of Providence', the deaths of Juliet and Cordelia arouse in the mind 'the gloomy notion of chance' (No. 193). Kames is quite explicit about the Platonic concept of literary censorship which he believes in: 'Chance, giving an impression of anarchy and misrule, produces always a damp upon the mind', and the sense of unease which results is 'a sufficient reason for excluding stories of that kind from the theatre'. The critical system of Neo-classicism could only tolerate evil when it was unequivocally punished within the literary work; and even then there were strong pressures against representing it at all. Earlier Shakespeare critics had pronounced some of Shakespeare's most celebrated characters—including Macbeth, Lady Macbeth, Iago, Richard

III, Shylock, and Brutus—to be 'too monstrous for the stage'.[13] Kames is so horrified by Lady Macbeth's soliloquy arousing herself to the murder of Duncan that he twice describes it as 'not natural', and concludes with the hope that 'there is no such wretch to be found as is here represented'. That is, Shakespeare must be wrong: people of such evil simply do not exist. Or if such evil does exist it ought not to be represented. William Kenrick, not otherwise a squeamish man, approved of William Hawkins's adaptation of *Cymbeline* for having 'judiciously left out . . . the abandoned character of the queen' (No. 177). Predictably, perhaps, Mrs Lennox expresses outrage at the 'more than shocking Absurdity' of Queen Margaret joining in the murder of York in *3 Henry VI*, but even that liberal critic and Shakespeare lover Joseph Warton finds that he cannot defend the character of Richard III since 'there is no person, probably, however vicious and depraved, but who hath some spark of virtue, and some good qualities in his heart'. (*Virgil, ed. cit., IV*, pp. 190f.) The presence of evil was a threat to the optimistic theodicy which underpinned this critical system.

In addition to these relatively limited areas the canons of Neoclassicism were invoked to deal with an issue that had much wider implications, Shakespeare's failure to observe the Unities. This criticism is so often expressed by Mrs Lennox in her strictures on Shakespeare's fables lacking design, or regularity, or—the most severe criticism—being so unorganised that they have 'no plot' at all, that there seems no need to illustrate it further here. It becomes commonplace to observe (as the writer in the *Universal Museum* does of *Cymbeline*, for instance) that 'in Shakespeare's plays we are not to look for an observance of the unities' (No. 191), and it is commonplace to pass on and find other, compensating, beauties. What is surprising now is the movement (which may claim Farquhar as its ancestor: see Vol. 2, No. 45) towards arguing out the criteria of the Unities in general terms, and denying their relevance. This tradition (from which Dr Johnson learned much and to which he gave an individual and not altogether satisfactory turn) is best outlined chronologically.

In 1702 Farquhar had attacked the convention whereby the total time taken by the action represented was allowed to be longer than the time it took to present it:

Now is it feasible in *rerum natura*, that the same Space or Extent of Time can be three Hours by your Watch, and twelve Hours upon the Stage, admitting the same Number of Minutes, or the same Measure of Sand to both? I'm afraid, Sir, you must allow this for an Impossibility too; and you may with as much Reason allow the Play the Extent of a whole Year. And if you grant me a Year, you may give me seven, and so to a thousand. For that a thousand Years should come within the Compass of three Hours is no more an Impossibility than that two Minutes should be contain'd in one. (Vol. 2, p. 186)

The argument that once you allow any disproportion between time represented and time acted then you cannot subsequently limit the first was made in challenging terms by Fielding in *Tom Jones* (1749), in a prefatory chapter headed 'Of THE SERIOUS in writing, and for what purpose it is introduced':

Who ever demanded the reasons of that nice unity of time or place which is now established to be so essential to dramatic poetry? What critic has ever been asked, why a play may not contain two days as well as one? Or why the audience . . . may not be wafted fifty miles as well as five?

Thanks to the 'dogmatical rules' laid down 'peremptorily' by the critic turned 'legislator', accidental elements in some writers who were taken as critical models have been elevated to the status of unbreakable laws, 'and thus many rules for good writing have been established which have not the least foundation in truth or nature, and which commonly serve for no other purpose than to curb or restrain genius' (Book V, Chapter 1). Two years later, in *Rambler* 156 (24 September 1751) Dr Johnson attacked 'the accidental Prescriptions of Authority' over the drama, such as the limiting the number of acts to five and the confining 'the dramatic Action to a certain Number of Hours. Probability indeed requires that the Times of Action should approach somewhat nearly to that of Exhibition. . . . But since it will frequently happen that some Delusion must be admitted I know not where the Limits of Imagination can be fixed.' Open-minded theatre-goers, Johnson declares, are not offended by 'the Extension of the Intervals between the Acts, nor can I conceive it absurd or impossible that he who can multiply three Hours into twelve or twenty-four might image with equal Ease a greater Number' (Vol. 3, p. 434). These arguments are fully in tune with the more liberal, less restrictive attitudes of the mid-century.

The clash between the orthodox and the liberal approach to the Unities was often expressed as one between England and France. Thus John Berkenhout, reviewing Voltaire's play *The Orphan of China* in the *Monthly Review* for December 1755, quotes the French dramatist's discussion of his original source-play, with his sneering comment that 'the time of action of this *Chinese* dramatic poem continues twenty-five years, as in the monstrous farces of *Shakespeare* and *Lope de Vega*, called tragedies'. Berkenhout, like Farquhar, challenges the status of Aristotle's *ipse dixit*, and, like both Farquhar and Fielding, stresses the separate time-scales of 'historical' and 'fabulous' time:

I am sorry for Mr. *Voltaire*'s reputation to hear him talk so much at random. *Aristotle* says that the time of action of a dramatic poem should continue about as long as whilst the sun is moving once round the earth. In compliance with this rule a *French* tragedy is strictly confined to twenty-four hours: but why just twenty-four hours? Why, because *Aristotle* chose to fix that time. *Aristotle* talks too of the sun moving round the earth. I wonder the *French* do not maintain the same thing, since they have his authority for it.

That this stated time hath no foundation in nature is self-evident. Nature would, with more propriety, tell us that the time of action ought to continue no longer than while the play is acting; but if we must needs have recourse to supposition we may as well suppose a whole day, as five hours, between each act.

Surely Mr. *Voltaire* is but little acquainted with *Shakespeare*, or he who has so much taste for poetry would have mentioned the greatest genius that any nation ever produced with a little more respect. By their own *Aristotle*'s rules neither the epic nor dramatic poet are confined to historical truth. They are at liberty to select any part or parts of history, and to unite events which really happened at distant periods of time, provided they be so united as to preserve *probability*: I mean, as *Shakespeare* has done in some of his historical plays, wherein he has connected the remarkable events of a whole reign, all of which might have been transacted in much less time. Considered in this light the time of action in *Shakespeare*'s tragedies seldom continues more than a few days. I wonder that Mr. *Voltaire* should mistake the historical for the fabulous time. (xiii, 494–5)

Berkenhout's discussion, if not entirely original, is succinct and to the point.

In his lively satire on critical rules (No. 184), written in 1760, Robert Lloyd expresses not disgust but, on the contrary, pleasure at Shakespeare's power in the flexibility of movement and the unification of design:

> When Shakespeare leads the mind a dance,
> From France to England, hence to France,
> Talk not to me of time and place;
> I own I'm happy in the chace.
> Whether the drama's here or there,
> 'Tis nature, Shakespeare, everywhere.
> The poet's fancy can create,
> Contract, enlarge, annihilate,
> Bring past and present close together,

In spite of distance, seas, or weather;
And shut up in a single action,
What cost whole years in its transaction.

Lord Kames attacked the topic in 1762, first from a historical view-point, arguing that the Unities of Time and Place were a necessity in the Greek theatre, and second from a purely theoretical one. His second line of argument gives great prominence to the imagination, which, in the intervals between the actions, 'can with the greatest facility suppose any length of time or any change of place'. Kames goes on to make the crucial distinction between imagination and reflection, that is, between involvement in the world of fiction and detachment from it:

the spectator, it is true, may be conscious that the real time and place are not the same with what are employed in the representation: but this is a work of reflection; and by the same reflection he may also be conscious that Garrick is not King Lear, that the playhouse is not Dover Cliffs, nor the noise he hears thunder and lightning.

Once a critic has conceded the imaginative existence of the world before him in the theatre, once he 'is willing to hold candle-light for sun-shine, and some painted canvasses for a palace or a prison', then it is absurd for him to wish to impose quasi-naturalistic limitations on place or time. Although Kames made a cogent attack on the rules he nevertheless had some reservations about the dramatist's liberty of representation, and felt that works which were set in one place were likely to be 'the more perfect' since that would automatically ensure unity of action.

Further valuable arguments were made by Daniel Webb (No. 195) from the standpoint of the dramatic work itself. The beauties of Shakespeare, so much admired, derive precisely from 'the promptness and vivacity of his genius' in breaking through rules: the 'commanding energy' of the plays 'transports the heart in defiance of the understanding'. When the Unities are observed the consequences for the play are monotony of feelings, and an action presented at one remove, not directly but by narration:

as no one simple and confined action can furnish many incidents, and those, such as they are, must tend to one common point, it necessarily follows that there must be a sameness and uniformity in the sentiments. What must be the result of this? Why, narration is substituted in the place of the action, the weakness in the manners supplied by elaborate descriptions; and the quick and lively turns of passion are lost in the detail and pomp of declamation.

And to crowd into four hours events 'which, in the natural course of things, would have taken up as many days' is to commit 'a violence on nature, in order to come nearer to truth'. Similarly John Langhorne, translator of Plutarch and prolific writer for the *Monthly Review*, attacked the cramping effect of the rules both in theory and in practice. Letter XXX of his epistolary novel, *Effusions of Friendship and Fancy* (1763),[14] rebukes its addressee, 'a friend to the theatres,' for never lifting up his voice

against those formal figures called *the three* UNITIES. They have amused the town with the words *truth* and *nature* and *probability*, till they have appointed such narrow limits to dramatic composition that *genius* dares not give free scope to his wing, for fear he should soar beyond them. *Imagination* feels herself confined, and ventures not to exert her powers while she beholds the finger of art limiting the sphere and describing the circle in which she is to move. Such consequences has the reign of these petty tyrants. And what have we gained by giving up so much? A dull regularity, an insipid consistency. The bold flights of gothic genius are no more, and all is symmetry and exactness and proportion.

The system is supposed to aid 'the credibility of the plot', Langhorne observes, yet its effect is to deny the fictional existence of a work of art, which is the justification for the plot as for everything else.

What occasion for the scene to be altogether *in one apartment*? We must be sensible, if we are awake at all, that the whole representation is a fiction. And why cannot we as well follow the imagination of the poet from region to region? It is still but fiction, and, if it be *spirited* fiction, I am sure it will not be without its effect. It is the same with regard to time.

Langhorne now moves to the practical effects of the observation of the rules: like Webb, he has a good eye for the deformations of drama that result.

But I have yet more to say against these Unities. Far from aiding probability, they generally wound it. It is amazing to see what a hubbub of wonderful events are crowded in every modern play, into the short space of three hours. I remember, in a late comedy, there were two or three courtships projected, begun, carried on, and finished; writings were drawn for which an attorney would have charged ten pounds, as the reward of manual labour; and the whole state and sentiments of a family were as much changed in three hours as they could have been in three years.

We may by now agree with Langhorne's conclusion, 'that the accuracy of art has always been prejudicial to works of genius, and what they have gained in correctness they have lost in spirit'.

Yet new ideas do not displace old ones easily, nor universally. This we see from the example of Adam Smith, who discussed the Unities in some lectures which he gave in the University of Glasgow in 1762–3, and which were first printed by J. M. Lothian in 1963. The 'reason generally given for the bad effect' of several days elapsing between one scene and another 'is that it prevents our deception', in that after only 'half an hour in the playhouse' we cannot suppose that 'two or three years have passed'. An unexceptionable beginning: but Smith went on to reject this explanation, and also, alas, the concept of imaginative involvement that it presupposed:[15]

But in reality we are never thus deceived. We know that we are in the play-house, that the persons before us are actors, and that the thing represented either happened before, or perhaps never happened at all. The pleasure we have in a dramatical performance no more rises from deception than that which [we] have in looking at pictures. No one ever imagined that he saw the sacrifice of Iphigenia; no more did anyone imagine that he saw King Richard the Third. Everyone knows that at one time he saw a picture, and at the other Mr. Garrick, or some other actor. 'Tis not, then, from the interruption of deception that the bad effect[s] of such transgression of the unity of time proceed: 'tis rather from the uneasiness we feel in being kept in the dark with regard to what happened in so long a time.

However, Smith has failed to conceive of the distinction made by Kames between imagination and reflection, and—as Dr Johnson was to do two years later—failing to make this he is forced to reject the whole concept of illusion. Subsequently he recommends that the action should be fixed 'to one place if possible, as Racine and Sophocles have done', or else confine the action 'to the same house or thereabouts' (p. 119). It is disappointing to find Adam Smith in effect reaffirming the concept of the Unities after the fresh and cogent criticisms of it made by Webb, Kames, Lloyd, Berkenhout, and Langhorne. A re-establishment of a more enlightened viewpoint came at the end of this period from Benjamin Heath (No. 203), who mocked 'all that critical parade concerning the dramatick unities, the hackneyed topick of every Italian, French, and English critick for above a century'. Shakespeare, Heath argued, never thought about the Unities, and was certainly ignorant of any advantages to be gained from observing them. The example of *The Tempest* is misleading, for 'the constitution of the fable was such, by the whole transaction being confined within a little desolate island, as not to admit of a violation of the unities of time and place'. And Shakespeare had 'the superior knowledge' and 'unrivalled ascendancy of his genius' to have scorned the taste of his age. Here, as on several other issues, Heath challenges eighteenth-century orthodoxy with great vigour.

II

The plan of this collection, embracing as many aspects of the reaction to Shakespeare as can be illustrated in print, allows us now to move from literary criticism to the theatre, and to the adaptations of Shakespeare's plays. Here we find the older Neo-classic concept of the Unities still in undisputed possession, and having seen the debate on the Unities as it took place in the journals and books of the 1750s and 1760s we can begin to understand the remarkable fact that in this period the adapters almost without exception give as their main reason for altering the plays Shakespeare's failure to observe the Unities. If we look at the similar claims made by Dryden or Tate in the 1670s and 1680s we see again the persistence of Neo-classical canons. Mrs Lennox had echoed Dryden and Rymer: Thomas Sheridan echoed Mrs Lennox, justifying his curious mixture of Thomson's *Coriolanus* with Shakespeare's on the grounds that 'Shakespeare's play was purely historical, and had little or no plot' (No. 144)—that is, it seemed to his eyes to be merely a succession of incidents with no design. Another tragedy that caused critical difficulty was *Romeo and Juliet*. Garrick's adaptation had cut many of the quibbles, but Charles Marsh for one was not satisfied, and records that in 1752 he had prepared 'an Alteration of *Romeo and Juliet* wherein I had separated the Tragedy from the Comedy, and thrown the latter quite away' (Preface to No. 176). Shakespeare's mingling of the two genres had given offence to the first generation of Neo-classics, and we must remember that throughout this period *King Lear* was acted in Tate's adaptation, without the Fool. Horace Walpole justified Shakespeare's practice in *Hamlet* and *Julius Caesar* (No. 202), but a reviewer objected that in those tragedies Shakespeare had 'blended humour and clumsy jests with dignity and solemnity', and was confident that 'if Shakespeare had possessed the critical knowledge of modern times he would have kept those two kinds of writing distinct, if the prepossessions and habits of the age could have suffered him'.[16] Indeed Walpole himself had written to a friend in 1755 congratulating him for some 'most delightful' criticism on the Queen in *Hamlet*, 'so artful a banter' on Shakespeare 'for so improperly making her Majesty deal in *doubles entendres* at a funeral!'[17]

Shakespeare's tragedies had already been 'regularized' by Tate and Co.; in this period it was the turn of the Romances, especially *The Winter's Tale* and *Cymbeline*. A glance at the stock Neo-classical rejection of the 'absurdities' and 'improbabilities' of these plays, as expressed by Pope, for instance, in Vol. 2 of this collection (pp. 413, 418) or Gildon (*ibid.*, pp. 245, 261), or by Mrs Lennox in this volume, will show what their sensibilities were offended by and what the adapters set out to excise. Garrick's abbreviation of *The Winter's Tale* (1756: No. 150) dealt with the embarrassing gap of sixteen years between Act III and Act IV by simply omitting Acts I to III, and devoting his opening scene to a recapitulation of the action up to that point. His Prologue draws attention to this feature:

> The five long Acts, from which our Three are taken,
> Stretch'd out to sixteen Years, lay by, forsaken.
> Lest then this precious Liquor run to waste,
> 'Tis now confin'd and bottled for your Taste.
> 'Tis my chief Wish, my Joy, my only Plan,
> To lose no *Drop* of that immortal Man.

The unity of place is achieved by setting the action in Bohemia, and having Leontes arrive there by ship. Unfortunately, both the resulting scenes more than bear out Daniel Webb's contention that reducing action to narration results in dull and monotonous drama. When Charles Marsh made his adaptation he chose the same solution (No. 153). A new expository scene tells us of the earthquakes that have struck Sicily, that Hermione has been in prison for fifteen years, and so on. In both cases we see the rather desperate measures the adapters were forced into by the desire to retain parts of Shakespeare's plot while rejecting others. It is perhaps easier to think of Hermione filling up that long period in prison for fifteen years than being secretly tended by Paulina ('a mean and absurd Contrivance', Mrs Lennox called it), but it does mean that Leontes, instead of being given a manic irruption of jealousy (as in Shakespeare) and an equally sudden return to sanity and remorse, has persisted in his mania all this time. It is even less likely, therefore, that he will be brought round to forgiveness and reunion within the short space of the play. What was a state of mind in Shakespeare has been transformed into a way of life, permanent, inflexible.

The reviewer's reactions to these adaptations shows the uniformity of taste and critical principle within the Neo-classicist tradition. Smollett, writing in the *Critical Review*, approved of Marsh's restoring the Unity of Time, and so removing 'in some measure . . . the improbability that shocks the imagination of a person that sees the performance acted', but complained that Marsh had not only failed to restore the Unity of Place, 'for the scene is still shifted from one Kingdom to another', but had also retained the deaths of Mamilius, Antigonus, and the ship's crew, 'which create a confusion of tragedy and comedy, and destroy the propriety of the composition' (No. 154)—that is, cause a mixture of genres and so destroy Unity of Action. Berkenhout, in the *Monthly Review*, agreed: the play is 'one of the most *unalterable*', owing to its offending two of the Unities, and while 'the first of these absurdities is lopt by the pruning knife of Mr. Marsh . . . he has suffered the other, tho' equally monstrous, to remain' (No. 155). Garrick's *Winter's Tale* adaptation had a better reception, although we must take into account the peculiar mixture of panegyric and denigration that accompanied all of Garrick's doings with Shakespeare. Thus the notice in the *Critical Review* for February 1762 (No. 190), written by Smollett[18] (who had been given a presentation copy in January and wrote thanking Garrick for it), praised the now 'regular, connected, and consistent entertainment'. The *Monthly Review* was equally flattering to Garrick and critical of Shakespeare's original:

The meanness of the Fable, and the extravagant conduct of it, has been the chief objections to this Play . . . The *Action* of this piece, as Shakespeare left it, comprehends the monstrous space of sixteen years. Mr. Garrick has cleared it of this absurdity; reduced it from *five* to a more regular piece of three acts; added a pretty song in the festive scene of Sheep-sheering; and to the whole has prefixed a very humorous Prologue. (xxvi, 151)

In his theatre column in the *London Chronicle* Arthur Murphy also welcomed Garrick's version as being 'more compact', with Shakespeare's 'Absurdities . . . retrenched' (No. 161l).

With *Cymbeline* the adapters took much the same course. Charles Marsh's version (No. 176) set out 'to amend the *Conduct* of the *Fable*, by confining the Scenes, at least, to this Island'. Whereas in Shakespeare Posthumus Leonatus is banished from Britain, and the action subsequently alternates between Britain and Italy, Marsh wrote a new scene (II, i) which transported him back to Britain immediately after he had left it. When William Hawkins adapted the play he had the same objections to the original, 'one of the most irregular productions of Shakespeare' (No. 175). But in addition to its beauties there was 'something so pleasingly romantic, and likewise truly *British* in the subject of it' that he had attempted 'to new-construct this Tragedy, almost upon the plan of *Aristotle* himself, in respect of the *unity* of *Time*'. The task proved more difficult than he expected, for he had to omit characters, scenes, and incidents, 'or rather to bring the substance and purport of them within the compass of a few short narrations'. Webb's diagnosis of the effects of regularisation is again validated, for whereas Marsh brought Posthumus back to England in order to avoid a change of place, Hawkins allows him to proceed to Italy yet then brings Pisanio (his name for Shakespeare's Iachimo) back to report on what happened there. So the vigorous scenes of Posthumus's wager, his jealousy, and so on, are now narrated at second hand, not presented directly. William Kenrick, reviewing the adaptations in the *Monthly Review* (No. 177), preferred Hawkins to Marsh. He found Hawkins completely successful in turning 'a parcel of loose incoherent scenes' into 'a beautiful and correct piece of dramatic poesy', and removing 'its principal defects'. Marsh, however, offended decorum by retaining the evil Queen and by allowing the characters to 'speak indifferently [*sic*] either in prose or verse'. Hawkins's version was evidently more 'polite'.

David Garrick produced his version of *Cymbeline* on 28 November 1761 and published it in the following year with an advertisement which reveals a new conservatism in his approach to Shakespeare adaptations:

The admirers of *Shakespeare* must not take it ill that there are some Scenes, and consequently many fine Passages omitted in this Edition of CYMBELINE. It was impossible to retain more of the Play and bring it within the Compass of a Night's Entertainment. The chief Alterations are in the Division of the Acts, in the Shortning many parts of the Original, and some Scenes. As the Play has met with so favourable a Reception from the Publick, it is hop'd that the Alterations have not been made with great Impropriety.

G.C.D. Odell, that indefatigable historian of Shakespeare in the theatre, did 'not hesitate to pronounce it . . . the most accurate of Eighteenth-Century acting versions'.[19] Yet the cuts have more significance than mere theatrical convenience. In his edition of Shakespeare Pope had written of Act V, scene iii: 'Here follows a *Vision*, a *Masque*, and a *Prophecy*, which interrupt the Fable without the least necessity and unmeasurably lengthen this Act. I think it plainly foisted in afterwards for meer show, and apparently not of *Shakespeare*' (*Shakespeare: The Critical Heritage*, Vol. 2, p. 418). That note was reprinted with approval by Dr Johnson in his edition of 1765,[20] and it is significant that in Garrick's version the vision that appears to Posthumus in his dream is cut, including the appearance of Jupiter (5.4.30-122), as is the densely-quibbling scene with the Soothsayer (5.5.425-55). Nor do these scenes appear in Hawkins's version, nor Marsh's. Evidently the eight-eenth century, although it could digest pantomime, had difficulties with the Jacobean masque. In the acting version of *The Tempest* preserved in Bell's edition of Shakespeare (1773) we are informed that 'the following Masque is altered from *Shakespeare*, and judiciously made half as short again as the original' (III, p. 47n.), while that in *Cymbeline* is silently cut.

The claim that an adaptation has been performed in order to restore the Unities of Time and Place was even made by Benjamin Victor for his version of *The Two Gentlemen of Verona* in 1762 (No. 196), in which his design was 'to give a greater uniformity to the scenery, and a connection and consistency to the fable (which in many places is visibly wanted) . . .'. Kenrick, in the *Monthly Review* for January 1763, approved of the 'careful and skilful hand' of the adapter in regularising a comedy which 'is generally reckoned as one of Shake-speare's worst Performances, and even by many thought so meanly of as to be deemed the Work of some inferior hand, in which Shakespeare bore but a very small part' (xxviii, p. 75).

The agreement between adapters and reviewers held, then, for a number of new adaptations made in this period, which patently appealed to surviving Neo-classic taste. On the older adaptations, though, opinions differed. Most of those who approved of the adaptations were actors or men of the theatre, evaluating them purely as theatrical vehicles. So MacNamara Morgan praised the Otway-Garrick alteration of the death-scene in *Romeo and Juliet* (No. 137), a preference shared by Arthur Murphy (No. 161c). Murphy, again, believed that *King Lear* 'as altered by *Tate* will always be more agreeable to an audience' (No. 140), and the theatre reviewer in the *Gazetteer and London Daily Advertiser* on 9 January 1765, comparing *King Lear* at the two theatres, was dis-appointed with the production at Drury Lane since it was 'a mixture of Shakespeare's and Tate's, the whole part of the Bastard (which is far the least interesting in the piece) being injudiciously restored'. He believed that 'candid judgment will allow . . . Tate's *Lear* (as at Covent-Garden) the best and most agreeable alteration'. Garrick had presented his version of *Lear* at Drury Lane on 28 October 1756.[21] It restores the first three acts of Shakespeare 'almost verbatim', as C. B. Hogan puts it,[22] but the later stages revert more and more to Tate. However, 'almost verbatim' means that Garrick still follows the major changes of

Tate: the Fool is omitted, Edgar and Cordelia have their love-affair, and the play ends with Lear, Edgar and Cordelia alive and happily reunited. It is to be regretted that Garrick's courage failed him, for perhaps he alone, as Richardson told him in 1748,[23] would have had enough influence over the public to convert them.

It is common to find writers quoting from Tate's *Lear* (e.g. Nos 148, 157, 165, 173, 191) or Cibber's *Richard III* (e.g. Nos 157, 165, 173, 191) since both were the current acting versions. Yet these accepted adaptations had their opponents. Frances Brooke, writing in 1756 (No. 156), expressed surprise that both companies should prefer Tate's version, and turned Garrick's metaphor of losing 'no drop' of Shakespeare against him, deploring that he 'should yet prefer the adulterated cup of *Tate* to the pure genuine draught offered him by the master he avows to serve with such fervency of devotion'. George Colman exclaimed with disgust at the Edgar-Cordelia scenes in *Lear*: 'with what a Philosophical Calmness do the audience doze over the tedious and uninteresting Love-Scenes with which the bungling hand of Tate has coarsely pieced and patched that rich Work of Shakespeare!' (No. 187). We find similarly sharp attacks on the Sheridan–Thomson–Shakespeare *Coriolanus* from Arthur Murphy for pounding together 'two things so heterogeneous', resulting in a 'fantastical mixture' (No. 170c), and from Benjamin Victor in 1761 (No. 188). Theophilus Cibber, reviewing the production in the *Monthly Review* for January 1755, wrote that in this 'motley tragedy' Sheridan had 'joined *Shakespeare* and *Thomson* as awkwardly together as if a man should tack to the body of one picture the limbs of another, without considering what an uncouth figure they might make together, how well soever they appeared separate'.[24] In such criticism we see an increasing sense of the integrity of Shakespeare's plays, a unity which could only be destroyed by the hand of the adapter.

All the adaptations so far considered were regular theatrical versions, the main item in the evening's entertainment, to be acted, not sung. Yet another group of adaptations, mostly emanating from Garrick, adapt Shakespeare to other purposes, spectacle, music, farce. Just as his adaptation of *Romeo and Juliet* (No. 117 in Vol. 3) had made the Funeral Procession an event in its own right, so in his version of *King Henry VIII* in 1762, among other smaller changes,[25] Garrick constructed an enormous procession (No. 192), which became a famous spectacle in the London theatre. Such spectacles (as with the 'Ovation' in the Sheridan–Thomson *Coriolanus*) became great crowd-pullers, and were often the main advertising point on the play-bills. The modern reader may not greatly mind about this procession, since it is merely a larger version than the one by Shakespeare himself. Yet the other two new modes of adaptation seem to me unequivocally disastrous.

For his 'musical' versions of *The Tempest* and *A Midsummer Night's Dream* Garrick reverted to the practice of the 1670s (compare the 1674 *Tempest*, No. 13 in Vol. 1, and the 1692 *Midsummer Night's Dream*, No. 28). Shakespeare's text is cut to shreds, shortened and simplified so that there is not too much (nor too difficult) dialogue in between the musical numbers. (These are just the principles of the modern musical comedy: Garrick may be said to have produced the first Hollywood 'musicals' of Shakespeare.) The text of the arias, whatever their musical merit may have been, is unbearably banal, as in the closing duet of *The Tempest* (p. 228) or in Prospero's memorable exclamation just after Ferdinand sees Miranda for the first time:

> In tender sighs he silence breaks,
> The fair his flame approves,
> Consenting blushes warm her cheeks,
> She smiles, she yields, she loves. (II,i; p. 19)

One is appalled to find Ben Jonson's 'Have you seen but a bright lily grow' pitched into the text, a form of plagiarism. The facetiousness of the prologue to *The Fairies* (No. 146), and the Dialogue on *The Tempest* (No. 151) with its crude victory for the Actor over the Critic, show the low level at which Garrick was operating. As for the *Midsummer Night's Dream* adaptation, the three versions it went through show the kind of structureless reshuffling that Garrick and his collaborators were capable of:

(a) 1755, Garrick: *The Fairies*. An Opera. 28 songs

(b) 1763, Garrick and Colman: *A Midsummer Night's Dream*. 33 songs

(c) 1763, Colman: *A Fairy Tale*. 13 songs

Version (a) included the lovers and the fairies from Shakespeare's plot, but not the clowns; (b) included lovers, fairies, and clowns; (c) included fairies and clowns, but no lovers. All three versions are so silly that it would have been pointless to include them here. Equally disposable, were it not for the great vogue they enjoyed as after-pieces in the eighteenth century, were the Garrick *Winter's Tale* (*Florizel and Perdita*, No. 150) and his *Catharine and Petruchio*, a much-potted version of *The Taming of the Shrew* first performed with *Florizel and Perdita* on 21 January 1756, which held the stage until 1886 (Odell, *op cit.*, I, 362).

I have selected one example from each category of Garrick's adaptations in this period (spectacle, music, and after-piece) to show the direction taken by the theatre-manager who professed to revere Shakespeare. To the modern student, horrified at such mangling, it is rather heartening to discover that many of Garrick's contemporaries felt the same about them. Writing in the *Critical Review* Samuel Derrick (who took a much sharper attitude towards Garrick than did his collaborator Smollett) could not 'remember to have seen a more flagrant imposition of the kind' than *Catharine and Petruchio*, and recorded sarcastically that 'he must have a great taste and infinite veneration for *Shakespeare,* who thus fritters his plays into farces' (No. 154b). He viewed with regret Shakespeare 'cruelly mangled and unhappily pieced' in the operatic *Tempest*, and perceptively noted that the need to abbreviate the recitatives as much as possible had made them 'rough and dissonant' (No. 154c). In 1758 William Shirley also recalled Garrick's claim to revere Shakespeare while juxtaposing this 'pious regard for the venerable father of the stage' with its consequence, that he is 'sacrilegiously frittered and befribbled' (No. 166). Goldsmith's pessimistic survey of the stage in 1759 is clearly directed at Garrick and the cult of the actor, 'who thinks it safest acting in exaggerated characters' and therefore creates comic vehicles for himself out of Shakespeare's weaker pieces, producing 'strange vamp'd comedies, farcical tragedies, . . . speaking pantomimes' (No. 174): Goldsmith is presumably referring to *Catharine and Petruchio*. The *Midsummer Night's Dream* adaptations came in for sharp criticism, too. The *Critical Review* (a notice not written by Smollett, who was abroad, but perhaps by Samuel Derrick) said of *A Fairy Tale* that it was Shakespeare's play 'curtailed into a kind of sing-song farce, which has been lately played by *little* children for the entertainment of *great* ones' (March, 1764; xvii, p. 238). Horace Walpole wrote to a friend in February 1755 that 'Garrick has produced a detestable English opera [*The Fairies*] which is crowded by all true lovers of their country. To mark the opposition to Italian operas, it is sung by cast [i.e. worn-out] singers, two Italians and a French girl, and the chapel boys; and to regale us with sense, it is Shakespeare's *Midsummer Night's Dream,* which is forty times more nonsensical than the worst translation of any Italian opera-books.—But such sense and such harmony are irresistible!'[26]

The most perceptive criticisms of Garrick's adaptations of Shakespeare came from Theophilus Cibber, in his two theatrical 'dissertations' (No. 157). Cibber conceded that *The Winter's Tale* is irregular but argued that it was none the less beautiful, full of imaginative touches.

Garrick, owing to his desire to restore Unity of Time, had entirely omitted many of the best-written and most moving scenes, 'such as the Jealousy of *Leontes*, the Trial of *Hermione*'. Those parts retained from the first three Acts 'are crowded into a dull narrative', 'two long-winded Relations' of events which 'we might have expected to have seen represented'. Anticipating Webb there, Cibber then poured scorn on the disjointed nature of the resulting work, a 'gallimaufry', 'such a Mixture of piecemeal, motley Patchwork that *The Winter's Tale* of *Shakespeare*, thus lop'd, hack'd, and dock'd, appears without Head or Tail'. He joins Goldsmith in deploring the lack of choice before the London theatre audience—'they must have that or nothing'—and ends with a vigorous and witty attack on Garrick:

Were *Shakespeare*'s Ghost to rise, wou'd he not frown Indignation on this pilfering Pedlar in Poetry, who thus shamefully mangles, mutilates, and emasculates his plays? The *Midsummer Night's Dream* has been minc'd and fricasee'd into an indigested and unconnected Thing call'd *The Fairies*; *The Winter's Tale* mammoc'd into a Droll; *The Taming of the Shrew* made a Farce of; and *The Tempest* castrated into an opera.

O Tempora! O Mores!

III

As an adapter of Shakespeare Garrick has nothing to recommend him to posterity. His influence was pernicious, for not only did he further the work of Tate and others but also, in his own person, he set new and bad fashions which were to persist for many generations. As an actor and theatre-manager he had an enormous pull—it is not too much to say that Garrick's Shakespeare had more influence on more people than that of any editor, critic, or commentator. Although, as we have seen in the preceding volume in this collection (Vol. 3, pp. 11ff.), he can no longer be thought to have started the vogue for Shakespeare in the theatres, he certainly did much to consolidate it. Yet, equally, we must repeat the point made there (p. 13) that a taste for Shakespeare was a conservative taste, a safe-choice vehicle for actors or actresses. While Shakespeare held both stages there was hardly any room for new drama: it is significant that a number of the critics of the 1750s selected here complain of the difficulty of getting new plays accepted, of the monotonous diet and lack of choice in the theatres: Cibber, Shirley, Goldsmith,

Kelly, Hawkins, Marsh, Kenrick. All were critical of Garrick's role in this context. Within the Shakespeare repertoire, too, there was little adventure. As Cecil Price has put it, mid-eighteenth-century taste 'was very conservative. Almost a third of all the plays given at Drury Lane in the whole of the season were by Shakespeare. . . . The same comedies and tragedies went on appearing year by year' (*Theatre in the Age of Garrick*, p. 196). The statistics of H. W. Pedicord[27] and G. W. Stone (*The London Stage, 1747–1776*, I, pp. clxii ff.) for the period 1747 to 1776 show that Shakespeare was by far the most popular dramatist at both theatres. Of the 5,363 performances at Drury Lane 1,065 (approximately 20 per cent of the total) were of Shakespeare: yet only nine plays were performed. At Covent Garden the figures are 5,192, of which 852 (approximately 16 per cent) were of Shakespeare, but of only eight plays. Beyond the bare figures, however apparently gratifying to Shakespeare lovers, was the fact that Garrick, who knew the nature of his audience, used to 'prop-up' his tragedies soon after their first appearance with a sure-draw after-piece, such as the 'new masquerade dance' which followed *Romeo and Juliet* in November, 1748 (Pedicord, pp. 138ff.), or the 'vocal parts and solemn dirge sung at Juliet's funeral procession' for the January 1763 production (Stone, p. cxxxiv). G. W. Stone records neutrally that one reason 'for the popularity of a number of Shakespeare's plays lay in their dance possibilities' (pp. cxli f.), and Kalman Burnim has commented, more critically, that although Garrick 'made the age "Shakespeare conscious"', often the play was not the main attraction, rather the dances or pantomimes.[28]

These facts necessarily qualify the traditional image of Garrick as the great reviver of Shakespeare. The version of history put about by Garrick's supporters at the time was that until he came Shakespeare lay in neglect. A convenient statement of this myth can be found in the Poet Laureate William Whitehead's 'Verses dropt in Mr. Garrick's Temple of Shakespeare at Hampton', in which, while Garrick is one day offering thanks to the statue of Shakespeare, it suddenly speaks. The 'marble God' points to 'his laurel'd brow' and cries

> 'Half this wealth to you I owe.
> Lost to the Stage, and lost to Fame,
> Murder'd my scenes, scarce known by name,
> Sunk in oblivion and disgrace
> Among the common scribbling race,
> Unnotic'd long thy Shakespeare lay,
> To Dullness and to Time a prey;

But lo! I rise, I breathe, I live
In you, my representative!'

Garrick modestly refuses half the garland and would settle for a 'single leaf', yet the poem ends with wreaths being distributed to both:

Each matchless, each the palm shall bear;
In heav'n, the Bard; on earth, the Play'r.

Similarly George Colman, in his mock-satire called *A Letter of Abuse, to D—d G—k Esq.* (1757) wrote, 'I will not deny that many Parts, even of the divine *Shakespeare*, were no more than a dead Letter, until your animating Genius enlivened their Beauties, and enforced their Energy' (p. 5). Modern theatrical historians (especially A. H. Scouten) have shown how false that picture is, yet it is just as important to note that in this period it was generally accepted, and that the names of Garrick and Shakespeare were constantly linked. At the beginning of the period represented here Arthur Murphy described Garrick as Shakespeare's 'best commentator' (No. 140), and that association holds constant, as we see in Lyttelton's *Dialogues of the Dead* (1760, 1765), where Garrick is said to have 'shewn the English nation more excellences in Shakespeare than the quickest wits could discern' (No. 181).

Yet in the more extended accounts of Garrick as an actor of Shakespeare adverse criticism at least balances praise. In the selections collected here there are six substantial items on the credit side, the essays by Shebbeare (No. 148: heavily plagiarised by Pittard in No. 165), those by Thomas Wilkes (No. 173), and the reviewer in the *Universal Museum* (No. 191), together with the poems by Lloyd (No. 184) and Churchill (No. 186); while on the debit page we have the anonymous criticisms by 'Telemachus Lovet' (No. 163) and the essays by Cibber (No. 157), Shirley (No. 166), Fitzpatrick (No. 185) and Kelly (No. 189). The Shebbeare–Pittard essay on Garrick's Lear is wholly panegyrical, and gives an enthusiastic account of Garrick's dignity and forcefulness in the part, especially in the curse on Goneril ('I could not avoid expecting a paralytic Stroke would wither every Limb of Goneril') and in the storm-scenes, with their rapid oscillation of feeling. In the account of the madness and recovery scenes, unfortunately, Shebbeare becomes vaguer, and tries to evoke the feeling Garrick produced in him without substantiating the details of gesture and speech which made up that feeling. This was the occupational hazard of Garrick's supporters, as we see from Lloyd's poem (No. 184) and dozens like it, or from Churchill's *Rosciad* (No. 186): it is frustrating to be told only that Garrick could represent Nature or appeal to the heart. Not much more helpful is the essayist in the *Universal Museum* (No. 191), for whom 'nothing could be finer spoke' than Garrick's soliloquy as Macbeth, 'Nothing could possibly be greater than Macbeth's seeing the daggers in the air', while in *King Lear* Garrick was 'inimitable', 'never greater', 'almost inconceivable', 'amazingly great', 'very great', 'extremely moving'. This writer seems unable to translate his enthusiasm into description or analysis, and we catch only a few glimpses of specific gesture or posture: such as Garrick's Macbeth, 'when he looked on his bloody hands, we saw the sad condition of his soul in his eyes'; or his Lear, the emphatic way he spoke the prayer against his daughters, kneeling; or the mixture of emotions with which he confronted Goneril and Regan, 'ready to choke with passion'; or the moment (albeit from Tate's version) when 'tired with the fray, [he] leans against the wall'. More articulate is the appreciation by Thomas Wilkes (No. 173), who stresses the anger and pathos of his Lear, Richard III's resentment at his deformity (although this contradicts other accounts), the graphically rendered emotional confusion of Macbeth or Hamlet—it would seem as if Garrick excelled at depicting strongly contrasting emotions, or drastic changes of mood. Despite their vaguenesses, from these accounts we get at least some idea of the intensity and involvement with which Garrick performed.

Yet these energies were not without excesses. The criticisms of Garrick's acting in this period are far more detailed than the panegyrics, and even though we must discount part of their animus (since some of the authors had quarrelled with Garrick or criticised his policies and practices as theatre-manager)—just as we must discount part of the praise from his friends—the explicitness of the documentation leaves no doubt that he was guilty of some of these offences. William Shirley (No. 166) claimed that Garrick employed 'abundance of false action, such as . . . grasping the side of his robe', and used 'pantomime tricks in affected agitations, tremblings and convulsions; he over-agonizes dying'. Theophilus Cibber (No. 157) also objected to Garrick's 'pantomimical acting every Word in a Sentence', and the examples he gives from the roles of Benedick and Richard III do seem excessive. It was most 'theatrical' of Garrick to change into black in the interval before the tomb-scene in *Romeo and Juliet*, and his start of surprise at seeing the tomb, like his fighting Paris with a massive-seeming crow-bar, are both exaggerated bits of theatre. The hero of an epistolary novel (No. 163) also criticised the 'extravagant attitudes'—postures and gestures—of Garrick's Romeo in the tomb-scene. Even more displeasing is Cibber's account of Garrick's acting in *King Lear*, at the end of the scene where Lear (with his hundred knights) is refused hospitality by his daughters. Instead of sweeping off stage in anger Garrick collapsed 'almost lifeless, into the Arms of his Attendants', and in an unnaturally contorted posture—which contradicts the appearance of a faint—walked off stage supported, with his head and body 'thrown extravagantly behind, as if his Neck and Back were broke'.

Cibber's criticisms were partly directed against the audience who lacked the judgment to detect these excesses, and in his more moderate account Hugh Kelly (No. 189) also stated that 'no inconsiderable share of [Garrick's] infallibility exists in the good-nature or ignorance of his auditors'. Kelly agreed that although Garrick's 'action'—gesture, posture, movement—'may be extremely easy, it is very frequently unnatural', especially as Richard III. He found Garrick most suited to tragic roles needing 'weight and dignity', such as Henry IV and above all Lear, where 'the circumstances of age and infirmity are more happily suited to the weakness of his powers'. (Garrick was forty-five at the time.) One of the great problems in writing the history of the theatre is to reconcile the conflicting impressions that the same performance makes on different spectators. Kelly approved of Garrick's Henry IV, and when Boswell went to see it on 10 January 1763 he recorded that 'Mr. Garrick in the pathetic scene between the old King and his son drew tears from my eyes'. Yet at dinner two days later Thomas Sheridan 'showed to my conviction that Garrick did not play the great scene in the Second Part of *King Henry IV* with propriety. . . . Now Mr. Garrick in that famous scene whines most piteously when he ought to upbraid'. The King should be 'anxious and vexed', should be 'fired with rage' to discover that 'the Prince had taken the crown from his pillow', and thus desires his death. 'His anger animates him so much that he throws aside his distemper. Nature furnishes all her strength for one last effort. He is for a moment renewed. He is for a moment the spirited Henry the Fourth. He upbraids him with bitter sarcasm and bold figures'. (Boswell, *London Journal, 1762–3, ed. cit.,* pp. 135–6.) Kelly found 'weight and dignity' in Garrick's performance: to Sheridan he 'whined'.

Apart from Garrick's over-expressive gestures, he was often criticised for his eccentric speaking of Shakespeare, and there is a striking agreement between four of the observers recorded here. William Shirley complained that 'he lays frequent clap-traps, in false pauses, stammerings, hesitations and repetitions', while Theophilus Cibber referred specifically to Lear's curse, and made the acute point that the delivery ought to be rapid, without 'long Pauses' to 'damp the Fire of it, like Cold Water dropp'd thereon', since the vehemence is a representation of Lear's deeper character:

'Tis hasty, rash, and uttered in the Whirlwind of his Passion;—too long a Preparation for it seems not consistent with *Lear*'s Character: 'Tis here un-natural. Such long Pauses give him Time to reflect, which the hasty *Lear* is not apt to do, 'till 'tis too late.—This philosophic Manner would become a Man who took Time to recollect; which if *Lear* did, would not the good King, the o'er-kind Father, change this dire Curse into a fervent Prayer for his Child's Repentance and Amendment?

Hugh Kelly also felt that Garrick's 'pauses at the conclusion of his lines are so improper and injudicious that nothing but the high opinion of the town could possibly excuse such an error in *his* performance, as they must absolutely condemn in anybody else', and he gives an example of an unnatural pause and stress in a line from *Richard III*, which Garrick used in order to 'roar out' the line (a trait that Cibber also observed). The fourth of these observers was also the most thorough, and Thady Fitzpatrick's list of examples from Garrick's Hamlet[29] and Richard III of pauses and stresses quite against the flow of the sense (No. 185: he lists twenty for each play) document beyond dispute the counterpart in speech to Garrick's excessive emphases in gesture.

As I have remarked earlier, Garrick seemed to excite either panegyric or denigration, and the truth about his Shakespeare interpretation must lie somewhere between those two extremes. This collection will reprint more accounts of Garrick's Shakespeare than have ever been assembled, and ultimately every reader will be in the position to judge for himself where the emphasis should be laid. But it will not do to ignore the criticisms, or to cast his critics as villains or personal enemies releasing their malice by inventing fantasies about him. The critical evaluations may not be the whole truth, yet what we know of the taste of the mid-eighteenth-century London theatre audience hardly encourages us to rate their judgment and discrimination highly. Such a cogent account as that by Theophilus Cibber, which manifests a much more enlightened sense of the integrity of Shakespeare's text and a balanced theatrical interpretation of it than any of Garrick's panegyrists known to me, cannot be written off as the effusion of envy or spleen. If we are to gain an accurate picture of Garrick's dominance as an interpreter of Shakespeare in his three roles as impresario, adapter, and actor, we must weigh all the evidence.

The other theatrical criticism represented here, dealing with Barry as Lear (Nos 156, 157, 170) and the Othellos of Barry (No. 161j) and Barton Booth (No. 188), is less controversial, and illuminates a more traditional actor's approach to the major roles. Yet even here Garrick is in the picture. Theophilus Cibber's 1753 *Life of Barton Booth* includes an account of his Othello which seems an implicit criticism of Garrick's emotionalism (compare the very similar language of his 1756 'Dissertation', No. 157 below):[30]

In *Othello* the heart-breaking anguish of his Jealousy would have drawn Tears from the most obdurate; yet all his Grief, though most feelingly expressed, was never beneath the Hero. When he wept, his Tears broke from him perforce:—He never whindled, whined, or blubbered. In his Rage he never mouthed or ranted.

In recording his appreciation of Booth's Lear, however, Cibber focused on the man himself:

Mr. *Booth*'s general Deportment was Majestic, yet he used no more of that Stateliness than became the Character, and he had the Art of diversifying his Tragic Characters in a most masterly Manner.—His Madness in *Lear* is hardly to be described:—He there shewed the throws and Swellings of the Heart of an unhappy, proud, disappointed Monarch with an Enthusiasm of Passion which elated him;—shook off a while the Infirmity of Age, and expanded his whole frame. He then displayed the Furor of Majesty—and when crowned with Poppies, &c., the Monarch, jealous of his Power, seemed to rise above himself, took more majestic State in his Distress—assumed the God, and grasped his Scepter of Straw like the Thunder-bolt of a *Jupiter Tonans*. Never did Pity or Terror more vehemently possess an Audience than by his judicious and powerful Execution in this Part. (*Ibid.*, pp. 52–3)

It is notoriously difficult to give an adequate verbal record of the totality of an actor's performance, yet I hope the attempts included here will at least illuminate how mid-eighteenth-century critics thought that Shakespeare ought to be interpreted. Their work has more than historical value, however: it will soon be apparent that in the work of such men as Cibber, Arthur Murphy and Hugh Kelly theatrical criticism in this period shows an intelligence and concern for dramatic values far above anything we have yet seen. Would that our own were always of such quality.

IV

In literary criticism we note a partial step forward. This is not to be located at the level of critical method, however, for we find as yet little or no analysis of Shakespeare's plays as dramatic structures. In discussing *King Lear*, for instance, it is thought sufficient to work through the play, quoting only Lear's speeches. Joseph Warton does so to prove that Lear's madness is due to the loss of his royalty (No. 139), Arthur Murphy does so to argue that it is caused by his daughters' ingratitude (No. 140), Mrs Lennox does so to point up Lear's faults of character (No. 141). All three are making different points, but all three merely illustrate one role. No one in this period gives an adequate account of the interplay between characters, or the structure and dynamics of a whole scene.

Indeed, in their awareness of form and meaning in the plots of Shakespeare's plays the critics of this period are less perceptive than their predecessors. The Neo-classic preference for a single plot and an obviously moralised unified design not only resulted in the rejection of several plays as having 'no plot', but it also blinded critics to the significance of meaningful plot-parallelism. Thus Mrs Lennox complained that as Laertes is 'a subordinate character' in *Hamlet*

it seems to be a fault in *Shakespeare* to shew him with a Similitude of Manners, under the same Circumstances, and acting upon the same Principles as *Hamlet*, his Hero. . . . This Sameness of Character, and Parity of Circumstances with the Hero, lessens his Importance, and almost divides our Attention and Concern between them.

That otherwise perceptive critic, Benjamin Heath, complained that Shakespeare had 'violated' the Unity of Action in *The Tempest* 'by the introduction of those episodick scenes of Trinculo, Stephano and Caliban, which may be all struck out without the least injury or inconvenience to the main action' (No. 203). It was clearly with such an unawareness of plot-parallelism that Colman and Garrick shuffled around the various levels of action in *A Midsummer Night's Dream*. Some critics even confused the adaptation and the original: the *Universal Museum* reviewer said that *The Winter's Tale* had a 'plot . . . indifferently contrived', apparently unaware that he was seeing Garrick's mutilation of it (he did note that Hermione's part 'is so very short . . . she hardly speaks ten words'). Arthur Murphy (No. 161h) complained that the plot of *Measure for Measure* was overcrowded with incidents and with 'episodical' characters (that is, characters who supposedly do not contribute to the main design), and Dr Johnson (inspired, regrettably, by Mrs Lennox) stated that Shakespeare had followed his authors so unimaginatively that 'he often combines circumstances unnecessary to his main design, only because he happened to find them together. Such passages can be illustrated only by him who has read the same story in the very book which SHAKESPEARE consulted' (No. 160). Murphy's correspondent, Thomas Fitzpatrick, was one of the few readers to see the significant duplication of experience in *King Lear*: '*this same folly of parents* is also touched with great judgment in the underplot of *Glo'ster*. The characters of *Lear*'s two daughters are finely contrasted with those of *Cordelia* and *Edgar*' (No. 140d). In reply Murphy rather grudgingly conceded that the episode 'in which the *bastard* acts the same unnatural part as *Lear*'s legitimate daughters is not entirely detached from the main subject' (No. 140e). One other exception to the general lack of insight into Shakespeare's dramatic structure is George Colman, who ended a discussion of the source for *The Merchant of Venice* with this paragraph:[31]

I cannot conclude without remarking with what art and judgment *Shakespeare* has wove together these different stories of the *Jew* and the *Caskets*; from both of which he has formed one general fable, without having recourse to the stale artifice of eking out a barren subject with impertinent underplots.

If the critics of this period disappoint in their understanding of dramatic form, they exceed expectations in their response to Shakespeare's language and poetry. The same generosity which excused his faults in the 'petty' areas of the Unities is found in a warm response to the 'profusion' or 'impetuosity' of Shakespeare's poetry, which is said to blot out any thought of 'correctness'. Thus Burke in 1759:[32]

There are also many descriptions in the poets and orators which owe their sublimity to a richness and profusion of images, in which the mind is so dazzled as to make it impossible to attend to that exact coherence and agreement of the allusions, which we should require on every other occasion. I do not now remember a more striking example of this than the description which is given of the king's army in the play of *Henry the fourth*:

> All furnished, all in arms ... [1 Henry IV, 4.1.97ff.]

Similarly Benjamin Heath in 1765, pointing to Shakespeare's deliberate use of the figure *anacolouthon* (breaking off the sense) preferred 'the impetuosity of the poet's genius' to 'the timid regularity' of his editors, who correct what they take to be faults (No. 203). Attacking an unimaginative correction by Warburton, Heath praised 'Shakespeare's English, the energy of whose language not unfrequently soars . . . beyond the comprehension of the verbal critick'. Another pronouncement by Warburton which Heath rejects is that editor's astonishing claim that Shakespeare 'entirely neglected the metre of his verse', a judgment shared by many eighteenth-century commentators. Heath replies that Shakespeare has not 'confined himself, like our modern tragick poets, to metre of one kind only. His is very various, and of very different kinds, but it is in general regular', and where there are incomplete verses they 'ought to be regarded with the same indulgence as the hemistichs of Virgil'.

The issue of correctness is more important than it might seem, for while Shakespeare was thought of as an untutored natural genius, warbling his wood-notes wild without knowledge of the conventions of grammar, syntax and metrics, there was no incentive to examine his language any more closely for what it was in itself. External Neo-classic criteria of correctness were swiftly applied, it was declared irregular, and either relegated to the 'Faults' table or regarded as free game for editorial alteration. The first step towards justifying Shakespeare's language as a system in its own right, with its own consistent rules and procedures, was made by John Upton in 1746 (No. 114 in Vol. 3), who provided an outline of Shakespeare's characteristic uses of grammar syntax and metrics. In the period considered here, that approach was continued (albeit without acknowledgment) by Richard Hurd (No. 162a), who listed eleven ways in which Shakespeare innovated in vocabulary, including the formation of compound epithets ('armgaunt steed'), compound verbs ('discandy, dislimn'), the conversion of adjectives, verbs and participles into substantives, and so on. Hurd singles out Shakespeare's ability to apply *figurative terms* . . . , those innumerable terms in Shakespeare which surprize us by their novelty; and which surprize us generally on account of his preferring the *specific* idea to the *general* in the *subjects* of his Metaphors', as in the lines

> This common Body
> Like to a vagabond flag, upon the stream,
> Goes to, and back, *lacquying* the varying tide.

In defining some characteristics in Shakespeare's style it is significant that Hurd takes many of his examples from the late plays—*Cymbeline*,

33

Antony and Cleopatra, Coriolanus—where Shakespeare is at his most inventive and idiosyncratic.

The direction of Hurd's work is analytical, but it clearly implies that these innovations in Shakespeare are systematic, not random, and this attitude is not inconsistent with a new image of Shakespeare as a writer who worked according to art. It was that pioneer John Upton, again, who in 1746 had first stressed that Shakespeare's verse was the product of 'art', that is, of a system of rules and conventions governing prosody, and by a detailed (if rambling) analysis Upton tried 'to do justice to Shakespeare as an artist in dramatic poetry' (Vol. 3, pp. 317ff.). Apart from his influence on Hurd, the analytical method of Upton is seen at about the same time in Richard Roderick's important discussion of the irregular verse in *Henry VIII* (No. 169). Roderick noticed something 'peculiar' about 'the measure' in this play: there are more verses ending 'with a redundant syllable' (that is, lines of eleven syllables) than in any other play by Shakespeare; further, in many of these lines the caesura comes at the seventh rather than the fifth or sixth, syllable; and, stranger still, 'the emphasis arising from the sense of the verse very often clashes with the cadence that would naturally result from the metre'. Roderick gives well-chosen examples of 'all these peculiarities', and concludes that they 'were done by [Shakespeare] advertently, and not by chance'. The further significance for contemporary criticism, as he immediately sees, is that 'if then Shakespeare appears to have been careful about measure, what becomes of that heap of emendations founded upon the presumption of his being either unknowing or unsollicitous about it?' Roderick's pioneering analyses are in effect the first attempt to define the style of a single play. His findings can of course be related to the development of Shakespeare's verse over-all, or to the distinguishing of authentic Shakespearian verse from that of a collaborator in the writing of the play, two approaches which Victorian critics were to pursue with a great rash of statistics. The importance of Roderick's findings for this period, however, lies rather in their demonstration of the existence of Shakespeare's 'design'.

This new awareness of Shakespeare's deliberate art in metre and versification is seen in various ways. The compiler of a new 'Poetical Scale' in 1758 (No. 167) gives Shakespeare the maximum points for versification (in the 1746 version by Mark Akenside, No. 106 in Vol. 3, he received only ten out of a possible eighteen), and he now shares first place among the English poets, with Pope. In the same year John Armstrong praised Shakespeare for having 'the most musical ear of all the *English* poets', and defended his irregularities on the grounds that they 'give his verse a spirit and variety which prevents its ever cloying' (No. 164). Four years later Daniel Webb, in his *Beauties of Poetry* (No. 195) produced the first detailed appreciation of Shakespeare's verse, basing his whole argument on the view that Shakespeare worked not by accident but by design, for as the poet 'has time to select his images and sentiments, so he has likewise to accommodate the movement of his numbers to the nature of those ideas he means to express'. Webb explicitly rejects 'the common notions concerning Shakespeare', that he composed great poetry by accident, or was merely the 'instrument of nature' (Pope's earlier Neo-classic explanation is thus refuted). That his verse appears the work of nature is due to the great art that has gone into its shaping:

The beauties of Shakespeare's versification appear accidental when they are most artificial: for the mechanism of his verse, however carefully formed to have this effect, is so fashioned to the temper of the speaker and nature of the subject that we overlook the artifice, and it passes along unheeded, as the casual flow of an unstudied eloquence.

Having established Shakespeare's deliberate artistry, Webb is free to go on and analyse its workings. In doing so he has two main categories. The first is 'sentimental harmony', by which he means the agreement between the meaning of the verse, its sound, and its movement. Although not all of his examples are convincing (he seems to have misjudged the tone of Othello's 'Farewell the plumed troops' speech when he describes it as 'a languid monotony'[33]) the argument is performed with confidence and skill. The second category is imagery, under which Webb expects to judge the merit of a comparison or simile 'by the degree of our surprize, which arises from a combined admiration of its justness, its novelty, and beauty', while the purpose of metaphor 'is either to illustrate or aggrandize our ideas'. There are times when we could wish Webb to have been more clear-cut in his terminology (as with such concepts as the Sublime, the Beautiful, the Pathetic), but this enthusiastic and generously illustrated account is a significant step forward in the understanding of Shakespeare's imaginative art.

An equally long discussion of Shakespeare's style, just as fully illustrated (indeed it contained so many quotations that it was in effect a Shakespeare anthology, to which feature it may have owed much of its popularity[34]), appeared in the same year as Webb's essay, Lord Kames's *Elements of Criticism* (No. 193). Of all the eighteenth-century works in the 'Beauties and Faults' mode, this is the most thorough. Kames was writing a theoretical system, giving prescriptions of what, for him, constituted good or bad writing, and at every turn he illustrated his argument from Shakespeare. The result is a curious mixture of persisting Neo-classic taste with some personal and original aspects. Kames was especially bothered by Shakespeare's word-play, even though in addition to the historical argument (punning was the 'taste of the age') he formulated a theory of verbal play which is by no means despicable. Yet although he dismissed playing on words as a 'bastard wit', 'low and childish', and playing with 'the sound of words' as 'the meanest of all conceits', he still had enough independence to see that Shakespeare can use punning 'to denote a peculiar character', such as the Bastard in *King John*. He praised Shakespeare as being 'superior to all other writers in delineating passion', and held up his soliloquies as models of the spontaneous expression of emotion. He also (like Hurd) praised Shakespeare for avoiding generalities and abstractions ('every article in descriptions is particular'), but when he got down to a detailed discussion of simile and metaphor he found more to blame in Shakespeare than to praise. The fallacies in his theories that metaphor is not to be used to depict 'a man in his ordinary state of mind', and that similes are not to be used to express 'grief, deep anguish, terror, remorse, despair, and all the severe dispiriting passions', will be evident to all modern readers (and were to some of his contemporaries).[35] Yet whenever we feel tempted to dismiss Kames he can surprise by his cogency, as in the discussion of the Unities, or the truly original insight into the 'rule' which Shakespeare has followed, 'to intermix prose with verse, and only to employ the latter where it is required by the importance or dignity of the subject'. It was to be a long time before critics rediscovered that point.

Kames, with his mixture of original and inherited attitudes, is typical of the discussion of Shakespeare's language in this period. His contempt for rhyme, for instance, ('unnatural and disgustful in dialogue'), is shared by George Colman (No. 187)—both rejoice that it has been 'banished from our theatre', Colman seeing it as 'a Gothick practice' still found in France but which England rejected 'long ago' (as recently as midway through Dryden's career, in fact). Neither of them discusses Shakespeare's use of rhyme, and had they done so we might expect them to have expressed something of the distaste of David Hume:[36]

Sir John Denham in his *Cooper's Hill* (for none of his other poems merit attention) has a loftiness and vigour, which had not before him been attained by any

English poet who wrote in rhyme. The mechanical difficulties of that measure retarded its improvement. Shakespeare, whose tragic scenes are sometimes so wonderfully forcible and expressive, is a very indifferent poet when he attempts to rhyme.

A similarly cool disapproval can be found in the lectures of Adam Smith, guarding his students 'against using epithets that are contradictory or not applicable to the object', a fault that Shakespeare is guilty of 'almost continually'. Nor, Smith laid down, should 'two metaphors' ever 'be run and mixed together, as in that case they can never be just. Shakespeare is often guilty of this fault'.[37]

To set against these chilling orthodoxies, we have not only the work of Roderick, Hurd, Webb and Kames, but also some perceptive observations by Arthur Murphy in his *London Chronicle* reviews. Murphy observed (perhaps silently criticising Garrick) that the soliloquies of Richard III 'are mostly Situations of dark, cool, and deliberate Wickedness, and should be uttered with deep and grave Tones of Voice, and a gloomy Countenance'. The peculiar feature of Richard's humour is that his 'Pleasantry never rises to Mirth' but is ever 'a mixed Emotion of Joy and Malice', a humour which never 'takes off the Mask'. Thus in his wooing of Anne his dissimulation utters 'Words . . . [that] come from him like Flakes of feathered Snow, that melted as they fell' (No. 161b). This sensitivity to language in its dramatic context is shown again in Murphy's comments on *Macbeth*, where he is one of the very few eighteenth-century critics to see the way Shakespeare's language is affected by, recreates, his subject-matter:

The Stile of *Macbeth* is indeed peculiar, abounding in Words infrequent in their Use, but remarkably strong and picturesque. The Language takes a Tincture from the Subject, which being dark and gloomy, it thence follows that the Poet's Choice of Words, and their Arrangement, are calculated to fill the Mind with Imagery of the most solemn and awful Aspect. In Consequence of this the Writing of *Macbeth* is distinguished from the Poet's general Stile.

Here Murphy perceives the individual stylistic unity of a play (as did Roderick with *Henry VIII*). Perhaps even more striking is his sensitivity to the individual style of Othello in the third Act, when jealousies 'burst out into an amazing Wildness of Rage. . . . The Extravagance of all his Ideas, and of the Emotions attendant on them, is perfectly characteristic. . . . The whole is vented with the impetuous Ferocity natural to one of Othello's Complexion, still improved with the wildest Harmony of Voice.' Murphy is writing in part about Barry's performance, but in his characterisation of Othello's language as an 'Extravagance' of ideas and emotions he looks a long way forward, to Wilson Knight's essay on 'The Music of Othello'.

V

Turning finally to the state of Shakespeare scholarship in this period, we can observe much less forward movement than in the best of the literary or theatrical criticism. The concept of historical scholarship itself—the need to reconstruct the vocabulary, taste, ideas and attitudes of a period as the prerequisite for evaluating the literary works produced in that period—was generally accepted (there were, at any rate, no opponents of it). The most convincing formulation of it was given, as one might have expected, by Dr Johnson, in his description of the edition of Shakespeare that he was planning:

When a writer outlives his contemporaries, and remains almost the only un-forgotten name of a distant time, he is necessarily obscure. Every age has its modes of speech, and its cast of thought; which, though easily explained when there are many books to be compared with each other, becomes sometimes un-intelligible, and always difficult, when there are no parallel passages that may conduce to their illustration. . . .

It is the great excellence of SHAKESPEARE, that he drew his scenes from nature, and from life. He copied the manners of the world then passing before him, and has more allusions than other poets to the traditions and superstition of the vulgar; which must therefore be traced before he can be understood (No. 160).

Johnson writes from the standpoint of an editor, who is concerned with elucidating rather than evaluating. Other writers in this period took up the question of judgment and endorsed the point already made by Dryden, Gildon, Rowe, Shaftesbury, Addison, Dennis and others (see Vol. 2, pp. 8–9), that if Shakespeare worked according to other principles then we ought not to judge him by ours. This argument, used mostly to excuse his punning, is found in works by Murphy (Nos 140, 161a), Grey (No. 142), 'K.L.' (No. 197), and Lyttelton (No. 181), while Hume gives it full expression as part of a larger account of literary 'decadence', comparing the late Renaissance with the (traditionally conceived) decline of Attic style into Asiatic (No. 145). This interesting essay in the periodisation of literary taste results in a judgment of Shakespeare which, unlike the other apologias for the 'taste of the age', refuses to grant him total amnesty. (Hume is nearer to the tone and attitudes of French Neo-classicism than any other critic in this period.) Finally, Bishop Percy translated the general point into a specific plea for a genre which appeared long after the tenets of Aristotle and Horace, the English History play (No. 201).[38]

The concept of historical scholarship was widely accepted, then. Yet it was accepted in theory only: the corollary, that one ought systematically to reconstruct the taste of the previous age, was a project which had been vigorously pursued by Theobald in his edition (No. 82 in Vol. 2) and which Dr Johnson was furthering at the level of vocabulary in his great work on the *Dictionary*. Otherwise, though, no one attempted to reconstruct the Renaissance's dramatic theory, its concept of language and style (there is a significant drop in the awareness of Shakespeare's use of rhetoric in this period compared to the preceding ones), Elizabethan dramatic conventions, or any of several other important topics. Nor does anyone try to solve the controversial problem of Shakespeare's knowledge of classical literature by investigating the curriculum of the Elizabethan grammar-school. Indeed the discussion of Shakespeare's learning in the 1750s and 1760s added little to the traditional picture. Edward Young follows an old *topos* (see Vol. 1, p. 13) in claiming that Shakespeare's ignorance of the classics guaranteed his originality (No. 179), but the majority of critics claim that Shakespeare knew the classics well, without, however, being able to show how this came about. Daniel Webb asserts (not unfairly, too) that Shakespeare's 'classical images are composed of the finest parts, and breathe the very spirit of the antient Mythology' (No. 195), and Zachary Grey casts his vote on this side, if rather perfunctorily (No. 142). The fullest theoretical discussion comes from Richard Hurd, part of an attempt to formulate a general theory of imitation in literature (No. 162b) and, although there are some sensible arguments on both sides of the issue, Hurd does not have a good enough knowledge of the Elizabethan period to enter into details convincingly (he is quite wrong about the chronology of Jonson's masques, for instance, most of which date after Shakespeare's career was over, and from which he could have learned nothing). Similarly, the only extended list of parallel passages, that by Christopher Smart (No. 149), is a mixed bag of which some are likely (Virgil on bees, for instance, which was a well-known text to the Elizabethans), others not (the instances from Homer and Propertius). Modern scholarship would, in fact, endorse Smart's claim that Shakespeare was 'a good scholar' but not an accurate one, yet the whole problem of the cultural context of the Elizabethan grammar-school, the modes in which the Renaissance transmitted the classics, was yet to be raised.

In the field of editing and textual scholarship there was again no great development. The major figure in these discussions continues to be William Warburton, the absurdities of whose edition (No. 111 in Vol. 3) are by now fully documented. Much of the reaction against Warburton was coarsely polemical, not revealing anything new about Shakespeare, and I have not included such pieces. The great exposure of Warburton had been Thomas Edwards's *The Canons of Criticism, and Glossary* (No. 127 in Vol. 3), first published in 1748 and reaching its sixth edition by 1758, some of the new material from which is included here (No. 168). Edwards shows the absurd contradictions in Warburton's estimates of Shakespeare's character—a curiously thoughtless arrogance, pontificating on without remembering that it had pontificated the opposite view just before—and adds further instances of Warburton's irresponsible practice of misrepresenting or corrupting Shakespeare in order to emend him. What was so astonishing about Warburton was his perverse failure to understand even the simplest passages, and his contemporaries pointed this out while applauding Edwards. Theophilus Cibber, defending his father (Colley Cibber) against the attacks of Warburton and Pope, recommended to his readers *The Canons of Criticism*, 'in the Perusal of which they'll be agreeably entertained and instructed, and find more Justice done to *Shakespeare* in a few Pages than *Warburton* has been able (or he was unmercifully or strangely unwilling) to bestow on him through all that motley Work which he modestly stiles a Compleat Edition of that inimitable Poet'.[39] The reaction to Warburton is important not only because it demonstrates an increasingly enlightened conception of textual criticism but also because, in answering him, critics were in fact engaged in the process of restoring Shakespeare's text. In the exuberant language of Cibber, Thomas Edwards's learning 'is demonstrable in his Remarks, where (like the good *Samaritan*) he heals the deadly Wounds the Poet suffered under the Claws of this unmerciful Editor, who, Tinker-like, makes many Holes for one he mends' (*op cit.*, p. liii).

The two original essays in textual criticism in our period are both very substantial, but vary greatly in quality: from Zachary Grey (740 pages) I fear that I have included too much, and from Benjamin Heath (573 pages) I have perhaps not given enough. Grey (No. 142), an industrious editor of *Hudibras*, had read widely in Jacobean and Caroline drama (the dramatists he quotes from include Jasper Mayne, Brome,

Shirley, Quarles, Massinger, Cartwright, Randolph) but he had no gift for apt illustration, and no sense of the textual principles involved. Among this mass of isolated and sporadic suggestions, the best come from friends who contributed notes, although even these lack intelligence (as with the anonymous writer who rightly observes that Shakespeare gives Caliban verse in scenes otherwise in prose,[40] but then treats all that Caliban says in terms of a rigid pentameter line). Grey deserves some credit for finding a parallel source of *As You Like It*, but otherwise we must concur with the verdict of the *Monthly Review* for July, 1754, which could find little to praise in the book (xi, p. 80).

Benjamin Heath (No. 203), by contrast, is full of intelligent observations on many aspects of Shakespeare. Working in the tradition of Theobald, Upton, and Edwards, he urges that the editor's task is to understand the text before he emends it, and to restore the original reading whether or not it offends his critical sensibilities. I have already quoted Heath's defence of the energies of Shakespeare's language, his reinstatement of Shakespeare's artistry in verse, and his cogent attack on the Unities. He shows comparable good sense and independence in his challenge to the received idea (dating from before Dryden) of Caliban's language being 'antique' and 'savage', and in his exposure of Warburton's *idée fixe* that metaphors should have an 'integrity' which Shakespeare's often lack.[41] In commenting directly on Shakespeare he is the first writer to express disgust at the betrayal of the rebels in *2 Henry IV*, and sees that our shock at this event must lower our liking for Prince John (he might have gone on to consider that Shakespeare may have intended this abreaction). He observes acutely that Lear recognises his folly yet is unable to sustain the recognition and takes refuge in fantasy, and that Lear is too involved in his own grievances to be capable of irony; and he has some perceptive notes on *Macbeth*. Some weaknesses of his book were pointed out by the reviewers,[42] yet Dr Johnson thought highly enough of it to borrow a number of notes from it, some of them silently.[43]

Heath was a commentator on Shakespeare, rather than an editor of him. On the fly-leaf of his copy of Heath's *Revisal* (now in the Folger Shakespeare Library) Dr Johnson made the following judgment on the commentators, a judgment that must be taken to include Heath although Johnson (oddly enough, to my mind) writes the name of Grey:[44]

Such critics of Shakespeare as Theobald and Grey perceive matters that eluded Pope and Warburton. This phenomenon is only to be explained by the fact that we editors have attempted to restore, that is, to emend the text instead of explain it.

Johnson had published his notes on *Macbeth* in 1745 (No. 105 in Vol. 3), as a specimen of a proposed new edition of Shakespeare 'with Notes Critical and Explanatory',[45] and in 1756 issued a more detailed set of proposals for his own edition (No. 160). In this magisterial document Johnson surveys, first, the causes of the corruption of Shakespeare's text. Following the work of Theobald and others inspired by Pope's slander on the actors in his edition (see, in Vol. 2, Nos 71, 77, 78, 82), he gives a coherent account of the factors which affected the textual transmission of play-texts, a sequence (paragraphs 3 and 4) in which his wonderfully inventive prose even exaggerates the misfortunes endured by Shakespeare's text. But one is impressed still by Johnson's grasp of the whole situation, as too by his remedies for it:

The corruptions of the text will be corrected by a carefull collation of the oldest copies, by which it is hoped that many restorations may yet be made: at least it will be necessary to collect and note the variations as materials for future crickts, for it very often happens that a wrong reading has affinity to the right.

Johnson therefore promises to list all variants from 'all the copies that can be found', so that the reader will have at hand all the materials from which to select.[46] Emendation, Johnson promises, will only be indulged in when it proves impossible to decipher the original text or to explain the received ones.

Johnson's grasp of the whole rationale of editing, although it does not add anything to the methods already practised with such success by Lewis Theobald, is impressive for the cogency and solidity with which it is formulated. Equally impressive is his proposal to elucidate Shakespeare's language and allusions by reading 'the books which the authour read', by tracing 'his knowledge to its source', and by comparing 'his copies with their originals'. Here again Johnson restates in theory the principles already put into operation by Theobald, and it is disappointing to find here the first of Johnson's many disparaging remarks about that editor, who is said to have 'considered learning only as an instrument of gain' and to have regarded annotation of Shakespeare as a form of decoration of the page. As for Johnson's project for illustrating Shakespeare's 'obsolete or peculiar diction', he writes with justifiable self-authorisation as 'having had more motives to consider the whole extent of our language than any other man from its first formation', and his plan to elucidate Shakespeare by establishing Elizabethan usage (as

Theobald had done) is obviously sound. We can only support, too, his decision not to follow Pope, Hanmer and Warburton in singling out 'beauties' in the text with asterisks and in rejecting 'faults' to the foot of the page. Johnson ends with the admirable statement that he

does not however intend to preclude himself from the comparison of SHAKE-SPEARE's sentiments or expression with those of ancient or modern authors, or from the display of any beauty not obvious to the students of poetry; for as he hopes to leave his authour better understood, he wishes likewise to procure him more rational approbation.

The formulation of what needed to be done was so masterly that it is no wonder that Johnson's contemporaries were impressed, and awaited publication-date so impatiently. In the next volume of this series readers will be able to judge for themselves the extent to which Johnson made good his contract.

NOTES

1 See *Shakespeare: The Critical Heritage*, Vol. 3, pp. 2ff.
2 *Gibbon's Autobiography*, ed. M. M. Reese (London, 1971), p. 54.
3 *The Works of Virgil, in Latin and English*, 4 vols (1753), IV, p. 420.
4 Rogers, 'An ars naturâ sit perfectior', in *St James's Magazine*, ii (March 1763), p. 63. Stanza 1 was also quoted from Rogers's *Poems on Several Occasions* when that volume was reviewed in *Critical Review* xviii (1764), p. 381.
5 Burke, *A Philosophical Enquiry into the Origin of our Ideas of the Sublime and Beautiful*, second edition, 1759, pp. 25–6; 'Introduction: On Taste'.
6 As W. K. Wimsatt has observed, 'the first half of this curiously balanced or self-cancelling critical document argues that the most important thing to know about an author is the degree of originality in his plot. The second half assures us that Shakespeare's merits are of a different order': Wimsatt, ed., *Samuel Johnson on Shakespeare* (Harmondsworth, 1961) p. xviii n. The Preface is reprinted in Arthur Sherbo (ed.), *Johnson on Shakespeare* (New Haven, 1968), VII, pp. 47ff.: I have not thought it worth including, since Johnson repeats the more valuable points in the preface to his edition of 1765 (see Vol. 5, No. 205).
7 *Monthly Review* ix, p. 145 (August 1753) and x, p. 309 (April 1754). Even John Nichols, no enemy of Shakespeare, could record that Mrs Lennox was 'a lady of considerable genius, and who was long distinguished for her literary merit', and accepted the claims of her book: *Literary Anecdotes of the Eighteenth Century*, 6 vols (London, 1812), III, pp. 200f. Identification of contributors to the *Monthly Review* derives from the set of that journal

annotated by the editor Ralph Griffiths, now in the Bodleian, and meticulously edited by Benjamin C. Nangle, *The Monthly Review. First Series, 1749–1789. Indexes of Contributors and Articles* (Oxford, 1934).

8 Cited in T. C. Duncan Eaves and Ben D. Kimpel, *Samuel Richardson. A Biography* (Oxford, 1971), p. 573.

9 The leading authority on the Goldsmith canon, Arthur Friedman (editor of the Clarendon Press edition of his *Works*, 5 vols, 1966) has convincingly ascribed to Goldsmith a review of *The Works of Massinger* in the *Critical Review* for July, 1759, which describes Shakespeare as 'a man whose beauties seem rather the result of chance than design; who, while he laboured to satisfy his audience with monsters and mummery, seemed to throw in his inimitable beauties as trifles into the bargain', and invokes the historical argument rather cuttingly: 'Nothing less than a genius like Shakespeare's could make plays wrote to the taste of those times, pleasing now' (viii, pp. 86–7). See Friedman, 'Goldsmith's Contributions to the *Critical Review*', *Modern Philology* 44 (1946), pp. 23–52, at p. 30. These remarks, similar in tone to those in the *Enquiry*, put Goldsmith close to Hume on the side of those critics who judge Shakespeare by more severe standards, though neither is as disapproving as Smollett.

10 Smollett's authorship of the *Critical Review* piece on Warton (No. 159) was established by the identification list of contributors to the first two volumes of that journal recently discovered in the University of Oregon library by Mr R. M. McCollough: see Derek Roper, 'Smollett's "Four Gentlemen": the first contributors to the *Critical Review*', *Review of English Studies* n.s. 10 (1959), pp. 38–44. (These annotated copies also identify Smollett as the author of the review of Marsh's adaptation of *The Winter's Tale* in March 1756 (No. 154a), with its qualified approval of Marsh's only partial success in removing the 'absurdity' of an anachronism, the 'improbability' of the fifteen-year period of the original play, and its lack of 'propriety' in mingling tragedy and comedy.) Strong internal resemblances between the Warton piece and the *British Magazine* articles (No. 196) led me to conclude that they were by the same hand, and I was encouraged to find that this ascription had been made independently, before the discovery of the annotated *Critical Review* file, by Caroline F. Tupper, 'Essays Erroneously Attributed to Goldsmith', *PMLA* 39 (1924), pp. 325–42, at pp. 338ff. Miss Tupper showed that the section on versification in the *British Magazine* series repeated passages from a review of John Armstrong's *Sketches* in the *Critical Review* for May, 1758 (v, p. 300). Armstrong was one of the four founding contributors to the *Critical Review*, under Smollett's editorship, from 1756 on, and it seems certain that Smollett was the author of this review. Smollett was also, of course, editor of the *British Magazine* from 1760 to 1763, and published *The Adventures of Sir Launcelot Greaves* in it between January 1760 and December 1761: with such a busy journalistic career it is hardly surprising that he plagiarised himself. One other parallel between the *British*

Magazine articles and Smollett's other work was noted by Miss Tupper (p. 341), echoing also the attack on the 'broken, incongruous metaphors' of Hamlet's soliloquy in No. 159. In reviewing Voltaire's translation of 'To be, or not to be', Smollett criticised its accuracy, yet concluded: 'It must be owned, however, that M. de Voltaire has avoided the confusion of metaphors which is to be found in Shakespeare'. *The Works of M. de Voltaire. Translated from the French with Notes Historical and Critical* (1762), xiii, p. 137.

11 The defence of Coriolanus's simile for Valeria (pp. 503f. below) was repeated in the *Critical Review* xiii (1762), reviewing Kames: 'This comparison of Shakespeare, which hath been admired by some other critics, is specified by his lordship as an instance of bastard wit, but we think with too much rigour . . .' (p. 368). In an earlier instalment of this notice, the reviewer had written that 'Shakespeare may be thought to seek the occasion to put a fine speech in the mouth of a principal character, of which *Hamlet* affords a notorious instance' (p. 297), thus suggesting that Smollett was the author of this review as well as items 159 and 196.

12 *Boswell's London Journal, 1762–3* ed. F. A Pottle (London, 1950), pp 234–5.

13 See, e.g., Vol. 2, p. 6 (Gildon, Theobald, Dennis); Vol. 3, p. 296 (Upton).

14 Quoted by R. G. Noyes, *The Thespian Mirror*, pp. 20f.

15 Smith, *Lectures on Rhetoric and Belles Lettres*, ed. J. M. Lothian (London, 1963), p. 118.

16 *Critical Review* xix (1765), p. 469, discussing the second edition of *The Castle of Otranto*.

17 *Horace Walpole's Correspondence*, ed. W. S. Lewis *et al.*, vol. 35, p. 262; ed. P. Toynbee, vol. 3, p. 375; letter to Richard Bentley, 17 December 1755.

18 C. E. Jones, *Smollett Studies* (Berkeley and Los Angeles, 1942), p. 89, and 'Contributors to the *Critical Review*, 1756–1785', *Modern Language Notes* 61 (1946), pp. 433–41, at p. 440.

19 Odell, *Shakespeare from Betterton to Irving* (New York, 1920, 1966), I, p. 371. One spectator wrote a letter to the newspapers to express his approval: 'The Revival of *Cymbeline* at *Drury-Lane* Theatre, in which there are very few alterations, except the necessary Omissions, does Honour to the Taste and Judgement of the Manager, as it plainly shews, as well as in the Instance of *Romeo and Juliet*, that *Shakespeare* only wants to have his Excrescences pared away without adding the Patchwork of other Hands. The last scene of *Romeo and Juliet* is, indeed, an Exception, which I am not so willing to allow in the Case of the last Scene of *Lear*.' The correspondent (who signs himself 'B.T.') complains, however, that this production uses Warburton's text at one point, changing 'O disloyal Thing,/That should'st repair my Youth, thou heap'st/ A *Year's* Age on me' (1.1.131) into 'A *Yare* Age, i.e. sudden, precipitate old Age'. To 'render the Sense easy and conspicuous', the correspondent suggests, we should read 'heapest *many*/ A Year's Age on me'. Letter in *London Spy, and Read's Weekly Journal*, 12 December 1761, pp. 169–70.

20 Vol. VII, p. 377. Horace Walpole was also offended by *Cymbeline*, writing to Montagu on 8 December 1761: 'To change the dullness of the scene, I went t'other night to the play, where I had not been this winter. They are so crowded, that though I went before six I got no better place than a fifth row, where I heard very ill, and was pent for five hours without a soul near me that I knew. It was *Cymbeline*, and appeared to me as long as if everybody in it went really to Italy in every act, and came back again. With a few pretty passages and a scene or [two,] it is so absurd and tiresome, that I am persuaded Garrick . . . [rest missing]' (*Horace Walpole's Correspondence*, ed. W. S. Lewis *et al.*, I, p. 408).

21 See G. W. Stone, Jr, 'Garrick's Production of *King Lear*: A Study in the Temper of the Eighteenth-Century Mind', *Studies in Philology* 45 (1948), pp. 89–103. Two versions exist of Garrick's text: in Bell's *Shakespeare* (1773), and as a separate printing by C. Bathurst in 1786. The later version includes more Shakespeare and cuts more Tate, but there is no evidence for the date of its acting, if indeed it was ever performed.

22 C. B. Hogan, *Shakespeare in the Theatre, 1701–1800*, vol. 2 (Oxford, 1957), p. 334.

23 See *Shakespeare: The Critical Heritage*, Vol. 3, p. 326.

24 *Monthly Review* xii, p. 80. An equally caustic notice was that of Paul Hiffernan, who reviewed both productions. (As often happened in this period, when one theatre got wind of a new Shakespeare production being prepared by its rival it would try to scoop it by mounting its own production of the original play, or an adaptation, whichever the other house was not performing.) 'The original *Coriolanus*, as played at *Drury-Lane* Theatre, is the most mobbing, huzzaing, shewy, boasting, drumming, fighting, trumpeting Tragedy I ever saw:—As exhibited in *Covent-Garden*, it is the divine but nodding *Shakespeare*, put into his Night-Gown by *Messire Thomson*; and humm'd to Sleep by *Don Torpedo* [presumably Thomas Sheridan], infamous for the *Mezentian* Art of joining his *Dead* to the *Living*: For which he is most justly damned' (*Tuner*, no. iii, (1754), p. 22).

25 One small but significant feature may be noted here, Garrick's addition of a sententious and pious ending to Wolsey's speech at the close of Act III, scene ii (at line 457ff. in Shakespeare):

> Have left me naked to my enemies.
> But soft. Let me not murmur at the will of Heaven.
> Oh chastisement, thou wholesome physic to my soul
> Be witness Heaven, how willingly I bear thee.
>
> [*Exeunt.*

Similarly Marsh, in his adaptation of *Cymbeline*, added a number of moralising soliloquies at the ending of scenes (1759 text, pp. 28, 49, 63, 82). This is part of the process by which the 'moral' was made explicit.

26 *Horace Walpole's Correspondence*, ed. W. S. Lewis *et al.*, vol 35, pp. 209–10;

ed. P. Toynbee, vol. 3, p. 288; to Richard Bentley, 23 February 1755.

27 H. W. Pedicord, *The Theatrical Public In The Time of Garrick* (New York, 1954), pp. 137, 140f.

28 Burnim, *David Garrick, Director* (Pittsburgh, 1961), p. 9.

29 In Book III, chapter xii, of *Tristram Shandy*, published in 1761, Sterne mocked the pedantry of contemporary critics, with their heads 'stuck so full of rules and compasses ... that a work of genius had better go to the devil at once, than stand to be pricked and tortured to death by 'em'. The first example Sterne gives is in fact a parody of Thady Fitzpatrick's account of Garrick's pauses and ungrammatical stresses:

And how did Garrick speak the soliloquy last night?—Oh, against all rule, my Lord,—most ungrammatically! betwixt the substantive and the adjective, which should agree together in number, case, and gender, he made a breach thus,—stopping, as if the point wanted settling;—and betwixt the nominative case, which your lordship knows should govern the verb, he suspended his voice in the epilogue a dozen times three seconds and three fifths by a stop-watch, my Lord, each time.—Admirable grammarian!—but in suspending his voice—was the sense suspended likewise? Did no expression of attitude or countenance fill up the chasm? Was the eye silent? Did you narrowly look?—I looked only at the stop-watch, my Lord.—Excellent observer!

The parody is characteristically witty, and puts the critics in an absurd light, but it hardly answers the serious issue of the proper communication of Shakespeare's meaning.

30 T. Cibber, *Lives and Characters of the most Eminent Actors and Actresses of Great Britain and Ireland* ... (1753), p. 50.

31 Colman, *Connoisseur* no. 16, 16 May 1754.

32 Burke, *op. cit.*, pp. 141–2; from II, §xiii, 'Magnificence'.

33 Reviewing Webb's book in the *Monthly Review* for April 1762, Langhorne granted that many of the instances from Shakespeare 'are indeed very happy and much to his purpose', but took exception to his interpretation of Othello's speech: 'Our Author has justly remarked, that in all these passages the language is with great felicity adapted to the idea; but we do not think that the languid fall in the last quoted line [see pp. 507f. below], which he takes notice of as a beauty, is either natural or necessary' (xxvi, pp. 287, 289).

34 That the many quotations from Shakespeare made Kames's book popular was stated by John Gregory: see Forbes's *Life of Beattie* (1806), p. 110 (*cit.* H. S. Robinson, *English Shakespearian Criticism in the Eighteenth Century* (New York, 1932), p. 103 n.).

35 Some perceptive criticisms were made by Owen Ruffhead in the *Monthly Review* for July and August, 1762. To Kames's complaint that Othello's 'O my soul's joy' speech is too strong, Ruffhead replies:

Here his Lordship will pardon us if we cannot subscribe to the justice of his criticism. For we cannot conceive that a meeting after a storm at sea, even between indifferent persons, can, with any propriety, be termed a slight joy. But his Lordship's censure appears the more exceptionable when we consider the vehemence and enthusiasm of Othello's character; and that the meeting was between him and his beloved Desdemona, his new-married bride, who had escaped a dreadful tempest, and whom he did not expect to find on shore; for in the opening of the speech he says

> It gives me wonder, great as my content,
> To see you here before me.—My soul's joy, &c.   [2.1.181f.]

Surely if such high-flown expression as Shakespeare has put in his mouth is at any time justifiable it must be on such an occasion! (xxvii, pp. 19f.).

Although agreeing with Kames that Rutland's simile with the 'pent-up lion' is 'faulty by being improperly introduced' (and 'is, in itself, far from being apposite or well supported': xxvii, pp. 106f.), Ruffhead took exception to Kames's attack on Antony addressing the corpse of Julius Caesar as a 'bleeding piece of earth': 'it was no "bold delusion" of mind in Antony to bestow sensibility on the dead body of Caesar bleeding before him with recent wounds' (p. 108). Finally he criticised Kames for saying that there was no resemblance in Coriolanus's image for Valeria as being 'chaste as the icicle': 'We confess, however, that we cannot be displeased with the foregoing simile: and, indeed, if we attend to the physical causes of chastity the resemblance, with great deference to his Lordship, will appear to be more than verbal' (p. 107).

36 Hume, *History of Great Britain* (1756), chapter 62, 'The Commonwealth'; 1778 edition (London and Edinburgh, 8 vols), VII, p. 346. Another passing reference by Hume may be noted here, in the 'Appendix to the Reign of Elizabeth' (1754):

It is remarkable, that in all the historical plays of Shakespeare, where the manners and characters, and even the transactions of the several reigns are so exactly copied, there is scarcely any mention of *civil Liberty*; which some pretended historians have imagined to be the object of all the ancient quarrels, insurrections, and civil wars. In the elaborate panegyric of England contained in the tragedy of *Richard II*, and the detail of its advantages, not a word of its civil constitution as anywise different from or superior to that of other European kingdoms: An omission which cannot be supposed in any English author that wrote since the Restoration, at least since the Revolution. (V, p. 469 n.)

37 Smith, *Lectures on Rhetoric and Belles Lettres* ed. J. M. Lothian (London, 1963), pp. 73, 27. Smith's example of mixed metaphor is an unfortunately garbled reminiscence of *Hamlet*: '*or bravely arm ourselves and stem a sea of troubles.* Here there is a plain absurdity, as there is no meaning in one's putting on armour to stem the sea.' These lectures were first given at Edinburgh between

1748 and 1751 (Lothian, pp. xiii–xvi), and subsequently revised, when they were noted down by a student at Glasgow in 1762–3. Thus Smith adds later: 'Shakespeare's "sea of troubles" has been converted in a late edition [Pope's] into a "siege", but the former reading is so like Shakespeare's manner that I dare to say he wrote it so' (p. 27). True enough, but he might have checked the rest of the line.

38 There is evidence of an increasing historical interest in the theatre, as we see from the archaeological reconstruction of the Roman 'Ovation' in the Sheridan–Thomson *Coriolanus* (No. 144). As early as 1731 Aaron Hill had written to Wilkes (letter of 28 October 1731: *The Works of the Late Aaron Hill* (4 vols, 1753), I, pp. 89–91) suggesting that Hill's play *The Generous Traitor, or Aethelwold* should be acted in authentic Saxon costumes (*cit.* David Bartholomeusz, *Macbeth and the Players* (Cambridge, 1969), p. 84). On 26 December 1757 *Macbeth* was given at Edinburgh ' "with the characters entirely new dress'd after the manner of the Ancient Scots" ' (Cecil Price, *Theatre in the Age of Garrick*, Oxford, 1973, p. 52).

39 T. Cibber, *Lives and Characters*, pp. xxiiif. One writer who praised Warburton in this period was Hurd (whose career had been furthered by his patronage: cf. headnote to No. 120 in Vol. 3), and Horace Walpole, writing to the Revd Henry Zouch on 4 February 1760, complained of Hurd's dense style and of his weakness for Warburton: 'In his other work, the notes on Horace, he is still more absurd. He cries up Warburton's preposterous notes on Shakespeare,—which would have died of their own folly, though Mr. Edwards had not put them to death with the keenest wit in the world': *Horace Walpole's Correspondence*, ed. W. S. Lewis *et al.*, vol. 16, pp. 37f.; ed. P. Toynbee, vol. 4, pp. 356f.

40 This had already been pointed out by Upton: *Critical Observations on Shakespeare* (1748 ed.), p. 379 n.

41 Another attack on Warburton's demand for a 'consonance of metaphors' (which, alas, much influenced Theobald) was made by Paul Gemsege in a note on the word 'earing', contributed to the *Gentleman's Magazine* in May 1755. Gemsege shows that the word means 'to plough', and that Theobald was wrong to gloss its use in *Henry VIII* as 'to harrow' or 'weed up'. Theobald did so in order to preserve 'consonance': 'But this consonance of metaphors, which he mentions, and which these critical gentlemen are perpetually hunting after, are not always needful, because metaphors often occur singly' (xxv, pp. 212f.).

42 The *Critical Review* notice (No. 204), albeit in a rather shrill tone and very much pro-Warburton, has some sound corrections of errors and some good notes on Shakespeare's English, although it claims more than it can deliver. The *Gentleman's Magazine* (February and March 1765) included a number of favourable quotations from Heath's book (xxxv, pp. 65–7) but deplored its being 'an hyper-criticism on the criticisms of the present Bishop of Gloucester', rather than a work 'on a more general plan' (ibid., pp. 110f.). In

the *Monthly Review* William Kenrick wrote that 'This work may indeed be looked upon as a kind of supplement to *The Canons of Criticism*. It is not written, however, with equal spirit, nor is there an equal share of critical sagacity displayed in this, as in that famous performance. A laborious attention to the minutest alterations in Shakespeare's text is the characteristic of the present work.' Heath ought, however, Kenrick complained, to have communicated his findings 'to the Editor of the new edition of Shakespeare, so long impatiently expected, and now almost ready to make its appearance' (xxxii, pp. 482f.).

43 See Arthur Sherbo, *Samuel Johnson, Editor of Shakespeare* (Illinois Studies in Language and Literature, vol. 42; Urbana, Illinois, 1956), pp. 36, 39.

44 Quoted by Arthur Sherbo, *Johnson on Shakespeare*, VII, p. 101, n. 5.

45 *Ibid.*, illustrations preceding pp. 3, 47.

46 Upton had already made this suggestion, in 1746 and 1748: 'If the plan likewise here proposed were followed the world might expect a much better, at least a less altered edition from Shakespeare's own words, than has yet been published. In order for this, all the various readings of *authority* should faithfully and fairly be collated and exhibited before the reader's eyes; and with some little ingenuity the best of these should be chosen and placed in the text.' (Vol. 3, p. 320)

Note on the Text

The texts in this collection are taken from the first printed edition, unless otherwise stated. The date under which a piece is filed is that of the first edition, with two exceptions; plays, for which, usually, the first performance is used (for such information I have relied on *The London Stage* for the period 1660 to 1800); and those works for which the author gives a date of composition substantially earlier than its first printing. The place of publication is London, unless otherwise indicated.

Spelling and punctuation are those of the original editions except where they seemed likely to create ambiguities for the modern reader. Spelling has, however, been standardised for writers' names (Jonson not Johnson, Rymer not Rhimer), for play-titles, and for Shakespearian characters.

Small omissions in the text are indicated by three dots: [. . .]; larger ones by three asterisks.

Footnotes intended by the original authors are distinguished with an asterisk, dagger, and so on; those added by the editor are numbered. Editorial notes within the text are placed within square brackets.

Act-, Scene- and line-numbers have been supplied in all quotations from Shakespeare, in the form 2.1.85 (Act 2, Scene 1, Line 85). The text used for this purpose was the *Tudor Shakespeare* ed. P. Alexander (Collins, 1951).

Classical quotations have been identified, and translations added, usually those in the Loeb library.

137. MacNamara Morgan, *Romeo and Juliet* acted and adapted

1753

From *A Letter to Miss Nossiter Occasioned by Her first Appearance on the Stage: In which is contained Remarks Upon her Manner of Playing The Character of Juliet* . . . (1753).

MacNamara Morgan (d. 1762), dramatist, born in Dublin, was a friend of the actor Spranger Barry, through whose influence his tragedy *Philoclea* (taken from Sidney's *Arcadia*) was performed in January 1754, the main roles being taken by Barry and Miss Nossiter. Morgan also had performed that year *Florizel and Perdita, or the Sheepshearing*, a particularly mindless adaptation of *The Winter's Tale* which enjoyed, nevertheless, much success in the theatre. For his authorship of this pamphlet, and for biographical information about him and the actress, Maria Nossiter, see the articles by G. W. Stone, Jr and C. B. Hogan in *Shakespeare Quarterly* 3 (1952), pp. 69–70 and 284–5. Much of the pamphlet is a mere puff for the actress (a not uncommon form taken by theatre criticism in this period), and it included the allegation that Arthur Murphy was in the pay of Garrick. This aroused the anger of Murphy, who fought a duel with Morgan in the Bedford Coffee House on 2 November 1753, and subsequently criticised the work in the *Gray's-Inn Journal* (nos 6, 7, 16: Folio).

I look upon a good Player as the best Commentator; he calls forth latent Beauties from the Poet's Works that a common Reader, tho' deeply learned, cou'd never have imagined. (13)

*　　*　　*

And upon the Nurse's resenting her Warmth, she turns from her with Dissatisfaction,

Here's such a Coil! [2.5.65]

But instantly her native Sweetness returns,

Come, what says ROMEO? [2.5.65]

Nothing cou'd be acted with greater Propriety; every little Alteration in the Temper being clearly marked out and distinguished. And indeed it is in these Changes, making the whole body keep Pace with the Sentiments of the Soul, that the chief Excellence of Acting consists. There is not an Idea in a Sentence that should not have its peculiar Look and Tone of Voice. What then shall we say to some who speak twenty Lines in a String without the least Variation, when there cannot be produced in any Author four Lines together that can, with Propriety, be spoken with a Sameness? Will any one call a Recitative of this kind Acting? May we not say to one of this Class as *Julius Caesar* did once to a Reader in the same Stile, *Do you speak, or do you sing? If you sing, you sing very badly.*

SHAKESPEARE, who was the greatest Master of the Passions, generally heightens all his Distresses by some preceding Joy. Thus JULIET, before she is to receive the News of TYBALT's Death and ROMEO's Banishment, works up her Imagination to the highest Pitch of joyful Expectation of the Coming-on of Night, which is to bring ROMEO to her Arms. All which was finely expressed by Miss NOSSITER; she comes in with Fire,

> *Gallop apace, ye fiery-footed Steeds,*
> *To Phœbus' Mansion; such a Wagoner*
> *As* Phaëton, *wou'd whip you to the West*
> *And bring in cloudy Night immediately.* [3.2.1ff.]

Then in a lower Tone, still filled with the Thoughts of Joy,

> *Spread thy close Curtain, Love-performing Night,*
> *That the Run-away's Eyes may wink; and* ROMEO,
> *Leap to these Arms,* [3.2.5ff.]

With what Rapture did she hug the Thought of ROMEO's leaping to her Arms! (16-17)

* * *

The Reader, I hope, will indulge me with this Opportunity of making an Observation or two upon the Play itself as it is now altered and fitted for the Stage.

Nothing was ever better calculated to draw Tears from an Audience, than the last Scene, when it is happily performed. The Circumstance of JULIET's waking from her Trance before ROMEO dies, and he, in the Excess and Rapture of his Joy, forgetting he had drank Poison:[1]

She speaks, she lives, and we shall still be bless'd!

is perhaps the finest Touch of Nature in any Tragedy, ancient or modern. But, as SHAKESPEARE wrote it, when JULIET revives she finds ROMEO dead, and discovers the Manner of his Death by the Vial; therefore that Passage shou'd now be left out, for as ROMEO tells her himself that he had drank Poison she is not under a Necessity of gathering the Fact from Circumstances; yet, as Miss NOSSITER speaks it, I wou'd not wish it away. SHAKESPEARE's Conduct was not half so distressing as,

Within Sight of Heaven,
To be plunged in Hell.

It is very strange, therefore, that it has not been inquired into who the Author was that made so happy an Alteration. I have heard it attributed to one of the Players [Garrick]; and it passes current that his Knowledge of the Stage enabled him to do it. But that we may not learn to set too small a Value on the tragic Genius by imagining that every little Smatterer can, with such Delicacy, touch the human Heart; know, none but that Genius who comes next to SHAKESPEARE's self cou'd draw so fine a Stroke. It was OTWAY altered it. Compare the Tomb-Scene in *Romeo and Juliet* with that in *Caius Marius*, which is but another Alteration of the same Play,[2] and there you will find this noble Incident, and the very Words of the whole Scene, with very little Alteration. (49–50)

[1] See Otway's version, Vol. 1, p. 316 and Garrick's, Vol. 3, p. 338.
[2] Compare Vol. 1, pp. 315ff. (Otway) and Vol. 3, pp. 337ff. (Garrick).

138. George Colman, Shakespeare's self-criticism

1753

From the *Adventurer*, no. 90 (15 September 1753). In reprinting this essay in his *Prose on Several Occasions*, 3 vols (1787) Colman gave it the title 'Sacrifice by the authors of the exceptionable parts of their works: a vision'.

George Colman, the elder (1732–94), was educated at Westminster, Christ Church, Oxford, and Lincoln's Inn. While still at Oxford he conducted (with Bonnell Thornton) the *Connoisseur*, and subsequently contributed essays to *St James's Chronicle* (1761–2), *Terrae filius* (1763), and the *Monthly Review* (1764–89). He wrote poetry, translated Terence's comedies and Horace's *Ars Poetica*, and wrote or adapted over thirty plays. From 1767 to 1777 he was manager of the Covent Garden theatre (where he staged both of Goldsmith's comedies, which Garrick refused to perform), and from 1777 to 1789 of the Haymarket.

To the ADVENTURER.

SIR,

Nothing sooner quells the ridiculous triumph of human vanity than reading those passages of the greatest writers in which they seem deprived of that noble spirit that inspires them in other parts, and where, instead of invention and grandeur, we meet with nothing but flatness and insipidity.

The pain I have felt on observing a lofty genius thus sink beneath itself has often made me wish that these unworthy stains could be blotted from their works, and leave them perfect and immaculate.

I went to bed a few nights ago full of these thoughts, and closed the evening, as I frequently do, with reading a few lines in VIRGIL. I accidently opened that part of the sixth book where ANCHISES recounts to his son the various methods of purgation which the soul undergoes in the next world, to cleanse it from the filth it has contracted by its connection with the body, and to deliver the pure etherial essence from the vicious tincture of mortality. This was so much like my evening's speculation that it insensibly mixed and incorporated with it, and as soon as I fell asleep formed itself into the following dream.

I found myself in an instant in the midst of a temple which was built with all that magnificent simplicity that distinguishes the productions of the ancients. At the east end was raised an altar, on each side of which stood a priest who seemed preparing to sacrifice. On the altar was kindled a fire, from which arose the brightest flame I had ever beheld. The light which it dispensed, though remarkably strong and clear, was not quivering and dazzling but steady and uniform, and diffused a purple radiance through the whole edifice, not unlike the first appearance of the morning.

While I stood fixed in admiration my attention was awakened by the blast of a trumpet, which shook the whole temple; but it carried a certain sweetness in it's sound, which mellowed and tempered the natural shrillness of that instrument. After it had sounded thrice the being who blew it, habited according to the description of FAME by the ancients, issued a proclamation to the following purpose. 'By command of APOLLO and the MUSES, all who have ever made any pretensions to fame by their writings are injoined to sacrifice upon the altar in this temple those parts of their works which have hitherto been preserved to their infamy, that their names many descend spotless and unsullied to posterity. For this purpose ARISTOTLE and LONGINUS are appointed chief priests, who are to see that no improper oblations are made and no proper ones concealed; and for the more easy performance of this office they are allowed to chuse as their assistants whomsoever they shall think worthy of the function.'

As soon as this proclamation was made I turned my eyes with inexpressible delight towards the two priests; but was soon robbed of the pleasure of looking at them by a croud of people running up to offer their service. These I found to be a groupe of French critics; but their offers were rejected by both priests with the utmost indignation, and their whole works were thrown on the altar and reduced to ashes in an instant. The two priests then looked round and chose, with a few others, HORACE and QUINTILIAN from among the Romans, and ADDISON from the English as their principal assistants.

The first who came forward with his offering, by the loftiness of his demeanor was soon discovered to be HOMER. He approached the altar with great majesty, and delivered to LONGINUS those parts of his *Odyssey* which have been censured as improbable fictions, and the ridiculous narratives of old age. LONGINUS was preparing for the sacrifice, but, observing that ARISTOTLE did not seem willing to assist him in the office, he returned them to the venerable old bard with great deference, saying that 'they were indeed the tales of old age, but it was the old age of HOMER'.[1]

VIRGIL appeared next, and approached the altar with a modest dignity in his gait and countenance peculiar to himself; and to the surprise of all committed his whole ÆNEID to the flames. But it was immediately rescued by two Romans, whom I found to be TUCCA and VARIUS, who ran with precipitation to the altar, delivered the poem from destruction, and carried off the author between them, repeating that glorious boast of about forty lines at the beginning of the third *Georgic*.[2]

> —*Tentanda via est; qua me quoque possim*
> *Tollere humo, victorque virûm volitare per ora.*
> *Primus ego in patriam mecum,* &c.

After him most of the Greek and Roman authors proceeded to the altar, and surrendered with great modesty and humility the most faulty part of their works. One circumstance was observable, that the sacrifice always increased in proportion as the author had ventured to deviate from a judicious imitation of HOMER. The latter Roman authors, who seemed almost to have lost sight of him, made so large offerings that some of their works, which were before very voluminous, shrunk into the compass of a primer.

It gave me the highest satisfaction to see PHILOSOPHY thus cleared from erroneous principles, HISTORY purged of falsehood, POETRY of fustian, and nothing left in each but GENIUS, SENSE, and TRUTH.

I marked with particular attention the several offerings of the most eminent English Writers. CHAUCER gave up his obscenity, and then delivered his works to DRYDEN to clear them from the rubbish that encumbered them. DRYDEN executed his task with great address, 'and,'

---

[1] Longinus, *On the Sublime*, §21.

[2] 3.8ff.: 'I must essay a path whereby I, too, may rise from earth and fly victorious on the lips of men. I first, if life but remain, will return to my country, bringing the Muses with me in triumph from the Aonian peak.'

as ADDISON says of VIRGIL in his *Georgics*, 'tossed about his dung with an air of gracefulness:' he not only repaired the injuries of time but threw in a thousand new graces. He then advanced towards the altar himself, and delivered up a large pacquet, which contained many plays and some poems. The pacquet had a label affixed to it, which bore this inscription, 'To Poverty.'

SHAKESPEARE carried to the altar a long string of puns, marked 'The Taste of the Age,' a small parcel of bombast, and a pretty large bundle of incorrectness. Notwithstanding the ingenuous air with which he made this offering, some officiates at the altar accused him of concealing certain pieces, and mentioned *The London Prodigal, Sir Thomas Cromwell, The Yorkshire Tragedy*, &c. The poet replied, 'that as those pieces were unworthy to be preserved, he should see them consumed to ashes with great pleasure; but that he was wholly innocent of their original.' The two chief priests interposed in this dispute, and dismissed the poet with many compliments; LONGINUS observing, that the pieces in question could not possibly be his for that the failings of SHAKESPEARE were like those of HOMER, 'whose genius, whenever it subsided, might be compared to the ebbing of the ocean, which left a mark upon its shores to shew to what a height it was sometimes carried.' ARISTOTLE concurred in this opinion, and added 'that although SHAKESPEARE was quite ignorant of that exact œconomy of the stage which is so remarkable in the Greek writers, yet the meer strength of his genius had in many points carried him infinitely beyond them.'

MILTON gave up a few errors in his *Paradise Lost*, and the sacrifice was attended with great decency by ADDISON. OTWAY and ROWE threw their comedies upon the altar, and BEAUMONT and FLETCHER the two last acts of many of their pieces. They were followed by TOM D'URFEY, ETHEREGE, WYCHERLEY, and several other dramatic writers, who made such large contributions that they set the altar in a blaze.

139. Joseph Warton on *The Tempest* and *King Lear*

1753-4

From the *Adventurer*, nos 93, 97, 116, 132. This journal (published twice weekly, from 7 November 1752 to 9 March 1754; reissued 1753-4) was edited by John Hawkesworth: besides Colman and Warton other contributors included the Earl of Orrery, Bonnell Thornton, Dr Johnson, and Richard Bathurst.

Joseph Warton (1722-1800) was educated at Winchester (where he returned as headmaster from 1766 to 1793) and Oxford. A poet and critic, he wrote twenty-four essays for the *Adventurer*, translated Virgil (1753), edited Sidney's *Defence of Poetry* (1787), wrote an important essay on Pope (see No. 158), and edited Pope's works (1797). He was a friend of the poet Collins and of Dr Johnson and his circle.

---

[a] No. 93 (25 September 1753)

Writers of a mixed character, that abound in transcendent beauties and in gross imperfections, are the most proper and most pregnant subjects for criticism. The regularity and correctness of a VIRGIL or HORACE almost confine their commentators to perpetual panegyric, and afford them few opportunities of diversifying their remarks by the detection of latent blemishes. For this reason I am inclined to think that a few observations on the writings of SHAKESPEARE will not be deemed useless or unentertaining, because he exhibits more numerous examples of excellencies and faults of every kind than are, perhaps, to be discovered in any other author. I shall, therefore, from time to time examine his merit as a poet, without blind admiration or wanton invective.

As SHAKESPEARE is sometimes blameable for the conduct of his fables, which have no unity, and sometimes for his diction, which is obscure and turgid, so his characteristical excellencies may possibly be reduced to these three general heads: 'his lively creative imagination; his strokes of nature and passion; and his preservation of the consistency of his characters.' These excellencies, particularly the last, are of so much importance in the drama that they amply compensate for his transgressions against the rules of TIME and PLACE, which being of a more mechanical nature are often strictly observed by a genius of the lowest order; but to portraye characters naturally and to preserve them uniformly requires such an intimate knowledge of the heart of man and is so rare a portion of felicity as to have been enjoyed, perhaps, only by two writers, HOMER and SHAKESPEARE.

Of all the plays of SHAKESPEARE *The Tempest* is the most striking instance of his creative power. He has there given the reins to his boundless imagination, and has carried the romantic, the wonderful, and the wild to the most pleasing extravagance. The scene is a desolate island; and the characters the most new and singular that can well be conceived: a prince who practises magic, an attendant spirit, a monster the son of a witch, and a young lady who had been brought to this solitude in her infancy, and had never beheld a man except her father.

As I have affirmed that SHAKESPEARE's chief excellence is the consistency of his characters I will exemplify the truth of this remark by pointing out some master-strokes of this nature in the drama before us.

The poet artfully acquaints us that PROSPERO is a magician by the very first words which his daughter MIRANDA speaks to him:

> If by your art, my dearest father, you have
> Put the wild waters in this roar, allay them: [1.2.1f.]

which intimate that the tempest described in the preceding scene was the effect of PROSPERO's power. The manner in which he was driven from his dukedom of Milan and landed afterwards on this solitary island, accompanied only by his daughter, is immediately introduced in a short and natural narration.

The offices of his attendant Spirit ARIEL are enumerated with amazing wildness of fancy, and yet with equal propriety: his employment is said to be

> —To tread the ooze
> Of the salt deep;
> To run upon the sharp wind of the north;
> To do—business in the veins o'th'earth,

When it is bak'd with frost;
. . . to dive into the fire: to ride
On the curl'd clouds— [1.2.252ff., 191ff.]

In describing the place in which he has concealed the Neapolitan ship ARIEL expresses the secrecy of its situation by the following circumstance, which artfully glances at another of his services:

—In the deep nook, where once
Thou calld'st me up at midnight, to fetch dew
From the still-vext Bermudas— [1.2.227ff.]

ARIEL, being one of those elves or spirits, 'whose pastime is to make midnight mushrooms, and who rejoice to listen to the solemn curfew'; by whose assistance PROSPERO has 'bedimm'd the sun at noon-tide', [5.1.38ff.]

And 'twixt the green sea and the azur'd vault,
Set roaring war;— [5.1.43ff.]

has a set of ideas and images peculiar to his station and office; a beauty of the same kind with that which is so justly admired in the ADAM of MILTON, whose manners and sentiments are all Paradisiacal. How delightfully and how suitably to his character are the habitations and pastimes of this invisible being, pointed out in the following exquisite song!

Where the bee sucks, there lurk I. . . . [5.1.88]

Mr POPE, whose imagination has been thought by some the least of his excellencies, has doubtless conceived and carried on the machinery in his *Rape of the Lock* with vast exuberance of fancy. The images, customs, and employments of his SYLPHS are exactly adapted to their natures, are peculiar and appropriated, are all, if I may be allowed the expression, SYLPHISH. The enumeration of the punishments they were to undergo if they neglected their charge would, on account of its poetry and propriety, and especially the mixture of oblique satire, be superior to any circumstances in SHAKESPEARE's Ariel if we could suppose POPE to have been unacquainted with the *Tempest* when he wrote this part of his accomplished poem.

—She did confine thee
Into a cloven pine; [1.2.274f.]

> If thou more murmur'st, I will rend an oak,
> And peg thee in his knotty entrails, 'till
> Thou'st howl'd away twelve winters.   [1.2.294ff.]

> For this, be sure, to-night thou shalt have cramps,
> Side-stitches that shall pen thy breath up: [1.2.325f.]

> Whatever spirit, careless of his charge,
> Forsakes his post or leaves the Fair at large,
> Shall feel sharp vengeance soon o'ertake his sins,
> Be stopp'd in vials, or transfix'd with pins;
> Or plung'd in lakes of bitter washes lie,
> Or wedg'd whole ages in a bodkin's eye; . . . POPE.

The method which is taken to induce FERDINAND to believe that his father was drowned in the late tempest is exceedingly solemn and striking. He is sitting upon a solitary rock and weeping, over against the place where he imagined his father was wrecked, when he suddenly hears with astonishment aërial music creep by him upon the waters, and the SPIRIT gives him the following information in words not proper for any but a SPIRIT to utter:

> Full fathom five thy father lies. . . .   [1.2.396ff.]

And then follows a most lively circumstance;

> Sea-nymphs hourly ring his knell.
> Hark! now I hear them—Ding-dong-bell!   [1.2.401f.]

This is so truly poetical that one can scarce forbear exclaiming, with FERDINAND,

> This is no mortal business, nor no sound
> That the earth owns!—   [1.2.406f.]

The happy versatility of SHAKESPEARE's genius enables him to excell in lyric as well as in dramatic poesy.

But the poet rises still higher in his management of this character of ARIEL by making a moral use of it that is, I think, incomparable, and the greatest effort of his art. ARIEL informs PROSPERO that he has fulfilled his orders, and punished his brother and companions so severely that if he himself was now to behold their sufferings he would greatly compassionate them. To which PROSPERO answers,

                —Dost thou think so, Spirit?
ARIEL.   Mine would, Sir, were I human.
PROSPERO. And mine shall.   [5.1.19ff.]

He then takes occasion, with wonderful dexterity and humanity, to
draw an argument from the incorporeality of ARIEL for the justice and
necessity of pity and forgiveness:

> Hast thou, which art but air, a touch, a feeling
> Of their afflictions; and shall not myself,
> One of their kind, that relish all as sharply,
> Passion'd as they, be kindlier mov'd than thou art? [5.1.21ff.]

The poet is a more powerful magician than his own PROSPERO:
we are transported into fairy-land; we are wrapt in a delicious dream,
from which it is misery to be disturbed; all around is enchantment!

        —The isle is full of noises,
Sounds, and sweet airs, that give delight and hurt not. . . . [3.2.130ff.]

[b] No. 97 (9 October 1753)

'Whoever ventures,' says HORACE, 'to form a character totally original,
let him endeavour to preserve it with uniformity and consistency: but
the formation of an original character is a work of great difficulty and
hazard.'[1] In this arduous and uncommon task, however, SHAKESPEARE
has wonderfully succeeded in his *Tempest*: the monster CALIBAN is
the creature of his own imagination, in the formation of which he
could derive no assistance from observation or experience.

CALIBAN is the son of a witch, begotten by a demon. The sorceries
of his mother were so terrible that her countrymen banished her into
this desart island as unfit for human society: in conformity, therefore,
to this diabolical propagation he is represented as a prodigy of cruelty,
malice, pride, ignorance, idleness, gluttony and lust. He is introduced
with great propriety, cursing PROSPERO and MIRANDA (whom he
had endeavoured to defile), and his execrations are artfully contrived
to have reference to the occupations of his mother:

> As wicked dew, as e'er my mother brush'd
> With raven's feather from unwholsome fen,
> Drop on you both!—
>   —All the charms
> Of Sycorax, toads, beetles, bats, light on you! [1.2.321ff., 339f.]

[1] Horace, *Ars Poetica*, 119-27.

His kindness is, afterwards, expressed as much in character as his hatred, by an enumeration of offices that could be of value only in a desolate island, and in the estimation of a savage:

> I pr'ythee, let me bring thee where crabs grow;
> And I with my long nails will dig thee pig-nuts . . .
> I'll shew thee the best springs; I'll pluck thee berries;
> I'll fish for thee, and get thee wood enough.   [2.2.156ff., 150f.]

Which last is, indeed, a circumstance of great use in a place where to be defended from the cold was neither easy nor usual; and it has a farther peculiar beauty because the gathering wood was the occupation to which CALIBAN was subjected by PROSPERO, who therefore deemed it a service of high importance.

The gross ignorance of this monster is represented with delicate judgment. He knew not the names of the sun and moon, which he calls the bigger light and the less; and he believes that Stephano was the man in the moon, whom his mistress had often shewn him; and when PROSPERO reminds him that he first taught him to pronounce articulately, his answer is full of malevolence and rage:

> You taught me language; and my profit on't
> Is, I know how to curse:—   [1.2.363f.]

The properest return for such a fiend to make for such a favour. The spirits whom he supposes to be employed by PROSPERO perpetually to torment him, and the many forms and different methods they take for this purpose, are described with the utmost liveliness and force of fancy:

> Sometimes like apes, that moe and chatter at me,
> And after bite me; then like hedge-hogs, which
> Lie tumbling in my bare-foot way, and mount
> Their pricks at my foot-fall: sometimes am I
> All wound with adders, who with cloven tongues
> Do hiss me into madness.   [2.2.9ff.]

It is scarcely possible for any speech to be more expressive of the manners and sentiments than that in which our poet has painted the brutal barbarity and unfeeling savageness of this son of Sycorax by making him enumerate, with a kind of horrible delight, the various ways in which it was possible for the drunken sailors to surprize and kill his master:

    —There thou mayst brain him,
Having first seiz'd his books; or with a log
Batter his skull; or paunch him with a stake;
Or cut his wezand with thy knife—   [3.2.84ff.]

He adds, in allusion to his own abominable attempt, 'above all be sure to secure the daughter; whose beauty, he tells them, is incomparable.' The charms of MIRANDA could not be more exalted than by extorting this testimony from so insensible a monster.

SHAKESPEARE seems to be the only poet who possesses the power of uniting poetry with propriety of character; of which I know not an instance more striking than the image CALIBAN makes use of to express silence, which is at once highly poetical and exactly suited to the wildness of the speaker:

    Pray you tread softly, that the blind mole may not
    Hear a foot-fall.—   [4.1.194f.]

I always lament that our author has not preserved this fierce and implacable spirit in CALIBAN to the end of the play; instead of which he has, I think injudiciously, put into his mouth words that imply repentance and understanding:

    —I'll be wise hereafter
    And seek for grace. What a thrice double ass
    Was I, to take this drunkard for a God,
    And worship this dull fool?   [5.1.294ff.]

It must not be forgotten that SHAKESPEARE has artfully taken occasion from this extraordinary character, which is finely contrasted to the mildness and obedience of ARIEL, obliquely to satirize the prevailing passion for new and wonderful sights which has rendered the English so ridiculous. 'Were I in England now,' says TRINCULO on first discovering CALIBAN, 'and had but this fish painted, not an holiday fool there but would give a piece of silver.—When they will not give a doit to relieve a lame beggar, they will lay out ten to see a dead Indian.'   [2.2.25ff.]

Such is the inexhaustible plenty of our poet's invention that he has exhibited another character in this play entirely his own, that of the lovely and innocent MIRANDA.

When PROSPERO first gives her a sight of prince FERDINAND she eagerly exclaims

—What is't? a spirit?
Lord, how it looks about! Believe me, Sir,
It carries a brave form. But 'tis a spirit.   [1.2.409ff.]

Her imagining that as he was so beautiful he must necessarily be one of
her father's aërial agents is a stroke of nature worthy admiration as are
likewise her entreaties to her father not to use him harshly by the power
of his art:

Why speaks my father so ungently? This
Is the third man that e'er I saw; the first
That e'er I sigh'd for!—   [1.2.444ff.]

Here we perceive the beginning of that passion which PROSPERO was
desirous she should feel for the prince, and which she afterwards more
fully expresses upon an occasion which displays at once the tenderness,
the innocence, and the simplicity of her character. She discovers her
lover employed in the laborious task of carrying wood, which
PROSPERO had enjoined him to perform. 'Would,' says she, 'the
lightning had burnt up those logs that you are enjoined to pile!'

—If you'll sit down
I'll bear your logs the while. Pray give me that,
I'll carry't to the pile.
—You look wearily.   [3.1.23ff.]

It is by selecting such little and almost imperceptible circumstances that
SHAKESPEARE has more truly painted the passions than any other
writer: affection is more powerfully expressed by this simple wish and
offer of assistance than by the unnatural eloquence and witticisms of
DRYDEN, or the amorous declamations of ROWE.

The resentment of PROSPERO for the matchless cruelty and wicked
usurpation of his brother, his parental affection and sollicitude for the
welfare of his daughter, the heiress of his dukedom, and the awful
solemnity of his character as a skilful magician, are all along preserved
with equal consistency, dignity and decorum. One part of his behaviour
deserves to be particularly pointed out. During the exhibition of a
masque with which he had ordered ARIEL to entertain FERDINAND
and MIRANDA he starts suddenly from the recollection of the conspiracy of CALIBAN and his confederates against his life, and dismisses
his attendant spirits, who instantly vanish to a hollow and confused
noise. He appears to be greatly moved; and suitably to this agitation of
mind which his danger has excited he takes occasion from the sudden

disappearance of the visionary scene, to moralize on the dissolution of
all things:

> —These our actors,
> As I foretold you, were all spirits; and
> Are melted into air, into thin air:
> And, like the baseless fabric of this vision,
> The cloud-capt towers, the gorgeous palaces,
> The solemn temples, the great globe itself,
> Yea, all which it inherit, shall dissolve;
> And, like this unsubstantial pageant faded,
> Leave not a rack behind—   [4.1.148ff.]

To these noble images he adds a short but comprehensive observation
on human life, not excelled by any passage of the moral and sententious
EURIPIDES:

> —We are such stuff
> As dreams are made on; and our little life
> Is rounded with a sleep!—   [4.1.156ff.]

Thus admirably is an uniformity of character, that leading beauty in
dramatic poesy, preserved throughout *The Tempest*. And it may be
farther remarked that the unities of action, of place, and of time are in
this play, though almost constantly violated by SHAKESPEARE, exactly
observed. The action is one, great, and entire, the restoration of
PROSPERO to his dukedom; this business is transacted in the compass of
a small island and in, or near, the cave of PROSPERO (though indeed it
had been more artful and regular to have confined it to this single spot);
and the time which the action takes up is only equal to that of the
representation, an excellence which ought always to be aimed at in
every well-conducted fable, and for the want of which a variety of the
most entertaining incidents can scarcely attone.

[c] No. 113 (4 December 1753)

One of the most remarkable differences betwixt ancient and modern
tragedy arises from the prevailing custom of describing only those
distresses that are occasioned by the passion of love; a passion, doubtless,
which from the universality of its dominion may justly claim a large
share in representations of human life but which, by totally engrossing
the theatre, hath contributed to degrade that noble school of virtue into
an academy of effeminacy.

When RACINE persuaded the celebrated ARNAULD to read his PHÆDRA, 'Why,' said that severe critic to his friend, 'have you falsified the manners of HIPPOLITUS and represented him in love?' 'Alas!' replied the poet, 'without that circumstance how would the ladies and the beaux have received my piece?' And it may well be imagined that to gratify so considerable and important a part of his audience was the powerful motive that induced CORNEILLE to enervate even the matchless and affecting story of OEDIPUS by the frigid and impertinent episode of THESEUS's passion for DIRCE.

SHAKESPEARE has shewn us, by his *Hamlet, Macbeth*, and *Cæsar*, and above all by his *Lear*, that very interesting tragedies may be written that are not founded on gallantry and love, and that BOILEAU was mistaken when he affirmed

> —*de l'amour la sensible peinture,*
> *Est pour aller au cœur la route la plus sûre.*

The distresses in this tragedy are of a very uncommon nature, and are not touched upon by any other dramatic author. They are occasioned by a rash resolution of an aged monarch, of strong passions and quick sensibility, to resign his crown and to divide his kingdom amongst his three daughters. The youngest of whom (who was his favourite) not answering his sanguine expectations in expressions of affection to him, he for ever banishes, and endows her sisters with her allotted share. Their unnatural ingratitude, the intolerable affronts, indignities and cruelties he suffers from them, and the remorse he feels from his imprudent resignation of his power, at first inflame him with the most violent rage and by degrees drive him to madness and death. This is the outline of the fable.

I shall confine myself at present to consider singly the judgment and art of the poet in describing the origin and progress of the distraction of LEAR; in which, I think, he has succeeded better than any other writer, even than EURIPIDES himself, whom LONGINUS so highly commends for his representation of the madness of ORESTES.

It is well contrived that the first affront that is offered LEAR should be a proposal from GONERIL, his eldest daughter, to lessen the number of his knights, which must needs affect and irritate a person so jealous of his rank and the respect due to it. He is at first astonished at the complicated impudence and ingratitude of this design; but quickly kindles into rage, and resolves to depart instantly:

> —Darkness and devils!—
> Saddle my horses, call my train together—
> Degen'rate bastard, I'll not trouble thee.— [1.4.252ff.]

This is followed by a severe reflection upon his own folly for resigning his crown, and a solemn invocation to NATURE to heap the most horrible curses on the head of GONERIL, that her own offspring may prove equally cruel and unnatural;

> —That she may feel,
> How sharper than a serpent's tooth it is,
> To have a thankless child!— [1.4.287ff.]

When ALBANY demands the cause of this passion LEAR answers 'I'll tell thee!', but immediately cries out to GONERIL

> —Life and death! I am asham'd,
> That thou hast power to shake my manhood thus.
> —Blasts and fogs upon thee!
> Th'untented woundings of a father's curse,
> Pierce every sense about thee! [1.4.296ff.]

He stops a little and reflects:

> Ha! is it come to this?
> Let it be so! I have another daughter,
> Who, I am sure, is kind and comfortable.
> When she shall hear this of thee, with her nails
> She'll flea thy wolfish visage— [1.4.304ff.]

He was, however, mistaken; for the first object he encounters in the castle of the Earl of Gloucester (whither he fled to meet his other daughter) was his servant in the stocks, from whence he may easily conjecture what reception he is to meet with:

> —Death on my state! Wherefore
> Should he sit here? [2.4.110f.]

He adds immediately afterwards,

> O me, my heart! my rising heart!—but down. [2.4.118f.]

By which single line the inexpressible anguish of his mind, and the dreadful conflict of opposite passions with which it is agitated, are more forcibly expressed than by the long and laboured speech, enumerating the causes of his anguish, that ROWE and other modern tragic writers would certainly have put into his mouth. But NATURE, SOPHOCLES, and SHAKESPEARE represent the feelings of the heart in a different manner; by a broken hint, a short exclamation, a word, or a look:

> They mingle not, 'mid deep-felt sighs and groans,
> Descriptions gay, or quaint comparisons.
> No flowery, far-fetch'd thoughts their scenes admit;
> Ill suits conceit with passion, woe with wit.
> Here passion prompts each short, expressive speech;
> Or silence paints, what words can never reach.　　J.W.

When JOCASTA, in SOPHOCLES, has discovered that OEDIPUS was the murderer of her husband she immediately leaves the stage; but in CORNEILLE and DRYDEN she continues on it during a whole scene, to bewail her destiny in set speeches.

I should be guilty of insensibility and injustice if I did not take this occasion to acknowledge that I have been more moved and delighted by hearing this single line spoken by the only actor of the age who understands and relishes these little touches of nature, and therefore the only one qualified to personate this most difficult character of LEAR, than by the most pompous declaimer of the most pompous speeches in CATO or TAMERLANE.

In the next scene the old king appears in a very distressful situation. He informs REGAN (whom he believes to be still actuated by filial tenderness) of the cruelties he had suffered from her sister GONERIL, in very pathetic terms:

> Beloved Regan,
> Thy sister's naught.—O Regan! she hath tied
> Sharp-tooth'd unkindness, like a vulture, here.
> I scarce can speak to thee—thou'lt not believe,
> With how deprav'd a quality,—Oh Regan!　　[2.4.131ff.]

It is a stroke of wonderful art in the poet to represent him incapable of specifying the particular ill usage he has received and breaking off thus abruptly, as if his voice was choaked by tenderness and resentment. When REGAN counsels him to ask her sister forgiveness he falls on his knees with a very striking kind of irony, and asks her how such supplicating language as this becometh him:

> Dear daughter, I confess that I am old;
> Age is unnecessary: on my knees I beg
> That you'll vouchsafe me raiment, bed, and food.　　[2.4.152ff.]

But being again exhorted to sue for reconciliation the advice wounds him to the quick and forces him into execrations against GONERIL which, though they chill the soul with horror, are yet well suited to the impetuosity of his temper:

> She hath abated me of half my train;
> Look'd bleak upon me; struck me with her tongue,
> Most serpentlike, upon the very heart.
> All the stor'd vengeances of heaven fall
> On her ungrateful top! Strike her young bones,
> Ye taking airs, with lameness!
> Ye nimble lightnings, dart your blinding flames
> Into her scornful eyes! [2.4.157ff.]

The wretched king, little imagining that he is to be outcast from REGAN also, adds very movingly:

> 'Tis not in thee
> To grudge my pleasures, to cut off my train,
> To bandy hasty words, to scant my sizes.
> Thou better know'st
> The offices of nature, bond of childhood. . . .
> Thy half o'th'kingdom thou hast not forgot,
> Wherein I thee endow'd. [2.4.172ff.]

That the hopes he had conceived of tender usage from REGAN should be deceived, heightens his distress to a great degree. Yet it is still aggravated and increased by the sudden appearance of GONERIL, upon the unexpected sight of whom he exclaims;

> Who comes here? O heav'ns!
> If you do love old men, if your sweet sway
> Allow obedience, if yourselves are old,
> Make it your cause; send down and take my part! [2.4.188ff.]

This address is surely pathetic beyond expression; it is scarce enough to speak of it in the cold terms of criticism. There follows a question to GONERIL that I have never read without tears:

> Ar't not asham'd to look upon this beard? [2.4.192]

This scene abounds with many noble turns of passion, or rather, conflicts of very different passions. The inhuman daughters urge him in vain by all the sophistical and unfilial arguments they were mistresses of to diminish the number of his train. He answers them by only four poignant words;

I gave you all! [2.4.248]

When REGAN at last consents to receive him, but without any attendants, for that he might be served by her own domestics, he can no longer contain his disappointment and rage. First he appeals to the heavens, and points out to them a spectacle that is indeed inimitably affecting:

> You see me here, you Gods! a poor old man,
> As full of grief as age, wretched in both.
> If it be you that stir these daughters hearts
> Against their father, fool me not so much
> To bear it tamely! [2.4.271ff.]

Then suddenly he addresses GONERIL and REGAN in the severest terms and with the bitterest threats:

> No, you unnatural hags!
> I will have such revenges on you both
> That all the world shall—I will do such things—
> What they are yet, I know not— [2.4.277ff.]

Nothing occurs to his mind severe enough for them to suffer, or him to inflict. His passion rises to a height that deprives him of articulation. He tells them that he will subdue his sorrow, though almost irresistible, and that they shall not triumph over his weakness:

> You think I'll weep!
> No! I'll not weep: I have full cause of weeping;
> But this heart shall break into a thousand flaws,
> Or e'er I'll weep! [2.4.281ff.]

He concludes,

> O fool—I shall go mad! [2.4.285]

which is an artful anticipation that judiciously prepares us for the dreadful event that is to follow in the succeeding acts.

[d] No. 116 (15 December 1753)

Thunder and a ghost have been frequently introduced into tragedy by barren and mechanical play-wrights, as proper objects to impress terror and astonishment where the distress has not been important enough to render it probable that nature would interpose for the sake of the sufferers, and where these objects themselves have not been supported by suitable sentiments. Thunder has, however, been made use of with great judgment and good effect by SHAKESPEARE to heighten and impress the distresses of LEAR.

The venerable and wretched old king is driven out by both his daughters, without necessaries and without attendants, not only in the night but in the midst of a most dreadful storm and on a bleak and barren heath. On his first appearance in this situation he draws an artful and pathetic comparison betwixt the severity of the tempest and of his daughters:

> Rumble thy belly full! spit, fire! spout, rain!
> Nor rain, wind, thunder, fire, are my daughters.
> I tax not you, you elements, with unkindness;
> I never gave you kingdom, called you children;
> You owe me no subscription. Then let fall
> Your horrible pleasure. Here I stand your slave;
> A poor, infirm, weak, and despis'd old man!   [3.2.14ff.]

The storm continuing with equal violence, he drops for a moment the consideration of his own miseries and takes occasion to moralize on the terrors which such commotions of nature should raise in the breast of secret and unpunished villainy:

> Tremble thou wretch,
> That hast within thee undivulged crimes
> Unwhipt of justice! Hide thee, thou bloody hand. . . .   [3.2.51ff.]

He adds, with reference to his own case,

> I am a man
> More sinn'd against, than sinning.   [3.2.59f.]

KENT most earnestly entreats him to enter a hovel which he had discovered on the heath; and on pressing him again and again to take shelter there LEAR exclaims

> Wilt break my heart?   [3.2.4]

Much is contained in these four words; as if he had said, 'the kindness and the gratitude of this servant exceeds that of my own children. Tho' I have given them a kingdom, yet have they basely discarded

me, and suffered a head so old and white as mine to be exposed to this
terrible tempest, while this fellow pities and would protect me from its
rage. I cannot bear this kindness from a perfect stranger; it breaks my
heart.' All this seems to be included in that short exclamation, which
another writer less acquainted with nature would have displayed at
large: such a suppression of sentiments plainly implied is judicious and
affecting. The reflections that follow are drawn likewise from an
intimate knowledge of man:

> When the mind's free,
> The body's delicate: the tempest in my mind
> Doth from my senses take all feeling else,
> Save what beats there.   [3.2.11ff.]

Here the remembrance of his daughters behaviour rushes upon him and
he exclaims, full of the idea of its unparalleled cruelty,

> Filial ingratitude!
> Is it not, as this mouth should tear this hand
> For lifting food to't!   [3.2.14ff.]

He then changes his stile, and vows with impotent menaces, as if still in
possession of the power he had resigned, to revenge himself on his
oppressors and to steel his breast with fortitude:

> But I'll punish home.
> No, I will weep no more!   [3.2.16f.]

But the sense of his sufferings returns again, and he forgets the resolution
he had formed the moment before:

> In such a night,
> To shut me out?—Pour on, I will endure!
> In such a night as this?   [3.2.17ff.]

At which, with a beautiful apostrophe, he suddenly addresses himself to
his absent daughters, tenderly reminding them of the favours he had so
lately and so liberally conferred upon them:

> O Regan, Goneril,
> Your old kind father; whose frank heart gave all!
> O that way madness lies; let me shun that;
> No more of that!   [3.2.19ff.]

The turns of passion in these few lines, are so quick and so various, that

I thought they merited to be minutely pointed out by a kind of perpetual commentary.

The mind is never so sensibly disposed to pity the misfortunes of others as when it is itself subdued and softened by calamity. Adversity diffuses a kind of sacred calm over the breast, that is the parent of thoughtfulness and meditation. The following reflections of LEAR in his next speech, when his passion has subsided for a short interval, are equally proper and striking:

> Poor naked wretches, wheresoe'er ye are,
> That bide the pelting of this pityless storm!
> How shall your houseless heads and unfed sides,
> Your loop'd and window'd raggedness, defend you
> From seasons such as these! [3.2.28ff.]

He concludes with a sentiment finely suited to his condition, and worthy to be written in characters of gold in the closet of every monarch upon earth:

> O! I have ta'en
> Too little care of this. Take physic, pomp!
> Expose thyself to feel what wretches feel;
> That thou may'st shake the superflux to them,
> And shew the Heav'ns more just! [3.2.32ff.]

LEAR being at last persuaded to take shelter in the hovel, the poet has artfully contrived to lodge there EDGAR, the discarded son of Gloucester, who counterfeits the character and habit of a mad beggar haunted by an evil demon, and whose supposed sufferings are enumerated with an inimitable wildness of fancy: 'Whom the foul fiend hath led thro' fire and thro' flame, thro' ford and whirlpool, o'er bog and quagmire; that hath laid knives under his pillow, and halters in his pew; set ratsbane by his porridge; made him proud of heart, to ride on a bay trotting horse over four inch'd bridges, to course his own shadow for a traitor.— Bless thy five wits, Tom's a cold!' [3.2.51ff.] The assumed madness of EDGAR and the real distraction of LEAR form a judicious contrast.

Upon perceiving the nakedness and wretchedness of this figure the poor king asks a question that I never could read without strong emotions of pity and admiration:

> What! have his daughters brought him to this pass?
> Couldst thou save nothing? Didst thou give them all? [3.2.63f.]

And when KENT assures him that the beggar hath no daughters, he hastily answers:

> Death, traitor, nothing could have subdued nature
> To such a lowness, but his unkind daughters.   [3.4.69ff.]

Afterwards, upon the calm contemplation of the misery of EDGAR, he breaks out into the following serious and pathetic reflection: 'Thou wert better in thy grave, than to answer with thy uncovered body this extremity of the skies. Is man no more than this? Consider him well. Thou ow'st the worm no silk, the beast no hide, the sheep no wool, the cat no perfume. Ha! here's three of us are sophisticated. Thou art the thing itself: unaccommodated man is no more than such a poor, bare, forked animal as thou art. Off, off, you lendings! Come, unbutton here.' [3.4.100ff.]

SHAKESPEARE has no where exhibited more inimitable strokes of his art than in this uncommon scene; where he has so well conducted even the natural jargon of the beggar and the jestings of the fool, which in other hands must have sunk into burlesque, that they contribute to heighten the pathetic to a very high degree.

The heart of LEAR having been agitated and torn by a conflict of such opposite and tumultuous passions, it is not wonderful that his 'wits should now begin to unsettle.' The first plain indication of the loss of his reason is his calling EDGAR a 'learned Theban', and telling KENT that 'he will keep still with his philosopher.' [3.4.150ff.] When he next appears he imagines he is punishing his daughters. The imagery is extremely strong, and chills one with horror to read it.

> To have a thousand with red burning spits
> Come hizzing in upon them!   [3.6.15f.]

As the fancies of lunatics have an extraordinary force and liveliness, and render the objects of their frenzy as it were present to their eyes, LEAR actually thinks himself suddenly restored to his kingdom, and seated in judgment to try his daughters for their cruelties:

> I'll see their tryal first; bring in the evidence.
> Thou robed man of justice take thy place;
> And thou, his yoke fellow of equity,
> Bench by his side. You are of the commission,
> Sit you too. Arraign her first, 'tis GONERIL——
> And here's another, whose warpt looks proclaim
> What store her heart is made of.   [3.6.35ff.]

Here he imagines that REGAN escapes out of his hands, and he eagerly exclaims,

> Stop her there.
> Arms, arms, sword, fire—Corruption in the place!
> False justicer, why hast thou let her 'scape?   [3.6.54ff.]

A circumstance follows that is strangely moving indeed, for he fancies that his favourite domestic creatures that used to fawn upon and caress him, and of which he was eminently fond, have now their tempers changed and join to insult him:

> The little dogs and all,
> Tray, Blanch, and Sweet-heart, see! they bark at me!   [3.6.61f.]

He again resumes his imaginary power, and orders them to anatomize REGAN: 'See what breeds about her heart—Is there any cause in nature that makes these hard hearts! You, Sir,' speaking to EDGAR, 'I entertain for one of my HUNDRED;' [3.6.75ff.] a circumstance most artfully introduced to remind us of the first affront he received, and to fix our thoughts on the causes of his distraction.

General criticism is on all subjects useless and unentertaining; but is more than commonly absurd with respect to SHAKESPEARE, who must be accompanied step by step and scene by scene in his gradual *developments* of characters and passions, and whose finer features must be singly pointed out if we would do compleat justice to his genuine beauties. It would have been easy to have declared, in general terms, 'that the madness of LEAR was very natural and pathetic;' and the reader might then have escaped what he may, perhaps, call a multitude of well known quotations. But then it had been impossible to exhibit a perfect picture of the secret workings and changes of LEAR's mind, which vary in each succeeding passage, and which render an allegation of each particular sentiment absolutely necessary.

[e] No. 132 (5 January 1754)

Madness being occasioned by a close and continued attention of the mind to a single object, SHAKESPEARE judiciously represents the loss of royalty as the particular idea which has brought on the distraction of LEAR, and which perpetually recurs to his imagination and mixes itself with all his ramblings. Full of this idea, therefore, he breaks out abruptly in the Fourth Act: 'No, they cannot touch me for coining: I am the king himself.' [4.6.83f.] He believes himself to be raising recruits, and censures the inability and unskilfulness of some of his soldiers: 'There's your press money. That fellow handles his bow like a crow keeper: draw me a clothier's yard. Look, look, a mouse! Peace peace; this piece of toasted cheese will do it.' [4.6.87ff.] The art of our poet is transcendent in thus making a passage that even borders on burlesque strongly expressive of the madness he is painting. LEAR suddenly thinks himself in the field: 'there's my gauntlet—I'll prove it on a giant,' and that he has shot his arrow successfully: 'O well flown barb! i'th' clout, i'th' clout: hewgh! give the word.' [4.6.90ff.] He then recollects the falshood and cruelty of his daughters, and breaks out in some pathetic reflexions on his old age and on the tempest to which he was so lately exposed: 'Ha! Goneril, ha! Regan! They flattered me like a dog, and told me, I had white hairs on my beard, ere the black ones were there. To say ay, and no, to every thing that I said—ay and no too, was no good divinity. When the rain came to wet me once, and the wind to make me chatter; when the thunder would not peace at my bidding; there I found 'em, there I smelt 'em out. Go to, they're not men of their words; they told me I was every thing: 'tis a lie, I am not ague-proof.' [4.6.96ff.] The impotence of royalty to exempt its possessor, more than the meanest subject, from suffering natural evils is here finely hinted at.

His friend and adherent GLO'STER, having been lately deprived of sight, enquires if the voice he hears is not the voice of the king. LEAR instantly catches the word, and replies with great quickness,

> Ay, every inch a king:
> When I do stare, see how the subject quakes!
> I pardon that man's life. What was thy cause?
> Adultery? no, thou shalt not die: die for adultery!
>
> [4.6.107ff.]

He then makes some very severe reflections on the hypocrisy of lewd and abandon'd women, and adds, 'Fie, fie, fie; pah, pah! Give me an ounce of civet, good apothecary, to sweeten my imagination:' and as every object seems to be present to the eyes of the lunatic, he thinks he pays for the drug; 'there's money for thee!' [4.6.129ff.] Very strong and lively also is the imagery in a succeeding speech, where he thinks himself viewing his subjects punished by the proper officer:

> Thou rascal bedel, hold thy bloody hand:
> Why dost thou lash that whore? strip thy own back;
> Thou hotly lust'st to use her in that kind
> For which thou whip'st her!   [4.6.160ff.]

This circumstance leads him to reflect on the efficacy of rank and power to conceal and palliate profligacy and injustice; and this fine satire is couched in two different metaphors, that are carried on with much propriety and elegance:

> Through tatter'd cloaths small vices do appear;
> Robes and furr'd gowns hide all. Plate sin with gold,
> And the strong lance of justice hurtless breaks;
> Arm it in rags, a pigmy's straw doth pierce it.   [4.6.164ff.]

We are moved to find that LEAR has some faint knowledge of his old and faithful courtier:

> If thou wilt weep my fortunes, take my eyes.
> I know thee well enough; thy name is Glo'ster: [4.6.177f.]

The advice he then gives him is very affecting:

> Thou must be patient; we came crying hither:
> Thou knowst, the first time that we smell the air,
> We wawle and cry . . .
> When we are born, we cry that we are come
> To this great stage of fools!   [4.6.179ff.]

This tender complaint of the miseries of human life bears so exact a resemblance with the following passage of LUCRETIUS that I cannot forbear transcribing it:[1]

> Vagitûque locum lugubri complet, ut æquum est,
> Cui tantum in vitâ restet transire malorum.

It is not to be imagined that our author copied from the Roman; on such a subject it is almost impossible but that two persons of genius and sensibility must feel and think alike. LEAR drops his moralities, and meditates revenge:

> It were a delicate stratagem to shoe
> A troop of horse with felt. I'll put't in proof;
> And when I've stolen upon these sons in law,
> Then kill, kill, kill, kill, kill, kill.   [4.6.185ff.]

The expedient is well suited to the character of a lunatic; and the frequent repetitions of the word 'kill' forcibly represent his rage and desire

---

[1] 5.226ff: The new-born child lies naked on the ground, speechless; 'He fills the air with his piteous wailing, and quite rightly, considering what evils life holds in store for him.'

of revenge, and must affect an intelligent audience at once with pity and terror. At this instant CORDELIA sends one of her attendants to protect her father from the danger with which he is threatened by her sisters. The wretched king is so accustomed to misery, and so hopeless of succour, that when the messenger offers to lead him out he imagines himself taken captive and mortally wounded:

> No rescue? what a prisoner? I am e'en
> The nat'ral fool of fortune: use me well,
> You shall have ransom. Let me have surgeons;
> I am cut to th' brains.   [4.6.190ff.]

CORDELIA at length arrives. An opiate is administered to the king to calm the agonies and agitations of his mind, and a most interesting interview ensues between this daughter that was so unjustly suspected of disaffection, and the rash and mistaken father. LEAR, during his slumber, has been arrayed in regal apparel and is brought upon the stage in a chair, not recovered from his trance. I know not a speech more truly pathetic than that of CORDELIA when she first sees him:

> Had you not been their father, these white flakes
> Did challenge pity of them. Was this a face
> To be expos'd against the warring winds?   [4.7.30ff.]

The dreadfulness of that night is expressed by a circumstance of great humanity, for which kind of strokes SHAKESPEARE is as eminent as for his poetry:

> My very enemy's dog,
> Tho' he had bit me, should have stood that night
> Against my fire. And wast thou fain, poor father,
> To hovel thee with swine, and rogues forlorn,
> In short and musty straw?   [4.7.36ff.]

LEAR begins to awake; but his imagination is still distempered, and his pain exquisite:

> You do me wrong to take me out o'th' grave.
> Thou art a soul in bliss; but I am bound
> Upon a wheel of fire, that mine own tears
> Do scald like molten lead . . .   [4.7.44ff.]

When CORDELIA in great affliction asks him if he knows her, he replies,

You are a spirit, I know; when did you die? [4.7.49]

This reply heightens her distress: but his sensibility beginning to return, she kneels to him, and begs his benediction. I hope I have no readers that can peruse his answer without tears:

> Pray do not mock me:
> I am a very foolish fond old man,
> Fourscore and upward; and to deal plainly,
> I fear I am not in my perfect mind.
> Methinks I should know you, and know this man;
> Yet I am doubtful: for I'm mainly ignorant,
> What place this is.—Do not laugh at me;
> For as I am a man, I think this lady
> To be my child CORDELIA. [4.7.59ff.]

The humility, calmness and sedateness of this speech, opposed to the former rage and indignation of LEAR, is finely calculated to excite commiseration. Struck with the remembrance of the injurious suspicion he had cherished against this favourite and fond daughter the poor old man entreats her 'not to weep,' and tells her that 'if she has prepared poison for him, he is ready to drink it; for I know,' says he, 'you do not, you cannot love me, after my cruel usage of you: your sisters have done me much wrong, of which I have some faint remembrance; you have some cause to hate me, they have none.' [4.7.71ff.] Being told that he is not in France but in his own kingdom he answers hastily, and in connection with that leading idea which I have before insisted on, 'Do not abuse me:' [77]—and adds, with a meekness and contrition that are very pathetic, 'Pray now forget and forgive; I am old, and foolish.' [85]

CORDELIA is at last slain: the lamentations of LEAR are extremely tender and affecting; and this accident is so severe and intolerable that it again deprives him of his intellect, which seemed to be returning.

His last speech, as he surveys the body, consists of such simple reflections as nature and sorrow dictate:

> Why should a dog, a horse, a rat have life,
> And thou no breath at all? Thou'lt come no more;
> Never, never, never, never, never! [5.3.306ff.]

The heaving and swelling of his heart is described by a most expressive circumstance:

> Pray you undo this button. Thank you Sir:

Do you see this? Look on her, look on her lips,
Look there, look there . . .   (*Dies.*)   [5.3.309ff.]

I shall transiently observe, in conclusion of these remarks, that this drama is chargeable with considerable imperfections. The plot of EDMUND against his brother, which distracts the attention, and destroys the unity of the fable; the cruel and horrid extinction of GLO'STER's eyes, which ought not to be exhibited on the stage; the utter improbability of GLO'STER's imagining, though blind, that he had leaped down Dover Cliff; and some passages that are too turgid and full of strained metaphors are faults which the warmest admirers of SHAKESPEARE will find it difficult to excuse. I know not, also, whether the cruelty of the daughters is not painted with circumstances too savage and unnatural: for it is not sufficient to say that this monstrous barbarity is founded on historical truth, if we recollect the just observation of BOILEAU,[1]

Le vrai peut quelquefois n'etre pas vraisemblable.

[1] 'Some truths may be too strong to be believed.' [Somes]

83

140. Arthur Murphy, Essays on Shakespeare

1753–4

From the *Gray's-Inn Journal* (1753–4). The textual history of this journal is complex: apparently, fifty-two of the essays originally appeared in the *Craftsman: or Gray's-Inn Journal* between 21 October 1752 and September 1753. Murphy wrote another fifty-two for the *Gray's-Inn Journal* as a separate publication between 29 September 1753 and 21 September 1754: the essays selected here all come from this second set. The essays were reprinted in a two-volume edition in 1756, and again in Murphy's *Works*, 7 vols, 1786 (vols V–VI). In these reprints Murphy made large and small alterations, and changed the dates of the original essays: for this reason I have given to the essays here reprinted the titles which he added to them in 1756 and 1758. The first essay printed here on *Macbeth* was not reprinted in full, perhaps because it plagiarized Dr Johnson, with whom Murphy later became friendly. Apart from this item the text reprinted is from the last version revised by Murphy, that of 1786. The best study of the textual problem is R. B. Botting, 'The Textual History of Murphy's *Gray's-Inn Journal*', *Research Studies of the State College of Washington*, xxv (1957), pp. 33–48.

Arthur Murphy (1727–1805), for a brief period an actor, and for many years (1757–88) a lawyer, was also a dramatist, poet, journalist and critic of some repute. He wrote some sixteen plays, numerous poems and translations, edited Fielding's *Works* in 1762 and wrote a biography to accompany them, as he did when editing Dr Johnson's *Works* (12 vols, 1792). He edited and translated Tacitus and Sallust, and in 1801 published *The Life of David Garrick*. Of the *Gray's-Inn Journal* Walter Graham wrote that it contained 'some notable criticism which distinguished it . . . above the general level of its contemporaries' (*English Literary Periodicals* (New York, 1930) p. 124), and Arthur Sherbo has described him as being 'without doubt the ablest critic of contemporary drama and acting in the century' (*New Essays by Arthur Murphy* (East Lansing, Michigan, 1963) p. 185).

---

[a] Criticism on the Tragedy of *Macbeth*.[1]

My Friend Mr *Candid*, whom I have formerly introduced to my Readers as a Member of the Club to which I belong at the *Devil-Tavern* near *Temple-Bar*, called upon me the other Morning and informed me that having seen the Tragedy of *Macbeth* inimitably performed the Night before he had thrown together some cursory Observations on that Production, which he desired I would communicate to the Public through the Channel of this Paper. As I make no doubt but they will prove acceptable I shall submit them to the Perusal of the Critics in the loose Form which the Writer observed in putting them together.

'In order to calculate the Merit and Abilities of an Author with any Degree of Exactness it is highly necessary to consider the Genius of his Age, and to examine the Opinions of his Contemporaries.[2] If a Poet now-a-days should make the entire Action of his Tragedy depend upon Enchantment, and the principal Incidents result from the interposition of supernatural Agents, he would undoubtedly be censured as transgressing the Bounds of Probability. He would be banished from the Stage to the Nursery, and condemned to write Fairy Tales instead of Tragedies. But *Shakespeare* was in no Danger of such Censures; for if we survey the Notions that prevail'd when *Macbeth* was written it will appear that he only turned a System universally admitted to his Advantage; and did not in the least over burthen the Credulity of his Audience.

The Reality of Witchcraft and Enchantment has in all Ages been credited by the common People, and in many Countries even by the Learned. In Proportion as the Darkness of Ignorance was more gross these Phantoms have appeared more frequently, but the brightest Beams of Knowledge have never been sufficient to drive them throughout the World. In the Time of our great Dramatic Genius the Doctrine of Witchcraft was by the Law and Fashion equally established.[3] As Prodigies therefore are always seen whenever the Imagination is prepossessed

[1] This is no. 8 in the original edition, dated 17 November 1753.

[2] Compare Johnson's *Observations on Macbeth*, Vol. 3, pp. 165f.: Note 1. I have placed these borrowings from Johnson within inverted commas, as I have also done with the other authors Murphy draws on in this essay.

[3] Murphy now borrows from the later part of Johnson's Note, p. 167.

with them Witches were discovered daily, and in some Places increased so much that a learned Bishop takes notice of a Village in *Lancashire* where their Number exceeded the Number of Houses.

Upon this epidemical Phrenzy *Shakespeare* might well be permitted to Build a Play especially since he has with great Exactness followed the Histories, which were then deemed authentic, and I do not doubt but the Scenes of Enchantment were thought by himself and his Audience very awful and affecting.'

This Tragedy may be considered in a twofold View: with regard to the imaginary Existencies introduced, and likewise with respect to the Characters drawn from the Page of human Nature. In this latter Sense it must be allowed to teach a very important Lesson, *viz.* the intoxicating Power and rapid Progress of Vice. In the Person of *Macbeth* we see a Mind enriched with many noble Qualities, and, after a severe Conflict, subdued by Invincible Ambition, in spite of the Suggestions of a Conscience naturally tender and sensible. All his Sentiments of Loyalty, Gratitude, and Hospitality give place by imperceptible Degrees to his unbounded Lust of Power and to the Instigations of a wicked Woman, till at length he is transformed from a Man of many moral Virtues to as great a Monster of Iniquity as ever debased human Nature. Who is there that does not Startle at the Moral here inculcated? Who, though adorned with every amiable Quality, can reflect on *Macbeth's* unhappy Fate without Shuddering to think on what a precarious Tenure he holds the most valuable of all his Possessions?

'Macbeth (says an ingenious Author)[1] is the same in *Shakespeare* as in *Boethius* and *Buchanan*. The Poet conforms his Fable and Characters to the Traditions of his Historians. "Animus etiam *Macbethi* per se ferox, prope quotidianis conviciis conjugis (quæ omnium Consiliorum ei erat conscia) stimulabatur." "*Macbeth*, fierce of himself, was spurr'd on by the almost daily Reproaches of his Wife, his Bosom-Counsellor in all his Designs." How nobly has *Shakespeare* improved this Hint; and how finished are his Characters of this wicked Pair through every Stage of Guilt, unsteady and reluctant in the Man, ready and remorseless in the Woman!'

The Incantations in this Play have a Solemnity admirably adapted to the Occasion; they are part of the Story itself, and therefore properly used by the Poet in a Business of itself Dark, Horrid and Bloody. But Subjects of this Kind (which are perhaps in themselves disagreeable) cannot at any Time become Entertaining but by receiving a Tinge from

[1] William Guthrie, *An Essay upon English Tragedy*, 1747: see Vol. 3, p. 199.

an Imagination like *Shakespeare*'s; for which Reason Mr *Dryden* would not allow even *Beaumont* and *Fletcher* to imitate him in this Point.[4]

> *But* Shakespeare's *Magic could not copied be;*
> *Within that Circle none could walk but he.*

Our Author could not only bring his *Ariel* from the Ætherial Regions but could also summon Ghosts from below, and had an equal sway in the Upper and Lower World. 'The noble Extravagance of Fancy, which he had in so great Perfection, made him capable of succeeding where he had nothing to support him besides the Strength of his own Genius. There is something so wild, yet so solemn, in the Speeches of his imaginary Persons that we cannot help thinking them Natural, and must confess that if there are such Beings it is highly probable their Manners and Vocations, their Sports and Pastimes, their Delights and Resentments, must be such as he has represented.'[2]

'Through all the Scenes of Inchantment it is observable that *Shakespeare* has selected his infernal Ceremonies with the utmost Judgment. He artfully conforms to vulgar Opinions and Traditions, and multiplies the Circumstances of Horror upon an Occasion in which the Fate of a King is involved with the most amazing Solemnity. The *Babe* whose *Finger* is used must be *strangled* in its Birth; the *Liver* of a *blaspheming Jew* must make part; the *Grease* must not only be *human* but must have dropped from a *Gibbet*, and that too, the *Gibbet of a Murderer*; and even the *Sow* whose Blood is infused must have offended Nature by *devouring her own Farrow*. [4.1.26ff., 64ff.] These are touches of the greatest Judgment and Genius'.[3]

After this general View of *Macbeth* I must beg leave to mention some particular Passages which are always sure to strike very forcibly on my Imagination. The Scene wherein Lady *Macbeth* endeavours to work her Husband to the Execution of her treacherous Design on *Duncan*'s Life seems to deserve particular Notice. 'The Arguments which she urges evidently demonstrate the Poet's Knowledge of the human Heart. She artfully dwells on the Excellence and Dignity of Courage, which Ideas have in every Age dazled Mankind, and animated by turns the victorious Hero and the midnight Ruffian. *Macbeth* destroys the Fallacy by distinguishing between true Courage and false Spirit:

1 See Vol. 1, p. 79.
2 Compare Addison, *Spectator* 419: Vol. 2, p. 280.
3 See Johnson's Note XXXV: Vol. 3, pp. 179f., and below, pp. 282f.

> *I dare do all that may become a Man,*
> *Who dares do more is none.* [1.7.46f.]

The judicious Critic will perceive that this Topic is insisted upon with the utmost Propriety, for as Courage is the principal Virtue of a Soldier the Reproach of Cowardice cannot be borne from *a Woman* with any Degree of Patience.'[1]

When *Lady Macbeth* is confirming herself in her horrid Purpose she breaks out into a Wish (amidst the Violence of her Emotions) very natural to a Murderer:

> *Come thick Night,*
> *And pall thee in the* dunnest Smoke of Hell,
> *That my keen Knife* see not *the* Wound *it makes,*
> *Nor Heav'n peep thro' the Blanket of the Dark,*
> *To cry* — HOLD! — HOLD! [1.5.47ff.]

In this Passage is exerted all the Force of Poetry. The Night is invoked, not invested in common Obscurity but the *Smoke of Hell*; and we cannot but sympathize with the Horrors of a Wretch about to murder her King, her Friend, her Benefactor, and her Guest. Lady *Macbeth* dreads lest the Sight of the intended Wound should withold her Knife, and she proceeds to wish, in the Madness of her Guilt, that the very Inspection of Heaven may be intercepted and that she may (veiled in infernal Darkness) escape the Eye of Providence. This is the highest Extravagance of determined Wickedness.

When *Macbeth* is preparing for the Murder of *Duncan* his Imagination is big with the Horror of the Deed; *within*, his Soul is dismay'd at the Guilt of the Enterprize, and *without*, every thing is dismal and affrighting. His Eyes rebel against his Reason, and he starts at Images which have no Reality.

> *Is this a Dagger, which I see before me,*
> *The Handle tow'rd my Hand! come, let me clutch thee—*
> *I have thee not, and yet I see thee still.* [2.1.33ff.]

He then endeavours to summon his Reason to his Aid, but in vain; the Terror stamped on all his Powers will not be shaken off:

> *I see thee yet, in Form as palpable*
> *As this which now I draw.* [2.1.40f.]

[1] This paragraph is taken from Johnson's Note XVI: Vol. 3, pp. 172f.

Here ensues a new Attempt to reason himself out of the Delusion, but it is too strong:

> *I see thee still;*
> *And on thy Blade and Dudgeon gouts of Blood,*
> *Which were not there before.*   [2.1.45ff.]

At length the Chimera vanishes:

> *There's no such Thing.*   [2.1.47]

The whole Delusion is carried on in so skilful a Manner that the Audience start at the visionary Dagger, and share the Consternation. The Contrast between *Macbeth* and his Wife is finely marked by the Remorse of the Man and the hard-hearted Cruelty of the Woman. The least Noise, the very sound of their own Voices is affrighting, and the Mind is alarmed every instant with new Conjectures and fresh Ideas of Perturbation.—

> *Hark! Peace!*
> *It was the Owl that shrieked;—that fatal Bellman*
> *That gives the stern'st Good-night—he is about it*   [2.2.2ff.]

and again:

> *Alack! I am afraid they have awak'd;*
> *And 'tis not done;—th' Attempt, and not the Deed,*
> *Confounds us—hark!—I laid the Daggers ready,*
> *He could not miss them.*   [2.2.9ff.]

In short, the Murder is represented in the same affecting Horror which would seize the Heart upon actual Commission. Every Image seems Reality, and alarms the Soul; the very Blood curdles and runs cold through the utmost Horror and Detestation of the Deed.

Shakespeare is almost the only Poet who can boast the peculiar Art of inserting Poetical Description in the most serious Part of his Drama with Propriety. Passion, Sentiment, and Poetry are frequently united by him in the most agreeable Assemblage. Amidst *Macbeth*'s slaughterous Thoughts the following Lines are introduced with a solemnity suitable to the Occasion, and carry with them a pleasing kind of gloomy Imagery:

> *E're the Bat hath flown*
> *His cloyster'd Flight, e're to black Hecate's Summons*

The shard-born Beetle with his drowsy Hums
Hath rung Night's yawning Peal, there shall be done
A deed of dreadful Note. [3.2.40ff.]

It is impossible to reflect on the Character of *Macduff* without observing the singular Art with which the Author paints the domestic Virtues, or those Affections of the Soul which regard the Preservation of a Wife and Children. Such Sentiments as are there expressed result from the Suggestions of Nature, at all Times so uniform in her Workings that nothing but a perverse Affectation of pompous Language and luxuriance of Diction can hinder so many Writers from reaching a more exact Similitude in their Representations.

I shall conclude with observing that the first great Instance of a Dramatic Genius consists in the Formation of Characters. In this Field *Shakespeare* remains unrivalled. It is his great Excellence to mark every Character with Manners and Sentiments properly adapted, and to maintain the Propriety of each in all Circumstances of Action. 'Guilty Ambition moves in a Sphere so narrow in itself that it seems almost impossible to Diversify it; and yet we see it differently modified in four Characters of our Author. If we view *Hamlet*'s Father-in-Law how different is the Remorse of the *Dane* from the *Scot*'s Distraction? The Confusion of *King John* how distinguished from both? While the close, the vigilant, and the jealous Guilt of *Richard* is entirely peculiar to himself.'[1] (43–7)

[b] Shakespeare vindicated, in a letter to Voltaire[2]

*   *   *

I have observed, Sir, that you are disposed upon all occasions to censure the *English* stage with some degree of acrimony whenever it comes in your way. SHAKESPEARE stands at the head of our dramatic writers, perhaps at the head of all who have figured in that kind in every age and nation. With that great poet you have not hesitated to take unbounded liberty in a manner, if I am not mistaken, not consistent with that manly sense which seems to be your characteristic, and in a stile apparently destitute of your usual delicacy. Should I say that the boasted *bienséance*

1 This point is borrowed from Guthrie: see Vol. 3, p. 195, and compare the same idea in Murphy's *London Chronicle* essay, pp. 281f. below.

2 In the first edition this essay is numbered 12, and dated 15 December 1753; in the 1756 and 1786 editions it is numbered 41 and dated 28 July 1753.

of your country has deserted you in some of these passages, I flatter myself that upon a review of them you will not totally disavow it. The most striking of the various judgments which you have vented against our immortal bard is found in the discourse prefixed to your tragedy of *Semiramis*, and literally translated into *English* is as follows:

I do not mean to justify the tragedy of *Hamlet* in every particular; it is in fact a barbarous piece, abounding with such gross absurdities that it would not be tolerated by the vulgar of *France* and *Italy*. The hero of the play runs mad in the second act, and his mistress meets with the same misfortune in the third. The Prince takes *Ophelia*'s father for a rat, and kills him: in despair she throws herself into a river. Her grave is dug on the stage: the grave-digger, with a skull in his hand, amuses himself with a string of miserable jests, and the Prince answers them in language equally disgusting. *Hamlet*, his mother, and father-in-law drink together on the stage. They divert themselves with bottle songs, (*Chansons à boire*) they quarrel, they fight, they kill. One would imagine this play the production of a drunken savage. And yet among these absurdities, which render the *English* drama absolutely barbarous, there are some strokes in *Hamlet* worthy of the most exalted genius. This has always been matter of astonishment to me; it looks as if Nature, in pure sport, diverted herself with mixing in *Shakespeare*'s head every thing sublime and great with all that can be conceived low, mean and detestable.

It is thus the elegant and sensible *Voltaire* speaks of *Shakespeare*. I would ask yourself, Sir, is this criticism candid? Is it a fair analysis, a true account of the tragedy in question? We do not concern ourselves in this country with what is agreeable to the taste of the vulgar in *France* or *Italy*; we know that the *clinquant* of an opera, or a *comedie ballet*, is more acceptable to their refinement than the sterling bullion of an *English* performance; but we might expect from a writer of eminence a truer and more exact opinion. *Hamlet*, Sir, does not run mad: if he did, *King Lear* has proved what a beautiful distress might arise from it. *Hamlet* counterfeits madness, for his own private end. Nobody ever imagined that he thinks he is killing a rat when he says *Polonius*. If you will be pleased to recollect the passage you will find that he takes him for his better, meaning the King, and the rat is only mentioned to save appearances.

Ophelia does undoubtedly run mad. The desolation of her mind arises from filial piety: her virtue and her misfortunes make her respectable. Give me leave to add, her distress is perhaps the most pathetic upon any stage. It is true she sings in misery, and that is not usual in grave and serious tragedy; but it occurs in nature, and what *Shakespeare* saw in nature he transplanted into his drama. He knew of no rules to restrain him, and if he did he scorned the restraint. The beauty of *Ophelia*'s madness, Sir, consists in this: it gives the actings of the mind; it shews the course of the ideas in a disturbed imagination; and the poet who can thus turn the heart inside out does more than pompous declamation ever attained. That *Ophelia*'s grave is dug on the stage cannot be denied, but that very indecorum produces a string of beautiful reflections, and such a vein of morality as cannot be paralleled by the *Scene Francoise*. I cannot recollect that *Hamlet* ever shocked me with miserable jests upon this occasion; nor do I remember that any of the personages are such honest bottle companions as to carouse and sing merry catches on the stage. Pray consider, Sir, that our language, though no way inferior to the *French*, is not universally understood abroad. From your representation it may be inferred that our great poet is really the *drunken savage* you have thought proper to call him. This would be derogating from the greatest poet (*Milton* excepted) that the world has seen since the days of *Homer*, and, I believe you will grant, is dealing unfairly with a man whom you cannot but reverence.

When you confess that he has many flights of the highest elevation you make an approach towards justice, but I cannot help thinking that you are somewhat like a painter who lays on just and proper colouring and then instantly effaces it, when you add that you are astonished at his sublime excursions of fancy. I should have expected from your candour that you would rather have said, it is a pity that he who soared to such glorious heights should ever tire his eagle wing and fall beneath himself. You may remember that it is with this good temper *Longinus* talks of *Homer*; they are dreams, says he, but they are the dreams of *Homer*.[1] He might have given the appellation of a *drunken savage*; he might have called *Homer* an *old dotard*; he might have said, in the fury of criticism, that some of his long stories are detestable; but a candid critic forgives the imbecilities of human nature, and passes sentence like a mild and good-natured judge.

Cum tabulis animum censoris sumet honesti.[2]

HOR.

In one of your letters concerning the *English* nation you are pleased with a saying of the late Lord *Bolingbroke*, in relation to the Duke of

[1] Longinus, *On the Sublime*, §21: compare Colman above, p. 58.

[2] *Epistles*, 2.2.110: 'But the man whose aim is to have wrought a poem true to Art's rules, when he takes his tablets, will take also the spirit of an honest censor.'

Marlborough. 'He was,' replied that ingenious nobleman when his opinion was asked, 'so great a man that I have forgot his faults.' Something like this might have been your judgment upon *Shakespeare*: and give me leave to add, it was more particularly incumbent upon you to treat his memory with respect because, I apprehend, you owe very great obligations to him in many of your dramatic writings. We frequently perceive you lighting your torch at his fire; in your *Mahomet*, *Macbeth* 'marshals you the way that you are going'; in many other scenes we can catch your eye fixed upon our immortal bard; and in your *Semiramis* you have adventured to introduce a ghost, in imitation of the very play which has occasioned the severity already cited. The success you met with on that occasion might serve to convince you of *Shakespeare's* inimitable merit. The *Parterre*, if I mistake not, turned their backs to the stage, and blew their noses; while the ghost on our theatre never fails to impress an awful stillness on every mind. This, Sir, let me assure you, is not owing to the barbarity of our taste but to the amazing power of our poet's imagination, which could explore the undiscovered regions of eternity, and recall the fleeting spirit with a solemnity of ideas responsive to the occasion.

With us islanders *Shakespeare* is a kind of established religion in poetry. His bays will always flourish with undiminished verdure. When I say this I am far from maintaining that he is not guilty of transgressions; but for his transgressions he recompences his auditors with beauties which no art will ever equal. That the rules established by *Aristotle* and *Horace* are, for the most part, agreeable to nature, I am ready to allow. Men of inferior genius may think it their interest, and, if they will, their DUTY, to conform to those rules. They may, in that school, learn the œconomy of a just and well arranged fable. But fable is but a secondary beauty, the exhibition of character and the excitement of the passions justly claiming the precedence. With the rules which theoretical writers have drawn into a system *Shakespeare* appears not much acquainted. Of those rules some are valuable, because founded in NATURE; others are of positive institution only, and like many arbitrary acts of civil society they cease in time to have the force of obligation. In dramatic poetry SHAKESPEARE may be considered as one of the GENTILES, but of those GENTILES *who, having not the* LAW, DO BY NATURE the *things contained in the Law; which shews the work of the Law within their hearts, and they are* A LAW *unto themselves.*[1] This, Sir, was precisely the case of SHAKESPEARE. He had no written precepts, and

[1] Romans 2.14–15.

he wanted none: the light of Nature was his guide. In some instances he saw the beauty arising from the unity of his subject; in others he chose to follow the chain of historical events, and he felt, as his auditors always feel, that the warmth, the spirit, and rapidity of his genius could give even to wild variety all the graces of connection. He knew how to interest the affections, and that interest diffused through every piece hurries the mind in a stream of passion to new matter, without a pause to mark the transition. It is in dramatic composition as in gardening: where nature does not afford spontaneous beauties recourse must be had to the embellishments of slow endeavoring art, to the regularity of uniform vistas, the intricacy of elaborated mazes, and a studied insertion of evergreens. But when the country of itself presents attractive scenes on every side, when the trees branch out with free expansion, and the bold prospect surprizes with the heath, the lawn, the hill, and valley in wild variety, the littleness of tedious culture is unnecessary and trifling ornaments are unlooked for.

I shall conclude with a passage from your own works. 'Do not blush, Sir, to repent of your little inadvertencies: it is hard, but it is amiable to acknowledge our errors.' *Ne rougissez point, Monsieur, de vous repentir de vos petites inadvertances. Il est dur, mais il est beau d'avouer ses fautes.* (V, 348–58)

[c] Criticism on the Tragedy of King Lear[1]

At the last meeting of our club my friend Mr *Candid* informed us that he had lately seen the character of King *Lear* inimitably performed by Mr *Garrick*. The impression, he told us, left upon his mind by the united art of the poet and the actor kept all his passions in agitation for several days. He could not advert to any other subject till he discharged the fulness of his thoughts in an essay upon that excellent Tragedy, which he desired might be this day communicated to the readers of the *Gray's-Inn Journal*.

In order to criticise a great poet with any degree of perspicuity it is requisite to consider the nature of his fable and the moral scope of the

---

[1] This essay is no. 16 in the original edition, and is dated 12 January 1754; in the 1756 edition it was no. 65 (12 January 1754) and in 1786 it was no. 78 (13 April 1754). In the first edition it began as follows: 'Having lately seen in the *Adventurer* a Criticism upon the Tragedy of *King Lear*, in which that Writer, whom I have often admired upon other Occasions, seems to me to have mistaken the principal Idea in the old King's Mind while in a State of Madness, I hope it will be Unnecessary to make any Apology either to him, or to the Public, for offering my Thoughts on this Subject.' Compare a similar disagreement that took place in 1747, between Samuel Foote (Vol. 3, No. 109), who argued that Lear's madness derives from his frustrated desire for power, and an anonymous writer (No. 112) who urged the effects of ingratitude.

work. Order requires that in the next place we proceed to observe how he lays on his colouring, the disposition of each person, the expression of the passions, and which is the capital figure in the piece. *Lear* being examined in this manner it will appear that the author intended to exhibit in the most striking colours the horrid crime of filial ingratitude. To enforce this he represents an old monarch tired with the cares of state, and willing to distribute his possessions among his daughters in proportion to their affections towards his person. Accordingly the two that flatter him obtain all, the third sister being disinherited for her sincerity. The king is at length driven by the ingratitude of his two eldest daughters to an extreme of madness, which produces the finest tragic distress ever seen on any stage.[1]

This is the ground-work of the play. A different view of it has been of late displayed by a writer of known ability. He ascribes the madness of *Lear* to the loss of royalty. That this notion is not only fundamentally wrong but also destructive of the fine pathetic that melts the heart in every scene will, I think, appear from a due attention to the conduct of the poet throughout the piece. The behaviour of *Lear*'s children is always uppermost in the thoughts of the aged monarch. We perceive it working upon his passions, till at length his mind settles into a fixed attention to that single object. This, I think, is evident in the progress of the play.

Lear, in his first scene, shews himself susceptible of the most violent emotions. The poet has drawn him impetuous to a degree, proud, haughty, revengeful, and tender-hearted. In such a mind it is not to be wondered that ill-treatment should excite the most uneasy sensations. He takes fire at an imaginary appearance of disaffection in *Cordelia*.

> *But goes thy heart with this?*
> *So young and so untender!*   [1.1.104f.]

He is soon after alarmed with suspicions of disrespect from *Goneril*. 'I will look further into't.' [1.4.69]—He is soon convinced of her disregard. The effect it has upon him indicates a mind impotent, and liable to the worst perturbations.

> *Does* Lear *walk thus? speak thus? where are his eyes?*
> *Either his notion weakens, his discernings*
> *Are lethargy'd.*   [1.4.226ff.]

[1] The original edition continued, 'As this is the Groundwork of the Play, I am really surprized that the critic in the *Adventurer* should impute the Madness of *Lear* to the Loss of Royalty.'

His reflections shew what is nearest to his heart.

> *Ingratitude! thou marble-hearted fiend,*
> *More hideous, when thou shew'st thee in a child,*
> *Than the sea-monster.* [1.4.259ff.]

He observes that *Cordelia*'s fault was small; and when even that made such an impression on him what are we to expect from his fiery disposition when rejected by those to whom he had given all? His imprecation, though big with horror, is the natural result of his indignation and the tenderness and overflowings of softness which melt him in the midst of his vehemence produce a fine conflict of passions.

> *Th'untented woundings of a father's curse*
> *Pierce ev'ry sense about thee!—Old fond eyes,*
> *Beweep this cause again, I'll pluck ye out,*
> *And cast ye, with the waters that you lose,*
> *To temper clay.* [1.4.300ff.]

His haughtiness breaks out in a menace to his daughter:

> *Thou shalt find*
> *That I'll resume the shape, which thou dost think*
> *I have cast off for ever.* [1.4.308ff.]

His address to *Regan* is extremely tender and pathetic:

> *Thy tender-hefted nature shall not give*
> *Thee o'er to harshness.* [2.4.170f.]

And a little after:

> *Thou better know'st*
> *The offices of nature, bond of childhood,*
> *Effects of courtesy, dues of gratitude;*
> *Thy half o'th'kingdom thou hast not forgot,*
> *Wherein I thee endow'd* [2.4.176ff.]

There have been many poets acquainted in general with the passions of human nature. Accordingly we find them constantly describing their effects; but *Shakespeare*'s art shows their impulse and their workings without the aid of definition or flowery description. Besides the general survey of the heart, *Shakespeare* was more intimately versed in the various tempers of mankind than any poet whatever. We always find him making the passions of each person in his drama operate according

to his peculiar habit and frame of mind. In the tragedy in question there
are so many strokes of this nature that in my opinion it is his master-
piece. In every speech in *Lear*'s mouth there is such an artful mixture of
opposite passions that the heart-strings of an audience are torn on every
side. The frequent transition and shifting of emotions is natural to every
breast: in *Lear* they are characteristic marks of his temper:

> *I pr'ythee, daughter, do not make me mad.*
> *I will not trouble thee, my child. Farewel.*
> *We'll meet no more—no more see one another.*
> *But yet thou art my flesh, my blood, my daughter;*
> *Or rather a disease that's in my flesh, &c.*
> > *But I'll not chide thee;*
> *Let shame come when it will, I do not call it;*
> *I do not bid the thunder-bearer shoot,*
> *Nor tell tales of thee to high judging* Jove.   [2.4.217ff.]

In this speech every master passion in his temper rises in conflict, his
pride, his revenge, his quick resentment, and his tenderness. The
following passage has some of the finest turns in the world:

> *O let not woman's weapons, water-drops,*
> *Stain my man's cheeks—no, ye unnat'ral hags—*
> *I will have such revenges on ye both—I'll do such things—*
> *What they are I know not—but they shall be*
> *The terrors of the earth.—You think I'll weep—*
> *No—I'll not weep—I have full cause for weeping—*
> *This heart shall break into a thousand flaws—*
> *Or e'er I'll weep—O fool, I shall go mad.*   [2.4.276ff.]

Here the distressed monarch leaves his daughter's roof. The next time
we see him he is on a wild heath in a violent storm. In this distressful
situation all his reflections take a tincture from the gloomy colour of his
mind. We soon see what is the principal object of his attention.

> > *Thou all-shaking thunder,*
> *Crack nature's mould; all germins spill at once,*
> *That make* UNGRATEFUL MAN.   [3.2.6ff.]

And again:

> > *The tempest in my mind*
> *Doth from my senses take all feeling else*
> *Save what beats there—Filial ingratitude!*   [3.4.12ff.]

His sudden apostrophe to his daughters must draw tears from every eye:

> O Regan! Goneril!
> *Your old kind father, whose frank heart gave all.*   [3.4.19f.]

The break has a fine effect.

> *O! that way madness lies—let me shun that—*
> *No more of that—*   [3.4.21f.]

As yet the perturbation of his mind does not seem fixed to a point. He begins to moralize, but still with a view to his own afflictions. *Edgar* enters disguised like a madman, and this seems to give the finishing stroke. *Lear's* first question is, 'have his daughters brought him to this pass? couldst thou save nothing? didst thou give them all?' [3.4.63ff.] Here we have the first touch of fixed madness in the play. Will the resignation of his sceptre or the mere loss of regal power be any longer urged as the cause of *Lear's* distraction?

Madness opens a new field to the vast imagination of *Shakespeare*. He had before displayed every movement of the heart: the human understanding now becomes his province. In this, we shall find, he acquits himself with the most masterly skill. Mr *Locke* observes, that *madmen do not seem to have lost the faculty of reasoning; but having joined together some ideas very wrongly, they mistake them for truths; and they err as men do that argue right from wrong principles. For by the violence of their imaginations having mistaken their fancies for realities, they make right deductions from them.*[1]

Agreeably to this account *Lear*, upon the appearance of a madman, takes it for granted that it is owing to his daughters ill-treatment. When contradicted, he replies, 'Death! traitor! nothing could have subdued nature to such a lowness, but his unkind daughters.' [3.4.69ff.] He next takes him for a philosopher, and agreeably to that notion enquires 'what is the cause of thunder?' [3.4.151].

To a mind exasperated the desire of revenge is natural: accordingly we find him breaking out with the utmost rage.

> *To have a thousand with red burning spits*
> *Come hizzing in upon 'em!*   [3.6.15f.]

He proceeds to accuse his daughters in a court of justice. 'Arraign her

---

[1] Locke, *An Essay Concerning Human Understanding*, 2.11.13.

first, 'tis *Goneril*. I here make oath before this honourable assembly, she kicked the poor king her father. Here is another too, whose warpt looks proclaim what store her heart is made of.' [3.6.45ff.]—He continues to dwell in imagination upon the crime of ingratitude, which appears so shocking that he exclaims, 'Let them anatomize *Regan*; see what breeds about her heart. Is there any cause in nature for these hard hearts?' [3.6.75f.] This last stroke cannot fail to draw tears from every eye. The reader will please to observe, that all this time there is not a word said of his royalty; on the contrary, he says to *Edgar*, 'You, Sir, I entertain for one of my hundred; only, I do not like the fashion of your garment.' [3.6.77ff.]

How was *Shakespeare* to represent *Lear* again so as to keep up the passions and heighten the distress? By taking advantage of every circumstance in *Lear's* temper. He had said that he would reassume the shape he had cast off: this then remained untouched. Accordingly, in the next scene we perceive him actually putting it in execution. His fancy suggests to him that he is a king; from this idea he reasons, as from every other principle, always with an eye to his children: 'No, they cannot touch me for coining; I am the king himself.' 'There's my gauntlet—I'll prove it on a giant.' From this, his imagination wanders: 'Bring up the brown bills—O well flown barb! i'th' clout! i'th' clout —Hewgh, give the word.' [4.6.83ff.] From this rambling he soon returns, and the habitual ideas again take possession of him. 'Ha, *Regan! Goneril!* they flattered me like a dog!' [4.6.95f.] *Glo'ster* enquiring if it is not the king, he catches at the word, and answers, 'Ay, every inch a king.' [4.6.107] He proceeds to draw some inferences from that notion, till he reflects that *Glo'ster's* bastard son was kinder to his father than his own daughters, got in lawful sheets. From this he digresses into an invective against women, and continues raving till at length his spirit of revenge returns upon him. 'And when I've stolen upon these SONS-IN-LAW, then kill, kill, kill, kill.' [4.6.187f.]

It was *Shakespeare's* art to reserve his being crowned with straw for the last scene of his madness. Here we have a representation of human nature reduced to the lowest ebb. Had he lost his reason on account of his abdicated throne the emotions of pity would not be so intense as they now are, when we see him driven to that extreme by the cruelty of his own children. A monarch voluntarily abdicating and afterwards in a fit of lunacy resuming his crown would, I fear, border upon the ridiculous. Every topic of parental distress being now exhausted and the master-passions of the king appearing in his madness, the poet, like a

great master of human nature, shews him gradually coming to himself.
We see the ideas dawning slowly on his soul:

> *Where have I been?—where am I? fair day-light!*   [4.7.52]

In this recollection of his reason he never once mentions the loss of
royalty, but again touches upon the cause of his distress in his speech to
Cordelia.

> *I know you do not love me; for your sisters*
> *Have, as I do remember, done me wrong:*
> *You have some cause; they have none.*   [4.7.73ff.]

Upon the whole, before his madness, in it, and after it, *Lear* never
loses sight of the ideas which had worn such traces on his brain. He
must be unfeeling to the great art of our poet who can look for any
other cause of distress in scenes which are drawn so forcibly and strong,
and kept up with the most exquisite skill to the very dying words of the
unhappy monarch.[1] (VI, 233-44)

[d] Letter to the Author, occasioned by his Criticism on *King Lear*[2]

The following letter[3] is written with such a vein of candour and taste
that I cannot with-hold it from the public this day. I am highly obliged
to the author for so ingenious a piece, and though he seems to differ
from the commentary upon *King Lear* which I gave in last Saturday's
paper I hold it material that *Shakespeare* should be seen in every point of
view, especially when I am favoured with the sentiments of so elegant a
critic as my correspondent of this day. The reader will judge of the
matter for himself.

To CHARLES RANGER, Esq.

SIR,
To address a letter to you under the character of Mr *Ranger*, I am
persuaded, needs little apology; especially when it goes from one who
has a real regard to your reputation as an author, and, having often

---

[1] In the original edition the essay ended: 'I have purposely avoided saying any Thing
of the Under Plot of this Tragedy, as I foresaw a long Essay this Day. I shall take another
Opportunity to offer my Thoughts on that Head, and the Corner-Stone of *Lear*'s Madness
being now established, I think I shall be able to raise a Superstructure upon it, which I hope
will not be disagreeable to my Readers, and therefore I shall postpone these Reflections till
another Occasion.'

[2] This essay is no. 17 in the original edition (dated 19 January 1754), no. 66 in the 1756
edition (dated 19 January 1754), and no. 79 in the 1786 edition (dated 20 April 1754).

[3] According to Jesse Foot, *Life of Arthur Murphy* (1811), p. 68, the anonymous correspondent was Thomas Fitzpatrick.

received pleasure from your weekly essays, takes the liberty of throwing out his thoughts on a piece of criticism in which he differs with you in opinion.

Your paper of last *Saturday* contains an examen of *King Lear*. You seem to think that an ingenious critic who in the *Adventurer* has given a discourse upon that beautiful tragedy has intirely mistaken the principal idea in the old king's mind during his state of madness. After citing *Lear*'s exclamation on the ingratitude of his daughters, you add, 'this might lead any man to the cause of *Lear*'s madness, without thinking of the resignation of his sceptre.' But certainly, whoever considers *Lear*'s character with attention will from the very passage you quote, beside an hundred others, think there is much to be said on the other side of the question.

I have read with pleasure several of the remarks you make on the speeches in *Lear*, which are such as can arise only in the mind of a reader of taste; but I cannot agree that '*he must be unfeeling to the great art of our poet who can look for any other cause of distress*' in the madness of the king than the ingratitude of his daughters.

I know not in what manner you may treat the remarks I am about to make, but I can sincerely assure you they are only intended as hints to yourself on a subject which I think of some consequence to the admirers of *Shakespeare*.

The critic in the *Adventurer* was somewhat wanting in justice to the poet by mentioning the loss of royalty as the sole cause of *Lear*'s madness, without taking notice at the same time of the forcible idea he must have of the ingratitude of his two daughters. I think Mr *Ranger* also wrong in excluding intirely his opinion. What I purpose here is to point out *both the ideas* working strongly in his mind, and what the author intended as conducive to the moral of his play.

No critic on *Shakespeare* can better explain the characters he draws than the poet himself does in every speech. We not only see what his persons are during the scene represented but we are also made acquainted, by some nice touches in each play, with their former mode of thinking and acting. No poet ever understood nature better in the operation of the passions. The persons in *Shakespeare* always speak and act in the highest conformity to their characters: the poet's genius and judgment are in this respect every where equal to *Horace*'s precept.[1]

Ætatis cujusque notandi sunt tibi mores.

[1] *A.P.* 156: 'You must note the manners of each age.'

Lear's deportment and sentiments in regard to his daughters in the first act, and what *Goneril* says of him to *Regan* mark very plainly his character, which is that of *a haughty, passionate, inconstant, weak old man.* He does not resign his authority to his daughters so much out of love to them as to rid himself of the cares of government. He retains the name of king, with a suitable train of attendants: he still commands with his former impetuosity of temper, and is jealous even of trifles. This the ill-nature of the daughters will not suffer. We soon find them in consultation, in the most undutiful and unbecoming manner, to deprive him of his remaining shew of power: their behaviour and ingratitude soon appear in the most glaring instances and make the old king sorely sensible that he had *given them* ALL.

Nature was *Shakespeare*'s guide. He describes the imagination affected by concurring causes to pave the way for a scene of the highest distress. *Lear*, as a king and father, feels with great sensibility the shock of his daughters' ingratitude and unnatural treatment. He exhibits a moving picture of the feelings of the heart and the various conflicts of passion expressive of his character and circumstances. If the poet had nothing more in view he might have been well content with the masterly picture he has drawn of his distress, grief, and rage in every scene before the loss of his senses; but he has crowned the distress by making him at last fix his imagination on his own rashness and folly in giving away his ALL. He laments his want of power to avenge himself. It is this reflection chiefly that drives him to madness.

The jesting of the fool wholly turns upon his *unkinging himself* and retaining *nothing*, which *Lear* minutely attends to, and says, 'a bitter fool!' [1.4.135] After *Goneril*'s proposal to reduce his train, he breaks out, '*woe! that too late repents.*' [1.4.257] The ingratitude of his daughters, and his own folly, strike him deeply.

> O Lear, Lear, Lear!
> *Beat at this gate that let thy folly in,*
> *And thy dear judgment out.* [1.4.270ff.]

Afterwards he says to *Goneril*,

> *Thou shalt find,*
> *That I'll resume the shape which thou didst think,*
> *I have cast off for ever.*
> Gon. *Do you mark that?* [1.4.308ff.]

In the next scene, wrapt up in thought, he says,

To take 't again perforce!—*Monster Ingratitude!*   [1.5.37]

In this line the two ideas are strongly blended, and the *loss of power* foremost; for surely that was the obvious reason of the insults he had received. If he had still been in possession, they would have continued to sprinkle him with *court holy-water*: the fool whose phrase the last is, says,

> *Fathers that wear rags,*
> *Do make their children blind;*
> *But fathers that bear bags,*
> *Shall see their children kind.*   [2.4.47ff.]

I must here take notice of the different colouring used by our poet, and all good writers, in distinguishing the characters of men seemingly agitated by the same passions. *Lear's* idea of his folly, in divesting himself of his authority, is nicely and artfully disinguished by *Shakespeare* from that kind of regret which an imperious man of a different character would feel from the deprivation of power. He is full of the loss of his dignity only as it was the occasion of the ill treatment he met with, not from a thirst of rule. This idea, and that of the ingratitude of his daughters which he feels as the consequence of it, I cannot help thinking, are as closely united in his madness as two twigs twisted together and growing out of the same stem.

When he reproaches his daughters in that heart-piercing scene of distress on the heath he says,

> O Regan! O Goneril!
> *Your old kind father! whose frank heart gave all!*
> *O that way madness lies—Let me shun* THAT; *no more of* THAT.
>   [3.4.19ff.]

On his recollection that he *gave all* he breaks short, and immediately subjoins, 'O that way madness lies; let me shun *that*;' no more of *that*: let me not think that I have been guilty of so much folly as to have given *all* to such ungrateful wretches: the reflection will make me mad.

I know it may be insisted on by you, and perhaps by many others, that *Lear* makes use of the sentiment of *giving all* only to tax the ingratitude of his daughters in a higher degree; but it is possible you may be of a contrary opinion, if you can allow that the moral of this play does not expose the ingratitude of children more than the folly of parents. *This same folly of parents* is also touched with great judgment in the under-plot of *Glo'ster*. The characters of *Lear's* two daughters are finely con-trasted with those of *Cordelia* and *Edgar*; and the poet's design in marking out so strongly the folly and ill-judged partiality of parents is confirmed by the behaviour of *Edmund*.

When *Lear* sees the wretchedness of *Edgar* he pursues the same train of reasoning which before possest him and asks, '*didst thou* GIVE ALL *to thy daughters?—And art thou to come to this?*' [3.4.48f.] And immediately after,

> *What! Have his daughters brought him to this pass?*
> *Could'st thou* save nothing?—*Did'st thou* give them all? [3.4.63f.]

This is agreeable to his character. And from all that we hear in common life (for there are many stories) of old weak parents who have acted much in the manner of *Lear*, and to the reproach of human nature have met with ingratitude and disobedience; these, I say, in their feeling-hours of distress are reported to have reproached themselves with their folly in GIVING ALL as well as to have exclaimed against the ingratitude of their children.

There are many characters, I doubt not, now in the world who retain a heap of treasure useless to themselves from their children on no better motives than to ensure their duty and attention; and some who carry the moral of this play to a ridiculous height by denying their children an independence merely on the same parity of reasoning, without considering the difference between the prudence of parents and their folly.

I forbear making any quotations from *Lear's* speeches in his madness. I think the whole obvious enough, and that our immortal poet, who had a perfect knowledge of the workings of the human mind, has drawn *both the ideas* in *Lear's* madness agreeable to the representation he has made of him in the first act.

What I have hitherto said is entirely confined to the different opinions of Mr *Ranger* and the *Adventurer*. I do not expect that you will alter your's in conformity to my judgment. Let a diligent examination of the play determine you in the future criticisms you intend to give the public on this subject.

What has often occurred to me in reading over the several editions of our poet, and what has been said by you and many great geniusses, only serves to convince me of the difficulty of any one man's succeeding in a perfect criticism on *Shakespeare*. At least I have reason to think so from what I have seen of the several attempts that have been made by different commentators, from the time of Mr *Rowe* to the mutilated condition our poet was thrown into by subsequent editors.

Several persons have succeeded in pointing out occasionally some of the latent beauties; but, I believe, *'there is scarce one man alive* (to speak in the style of a very extraordinary address to a great man in last *Saturday's Inspector*), *who is even capable of calling all his beauties by their proper names,* much less of *exhibiting them all with advantage to the public*; whose property *they now are, if they will acquire a taste to enjoy them.'*

I cannot forbear mentioning the obligation which the public has to the genius of Mr *Garrick,* who has exhibited with great lustre many of the most shining strokes of *Shakespeare's* amazing art, and may be justly styled (as he was once called by you) his best commentator. For it is certain, he has done our poet more justice by his manner of playing his principal characters than any editor has yet done by a publication.

I shall conclude with the same freedom as I began by desiring you will consider my manner of treating this subject as the mere hints of a friendly letter, and not as an essay on the subject in dispute.

I am, Sir,

Your most obedient servant,

T.G.D. (VI, 245–55)

[e: Letter to the Editor, on *King Lear*[1]]

SIR,

In your paper of Saturday, April 20, you have given place to a letter written, indeed, with taste and great acuteness of argument, which seems intended as a refutation of the principles advanced by me in a late criticism on the tragedy of *King Lear*. Your correspondent seems to think that neither the papers in the *Adventurer* nor the essay in the *Gray's-Inn Journal* have settled with precision the true cause that brings on the madness of the distressed and aged monarch. The arguments on both sides taken together and consolidated into one might, in your friend's opinion, give a solution of the difficulty.

Notwithstanding what that gentleman has so ingeniously urged I cannot, after a review of the tragedy, find any reason to retract my assertion that the madness so finely drawn by *Shakespeare* is occasioned by the ingratitude of his daughters. The folly of a parent's putting himself in the power of his children must incidentally appear in a play

---

[1] This essay did not appear in the original edition; it is no. 87 in 1756 (15 June 1754) and no. 81 in 1786 (4 May 1754). The title here given it is mine.

founded on such a story, but had those children not proved ungrateful I apprehend there is no reason to imagine the king's mind would have taken that fatal turn. Let us, if you please, once more advert to the frame and temper of the old king. In the texture of the man the poet has, with great art, taken care to shew us the latent seeds which are likely to kindle into a blaze upon the revolt of his daughters. The impression which *Cordelia's* artless answer had upon him is described by himself.

> *O most small fault,*
> *How ugly didst thou in* Cordelia *shew,*
> *Which, like an engine, wrench'd my frame of nature*
> *From the fix'd place; drew from my heart all love,*
> *And added to the gall!* [1.4.266ff.]

Here we see where the old man's passions were most accessible, and how strong the inward-workings were likely to be when he should find a total disaffection. It is then no wonder that his frame of nature should be wrench'd from the fix'd place, and indeed his tendency that way soon discovers itself when he breaks out into these words.

> *I will forget my nature;—so* KIND *a father!* [1.5.31]

Were the loss of royalty uppermost in his thoughts his remarks would take their tincture from that idea: he would rather blame himself as a WEAK *father* who had given all to his children. But the circumstance of his having given all is never mentioned, unless it is to aggravate the ill-usage he has met with. When he says to himself *to take't again perforce*, it is plain that it is not merely for the sake of regaining lost grandeur but to avenge his wrongs; he immediately subjoins, *monster ingratitude!*—And a little after, *let me not be mad; not mad, sweet Heaven!* [1.4.37ff.] The fool, indeed, taunts him with the folly of his having divested himself of power and put the rod, as he calls it, in his children's hand. These ideas are so obvious that *Shakespeare* knew they would strike even the most superficial mind; but we find it is no consideration with the father. He never dwells upon it, though suggested to him so frequently. On the other hand, how acute are his feelings whenever he recurs to his daughter's want of filial piety! He that can read the following lines without being softened into tears must, as Mr *Addison* has said upon another occasion, have either a very good or a very bad head.

> *Oh!* Regan! *she has tied*
> *Sharp-tooth'd* UNKINDNESS *like a* VULTURE *here!*

—I scarce can speak to thee—thou'lt not believe
With how deprav'd a quality—Oh! Regan! [2.4.132ff.]

What a picture of a mind is here presented to us!—The struggle with his sorrows, the breaks of passion, the attempt to speak, and the instant suppression of his powers are the most natural and pathetic touches. Can the human imagination, in all her treasury of language, find words to express at once the detestable crime of filial ingratitude and the exquisite feelings of an injured father like the following passage?

She has struck me with her tongue
Most serpent-like upon the very heart! [2.4.158f.]

Who is there that does not instantaneously find himself in a gush of tears on reading those lines when, a little afterwards, he comes to the speech which closes with

You think I'll weep;
No, I'll not weep—tho' I have full cause of weeping
—This heart shall break into a thousand flaws
Or e'er I'll weep—O fool! I shall go mad! [2.4.281ff.]

The last touch in this speech is the finest close of a climax of passion that can be conceived. To prepare us for what is to follow we are here told that his *wits begin to turn*. For this melancholy situation *Shakespeare* all along finely prepares us.

I have dwelled thus long on the cause of *Lear*'s distraction because the arguments offered by your ingenious correspondent are not without plausibility; but from what has been premised, together with what I have urged in my former paper, there cannot, I think, remain a moment's doubt. To those who are not satisfied with this reasoning it may be proper to recommend the noblest commentary this or any poet ever had. I mean Mr *Garrick*'s performance of *Lear*, in which there is displayed so just a knowledge of the human mind under a state of madness, together with such exquisite feelings of the various shiftings of the passions, so finely at the same time enfeebled with the debility of age, that I believe whenever this admirable actor ceases to play this part the unhappy monarch will lose more than *fifty of his followers at a clap*.

Though our great poet pays us amply for all his transgressions against the laws of *Aristotle* yet I have frequently wished that the noble wilderness of his genius had not rendered him so unbounded and irregular in his fables. Had this tragedy been planned with more art, and without that multiplicity of incidents which draw off our affections from the principal object, it had been a piece for the united efforts of *Greece* to envy. The episode, however, in which the *bastard* acts the same unnatural part as *Lear*'s legitimate daughters is not entirely detached from the main subject: the misfortunes of the good old *Glo'ster*, who endeavours to assist the forlorn king, must touch every breast, and the character of *Edgar* is sure to be amiable in every eye.

The close of this tragedy is full of terror and commiseration. Our great poet has here given us a death not often to be found in the play-house bill of mortality; I mean, the death of *Lear* without the dagger or the bowl. But perhaps, after the heart-piercing sensations which we have endured through the whole piece, it would be too much to see this actually performed on the stage: from the actor whom I have already named I am sure it would. I should be glad, notwithstanding, to see the experiment made, convinced at the same time that the play as altered by *Tate* will always be more agreeable to an audience. The circumstances of *Lear*'s restoration, and the virtuous *Edgar*'s alliance with the amiable *Cordelia*, can never fail to produce those gushing tears which are swelled and ennobled by a virtuous joy. The alteration is justified by another reason, which is that *Lear* was really restored to his crown, if we may believe *Spenser*, who gives the following remarkable narrative with which I shall close this letter. To see *Shakespeare*'s story related by so great a poet as *Spenser*, in his tenth canto of the *Faerie Queene*, may prove amusing to the reader.

I am, sir, &c.

CANDID.

[Quotes *Faerie Queene*, 2,10, 27-32.] (VI, 265-71)

[f: On love in the drama¹]

*   *   *

Notwithstanding the extensive influence of this soft infection it is somewhat surprizing that among all the writers who have endeavoured to describe it very few have succeeded in any tolerable degree. What numbers of *English* Tragedies have been sunk into an insipid languor by the ineffectual whine of episodic love? The Tragedy of *Romeo and Juliet*, excepting now and then some glittering conceits (which we may suppose to be translations from the *Italian Novelist* who furnished *Shakespeare* with the story) affords a beautiful representation of two young minds touched with this tender sympathy. (VI, 277)

*   *   *

¹ This essay was no. 85 in the 1756 edition (dated 1 June 1754) and no. 82 in 1786 (dated 11 May 1754).

[g] On Tragedy[1]

*   *   *

Virgil was as skilful a master of the passions as any writer, ancient or modern. . . . I believe, notwithstanding, that *Shakespeare's Lear* and *Othello* have made deeper impressions upon the minds of an audience. . . .

Shakespeare is almost the only poet who has excelled in a masterly power of striking the *imagination*, the *heart*, and our *reason* all at once. Poetry, sentiment, and passion are combined in the most agreeable assemblage. In his Tragedy of *Macbeth* there are several strokes of this *nature*. The following lines are introduced with a solemnity suitable to the occasion, and have a pleasing kind of gloomy imagery.

> Ere the bat hath flown
> His cloister'd flight; ere to black Hecate's summons
> The shard-borne beetle with his drowsy hums
> Hath rung night's yawning peal, there shall be done
> A deed of dreadful note.   [3.2.40ff.]

To conclude: *Aristotle* tells us that fable is the soul of tragedy, and there can be no doubt but the great critic is right. Tragedy represents the misfortunes of the great, and misfortune is the consequence of human actions. *Shakespeare*, with all his rudeness, was fully aware of the doctrine, and accordingly we find that no man better knew the art of bringing forward great and striking situations. He was not versed in *Aristotle's* art of poetry; but he had what was better than art; a genius superior to all mankind.[2] [VI, 336–8]

[1] This essay was no. 48 in the first edition (dated 24 August 1754), no. 94 in 1756 (dated 3 August 1754), and no. 89 in 1786 (dated 3 August 1754).

[2] In the original and in the second (1756) version the penultimate paragraph is substantially the same, but after the *Macbeth* quotation it reads as follows: 'The Soliloquy in the Tent Scene of *Richard the Third* is also a further Instance of the same Beauty, though by the Way it may not be improper to observe, notwithstanding we must allow that Mr *Cibber* was in the right to transplant *Shakespeare's* own Words, that they are not perfectly suitable to the Character of *Richard*; and I believe had our great Poet thought of shewing his Hero in this Situation, he would have shewed *Richard's* Feelings quite otherwise on such an Occasion.

To conclude: *Aristotle* was certainly mistaken when he called the Fable the Life and Soul of Tragedy; the Art of constructing the dramatic Story should always be subservient to the Exhibition of Character. Our great *Shakespeare* has breathed another Soul into Tragedy, which has found the Way of striking an Audience with Sentiment and Passion at the same Time.'

141. Charlotte Lennox, Shakespeare's misuse of his sources

1753-4

From *Shakespear Illustrated: or the Novels and Histories, On which the Plays of Shakespear are Founded, Collected and Translated from the Original Authors, with Critical Remarks*, vols I and II (1753); vol. III (1754).

Charlotte Lennox, Mrs Ramsay (1720–1804), poet, novelist and translator, is best known for her novel *The Female Quixote* (1752), a satire on the vogue for romances. She was born in America, and was a friend of Dr Johnson for over thirty years: among Johnson's many good deeds on her behalf he wrote the Dedication to John, Earl of Orrery for this volume (see Introduction, pp. 6, 43). Orrery, in turn, wrote the preface for the translation of Brumoy which she edited (see No. 172). On Charlotte Lennox and her relationship with Dr Johnson, see Karl Young, *Samuel Johnson on Shakespeare, One Aspect*, University of Wisconsin Studies in Language and Literature, No. 18 (Madison, 1924), pp. 147–227.

[On *Measure for Measure* and its source]

*   *   *

Angelo hereupon confesses his Crime; the Duke orders him to marry *Mariana* immediately, which being done he condemns him to Death. At the Intercession of *Mariana* and *Isabella* he is pardoned; and the Duke, charmed with the Virtue and Beauty of *Isabella*, offers himself to her for a Husband.

The rest is all Episode, made up of the extravagant Behaviour of a wild Rake, the Blunders of a drunken Clown, and the Absurdities of an ignorant Constable.

There are a greater Diversity of Characters and more Intrigues in the Fable of the Play than the Novel of *Cinthio*; yet I think wherever *Shakespeare* has invented, he is greatly below the Novelist, since the Incidents he has added are neither necessary nor probable.

The Story of *Juriste* and *Epitia*, of itself, afforded a very affecting Fable for a Play; it is only faulty in the Catastrophe. The Reader, who cannot but be extremely enraged at the Deceit and Cruelty of *Juriste*, and very desirous of his meeting with a Punishment due to his Crime, is greatly disappointed to find him in the End not only pardoned but made happy in the Possession of the beautiful *Epitia*.

Shakespeare, though he has altered and added a good deal, yet has not mended the Moral, for he also shews Vice not only pardoned but left in Tranquility.

The cruel, the vicious and hypocritical *Angelo* marries a fair and virtuous Woman who tenderly loved him, and is restored to the Favour of his Prince. (I, 24–5)

[An alternative plot, based on Cinthio, outlined]

Here the Novelist should be dropt and the Catastrophe, according to poetical Justice, might be thus wound up.

The Lady having performed her Duty in saving the Life of a Man who, however unworthy, was still her Husband, should devote herself to a Cloister for the remainder of her Life; and the wretched *Juriste* deprived of his Dignity, in Disgrace with his Prince and the Object of Universal Contempt and Hatred, to compleat his Miseries he should feel all his former Violence of Passion for *Epitia* renewed, and falling into an Excess of Grief for her Loss (since the Practice is allowed by Christian Authors), stab himself in Despair.

The Fable thus manag'd takes in as great a Variety of Incidents as with Propriety can be introduced in a Play, and those Incidents naturally rising out of one another, and all dependant on the principal Subject of the Drama, forms that Unity of Action which the Laws of Criticism require.

This Fable also, would not be destitute of a Moral, which as *Shakespeare* has managed it is wholly wanting. The fatal Consequence of an irregular Passion in *Claudio*, the Danger of endeavouring to procure Good by indirect Means in *Isabella*, and the Punishment of lawless Tyranny in the Governor convey Instruction equally useful and just.

Since the Fable in *Cinthio* is so much better contrived than that of *Measure for Measure* on which it is founded, the Poet sure cannot be defended for having altered it so much for the worse; and it would be but a poor Excuse for his want of Judgment to say that had he followed the Novelist closer his Play would have been a Tragedy, and to make a Comedy he was under a Necessity of winding up the Catastrophe as he has done.

The comic Part of *Measure for Measure* is all Episode, and has no Dependance on the principal Subject, which even as *Shakespeare* has managed it has none of the Requisites of Comedy. Great and flagrant Crimes, such as those of *Angelo* in *Measure for Measure*, are properly the Subject of Tragedy, the Design of which is to shew the fatal Conse-quences of those Crimes and the Punishment that never fails to attend them. The light Follies of a *Lucio* may be exposed, ridiculed and corrected in Comedy.

That *Shakespeare* made a wrong Choice of his Subject, since he was resolved to torture it into a Comedy, appears by the low Contrivance, absurd Intrigue, and improbable Incidents he was obliged to introduce in order to bring about three or four Weddings instead of one good Beheading, which was the Consequence naturally expected.

The Duke (who, it must be confess'd, has an excellent plotting Brain) gives it out that he is going *incog.* to *Poland* upon weighty Affairs of State, and substitutes *Angelo* to govern till his Return. To Friar *Thomas* his Confidant, however, he imparts his true Design, which is in his Absence to have some severe Laws revived that had been long disused. Methinks this Conduct is very unworthy of a good Prince; if he thought it fit and necessary to revive those Laws why does he commit that to another which it was his Duty to perform?

The Friar's Answer is very pertinent.

> It rested in your Grace
> T' unloose this tied-up Justice when you pleas'd;
> And it in you more dreadful would have seem'd
> Than in Lord *Angelo*. [1.3.31ff.]

The Duke replies,

> I do fear, too dreadful. [1.3.34]

In short, the poor Duke is afraid to exert his own Authority by enforcing those Laws notwithstanding he thinks them absolutely necessary, and therefore as he says:

> I have on *Angelo* imposed the Office;
> Who may in the Ambush of my Name strike home. [1.3.40f.]

However, in Fact it is the Duke who strikes in the Ambush of *Angelo*'s Name; for it is he who causes *Angelo* to put those severe Laws in Execution while he skulks in Concealment to observe how they are received: if ill, *Angelo* must stand the Consequence; if well, he will enjoy the Merit of it. And in order to discover how Things are carried on in the Commonwealth he makes the Friar procure him a Habit of the Order, and thus disguised, where does he go: Why, to the common Jail, among the condemned Malefactors. His Speculations are wholly confined to this Scene.

Here, entirely taken up with the Affairs of the Prisoners, his Highness ambles backwards and forwards from the Prison to *Mariana*'s House, fetching and carrying Messages, contriving how to elude those very Laws he had been so desirous of having executed; corrupting one of the principal of his Magistrates, and teaching him how to deceive his Delegate in Power.

How comes it to pass that the Duke is so well acquainted with the Story of *Mariana*, to whom *Angelo* was betrothed but abandoned by him on Account of the Loss of her Fortune? She speaks of the Duke as of a Person she had been long acquainted with.

> *Mariana.* Here comes a Man of Comfort, whose Advice
> Hath often still'd my brawling Discontent.   [4.1.8f.]

Yet this could only happen while he assumed the Character of a Friar, which was but for two or three Days at most; he could not possibly have been acquainted with her Story before. If he had, the Character of *Angelo* would have been also known to him, and consequently it was unnecessary to make him his Deputy in order to try him further, which was one of his Reasons, as he tells Friar *Thomas*, for concealing himself.

If it is granted that the Duke could not know *Mariana*'s Affair before his Disguise, what Opportunities had he of learning it afterwards? For notwithstanding what *Mariana* says, which intimates a long Acquaintance, it is certain it could have been but a very short one. Some extraordinary Accident therefore must have brought her Story to his Knowledge, which we find was known to no one else; for *Angelo*'s Reputation for Sanctity was very high, and that could not have been if his Wrongs to *Mariana* were publickly known.

But why does not the Poet acquaint us with this extraordinary Accident, which happens so conveniently for his Purpose? If he is accountable to our Eyes for what he makes us see is he not also accountable to our Judgment for what he would have us believe? But, in short, without all this Jumble of Inconsistencies the Comedy would have been a downright Tragedy, for *Claudio's* Head must have been cut off if *Isabella* had not consented to redeem him, and the Duke would have wanted a Wife if such a convenient Person as *Mariana* had not been introduced to supply her Place and give her Honour.

As the Character of the Duke is absurd and ridiculous, that of *Angelo* is inconsistent to the last Degree. His Baseness to *Mariana*, his wicked Attempts on the Chastity of *Isabella*, his villainous Breach of Promise and Cruelty to *Claudio* prove him to be a very bad Man, long practised in Wickedness; yet when he finds himself struck with the Beauty of *Isabella* he starts at the Temptation, reasons on his Frailty, asks Assistance from Heaven to overcome it, resolves against it, and seems carried away by the Violence of his Passion to commit what his better Judgment abhors.

Are these the Manners of a sanctified Hypocrite, such as *Angelo* is represented to be? Are they not rather those of a good Man overcome by a powerful Temptation? That *Angelo* was not a good Man appears by his base Treatment of *Mariana*; for certainly nothing can be viler than to break his Contract with a Woman of Merit because she had accidentally become poor and, to excuse his own Conduct, load the unfortunate Innocent with base Aspersions and add Infamy to her other Miseries. Yet this is the Man who, when attacked by a Temptation, kneels, prays, expostulates with himself, and while he scarce yields in Thought to do wrong his Mind feels all the Remorse which attends actual Guilt.

It must be confessed indeed, that *Angelo* is a very extraordinary Hypocrite, and thinks in a Manner quite contrary from all others of his Order; for they, as it is natural, are more concerned for the Consequences of their Crimes than the Crimes themselves, whereas he is only troubled about the Crime and wholly regardless of the Consequences.

The Character of *Isabella* in the Play seems to be an Improvement upon that of *Epitia* in the Novel, for *Isabella* absolutely refuses, and persists in her Refusal, to give up her Honour to save her Brother's Life; whereas *Epitia*, overcome by her own Tenderness of Nature and the affecting Prayers of the unhappy Youth, yields to what her Soul abhors to redeem him from a shameful Death. It is certain, however, that *Isabella* is a mere Vixen in her Virtue. How she rates her wretched Brother, who gently urges her to save him!

> *Isabella.* Oh, you Beast!
> Oh faithless Coward! Oh dishonest Wretch!
> Wilt thou be made a Man out of my Vice?
> Is't not a Kind of Incest, to take Life
> From thine own Sister's Shame? . . .
> Thy Sin's not accidental, but a Trade;
> Mercy to thee wou'd prove itself a Bawd:
> 'Tis best that thou dy'st quickly.   [3.1.138–52]

Is this the Language of a modest tender Maid, one who had devoted herself to a religious Life, and was remarkable for an exalted Understanding and unaffected Piety in the earliest Bloom of Life?

From her Character, her Profession, and Degree of Relation to the unhappy Youth, one might have expected mild Expostulations, wise Reasonings, and gentle Rebukes. His Desire of Life, though purchased by Methods he could not approve, was a natural Frailty which a Sister might have pitied and excused, and have made use of her superior Understanding to reason down his Fears, recall nobler Ideas to his Mind, teach him what was due to her Honour and his own, and reconcile him to his approaching Death by Arguments drawn from that Religion and Virtue of which she made so high a Profession. But that Torrent of abusive Language, those coarse and unwomanly Reflexions on the Virtue of her Mother, her exulting Cruelty to the dying Youth, are the Manners of an affected Prude, outragious in her seeming Virtue, not of a pious, innocent and tender Maid.

I cannot see the Use of all that juggling and Ambiguity at the winding up of the Catastrophe. *Isabella* comes and demands Justice of the Duke for the Wrongs she had received from his Deputy, declaring she had sacrificed her Innocence to save her Brother's Life whom *Angelo* had, notwithstanding his Promise to the contrary, caused to be executed.

Upon the Duke's telling her that he believed her Accusation to be false she goes away in Discontent, without saying a Word more: is this natural? Is it probable that *Isabella* would thus publicly bring a false Imputation on her Honour and, though innocent and unstained, suffer the World to believe her violated?—She knows not that the honest Friar who advised her to this extraordinary Action is the Duke to whom she is speaking; she knows not how the Matter will be cleared up.

She who rather chose to let her Brother die by the Hands of an Executioner than sacrifice her Virtue to save his Life, takes undeserved Shame to herself in public without procuring the Revenge she seeks after.

Mariana's evasive Deposition, Friar *Peter*'s enigmatical Accusation of *Isabella*, the Duke's winding Behaviour: what does it all serve for but to perplex and embroil plain Facts, and make up a Riddle without a Solution?

The Reader can easily discover how the Plot will be unravelled at last, but the unnecessary Intricacies in unravelling it still remain to be accounted for.

The Play sets out with the Moral in the Title, *Measure for Measure*; but how is this made out? the Duke speaking of *Angelo* to *Isabella*, says . . .:

> An *Angelo* for *Claudio*; Death for Death.
> Haste still pays Haste, and Leisure answers Leisure;
> Like doth quit Like, and *Measure* still for *Measure*.
> [5.1.407ff.]

Thus it should have been, according to the Duke's own Judgment to have made it *Measure for Measure*; but when *Angelo* was pardoned and restored to Favour how then was it *Measure for Measure*?

The Case is not altered because *Claudio* was not put to death and *Isabella* not violated: it was not through *Angelo*'s Repentance that both these Things did not happen; a Woman he was engaged to supplied the Place of *Isabella*, and the Head of another Man was presented to him instead of *Claudio*'s. *Angelo* therefore was intentionally guilty of perverting Justice, debauching a Virgin, and breaking his Promise in putting her Brother to death, whose Life she had bought by that Sacrifice. *Isabella*, when pleading for him, says:

> My Brother had but Justice,
> In that he did the Thing for which he dy'd;
> For *Angelo*, his Act did not o'ertake his bad Intent,
> And must be buried but as an Intent,
> That perish'd by the Way; Thoughts are no Subjects:
> Intents, but meerly Thoughts. [5.1.446ff.]

This is strange Reasoning of *Isabella*; her Brother deserved Death, she says, because *he did the Thing for which he died*; he intended to do it, and his doing it was the Consequence of his Intention.

Angelo likewise intended to debauch her and murder her Brother, and he did both in Imagination; that it was only Imagination was not his Fault, for so he would have had it, and so he thought it was. It is the Intention which constitutes Guilt, and *Angelo* was guilty in Intention, and, for what he knew, in fact; therefore as far as lay in his Power he was as guilty as *Claudio*.

This Play therefore being absolutely defective in a due Distribution of Rewards and Punishments, *Measure for Measure* ought not to be the Title since Justice is not the Virtue it inculcates. Nor can *Shakespeare's* Invention in the Fable be praised, for what he has altered from *Cinthio* is altered greatly for the worse. (1, 27–37)

*   *   *

[On *Othello*]

*   *   *

In *Cinthio* the Moor is mentioned without any Mark of Distinction; *Shakespeare* makes him descended from a Race of Kings. His Person is therefore made more considerable in the Play than in the Novel, and the Dignity which the *Venetian* Senate bestows upon him is less to be wondered at.

In the Play *Cassio*, the Person of whom *Othello* is jealous, is represented to be a young amiable Officer, remarkable for the Agreeableness of his Person and the Sweetness of his Manners, and therefore likely enough to inspire *Desdemona* with a Passion for him.

In the Novel these Qualities are all ascribed to the Villain who betrays the Moor to the Murder of his Wife, and the suspected Rival is no more than an ordinary Person.

Cinthio might perhaps think it necessary to give his Villain a pleasing Person and insinuating Address in order to make his Artifices less suspected, but to give Probability to the Jealousy of the Moor was it not also as necessary to make the suspected Rival possess some of those Qualities with which the Minds of young Ladies are soonest captivated?

Shakespeare therefore paints *Cassio* young, handsome and brave; and *Othello*, who feeds his Jealousy by reflecting that he himself is neither young nor handsome, by the same Train of Thought falls naturally into a Suspicion that what he loses for want of those Qualities will be gained by another who possesses them.

But on the other Hand *Shakespeare* has made a very ill Use of the Lieutenant's Wife.

Cinthio shews this Woman privy, much against her Will, to the Design on *Desdemona*; and though she dares not discover it to her for fear of her Husband's Resentment yet she endeavours to put her upon her Guard, and gives her such Advice as she thinks will render all his Schemes ineffectual.

Shakespeare calls this Woman *Emilia*, and makes her the Attendant and Friend of *Desdemona*; yet shews her stealing a Handkerchief from her which she gives her Husband, telling him at the same Time that the Lady will run mad when she misses it, therefore, if it is not for some Purpose of Importance that he wants it, desires him to return it to her again.

If her Husband wants it for any Purpose of Importance that Purpose cannot be very good. This Suspicion, however, never enters her Mind, but she gives it him only upon that very Condition which ought to have made her refuse it.

Yet this Woman is the first who perceives *Othello* to be jealous, and repeats this Observation to her Mistress upon hearing him so often demand the Handkerchief she had stolen, and fly into a Rage when he finds his Wife cannot produce it.

Emilia pronounces him jealous, perceives the Loss of that fatal Handkerchief, confirms some Suspicions he had entertained, and though she loves her Mistress to Excess chuses rather to let her suffer all the bad Consequences of his Jealousy than confess she had taken the Handkerchief, which might have set all right again. And yet this same Woman, who could act so base and cruel a Part against her Mistress, has no greater Care in dying than to be laid by her Side.

Mr. *Rymer*, in his Criticisms on this Play, severely censures the Characters as well as the Fable and Conduct of the Incidents.

That of *Emilia*, though more inconsistent than any, he has taken no Notice of; and most of the Charges he brings against the others have little or no Foundation.

The Character of *Iago*, says this Critic, is against common Sense and Nature. '*Shakespeare* would pass upon us a close, dissembling, false, insinuating Rascal, instead of an open-hearted, frank plain dealing Soldier; a Character constantly worn by them for some Thousands of Years in the World.'[1]

The Soldiers are indeed greatly obliged to Mr. *Rymer* for this Assertion, but though it may in general be true yet surely it is not absurd to suppose that some few Individuals amongst them may be close dissembling Villains.

Iago was a Soldier, it is true, but he was also an *Italian*; he was born in a Country remarkable for the deep Art, Cruelty, and revengeful

[1] See Vol. 2, p. 30.

Temper of its Inhabitants. To have painted an *Italian* injured, or under a Suspicion of being injured, and not to have shewn him revengeful, would have been mistaking his Character.

It is with Justice indeed that Mr. *Rymer*[1] condemns *Shakespeare* for that unnecessary and diabolical Cruelty he makes *Iago* guilty of in urging *Othello* to the Murder of the innocent Lady who had never offended him; his Point was gained by making *Othello* jealous, and procuring his Consent to the Death of *Cassio*, who stood in his Way to Preferment. But the Murder of *Desdemona* was such an Excess of wanton Cruelty that one can hardly conceive it possible a Man could be so transcendently wicked.

Cinthio indeed makes *Iago* not only urge *Othello* to the Murder of his Wife but is himself the Perpetrator of it. This seems still more absurd, but he tells us that he had been violently in love with *Desdemona*, and the Indifference she had discovered towards him converted his Love into a settled Hatred.

Shakespeare injudiciously copies *Cinthio* in making *Iago* confess a Passion for *Desdemona*, as it rendered his urging on her Murder less probable, since in the Play *Iago* had no Opportunity of declaring that Love to her and consequently could not be stimulated by her Contempt of him to act so cruel a Part against her.

But he has greatly improved on the Novelist by making him jealous of the Moor with his own Wife; this Circumstance being sufficient, in an *Italian* especially, to account for the Revenge he takes on *Othello*, though his Barbarity to *Desdemona* is still unnatural.

Upon the whole there is very little Difference between the Character of the Lieutenant as it is drawn in the Novel and *Iago* as managed in the Play. His ambiguous Questions, dark Hints, and villainous Arts to raise Suspicions in the Mind of *Othello* are the same in the Novel as in the Play; and the Scene where *Othello* is made to observe the Gestures of *Cassio* while he is talking to *Iago* is exactly copied from *Cinthio*, as is likewise a preceding one where *Othello*, tormented with Doubts about his Wife, threatens *Iago* with Destruction unless he gives him ocular Proof of her Dishonesty.

This Demand, with *Iago*'s Expostulations, Arguments, and satisfactory Replies, are also the same with those in the Novel.

The Character of *Desdemona* fares no better in Mr. *Rymer*'s Hands than that of *Iago*; her Love for the Moor, he says, is out of Nature.[2]

[1] Vol. 2, p. 47.
[2] Vol. 2, p. 34.

Such Affections are not very common indeed, but a very few Instances of them prove that they are not impossible, and even in *England* we see some very handsome Women married to Blacks, where their Colour is less familiar than at *Venice*. Besides, the *Italian* Ladies are remarkable for such Sallies of irregular Passions.

Cinthio, it is true, says that *Desdemona* was not overcome by a womanish Appetite but represents her, as *Shakespeare* does likewise, subdued by the great Qualities of the Moor.

Courage in Men has always had an invincible Charm for the Ladies. *Desdemona* admired the Moor for his Valour, and the Transition from extreme Admiration to Love is very easy in a female Mind.

Mr. *Rymer* alledges[1] that *Shakespeare* makes *Desdemona* a Senator's Daughter instead of a simple Citizen, and this he imputes to him as a Fault, which is perhaps a great Instance of his Judgment.

There is less Improbability in supposing a noble Lady, educated in Sentiments superior to the Vulgar, should fall in love with a Man merely for the Qualities of his Mind than that a mean Citizen should be possessed of such exalted Ideas as to overlook the Disparity of Years and Complexion, and be enamoured of Virtue in the Person of a Moor.

However, it is not true that *Shakespeare* has changed a simple Citizen into a Lady of Quality, since *Desdemona* in the Novel is mentioned as a Woman of high Birth.

Cinthio calls her *Cittadina*, which Mr. *Rymer* translates a simple Citizen,[2] but the *Italians* by that Phrase mean a Woman of Quality.

If they were, for Example, to speak of a Woman of the middle Rank in *Rome* they would say *Una Romana*; if of a noble Lady *Una Cittadina Romana*. So in *Venice* they call a simple Citizen *Una Venitiana*, but a Woman of Quality *Una Cittadina Venitiana*.

That Simplicity in the Manners of *Desdemona*, which Mr. *Rymer* calls Folly and Meanness of Spirit,[3] is the Characteristic of Virtue and Innocence.

Desdemona was conscious of no Guilt and therefore suspected no Blame. She had so lately given the Moor an incontestable Proof of her Affection that it was not unnatural for her to impute his sudden Starts of Passion to some other Cause than Jealousy.

The whole Stress of the Proof against *Desdemona* is laid upon the Handkerchief, as well in the Novel as the Play; though I think in the

[1] Vol. 2, p. 27.
[2] Vol. 2, p. 27.
[3] Vol. 2, pp. 28ff.

Novel it is more artfully managed. There the Moor insists upon seeing it in the Captain's Possession e'er he will resolve any Thing against his Wife, and the Lieutenant contrives to give him this Satisfaction.

Othello, in the Play, has not the least Appearance of Proof against his Wife but seeing the Handkerchief in the Lieutenant's Possession, yet this is brought about by mere Accident.

Bianca, to whom *Cassio* had given it to have the Work copied (which, by the way, was an odd Whim for a Soldier), comes to him while he is engaged in a private Discourse with *Iago*; and *Othello* observing them concealed, and in a Fit of Jealousy, throws the Handkerchief at his Head.

This happens well for *Iago*'s Plot; but as he did not, and indeed could not foresee this lucky Accident, methinks it would have been more natural, since every Thing depended upon that, to have made it the Effect of some Contrivance of his.

The Outlines of *Iago*, *Desdemona*, and *Cassio*'s Characters are taken from the Novel; but that of *Othello* is entirely the Poet's own.

In *Cinthio* we have a Moor valiant indeed, as we are told, but suspicious, sullen, cunning, obstinate and cruel.

Such a Character married to the fair *Desdemona* must have given Disgust on the Stage; the Audience would have been his Enemies, and *Desdemona* herself would have sunk into Contempt for chusing him.

With what Judgment then has *Shakespeare* changed the horrid *Moor* of *Cinthio* into the amiable *Othello*, and made the same Actions which we detest in one excite our Compassion in the other!

The Virtues of *Shakespeare*'s *Moor* are no less characteristic than the Vices of *Cinthio*'s; they are the wild Growth of an uncultivated Mind, barbarous and rude as the Clime he is born in. Thus his Love is almost Phrensy, his Friendship Simplicity, his Justice cruel and his Remorse Self-Murder. (I, 127–34)

* * *

[On *Cymbeline*]

* * *

It would be an endless Task to take Notice of all the Absurdities in the Plot, and unnatural Manners in the Characters of this Play.

Such as the ridiculous Story of the King's two Sons being stolen in their Infancy from the Court, and bred up in the Mountains of Wales till they were twenty Years of Age.

Then, at their first Essay in Arms, these Striplings stop the King's Army, which is flying from the victorious *Romans*, oblige them to face their Enemies, and gain a compleat Victory.

With Inconsistencies like these it everywhere abounds. The whole Conduct of the Play is absurd and ridiculous to the last Degree, and with all the Liberties *Shakespeare* has taken with Time, Place and Action the Story, as he has managed it, is more improbable than a Fairy Tale. (I, 166)

*　　*　　*

[On *The Winter's Tale*]

*　　*　　*

It has been mentioned as a great Praise to *Shakespeare* that the old paltry Story of *Dorastus and Fawnia* served him for *A Winter's Tale*, but if we compare the Conduct of the Incidents in the Play with the paltry Story on which it is founded we shall find the Original much less absurd and ridiculous.

If *Shakespeare* had even improved the Story and cleared it of great Part of its Inconsistencies yet he would still have been accountable for what remained, for why indeed did he chuse a Subject so faulty for the Story of a Play? His Claim to Praise would have been but very small by making what was bad better, since he was free in the Choice of his Subject; but certainly he can have no Pretensions to it at all by changing bad to worse. That he has done so will be easily proved by examining some of the principal Incidents as they are differently managed by the Novelist and the Poet.

The King's Jealousy is the Foundation of all the Adventures that followed, but extravagant as its Consequences are in both yet the Rise and Progress of this terrible Passion is better accounted for in the Novel than the Play. In the first we are told that *Pandosto*, charmed with the friendly Visit *Egistus* paid him in his Dominions, desired the Queen to treat her royal Guest with the Respect and Esteem that was due to his Merit and the Friendship he had for him. The Queen, like an obedient Wife, complies with her Husband's Directions, and perhaps over-acts her Part. The King begins to think he has been too officious. The innocent Familiarity between his Wife and Friend creates Suspicions, which, meeting with a Mind prepared by a natural Distrustfulness to receive them, produces those Sparks of Jealousy which his interested Observations on all their Looks, Words, and Actions, afterwards blew into a Flame.

This Account of the King's Jealousy does not absolutely clash with Probability. But let us see how *Shakespeare* manages it in the Play. The two Kings make their first Appearance in the second Scene in high Friendship and Confidence. *Polixenes*, reminding his Friend of the Length of his Visit, tells him he is now resolved to be gone.

Leontes, not able to part with him, presses him earnestly to stay longer. *Polixenes* urges the Necessity of his speedy Departure, and truly, as he observes, nine Months is a great while for a good King to be out of his own Dominions.

Leontes, after many fruitless Intreaties, reproaches his Queen for not endeavouring to detain *Polixenes*; she, in obedience to his Commands, presses him to gratify her Lord by a little longer Stay; *Polixenes* complies at her Request, and certainly he must be a very illbred Monarch had he done otherwise.

All this Conversation passes in the Presence of *Leontes*, who from hence takes Occasion to be jealous, and passes in an Instant from the greatest Confidence, Security, and Friendship imaginable to the last Extremity of Jealousy and Rage. What wonderful Contrivance is here! The Legerdemain, who shews you a Tree that buds Blossoms and bears ripe Fruit in the Space of five Minutes, does not put so great a Cheat on the Senses as *Shakespeare* does on the Understanding. For this Jealousy of one Minute's Growth we see take Root before our Eyes, and so far from there being the smallest Progression in the several Actions of budding, blossoming, and bearing ripe Fruit, that we have the first and the last at one and the same Instant.

The extravagant Effects of the King's Rage and Jealousy are carried far enough in all Conscience in the Novel, and *Shakespeare* is not a Whit more moderate; only he has altered a Circumstance which entirely destroys the little Probability the Novelist had preserved in the Relation.

In the Story the King, being in his own Mind firmly persuaded of the Queen's Guilt, orders her to be imprisoned, and the Daughter that she was delivered of in Prison to be burnt. At the Intreaties of his Courtiers he reverses the Sentence past on the Child and commands it to be exposed in a Boat, but declares that his Queen shall die.

She insists upon being confronted with her Accusers, whereupon she is brought to a Tryal. But finding she was likely to meet with no Justice in a Court over-ruled by the Power of her Husband, she on her

Knees protests her Innocence and intreats the King to consult the Oracle of *Apollo* concerning the Crimes of which she was accused. This so reasonable a Request being made in open Court, the King could not refuse it, and therefore sends Ambassadors to *Delphos*, who return with the Answer of the God; which, being read, declares her Innocence, and the King is satisfied.

Shakespeare makes the King in the Heighth of his Frenzy of Jealousy send himself to the Oracle of *Apollo*, and in the mean Time commit the most barbarous Cruelties on his Queen and Child. How inconsistent is this! Why does he consult the Oracle if he is resolved to proceed to Extremities before the Answer arrives? The Request comes very naturally from the Queen in the Novel, and the King's Compliance with it is very well accounted for, but in the Play nothing can be more absurd than that the King should be reasonable enough to consult voluntarily the Gods concerning the Infidelity of his Wife, and while the Answer was expected, and her Guilt yet doubtful, punish her with as much Rigour as if the Oracle had declared her an Adultress. Here again the paltry Story has the Advantage of the Play. Let us go on to examine a few more of the Incidents.

In the Novel the Persons who perform the hateful Office of exposing the Infant Princess are some of the King's Guards.

In the Play it is a Nobleman of high Rank, who had Courage enough to reprove the King for his violent and unjust Jealousy, yet basely submits to take an Oath to perform his Commands (though he had Reason to think they would not be very mild), and still more basely keeps that Oath, though it enjoins him to carry the innocent Babe to a Desert and there leave it to the Mercy of the wild Beasts.

In the Novel the Accidents that happen to the exposed Infant are governed by Chance; the Boat, into which it was put, being left in the midst of the Ocean is driven by the Winds to the Coast of *Bohemia*, and being spied by a Shepherd is drawn to Land.

In the Play *Antigonus*, who is bound by Oath to leave the Child in some desert Place quite out of its Father's Dominions, is warned in a Dream by its unhappy Mother to call the Infant *Perdita* and carry it to *Bohemia*, and there leave it.

Antigonus obeys, and this done, it is absolutely necessary he should never return to *Sicily*, otherwise it may be discovered where the Princess is left and all the future Adventures would fall to the Ground: therefore a Bear rushes out of the Woods and devours him. The good-natured Bear (as it should seem), resolved not to spoil the Story, passes by the little Princess who is to make so great a Figure hereafter; and a convenient Storm arising, splits the Ship in which she was brought thither, so that all the Sailors perishing—though they were near enough the Shore to have saved themselves—no-one is left to carry back any Account of the Affair to *Sicily* and thereby prevent the Adventures which are to follow.

All this is very wonderful. *Shakespeare* multiplies Miracle upon Miracle to bring about the same Events in the Play which Chance, with much more Propriety, performs in the Novel. . . . (II, 75–80)

[The Florizel-Perdita plot in Greene's *Pandosto* is summarised]

Thus these Circumstances are altered by *Shakespeare*.—The Prince, having changed Cloaths with a cheating Pedlar, escapes with his Mistress to the Ship. The Pedlar immediately over-hears a Conversation between the reputed Father of *Perdita* and his Son, in which it is resolved that he shall carry the Jewels to the King and declare how he found *Perdita*. The Pedlar, supposing it would be an Advantage to the Prince to know this, decoys the old Shepherd and his Son aboard. Now one would imagine that all must come out: but see what strange Accidents conspire to hinder it.

The Pedlar, though he over-heard the old Shepherd say that *Perdita* was a Foundling and not his Daughter, neglects to tell the Prince this important Circumstance, though it was with that very Design he came and forced the two Clowns along with him.

Perdita, though her Father and Brother are in the same Vessel with her, never sees or speaks to them; the old Shepherd and his Son make no Attempts to speak to her; and the Prince has so little Consideration for the Father and Brother of his Beloved that he takes no Notice of them: how wonderful is all this! The most unlikely Things imaginable fall out to postpone the Discovery of *Perdita* till their Arrival at *Sicily*.

The Novel makes the Wife of the jealous King die through Affliction for the Loss of her Son. *Shakespeare* seems to have preserved her alive for the sake of her representing her own Statue in the last Scene, a mean and absurd Contrivance, for how can it be imagined that *Hermione*, a virtuous and affectionate Wife, would conceal herself during sixteen Years in a solitary House, though she was sensible that her repentant Husband was all that Time consuming away with Grief and Remorse for her Death? And what Reason could she have for chusing to live in such a miserable Confinement when she might have been happy in the Possession of her Husband's Affection and have shared his Throne? How ridiculous also in a great Queen, on so interesting an Occasion, to submit to such Buffoonery as standing on a Pedestal, motionless, her Eyes fixed, and at last to be conjured down by this magical Command of *Paulina*:

> Music, awake her; strike;
> 'Tis Time, descend; be Stone no more; approach;
> Strike all that look upon with Marvel; Come
> I'll fill your Grave; up stir; nay, come away;
> Bequeath to Death your Numbness, for from him
> Dear Life redeems you.   [5.3.98ff.]

After this solemn Incantation her Majesty comes down from the Pedestal and embraces her Husband and her new found Daughter, for whose Sake she declares she had preserved her Life.

To bring about this Scene, ridiculous as it is, *Shakespeare* has been guilty of many Absurdities, which would be too tedious to mention and which are too glaring to escape the Observation of the most careless Reader.

The Novel has nothing in it half so low and improbable as this Contrivance of the Statue; and indeed, wherever *Shakespeare* has altered or invented, his *Winter's Tale* is greatly inferior to the old paltry Story that furnished him with the Subject of it. (II, 84–7)

*   *   *

[On *Hamlet*]

*   *   *

The Translation of the Story of *Amleth* from the *Danish* History of *Saxo-Grammaticus*, I was favoured with by a Friend; the Story itself is full of ridiculous Fancies, wild and improbable Circumstances, and as it is conducted has more the Appearance of a Romance than an Historical Fact.

That *Shakespeare* founded his *Tragedy of Hamlet* upon it is very plain, but it is uncertain whether he saw a literal Translation of it or met with the Incidents drest up like a Novel, and perhaps with those Alterations which he has adopted in his Play. All the principal Circumstances are the same in the Play as the History. In both a Prince murders his Brother, usurps his Dignity, and marries his Widow; the Son of the murdered Prince resolves to revenge his Father; for that Purpose he feigns himself mad, and at last accomplishes his Design. Several of the lesser Circumstances are also as exactly copied, and others have afforded Hints for new ones.

Amleth has a private Interview with his Mother and kills the Spy who had been appointed to overhear their Conversation. *Hamlet* likewise visits the Queen in her Apartment and kills *Polonius*, who had concealed himself behind the Hangings.

When the Spies are removed the Discourse of the two Princes is much the same: they reproach their Mothers with their incestuous Marriage, sharply reprove them for their Crimes, declare their Madness to be feigned, and enjoin them to Secrecy.

The Embassy to *England* is designed after the History. *Shakespeare* indeed makes *Hamlet* after two Days Absence be set on shore again at *Denmark*; and *Amleth* in the History arrives in *England*, has his Companions hanged, and marries the King's Daughter before he comes back. But *Shakespeare's* Plan required the immediate Return of *Hamlet*; however, the Contrivance of changing the Letters are the same, and of punishing the treacherous Bearers of them. *Shakespeare* makes those Bearers the Schoolfellows and profest Friends of *Hamlet*, a Circumstance which heightens their Baseness, and justifies the Artifice he uses to procure their Punishment.

The Design of entrapping *Amleth* by means of a Girl has not been wholly neglected by *Shakespeare*, though he manages this Incident much more decently. *Ophelia*, with whom he is in Love, is ordered to throw herself in his way and the King and his Confident listen to their Conversation. 'Tis very easy to see he took the Hint of this Stratagem from the Story, though it is very differently conducted, for *Ophelia* is not a loose Wanton, as in the History, but a Woman of Honour with whom he is in love. The accidental killing of her Father, and her Distraction which was caused by it, is all his own Invention, and would have made a very affecting Episode if the Lady had been more modest in her Frenzy and the Lover more uniformly afflicted for her Death. For at his first hearing it he expresses only a slight Emotion; presently he jumps into her Grave, fiercely demands to be buried with her, fights with her Brother for professing to love her, then grows calm and never thinks of her any more.

The Ghost is wholly the Invention of *Shakespeare*, as is likewise the King's concerted Scheme with *Laertes* to kill *Hamlet* treacherously as they fenced, or if he failed, to poison the Wine. The King is killed by *Hamlet* both in the History and the Play, but in the Play he is stabb'd in the midst of his Friends, Guards, and Attendants; in the History as he is rising in Confusion from his Bed, and unable to draw his Sword to defend himself.

Here the Historian, romantic as his Relation seems, has the Advantage of the Poet in Probability. After *Amleth* has secured his Uncle's Attendants, taken away his Sword from him, and placed his own (which was fastened to the Scabbard) in its stead, it was not difficult for him to kill him disarmed, and without any Assistance.

But *Shakespeare* makes *Hamlet* execute his Vengeance on the King in a public Hall, crouded with his Attendants and Guards, and surrounded by his Friends. None of these offer to assist him, and *Hamlet* has leisure enough after he has stabbed him to make him drink some of the Wine he had poisoned, lest his Sword had not compleated the Work.

The Queen's Death, by drinking ignorantly of the poisoned Wine, is a beautiful Stroke of the Poet's. The History shews her unfortunate, but *Shakespeare* makes the same Man who seduced her to Wickedness be her involuntary Murderer, and at once the Cause and Punisher of her Guilt.

Shakespeare has with Reason been censored for the Catastrophe of this Tragedy. The brave, the injured *Hamlet* falls with the Murderers he punishes; one Fate overwhelms alike the innocent and the guilty. In the History we find he did not live long after the severe Revenge he took for his Father's Murder, but was unfortunately killed in Battle. *Shakespeare* would not so far deviate from the History as to leave him happy and in Peace, though he has hastened his Death as well as changed the Manner of it. He is killed by the treacherous Contrivance of the King, and *Laertes* is the Instrument of that Treachery, which is afterwards turned upon himself.

As *Laertes* is a subordinate Character in the Play, it seems to be a Fault in *Shakespeare* to shew him with a Similitude of Manners, under the same Circumstances, and acting upon the same Principles as *Hamlet*, his Hero. *Laertes* is brave and generous, his Father is murdered basely, as he is informed, Duty and Honour incite him to revenge his Death, and he does so.

This Sameness of Character and Parity of Circumstances with the Hero lessens his Importance, and almost divides our Attention and Concern between them; an Effect which *Shakespeare* certainly did not intend to produce. Nor can it be lessened by the Consideration of the treacherous Measures *Laertes* was prevailed upon to enter into against

Hamlet, who had murdered his Father. In this he does not differ much from *Hamlet*, who did not attempt by open Force to revenge his Father's Murder on his Uncle, but designed to accomplish it by Subtilty and Craft.

The same Equality is preserved in their Deaths and in their Actions throughout the Play. *Laertes* wounds *Hamlet* with the poisoned Weapon, in the Scuffle they change Rapiers and *Hamlet* wounds *Laertes*; and they exchange Forgiveness with each other before they die.

Thus has *Shakespeare*, undesignedly no doubt, given us two Heroes instead of one in this Play; the only Difference between them is that one of them is a Prince, the other a Nobleman, and but for this slight Distinction the Play might have been as well called the *Tragedy of Laertes* as *Hamlet*.

It ought to be observed that *Shakespeare* has not been led into this Error by the History: the Character of *Laertes* and all the Circumstances relating to him is his own, which he has introduced by making the Spy who is killed Father of *Laertes*.

The Madness of *Hamlet* seems to be less essential to the Play than the History. In the latter it affords him the Means of executing a Contrivance which, absurd as it is, secures the Accomplishment of his Revenge, but in the Play it is of no other Use than to enliven the Dialogue, unless its Usefulness may be deduced from its bringing on such Accidents as it was assumed to prevent. For *Hamlet*'s Madness alarms the King's Suspicion, and that produces the treacherous Embassy to *England*, which failing, the Contrivance of the poisoned Rapier followed, and that does the Business.

But since the King's conscious Guilt and Terror might reasonably have created a Distrust of *Hamlet*, and that Distrust and a Desire of Security induced him to seek his Death, what need had *Shakespeare* to make his Heroe's Sense and Discretion appear doubtful by shewing him feigning a Madness destructive to his Safety, and which he himself knows to be so, and yet persists in?

Shakespeare has indeed followed the History in making *Hamlet* feign himself mad; but that Madness being of no Consequence to the principal Design of the Play (as it is in the History), or if of Consequence, it hurts the Reputation of his Heroe, 'tis certainly a Fault; for at least he only produces the same Events by a Blunder which might have happened without it.

The Violation of poetical Justice is not the only Fault that arises from the Death of *Hamlet*. The revenging his Father's Murder is the sole End of all his Designs and the great Business of the Play, and the noble and fixed Resolution of *Hamlet* to accomplish it makes up the most shining Part of his Character; yet this great End is delayed till after *Hamlet* is mortally wounded. He stabs the King immediately upon the Information of his Treachery to himself! Thus his Revenge becomes interested, and he seems to punish his Uncle rather for his own Death than the Murder of the King, his Father. (II, 267–74)

★　　★　　★

[On *The Two Gentlemen of Verona*]

★　　★　　★

The Story, indeed, is highly romantic and improbable, and *Shakespeare's* Judgment in rejecting many of the Circumstances might be praised if those he has invented were not equally absurd: 'tis generally allowed that the Plot, Conduct, Manners, and Sentiments of this Play are extreamly deficient.

The Court and Palace of the Duke of *Milan*, to which first Sir *Valentine*, and then Sir *Protheus* are sent to improve their Politeness in, has less Dignity and Decorum in it than the House of a private Gentleman. *Silvia*, the Duke's Daughter, notwithstanding we are told with wonderful Simplicity in different Passages of the Play that she is *a virtuous civil Gentlewoman*, yet behaves with all the rustic Smartness and awkward Gaiety of a Village Coquet.

She is introduced flirting from Room to Room, followed by two of her Lovers, and laughing equally at the Man she favours and him she rejects, slyly inciting them to quarrel; and when she has set them together by the Ears, enjoys the Jest 'till the good Prince, her Father, comes in to part them.

Sir *Valentine's* Courtship of this Princess, it must be confessed, is extreamly singular, and the Appearance of his dirty Footman, *Speed*, in the *Presence-Chamber*, breaking Jests upon his Master and her Highness while they are discoursing has something in it very new and uncommon. . . . (III, 24–5)

Nothing can be more inconsistent than the Character of *Valentine*; nothing more improper than the Manners attributed to him as a Lover.

Passionately enamoured as he is with *Silvia*, he recommends a new Lover to her with the utmost Earnestness, and will not be satisfied 'till she promises to entertain him.

When he is banished to *Milan*, and in the extreamest Despair for the Loss of his Mistress, the Fear of Death prevails upon him to become the

Head of a Gang of Banditti, and having in this Situation fortunately rescued his beloved *Silvia* from the Violence of his treacherous Friend who was going to ravish her, a few repentant Words uttered by that Friend makes him resolve to resign her to him, notwithstanding the generous Proof she had given him of her Tenderness in running so many Hazards to be with him.

> *Protheus.* Forgive me, *Valentine*; if hearty Sorrow
> Be a sufficient Ransom for Offence
> I tender't here; I do as truly suffer
> As e'er I did commit.
> *Valentine.*   Then I am paid:
> And once again I do receive thee honest.
> Who by Repentance is not satisfied
> Is nor of Heaven, nor Earth; for these are pleas'd;
> By Penitence the Eternal's Wrath's appeas'd.
> And that my Love may appear plain and free,
> All that was mine in *Silvia* I give thee.   [5.4.74ff.]

This Part of the Intrigue of the Play, such as it is, that relates to the Loves of *Silvia* and *Valentine* is probably the Poet's own Invention; but the Adventure of *Julia* and *Protheus* are copied closely from the Pastoral Romance.

The Poet drops the Story at the Flight of *Silvia*, and adds all the remaining Circumstances.

He also paints *Protheus* in much more disadvantageous Colours than he is represented in the Original; there we find him indeed inconstant to his Mistress, who loves him passionately, and forsaking her for one that treats him with the utmost Disdain. But *Shakespeare* shews him treacherous in the highest Degree to his Friend, base and ungrateful to the Duke his Benefactor, and guilty of intended Violence towards the Woman he professes to love. Yet, wicked as he is, he escapes not only without Punishment but is made as happy as the renewed Tenderness of his injured Friend and the inviolable Fidelity of his once loved *Julia* can make him. . . . (III, 32–3)

The Wit in this Play consists in Puns, Quibbles, Antitheses's and playing upon Words, and the Humour is all divided between *Launce* and his Dog. The last of these Personages is indeed a Mute, which those who contend for the Learning of *Shakespeare* may say, he introduced in Imitation of the Ancients. . . . (III, 46)

★   ★   ★

[On *Troilus and Cressida*]

*   *   *

The Story of this Play is partly taken from Chaucer's Poem of *Troilus and Cressida*, and partly from an old Story Book called *The three Destructions of Troy*.

The first furnished *Shakespeare* with the Love Plot, and the second with all the Incidents that relate to the War.

This Play has been severely censured on account of the Faults of its Plot (if that can be called a Plot which is only a Succession of Incidents without Order, Connexion, or any Dependance upon each other) as well as the Inequality of the Manners the Poet has given to his Persons.

The Loves of *Troilus* and *Cressida* are, in all the Circumstances, exactly copied from *Chaucer*, but these Circumstances are intirely detached from the rest of the Play and produce no Event worthy our Attention.

Troilus and *Cressida* give Name to the Tragedy, and by Consequence are the most considerable Persons in it; yet *Troilus* is left alive, and *Cressida*, too scandalous a Character to draw our Pity, does not satisfy that Detestation her Crimes raise in us by her Death, but, escaping Punishment, leaves the Play without a Moral and absolutely deficient in poetical Justice.

The Manners of these two Persons, however, ought to escape the general Charge of Inequality.

Troilus, who is drawn exactly after *Chaucer*, is every where consistent with his Character of a brave Soldier and a passionate and faithful Lover. From *Cressida*'s first and second Appearance we may easily guess what her future Conduct will be. The deep Art with which she conceals her Passion for *Troilus*, her loose Conversation with her Uncle, her free Coquettry with the Prince, and her easy yielding to his Addresses prepare us for her Falsehood in the succeeding Part of the Play, and all together make up the Character of a compleat Jilt. Her not being punished is indeed an unpardonable Fault and brings the greatest Imputation imaginable upon *Shakespeare*'s Judgment, who could introduce so vicious a Person in a Tragedy and leave her without due Reward of her Crimes.

The Character of *Cressida* is much more consistent in *Shakespeare* than *Chaucer*; the latter represents her wise, humble, and modest, nicely sensible of Fame, fond of her Country, not easily susceptible of Love, hard to be won, and rather betrayed than yielding to the Desires of her

Lover. With all these amiable Qualities to engage our Esteem and those alleviating Circumstances that attended her Fall with *Troilus*, we cannot, without Surprize, see her so soon changing her Love, violating her Vows, and basely prostituting her Honour to *Diomede*. The inequality of Manners here is very observable; but *Shakespeare* in drawing her Character has avoided falling into the same Fault by copying *Chaucer* too closely, and *Cressida* throughout the Play is always equal and consistent with herself.

That the old Story Book, called *The three Destructions of Troy*, furnished *Shakespeare* with the other Part of the Plot, is plain from several of the Incidents being exactly copied from thence. Thus he makes *Achilles* to be in Love with *Polyxena* the Daughter of *Priam*, and this Passion to be the Cause of his refusing to fight against the *Trojans*; and *Hector* to be cowardly killed by *Achilles*, as he was intent on spoiling a *Greek* of his Golden Armour, which he had eagerly sought after in the Battle.

This Circumstance, however, *Shakespeare* has altered greatly for the worse. The Story says that *Hector* having slain *Patroclus* and performed many wonderful Acts of Valour, satisfied with the Slaughters of the Day, was going to quit the Field when happening to see a *Greek* with a compleat Suit of Golden Armour on, his Avarice was awakened and he resolved not to quit the Battle till he had gained this rich Prize; accordingly he assaulted the *Greek*, took him Prisoner, and to lead him more easily out of the Throng, cast his Shield behind him. *Achilles*, whom the Death of *Patroclus* had brought into the Field burning with a Desire of Revenge on *Hector*, hastened to seize him at this Disadvantage and gave him a Blow with his Spear which killed him.

Shakespeare makes *Hector* in the same Manner eager to win this Suit of Armour, but after he has slain the *Greek* who owned it he disarms himself in the Field of Battle, and *Achilles* and his Myrmidons coming up they all surround him, fall upon him and kill him. Thus has *Shakespeare* made *Achilles* a greater Coward than the old Story Writer, for in the latter he only takes Advantage of his Enemy's Shield being thrown behind him to give him a Wound, but *Shakespeare* makes him employ all his Myrmidons to kill one Man, and he disarmed and calling for Mercy.

The Absurdity of *Hector's* unarming himself in the Field of Battle, with all his Foes about him, in order to facilitate this wonderful Enterprize, is too gross to need any Remark.

Hector's challenging any of the *Grecian* Princes to single Combat in

Honour of their Ladies Beauty is a Circumstance borrowed from the Story Book, but surely very injudiciously. The following Message from the Defender of *Troy*, a City almost ruined by a War of nine Years Continuance, can hardly be read without a Smile. . . . [quotes 1.3.26off.]. (III, 91-5)

Tho' *Shakespeare* consulted this Book for Part of his Plot, yet in drawing the Characters of his *Grecian* Princes I cannot help thinking he had *Homer* in his Eye; and probably saw some old Translation of that Poet, for there was one in his Time. *Achilles*, indeed, is a Character of his own Invention, ridiculous and inconstant to the last Degree, Brave, and a Coward; a Fool, yet a deep and accurate Reasoner. But in the others he seems to have endeavoured at an Imitation of *Homer*. Thus he makes *Diomede* bold and enterprizing; *Ulysses* wise and artful; *Nestor* narrative, and ever ready to expatiate on his past Exploits; *Thersites* cowardly, satyrical, witty, and malicious. In the Interview between the *Greek* and *Trojan* Princes he makes them all speak with great Propriety, and suitable to their respective Characters. *Hector*, indeed, by mentioning *Helen* ludicrously to the injured *Menelaus*, who had given him a free and soldier-like Greeting [4.5.174ff.] discovers in that Instance neither the Manners of a Prince or Warrior; but this is only a Slip, for his Discourse both before and after it is quite agreeable to his Character.

The Silence of *Troilus* in this Scene is beautifully imagined. The Poet makes this passionate Prince attend *Hector* to the *Grecian* Tents, whither he is invited only with a Design of seeing his beloved *Cressida*. But his Resentment towards the Enemies of his Country being heightened by the Consideration of their having deprived him of his Mistress, he is incapable of mixing in the Conversation or even of returning the Civilities of the *Grecian* Princes; he stands at a Distance, pensive, silent, wholly absorb'd in mellancholly Reflections. The Grief of this young Lover is finely marked by *Agamemnon*, in that short Question to *Ulysses* pointing him out:

> What *Trojan* is that same that looks so heavy? [4.5.95]

However ridiculous, inconsistent, and contrary to general Opinion *Shakespeare* has drawn the Character of *Achilles* in this Play; yet in the following Lines he must have had *Homer* in his View. The *Grecian* Army is almost routed by the *Trojans*, the Commanders in the utmost Consternation, when *Ulysses* enters and thus reassures them:

> Oh Courage, Courage, Princes! great *Achilles*

Is arming, weeping, cursing, vowing Vengeance!
Patroclus' Wounds have rous'd his drousy Blood.   [5.5.30ff.]

Here *Achilles* is made of so much Importance to the *Grecians* that,
vanquished as they were and flying from the Field, they no sooner
heard that *Achilles* is arming and coming to join them than their
Courage is reanimated; they renew the Fight and Victory declares for
them. Only *Homer* could have furnished *Shakespeare* with this Thought,
nor with an Idea of *Achilles*'s Grief for the Death of *Patroclus*, which in
two Lines he has so pathetically described. The old Story which in
many Places he has faithfully copied is absolutely silent here.

The Speech of *Calchas* to the *Grecian* Princes, demanding their
Trojan Prisoner *Antenor* to be exchanged for his Daughter, *Cressida*, is
almost literally taken from *Chaucer*.

The Character of *Pandarus*, also, is borrowed from him, but much
heightened by *Shakespeare*. Part of the Conversation between *Pandarus*
and his Niece is copied exactly from *Chaucer*. (III, 98–100)

*   *   *

[On *Richard II*]

*   *   *

This Play affords several other Instances in which *Shakespeare*'s Inattention to the History is plainly proved, and is therefore the less
pardonable as the Subject of it is not one entire Action, wrought up
with a Variety of beautiful Incidents, which at once delight and instruct
the Mind, but a Dramatick Narration of Historical Facts, and a successive
Series of Actions and Events which are only interesting as they are true,
and only pleasing as they are gracefully told.

The Manner of *Bolingbroke*'s appealing the Duke of *Norfolk*, the
Order of the intended Combat, the very Words of the Appellant and
Defendant, the Behaviour and Speech of the King on that Occasion, are
exactly copied from *Holinshed*, as is likewise the Appeals of the Lords in
the first Scene of the fourth Act.

The Duke of *York*'s Conduct throughout the Play is the same as the
History represents it, only *Shakespeare* has aggravated his Zeal to the
new-made King by introducing him eager and solicitous to procure the
Death of his Son *Aumerle* for having engaged in a Conspiracy against
him. The Impropriety of making a Father press so ardently the Execution of a beloved Son because that Son had joined with a Party that had

resolved to dethrone an Usurper and restore the lawful King, is too glaring to need any Animadversion. . . . (III, 108-9)

That little Fiction which *Shakespeare* has introduced into this Play is imagined with his usual Carelesness and Inattention to Probability. The Queen who, more than any other Person, is interested in every thing that relates to the King her Husband is, nevertheless, the last that hears of the Seizure of her Lord.

In the second Act she is informed of *Bolingbroke*'s Invasion and the Disaffection of almost all the Nobility, and in the fourth this sorrowful Queen is introduced in her Garden with two Ladies, who press her to dance. The Gardener and two Workmen entering, she retires behind the Trees in Hopes of learning some News of the State from them, nor is she deceived. From them she first hears of the Imprisonment and intended Deposition of the King her Husband.

One might be surprised, perhaps, to hear from a Gardener's Mouth a beautiful System of Politics, couched in a close and well-conceived Allegory, drawn from such Images as his Profession furnished him with [3.4.29ff.], if the poor Fellow who works under his Directions did not allegorize as well as his Master, and lessen the Wonder. (III, 114-15)

*   *   *

[On *1 Henry IV*]

*   *   *

Shakespeare has copied *Holinshed* very closely, as well in the Historical Facts as the Characters of his Persons; *Percy*'s and *Glendower*'s are indeed greatly heightened, but both with wonderful Propriety and Beauty. The Episodical Part of the Drama, which is made up of the extravagant Sallies of the Prince of *Wales* and the inimitable Humour of *Falstaff*, is entirely of his own Invention. The Character of Prince *Henry*, tho' drawn after the Historians, is considerably improved by *Shakespeare*, and through the Veil of his Vices and Irregularities we see a Dawn of Greatness and Virtue that promises the future Splendor of his Life and Reign.

The Poet has indeed deviated from History in making this young Prince kill the gallant *Percy* at the Battle of *Shrewsbury*. According to them it is uncertain by whom he fell; however, this Circumstance is beautifully imagined by *Shakespeare* in order to exalt the Character of

Prince *Henry*, which had before been obscured by the Glory of that Heroe. (III, 125)

★   ★   ★

[On Henry V]

★   ★   ★

In the first Act of this Play the Dauphin of *France* sends an insulting Message to King *Henry* accompanied with a Present of Tennis Balls as a Reproach for the wild Sallies of his Youth. There is no Foundation either in *Hall* or *Holinshed* for this Circumstance. *Shakespeare* indeed took the out-lines of the Dauphin's Character from these Historians, who represent him to be a light, arrogant, and vain-glorious Prince, but he has painted at full Length what they only drew in Miniature; and by adding with great Propriety some of the Characteristic Follies of his Nation given us a lively and humorous Picture of a Coxcomb Prince.

The absurdity of making the Princess *Catharine* the only Person in the *French* Court who does not understand *English*, has been already taken Notice of, and it must be confessed that the great *Henry* makes but a miserable Figure as a Lover; no Language can be coarser than that in which he addresses the Princess the first Time he sees her: *Do you like me* Kate, &c. [5.2.107]. Yet the Dialogue is not without wit, liveliness, and humour but so utterly void of Propriety that we lose all Idea of the Dignity of the Persons who manage it, and are readier to imagine we hear a common Soldier making love to an aukward Country Girl than a King of *England* courting a Princess of *France*. (III, 136–7)

★   ★   ★

[On Henry VI, Parts 1–3]

★   ★   ★

Shakespeare has given the same inconsistent and improper Manners to all the chief Persons in this Play. The brave old Duke of *York*, the gallant *Edward* his Son, afterwards King, the heroic *Warwick*, whom the Poet so often styles the Maker and Subduer of Kings, are all Murderers; at once the Heroes and the Villains of the Scene, equally exciting our Praise and Detestation. The Poet, in order to display this predominant Passion, Cruelty, in Characters where it is least expected to be found, the Heroe and the Prince, has not scrupled to violate sometimes the Truth of History. . . . (III, 156)

[On Queen Margaret's urging the death of York]

Off with the Crown, and with the Crown his Head;
And whilst we breathe, take Time to do him dead,

[*3 Henry VI*, 1.4.107f.]

With this more than fiendlike Cruelty has *Shakespeare* represented a Queen whose Motives for taking Arms were far from being unjust: the recovery of her Husband's Liberty and Crown and the restoring her Son to the Rights and Privileges of his Birth. And for the Sake of this shocking Absurdity in the Manners of a Female Character in so high a Rank he contradicts a known Fact in History, and makes one of the greatest Captains of the Age die by the cowardly Stabs of a Woman and a Ruffian, who according to the Chronicles, fell in the Field of Battle, covered with Wounds and Glory. (III, 158)

* * *

[On *Richard III*]

* * *

The historical Facts are all taken from *Holinshed*, and the Characters all closely copied from that Author; that of *Richard* the third has been censured as monstrous, the Picture of a Fiend and not a Man; and too exquisitely wicked to be represented on the Stage.[1] 'Tis certain however, that *Shakespeare* has not aggravated the Vices and Cruelty of this Prince. He paints him such as History has transmitted him to us, and if his Character shocks us more in the Scene than the Story 'tis because the Colours of the Poet are more lively, his Expression stronger, and the Lights he shews him in more diversified; but the Subject in both is the same. The qualities of his Mind and Person are thus summed up by *Holinshed*:

'As he was small and little of Stature, so was he of Body greatly deformed, the one Shoulder higher than the other, his Face was small, but his Countenance cruel, and such that the first Aspect a Man would judge it to smell and savour of Malice, Fraud and Deceit; when he stood musing, he would bite and chaw his nether Lip; as who said, that his fierce Nature always chafed, stirred and was ever unquiet: beside that, the Dagger which he wore, he would (when he studied) with his Hand pluck up and down in the Sheath to the mid'st, never drawing it fullie

---

1 Compare Vol. 2, p. 6, Vol. 3, p. 296, and Introduction above, pp. 9f.

out. He was of a ready, pregnant and quick Wit, wilie to feire, and apt to dissemble. . . .'

This Character is the very same with that drawn of him by *Shakespeare*, but the latter is made more striking by the wonderful Propriety of the Manners and Sentiments he every where, throughout the Play, attributes to him. If *Shakespeare* is in any Instance to be blamed for keeping too close to the Historian, it is for dignifying the last Moments of this bloody Tyrant with such shining Proofs of Fortitude and Valour as, notwithstanding the Detestation we conceived at his cruelties, must force from us an involuntary Applause. The History tells us he fought bravely in that Battle which decided his Fate and, overpowered as he was by Numbers, disdained to save his Life by Flight. *Shakespeare* improved this into the following noble Description, which has indeed this improper Effect that our hatred of the Tyrant is wholly lost in our Admiration of the Heroe.

Alarm. Excursions. Enter Catesby.
Catesby. Rescue, my Lord of *Norfolk*, rescue, rescue:
The King enacts more wonders than a Man,
Daring an Opposite to every Danger!
His Horse is slain and all on Foot he fights
Seeking for *Richmond* in the Throat of Death.
Alarm. Enter King Richard.
K. Richard. A Horse! a Horse! my Kingdom for a Horse!
Catesby. Withdraw, my Lord, I'll help you to a Horse.
K. Richard. Slave, I have set my Life upon a Cast,
And I will stand the Hazard of the Dye. [5.4.1.ff.]

There are several of *Shakespeare*'s historical Plays which take in a greater Compass of Time than this, but none in which the absurdity of crowding the Events of many Years into a Representation of three Hours is made so glaring. This, no doubt, is occasioned by the very unartful Disposition of the Incidents which, though made up of distant Events, follow one another without the least Preparation, without the Intervention of an Act, or Change of Scene, to give the Spectator's Imagination room to cheat itself agreeably, by supplying that Distance of Time necessary for the giving any Probability to the Story. . . .
(III, 163–6)

*　　*　　*

[On *Henry VIII* and Shakespeare's treatment of the tragedy of
Queen Catherine]

*　　*　　*

After this we see her despised, neglected, banished from his Bed, the Name and Character of Wife taken from her, divorced, unqueen'd, and shutting up all her Sorrows in Death. The Fate of this Queen, or that of Cardinal *Wolsey*, each singly afforded a Subject for Tragedy. *Shakespeare*, by blending them in the same Piece, has destroyed the Unity of his Fable, divided our Attention between them, and, by adding many other unconnected Incidents all foreign to his Design, has given us an irregular historical Drama instead of a finished Tragedy. (III, 226)

*   *   *

[On *Much Ado About Nothing*]

*   *   *

This Fable, absurd and ridiculous as it is, was drawn from the foregoing Story of *Genevra* in *Ariosto*'s *Orlando Furioso*, a Fiction which, as it is managed by the Epic Poet, is neither improbable nor unnatural; but by *Shakespeare* mangled and defaced, full of Inconsistencies, Contradictions and Blunders. The defaming a Lady by means of her Servant personating her at her Chamber-window is the Subject pursued by both.

Shakespeare, by changing the Persons, altering some of the Circumstances and inventing others has made the whole an improbable Contrivance, borrowed just enough to shew his Poverty of Invention, and added enough to prove his want of Judgment.

The Scheme for ruining the Lady in the Original is formed and executed by a rejected Lover who sees a Rival, his inferior in Rank and Fortune, preferred before him, and loses at once the Object of his Wishes and the Prospect of increased Honours by that Preference. Ambition and the Desire of Revenge are Passions strong enough in a Mind not very virtuous to produce Acts of Baseness and Villainy. *Polynesso*, urged by those powerful Incentives, contrives to blacken *Genevra*'s Fame, which produces a Separation between her and her Lover and prevents a Stranger from marrying this Princess, and consequently enjoying those Honours he so ardently desired himself.

Don *John* in the Play is a Villain merely through the Love of Villainy, and having entertained a capricious Dislike to *Claudio* closes eagerly with his Confident's horrid Scheme for breaking off his Marriage with *Hero*.

To prevent the multiplying such outrageously wicked and therefore unnatural Characters Don *John* himself might have been the Proposer of that black Contrivance against the innocent *Hero*, and *Borachio*, for the sake of the thousand Ducats that was afterwards given him by Don *John*, be induced to execute it. But here we have two Villains equally bad, both governed by the same detestable Principles, acting upon the same Motives, and such a perfect Parity in their Manners that they are only distinguished from each other by their Names.

When *Borachio* tells Don *John* to go to his Brother and maintain confidently that *Hero* is a loose Wanton, Don *John* asks what Proof he shall make of that? 'Proof enough, says the other, to misuse the Prince, vex *Claudio*, undo *Hero*, and kill *Leonato*, look you for any other Issue?' [2.2.25ff.]

Claudio only is the Object of Don *John*'s Hatred, yet the chief Force of the intended Injury is to fall on *Hero* and *Leonato* her Father, towards whom he has no Malice; and he is made to engage in this wicked Enterprize to procure the Ruin and Death of two Persons he hates not, to give a little Vexation to one he does. These Absurdities have their Rise from the injudicious Change of the Characters. The Contrivance to slander *Hero* is not less ridiculous, and this also is occasioned by the Poet's having deviated from the Original to introduce his own wild Conceits.

Borachio tells Don *John* that he is highly favoured by *Margaret*, *Hero*'s waiting Woman; that he will persuade her to dress in her Lady's Cloaths, assume her Name, and talk to him out of her Chamber-window, all which Don *Pedro* and *Claudio* being Witnesses of would effectually convince them that *Hero* was dishonoured.

But *Borachio* does not acquaint Don *John*, and through him the Audience, what Colour he will give to this strange Request in order to induce *Margaret* to grant it. *Margaret* is all along represented as faithful to her Mistress; it was not likely she would engage in a Plot that seemed to have a Tendency to ruin *Hero*'s Reputation unless she had been imposed on by some very plausible Pretences. What those Pretences were we are left to guess, which is indeed so difficult to do that we must reasonably suppose the Poet himself was as much at a Loss here as his Readers, and equally incapable of solving the difficulty he had raised. (III, 261–3)

*   *   *

[On *King Lear*]

*   *   *

This Fable, although drawn from the foregoing History of King *Leir*, is so altered by *Shakespeare* in several Circumstances, as to render it much more improbable than the Original. There we are sufficiently disgusted with the Folly of a Man who gives away one Half of his Kingdom to two of his Daughters because they flatter him with Professions of the most extravagant Love, and deprives his youngest Child of her Portion for no other Crime but confining her Expressions of Tenderness within the Bounds of plain and simple Truth. But *Shakespeare* has carried this Extravagance much farther. He shews us a King resigning his Kingdom, his Crown and Dignity to his two Daughters, reserving nothing to himself, not even a decent Maintenance, but submitting to a mean Dependance on the Bounty of his Children, whom, by promising Rewards proportionable to the Degree of Flattery they lavish on him, he has stimulated to outvie each other in artful Flourishes on their Duty and Affection toward him.

> *Lear.* Tell me, Daughters,
> (Since now we will divest us, both of Rule,
> Int'rest of Territory, Cares of State)
> Which of you, shall we say, doth love us most?
> That we our largest Bounty may extend
> Where Nature doth with Merit challenge. *Goneril*,
> Our eldest born, speak first. [1.1.47ff.]

What Wonder, when thus bribed *Goneril* should answer

> I love you, Sir,
> Dearer than Eye-sight, Space and Liberty. [1.1.54f.]

Lear does not run mad till the third Act. Yet his Behaviour towards *Cordelia* in this first Scene has all the Appearance of a Judgment totally depraved: He asks *Cordelia* what she has to say to draw a Dowry more opulent than her Sisters. Thus he suggested to her a Motive for exceeding them in Expressions of Love. The noble Disinterestedness of her Answer afforded the strongest Conviction of her Sincerity, and that she possessed the highest Degree of filial Affection for him, who hazarded the Loss of all her Fortune to confine herself to simple Truth in her Professions of it. Yet for this *Lear* banishes her his Sight, consigns her over to Want, and loads her with the deepest Imprecations. What less than Phrenzy can inspire a Rage so groundless and a Conduct so absurd! *Lear*, while in his Senses, acts like a mad Man, and from his first Appearance to his last seems to be wholly deprived of his Reason.

In the History *Lear* Disinherits *Cordelia*, but we read of no other kind of Severity exerted towards her. The King of *France*, as well in the

History as the Play, charm'd with the Virtue and Beauty of the injured *Cordelia*, marries her without a Portion. *Shakespeare* does not introduce this Prince till after the absurd Trial *Lear* made of his Daughters' Affection is over. The Lover who is made to Marry the disinherited *Cordelia* on account of her Virtue is very injudiciously contrived to be Absent when she gave so glorious a Testimony of it, and is touch'd by a cold Justification of her Fame, and that from herself, when he might have been charm'd with a shining Instance of her Greatness of Soul and inviolable Regard to Truth.

So unartfully has the Poet managed this Incident that *Cordelia*'s noble Disinterestedness is apparent to all but him who was to be the most influenced by it. In the Eyes of her Lover she is debased, not exalted; reduced to the abject Necessity of defending her own Character, and seeking rather to free herself from the Suspicion of Guilt than modestly enjoying the conscious Sense of superior Virtue.

Lear's Invective against her to the King of *France* is conceived in the most shocking Terms:

> I would not from your Love make such a stray,
> To Match you where I Hate; therefore beseech you,
> T'avert your Liking a more worthy Way,
> Than on a Wretch, whom Nature is asham'd
> Almost t'acknowledge her's.   [1.1.209ff.]

Well might the King of *France* be startled at such Expressions as these from a Parent of his Child. Had he been present to have heard the Offence she gave him to occasion them, how must her exalted Merit have been endeared to him by the extream Injustice she suffered! But as it is, a bare Acquittal of any monsterous Crime is all the Satisfaction she can procure for herself, and all the Foundation her Lover has for the Eulogium he afterwards makes on her.

> *Cordelia.* I yet beseech your Majesty,
> (If, for I want that glib and oily Art,
> To speak and purpose not; since what I well intend,
> I'll do't before I Speak) that you make known
> It is no vicious Blot, Murther, or Foulness,
> No unchast Action, or dishonour'd Step,
> That hath depriv'd me of your Grace and Favour.
> But ev'n for want of that, for which I'm richer,
> A still soliciting Eye, and such a Tongue,

That I am glad I've not; though not to have it
Hath lost me in your Liking.
   Lear.   Better thou
Hadst not been Born, than not to have pleased me better. [1.1.223ff.]

From this Speech of *Cordelia*'s, and *Lear*'s Answer, *France* collects
Matter for extenuating a supposed Error in his Mistress, not for Admiration of her Worth.

> *France.* Is it but this? a Tardiness in Nature,
> Which often leaves the History unspoke,
> That it intends to do.   [1.1.235ff.]

Yet a Moment after, without knowing any more of the Matter, he
lavishes the warmest Praises on her Virtues and offers to make her
(loaded as she is with her Father's Curses, and deprived of the Dower he
expected with her) Queen of *France*. This Conduct would be just and
natural had he been a Witness of her noble Behaviour, but doubtful as
it must have appeared to him in such perplexing Circumstances 'tis
extravagant and absurd.

Shakespeare has deviated widely from History in the Catastrophe of
his Play. The Chronicle tells us that King *Lear*, having been dispossessed
by his rebellious Sons-in-Law of that Half of the Kingdom which he
had reserved for himself, and forced by repeated Indignities from his
Daughters to take Refuge in *France*, was received with great Tenderness
by *Cordelia*, who prevailed upon her Husband to attempt his Restoration. Accordingly an Army of *Frenchmen* pass'd over into *Britain*, by
which, the Dukes of *Cornwal* and *Albany* being defeated, King *Lear* was
restored to his Crown, died in Peace two Years after, and left his Kingdom to *Cordelia*. In *Shakespeare* the Forces of the two wicked Sisters are
victorious, *Lear* and the pious *Cordelia* are taken Prisoners, she is hanged
in Prison and the old King dies with Grief. Had *Shakespeare* followed the
Historian he would not have violated the Rules of poetical Justice: he
represents Vice punished, and Virtue rewarded. In the Play one Fate
overwhelms alike the Innocent and the Guilty, and the Facts in the
History are wholly changed to produce Events neither probable,
necessary, nor just.

Several Incidents in this Play are borrowed from the History of the
old Prince of *Paphlagonia* in *Sidney*'s *Arcadia*, which I shall here
Transcribe. . . . (III, 286–91)

The under Plot of *Gloster* and his two Sons in the Tragedy of King

Lear is borrowed from this foregoing short History of *Leonatus*; several of the Circumstances closely copied, and the Characters of the Brothers nearly the same. The Adventure of the Rock is heightened by *Shakespeare*, perhaps with too little Attention to Probability. *Gloster*, though deprived of Sight, might easily be sensible of the Difference between walking on a level Plain and ascending a steep and craggy Rock; nor could he possibly suppose, when he fell gently on that Plain, that he had precipitated himself from an immense Height to the Margin of the Sea.

Shakespeare, in the pathetic Description he makes *Edgar* give of his Father's Death, had certainly the following Passage of the *Arcadia* in his Eye:

The blind King having in the chief City of his Realm set the Crown upon his Son *Leonatus*'s Head, with many Tears, both of Joy and Sorrow, setting forth to the People his own Fault, and his Son's Virtue; after he had kissed him, and forced his Son to accept Honour of him, as of his new become Subject, even in a Moment died, as it should seem, his Heart broken with Unkindness and Affliction, stretched so far beyond his Limits with his Excess of Comfort, as it was able no longer to keep safe his vital Spirits. *Sidney*

> *Edgar.* I met my Father with his bleeding Rings,
> Their precious Gems new lost; became his Guide;
> Led him, begg'd for him, sav'd him from Despair;
> Never (O Fault!) reveal'd myself unto him,
> Until some half Hour past, when I was arm'd,
> Not sure, though hoping, of this good Success,
> I asked his Blessing, and from first to last
> Told him my Pilgrimage: but his flaw'd Heart,
> Alack, too weak the Conflict to support,
> 'Twixt two Extremes of Passion, Joy and Grief,
> Burst smilingly.   [5.3.189ff.]

The Chronicle of *Holinshed*, and *Sidney*'s *Arcadia* are not the only Resources *Shakespeare* had for his Tragedy of *Lear*, if we may believe the Editor of a Collection of old Ballads[1] published in the Year 1726. In his Introduction to an old Ballad called, *A Lamentable Song of the Death of King Lear and his three Daughters*, he has these Words:

I cannot be certain directly as to the Time when this Ballad was written; but that it was some Years before the Play of *Shakespeare* appears from several

---

[1] See *A Collection of old Ballads*, edited by Ambrose Phillips (1723), Vol. 2, pp. 12–17; the ballad was first printed in *The Golden Garland of princely pleasures and delicate delights*, 1620, and is evidently later than the play.

Circumstances, which to mention would swell my Introduction too far beyond its usual Length.

It is to be wished that this Writer, since he was resolved not to exceed a certain Length in his Introduction, had omitted some Part of it in order to introduce those Circumstances that were of infinitely more Consequence than any thing else he has said on the Subject of that old Ballad: if it was really written before *Shakespeare*'s Play that great Poet did not disdain to consult it, but has copied it more closely than either the Chronicle or *Sidney*. From thence (for 'tis mentioned no where else) he took the Hint of *Lear*'s Madness, and the extravagant and wanton Cruelty his Daughters exercised on him; the Death of King *Lear* is also exactly copied.

Spenser seems to have furnished *Shakespeare* with the Hint of *Cordelia*'s Manner of Death. In the tenth Canto of the second Book of his *Faerie Queene* he relates the Story of King *Lear* and his three Daughters. *Cordelia*, he tells us, after having restored her Father to his Crown and succeeded to it after his Death, was by her Sister's Children dethroned and confined a long Time in Prison, so that, overcome by Despair, she hanged herself. In *Shakespeare Cordelia* does not hang herself but is hanged by a Soldier, a very improper Catastrophe for a Person of such exemplary Virtue. (III, 300–2)

142. Zachary Grey and others, Notes on Shakespeare

1754

From *Critical, Historical and Explanatory Notes on Shakespeare with Emendations of the Text and Metre* (2 vols, 1754).

Zachary Grey (1688–1766), a Cambridge clergyman, an antiquary and scholar, wrote various historical and theological works. He was best known for his edition of Butler's *Hudibras* (2 vols, 1744; additional notes, 1752) which was savagely abused by Warburton, and Grey may have been the author of some anonymously published works attacking Warburton's *Shakespeare*, and defending Sir Thomas Hanmer's, which appeared between 1746 and 1752. His collection of notes on Shakespeare, a long and diffuse book (it totals 740 pages), is the weakest of all the essays in textual criticism in this period.

[From the *Preface*]

How he [Warburton] has succeeded must be left to the reader to judge from the* *Remarks* of two learned and very ingenious gentlemen, *Thomas Edwards* Esq; *Barrister of Lincoln's Inn*, and the reverend Mr. *Upton, Prebendary of Rochester*. And I shall despair of seeing the genuine text of *Shakespeare* restored till the publication of his works is undertaken by one or both these gentlemen, who, from what they have publish'd upon the subject, have shewn that they are duly qualified to perform the task with great credit to themselves and advantage to their readers.

* The first, intitled *Canons of Criticism, and a Glossary. Being a supplement to Mr. Warburton's edition of Shakespeare*.[1] The fifth edition was publish'd in 1753.

The second, intitled, *Critical Observations on Shakespeare*.[2] See *Preface* to the second edition.

[1] See Vol. 3, No. 127, and below, No. 168.
[2] See Vol. 3, No. 114.

I have never heard any other objections made to the writings of this excellent poet but that he has here and there an *obscene expression*, or for his unskilfulness in the *dead languages*, remarkable *anachronisms* or blunders in *chronology*, and the *jingles*, *puns*, and *quibbles* which frequently occur in his *plays*.

As to the first, he is certainly indefensible, and cannot by any means be justified; though *Ovid, Horace* and others of the antient *poets*, and *Ben Jonson* and other contemporary writers have taken as great (if not greater) liberties in that respect. As to his ignorance in the *Greek* and *Latin tongues*, though that point has been more than once discussed and much said on both sides of the question, I cannot but think from his exact imitation of many of the antient *poets* and *historians* (of which there were no tolerable translations in his time), that his knowledge in that respect cannot reasonably be call'd in question. Nay, from the single play of *Hamlet*, which seems in many places to be an exact translation of *Saxo Grammaticus* (which I believe was never translated into any other language), it cannot be doubted but that he had a competent skill in the *Latin tongue*.

His mistakes in *chronology* are so notorious and numerous that I shall not pretend to vindicate them.

And as to the last particular, his *jingles, puns,* and *quibbles,* they were certainly owing to the false taste of the times in which he lived.

King *James* the *First* was by some persons thought to be a Prince of great learning, but he affected to shew it so much in his *speeches* that by others he has been charged with *pedantry,* which I suppose occasioned *Gondomar*'s saucy freedom, in telling his *Majesty* that *he* spoke *Latin* like a *pedant* but *he himself* like a *gentleman.*

Nay, this Prince discover'd in his writings so much of this low (but then fashionable) kind of wit that it is not to be wondered at if he was follow'd by the generality of writers of those times.

Bishop *Andrewes,* the most learned *Prelate* of that age, in all his sermons before the *King* abounds but too much in jingles, *&c.* I shall exhibit to the reader a few passages out of many in proof.

In his sermon before the King at *White-Hall* on *Christmas Day,* 1607, on 1 *Timothy,* vi. 1, he begins with the following words.

P. 17. The mystery (here mentioned) is the *mystery* of this *feast,* and this *feast* the *feast* of this *mystery*: for, as at this *feast* God was *manifested in the flesh,* in that it is a great *mystery,* it maketh the *feast* great; in that it is a *mystery of godliness,* it should likewise make it a *feast of godliness*; *great* we grant, and *godly* too we trust: would God, as *godly* as great, and no more controversie of one, than of the other.

In another sermon before the King, on *Christmas Day* 1623, on *Ephesians*. i. 10:

P. 148. Seeing the *text* is of *seasons*, it would not be out of *season* itself: and tho' it be never out of *season* to speak of Christ, yet Christ hath his *seasons*. *Your time is always* (saith he, *John* vii.) so is not myne; I have my *seasons*, one of which *seasons* is this, the *season* of his birth, by which all were recapitulate in *heaven and earth*; which is the *season* of the *text*, and so this a *text* of the *season*. . . .

I come now to give an account of what I have done in the following notes.

I have with tolerable care collated the two first folio editions of 1623 and 1632 (especially the latter) with Mr. *Theobald's*, Sir *Thomas Hanmer's*, and Mr. *Warburton's* (whose text I have generally made use of): by which I think it will appear that there are many alterations for the worse in these *modern editions*. I have read over the works of *Chaucer, Skelton*, and *Spenser*, and have endeavoured to point out those passages which *Shakespeare* probably borrowed from thence, and to shew what things have been copied from him by the *dramatic* writers who lived in or near his own time. (I, vi–ix)

*   *   *

[On *The Tempest*, 2.2.75ff.]

Cal. *Thou do'st me yet but little hurt, &c.*]

This is the first speech of *Caliban* in prose: I am apt to believe that every thing that *Caliban* says, not only in this scene but through the whole play, was design'd by the author for metre, either for verse or *Hemistics*. Certainly most of it is: for this reason it may be reduced to verse in the following manner.

> Thou do'st me yet but little hurt, thou wilt
> Anon: I know, it by thy *trembleing*,
> Now *Prospero* works so on thee.

Trembleing of three syllables, to which the editors not attending, jumbled this into prose. *Anon*.[1] (I, 19)

*   *   *

[1] In his preface Grey acknowledges quoting from 'the notes of a *learned* and *ingenious* person, dead some time ago, whom I have distinguished with the title of *Anonymous*' (p. xii).

[On *The Tempest*, 2.2.108ff.]

Cal. *These be fine things, an if they be not sprights, that's a brave god, and bears celestial liquor, I will kneel to him.*]

This speech of *Caliban's* plainly consists of two verses, and an *Hemistic*, thus.

> These be fine things, and if they be not sprights,
> That's a brave god, and bears celestial liquor,
> I will kneel to him. (I, 20)

* * *

[On *The Tempest*, 3.2.29f.]

> Cal. *Lo, how he mocks me, wilt thou let him,*
> *My lord?*

Here is a syllable too much for the verse, for (as is before observ'd) all *Caliban's* speeches are design'd to be metre; we should correct, I think, by striking out *my* before *lord*, as *Trinculo* immediately repeats it.

Trin. *Lord quoth he?* that a monster should be such a natural. *Anon.*

[On *The Tempest*, 3.2.36ff.]

Cal. *I thank my noble lord, wilt thou be pleas'd to hearken once again to the suit I made thee?*]

This speech comes into two verses.

> I thank my noble lord, wilt thou be pleas'd
> To hearken once again, to th' suit I made thee. *Anon.* (I, 24)

* * *

[On *A Midsummer Night's Dream*, 3.2.448ff.]

> Puck. *On the ground, sleep thou sound,*
> *I'll apply to your eye, gentle lover remedy.*]

A friend observes that the humour of *Puck's* fairy charm is lost by the present manner of writing the verses.

If they were thus ordered (as in Mr. *Warburton*)

> On the ground,
> Sleep thou sound, [Sleep sound. *Warb.*]
> I'll apply
> To your eye,
> Gentle lover remedy.
> When thou wak'st

> *Next, thou tak'st*
> *True delight*
> *In the sight*
> *Of thy former ladies eye.*

They would appear to as great advantage as the *Namby Pamby* stile, or the *poet-laureat*'s encomium upon the *man-mountain*. For sure *fairy verses* ought to be as short as *infantine*, or *liliputian*. [See *Rabelais*'s Work's, Book 5. ch. 35.]

But I rather think they should be wrote,

> On the ground, sleep thou sound,
> I'll apply to your eye,
> Gentle lover remedy, &c.

Because verses with the middle rhime, which were call'd *leonine* or *monkish* verses, seem to have been the ancient language of *charms* and *incantations,* as appears from several footsteps of it in *Virgil*'s *Pharmaceutria,* but particularly in this line, *Eclog.* 8, 80:[1]

> *Limus ut hic durescit, et hæc ut cera liquescit,*

And there are some traces of the same kind in that of *Theocritus* which *Virgil* here imitates, but none, it must be own'd, so strong as the example before us. Dr. *T.*[2] (I, 62–3)

*   *   *

[On the sources for *As You Like It*]

Several passages in this play were certainly borrowed from the *Coke's Tale of Gamelyn* in *Chaucer,*[3] as will appear I hope from the following abstract, &c.

Sir *John Boundis* an antient knight, finding himself in a declining state of health, by will devised his fortunes to his three sons, *John, Otis,* [or *Ote*] and *Gamelyn:* and as *Gamelyn* was very young he intreated his friends (knowing his eldest son to be of a barbarous and unnatural disposition) that they would take care, that *Gamelyn*'s share should be made secure to him.

But after the old knight's death they neglecting their promise;

[1] 'As this clay hardens, and as this wax melts / in one and the same flame. . . .'

[2] In the preface Grey acknowledges help from 'Dr. Tathwell, a learned and ingenious *physician* at *Stamford* in *Lincolnshire*' (p. xii).

[3] This poem, first printed in 1721, was erroneously ascribed to Chaucer. Shakespeare's main source was the story as re-told by Lodge in his *Rosalynde* (1590), but 'Lodge must have seen [the poem] and maybe Shakespeare did so too': G. Bullough, *Narrative and Dramatic Sources of Shakespeare* II (London, 1958), p. 143.

Gamelyn's eldest brother seiz'd upon his whole fortunes, committed great waste upon his parks and woods, suffering his houses at the same time to run to ruine, using *Gamelyn* much worse than he did the lowest of his menial servants.

Gamelyn resented his usage, and insisted that he might be put in possession of his fortunes left him by his father. But his brother, instead of complying with his request, ordered his servants to cudgel him into better manners, which they immediately attempted. But *Gamelyn*, by good fortune meeting with a *pestle*, turned it into a weapon of offence, and drove his brother and his servants before him. The brother then offered to accommodate the difference, telling him that the attempt made upon him by his servants was not with any intention of doing him harm but only to make trial of his strength and courage, promising at the same time to restore to him his lands and other possessions in as good condition as when they first came into his hands: which brought about a reconciliation, sincere on *Gamelyn*'s part but not so on the other's.

A wrestling having been proclaimed at some distance from his brother's house, *Gamelyn* intreated of him to lend him a horse to carry him to the place appointed, with which he complied.

At his first approach he heard a *frankline* [freeholder] passionately bewailing the loss of three sons who had unfortunately lost their lives, by rashly engaging with a celebrated wrestler. *Gamelyn* endeavoured to moderate his grief by promising that he would have a trial of skill with the wrestler, hoping by his defeats to revenge his cause. After he had prepared himself for the engagement and had entred the lists the champion enquired his name, and seemed to hold him in high contempt on account of his youth and inexperience. But that vain-glorious person had no reason to boast long, for after a short engagement *Gamelyn* gave him a fall and broke three of his ribs and his left arm, by which means being absolutely disabled for a second trial, the prize (which was a *goat* and a ring) was adjudged in favour of *Gamelyn*.

He returned immediately to his brother's house with several of his companions, thinking that they should be graciously received on account of his success at the *wrestling*. But instead thereof his brother ordered his porter to lock his gates against them, and not to admit them upon any consideration whatsoever. *Gamelyn*, resenting this usage, broke open one of the gates, pursued the porter, caught him in his arms, brake his neck and threw him into a well of water which was (according to *Chaucer*) 700 fathoms deep.

He told the other servants that when he went to the wrestling he left behind him a large quantity of wine, and if either they or his brother found fault with this entertainment of his friends they should undergo the porter's fate.

His brother concealed himself during their stay, but when *Gamelyn* had dismissed his companions he ventured out of his lurking hole and reproached him for having wasted his goods in so riotous a manner. But *Gamelyn* assigning reasons for what he had done he seemed to be reconciled, and told him at the same time that as he was a batchelour and had no children at his death he would leave him his whole fortunes, requesting only one favour at his hands, that he would suffer himself to be bound with chains to satisfy a rash vow which he had made when he threw his porter into the well. With which when *Gamelyn* had complied he had him chain'd to a large post in his hall, where he continued for the space of two days and two nights without meat or drink, exposed at the same time to the scorn and ridicule of all such as passed that way.

His brother in the mean time receiving a visit from an *abbot*, some *priors*, and others of the regular clergy, *Gamelyn* applied to them to favour his release, but they rather encouraging his brother in his ill treatment of him, he was privately, by the help of *Adam le Dispenser*, one of his brother's servants, freed from his bonds; and when the *religious* and his brother had dined he, by the help of his friend *Adam*, drove them forcibly out of the hall, made many of them cripples, and treated his brother in a manner by no means more favourable.

But being apprehensive that his brother would apply to the *sheriff* for relief he immediately decamp'd, and fled with *Adam le Dispenser* into a forest, where after enduring some hardships they were kindly received by a band of outlaws, with their King at their head; and the King of the outlaws being restored to favour and the fortunes of which he had been dispossessed, *Gamelyn* was unanimously chosen King.

His brother, not long after being made *high sheriff*, prevailed to have *Gamelyn* indicted for the violent outrage committed upon his person.

Gamelyn, having leave from the outlaws, made his personal appearance, upon which he was attach'd and committed to prison; but Sir *Ote* [or *Otis*] offering bail for his appearance to take his trial he was released and returned to the *outlaws*.

Gamelyn not appearing precisely at the time appointed, his eldest brother pack'd a jury to his mind with two corrupt Judges, and they were very near passing sentence of death upon Sir *Otis* for *Gamelyn*'s non-appearance. But he came opportunely with his *outlaws* to save his brother's life.

Gamelyn ascended the place of judicature, ordered the *Chief Justice* to give place to him, and upon his refusal he with his sword cleft his jaw bone, threw him over the bar, and broke his arm. After that he ordered the other Judge, his brother, and the *jurors* to be set to the bar, where after a short trial he passed sentence of death upon them all, which was immediately put in execution.

After which he and his outlaws made the best of their way towards the King; who pardoned them all, promoted Sir *Otis* and *Gamelyn* to great honours, and received the outlaws into favour.

The conclusion of the quarrel betwixt *Oliver* and *Orlando* proved much more favourable. For by a remarkable act of generosity in *Orlando*, who saved his brother's life from a lioness, which he killed, *Oliver* relented his former ill usage of him, and a thorough reconciliation by that means was brought about. (I, 156–61)

*   *   *

[On *Henry V*, 2.3.15ff.]

Quickly. *For his nose was as sharp as a pen on a table of green fields.*]

Here our editors, not knowing what to make of a *table* of *green fields*, Mr *Pope* and Mr *Warburton* have cast it out of the text; others have turn'd it into 'and have *babbled* of *green fields*.'

But had they been appriz'd that* *table* in our author signifies a pocket book, I believe they would have retained it, with the following alteration.

'For his nose was as sharp as a *pen* upon a *table* of *green fells*.'

On *table-books* silver or steel pens, very sharp-pointed, were formerly and are still fix'd either to the backs or covers.

Mother *Quickly* compares *Falstaff*'s nose, (which in dying persons grows thin and sharp) to one of those *pens* very properly, and she meant probably to have said on a *table-book* with a *shagreen* cover, or *shagreen table*; but in her usual blundering way she calls it a *table of green fells*, or a table cover'd with *green skin*, which the blundering transcriber turn'd into *green fields*: and our editors have turn'd the prettiest blunder in *Shakespeare* quite out of doors.

Mr *Smith*.[1] (I, 381–2)

---

* So it is used in the First Part of *King Henry* the *Fourth*. [i.e., *2 Henry IV*, 2.4.289]

    And in *Hamlet* Prince of *Denmark* (1.5.107).

[1] In the preface Grey acknowledges help from the 'Rev. Mr. *Smith*, of *Harleston* in Norfolk (p. xii) the most friendly and communicative man living.'

*   *   *

[On *King Lear*, 1.1.71ff.]

> Reg. *Only she comes too short: that I profess*
> *Myself an enemy to all other joys,*
> *Which the most precious square of sense possesses,*
> *And find I am alone felicitate,*
> *In your dear Highness' love.*

The want of an apostrophe over *sense* seems to have confounded our editors.

Goneril had pointed out two fours, or squares, not of sense, but of the joys or pleasures of sense; the first, eye-sight, space, and liberty, with what could be valued rich and rare, and declares the King was dearer to her than any thing contained in it, tho' it was a square of the joys of sense, comparatively speaking, vastly more agreeable to the female sex than any other square of joys of a lower, inferior nature.

The second square that *Goneril* names of the joys or pleasures of sense, is grace, health, beauty, honour.

But then she says she loves the King no less than these, and consequently she loves these as much as she does the King. And this is the point in which *Regan* says she falls short of her.

The second square is of the superlative kind of joys, the most precious to womankind. And *Regan* professes herself an enemy to three of the joys, *viz.* health, beauty, and honour, *i.e.* she has no relish, no manner of affection for them, which are of all the other joys the most precious square of sense [*i.e.* sense's joys] possesses; and declares that she finds herself alone felicitate in his dear Highness's love or grace, which is the only joy of the *square* which she values; and so long as she enjoys that all the others are nothing to her, she is as happy as her heart can wish. And in this it is plain that she outdoes her sister *Goneril*, and might well say, 'Only in this she comes too short of her.'

Mr Smith. (II, 102–3)

143. Arthur Murphy on Shakespeare's ghost-scenes

1754

From the *Entertainer*, no. 11 (12 November 1754). This journal, edited by 'Charles Mercury', appeared between 3 September and 19 November 1754. For the ascription to Murphy see Arthur Sherbo (ed.), *New Essays by Arthur Murphy* (East Lansing, Michigan, 1963), p. 11, who compares *Gray's-Inn Journal* 8 (No. 140a above) and the *London Chronicle* review of 16–19 April 1757 (No. 161a below).

On Murphy see the headnote to No. 140 above. In addition to his work for the *Entertainer* and the *Gray's-Inn Journal* Murphy contributed to the *Test* (1756–7) and the *Auditor* (1762–3).

This nation has in all ages been much more addicted to folly and superstition than any other whatever. The belief of GHOSTS and APPARITIONS is at present as strongly implanted in the minds of the major part of the inhabitants of this kingdom as it was in the days when ignorance and want of knowledge and experience blinded the eyes of men. I have always looked upon this foible as the creation of guilt or weakness. FEAR is the centre of both, and this continually fills our thoughts with unreal objects, full of darkness and horror. I have had frequent opportunities to realize this remark: several times have I gone through a CHURCH-YARD by night in company with persons whom I knew to be much given to melancholy and horrid thoughts. I have oft seen them start at the least noise, and when the glimpses of the MOON formed their own shadow upon the ground I could behold them suddenly stop and gaze at it with looks full of wildness and amazement.

SHAKESPEARE seems to have selected his *Hamlet* chiefly to shew the horrors and gloomy sights that continually croud upon the mind of a weak or melancholy person. FEAR and SADNESS are the characters of

HAMLET, and the black suggestions of his imagination appear in several scenes of that PLAY, especially when he goes to see his MOTHER by night and breaks out in this reflection:

> *'Tis now the very witching time of night,*
> *When church-yards yawn, and hell itself breaths out*
> *Contagion to the world:* [3.2.378ff.]

This short passage alone is sufficient to demonstrate whence proceed all the frightful objects that appear before us when our hearts are stung with SORROW and overwhelmed with GRIEF.

In the tragedy of *Macbeth* the bard has finely pictured the condition of a guilty mind, and the scene when MACBETH goes to murder DUNCAN is one of the strongest proofs that a GHOST or APPARITION proceeds either from GUILT or FEAR, or is a mixture of both. The thoughts of MACBETH are solely engaged by the deed he is going to act. That unhappy prince, we are told, was a virtuous man until, corrupted by his wife and misled by AMBITION, he is prompted to murder the KING, his benefactor. His forsaken virtue fills him with fear, and makes him sensible of his guilt; it presents to his view a DAGGER in the AIR leading him to DUNCAN, at which he starts and addresses it thus:

> *Is this a dagger which I see before me,*
> *The handle tow'rd my hand? come, let me clutch thee.*
> *I have thee not, and yet I see thee still.*
> *Art thou not, fatal vision, sensible*
> *To feeling, as to sight? or art thou but*
> *A dagger of the mind, a false creation*
> *Proceeding from the heat-oppressed brain?*
> *I see thee yet in form as palpable*
> *As this which now I draw—*
> *Thou marshal'st me the way that I was going;*
> *And such an instrument I was to use.*
> *Mine eyes are made the fools o'th' other senses,*
> *Or else worth all the rest—I see thee still;*
> *And on thy blade and dudgeon, gouts of blood,*
> *Which was not so before.* [2.1.33ff.]

Then he summons his reason to his aid, and prevails upon himself to believe it is the bloody purpose only that works upon his imagination; after which a secret horror takes possession of his SOUL, and he says

> *Now o'er one half the world*
> *Nature seems dead, and wicked dreams abuse*
> *The curtain'd sleep; now witchcraft celebrates*
> *Pale Hecate's offerings: and wither'd murder,*
> *(Alarm'd by his sentinel, the wolf,*
> *Whose howl's his watch) thus with his stealthy pace,*
> *With* Tarquin's *ravishing strides; tow'rds his design*
> *Moves like a ghost—* [2.1.49ff.]

Then he goes to murder DUNCAN; and LADY MACBETH enters, full of the same guilty thoughts as her husband, her imagination filled with BLOOD and DEATH, and as she comes forth every noise appalls her and engages her attention. Then she cries out

> *Hark!—peace?—*
> *It was the owl that shriek'd, the fatal bell-man,*
> *Which gives the stern'st good-night.—* [2.2.2ff.]

All this is finely imagined, and worthy of SHAKESPEARE. The whole is natural, and when I see Mr. GARRICK in the character of MACBETH I cannot help starting with him at the visionary DAGGER, and partake of his amazement. . . .

144. Thomas Sheridan, Thomson's
Coriolanus conflated with Shakespeare's

1754

From *Coriolanus: or, The Roman Matron. A Tragedy. Taken from Shakespeare and Thomson* (1755).

James Thomson (1700–48), the poet of *The Seasons*, wrote an original play on the Coriolanus story, which was produced at Covent Garden on 13 January 1749, and printed in that year. Thomas Sheridan (1719–88), actor and teacher of acting and elocution, father of Richard Brinsley Sheridan, had a successful career as an actor and theatre-manager. Subsequently he became a respected lecturer on rhetoric and elocution, wrote numerous works on education, and was incorporated M.A. of both Oxford and Cambridge. His conflation of Thomson's and Shakespeare's versions was performed on 10 December 1754. Shakespeare's Volumnia is renamed Veturia, and Virgilia becomes Volumnia. The old man who once befriended Coriolanus in Corioli (1.9.82ff.) appears as Galesus, while Aufidius is given a confidant, Volusius. See E. K. Sheldon, 'Sheridan's *Coriolanus*: An Eighteenth-Century Compromise', *Shakespeare Quarterly* 14 (1963), pp. 153–61.

Advertisement.

The person who undertook to alter and adapt the following piece to the stage did it with a view to preserve to the theatre two characters which seemed to be drawn in as masterly a manner as any that came from the pen of the inimitable *Shakespeare*. These he found were likely to be admired in the closet only; for the play in general seemed but ill calculated for representation. Upon examining a play of *Thomson's* upon the same subject, tho' he saw great beauties in it, he could not but perceive that it was defective in some essential points and must always appear tedious in the acting. From a closer view of both he thought they might mutually assist one another, and each supply the other's wants. *Shakespeare's* play was purely historical, and had little or no plot. *Thomson's*

159

plot was regular. but too much of the epic kind, and wanted business. He thought by blending these a piece might be produced which, tho' not perfect, might furnish great entertainment to, and keep up the attention of an audience. The success it has met with in both kingdoms (for it was first performed on the *Dublin* stage) has more than answered his expectation.

And he has good reason to hope that he has been the means of adding one play to the stock which is likely to live in any company where the characters of *Coriolanus* and *Veturia* can be properly supported.

As the military entry in this play, representing a *Roman* Ovation, has been universally admired, it is judged not unnecessary for the use of such as are not acquainted with the *Roman* customs to give the following account of that ceremony, together with the order of the procession as it was exhibited at the Theatre-royal in *Covent-garden*.

Ovation was a lesser sort of triumph. It had its name from *ovis*, a sheep, which was sacrificed on this occasion instead of a bull, used in the great triumph. The ovation was granted upon any extraordinary success against the enemy, in gaining a battle, taking a town, some remarkable exploit, or making an advantageous peace to *Rome*. But a triumph was never obtained unless a kingdom was entirely subdued and added to the *Roman* territories. They differed in form from each other principally in this, that in the Ovation all marched on foot, but in the triumph the victor was carried in a chariot drawn by horses and followed by horse-men, which makes the representation of the latter on the stage impracticable.

Underneath is the order of the Ovation as it was exhibited.

But previous to that there was a civil procession from the town, consisting of Priests, Flamens, Choristers, Senators, Tribunes, Virgins, Matrons, and the Mother, Wife, and Child of *Coriolanus*. These walked to the sound of flutes and soft instruments, and lined the way to behold the military entry and congratulate the victor. The Ovation was performed to the sound of drums, fifes and trumpets, in the following order.

The Order of the OVATION.

Six Lictors.
One carrying a small Eagle.
Six Incense-bearers.
Four Souldiers.
Two Fifes.
One Drum.

Two Standard-bearers.
Ten Souldiers.
Two Fifes.
One Drum.
Two Standard-bearers.
Six Souldiers.
Two Standard-bearers.
Four Serpent Trumpets.
Four carrying a Bier with Gold and Silver Vases,
    Part of the Spoil.
Two Souldiers.
Two Standard-bearers.
Two Souldiers.
Four carrying another Bier with a large Urn and
    Four Vases.
Four Souldiers carrying a Bier loaden with Trophies,
    Armour, Ensigns, &c. taken from the Enemy.
Five Souldiers with mural and civick Crowns.
Four Captive Generals in Chains.
One carrying a small Eagle.
Twelve Lictors preceding the two Consuls.

M. MINUCIUS.   C. COMINIUS.

CORIOLANUS.

A Standard-bearer,   Another Standard-bearer,
with a Drawing of   with the name of *Corioli*
Corioli.   wrote on the Banner.

Two carrying a large Eagle.
Four Standard-bearers.
Twelve Souldiers.

In the military Procession alone, independent of the Civil, there were an hundred and eighteen persons.

*   *   *

[Act V, Scene 1]

SCENE: *a Camp with* Volscian *Soldiers, as before.*

Enter CORIOLANUS, TULLUS, GALESUS, VOLUSIUS; *The* Roman *Ladies advance slowly, with* VETURIA *and* VOLUMNIA, *all clad in mourning.* CORIOLANUS *sits on his tribunal; but seeing them, advances, and goes hastily to embrace his mother.*

161

Coriolanus. Lower your fasces, Lictors—
O Veturia!
Thou best of parents!
 Veturia. Coriolanus, stop.
Whom am I to embrace? a son, or foe?
Say, in what light am I regarded here?
Thy mother, or thy captive?
 Coriolanus. Justly, madam,
You check my fondness, that, by nature hurry'd,
Forgot, I was the general of the Volsci,
And you a deputy from hostile Rome.

        [He goes back to his former station.

I hear you with respect. Speak your commission.
 Veturia. Think not I come a deputy from Rome.
Rome, once rejected, scorns a second suit.
You have already heard whate'er the tongue
Of eloquence can plead, whate'er the wisdom
Of sacred age, the dignity of senates,
And virtue can enforce. Behold me here
Sent by the shades of your immortal fathers,
Sent by the genius of the Marcian line,
Commission'd by my own maternal heart,
To try the soft, yet stronger powers of nature;
Thus authoriz'd, I ask, nay, claim a peace,
On equal, fair, and honourable terms,
To thee, to Rome, and to the Volscian people.
Grant it, my son! Thy mother begs it of thee;
Thy wife, the best, the kindest of her sex,
And these illustrious matrons, who have sooth'd
The gloomy hours thou hast been absent from us.
We, by whate'er is great and good in nature,
By every duty, by the Gods, conjure thee,
To grant us peace! and turn on other foes
Thy arms, where thou may'st purchase virtuous glory.
 Coriolanus. I should, Veturia, break those holy bonds
That hold the wide republic of mankind,
Society, together; I should grow
A wretch unworthy to be call'd thy son;
I should, with my Volumnia's fair esteem,
Forfeit her love; these matrons would despise me—

Could I betray the Volscian cause, thus trusted,
Thus recommended to me—no, my mother,
You cannot sure, you cannot ask it of me!
    Veturia. And does my son so little know me? Me!
Who took such care to form his tender years,
Left to my conduct by his dying father?
Have I so ill deserv'd that trust? Alas!
Am I so low in thy esteem, that thou
Should'st e'er imagine I could urge a part
Which in the least might stain the Marcian honour?
No, let me perish rather! perish all!
Life has no charms compar'd to spotless glory!
I only ask, thou woud'st forbid thy troops
To waste our lands, and to assault yon city,
'Till time be giv'n for mild and righteous measures.
Grant us but one year's truce: Mean while thou may'st,
With honour and advantage to both nations,
Betwixt us mediate a perpetual peace.
    Coriolanus. Alas! my mother! That were granting all.
    Veturia. Canst thou refuse me such a just petition,
The first request thy mother ever made thee?
Canst thou to her intreaties, prayers, and tears,
Prefer a savage obstinate revenge?
Have love and nature lost all power within thee?
    Coriolanus. No—in my heart they reign as strong as ever.
Come, I conjure you, quit ungrateful Rome,
Come, and complete my happiness at Antium,
You, and my dear Volumnia—There, Veturia,
There you shall see with what respect the Volsci
Will treat the wife and mother of their general.
    Veturia. Treat me thyself with more respect, my son;
Nor dare to shock my ears with such proposals.
Shall I desert my country, I who come
To plead her cause? Ah no!—A grave in Rome
Would better please me than a throne at Antium.
How hast thou thus forsaken all my precepts?
How hast thou thus forgot thy love to Rome?
O Coriolanus, when with hostile arms,
With fire and sword, you enter'd on our borders,
Did not the fostering air that breathes around us,

Allay thy guilty fury, and instil
A certain native sweetness thro' thy soul?
Did not your heart thus murmur to itself?
'These walls contain whatever can command
Respect from virtue, or is dear to nature,
The monuments of piety and valour;
The sculptur'd forms, the trophies of my fathers,
My houshold Gods, my mother, wife, and children!'
   Coriolanus. Ah! you seduce me with too tender views!
These walls contain the most corrupt of men,
A base seditious herd; who trample order,
Distinction, justice, law, beneath their feet,
Insolent foes to worth, the foes of virtue!
   Veturia. Thou hast not thence a right to lift thy hand
Against the whole community, which forms
Thy ever sacred country—That consists
Not of coeval citizens alone:
It knows no bounds; it has a retrospect
To ages past; it looks on those to come;
And grasps of all the general worth and virtue:
Suppose, my son, that I to thee had been
A harsh obdurate parent, even unjust;
How wou'd the mon'strous thought with horror strike thee,
Of plunging, from revenge, thy raging steel
Into her breast who nurs'd thy infant years!
   Coriolanus. Rome is no more! that Rome which nurs'd my youth;
That Rome, conducted by patrician virtue,
She is no more! my sword shall now chastise
These sons of pride and dirt! her upstart tyrants!
Who have debas'd the noblest state on earth
Into a sordid democratic faction;
Why will my mother join her cause to theirs?
   Veturia. Forbid it, Jove! that I should e'er distinguish
My interest from the general cause of Rome;
Or live to see a foreign hostile arm
Reform th' abuses of our land of freedom.

                                 [Pausing.

But 'tis in vain, I find, to reason more.
Is there no way to reach thy filial heart,
Once fam'd as much for piety as courage?

Oft hast thou justly triumph'd, Coriolanus;
Now yield one triumph to thy widow'd mother;
And send me back amidst the loud acclaims,
The grateful transports of deliver'd Rome,
The happiest far, the most renown'd of women!
 Coriolanus. Why, why, Veturia, wilt thou plead in vain?
 Tullus (*aside to* Volusius). See, see, Volusius, how the strong emotions
Of powerful nature shake his inmost soul!
See how they tear him—If he long resists them,
He is a God, or something worse than man.
 Veturia. O Marcius, Marcius! canst thou treat me thus?
Canst thou complain of Rome's ingratitude,
Yet be to me so cruelly ungrateful?
To me! who anxious rear'd thy youth to glory?
Whose only joy these many years has been,
To boast that Coriolanus was my son?
And dost thou then renounce me for thy mother?
Spurn me before these chiefs, before those soldiers,
That weep thy stubborn cruelty? Art thou
The hardest man to me in this assembly?
Look at me! speak!
       [*Pausing, during which he appears in great agitation.*
Still dost thou turn away?
Inexorable? silent?—Then, behold me,
Behold thy mother, at whose feet thou oft
Hast kneel'd with fondness, kneeling now at thine,
Wetting thy stern tribunal with her tears.
 Coriolanus. Veturia, rise; I cannot see thee thus.   [*Raises her.*
It is a sight uncomely to behold
My mother at my feet, and that to urge
A suit, relentless honour must refuse.
 Volumnia (*advancing*). Since, Coriolanus, thou dost still retain,
In spite of all thy mother now has pleaded,
Thy dreadful purpose, ah! how much in vain
Were it for me to join my supplications!
The voice of thy Volumnia, once so pleasing,
How shall it hope to touch the husband's heart,
When proof against the tears of such a parent?
I dare not urge what to thy mother thou
So firmly hast deny'd—But I must weep—

Must weep, if not thy harsh severity,
At least thy situation. O permit me   *[Taking his hand.*
To shed my gushing tears upon thy hand!
To press it with the cordial lips of love!
And take my last farewell!
    Coriolanus. Yet, yet, my soul,
Be firm, and persevere—
    Volumnia. Ah, Coriolanus!
Is then this hand, this hand to me devoted,
The pledge of nuptial love, that has so long
Protected, bless'd, and shelter'd us with kindness,
Now lifted up against us? yet I love it,
And, with submissive veneration, bow
Beneath th' affliction which it heaps upon us.
But oh! what nobler transports would it give thee!
What joy beyond expression! could'st thou once
Surmount the furious storm of fierce revenge,
And yield thee to the charms of love and mercy.
Oh make the glorious trial!
    Coriolanus. Mother! wife!
Are all the powers of nature leagu'd against me?
I cannot!—will not!—Leave me, my Volumnia!
    Volumnia. Well, I obey—How bitter thus to part!
Upon such terms to part!—perhaps, for ever!—
But tell me, ere I hence unroot my feet,
When to my lonely home I shall return,
What from their father, to our little slaves,
Unconscious of the shame to which you doom them,
What shall I say?   *[Pausing, he highly agitated.*
Nay—tell me, Coriolanus!
    Coriolanus. Tell thee! what shall I tell thee? See these tears!
These tears will tell thee what exceeds the pow'r
Of words to speak, whate'er the son, the husband,
And father, in one complicated pang,
Can feel—But leave me;—ev'n in pity leave me!
Cease, cease, to torture me, my dear Volumnia!
You only tear my heart; but cannot shake it:
For by th' immortal Gods, the dread avengers
Of broken faith!—
    Volumnia [*Kneeling*]. Oh swear not, Coriolanus!

Oh vow not our destruction!
   Veturia. Daughter, rise,
Let us no more before the Volscian people
Expose ourselves a spectacle of shame.
It is in vain we strive to melt a breast,
That, to the best affections nature gives us
Prefers the worst—Hear me, proud man, I have
A heart as stout as thine. I came not hither
To be sent back rejected, baffled, sham'd,
Hateful to Rome, because I am thy mother:
A Roman Matron knows, in such extremes,
What part to take—And thus I came provided.
                      [*Drawing forth a conceal'd dagger.*
Go! barbarous son! go! double parricide!
Rush o'er my corse to thy belov'd revenge!
Tread on the bleeding breast of her to whom
Thou ow'st thy life—Lo, thy first victim!
   Coriolanus. Ha!   [*Seizing her hand.*
What do'st thou mean?
   Veturia. To die, while Rome is free,
To seize the moment e're thou art her tyrant.
   Coriolanus. Oh use thy pow'r more justly! set not thus
My treach'rous heart in arms against my reason,
Here! here! thy dagger will be well employ'd;
Strike here, and reconcile my fighting duties.
   Veturia. Off—set me free!—think'st thou that grasp which binds
My feeble hand, can fetter too my will?
No, my proud son! thou can'st not make me live,
If Rome must fall!—No pow'r on earth can do it!
   Coriolanus. Pity me, generous Volsci!—You are men!—
Must it then be?—Confusion! Do I yield!
What is it? is it weakness? is it virtue?—
Well!—
   Veturia. What? Speak!
   Coriolanus. O, no!—
   Veturia. Nay, if thou yieldest, yield like Coriolanus;
And what thou do'st, do nobly!
   Coriolanus. There!—'Tis done!   [*Quitting her hand.*
Thine is the triumph, nature!
Ah, Veturia!   [*To* Veturia, *in a low tone of voice.*

Rome by thy aid is sav'd—But thy son lost.

Veturia. He never can be lost, who saves his country.

Coriolanus. Ye matrons!   [*Turning to the Roman ladies.*
Guardians of the Roman safety,
You to the senate may report this answer,
We grant the truce you ask, but on these terms:
That Rome, mean time, shall to a peace agree,
Fair, equal, just, and such as may secure
The safety, rights, and honour of the Volsci.
Volsci, we raise the siege. Go, and prepare,   [*To the troops.*
By the first dawn, for your return to Antium.

   [*As the troops retire, and* Coriolanus *turns to the Roman ladies,* Tullus
                            to Volusius *aside.*

Tullus. 'Tis as we wish'd, Volusius, to your station—

                  *   *   *

Coriolanus. Hear'st thou, Mars!

Tullus. Name not the God, thou boy of tears!

Coriolanus. Measureless liar, thou hast made my heart
Too great for what contains it. Boy! O slave!
If you have writ your annals true, 'tis there,
That like an eagle in a dove-coat, I
Flutter'd your Volscians in Corioli.
Alone I did it. Boy!—But let us part—
Lest my rash hand should do a hasty deed,
My cooler thought forbids.

Tullus. Begone—Return—
To head the Roman troops. I grant thee quittance,
Full and complete, of all those obligations,
Thou hast so oft insultingly complain'd
Fetter'd thy hands. They now are free. I court
The worst thy hand can do; whilst thou from me
Hast nothing to expect, but sore destruction.
Quit then this hostile camp. Once more I tell thee,
Thou art not here one single hour in safety.

Coriolanus. Think'st thou to fright me hence?

Tullus. Thou wilt not then?
Thou wilt not take the safety which I offer?

Coriolanus. 'Till I have clear'd my honour in your council,
And prov'd before them all, to thy confusion,

The falshood of thy charge; as soon in battle
I would before thee fly, and howl for mercy,
As quit the station they have here assign'd me.
    Tullus. Volusius! ho!
Enter Volusius *and* Conspirators, *with their swords drawn.*
Seize, and secure the traitor.
    Coriolanus. Who dares.   [*Laying his hand on his sword.*
Approach me, dies!
    Volusius. Die thou!
      [*As* Coriolanus *draws his sword,* Volusius *and the rest rush upon him*
        and stab him. Tullus *stands, without drawing.*
    Coriolanus. Off!—Villains.   [*Endeavours to free himself, falls.*
Oh murdering slaves! assassinating cowards.   [*Dies.*
Enter Galesus, *the Volscian states, officers and friends of* Coriolanus, *and*
    Titus, *with a large band of soldiers,* &c.
    Galesus. Are we a nation rul'd by laws, or fury?
How! whence this tumult?
Gods! what do I see?
The noble Marcius slain!
    Tullus. You see a traitor
Punish'd as he deserv'd, the Roman yoke,
That thrall'd us, broken, and the Volsci free.
    Galesus. Hear me, great Jove! Hear all you injur'd powers
Of friendship, hospitality and faith!
By that heroic blood, which from the ground
Reeking to you for vengeance cries, I swear!
This impious breach of your eternal laws,
This daring outrage of the Volscian honour,
Shall find in me a rigorous avenger!
On the same earth, polluted by their crime,
I will not live with these unpunish'd ruffians.
    Tullus. My rage is gone,
And I am struck with sorrow.
Tho' he has been our foe,
Yet as a soldier, brave, unmatch'd in arms,
With martial pomp, let these his sacred reliques
Be consecrate to the dread god of war,
Whose favourite he liv'd. His noble memory,
His deathless fame remain; but be his faults,
Be our resentments bury'd with his dust.

Galesius (*standing over the body of* Coriolanus, *after a short pause*).
Ye noble Volscians,
And ye, brave soldiers, see an awful scene,
Demanding serious, solemn meditation.
This man was once the glory of his age,
Disinterested, just, with every virtue
Of civil life adorn'd, in arms unequal'd.
His only blot was this; that, much provok'd,
He rais'd his vengeful arm against his country.
And lo! the righteous gods have now chastis'd him,
Even by the hands of those for whom he fought.
Whatever private views and passions plead,
No cause can justify so black a deed.
Then be this truth the star by which we steer,
Above ourselves our country should be dear.

145. David Hume, Shakespeare and Jacobean taste

1754

From *The History of Great Britain. Vol. 1, Containing The Reigns of James I and Charles I* (Edinburgh, 1754), chapter vi.

David Hume (1711–76), philosopher and historian, was educated at Edinburgh University, spent several years in France, and held various administrative posts. His literary criticism includes an essay on tragedy (which has a passing reference to Iago's working-up of Othello's jealousy), and two important essays on taste (1757).

The endeavors of James, or more properly speaking, those of the nation, for the promotion of trade were attended with greater success than those for the encouragement of learning. Tho' the age was by no means destitute of eminent writers a very bad taste in general prevailed during that period, and the monarch himself was not a little infected with it.

On the first origin of letters among the Greeks the genius of poets and orators, as might naturally be expected, was distinguished by an amiable simplicity which, whatever rudeness might sometimes attend it, is so fitted to express the genuine movements of nature and passion that the compositions possessed of it must for ever appear valuable to the discerning part of mankind. The glaring figures of discourse, the pointed antithesis, the unnatural conceit, the jingle of words: such false ornaments are not employed by early writers, not because they were rejected but because they scarce ever occurred to them. An easy, unforced strain of sentiment runs thro' their compositions; tho' at the same time we may observe that, amid the most elegant simplicity of thought and expression, one is sometimes surprised to meet with a poor conceit, which had presented itself unsought for and which the author had not

acquired critical observation enough to condemn.* A bad taste seizes
with avidity these frivolous beauties, and even perhaps a good taste, 'ere
surfeited by them. They multiply every day more and more, in the
fashionable compositions: Nature and good sense are neglected, laboured ornaments studied and admired, and a total degeneracy of style
and language prepares the way for barbarism and ignorance. Hence the
Asiatic manner was found to depart so much from the simple purity of
Athens; hence that tinsel eloquence which is observable in many of the
Roman writers, from which Cicero himself is not wholly exempted,
and which so much prevails in Ovid, Seneca, Lucan, Martial, and the
Plinys.

On the revival of letters, when the judgment of the public is as yet
raw and unformed, this false glister catches the eye and leaves no room,
either in eloquence or poetry, for the durable beauties of solid sense and
lively passion. The reigning genius is then diametrically opposite to that
which prevails on the first origin of arts. The Italian writers, 'tis evident,
even the most celebrated, have not reached the proper simplicity of
thought and composition, and in Petrarch, Tasso, Guarini, frivolous
witticisms and forced conceits are but too predominant. The period
during which letters were cultivated in Italy was so short as scarce to
allow leisure for correcting this adulterated relish.

The more early French writers are liable to the same reproach.
Voiture, Balzac, even Corneille have too much affected those ambitious
ornaments of which the Italians in general, and the least pure of the
antients, supplied them with so many models. And 'twas not till late,
that observation and reflection gave rise to a more natural turn of
thought and composition among that elegant people.

A like character may be extended to the first English writers; such
as flourished during the reign of Elizabeth and James, and even till long
afterwards. Learning, on its revival in this island, was attired in the
same unnatural garb which it wore at the time of its decay among the
Greeks and Romans. And, what may be regarded as a misfortune, the

---

* The name of Polynices, one of Oedipus's sons, means in the original *much quarrelling*. In
the altercations betwixt the two brothers, in Æschylus, Sophocles, and Euripides, this conceit is employed; and 'tis remarkable that so poor a conundrum could not be rejected by
any of these three poets, so justly celebrated for their taste and simplicity. What could
Shakespeare have done worse? Terence has his *inceptio est amentium, non amantium*.[1] Many
similar instances will occur to the learned. 'Tis well known that Aristotle treats very
seriously of puns, divides them into several classes, and recommends the use of them into
orators.

[1] Terence, *Andria*, 219: *inceptiost amentium, haud amantium*, 'theirs is more like a scheme
of lunatics than of lovers.'

English writers were possessed of great genius before they were endued with any degree of taste, and by that means gave a kind of sanction to those forced turns and sentiments which they so much affected. Their distorted conceptions are attended with such vigor of mind that we admire the imagination which produced them, as much as we blame the want of judgment which gave them admittance. To enter into an exact criticism of the writers of that age would exceed our present purpose. A short character of the most eminent, delivered with the same freedom which history exercises over kings and ministers, may not be improper. The national prepossessions which prevail may perhaps render the former liberty not the least perilous for an author.

If Shakespeare be considered as a MAN, born in a rude age and educated in the lowest manner, without any instruction either from the world or from books, he may be regarded as a prodigy. If represented as a POET, capable of furnishing a proper entertainment to a refined or intelligent audience, we must abate somewhat of this eulogy. In his compositions we regret that great irregularities, and even sometimes absurdities, should so frequently disfigure the animated and passionate scenes intermixt with them; and at the same time we perhaps admire the more those beauties on account of their being surrounded with such deformities. A striking peculiarity of sentiment, adapted to a singular character, he frequently hits, as it were by inspiration, but a reasonable propriety of thought he cannot for any time uphold. Nervous and picturesque expressions, as well as descriptions, abound in him, but 'tis in vain we look either for continued purity or simplicity of diction. His total ignorance of all theatrical art and conduct, however material a defect, yet as it affects the spectator rather than the reader, we can more readily excuse than that want of taste which often prevails in his productions and which gives way, only by intervals, to the irradiations of genius. A great and fertile genius he certainly possessed, and one enriched equally with a tragic and comic vein; but he ought to be cited as a proof how dangerous it is to rely on these advantages alone for the attaining an excellence in the finer arts.* And there may even remain a suspicion that we over-rate, if possible, the greatness of his genius; in the same manner as bodies often appear more gigantic on account of their being disproportioned and mishapen. He died in 1617, aged 53 years.

* *Invenire etiam barbari solent, disponere et ornare non nisi eruditus.* PLIN.[1]

[1] *Epistle* 3.13 (adapted): 'Brilliant content and impressive expression are sometimes within the capacities even of the uncivilized: only the expert can arrange with propriety and give variety to his figures' (tr. B. Radice, Penguin).

Jonson possessed all the learning which was wanting to Shakespeare, and wanted all the genius of which the other was possessed. Both of them were equally deficient in taste and elegance, in harmony and correctness. A servile copyist of the antients, Jonson translated into bad English the beautiful passages of the Greek and Roman authors, without accommodating them to the manners of his age and country. His merit has been totally eclipsed by that of Shakespeare, whose rude genius prevailed over the rude art of his cotemporary. The English theatre has ever since taken a strong tincture of Shakespeare's spirit and character; and thence it has proceeded that the nation have undergone, from all their neighbors, the reproach of barbarism, from which their many valuable productions in other parts of learning would otherways have exempted them. (I, 135-8)

146. David Garrick, in defence of Shakespeare musicals

1755

The Prologue to *The Fairies, An Opera* (1755). Garrick's adaptation of *A Midsummer Night's Dream*, with music by J. C. Smith, was first performed on 4 February 1755.

David Garrick (1717–79) made his debut as an actor in 1741 (see Vol. 3, p. 13 and Nos 99, 100, 101, 117) and on 15 September 1747 took over the management of the Drury Lane theatre, a position which he held until 1776, when he retired from the stage. No one has ever had so long and so powerful an influence on the English theatre. This adaptation brought him over £1,500 in ten performances.

PROLOGUE,

Written and spoken by Mr. GARRICK.

Enter—Interrupting the Band of Music.

A Moment stop your tuneful Fingers, pray,
While *Here*, as usual, I my Duty pay.   [*To the Audience.*]
Don't frown, my Friends [*to the Band*], you soon shall melt again;⎫
But, if not *There*, is felt each dying Strain,   ⎬
Poor I shall *Speak* and you will *Scrape* in vain.   ⎭
To see me *Now*, you think the strangest Thing!
For, like Friend *Benedick*, I cannot sing!
Yet in this Prologue, cry but you, *Coraggio*!
I'll *Speak* you both a *Jig*, and an *Adagio*.
  A *Persian* King, as *Persian* Tales relate,
Oft' went disguis'd to hear the People prate;
So, curious I, sometimes steal forth, *incog.*,

To hear what Critics croak of me—King *Log*.
Three Nights ago, I heard a *Tête à Tête*
Which fix'd, at once, our *English Opera's* Fate:
One was a Youth born here, but flush from *Rome*,
The *other* born abroad, but here his Home;
And first the *English Foreigner* began,
Who thus address'd the *foreign Englishman*:
An *English Opera!* 'tis not to be borne; ⎫
I, both my Country, and their Music scorn, ⎬
Oh, damn their *Ally Croakers*, and their *Early-Horn*. ⎭
Signor si—bat sons— woss recitativo;
Il tutto, è bestiale e cativo.
This said, I made my *Exit*, full of Terrors!
And now ask Mercy, for the following Errors:
   Excuse us first, for foolishly supposing,
Your *Countryman* could please you in composing;
An *Op'ra* too!—play'd by an *English* Band,
Wrote in a Language which you understand—
I dare not say, WHO wrote it—I could tell ye,
To soften Matters—Signor *Shakespearelli*:
This awkward *Drama*—(I confess th' Offence)
Is guilty too, of Poetry and Sense:
And then the Price we take—you'll all abuse it, ⎫
So low, so unlike *Op'ras*—but excuse it, ⎬
We'll mend that Fault, whenever you shall chuse it. ⎭
Our last Mischance, and worse than all the rest, ⎫
Which turns the whole Performance to a Jest, ⎬
OUR Singers all are well, and all will do their best. ⎭
But why would this rash Fool, this *Englishman*,
Attempt an *Op'ra*?—'tis the strangest Plan!
   Struck with the Wonders of his Master's Art,
Whose *sacred Dramas* shake and melt the Heart,
Whose Heaven-born Strains the coldest Breast inspire,
Whose *Chorus-Thunder* sets the Soul on Fire!
Inflam'd, astonish'd! at those magic Airs,
When *Samson* groans, and frantic *Saul* despairs;
The Pupil wrote—his Work is now before ye,
And waits your Stamp of Infamy, or Glory!
Yet, ere his Errors and his Faults are known,
He says, those Faults, those Errors, are his own:

If through the Clouds appear some glimm'ring Rays,
They're Sparks he caught from his great Master's Blaze!

* * *

ADVERTISEMENT.

Many Passages of the first Merit, and some whole Scenes in the *Midsummer Night's Dream*, are necessarily omitted in this *Opera*, to reduce the Performance to a proper length; it was feared that even the best Poetry would appear tedious when only supported by *Recitative*. Where *Shakespeare* has not supplied the Composer with Songs, he has taken them from *Milton, Waller, Dryden, Lansdowne, Hammond, &c.* and it is hoped they will not seem to be unnaturally introduced.

147. John Gilbert Cooper, *The Tomb of Shakespeare. A Poetical Vision*

1755

John Gilbert Cooper (1723–69), poet and miscellaneous writer, was a disciple of Shaftesbury and an opponent of Warburton. He was a frequent contributor to Dodsley's *Museum* from 1746 onwards, under the pseudonym 'Philaretes'. His works included *Letters on Taste* (1754), praised by Dr Johnson, *Epistles to the Great from Aristippus in Retirement* (1758), and *Poems on several subjects* (1764).

What time the jocund rosie-bosom'd HOURS
    Led forth the train of PHOEBUS and the SPRING,
And ZEPHYR mild profusely scatter'd flowers,
    On Earth's green mantle from his musky wing,

The MORN unbarr'd th' ambrosial gates of light,
    Westward the raven-pinion'd Darkness flew,
The Landscape smil'd in vernal beauty bright,
    And to their graves the sullen Ghosts withdrew:

Done had the nightingale to swell her throat
    With love-lorn lays trill'd tremulously slow,
And on the wings of Silence ceas'd to float
    The gurgling notes of her melodious woe:

Then sportive dreams mysterious visions led
    O'er the charm'd optics of the mental eye,
Or my free'd soul awhile her mansion fled,
    To try her plumes for immortality.

Thro' fields of air, methought, I took my flight,
    O'er ev'ry region of the globe I pass'd,
No paradise or ruin 'scap'd my sight,
    HESPERIAN garden or CIMMERIAN waste.

I lit on AVON's banks, whose streams appear
   To wind with eddies fond round SHAKESPEARE's tomb,
The year's first feath'ry songsters warble near,
   And vi'lets breathe, and earliest blossoms bloom.

Here FANCY sat, her dewy fingers cold
   Decking with flow'rets fresh th' unsullied sod,
And bath'd with tears the sad sepulchral mold,
   Of her lov'd son's clay corse the last abode.

Ah! what avails, she cry'd, a Poet's name?
   Ah! what avails th' immortalizing breath
To snatch from dumb Oblivion others' fame?
   My darling child has fall'n a prey to death!

Let gentle OTWAY, white-rob'd PITY's priest,
   From grief domestic teach the tear to flow,
Or SOUTHERNE captivate th' impassion'd breast
   With heart-felt sighs and sympathy of woe:

For not to these *his* genius was confin'd,
   Nature and I each museful pow'r had given,
Poetic transports of the madding mind,
   And the wing'd words that waft the soul to heaven;

The fiery ken of th' intellectual eye,
   Piercing all objects with it's eagley view,
Which in the wide world's whole existence lie;
   And plastic thought that still created new.

Whilst I attendant thro' my magic glass,
   Ere he portray'd, display'd in airy show,
Then made each image in review to pass,
   And dipt his pencil in the watry bow.

O grant, with eager rapture I reply'd,
   Grant me, great goddess of the changeful eye,
To view each being in poetic pride,
   To whom thy son gave immortality.

Sweet FANCY smil'd, and wav'd her mystic rod,
   When strait these visions felt the pow'rful charm,
And one by one succeeded at her nod,
   Like vassal sprites beneath the wizard's arm.

First a celestial form★ (of azure hue
   Whose mantle, bound with brede ætherial, flow'd
To the soft breath of ev'ry wind that blew)
   Swift down the sun-beams of the noon-tide rode.

Obedient to the necromantic sway
   Of an old sage, to solitude resign'd,
With fenny vapors he obscur'd the day,
   Volley'd the lightning, and unloos'd the wind.

He whirl'd the tempest thro' the howling air,
   Rattled the dreadful thunderclap on high,
And rais'd a roaring elemental war
   Betwixt the sea-green waves and azure sky.

Then, like heav'n's mild embassador of love
   To man repentant, bade the tumult cease,
Smooth'd the blue bosom of the realms above,
   And hush'd the rebel elements to peace.

Unlike to this in spirit or in mien
   Another form† succeeded to my view,
A two-legg'd brute which Nature made in spleen,
   Or from the loathing womb unfinish'd drew.

Scarce could he syllable the curse he thought,
   Prone were his eyes to earth, his mind to evil,
A carnal fiend to imperfection wrought,
   The mongrel offspring of a Witch and Devil.

Next bloom'd, upon an ancient forest's bound,
   The flow'ry margin‡ of a strolling stream,
O'er-arch'd by oaks with ivy mantled round,
   And gilt by silver CYNTHIA's maiden beam.

On the green carpet of th' unbended grass,
   A dapper train of female fairies play'd,
And ey'd their gambols in the watry glass,
   That smoothly stole along the gleamy glade.

Thro' these the queen TITANIA pass'd ador'd,
   Mounted aloft in her imperial car,

★ Ariel in *The Tempest*.
† Caliban in *The Tempest*.
‡ Fairy-land from the *Midsummer night's dream*.

Journeying to meet fierce OBERON her lord,
 Returning victor from a rear-mouse war.

Her chariot was a snail's embroider'd shell,
 The traces of the finest cobweb were,
Her canopy a cowslip's speckled bell,
 Her horses flies, a bee her charioteer.

Upon six gnats six glow-worms went before,
 Upon six grasshoppers six wasps behind,
These were her torch-men, those her armor bore,
 And gallop'd swifter than the eastern wind.

Arm'd cap-a-pee forth march'd the fairy king,
 A stouter warrior never took the field,
His long lance was a hornet's horrid sting,
 The sharded beetle's scale his sable shield.

Upon an earwig mounted gallantly,
 The mighty monarch rode in royal state,
Nodding his horse-hair crest tremendously,
 Of all the Fays the greatest 'mong the great.

Around their king the elfin host appear'd,
 'Gainst the moon's rays their helmets cast a glare,
And their sharp spears in pierceless phalanx rear'd,
 A grove of thistles, glitter'd in the air.

The scene then chang'd, from this romantic land,
 To a bleak waste by bound'ry unconfin'd,
Where three swart sisters* of the *weyward* band
 Were mutt'ring curses to the troublous wind.

Pale Want had wither'd every furrow'd face,
 Bow'd was each carcass with the weight of years,
And each sunk eye-ball from its hollow case
 Distill'd cold rheum's involuntary tears.

Hors'd on three staves they posted to the bourn
 Of a drear island, where the pendant brow
Of a rough rock, shagg'd horribly with thorn,
 Frown'd on the murmurs of the deeps below.

* The witches in *Macbeth*.

In an adjacent grot remote from day,
　　Where smiling Comfort never shew'd her face,
Nor light e'er enter'd, save one rueful ray
　　Discov'ring all the terrors of the place,

They held damn'd myst'ries with infernal state,
　　Whilst ghastly goblins grimly glided by,
The scritch-owl scream'd the dying call of fate,
　　And ravens croak'd their awful augury.

No human footstep chear'd the dread abode,
　　Nor sign of living creature could be found,
Save where the reptile snake, or sullen toad,
　　With slimy froth had soil'd th' envenom'd ground.

Here lay the bones of some ill-fated wretch,
　　Who wand'ring from the hated haunts of men,
Lur'd by the kindred Echo's mournful speech,
　　Came, saw, and dy'd within this dismal den.

Sudden I heard the whirlwind's hollow sound,
　　Each *weyward* sister vanish'd into smoke.
Now a dire yell of spirits* underground
　　With discontent earth's yawning surface broke,

Thro' which each injur'd apparition rose;
　　A murd'rer started from his regal bed;
Pale Guilt's cold breath his heart's red current froze,
　　And Horror's dew-drops bath'd his frantic head.

More had I seen—but now the God of day
　　O'er earth's broad breast his flood of light had spread,
When fickle Morpheus call'd his dreams away,
　　And on their wings each bright illusion fled.

Yet still the dear ENCHANTRESS of the brain
　　My waking eyes with wishful wand'rings sought,
Whose wizard will controuls th' ideal train,
　　That ever restless progeny of THOUGHT.

Sweet pow'r, said I, for others gild the ray
　　Of Wealth, or Honor's folly-feather'd crown,
Or lead the madding multitude astray
　　To grasp at air-blown bubbles of renown.

* Ghosts in *Macbeth, Richard the III*, &c.

My humbler lot let blameless bliss engage,
   Free from the noble mob's ambitious strife,
Free from the muck-worm miser's lucrous rage,
   Safe in Contentment's cottag'd vale of life.

If frailties there (for who from them is free?)
   Thro' Error's maze my devious footsteps lead,
Let them be frailties of humanity,
   And my heart plead the pardon of my head.

Let not my reason impiously require
   What heav'n has plac'd beyond it's mortal span,
But teach it to subdue each fierce desire,
   Which wars within it's own small empire man.

Teach me, what all believe, but few possess,
   The learned'st science is ourselves to know,
The first of human blessings is to bless,
   And he the best who feels another's woe.

Thus cheaply wise, and innocently great,
   While Time's smooth sand shall regularly pass,
My destin'd atoms trickling course I'll wait,
   Nor rashly break, nor wish to stop the glass.

And when in death my peaceful ashes lie,
   If e'er some tongue congenial speaks my name,
Friendship shall never blush to breathe a sigh,
   And great ones envy such an honest fame.

148. John Shebbeare, *Othello* and *King Lear* in the theatre

1755

From *Letters on the English Nation, by Batista Angeloni, a Jesuit resident in London* (1755).

John Shebbeare (1709–88) was a political writer and polemicist who frequently attacked the Crown and the governments of the day (he was sentenced to three years' imprisonment for libel in 1758, and was placed in the pillory). He also attacked Smollett, who in turn made him 'Ferret' in *The Adventures of Sir Launcelot Greaves*. Shebbeare's *Letters on the English Nation* began as an attack on the Duke of Newcastle; subsequent letters were issued in 1757, 1758, and 1770. See J. R. Foster, 'Smollett's Pamphleteering Foe Shebbeare', *PMLA* 57 (1942), pp. 1053–100.

LETTER LIV.
To the Countess of **** *at Rome.*

Madam,

Amongst the many works of literature in which this nation and the French are rivals, that of theatrical entertainments has been as much controverted as any whatever: each in its turn has asserted the superiority of its writers above the other.

Shakespeare by the English, and Corneille by the French, are cited as proofs of the superiority of English and French genius, and each advocate equally hardy in sustaining the glory of his nation.

Yet, Madam, after as candid and impartial a disquisition of that which constitutes genius as I am capable of making, I frankly confess, to me it appears that Shakespeare was the more exalted being in all that constitutes true superiority of soul. Regularity of plan in dramatic performances is the work of art; conception of character, and their support thro' a whole theatric piece, the child of genius. Many men, nay all the French writers in tragedy, have reduced their productions for the stage to the rules of the drama; yet how few of them, or of any nation, have exalted and finished the ideas of personage in their pieces to any degree of sublimity and perfection.

From this difference we must necessarily conclude that the power of conceiving and preserving just characters in writing is more rarely found than that of planning a play; rules can teach one which can effectuate nothing in the other, and many men may design what not one in a million can execute.

From this must it not be concluded that if Shakespeare exceeded the French writers in conceiving and justly sustaining characters in tragedy, that he was of a superior genius to the greatest of the French nation?

This you, madam, who understand both languages, shall decide; but permit me to point out such characters as have never been conceived by any French tragic writer, conducted and sustained in a manner which no other nation has ever seen, ancient or modern.

In the tragedy of *Othello* the Moor, all artless, open, and brave, is reduced by the wiles and subtilty of the hypocritic Iago.

The seeming simplicity of an honest heart is so exquisitely supported and practised by him on the unsuspecting disposition of a virtuous, valiant, and ingenuous mind, that no instance is to be produced of any thing parallel in any theatrical production.

In each of these characters there is not one mistaken deviation; every spectator excuses the Moor in his being deceived, and pities with sincerest sorrow the fate of open honesty seduced by artifice and wiles.

The difficulty is not easily imagined which attends the preservation of these two characters. The Moor must be supported as brave, sensible, and honest; the skill lay in preserving all these from the imputation of weakness in Othello, thro' the conducting the imposition which was to be play'd upon him.

The simple, plain, and seemingly artless cunning of Iago was attended with no less difficulty: to preserve the separate characteristics of this personage without deviating into one instance which might betray his design to a man of sense is of all things the most difficult. Yet thro' the whole conduct of both characters there appears no one violation of the intended and original design of the poet.

In this consistency of character the superiority of the English poet appears above all others, unless the critics devoted to the Greek and antiquity should contest it in favour of Homer; you, madam, will allow that the great Corneille affords no instance of this nature comparable to the English author.

His management of Cassio and Roderigo is in the same simple, natural, and apparent honest strain; we see that the deceit must be invisible to such men. The scene in the third act between Othello and Iago, where the latter first insinuates the idea of jealousy into the mind of the Moor, that timidity of accusing the innocent, that regard for the reputation of Desdemona, with the insinuation against her fidelity, are so artfully mixt that it is impossible but that Othello must have been insnared by his manner of conducting the conversation. How inimitable is his pretended love for Othello, his conjuring up the Moor's resolution to know his sentiments by distant hints and suggestions; and when Othello breaks out

> I'll know thy thoughts [3.3.166]

he answers

> You cannot, if my heart were in your hand:
> Nor shall not, whilst 'tis in my custody. [3.3.167f.]

At this seemingly determined secrecy, the Moor pronouncing 'ha!', Iago with all possible art cries out

> Oh! beware, my lord, of jealousy;
> It is a green-eyed monster, which doth mock
> The meat it feeds on. That cuckold lives in bliss
> Who, certain of his fate, loves not his wronger:
> But oh! what damned minutes tells he o'er
> Who doats yet doubts, suspects yet strongly loves? [3.3.169ff.]

This speech necessarily turns the thoughts of Othello on the idea of jealousy with all the appearance of nature and refined art; and then by proceeding in the same manner he leads him to examine the conduct of Desdemona, and creates a suspicion of her infidelity to the Moor from her having chosen him, and refused those

> Of her own clime, complexion, and degree. [3.3.234]

From this he draws an inference which reflects on the character of Desdemona; this almost convinces the Moor of her being false to his bed, and he desires Iago to set his wife to watch Desdemona. In answer to this the subtle villain pretends to intreat Othello to think no more of what he had told him, to attempt discovering Desdemona's true disposition by the vehemence of her suit to him for restoring Cassio, and to believe his fears for his honour had been too importunate in the affair; with this he leaves him. In all this scene there appears nothing which can discover the Moor weaker than an honest, plain, brave man may be allowed to be; not one step carried beyond the truth in nature by Iago.

The knowledge of the promptness of jealousy in the bosom of man which the author shews in the character of Iago is beyond all comparison; when he has possest the handkerchief which Desdemona drops, he says

> I will in Cassio's lodgings lose this napkin,
> And let him find it. Trifles light as air
> Are to the jealous confirmations strong
> As proofs of holy writ. [3.3.325ff.]

At seeing Othello enter he continues:

> Look where he comes! not poppy nor mandragora,
> Nor all the drowsy syrups of the world,
> Shall ever medicine thee to that sweet sleep
> Which thou hadst yesterday. [3.3.334ff.]

The operations which the jealous mind undergoes were never so truly described by any author. The trifles light as air, the tasteless poison of a hint becoming mines of burning sulphur to the soul, and the irrevocable power of sweet slumber to a mind haunted with jealousy are beyond all conception just, great and sublime, and I think to be found in no other author.

The Moor enters with a conviction of the truth of what Iago had said in the above soliloquy; his mind now burning with suspicion, lighted up from those sparks which Iago had thrown upon it, without seeing him he says

> Ha! false to me. [3.3.337]

to which Iago replies

> Why, how now, general? no more of that.
>   *Oth.* Avant! begone! thou'st set me on the rack.
> I swear 'tis better to be much abused
> Than but to know a little. [3.3.338ff.]

This answer shews that the revealing this infidelity of Desdemona had made Iago insufferable to his eyes. The combat between the violation of his bed and the love of Desdemona working strongly in him, he therefore swears 'tis better to be much abused in secret than not to know what may be avowed to be sufficient to vindicate the vengeance which an injured man should take upon the author of his dishonour. At this Iago, fearing lest he should retreat from the degree to which he had brought him, delay the pursuit, and relapse to love, cries

How, my lord!   [3.3.341]

Othello answers

> What sense had I of her stol'n hours of lust?
> I saw't not, thought it not, it harm'd not me;
> I slept the next night well; was free and merry:
> I found not Cassio's kisses on her lips:
> He that is robb'd, not wanting what is stol'n,
> Let him not know't, and he's not robb'd at all. [3.3.342ff.]

In this speech the whole bent of his mind is turned on the mischief and disquiet which Iago's discovery had brought upon his soul; without revealing it he had been happy, untouched by pangs of injury. Iago's answer is,

I am sorry to hear this.   [3.3.348]

Othello proceeds still in the same sentiment, exclaiming

> I had been happy if the general camp
> (Pioneers and all) had tasted her sweet body,
> So I had nothing known. Oh now, for ever
> Farewell the tranquil mind! farewell content;
> Farewell the plumed troops, and the big war,
> That make ambition virtue! Oh! farewell,
> Farewell the neighing steed, and the shrill trump,
> The spirit-stirring drum, th'ear-piercing fife,
> The royal banner, and all quality,
> Pride, pomp, and circumstance of glorious war.
> And oh! you mortal engines, whose rude throats
> Th' immortal Jove's dread clamours counterfeit,
> Farewell! Othello's occupation's gone!   [3.3.349ff.]

These reflections bring back on his soul, like the returning tide, the wretched change of situation which Iago's discovery had produced in him; upon which Iago asks

Is't possible, my Lord?   [3.3.362]

Othello, still improving the former sentiment, and feeling his fallen state with infinite sensibility, flies impetuously into rage and, seizing Iago, cries

> Villain, be sure thou prove my love a whore;
> Be sure of it; give me the ocular proof;
> Or, by the worth of mine eternal soul,
> Thou hadst been better have been born a dog
> Than answer my wak'd wrath.   [3.3.363ff.]

When, proceeding in the same passionate manner, Iago answers

> Oh grace! oh heaven defend me!
> Are you a man? have you a soul? or sense?
> God be w'you; take mine office. O wretched fool,
> That liv'st to make thine honesty a vice!
> Oh monstrous world! take note, take note, oh world!
> To be direct and honest is not safe.
> I thank you for this profit; and from hence
> I'll love no friend, sith love breeds such offence.   [3.3.377ff.]

This speech contains as much art as ever entered into the conception of human nature. He first appeals to Othello's humanity and understanding; then at that instant, as intending to leave him, he says 'God be with you' and throws up his commission. He then exclaims at his own folly that has thus converted his honesty into vice; when, throwing a sarcastic reflexion on the world and thanking Othello for this information of what is to be expected from man, he determines to renounce all love for human nature. What ideas are there to be imagined which can be thrown together with more judgment and propriety to reclaim Othello from that outrage which he has committed?

It has its proper effect; the mind of man, strongly agitated between two passions, suddenly veers from one to the other like the uncertain blowings of a storm. In consequence of which Othello comes about to believe that Iago is honest, and says

> Nay stay—thou should'st be honest.   [3.3.385]

Iago, who perceives this approaching change, answers

> I should be wise, for honesty's a fool,
> And loses what it works for.   [3.3.386f.]

After this Othello, reduced to the æquipoise between the love of his Desdemona and the truth of Iago's story, cries out

> By the world,
> I think my wife is honest, and think she is not:
> I think that thou art just, and think thou art not.
> I'll have some proof.   [3.3.387ff.]

This suspence Iago seizes to fix him in the firm opinion of her being false to his bed; when Othello says

> Give me a living reason she's disloyal.   [3.3.413]

At this Iago recounts what Cassio said in a dream, and wins upon the mind of the Moor entirely; at which he cries

> I'll tear her all to pieces—   [3.3.435]

Iago, not content with this, most artfully mentions to him the handkerchief in the hands of Cassio, which he had formerly given to Desdemona. This rivets him in the belief of his being dishonored by Cassio, at which he exclaims

> Oh that the slave had forty thousand lives!
> One is too poor, too weak for my revenge.
> Now do I see 'tis true.—Look here, Iago,
> All my fond love thus do I blow to heaven.
> 'Tis gone—
> Arise black vengeance from the hollow hell.
> Yield up, oh love! thy crown and hearted throne
> To tyrannous heat! swell bosom, with thy fraught,
> For 'tis of Aspic's tongues.
>   *Iag.* Yet be content.
>   *Oth.* Oh blood, blood, blood!
>   *Iag.* Patience, I say; your mind perhaps may change.
>   *Oth.* Never, Iago. Like to the Pontic sea,
> Whose icy current and compulsive course
> Ne'er feels retiring ebb, but keeps due on
> To the Propontic and the Hellespont;
> Even so my bloody thoughts with violent pace
> Shall ne'er look back, ne'er ebb to humble love,
> Till that a capable and wide revenge
> Swallow them up.—Now by yonder marble heaven,
> In the due reverence of a sacred vow,
> I here engage my words.   [3.3.446ff.]

Having thus wrought him up to his purpose, Iago swears that he will give himself up entirely to the service and revenge of Othello's injury.

In these last quotations it is easy to see that figurative expressions, when they arise from the subject unforced and unsought after, are the most naturally expressive of passion; the mind, dilated and carried on by the desire of revenge, rises into metaphor and simile with the utmost propriety; the occasion is equal to the conception and ideas, and not the least colour of bombast or false expression appears thro' the whole.

In all the French theatre I know of no play in which equal knowledge in human nature is manifested, where two characters so justly drawn, so nicely contrasted, and so well sustained are to be found. A common genius would have erred a thousand times in writing such parts: Othello would have manifested a thousand marks of being a fool in not seeing Iago's designs, and Iago betrayed himself by too bare-faced a conduct of his intention: as it is managed by Shakespeare there is no one slip or deviation of character in either, in one single instance.

Another letter, Madam, may probably bring you farther thoughts on this play; let me here remark, however, that great geniuses being difficultly imitated, Shakespeare has been the cause of two vast mistakes in the succeeding authors of this nation.

The first is, that they have copied his diversity of scenery and not possessed the power of conceiving or sustaining their characters as they ought. For this reason the plays which appear alert, active, and enter-taining to the eye on the stage by dint of stage-trick, and win some applause in the first presentations, are damned in the closet, and never more revived on the theatre.

The other is the admiration of that figurative style in Shakespeare, so natural, becoming, and just, as he uses it, filled with ideas answering the words. This has created a manner of writing consisting entirely of verbage without imagery to sustain it, a cold altisonant, gigantesque shadow, inane and puerile.

This, Madam, tho' I fear it may appear to have the air of dictating, has nothing of that in its intent. Permit me then the honor to know whether you confirm me in this opinion? Whether I ought to deem myself a judge in matters of genius, when I place the author of this above any writer which the French, or any nation, has hitherto pro-duced: your opinion will determine me. I am,

Your most obedient servant.
(II, 232–48)

*   *   *

LETTER LIX.

To the Countess of *****, at Rome.

Dear Madam,

Shall I meet your approbation when I dare assert that acting the part of a person of superior life, sublimely conceived and pathetically written, requires more genius than writing a tragedy where five acts of undistinguishable characters and regular mediocrity make its whole merit? I flatter myself that your opinion will not be different from mine in this instance, when I have laid before you all that I have to say on this occasion.

It has always appeared to me that, notwithstanding the apparent raptures with which men pretend to feel those passages of an author which place him above humanity, if their own performances in a like nature fall much short of it, that they have never reached in their conception the true spirit of the author which they have praised.

Whereas a player, who personates in every part the living manners of a superior character, manifests beyond contradiction that he has conceived the true idea of the author.

A poet, therefore, in raptures with the character of Lear as Shakespeare has drawn it, who in his writings should attempt something of a similar nature, instead of the sovereign of unfixt temper, choleric and sudden, whose ideas and conceptions express royalty in every part of his anger, should draw a porter in rage, replete with every Gothic grossness, will be infinitely inferior in genius to him that fills up this character with all that fire and majesty which becomes the personage as Shakespeare has completed it.

This a player on the English stage perfectly accomplishes: his name is Garrick.

It may be a vanity, but you, Madam, will pardon even that in a private letter not designed for the public eye. In the action of all other men I have imagined something yet farther than has been exprest by them; in this player and in this part this man has exceeded all my imagination; and as Poussin is considered the painter of men of taste so in like manner Mr Garrick is the player.

He is the only man on any stage where I have been, who speaks tragedy truly and natural. The French tragedians mouth it too much, and to appear something more than men they lose the resemblance of humanity. A hero on that stage, in dress and expression is a complete exotic of all nations, and seems a creature just arrived from some distant planet.

It must be allowed, however, that the passion of anger is the easiest to be imitated of all those which the human mind is subject to; but to be angry with superior sovereignty is as difficult to attain as any part, to be executed with that dignity which this English actor imparts to it.

In the first act of the tragedy of *Lear*, when Cordelia has displeased him by that which ought to have had a contrary effect, his anger is shewn by very great expression, very just tone of voice, and propriety of action; yet it still augments, and becomes more energic as the rising occasions require it, till at length, when Goneril refuses him his hundred followers, and says[1]

> Be then advised by her, that else will take
> That which she begs, to lessen your attendance:
> Take half away, and see that the remainder
> Be such as may befit your age, and know
> Themselves and you.

After these words of insolence, Lear replies,[2]

> Darkness and devils!
> Saddle my horses, call my train together.
> Degenerate viper, I'll not stay with thee:
> I yet have left a daughter—Serpent, monster!
> Lessen my train, and call them riotous!
> All men approved of choice and rarest parts,
> That each particular of duty know—
> How small, Cordelia, was thy fault? Oh Lear!
> Beat at that gate which let thy folly in,
> And thy dear judgment out; go, go, my people.

This all other actors speak with that kind of rage with which a drunken shoemaker curses his daughter that has secretly taken his money from him, and prevented his going to the ale-house; it is indeed a sheer scolding. In Mr Garrick it is a prince in anger, and every accompaniment expresses it thro' the whole passage. 'How small, Cordelia,' &c. This reflection, so natural to human minds, and parents in particular, to compare what they think a less fault in one child whilst they are suffering under the influence of a greater in another, is as truly exprest by the actor as imagined by the poet; and then reverting on himself at the words which follow, 'Oh Lear,' he absolutely imparts

[1] From Nahum Tate's adaptation, 1.2.56f.; corresponding to *King Lear*, 1.4.246f.
[2] Tate, 1.2.60ff.; *King Lear*, 1.4.252ff., 262ff.

a power to them which cannot be conceived but with much difficulty by those who have never beheld him. The whole bitter tide of resentment pours back on himself, and is as fully exprest from the fingers to the toes, thro' the flashing eye and keen feature, as Raphael has exprest the being possest in his demoniac (in his picture of the transfiguration); and in these words the soul of every hearer shivers as he pronounces them:[1]

> Blasts upon thee;
> Th' untainted woundings of a father's curse
> Pierce ev'ry sense about thee.

Indeed, I could not avoid expecting a paralytic stroke would wither every limb of Goneril, the power of expression seemed as if of necessity it must prevail over heaven.

Then follows that which is so natural to the soul of man in excessive anger, when it suffers equally from the faults of others and itself. Turning back with threats upon this weakness which had made him weep, he utters with the utmost internal sensibility, and yet weeps in opposition to his own resolution:[2]

> Old fond eyes,
> Lament this cause again, I'll pluck ye out,
> And cast you with the waters that ye lose
> To temper clay.

It is not possible to decide which is superior in the knowledge of nature, the poet who wrote, or the player who animates, these passages. Afterwards when he begins 'Hear, nature,'[3] and passes on to that most beautiful of all expressions,[4]

> How sharper than a serpent's tooth it is,
> To have a thankless child!

All is so firmly and interestingly exprest, with attitude and action so becoming the occasion, that, forgetting where I am, astonishment seizes me that Goneril has power to go off the stage unblasted at this imprecation: so perfectly the character is realized by every part of the player.

I thought to have instanced nothing of his powers in the second act, but it is impossible to omit those starts of expression which accompany

---

1 Tate, 1.2.74ff.; *King Lear*, 1.4.299ff.
2 Tate, 1.2.67ff.; *King Lear*, 1.4.301ff.
3 Tate, 1.2.82; *King Lear*, 1.4.275.
4 Tate, 1.2.95f.; *King Lear*, 1.4.288f.

so perfectly the ideas of the poet in answer to the following words of Gloster:

> You know the firey quality of the duke.

Lear replies,[1]

> Vengeance, death, plague, confusion!
> Firey! What quality—why Gloster, Gloster,
> I'd speak with the duke of Cornwall and his wife.

These, and many other passages, are spoken so justly and with so much emphasis that their influence on the hearer is amazing. They appear amidst the tempest of his mind like flashes of lightening in a stormy night, making the horrors more visible.

In the third act, Shakespeare—into whose hand nature had given the clue that leads thro' all her labyrinth of variety, reserving the other end to herself—has placed Lear amidst thunder-storms, whirlwind, rain, and fire; in this part he shews how every object finds some connection with those of a mind in deep distress. Lear says[2]

> Rumble thy fill; fight whirlwind, rain, and fire;
> Not fire, wind, rain, or thunder, are my Daughters.
> I tax not you, ye elements, with unkindness;
> I never gave you kingdoms, call'd ye children;
> You owe me no obedience; then let fall
> Your horrible pleasure; here I stand your slave,
> A poor infirm, weak, and despis'd old man.

Till the last line he agrees that these elements owe him no gratitude or obedience because unallied to him by birth or duty; yet, the last line recalling his present condition to his own imagination, he immediately conceives it a kind of mean cruelty to join with two disobedient daughters, and says[3]

> Yet will I call you servile ministers,
> That have with two pernicious daughters join'd
> Their engendered battle, against a head
> So old and white as mine; oh! oh! 'tis foul.

This speech is spoken at first with defiance; then, as the sense changes,

---

[1] Tate, 2.2.181ff.; *King Lear*, 2.4.90, 93ff.
[2] Tate, 3.1.10ff. (Vol. 1, pp. 355f.); *King Lear*, 3.2.14ff.
[3] Tate, 3.1.17ff. (Vol. 1, p. 356); *King Lear*, 3.2.21ff.

the player falls into an acquiescence with this suffering till, coming to the last part, he feels with much contempt that coward cruelty of basely joining with the perpetrators of filial disobedience. This is performed with such natural and easy transition, as if his soul conceived originally every sensation as they follow one another in the poet.

As the madness advances in the character of Lear it increases in the action and expression of the player. You scarce see where he first begins, and yet find he is mad before Kent says[1]

> I fear'd 'twould come to this; his wits are gone.

It steals so gradually and imperceptibly, the difference grows like a colour which runs on from the lightest to the darkest tint, without perceiving the shades but by comparing them at different parts of the whole. When he enters mad in the fourth act, with the mock ensigns of majesty on him, thro' this whole scene that which the poet has marked so strongly the player has also preserved: that satyric turn which accompanies madness arising from wrongs is inimitably conceived by the poet and sustained by the player; that vague and fugitive manner of pronouncing, mixt with the sarcastic touches of expression, is truly exhibited. And as in the poet's writings so in the player's behaviour, the king is never one moment forgotten: it is royalty in lunacy. To quote every passage would make a letter a whole play.

In that part of the fourth act where Lear recovers from his sleep, as the poet, who knew that sound intellect must not appear too suddenly in such instances of lunacy, so the player recovers his mind as gradually as he lost it; and at length distrusting his being recovered, he says[2]

> I will not swear these are my hands.

Cordelia answers,[3]

> O look upon me, Sir,
> And hold your hands in benediction o'er me.
> No Sir, you must not kneel.

When, Lear kneeling, the player pronounces with such pathetic simplicity[4]

> Pray do not mock me,
> I am a very foolish, fond old man,

[1] Tate, 3.3.99.
[2] Tate, 4.5.28 (Vol. 1, p. 372); King Lear, 4.7.55.
[3] Tate, 4.5.28ff. (Vol. 1, p. 372); King Lear, 4.7.57ff.
[4] Tate, 4.5.30ff. (Vol. 1, p. 372); King Lear, 4.7.59ff.

> Fourscore and upwards; and to deal plainly with you,
> I fear I am not in my perfect mind.

Whoever, at the uttering of these words as Mr Garrick speaks them, can avoid joining with Cordelia, must be more hardened than Goneril or Regan. She says:[1]

> Then farewell to patience: witness for me,
> Ye mighty powers, I ne'er complain'd till now.

With what knowledge of human nature was this written! When a mind exhausted by its former wildness recovers, nothing is so weak and vacillating: the unornamented simplicity of Lear's words, therefore, has more sublimity and pathos than all the powers of figure and metaphor could impart to them. And as it was imagined by Shakespeare it is spoken by Mr Garrick: my tears have ever testified this approbation.

The remaining part of this act is equally inimitable. Pray tell me, Madam, what art is this which, running from anger to rage to madness, then softens and sinks into the timid and suppliant, in poet and player? What compass and what power of nature must those possess who are equal to this variety and force?

In the fifth act, where the old king sleeps in the lap of Cordelia, he breaks out[2]

> Charge, charge upon their flank, their last wing halts.
> Push, push the battle, and the day's our own;
> Their ranks are broke: down with Albany.
> Who holds my hands?

This he pronounces in that imperfect and indistinct manner which attends those who talk in their sleep with expression of anger, yet different from that of madness or a sound mind; then wakes with a gentle exclamation:[3]

> Oh thou deceiving sleep!
> I was this very minute on the chace,
> And now a prisoner here.

This play terminates happily, as it is acted different from the manner in which Shakespeare wrote it. Cordelia is made Queen, and Lear retires to pass away his life in quietness and devotion. Many of the

[1] Tate, 4.5.34ff. (Vol. I, p. 372).
[2] Tate, 5.6.15ff. (Vol. I, p. 382).
[3] Tate, 5.6.18ff. (Vol. I, p. 382).

passages are transposed from the order they stand in the original; for that reason I have sent you the alteration, that you may see it as it is played. The words which express the joy at the thoughts of Cordelia's being a queen are spoken with an emphasis and energy which is peculiar to Mr Garrick only; and tho' the poet is no longer visible in this place the player sustains his character in this also.

Thus in anger, in grief, in madness, in revenge, in weakness, in contempt, in joy, all is equally natural and amazing. The same poet fancies all these; the same player follows him with equal justice.

Does it not seem probable then, Madam, that the genius of a player is more analogous to the painter and musician than to the poet? He rather knows with what attitude, tone of voice, and expression, characters already written should be expressed and acted, than conceives with what words the characters in a story painted by Dominiquino, Poussin, or other eminent artists should be animated. He can better adjust sounds to poetical compositions, than invent poetry for airs already made.

The mind of man, then, which is uncontaminated in action and expression with the borrowed aid of mimickry, is real genius; and, if it was not unpolite in writing to a lady, I could end with a syllogism, that this actor whom I have too imperfectly described in this letter, is undoubtedly so, and of a much superior nature to a *mediocre* poet; indeed, on a level with great painters and great musicians, a Raphael or Corelli. I am,

Your most obedient servant. (II, 283–96)

149. Christopher Smart on Shakespeare's learning

1756

'A Brief Enquiry into the Learning of Shakespeare', from the *Universal Visiter and Monthly Memorialist*, January 1756. This essay is signed 'S', the usual key to Smart's contributions to this journal, and confirmed by the file-copy discovered in the British Museum by R. B. Botting (see *Modern Philology* 36 (1939), pp. 293ff.) which has the authorship of most items marked by Ann Gardner, daughter of its publisher.

This journal appeared between January 1756 and December 1758 and was edited by Smart (up to April 1756) and Richard Rolt (1725?–70): see C. Jones in the *Library* (1937) and Arthur Sherbo, *ibid.* (1955). Christopher Smart (1722–71), poet and translator, friend of Dr Johnson and Gray, was undergraduate and Fellow of Pembroke Hall, Cambridge from 1740 to 1749, before moving to London, where he lived on his meagre earnings as a miscellaneous writer for the publisher, John Newbery, and various booksellers.

According to the biographical plan we originally proposed to ourselves, this would be the proper place to give some account of the life of our inimitable *Shakespeare*; but on examining what materials we were possessed of for this purpose we found them so very scanty and unsatisfactory that we were presently induced to lay aside all thoughts of such an attempt. Whatever material circumstances could be got together in relation to this matter Mr *Rowe* has already collected, and to give an abridgment of a work that is in every body's hands we thought would be impertinent and superfluous. We have been at a good deal of pains to acquire some anecdotes concerning this great genius, but tradition has failed us; and we have applied to our friends at both theatres, and elsewhere, in vain. The very few particulars that are handed down to us about *Shakespeare* are a strong confirmation of Mr *Pope*'s assertion, *viz.* that '*Shakespeare* and *Ben Jonson* may truly be said not much to have thought on immortality.'[1]

> Shakespeare (*whom you, and every play-house bill,*
> *Style the divine, the matchless, what you will*)
> *For gain, not glory, wing'd his roving flight,*
> *And grew immortal in his own despight.*

Shakespeare was very far from having an immoderate share of reputation amongst his *contemporaries, who left the extolling his works and the erecting of statues to him as a legacy for posterity. The *English*, who have ever been famous for ill-tim'd gratitude and post-humous generosity, have at length done that justice to his memory which their forefathers would not do to his merit. But, alas! what is a man the better for the tributes that are paid to his ashes? The writers of lives, erectors of monuments, and other favourers of defunct excellence are rather the oppressors than† encouragers of living worth. But this by the bye.

—Amongst all *Shakespeare*'s innumerable admirers there has not been, perhaps, one but has given into that extreme vulgar error of his being a man of no letters, and absolutely unindebted to any of the ancients even for a single thought. That nothing is more remote from truth than this notion will fully appear from the specimens annexed, and it is beyond measure amazing that such manifest imitations should have escaped the attention of so many critics and scholars.—It may be fairly said of our *Shakespeare* as it was of an eminent *Roman, Contemnebat*

---

* Had *Shakespeare*, and his works, been as much the subject of conversation in his life-time as they are at this day there must have been great materials for oral tradition, at least, concerning him; and, it is most probable, memoirs of his life and character would have been written by many authors who survived him.

† It must be allowed that there is a noble exception to this too general rule, subsisting in a society lately constituted to do honour to the memory of *Shakespeare*. It is formed by a number of very ingenious gentlemen, adepts in the polite arts and patrons of merit, who intend annually to exhibit some patterns of their own excellence at the same time that they assemble to commemorate that of the divine poet. Mr *Roubilliac* and Mr *Havard*, at the last meeting, gave universal satisfaction; the former by a fine model of a bust for *Shakespeare*, and the latter by an animated ode intended for music.[2]

1 Pope, *Imitations of Horace, Epistle II, i* (1737), 69ff. The note added by Pope continues after 'immortality': 'the one in many pieces composed in haste for the Stage, the other in his Latter works in general, which *Dryden* called his *Dotages.*'

2 Murphy reprints this ode in the *London Chronicle*: below, pp. 289ff.,

literas potius quam nesciebat;[1] He rather affected to contemn learning than remain'd in ignorance of it. Of his contempt for learning he gives us the following proof under his own hand.

> *Study is like the heaven's glorious sun,*
> > *That will not be deep-search'd with sawcy looks;*
> *Small have* continual plodders *ever won,*
> > Save base authority from others books,
> *Those* EARTHLY GODFATHERS *of heaven's lights,*
> > *That give a name to every fixed star,*
> *Have no more profit of the shining nights,*
> > *Than those who walk and wot not what they are.*
>
> *Love's Labour's Lost* [1.1.84ff.]

He was nevertheless, upon the whole, a good scholar; but in his learning as well as every thing else he was NEGLIGENTLY GREAT, and ADMIRABLE WITHOUT ACCURACY. He had little if any knowledge of the *Greek* and *Roman* prosody, which sufficiently appears in many instances. Throughout the whole play of *Cymbeline* it is evident from the structure of his versification that he mistook *Posthŭmus* for *Posthūmus.* In *Hamlet* he calls *Hyperīon, Hyperĭon;* and in another play he makes *Andronīcus, Andronĭcus.* But it may be he disdained these little niceties or thought, perhaps, if he made the words more musical it would justify his inaccuracy.

Having premised these few observations, we shall present our readers with several passages which *Shakespeare* has borrowed from the ancients. —We could have greatly increased the number, but what is here produced will sufficiently answer the end proposed.

> *Richard II.* [3.2.6ff.]

> *Dear earth, I do salute thee with my hand,*
> *Tho' rebels wound thee with their horses hoofs:*
> *As a long parted mother, with her child,*
> > *Plays fondly with her tears, and smiles in weeping,*
> *So weeping, smiling, greet I thee.*

This is a manifest (and perhaps the only) imitation of that most beautiful passage in the VIth book of the *Iliad,* verse 484.[2]

---

[1] Tacitus, *Dialogus (Dialogue on Orators)* 2.2: 'Aper by no means lacked learning—he wasn't without letters, he merely despised them' (tr. M. Winterbottom).

[2] '[Andromache] was smiling through her tears, and when her husband saw this he was moved' (tr. E. V. Rieu).

Ὡς εἰπὼν ἀλόχοιο φίλης ἐν χερσὶν ἔθηκε
παῖδ᾽ ἑόν· ἡ δ᾽ ἄρα μιν κηώδεϊ δέξατο κόλπῳ
δακρυόεν γελάσασα·

Mr *Pope*, in his version of this place, has fallen greatly short of his original.

Richard II. [3.4.84ff.]

Their fortunes both are weigh'd.
In your lord's scale, *is nothing but himself,*
And some few vanities, that make him light;
But, in the ballance of great Bolingbroke,
Besides himself, are all the English *peers,*
And with that odds he WEIGHS *king* Richard DOWN.

The hint of these lines was taken from the VIIIth book of the *Iliad*, ver. 69.[1]

καὶ τότε δὴ χρύσεια πατὴρ ἐτίταινε τάλαντα·
ἐν δὲ τίθει δύο κῆρε τανηλεγέος θανάτοιο,
Τρώων θ᾽ ἱπποδάμων καὶ Ἀχαιῶν χαλκοχιτώνων,
ἕλκε δὲ μέσσα λαβών. ῥέπε δ᾽ αἴσιμον ἦμαρ Ἀχαιῶν.
αἱ μὲν Ἀχαιῶν κῆρες ἐπὶ χθονὶ πουλυβοτείρῃ
ἑζέσθην, Τρώων δὲ πρὸς οὐρανὸν εὐρὺν ἄερθεν.

It is observable, however, that there is much more propriety in *Shakespeare* than in *Homer* with regard to this allusion, for the latter makes the fate of the *Greeks* preponderating, a sign of their being discomfited.

[2] King Henry IV. [4.5.23ff.]

O polish'd perturbation! golden care,
That keep'st the ports of slumber open wide
To many a watchful night: sleep with it now!
Yet not so sound, and half so deeply sweet,
As he, whose brow with homely biggen bound,
Snores out the watch of night.

Horace, Carm. Lib. III. Ode xiii. [i.e., 3.1.21ff.]
Somnus agrestium,

[1] 'But at high noon the Father held out his golden scales, and putting sentence of death in either pan, on one side for the horse-taming Trojans, on the other for the bronze-clad Achaeans, raised the balance by the middle of the beam. The beam came down on the Achaeans' side, spelling a day of doom for them. Their sentence settled on the bountiful earth, while that of the Trojans went soaring up to the broad sky' (tr. E. V. Rieu).

Lenis virorum non humiles domos
Fastidit.[1]

King Henry V. [1.2.187ff.]

So work the honey bees;
Creatures, that, by a rule in nature, teach
The art of order to a peopled kingdom.
They have a king, and officers of sort;
Where some, like magistrates, correct at home;
Others, like merchants, venture trade abroad;
Others, like soldiers, armed in their stings,
Make boot upon the summer's velvet buds:
Which pillage, they, with merry march, bring home
To the tent-royal of their emperor;
Who, busied in his majesty, surveys
The singing mason building roofs of gold;
The civil citizens kneading up the honey;
The poor mechanic porters crouding in
Their heavy burthens at the narrow gate:
The sad-ey'd justice with his surly hum,
Delivering o'er to executors pale
The lazy, yawning drone.

This is almost a translation of *Virgil, Georg.* IV. ver. 153.[2]

Solæ communes natos, consortia tecta
Urbis habent, magnisque agitant sub legibus ævum,
Et patriam solæ, & certos novere penates:
Venturæque hyemis memores æsta te laborem
Experiuntur, & in medium quæsita reponunt.
Namque aliæ victu invigilant, & fædere pacto

---

[1] 'Soft slumber scorns not the humble cottage of the peasant' (Loeb).

[2] 'They [the bees] alone have children in common, hold the dwellings of their city jointly, and pass their life under the majesty of law. They alone know a fatherland and fixed home, and in summer, mindful of the winter to come, spend toilsome days and garner their gains into a common store. For some watch over the gathering of food, and under fixed covenant labour in the fields; some, within the confines of their homes, lay down the narcissus' tears and gluey gum from tree-bark as the first foundation of the comb, then hang aloft clinging wax; others lead out the full-grown young, the nation's hope; others pack purest honey, and swell the cells with liquid nectar. To some it has fallen by lot to be sentries at the gates, and in turn they watch the rains and clouds of heaven, or take the loads of incomers, or in martial array drive the drones, a lazy herd, from the folds' (Loeb).

Exercentur agris: pars intra septa domorum
Narcissi lacrymam, & lentum de cortice gluten
Prima favis ponunt fundamina; deinde tenaces
Suspendunt ceras: aliæ, spem gentis, adultos
Educunt fætus: aliæ purissima mella
Stipant, & liquido distendunt nectare cellas.
Sunt quibus ad portas cecidit custodia sorti,
Inque vicem speculantur aquas & nubila cæli;
Aut onera accipiunt venientum, aut agmine facto
Ignavum fucos pecus a præsepibus arcent.

Midsummer Night's Dream, [1.1.234ff.]

Love looks not with the eyes, but with the mind;
And, therefore, is wing'd Cupid painted blind.
Nor hath love's mind of any judgment taste;
Wings, and no eyes, figure unheedy haste:
And, therefore, is love said to be a child,
Because, in choice, he is so oft beguil'd.
As waggish boys, themselves in game forswear,
So the boy love is perjur'd every where.

Shakespeare had this picture from *Propertius*, Lib. II.[1]

Quicunque ille fuit puerum qui pinxit amorem,
    Nonne putas miras hunc habuisse manus!
Hic primùm vidit sine sensu vivere amantes,
    Et levibus curis magna perire bona.
Idem non frustra ventosas addidit alas,
    Fecit & humano corde colare deum.
Scilicet alternâ quoniam jactamur in undâ,
    Nostraque non ullis permanet aura locis.
Et meritò hamatis manus est armata sagittis,
    Et pharetra ex humero Gnossa utroque jacet.
Ante ferit quoniam, tuti quam cernimus hostem,
    Nec quisquam ex illo vulnere sanus abit.

[1] 2.12: 'Whoever he was that painted Love a boy, do you not think that he had skilful hands? He saw first of all that lovers live without sense, and that great benefits are lost through trifling cares. The same man, not without reason, added swift wings and made the god fly about the human heart; for certainly we are tossed on one wave after another and our wind never sits in one quarter. Love's hand is also rightly armed with barbed arrows, and a Cretan quiver hangs from both his shoulders, because he strikes before we, feeling safe, see our enemy, nor does anyone go away uninjured by that wound' (tr. F. Brittain, Penguin).

Much Ado about Nothing, [4.1.217ff.]

> *It so falls out,*
> *That which we have, we prize not to the worth*
> *While we enjoy it; but being lack'd and lost,*
> *Why then we rack the value; then we find*
> *The virtue that possession wou'd not show us,*
> *While it was ours.*

Exactly from *Horace,* Carm. Lib. III. Ode xv.[1]

> Heu! nefas!
> Virtutem incolumem odimus
>   Sublatam ex oculis quærimus invidi.

Timon of Athens, [4.3.433ff.]

> *I'll example you with thievery.*
> *The sun's a thief, and with his great attraction*
> *Robs the vast sea. The moon's an arrant thief,*
> *And her pale fire she snatches from the sun.*
> *The sea's a thief, whose liquid surge resolves*
> *The mounds into salt tears. The earth's a thief,*
> *That feeds and breeds by a composture stol'n*
> *From general excrements.*

A very remarkable parody from *Anacreon.* Ode xix.[2]

> Πηγὴν μὲν αἶα πίνει,
> πίνει δὲ δένδρε' αἶαν·
> πίνει θάλασσ' ἀναύρους,
> ὁ δ' ἥλιος θάλασσαν,
> τὸν δ' ἥλιον σελήνη·
> τί μοι μάχεσθ', ἑταῖροι,
> καὐτῷ θέλοντι πίνειν;

In the second part of *Henry the VIth,* act the ivth, scene the 1st [4.1.116]
Shakespeare quotes a Latin poet in the character of *Suffolk,*[3] and in scene

---

[1] *Odes* 3.24.30ff.: 'Since we (alas, the shame!) with envy filled, hate virtue while it lives and mourn it only when snatched from sight'.

[2] *Anacreontea* 21 (Bergk): 'The black earth drinks, the trees drink the earth, the sea drinks the air, the sun drinks the sea, and the moon drinks the sun. Why then, my friends, do you stop me from drinking?' This parallel had already been drawn by William Dodd.

[3] Suffolk quotes the line *Gelidus timor occupat artus,* apparently a conflation of *Aeneid* 7.446 with Lucan, *Pharsalia* 1.246 (New Arden edition, *ad. loc.*).

the 1st, of the vth act in the same play, he alludes to the Αιασ Μαστιγο-
φορος of *Sophocles*.

> *And now, like* Ajax Telamonius,
> *On sheep and oxen cou'd I spend my fury.*   [5.1.26f.]
> &c. &c. &c.

150. David Garrick, from his adaptation of *The Winter's Tale*

1756

From *Florizel and Perdita. A Dramatic Pastoral, In Three Acts. Alter'd from The Winter's Tale of Shakespeare*, 1758; first performed 21 January 1756.

On the reception of Garrick's adaptation see above, p. 18. One contemporary who approved of it without reservation was William Warburton, who wrote to Garrick on 12 June 1758: 'As you know me to be less an idolizer of Shakespeare than yourself, you will less suspect me of compliment when I tell you that besides your giving an elegant form to a monstrous composition, you have in your additions written up to the best scenes in this play, so that you will easily imagine I read the "Reformed Winter's Tale" with great pleasure. You have greatly improved a fine prologue, and have done what we preachers are so commonly thought unable to do—*mend ourselves while we mend others*.' (*The Private Correspondence of David Garrick*, ed. James Boaden, 2 vols, 1831, I. p. 88).

PROLOGUE
TO THE
WINTER's TALE,
AND
CATHERINE and PETRUCHIO.
(Both from SHAKESPEARE)
Written and Spoken by
Mr. *GARRICK*.

To various Things the Stage has been compar'd,
As apt Ideas strike each humorous Bard:
This Night, for want of better Simile,

Let this our *Theatre* a *Tavern* be:
The Poets Vintners, and the Waiters we.
So (as the Cant, and Custom of the Trade is)
You're welcome *Gem'min*, kindly welcome *Ladies*.
To draw in Customers, our *Bills* are spread; [*Shewing a Play Bill.*
You cannot miss the Sign, 'tis *Shakespeare's Head*.[1]
From this same Head, this Fountain-head divine,
For different Palates springs a different Wine!
In which no Trick, to strengthen, or to thin 'em—
Neat as imported—no *French* Brandy in 'em—
Hence for the choicest Spirits flow *Champaign*;   }
Whose sparkling Atoms shoot thro' every Vein,   }
Then mount in magic Vapours, to th' enraptur'd Brain!   }
Hence flow for martial Minds Potations strong;
And sweet Love Potions, for the Fair and Young.
For you, my Hearts of Oak, for your Regale,
                              [*To the Upper Gallery.*
There's good old *English Stingo*, mild and stale.
For high, luxurious Souls with luscious smack,
There's *Sir John Falstaff*, is a Butt of Sack:
And if the stronger Liquors more invite ye,
Bardolph is Gin, and *Pistol* Aqua Vitæ.
But shou'd you call for *Falstaff*, where to find him,
* He's gone—nor left one Cup of Sack behind him.
Sunk in his Elbow Chair, no more he'll roam;   }
No more, with merry Wags, to *Eastcheap* come;   }
He's gone,—to jest, and laugh, and give his Sack at Home. }
As for the learned Critics, grave and deep,
Who catch at Words, and catching fall asleep;
Who in the Storms of Passion—hum,—and haw!
For such, our Master will no Liquor draw—
So blindy thoughtful, and so darkly read,
They take *Tom D'Urfey's*, for the *Shakespeare's* Head.
   A Vintner once acquir'd both Praise and Gain,
And sold much *Perry* for the best *Champaign*.
Some Rakes, this precious Stuff did so allure;
They drank whole Nights—what's that—when Wine is pure?
'Come fill a Bumper, *Jack*—, I will my Lord—

[1] The name of a famous tavern in London.
* Mr. *Quin* had then left the Stage.

Here's Cream!—Damn'd fine!—immense!—upon my Word!
Sir *William*, what say you?—The best, believe me—
In this—Eh *Jack!*—the Devil can't deceive me.'
Thus the wise Critic too, mistakes his Wine,
Cries out with lifted Hands, 'tis great!—divine!
Then jogs his Neighbour, as the Wonders strike him;
This *Shakespeare! Shakespeare!*—Oh, there's nothing like him!
In this Night's various, and enchanted Cup,
Some little *Perry*'s mixt for filling up.
The five long Acts, from which our Three are taken,
Stretch'd out to* sixteen Years, lay by, forsaken.
Lest then this precious Liquor run to waste,
'Tis now confin'd and bottled for your Taste.
'Tis my chief Wish, my Joy, my only Plan,
To lose no *Drop* of that immortal Man!

[Act I, Scene i]

SCENE: *The court of* BOHEMIA.

Enter CAMILLO *and a* GENTLEMAN.

Cam. The gods send him safe passage to us, for he seems embarked in a tempestuous season.

Gent. I pray thee, Lord *Camillo*, instruct me, what concealed matter there is in the coming of *Leontes* to *Bohemia*, shou'd so wrap our king in astonishment?

Cam. Good sign your knowledge in the court is young, if you make that your question.

Gent. I wou'd not be thought too curious, but I prithee, be my tutor in this matter.

Cam. To be short then—Give it thy hearing, for my tale is well worthy of it; these two kings, *Leontes* of *Sicily*, and *Polixenes* of *Bohemia*, were train'd together in their childhoods, and there rooted betwixt 'em such an affection as cou'd not chuse but branch as it grew up. One unhappy summer (and full sixteen as unhappy have follow'd it) our *Polixenes* went to repay *Sicily* the visitation which he justly ow'd him.— Most royally, and with the utmost freedom of society, was he entertain'd both by *Leontes*, and his queen *Hermione*; a lady, whose bodily accomplishments were unparallel'd, but by those of her own mind. The free strokes of youth and gaiety, in her extended civility to *Polixenes*

* The Action of the *Winter's Tale*, as written by *Shakespeare*, comprehends Sixteen Years.

(pleas'd as she was to see her lord delighted) bred in him suspicion of her conduct.

Gent. And that is an evil weed, that once taking root, needs no manure.

Cam. I then waited about the person of *Leontes*, and was alone thought worthy the participation of his jealousy. Into my bosom he disgorg'd his monstrous secret, with no tenderer an injunction than to take off his innocent, abused guest, by poison.

Gent. To kill *Polixenes!*

Cam. Even so.—What cou'd I do? What ran evenest with the grain of my honesty I did, and have not since repented me:—whisper'd *Polix.* of the matter—left my large fortunes, and my larger hopes in *Sicily*, and on the very wing of occasion flew with him hither, no richer than my honor; and have since been ever of his bosom.

Gent. I tremble for the poor queen, left to the injuries of a powerful king, and jealous husband.

Cam. Left too in her condition! for she had some while promis'd an heir to *Sicily*, and now, mark me, for the occasion—

Gent. Cannot surpass my attention.

Cam. Scarcely settled in *Bohemia* here, we are alarm'd with the arrival of *Paulina* (that excellent matron, and true friend of her unhappy queen) from whom we too soon learn how sad a tragedy had been acted in *Sicily*—the dishonor'd *Hermione* clapp'd up in prison, where she gave the king a princess—the child (the innocent milk yet in her innocent mouth) by the king's command, expos'd; expos'd even on the desarts of this kingdom;—our *Polixenes* being falsly deem'd the father.

Gent. Poor babe! unhappy queen! tyrant *Leontes!*

Cam. What blacker title will you fix upon him, when you shall hear that *Hermione*, in her weak condition (the child-bed privilege deny'd, which belongs to women of all fashion) was haul'd out to an open mockery of trial; that on this inhuman outrage (her fame being kill'd before) she died—in the very prison where she was deliver'd, died; and that on her decease, *Paulina* (whose free tongue was the king's living scourge, and perpetual remembrancer to him of his dead queen) fled with her effects, for safety of her life, to *Bohemia*, here—I tire you.

Gent. My king concern'd, I am too deeply interested in the event, to be indifferent to the relation.

Cam. All this did *Leontes*, in defiance of the plain answer of the oracle, by him consulted at *Delphi*; which now, after sixteen years occurring to his more sober thoughts, he first thinks it probable, then finds it true, and his penitence thereupon is as extreme, as his suspicions had been fatal. In the course of his sorrows he has, as we are inform'd, twice attempted on his life; and this is now his goad to the present expedition; to make all possible atonement to his injur'd brother *Bohemia*, and to us the fellow-sufferers in his wrongs—we must break off—the king and good *Paulina*—

Enter POLIXENES *and* PAULINA.

Polix. Weep not now, *Paulina*, so long-gone-by misfortunes; this strange and unexpected visit, from *Leontes*, calls all your sorrows up a-new: but good *Paulina*, be satisfied that heav'n has will'd it so. That sixteen years absence shou'd pass unnotic'd by this king, without exchange of gifts, letters, or embassies; and now!—I am amaz'd as thou art; but not griev'd—

Paul. Grudge me not a tear to the memory of my queen, my royal mistress; and there dies my resentment; now, *Leontes*, welcome.

Polix. Nobly resolv'd: of him think we no more 'till he arrives.

Cam. Hail, royal Sir. If the king of *Sicily* escape this dreadful tempest, I shall esteem him a favourite of the gods, and his penitence effectual.

Polix. Of that fatal country *Sicily*, and of its penitent (as we must think him) and reconcil'd king, my brother, (whose loss of his most precious queen and child are even now afresh lamented) I prithee, speak no more—say to me, when saw'st thou prince *Florizel*, my son? Fathers are no less unhappy, their issue not being gracious, than they are in losing 'em, when they have approv'd their virtues.

Cam. Sir, it is three days since I saw the prince; what his happier affairs may be, are to me unknown; but I have musingly noted, he is of late much retir'd from court, and is less frequent to his princely exercises than formerly he hath appear'd.

Polix. I have consider'd so much, *Camillo*, and with some care; so far, that I have eyes under my service, which look upon his removedness; from whom I have this intelligence, that he is seldom from the house of a most homely shepherd—A man, they say, that from very nothing, is grown rich beyond the imagination of his neighbours.

Paul. I have heard too of such a man, who hath a daughter of most rare note; the report of her is extended more than can be thought to begin from such a cottage.

Polix. That's likewise part of my intelligence, and I fear, the angle that plucks our son thither. Thou, *Camillo*, shalt accompany us to the place, where we will (not appearing what we are) have some question with the shepherd; from whose simplicity, I think it not uneasy to get the cause of my son's resort thither.

Cam. I willingly obey your command.

Polix. My best *Camillo!*—we must disguise ourselves.

Paul. Lest your royalty be discover'd by the attendance of any of your own train; my steward, *Dion,* shall provide disguises, and accompany your design with all secrecy.

Polix. It is well advis'd—I will make choice of some few to attend us, who shall wait at distance from the cottage—you instruct *Dion* in the matter, while we prepare ourselves.   [*Ex.* Polix. *and* Camillo.

Paul. (sola) What fire is in my ears! can it be so,
Or are my senses cheated with a dream?
Leontes in *Bohemia!*—O most welcome,
My penitent liege—my tears were those of joy.
—*Paulina,* for her royal mistress' sake,
Shall give thee welcome to this injur'd coast:
Such as the riches of two mighty kingdoms,
Bohemia join'd with fruitful *Sicily,*
Wou'd not avail to buy—*Leontes,* welcome.
Let thy stout vessel but the beating stand
Of this chaf'd sea, and thou art whole on land.   [*Exit* Paulina.

[Act I, Scene ii.]

The country by the sea-side. A storm.

Enter an OLD SHEPHERD.

Old Shep. I wou'd there were no age between thirteen and three and twenty; or that youth wou'd sleep out the rest: For there is nothing in the between, but getting wenches with child, wronging the ancientry, stealing, fighting.

*   *   *

Old Shep. Run, run, boy! thy legs are youngest.

Clown Stay, they have found the road to the beach, and come towards us.

Old Shep. Some rich men, I warrant 'em; that are poorer than we now.

Clown Lord, father! look—they are out-landish folk; their fine cloaths are shrunk in the wetting.

Enter LEONTES, *supported by* CLEOMENES.

Cleom. Bear up, my liege;—again welcome on shore.

Leon. Flatter me not—In death distinctions cease—
Am I on shore; walk I on land, firm land,
Or ride I yet upon the billows backs?
Methinks I feel the motion—who art thou?
    Cleom. Know you me not?—your friend *Cleomenes.*
    Leon. Where are my other friends?—What, perish'd all!
    Cleom. Not a soul sav'd! ourselves are all our crew,
Pilot, shipmaster, boatswain, sailors, all.
    Leon. Laud we the gods! Yet wherefore perish'd they,
Innocent souls! and I, with all my guilt,
Live yet to load the earth?—O righteous gods!
Your ways are past the line of man to fathom.
    Cleom. Waste not your small remaining strength of body
In warring with your mind. This desart waste
Has some inhabitants—Here's help at hand—
Good day, old man—
    Old Shep. Never said in worse time—a better to both your worships
—command us, Sir.
    Clown You have been sweetly soak'd; give the gods thanks that you
are alive to feel it.
    Leon. We are most thankful, Sir.
    Cleom. What desarts are these same?
    Old Shep. The desarts of *Bohemia.*
    Leon. Say'st thou *Bohemia?* ye gods, *Bohemia!*
In ev'ry act your judgments are sent forth
Against *Leontes!*—Here to be wreck'd and sav'd!
Upon this coast!—All the wrongs I have done,
Stir now afresh within me—Did I not
Upon this coast expose my harmless infant—
Bid *Polixenes* (falsly deem'd the father)
To take his child—O hell-born jealousy!
All but myself most innocent —and now
Upon this coast—Pardon, *Hermione!*
'Twas this that sped thee to thy proper heav'n;
If from thy sainted seat above the clouds,
Thou see'st my weary pilgrimage thro' life,
Loath'd, hated life, 'cause unenjoy'd with thee—
Look down, and pity me.
    Cleom.   Good Sir, be calm:
What's gone, and what's past help, shou'd be past grief;

213

You do repent these things too sorely.

    Leon. I can't repent these things, for they are heavier
Than all my woes can stir: I must betake me
To nothing but despair—a thousand knees
Ten thousand years together, naked, fasting,
Upon a barren mountain, and still winter,
In storms perpetual, could not move the gods
To look this way upon me.

    Clown What says he, pray? The sea has quite wash'd away the poor gentleman's brains. Come, bring him along to our farm; and we'll give you both a warm bed, and dry clothing.

    Cleom. Friends, we accept your offer'd courtesy.
Come, Sir—bear up—be calm—compose your mind;
If still the tempest rages there, in vain
The gods have sav'd you from the deep.

    Leon. I'll take thy council, friend,—Lend me thy arm—Oh,
Hermione!—   [*Leans on him.*

    Cleom. Good shepherd, shew us to the cottage.

*   *   *

[Act II, Scene i. *A prospect of a shepherd's cottage*]

*   *   *

Enter LEONTES and CLEOMENES, *from the farm-house.*

    Cleom. Why will you not repose you, Sir? these sports,
The idle merriments of hearts at ease,
But ill will suit the colour of your mind.

    Leon. Peace—I enjoy them in a better sort—
Cleomenes, look on this pretty damsel;   [*Pointing to* Perdita.
Haply such age, such innocence and beauty,
Had our dear daughter own'd, had not my hand—
O had I not the course of nature stop'd
On weak surmise—I will not think that way—
And yet I must, always, and ever must.

    Cleom. No more, my liege—

    Leon. Nay, I will gaze upon her; each salt drop
That tricles down my cheek, relieves my heart,
Which else wou'd burst with anguish.

    Polix. (*to* Camillo) Is it not too far gone? 'tis time to part 'em;

214

He's simple, and tells much—how now, fair shepherd;   [*To* Florizel.
Your heart is full of something that does take
Your mind from feasting. Sooth, when I was young,
And handed love as you do, I was wont
To load my she with knacks.

*   *   *

[Act III, Scene iv. PAULINA'S *House*]

*   *   *

   Paul. Music, awake her—strike—
'Tis time; descend—be stone no more—approach;
Strike all that look on you with marvel!
[*Music; during which she comes down.*
   Leon. (*Retiring*) Heav'nly pow'rs!
   Paul. (*to* Leontes) Start not—her actions shall be holy, as,
You hear, my spell is lawful; do not shun her,
Until you see her die again, for then
You kill her double; nay, present your hand;
When she was young, you woo'd her; now in age
She is become your suitor.
   Leon. Support me, gods!
If this be more than visionary bliss,
My reason cannot hold: my wife! my queen!
But speak to me, and turn me wild with transport.
I cannot hold me longer from those arms;
She's warm! she lives!
   Polix.   She hangs about his neck:
If she pertain to life, let her speak too.
   Perd. O *Florizel!*   [Perdita *leans on* Florizel's *bosom.*
   Flor.   My princely shepherdess!
This is too much for hearts of thy soft mold.
   Leon. Her beating heart meets mine, and fluttering owns
Its long-lost half: these tears that choak her voice
Are hot and moist—it is *Hermione!*   [*Embrace.*
   Polix. I'm turn'd myself to stone! where has she liv'd?
Or how so stolen from the dead?
   Paul.   That she is living,
Were it but told you, shou'd be hooted at

215

Like an old tale; but it appears she lives,
Tho' yet she speak not. Mark them yet a little.
'Tis past all utterance, almost past thought;
Dumb eloquence beyond the force of words.
To break the charm,
Please you to interpose; fair madam, kneel,
And pray your mother's blessing, turn, good lady,
Our *Perdita* is found, and with her found
A princely husband, whose instinct of royalty,
From under the low thatch where she was bred,
Took his untutor'd queen.

  Herm.   You gods, look down,
And from your sacred phials pour your graces
Upon their princely heads!

  Leon.   Hark! hark! she speaks—
O pipe, thro' sixteen winters dumb! then deem'd
Harsh as the raven's note; now musical
As nature's song, tun'd to th' according spheres.

  Herm. Before this swelling flood o'er-bear our reason,
Let purer thoughts, unmix'd with earth's alloy,
Flame up to heav'n, and for its mercy shewn,
Bow we our knees together.   [*Kneel.*

  Leon.   Oh! if penitence
Have pow'r to cleanse the foul sin-spotted soul,
Leontes' tears have wash'd away his guilt.
If thanks unfeign'd be all that you require,
Most bounteous gods, for happiness like mine,
Read in my heart, your mercy's not in vain.

  Herm. This firstling duty paid, let transport loose,
My lord, my king,—there's distance in those names,
My husband!

  Leon. O my *Hermione!*—have I deserv'd
That tender name?

  Herm. No more; be all that's past
Forgot in this enfolding, and forgiven.

  Leon. Thou matchless saint!—Thou paragon of virtue!

  Perd. O let me kneel, and kiss that honor'd hand.

  Herm. Thou *Perdita*, my long-lost child, that fill'st
My measure up of bliss—tell me, mine own,
Where hast thou been preserv'd? where liv'd! how found

Bohemia's court? for thou shalt hear, that I
Knowing, by *Paulina*, that the oracle
Gave hope thou wast in being, have preserv'd
Myself to see the issue.
    Paul.   There's time enough
For that, and many matters more of strange
Import—how the queen escap'd from *Sicily*,
Retir'd with me, and veil'd her from the world—
But at this time no more; go, go together,
Ye precious winners all, your exultation
Pertake to ev'ry one; I, an old turtle,
Will wing me to some wither'd bough, and there
My mate, that's never to be found again,
Lament 'till I am lost.
    Leon.   No, no, *Paulina;*
Live bless'd with blessing others—my *Polixenes!*
                   [*Presenting* Polixenes *to* Hermione.
What? look upon my brother: both your pardons,
That e'er I put between your holy looks
My ill suspicion—come, our good *Camillo*,
Now pay thy duty here—thy worth and honesty
Are richly noted, and here justified
By us a pair of kings; and last, my queen,
Again I give you this your son-in-law,
And son to this good king by heav'n's directing
Long troth-plight to our daughter.

Leontes, Hermione, *and* Polixenes *join their hands.*

    Perd.   I am all shame
And ignorance itself, how to put on
This novel garment of gentility,
And yield a patch'd behaviour, between
My country-level, and my present fortunes,
That ill becomes this presence. I shall learn,
I trust I shall with meekness—but I feel,
(Ah happy that I do) a love, an heart
Unalter'd to my prince, my *Florizel*.
    Flor. Be still my queen of *May*, my shepherdess,
Rule in my heart; my wishes be thy subjects,
And harmless as thy sheep.

Leon. Now, good *Paulina,*
Lead us from hence, where we may leisurely
Each one demand, and answer to his part
Perform'd in this wide gap of time, since first
We were dissever'd—then thank the righteous gods,
Who, after tossing in a perilous sea,
Guide us to port, and a kind beam display,
To gild the happy evening of our day.

[*Exeunt omnes.*

151. David Garrick, in defence of Shakespeare musicals

1756

'A Dialogue Between an Actor and a Critick, By way of Prologue to the *Tempest*, An Opera, by Mr. Garrick, acted at Drury-lane, Feb. 1756', from *The Poetical Works of David Garrick* (1785) I, pp. 143-9.

Enter *Heartly*, the Actor, and *Wormwood*, the Critic.

Worm. I say it is a shame, Mr Heartly; and I am amazed that you let your good-nature talk thus, against the conviction of your understanding.

Heart. You won't let me talk, sir; if you would but have patience, and hear reason a little.

Worm. I wish I could, sir; but you put me out of all patience, by having no reason to give me. I say that this frittering and sol fa-ing our best poets, is a damn'd thing. I have yet heard no reason to justify it, and I have no patience when I think of it.

Heart. I see you have not—

Worm. What! are we to be quivered and quavered out of our senses? Give me Shakespeare, in all his force, vigour, and spirit! What! would you make an eunuch of him? No *Shakespearelli's* for my money.

Heart. Nay but, dear sir, hear me in my turn; or the truth, for which we are, or ought to be, so warmly fighting, will *slip thro' our fingers.*

Worm. Will you hold it when you have it? I say, Mr Heartly, while you let your good-nature—

Heart. And I say, Mr Wormwood, while you are to be influenced and blown up by paragraphs in news-papers, and insinuations in coffee-houses, we can never come to a fair debate. They who write upon all subjects, without understanding any, or will talk about musick, without ears or taste for it, are but very indifferent judges in our dispute.

Worm. Well, come on, Mr *Sol-fa*, then—Let you and I fight it out; or, to speak in the musical phrase, let us have a *Duette* together; I'll clear up my pipes, and have at you.—Hem, hem—

Heart. With all my heart, tho' I'm afraid you'll make it a *Solo*, for you have not yet suffered the second part to come in.

Worm. Ho! play away, sir—I'll be dumb—

Heart. Let us calmly consider this complaint of your's: If it is well founded, I will submit with pleasure; if not, you will.

Worm. Not submit with pleasure, I assure you; I never do.

Heart. You will at least have this satisfaction, that the sentence which will be given, whether for or against you, will be as indisputable, as it will be just.

Worm. I don't know what you mean: Nothing's indisputable, that I please to contradict, and nothing's just, that I please to call in question.

Heart. Look round *upon* the court, and if you can reasonably except against any one of the jury, I will give up the cause before trial.

Worm. O, ho! what, you are bribing the court before-hand with your flattery, are you?

Heart. There you are out again: our countrymen in a body, are no more to be *flatter'd* than *bully'd*, which I hope their enemies (who can do both) will be convinced of before they have done with them. But I wander from the question. To the point, sir: what are your objections to this night's entertainment?

Worm. I hate an Opera.

Heart. I dislike tye-wigs; but should I throw your's into the fire, because I chuse to wear a bag?

Worm. Woe be to your bag if you did.

Heart. You hate musick, perhaps?

Worm. Damnably, and dancing too.

Heart. But why, pray?

Worm. They pervert nature. Legs are made for walking, tongues for speaking; and therefore capering and quavering are unnatural and abominable.

Heart. You like Shakespeare?

Worm. Like him! adore him! worship him! There's no capering and quavering in his works.

Heart. Have a care.

> The man that has no musick in himself,
> Nor is not mov'd with concord of sweet sounds,
> Is fit for treason, stratagems and spoils;
> The motions of his spirit are dull as night,
> And his affections dark as Erebus:
> Let no such man be trusted.

Worm. Fit for treason! dull as night! not to be trusted!—so you have proved me both a fool and a rebel.—Don't provoke me, Mr Heartly, Shakespeare never wrote such stuff as that; 'tis foisted in by some fiddler or other.

Heart. You pay the fiddlers (as you call them) a very great compliment.

Worm. Did I? I am sorry for it; I did not mean it: were I to pay 'em —crabstick's the word.

Heart. For shame, Mr Wormwood! Let me ask you a question: would you chuse your own country should be excelled in any thing by your neighbours?

Worm. In manufactures—no—from the casting of cannon, to the making of pins; from the weaving of velvets, to the making of hop-sacks; but your capering and quavering only spoils us, and make *us* the jests, who *should* be the terrors of Europe.

Heart. But English musick, Mr Wormwood—

Worm. English musick, or any musick, enervates the body, weakens the mind, and lessens the courage.

Heart. Quite the contrary.

Worm. Prove that, and I'll learn the gamut immediately; nay, be-speak me a pair of pumps, and I'll make one at the dancing academy for grown gentlemen.

Heart. Let us suppose an invasion!

Worm. Ha, ha, ha! an invasion!—musick and an invasion! they are well coupled, truly!

Heart. Patience, sir—I say, let us suppose ten thousand French landed.

Worm. I had rather suppose 'em at the bottom of the sea.

Heart. So had I—but that ten thousand are upon the coast.

Worm. The devil they are! What then?

Heart. Why then, I say, let but *Britons strike home,* or *God save the King,* be sounded in the ears of five thousand brave Englishmen, with a protestant prince at the head of 'em, and they'll drive every monsieur into the sea, and make 'em food for sprats and mackarel.

Worm. Huzza! and so they will!—'Egad you're right; I'll say no more: *Britons strike home!* You have warm'd me and pleas'd me; nay, you have converted me. I'll get a place in the house, and be as hearty as the best of 'em for the musick of Old England! Sprats and mackarel! ha, ha, ha! that's good! excellent! I thank you for it; musick for ever! *Britons strike home! God save the King!*

Heart. The last thing I have to say will touch you as nearly, Mr Wormwood—

Worm. You have touch'd me enough already; say no more; I am satisfy'd: I shall never forget sprats and mackarel.

Heart. We may boast, sincerely boast, of many excellent English composers; and would not you permit your countrymen to have the same encouragement as foreigners?

Worm. Encouragement! why I'll encourage them myself, man.

Heart. Where can they shew their talents, unless upon the English stages? and, if the managers of them will not give up a few nights to encourage English musick, our musical countrymen, Mr Wormwood, would be of the number of those persons of merit, who are undeservedly neglected in this kingdom.

Worm. But they shan't; I'll support 'em. I'll never more hearken to your club-speeches, and your dissertations, and news-paper essays. I see my error, but I'll make amends. Let us meet after it is over, and take a bottle to sprats and mackarel, eh, master Heartly, at the Shakespeare. I'll be with you. *Britons strike home.*   [*Exit singing.*

Heart. Ha, ha, ha! Mr Wormwood is now as much too violent in his zeal, as he was before in his prejudice. We expect not, ladies and gentlemen, that this night's performance should meet with success, merely because it is English. You would be as incapable of conceiving as we of urging, such false and contracted notions; yet, on the other hand, let not our musical brethren be cast off, because fashion, caprice, or manners, too refin'd, may have given you prejudices against them.

Musick is the younger sister of poetry, and can boast her charms and accomplishments. Suffer not the younger then to be turned out of doors, while the elder is so warmly and deservedly cherished.

> If worthy, you'll protect her, tho' distrest,
> 'Tis the known maxim of a British breast,
> Those to befriend the most, who're most opprest.

152. David Garrick, from his musical adaptation of *The Tempest*

1756

From *The Tempest. An Opera. Taken from Shakespeare* . . . *The Songs from Shakespeare, Dryden &c. The Music composed by Mr. Smith* (1756); performed 11 February 1756.

It is hoped that the Reader will excuse the omission of many passages of the first Merit, which are in the Play of The Tempest; it being impossible to introduce them in the plan of this Opera.

*   *   *

Act I, Scene i.

The Stage darkened—represents a cloudy sky, a very rocky coast, and a ship on a tempestuous sea.—ARIEL comes upon the stage.

AIR.

Arise, arise, ye subterranean winds,
Arise ye deadly blighting fiends;
Rise you, from whom devouring plagues have birth,

You that i' th' vast and hollow womb of earth
Engender earthquakes, make whole countries shake;
Ye eager winds, whose rapid force can make
All, but the fix'd and solid centre, shake:
Come, drive yon ship to that part of the isle
Where nature never yet did smile.

Myself will fly on board, and on the beak,
In the waste, the deck, in every cabin,
I'll flame amazement. Sometimes I'll divide,
And burn in many places. On the top-mast,
The yards, and bowsprit will I flame distinctly,
Then meet and join. *Jove's* lightnings, the precursors
Of dreadful thunder-claps, more momentary
And sight out-running, are the fire and cracks
Of sulph'rous roaring; the most mighty *Neptune*
Shall seem to siege, make his bold waves tremble,
Yea, his dread trident shake.

[*Exit.*

Repeated flashes of lightning, and claps of thunder.

[Act I], Scene ii.

A part of the island near PROSPERO'*s cell.*

Enter PROSPERO *and* MIRANDA.

Miranda. If by your art (my dearest father) you have
Put the wild waters in this roar, allay them.
O! I have suffer'd with those I saw suffer.
Had I been any god of pow'r, I would
Have sunk the sea within the earth, or e'er
It should the goodly ship have swallow'd, and
The freighting souls within her.

AIR.

Hark how the winds rush from their caves,
Hark how old ocean frets and raves,
From their deep roots the rocks he tears;
Whole deluges lets fly,
That dash against the sky,
And seem to drown the stars.

223

Prospero. Tell your piteous heart, there's no harm done;
I have done nothing, but in care of thee,
My child, who art ignorant of what thou art;
But I will now inform thee—pray attend:
'Tis twelve years since thy father was the duke
Of *Milan*—be not amaz'd, my daughter;
Thou art a princess of no less issue.
    Miranda. O the heav'ns, what foul play had we!
    Prospero. Mark me well.
I then neglecting worldly ends, all dedicated
To study, and the bettering of my mind,
Did cast the government on my brother,
Call'd *Anthonio.*—He, from substitution,
And executing the outward face of
Royalty, with all prerogative, did
Believe he was indeed the duke; hence his
Ambition growing, he confederates
With the king of *Naples*, my inveterate foe,
Who, for homage and certain tribute, agrees
To extirpate me from my dukedom, and
To confer fair *Milan* on my brother:
This settled, and an army levy'd; one night,
Fated to the purpose, did *Anthonio* open
The gates of *Milan*, and i' th' dead of darkness,
The ministers for the purpose, hurry'd thence
Me, and thy crying self; in fine, they forc'd us
Out to sea, in a rotten unrigg'd boat,
Where they left us to the mercy of the winds.

AIR.

> *In pity,* Neptune *smooths the liquid way,*
> *Obsequious* Tritons *on the surface play,*
> *And sportful dolphins with a nimble glance,*
> *To the bright sun their glitt'ring scales advance.*
> *In oozy bed profound the billows sleep,*
> *No clamorous winds awake the silent deep;*
> *With safety thro' the sea our boat is bore.*
> *In gentle gales we're wafted to the shore.*

Here in this island we arriv'd, and here
Have I, thy school-master, made thee more profit

Than other princes can, who have more time
For vainer hours, and tutors not so careful.
 Miranda. Heav'n thank you for't!
 Prospero. Know further, that fortune,
Now grown bountiful to this shore, hath brought
Mine enemies; and, by my prescience,
I find my zenith doth depend upon
A most propitious star, whose influence
If now I court not, but omit, my fortunes
Will ever after drop.—
Thou art inclin'd to sleep; 'tis a good dulness,
And give it way; I know thou can'st not chuse.

AIR.

Miranda.   *Come, O sleep, my eyelids close,*
         Lull my soul to soft repose.

* * *

Act III, Scene i.

PROSPERO's *cell.*

Enter PROSPERO, FERDINAND, *and* MIRANDA.

 Prospero. If I have too austerely punish'd you,
Your compensation makes amends; for I
Have giv'n you here a thread of mine own life,
Or that for which I live. O, *Ferdinand,*
Do not smile at me, that I boast her off;
For thou shalt find she will out-strip all praise.
 Ferdinand. I do believe it, against an oracle.

AIR.

Have you seen but a bright lily grow,
 Before rude hands have touch'd it?
Have you mark'd but the fall of the snow,
 Before the soil hath smutch'd it?
Have you felt the wool of the beaver?
 Or swan's down ever?
Or have smelt o' the bud o' the briar?
 Or the nard i' the fire?

Or have tasted the bag of the bee?
Oh, so white! Oh, so soft! Oh, so sweet is she!

Prospero. If thou dost break her virgin-knot before
All sanctimonious ceremonies may
With full and holy rite be minister'd,
No sweet aspersions shall the heav'ns let fall,
To make this contract grow: therefore take heed,
As *Hymen*'s lamps shall light you.

Ferdinand. Nothing shall melt mine honour into lust,
To spoil the edge of that day's celebration.

Prospero. Fairly spoken; *Miranda* is thine own.

*   *   *

[Act III, Scene iii]

Prospero. Look thou be true, and do not give dalliance
Too much the rein: the strongest oaths are straw
To th' fire i' th' blood: be more abstemious,
Or else, good night, your vow.

Ferdinand. I warrant you, Sir.
The white, cold virgin-snow upon my heart,
Abates the ardour of my passion.

AIR.

Miranda.   *Hope waits upon the flow'ry prime;*
           And summer, tho' it be less gay,
        Yet is not look'd on as a time
           Of declination, or decay;
        For, with a full hand, that does bring
        All that was promis'd by the spring.

                 [*Exeunt* Ferdinand *and* Miranda.

*   *   *

[Act III, Scene vi]

Opens to the entrance of PROSPERO*'s cell, and discovers* FERDINAND *and* MIRANDA *playing at chess.*

Miranda. Sweet lord, you play me false.

Ferdinand. No, my dear love,
I would not for the world.

Miranda. Yes, for a score of kingdoms you shall wrangle,
And I would call it fair play.

AIR.

Ferdinand.   *If on those endless charms you lay*
                            The value that's their due,
                    Kings are themselves too poor to pay,
                            A thousand worlds too few.
                    But if a passion without vice,
                            Without disguise or art,
                    Miranda, *if true love's your price,*
                            Behold it in my heart.

★   ★   ★

[Act III, Scene vii]

★   ★   ★

AIR.

Prospero (*to* Miranda).
                    With him thy joys shall be compleat,
                            Dissolv'd in ease, thy hours shall flow:
                    With love alone thy heart shall beat,
                            And his be all th' alarms you know.
                    Cares to sooth, and life befriend,
                    Pleasures on your nod attend.

   Prospero. Sir, I invite your highness and your train
To my poor cell, where you shall take your rest
For this one night, which (part of it) I'll waste
With such discourses, as I doubt not, will make it
Quickly pass away, and in the morning
I'll bring you to your ship, and so to *Naples*;
Where I hope to see the nuptials
Of these, our dear beloved, solemniz'd.
   Alonzo. I long to hear the story of your life.
   Prospero. In proper time, I will deliver all,
And promise you calm seas, auspicious gales,
And sail so expeditious, that shall catch
Your royal fleet far off: my *Ariel*, chick,
This is thy charge, then to the elements,
Be free, and fare you well.

DUETT.

Ferdinand.	*Love, gentle love, now fill my breast,*
	    The storms of life are o'er;
	In thee, my dear Miranda, *blest,*
	    What can I wish for more.

Miranda.	*Love, gentle love, and chaste desire,*
	    My breast shall ever move:
	Let me those heav'nly joys inspire,
	    And all our life be love.

Ferdinand.	*Thus ever kind,*
Miranda.	*Thus ever true,*
Ferdinand.	*May I, my sweet one, find,*
Miranda.	*May I be all in you,*
Both.	*And sacred Hymen shall dispense* *The sweets of love and innocence.*

CHORUS.

Let sacred Hymen now dispense
The sweets of love and innocence;
Let him his choicest blessings shed,
And nobly fruitful be their bed;
Virtue and love shall deck their crown,
With happy days and high renown.

[*Exeunt omnes.*

153. Charles Marsh, from his adaptation of *The Winter's Tale*

1756

From *The Winter's Tale, a Play. Alter'd from Shakespeare* (1756).

Charles Marsh (1735–1812), son of Charles Marsh, a London bookseller, was educated at Westminster and Trinity College, Cambridge. He was a clerk in the War Office for many years, and became fellow of the Society of Antiquaries. Having failed to have his Shakespeare adaptations performed, he printed them at his own cost.

*   *   *

SCENE, in the First, Second, and Fifth Acts, in *Sicilia*. In the Third, and Fourth, in *Bithynia*.

*   *   *

Act I, Scene i.

An Antichamber in the Palace of Leontes.

Enter Alcidales *and* Rogero.

  Alcid. Is it not strange, my Friend, this fatal Passion
So long shou'd prey upon a royal Mind?
O fall'n *Leontes*, once the boasted Pride
Of each *Sicilian* Tongue; for Justice fam'd,
For Prudence, Fortitude, and ev'ry Virtue
That swells the Annals of the best of Kings.
How art thou sunk!—become thy own poor Captive,
And Reason's Light extinguish'd in thy Soul!
  Rog. The Magnanimity with which the Queen
Sustains Imprisonment, can only flow
From conscious Innocence.

Alcid. From thence alone,
The Heart that by Injustice is oppress'd
Finds its Relief.

Rog. The Temper of the King
Of late seems strangely shaken.

Alcid. Need we wonder?
Have we not felt the Arm of *Jove* himself?
His own Right Hand hath wing'd th' avenging Bolts
That have transfix'd *Sicilia*'s hapless Sons!
' 'Tis for the King's Offence the People die:'
Why else, (since Heaven is just) this Visitation?
Why hath *Enceladus* thus shook our Isle?
Wherefore these fierce Irruptions? From the Mouth
Of thund'ring *Ætna*, fraught with raging Fires,
Volcanos, issuing with a Whirlwind's Force,
Tear up the seated Rocks.

Rog. Large Flakes of Embers
Involve in pitchy Clouds the dusky Air,
And where they fall, leave a sulphureous Stench,
Fatal to Man's frail Being.

Alcid. The Earth trembles,
As universal Ruin were at hand:
Happy the Dead! no more their Ears are wounded
With dreadful Sounds that bellow from the Deep,
As *all* the Elements with *all* their Force
Maintain'd within its Womb intestine War.

Rog. The King, with Gifts, has sought the *Delphian* God,
Exploring thence the Cause of this Destruction.

Alcid. He seems himself the Cause.—*Hermione!*
Thy Wrongs have sure alarm'd the mighty Gods!
For fifteen Years shut from the Light of Day;
Whilst Calumny with its nefarious Breath
Blasts thy good Name, and in thy Fate involves
Thy guiltless Offspring.

Rog. I was young at Court
When first *Hermione* began her Sufferings,
And but from Rumour took th' imperfect Tale;
You must have known it better.

Alcid. The good King,
Polixenes, who sways *Bithynia*'s Scepter,

From Infancy was train'd with our *Leontes*.
They were as twinn'd Lambs that did frisk i'the Sun,
And bleat the one at th' other. What they 'chang'd
Was only Innocence, for Innocence.
Thus growing up, cemented in their Loves,
There rooted 'twixt them such a fair Affection
As cou'd not chuse but branch, and blossom forth,
Mellow'd by Time into the strongest Friendship.
And the same Sun, that saw *Leontes* wiv'd,
Blest, with his Beams the Nuptials of *Polixenes*.
Tho' Seas divided them, yet did they seem,
In Absence, to embrace as 'twere; by Gifts,
By Letters, and by loving Embassies.—
At length *Bithynia* paid his Friend a Visit.

Rog. His Welcome at the Court is still a Theme,
When Men wou'd praise our King's Magnificence.

Alcid. He made a *July*'s Day short as *December*.
Nine Changes of the wat'ry Star had pass'd
Before *Bithynia* press'd his Home-Return.
At last he urg'd what Dangers to his State
Might grow in Absence—That his Royalty
Wou'd suffer, and his Throne, so long unfill'd
Might heat aspiring Minds.—*Leontes* still
Combats his Reasons, and commands *Hermione*
To use her Eloquence.—Th' unwary Queen
With Vehemence prefers her pious Suit;
Entreats him for a Month, a Week, a Day.
O'ercome by fair Persuasions, he delay'd
His fix'd Departure.—Sudden Jealousy
Then seiz'd *Leontes*' Bosom, and he swore
His Wife was an Adult'ress.

Rog. When the Brain
Is thus infected, the Imagination
Will to the Center stab; communicate with Dreams,
And make unreal things appear as strong
As sacred Verities.—Unhappy Queen!—

Alcid. I was in Presence when his flaming Eyes
Discover'd first his Rage. He call'd me to him:
Did'st thou not mark? he cry'd—*Bithynia* stays,
But not at my Entreaty: they're too hot,

To mingle Friendship far, is mingling Blood!
She arms her with the Boldness of a Wife,
To her allowing Husband.—Gone already;
Inch thick, Knee deep, o'er Head and Ears a fork'd one.
I then adjur'd him, by the Wounds he'd give
His Honour as a King, timely to think,
Before he plung'd himself in deep Despair.—
Nay, urg'd the Scandal to the Blood o' th' Prince,
His darling Son.

    Rog. Illustrious hapless Youth!
His Virtue suffers for his Father's Crimes.
Divided in his Duty, whilst his Heart
Acquits *Hermione*, and mourns in secret
The mighty Sorrows of that injur'd Saint;
The Thought infects, and preys upon his Health,
And will, 'tis fear'd, if not remov'd, prove fatal.

    Alcid. O Jealousy! how fatal is thy Rage?
Seated in private Breasts, it carries Ruin
Where-e'er its Influence spreads.
But when a pow'rful Monarch's Soul is tainted.
It scatters all around the vast Destruction,
And Numbers suffer for the Guilt of one.
Antigonus, who thinks upon thy Fate,
Without a melting Eye? Lost to thy Friends,
Thy Wife and native Clime, where dost thou wander?

    Rog. Mean you the Husband of the good *Paulina?*

    Alcid. I do. A Man full of the nicest Honour;
His Actions spoke him noble:—strictly honest;
Cautious to promise; but his Word once giv'n
Was irreversible.—This worthy Lord,
Leontes, in the Tempest of his Mind,
His frantick Bosom fraught with black Suspicion,
Commanded to destroy th' unhappy Fruit
Of his own Marriage-Bed.—On his Refusal,
He swore him, on the Peril of his Soul,
And on his Body's Torture, to convey it
Out of *Sicilia:* in some desart Place
To leave it to its Fortune—that blind Chance
Might either strangely rear it up, or end it.
But the Morn wastes.—By this, the King has left

His thorny Couch; where, to the Shades of Night,
Instead of tasting balmy, soft Repose,
Incessantly he pours out his Complaints.

Act I, Scene ii.

SCENE *opens and discovers the* King, *Attendants. Soft Musick.*

King. Nor Night, nor Day, no Rest;—it is but Weakness
To bear the Matter thus; mere weakness, if
The Cause were not in being; part o' the Cause,
She, the Adult'ress; for th' Adulterer,
Is quite beyond mine Arm; out of the Blank
And Level of my Brain, Plot proof; but she
I can hook to me: say, that she were gone,
Giv'n to the Fire, a Moiety of my Rest
Might come to me again.—But wherefore shakes
My Coward Soul, and startles at that Thought?
As she is guilty, Justice dooms her Death:
And yet,—these dreadful Heralds of the Gods,
Proclaiming Wrath divine, but newly wak'd,
Unnerve my Resolution,—and each Thought
That tends to Vengeance, with a strong Recoil
Bounds back, and strikes on my astonish'd Sense
With tenfold Horror!—Where's the Lord *Rogero?*
Rog. My Liege.
King. Have our Physicians yet discover'd
The secret Malady of Prince *Mamillius?*
Rog. They've try'd their utmost Skill, which yet seems baffled;
'Tis thought the working of his Mind enflames
His fev'rish Pulse.
King. His Mind, *Rogero?*—Ha!—
How sometimes Nature will betray its Folly!—
Its Tenderness!—And make itself a Pastime
To harder Bosoms.—O my Boy, so young,
And has already such a tender Sense
Of the Indignity thy Father suffers?
What wilt thou feel, when Manhood ripens thee,
And thou shalt know by Proof a Woman's Falshood?
For all are false;—as false as Winds, or Waters;
As Dice are to be wish'd, by one who fixes

233

No Bourne 'twixt his and mine.

    Alcid. Pardon me, Sir,
The Duty and Allegiance that I owe you
Unties my Tongue.—The Anguish you have felt,
Tormented by the Queen's imagin'd Falshood—

    King. Imagin'd Falshood!—Where, *Alcidales*,
Where were thy Eyes? Thou then wert of our Court,
And must have seen *Bithynia* and my Wife;
Have mark'd them, padling Palms, and pinching Fingers:
Have seen them stopping the Career of Laughter
With a sad sudden Sigh; a Note infallible
Of breaking Honesty.
Was Whisp'ring nothing?—Leaning Cheek to Cheek,
Kissing with inside Lip, and meeting Noses?
Sculking in Corners, wishing Clocks more swift;
Hours Minutes? the Noon Midnight, and all Eyes
Blind with the Pin and Web, but theirs; theirs only,
That wou'd unseen be wicked? Was this nothing?
Why then, the World, and all that's in't is nothing;
Nothing the cov'ring Sky—*Bithynia* nothing;
My Wife is nothing too, if this be nothing.

    Alcid. O that you had been cur'd by Times, my Liege,
Of this diseas'd Opinion.

    King. Dost thou think
That I am yet so muddy, and unsettled
T' appoint myself in this Vexation? sully
The Purity and Whiteness of my Sheets,
Which to preserve is Sleep; which being spotted,
Is Goads, Thorns, Nettles, Tails of Wasps,
Without ripe moving to't: cou'd I do this?
Cou'd Man so blench?—I tell thee, mindless Slave,
Were my Wife's Liver half so much infected,
As then was her lewd Life, she wou'd not live
The running of one Glass.

    Alcid. Still must I think,
(If 'tis Presumption, take my forfeit Head,)
The Queen and wrong'd *Polixenes* are honest.

    King. Villain, thou liest; he wore her like his Medal,
Hanging about his Neck.—*Bithynia* did!
Yet,—I but yoke with others:—there have been,

Or I am much deceiv'd, Cuckolds ere now;
And many a Man there is, ev'n at this present,
Now while I speak this, holds his Wife by th' Arm,
That little thinks how wanton she has been,
When he was absent. Nay, there's Comfort in't,
While other Men have Gates, and those Gates open'd
Like mine against their Will.—Shou'd all despair
That have revolted Wives, the tenth of Mankind
Wou'd hang themselves. And Physick for't there's none,
It is a powerful Planet, that will strike
Where 'tis predominant. There's Thousands of us
Have the Disease, and yet perceive it not.
    Rog. When you, dread Sir, shall come to clearer Proof
(As by *Apollo*'s Oracle we hope,)
How will you grieve, when what you now call Justice,
Be prov'd a Violence?
    King. Were you to swear *Hermione* is honest,
By each partic'lar Star that reigns in Heav'n,
By all their Influences; you may as well
Forbid the Ocean to obey the Moon,
As, or by Oath remove, or Counsel shake
My strong Suspicion.—There may be i'the Cup
A Spider steep'd, and one may drink, depart,
And yet partake no Venom; for his Knowledge
Is not infected: but if one present
Th' abhorr'd Ingredient to his Eye, make known
How he has drunk, he cracks his Gorge, his Sides
With violent Hefts.—I've drank, and seen the Spider.—
Trait'rous *Camillo* was his Fædary;
His Pander, and fled with him.—That false Villain!
And now they laugh secure, and loll the Tongue,
And cry, *Sicilia* is a soforth, a pinch'd Thing!
    Alcid. *Camillo* fled, 'tis true, my Sov'reign Liege;
And with *Polixenes*: Fear caus'd his Flight;
When Kings are angry, who can stand before 'em?
But let him not be burthen'd with a Crime
That taints the purest Blood;—call him not Traytor.
    King. *Alcidales*, thou know'st I've trusted thee
With all the things nearest my Heart,—with all
My Chamber-Councils, and therein, Priest-like,

Thou'st cleans'd my Bosom; I from thee departed,
Thy Penitent reform'd.—But I have been
Deceiv'd in thy Integrity.

   Alcid. Forbid it, Heav'n!

   King. Thou art not honest, or thou art a Coward:
Thou'rt sworn my Servant, in the nearest Trust,
Yet saw'st a false Game play'd, the rich Stake drawn,
And took it for a Jest. O had'st thou Eyes,
T' have seen alike, my Honour, as thy Profits,
Thine own particular Thrifts, thou'd'st have done that,
Which wou'd have paid the Villain in his kind;
Be-spic'd a Cup, and giv'n *Polixenes*
A lasting Wink;—which Draught to me were Cordial.

   Alcid. No, sacred Sir, cou'd I have found Examples
Of thousands that have struck anointed Kings,
And flourish'd after the atrocious Act,
Ev'n then my Soul wou'd have refus'd Consent;
But since nor Brass, nor Stone, nor Parchment bears
The Memory of one, let Villainy
Itself forswear it.—O ye righteous Pow'rs
Judge 'twixt the Royal Friends,—but spare, O spare
A sinking Land, that wastes beneath your Wrath!

   King. There, I am touch'd indeed!—to save my People
O that my Blood were an accepted Ransom!
Great *Smintheus!* Son of the divine *Latona*,
Bend, on *Leontes*, thy Death-darting Bow,
And with redoubled Rage, arm ev'ry Shaft;
But spare my poor *Sicilians*, they are guiltless.—
How am I torn! my violated Bed,
(For Heav'n is jealous of the Fame of Kings,)
Has brought Destruction on my wretched Subjects!

   Rog. Three great Ones suffer in this heavy Charge;
Yourself, your Queen, and Son.—Might I entreat,
Till, from the *Tripos*, the dread Answer comes
That must pronounce her Fate, yet hold her spotless.

   Alcid. I have three Daughters, Sir; but by mine Honour,
If it be prov'd *Hermione* is false,
They shall not live, to bring false Generations:
Their Beauty shall not bloom, this Hand shall slay 'em.—
For ev'ry Inch of Woman in the World

Is vile, if she be so.

 King. Peace, Peace, no more.
You smell this Business with a Sense as cold,
As is a dead Man's Nose.—*Camillo*'s Flight,
Added to their Familiarity,
Which was as gross as ever touch'd Conjecture;
That lack'd Sight only, all make up to th' Deed.
However, to give Rest to others Minds,
Whose Censure has fell on us, for the Heav'ns
Have with an Aspect of ill Favour look'd
Of late upon our Kingdom, we've dispatch'd
You know, to great *Apollo*'s Priest, at *Delphos*,
Cleomenes and *Dion*. By the *Oracle*
Their Doubts will be resolv'd.—I need no more
Than what I know, and what I feel within.—

Paulina entering, an Attendant stops her.

 Atten. Your pardon, Madam, 'tis the King's Command,
You must not enter.
 Paul. From the Queen I come.
And good my Lords, be you all Seconds to me;
Fear you his tyrannous Passion more alas,
Than the Queen's Life?—a gracious innocent Soul,
More free from his Attaints, than he is jealous.
 Attend. He has not slept to-night, and has commanded
Few shou'd come near his Presence.—You by Name
He has forbid.
 Paul. Not quite so hot, good Sir.
I come to bring him Sleep; 'tis such as you,
That creep like Shadows by him, and do sigh
At each his needless Heavings, such as you,
That nourish still the Cause of his awaking.
I come with Words, as med'cinal, as true;
To purge from him that Humour which makes Sleep
Fly from his Pillow.
 King. Hence, audacious Lady!
Have I not charg'd she shou'd not come about me?
 Paul. I come, my Liege, from Queen *Hermione*,
And I beseech you hear me! who profess
Myself your loyal Servant; your Physician,

Your most obedient Counsellor: yet that dares
Less appear so, in comforting your Evils,
Than such as most seem yours. I say, I come
From your good Queen.

 King. Good Queen?—

 Paul. Again I say
Good Queen, my Lord.—If e'er *Bithynia* touch'd her
Forbiddingly, let my best Blood now turn
To an infected Jelly, and my Name
Be rank'd with their's that have betray'd the best!
Where I arrive, may my Approach be shun'd;
Nay hated too, worse than the great'st Infection
That e'er was heard, or read of.

 King. Force her hence.

 Paul. Let him that makes but Trifles of his Eyes
First hand me.

 King. All conspire?—A Nest of Traytors!—

 Alcid. I am not one, my Liege.

 Paul. Nor I, nor any,
But one, that's here; and that's himself. For he
The sacred Honour of himself, his Queen,
His hopeful Son, and his lost Infant-Daughter
Betrays to Slander, whose envenom'd Sting
Is sharper than the Sword.
Full fifteen years have shed their leafy Honours
Since my *Antigonus*, by thee enjoin'd,
(O that he less had fear'd tyrannic Pow'r!)
On his Soul's peril swore he wou'd bear hence,
To some inhospitable desart Clime
The Issue of his King.

 King. 'Tis false, gross Hag!
My Issue! rather call it what it was,
The Bastard of the curst *Polixenes.*
I am a Feather for each Wind that blows;
Each bold intruding Tongue assaults my Fame.
Were I a Tyrant, where were now your Life?
But hence, away, while yet my Mercy lasts;
A Moment longer, and my rising Rage
May fatal prove.

 Paul. Your Rage may seize my Life,

For I am weary on't.—I an old Turtle
Wou'd wing me to some wither'd Bough, and there,
My Mate, that's never to be found again,
Lament, till I am lost.—*Antigonus!*
My dearest Lord, the Husband of my Youth,
Why, why did'st thou obey this cruel King?
I thought not to have wept, but O, thy Mem'ry
Forces this female Weakness from my Eyes.
   Alcid. Remove her, she'll but more incense the King.
   Paul. Unvenerable be the Hands that dare to touch me.
Once more, O King, I beg for Leave to speak.
I've heard, but not believ'd, the Spirits of the Dead
May walk again.—If such thing be, last Night
Did my *Antigonus*, who doubtless perish'd,
When by thy stern Command he left the Innocent,
Thy Daughter for a Prey to Kites and Vultures,
Appear to his *Paulina.*—Ne'er was Dream
So like a Waking. To me comes a Creature,
Sometimes his Head on one Side, sometimes th'other,
I never saw a Vessel of like Sorrow,
So fill'd, and so becoming; in pure white Robes,
Like very Sanctity he did approach me.—
   King. Boundless of Tongue!—once more I bid thee hence.
   Paul. My Story ended, take away my Life.
Thrice did the Spectre bow itself before me;
And gasping as it wou'd begin some Speech,
Instant his Eyes became two streaming Fountains.
Their Fury spent, at length these Words broke from him.
'I was thy Husband; in my Prime of Life
Torn from thy tender Side:—*Leontes* urg'd,
And by a fatal Oath enjoin'd my Service
Against my better Mind.—His Babe I left,
(What Time the Heav'ns, as angry at the Act,
In Peals of dreadful Thunder threaten'd Vengeance,)
Upon *Bithynia*'s Shore. Fate soon o'ertook me;
Pursu'd by rav'nous Bears, my quiv'ring Flesh,
And gushing Blood, yielded a dire Repast.'
   King. Cease, fabling Dreamer, babble to the Air,
To Echo tell the visionary Fears
That ride thee, in this Dotage of thy Soul.

Paul. Now by mine Honour, all I have deliver'd
Is strictly true. From Heav'n the Vision came,
To right the Injur'd, my afflicted Mistress,
When I inform'd her of this Visitation;
With Tears, she cry'd, *Paulina*, seek the King,
My dear, but cruel Lord. Let me embrace,
Instead of these vile Bonds, a bitter Death,
If on a legal, and an open Tryal,
My Innocency rises not triumphant,
O'er all th' insidious Malice of my Foes.

    King. Dare she abide th' impartial Test of Justice?
We mean to hold a free and solemn Session:
Our Messengers, that we dispatch'd to *Delphos*,
With ev'ry coming Hour we do expect.
Apollo judge betwixt us.

Enter Messenger.

    Messen. Please your Highness,
Posts are arriv'd from those you sent to th' *Oracle:*
Cleomenes, and *Dion*, are both landed,
And hast'ning to the Court.

    Alcid. Their Speed, my Liege,
Has been beyond Account.

    King. Scarce twenty Days
Have they been absent.—Lords, prepare you all;
Summon a session, that we may arraign,
In open Court, our most disloyal Lady.—
For as she hath been publickly accus'd,
So shall she have a just and open Tryal.
Whence these Misgivings?—wherefore is my Heart
Assaulted on a Sudden thus by Fear?
O, the inextricable Toil of Doubting!—
Unfold, great *Phœbus*, the mysterious Truth.
To thy Decision I my Cause will trust;
I have been cruel, or I have been just.   [*Exeunt.*

*   *   *

Act V, [Scene iii] Paulina's *House.*

Enter Leontes, Polixenes, Florizel, Perdita, Camillo, Paulina, *Lords,*
and Attendants.

*   *   *

Paul. Please you to interpose, fair Madam, kneel,
And pray your Mother's Blessing. Turn, good Lady,
Our *Perdita* is found.

                          [*Presenting* Perdita *to* Hermione.

Herm. You Gods, look down,
And from your sacred Vials pour your Graces
Upon my Daughter's Head. Tell me, mine own,
Where hast thou been preserv'd? where liv'd? how found
Thy Father's Court? for thou shalt hear, that I
Knowing by *Paulina* that the Oracle
Gave hope thou was't in being, have preserv'd
My self to see the Issue.

Perd. Gracious Powers!
What means this vast Profusion, this Extreme
Of heavenly Mercy?—

Flor. Thought is lost in Wonder!
Admiring Man may offer to the Gods
The tributary Sacrifice of Praise,
And grateful Thanks, for all their mighty Blessings,
But who presumes to scan th'impervious Ways,
By which they're wrought, proclaims aloud his Folly.

Leon. Have I been murm'ring, and with impious Rage
Cur'st ev'n my Being, wish'd myself extinct,
And number'd with the Dead; while Heav'n unseen,
With interposing Love, was kindly lab'ring
The full Completion of my earthly Bliss?
Pardon, *Hermione*; pardon me, Brother,
That e'er I put between your holy Looks
My ill Suspicion.

Herm. O, my dearest Lord!
This blessed Reconcilement overpays me,
For all the Agonies that rent my Heart
In the long Age of our sad Separation!—

Leon. Life of my Life! my Soul rejoices in thee,
As when in Youth, after three wasted Moons
Of cold Reluctance, with an amorous Sigh,
At last I made thee open thy white Hand,
And clepe thyself my Love. Prince *Florizel*,
And thou my long-lost *Perdita*, join Hands.

Brother, your Aid.—(My Queen smiles her Consent).
The Benediction of th'immortal Gods,
Thus supplicated by a Pair of Kings,
Descend from Heav'n upon you.

    Polix. Genial Love,
And Tenderness without Satiety,
Wait on your mutual Vows.

    Floriz. My Joys exceed
All that Imagination ever painted,
Ev'n when my raptur'd Fancy highest soar'd,
And swell'd my Bosom with the glorious Hope
That this blest Hour wou'd come.—My *Perdita*,
What shall I say?—But thou who know'st my Heart,
Know'st it's Recesses are all open to thee.

    Perd. My Prince! my *Florizel!*—I own my Soul
In secret long has languish'd: Why I knew not,
Or whence the Impulse came; but in my Cottage,
My Thoughts have hit the Palaces of Kings:
And now the golden Vision, like the Sun,
Has broke upon me, in full Streams of Glory;
And given me to reward thy faithful Passion,
Not with a Shepherd's Daughter, but a Princess.

    Floriz. Thou lovely Maid!—such is thy native Worth,
That I am richer, in possessing thee,
Than twenty Seas, if all their Sands were Pearl.

    Paul. Get ye together all, ye precious Winners;
Let each partake of th' other's Exultation;
Whilst I am happy in the gen'ral Joy.
No more my private Sorrows will I mourn,
Since this blest Day hath made a large Amends,
Ev'n for the Loss of my belov'd *Antigonus.*

    Leon. Thy Hand, *Hermione:* thou art a Proof
That only *Innocence* can be our Guard
Against the rude Assaults, and Shocks of Fortune.
'Tis that secures us the protecting Hand
Of gracious Providence. Hence learn, ye Fair,
That *Innocence* is Heaven's peculiar Care.

                           [*Exeunt omnes.*

154. Tobias Smollett and Samuel Derrick on the current adaptations of Shakespeare

1756

From the *Critical Review: or, Annals of Literature. By A Society of Gentlemen*, I (March 1756), pp. 144–8.

The first piece is assigned to Smollett in the annotated copy of the *Critical Review* in the University of Oregon library (D. Roper, *RES* n.s. 10 (1959), pp. 41–3), the other two to Samuel Derrick (1724–69), an unsuccessful actor turned miscellaneous writer ('the little Irishman' as Smollett called him, who 'was my Amanuensis and has occasionally been employed as a trash reader for the *Critical Review*'). Derrick (who edited Dryden's miscellaneous works in 1760, produced *The Dramatic Censor* in 1752 and *A Poetical Dictionary* in four volumes in 1761), figured in the London literary circle that included Johnson and Boswell, and in 1761 was appointed Master of the Ceremonies at Bath. Tobias Smollett (1721–71), surgeon, historian, novelist and translator, also led an active career as a journalist. Co-founder of the *Critical Review* in 1756, he was an editor and major contributor until 1763, when he set off (for reasons of health) on a two-year journey through France and Italy. He was also editor of the *British Magazine* from 1760 to 1763, of the *Briton* in 1762, and contributed to other periodicals.

---

[a] *The* WINTER'S TALE. *A play alter'd from* Shakespeare, by Charles Marsh.

The practice of altering *Shakespeare* is like that of mending an old *Roman* causeway by the hands of a modern paviour, tho' far less excusable, because not undertaken for use or convenience. A man of true taste will have more pleasure in seeing the ruins of a *Grecian* temple than in examining all the commodities of the neatest box in

Hackney, or in *Hammersmith*: even the irregularity of some *Gothic* edifices exhibits a rude, stupendous grandeur which, notwithstanding all its incorrectness, strikes the beholder with admiration and awe.

Mr *Marsh* has been very frugal in decorating the ground of *Shakespeare* with his own embroidery; and so far he is commendable. He has, by altering the word *Bohemia* into *Bithynia*, mended the geography of *Shakespeare*, who represents an inland country as situated on the sea coast; but he has retained an anachronism of equal absurdity in mentioning *Julio Romano* as a famous painter in the time of the *Delphian* oracle, whereas that artist lived above one thousand four hundred years after the oracle had ceased.

Instead of beginning the play with the jealous conceptions of *Leontes* before the birth of *Perdita*, and proceeding to represent the fate of *Antigonus* when he was sent to expose that infant, he cuts off fifteen years of the tale and opens the scene immediately before the arrival of the deputies from *Delphos*. This expedient of curtailing in some measure removes the improbability that shocks the imagination of a person that sees the performance acted, but even this improbability he has removed by halves, for the scene is still shifted from one kingdom to another, and he has concluded the third act in the middle of a scene.

Since he was resolved to alter *Shakespeare*, he might have suppressed the death of prince *Mamillius* and spared us the detail of the dreadful fate that befell *Antigonus* and the ship's crew, which create a confusion of tragedy and comedy and destroy the propriety of the composition; for since the garment of our *British Homer* was to be new cut it might have been reduced entirely to the fashion. (144-5)

[b] CATHARINE *and* PETRUCHIO. *A comedy in three acts. As it is performed at the theatre-royal in* Drury-lane. *Alter'd from* Shakespeare's Taming of the Shrew.

This title is of a piece with the scheme of the knavish hostler who pretended to shew an horse with his head where his tail should be, and when he had collected a pocket full of halfpence from the mob admitted them into a stable, where they saw a gelding standing with his tail towards the rack and manger. Tho' every individual had seen horses before there was not one in the crowd that would venture on his own judgment to declare that there was nothing extraordinary in this animal, and so the hostler kept his halfpence, and his skin whole. Our wits and managers may change *Shakespeare*'s position, or his perriwig, so they do not alter his features; tho' we do not remember to have seen a more flagrant imposition of the kind than the exhibition of this performance as a new entertainment on the stage.

He must have a great taste and infinite veneration for *Shakespeare* who thus fritters his plays into farces, and entertains the town with a single episode, spun out into three acts with so little contrivance that while a couple of short scenes are representing on the stage *Petruchio* and his bride mount their horse, ride a journey, in which they receive a fall and are accommodated at a farmhouse, get a horseback again, and arrive at a country seat which was at some distance from *Padua*, inasmuch as *Grumio* was almost frozen to death by the way. Such a genius in machinery might have supplied them from his own warehouse of wonders with a *Pegasus* or *Hypogriff* for their conveyance, and brought them souse from the clouds with great applause. (145–6)

[c] *The* TEMPEST, *an opera. Taken from* Shakespeare, *and performed at the theatre-royal in* Drury-lane. *The music composed by Mr.* Smith.

As an opera this performance does not come under our cognizance, and we have no doubt but Mr *Smith* has given sufficient proofs of his genius in the musical part; but as it is an alteration from *Shakespeare* we cannot overlook it. It is impossible for us to view the father of the *English* stage, thus cruelly mangled and unhappily pieced, without regret. Alterations, it seems, were necessary in order to adapt it to music, but if Mr *Garrick* finds that *Shakespeare* will not go down without music, an assertion which he will not undertake to advance, he surely may entrust the altering of him to somebody who, in abbreviating and curtailing will do more justice to the author than the manufacturer of the piece in hand, who seems to have studied making the Recitatives as rough and dissonant as possible by needless abbreviations, the avoiding which would certainly have given more general satisfaction to the public and more ease to the musical performer, as being more harmonious. The Airs of this opera are taken from *Shakespeare, Dryden, Cowley*, &c. (147–8)

155. John Berkenhout on Marsh's adaptation of *The Winter's Tale*

1756

From the *Monthly Review*, xiv (March, 1756), p. 270.

John Berkenhout (1730?–91), physician, naturalist and miscellaneous writer, was a frequent contributor to the *Monthly Review*, dealing mostly with military and medical topics. In 1777 he published *Biographia Literaria: or a biographical history of literature. . . .*, which was intended to cover all British authors up to that date, but of which only the first volume (reaching the end of the sixteenth century) ever appeared.

The Winter's Tale. A Play, altered from Shakespeare, by Charles Marsh.

The motto to this performance seems to intimate that the Author is out of humour with Mr Garrick for bringing upon the stage his own alteration of the same play in preference to this.

This tragi-comi-pastoral play is, of all Shakespeare's dramatic pieces, one of the most *unalterable*: the time of action being no less than sixteen years, and the scenes twice changed to very distant countries. The first of these absurdities is lopt by the pruning knife of Mr Marsh; but he has suffered the other, tho' equally monstrous, to remain. He has generally transposed the scenes, and frequently mingled his own poetry with that of Shakespeare, but the different muses are easily distinguished. To alter Shakespeare is a very bold undertaking. There is something so very great, and peculiar, in his manner that most of those who have hitherto dared to mix their compositions with those of our old inimitable bard have, instead of shewing their own genius to advantage, only convinced the world of Shakespeare's infinite superiority.

156. Frances Brooke on *King Lear*

1756

From the *Old Maid*, no. 18 (13 March 1756); this text from 'A New Edition, Revised and corrected by the Editor' (1764).

Frances Brooke (1724–89), poet, essayist, translator and novelist (*Lady Julia Mandeville*, 1763), also wrote a tragedy and two 'operas', one of which (*Rosina*, 1783) had a great success. She was co-editor of the *Old Maid*, a journal which appeared in thirty-seven numbers from 15 November 1755 to 24 July 1756.

> *This player here*
> *But in a fiction, in a dream of passion,*
> *Could force his soul so to his own conceit,*
> *That from her working, all his visage warm'd;*
> *Tears in his eyes, distraction in his aspect,*
> *A broken voice, and his whole function suiting*
> *With forms to his conceit*   [*Hamlet*, 2.2.544ff.]

I was prevailed upon by *Rosara* and my niece to go the other night to see *Barry* in *King Lear*, and I own myself obliged to them for the very great pleasure the representation gave me. I went with three of my six critical virgins into a part of the house where we enjoyed the double advantage of seeing the play and observing upon the audience, and I had the satisfaction of finding we were accompanied in our tears by almost the whole house. The young people, especially, showed such a becoming sensibility as gives me hopes virtue has a stronger party in the rising generation than those of my age in general are inclined to allow.

I think it a great mark of judgment in Mr *Barry* that he has thrown so strong and affecting a cast of tenderness into the character. He never loses sight of the Father, but in all his rage, even in the midst of his severest curses, you see that his heart, heavily injured as he is, and provoked to the last excess of fury, still owns the offenders for his children. Without this circumstance his concessions, when he meets with them at *Gloster*'s Castle, and his offering to return with *Goneril* with only fifty of his knights, would appear a degree of meanness; but we see in his whole manner that paternal fondness is combating his resentments, and that he endeavours, in spite of all appearances, to think them innocent. That this is the sense of the poet seems to me plain from the following passage, when on *Cornwall*'s and *Regan*'s refusal to see him he flies out into such a very just, though strong passion of anger:

> *The king wou'd speak with* Cornwall, *the dear father*
> *Wou'd with his daughter speak, commands her service:*
> *Are they inform'd of this? My breath and blood!*
> *Fiery? the fiery duke? Tell the hot duke that–* [2.4.99ff.]

This rage is no more than they merited, but the father's love checks him in all the heat of it:

> *No, but not yet, may be they are not well.* [2.4.103]

We see in this line that his fondness is forming an excuse for them, though their ill usage of his servant and almost every circumstance of their behaviour might have convinced him they were altogether fallen off from duty; and therefore this performer's manner of playing *Lear* appears perfectly consistent with the whole meaning of the poet.

His figure is so happily disguised that you lose Mr *Barry*, and have no other idea on his first appearance than that of a very graceful, venerable, kingly, old man. But it is not in his person alone he supports the character: his whole action is of a piece, and the breaks in his voice, which are uncommonly beautiful, seem the effect of real, not personated sorrow.

I am apt to imagine from his masterly performance of *Lear* that this actor is capable of playing a much greater variety of characters than he has yet attempted, and that he is yet far from knowing half his dramatic powers.

Though I am naturally much more inclined to praise than censure yet I cannot help taking notice of what I think a very extraordinary absurdity, which is the present manner of playing the Gentleman Usher. Whoever reads the play will, if I am not greatly mistaken, see in that character no more than a saucy, surly, impudent servant, vain of his lady's favour. But in the representation he is metamorphosed into a singing, dancing Fribble; and a comic character created contrary, as I apprehend, to the apparent meaning of the author. I allow that, taking it in that light, Mr *Shuter* is extremely well in it; but I think it treating the poet a little too cavalierly to new mould in this manner one of his characters. Especially as it answers no purpose but taking off our attention from the tender and noble sensations which are excited by the distresses of the principal personage, and disturbing the best emotions of the human heart by impertinent and ill-timed mirth.

I cannot conclude without taking notice of the applause Mr *Ryan* meets with in the counterfeited madness of *Edgar*. Applause which I heard with more pleasure because I am told he has played his part in the great drama of life in such a manner as not only to deserve but, what is more uncommon, to acquire universal approbation, and that he has been excelled by nobody in the real character of a worthy, deserving, and truly honest man.

It has always been matter of great astonishment to me that both the houses have given *Tate*'s alteration of *King Lear* the preference to *Shakespeare*'s excellent original, which Mr *Addison*, the most candid as well as judicious of critics, thinks so infinitely preferable as to bear no degree of comparison.[1] And one cannot help remarking particularly, and with some surprize, that Mr *Garrick*, who professes himself so warm an idolater of this inimitable poet and who is determined, if I may use his own words, in the prologue to the *Winter's Tale*,[2]

> *To lose no drop of this immortal man,*

should yet prefer the adulterated cup of *Tate* to the pure genuine draught offered him by the master he avows to serve with such fervency of devotion.

As to Mr *Barry*, I think he was perfectly right to take the *Lear* which is commonly play'd, that the competition between him and Mr *Garrick* in this trying part may be exhibited to the public upon a fair footing. I have not yet been so fortunate as to see the latter in it, whose performance, I doubt not, is no less justly than generally celebrated and admired. But the advantage Mr *Barry* has from his person, the variety of his voice, and its particular aptitude to express the differing tones which sorrow, pity, or rage naturally produce, are of such service to him in this character that he could not fail of pleasing, though he did not play it with all the judgment which in my opinion he does. (145–50)

[1] See Vol. 2, p. 273.
[2] See No. 152 above.

157. Theophilus Cibber, Garrick's Shakespeare

1756

From *Two Dissertations on Theatrical Subjects*, (1756); this text from the second edition (1759), which adds *An epistle from Mr. Theophilus Cibber to David Garrick esq.*, first published 1755.

Theophilus Cibber (1703–58), actor and dramatist, son of Colley Cibber (see Vol. 2, No. 38 and Vol. 3, No. 92) made adaptations of *Henry VI* in 1723 and *Romeo and Juliet* in 1744. His career included spells as patentee and manager of Drury Lane, and he acted at all the London theatres and in Dublin.

[From the first *Dissertation*]

The present Season is now above half over,* and what has been done?— Why, the Town has been entertained with a frequent Repetition of their old Plays and stale Farces; and one Farce, entitled the *Fair Quaker of Deal*, has been palm'd upon the Town as a reviv'd Comedy, and exhibited a greater Number of Nights than formerly better Plays, much better acted, were ever known to reign. As *Bartholomew Fair* has been some Years suppress'd the politic Manager contriv'd to introduce Drolls on the Stage at the Theatre Royal in *Drury-Lane*. 'Twas usual with the Masters of Droll Booths to get some Genius of a lower Class to supply 'em with Scenes, detach'd from our Plays, altered and adapted to the Taste of the holiday Audiences they were commonly perform'd to. This Hint the Manager has taken, and of this gallimaufry Kind was the Pastoral (as he call'd it) exhibited at *Drury's* Theatre.

The *Winter's Tale* of *Shakespeare*, tho' one of his most irregular Pieces, abounds with beautiful Strokes and touching Circumstances. The very Title (*A Winter's Tale*) seems fix'd on by the Author as an Apology for, and a bespeaking of, a loose Plan, regardless of Rule as to

* This Dissertation was first deliver'd towards the End of *January*, 1756.

250

Time or Place. The Story affected his Mind, and afforded a large Field for his lively Imagination to wander in. And here the Poet,[1]

> Fancy's sweetest Child,
> Warbles his native Wood-Notes wild.

In the Alteration many of the most interesting Circumstances, the most affecting Passages, and the finest Strokes in writing which mark the Characters most strongly and are most likely to move the Heart, are entirely omitted, such as the Jealousy of *Leontes*, the Trial of *Hermione*, &c. What remains is so unconnected, is such a Mixture of piecemeal, motley Patchwork that *The Winter's Tale* of *Shakespeare*, thus lop'd, hack'd, and dock'd, appears without Head or Tail.

In order to curtail it to three Acts the Story of the three first Acts of the original Play (and which contain some of the noblest Parts) are crowded into a dull Narrative, in the Delivery of which the Performer makes no happy Figure. So at the Beginning of the third Act the principal Parts of the Story, which in the Alteration we might have expected to have seen represented, were given in two long-winded Relations by two unskill'd Performers, whose Manner made 'em appear 'As tedious as a twice told Tale, vexing the dull Ear of a drowsy Man.' And this hasty Hash, or Hotch-potch, is call'd altering *Shakespeare*. Whenever *Shakespeare* is to be cut up let's hope, some more delicate Hand and judicious Head will be concern'd in the Direction.

> Let's carve him, like a Dish fit for the Gods!
> Not hew him, like a Carcass fit for Hounds.
> [*Julius Caesar*, 2.1.174]

I have heard of an Actor who humourously told one of his Brother Comedians, that, whenever he had a Part where the Redundancy of the Author run into too great a Length in the Scenes he had recourse to a whimsical Expedient for the shortning of 'em. He had the whole Part wrote out, and then gave it his Cat to play with. What Puss claw'd off the Actor left out, yet he generally found enough remain'd to satisfy the Audience.

In this frolicksome Manner seems Master *Davy* to have laid his wanton Claws on *Shakespeare*'s *Winter's Tale*. Or perhaps he follow'd the Actor's Example, and left the Laceration of it to his Cat. Sure, he was not so avaritiously unreasonable to demand of his Brother Manager

---

[1] Milton: cf. Vol. 1, p. 2.

the Profits of the Third, Sixth and Ninth Nights for the Benefit of his Cat.

However, his Houses were crowded, for what he designs to give must be receiv'd: it is *Hobson*'s Choice with the Town. These monopolising Venders of Wit, like Fellows that sell Wine in a Jail, consult not the Health or Pleasure of their Customers, but as it adds to their Profit, force a Sale of their Balderdash and then demand the Price of the best Wines, no Matter whether or no it pleases the Palates of the Purchasers, they must have that or nothing.

Were *Shakespeare*'s Ghost to rise, wou'd he not frown Indignation on this pilfering Pedlar in Poetry who thus shamefully mangles, mutilates, and emasculates his Plays? The *Midsummer's Night's Dream* has been minc'd and fricaseed into an indigested and unconnected Thing call'd *The Fairies*; *The Winter's Tale* mammoc'd into a Droll; *The Taming of the Shrew* made a Farce of; and *The Tempest* castrated into an Opera. Oh! what an agreeable Lullaby might it have prov'd to our Beaus and Belles to have heard *Caliban*, *Sycorax*, and one of the Devils trilling of Trios. And how prettily might the North-Wind (like the Tyrant *Barbarossa*) be introduc'd with soft Musick! To crown all, as the *Chinese* Festival prov'd the Devil of a Dance, how cleverly might it have been introduc'd in *The Tempest* new-vamp'd, as a Dance of frolicksome Devils!

Rouse *Britons*, rouse, for shame, and vindicate the Cause of Sense thus sacrific'd to Mummery! Think you see *Shakespeare's Injur'd Shade*, with Patriot-Anguish, sighing over your implicit Belief and Passive Obedience, your Non-Resistance to this Profanation of his Memory. He grieves to see your tame Submission to this merciless *Procrustes* of the Stage who wantonly, as cruelly, massacres his dear Remains. Are you not ready to cry out 'Ye Gods! what Havock does this Scribbler make among *Shakespeare*'s Works!' Yet this sly Prince would insinuate, all this ill Usage of the Bard is owing forsooth to his Love of him! Much such a mock Proof of his tender Regard as *The Cobler's Drubbing his Wife*.

In the two last Bellman-like nonsensical Lines of his absurd Prologue to the *Winter's Tale* he tells you[1]

> That 'tis his Joy, his Wish, his only Plan,
> To lose no Drop of that immortal Man!

Why truly, in the aforemention'd Pieces he does bottle him up with

[1] See above, No. 152.

a Vengeance! He throws away all the spirited Part of him, all that bears the highest Flavour. (i 32–7).

* * *

[On Garrick's over-literal acting.]

Of this Kind is the pantomimical acting every Word in a Sentence. When *Benedick* says 'If I do, hang me in a Bottle like a Cat, and shoot at me!' [1.1.222f.] methinks this slight short Sentence requires not such a Variety of Action as minutely to describe the Cat being clapp'd into the Bottle, then being hung up, and the farther painting of the Man shooting at it. But such Things we have seen, nay sometimes seen applauded. Observe the Golden Rule of not too much; this Rule every Actor shou'd pay regard to.

But how is this observed when *Richard* (as I have seen it played) in his very first Speech, wherein he describes his sullen Mood of Mind, his Restlessness of Spirit unemployed in War, his conscious Unfitness to join in the sportive, piping, medley Amusements of idle Peace, ironically says,[1]

> I have no Delights to pass away my Hours,
> Unless to see my Shadow in the Sun,
> And descant on my own Deformity.

This Idea of descanting on his own Deformity is what his hurt Imagination would naturally turn from the Moment it occurs to him. But for the Sake of an Attitude which is sure to be dwelt on 'till the Audience clap, this Sentence is commonly clos'd with an Action of pointing to the Ground and fixing the Eye thereon for some Time, as if *Richard* had a real Delight in ruminating on his uncouth Person. Again, after he has woo'd and (to his own Surprise) has won the Widow *Anne*, can we suppose that *Richard* is such a Fool as really to think himself comely of Person when he, exulting on his Success in wanton Pleasantry, breaks out:[2]

> My Dukedom to a Widow's Chastity,
> I do mistake my Person all this while.

Or when he says[3]

[1] Cibber's adaptation, 1.2.16ff. (Vol. 2, p. 109); *Richard III*, 1.1.25ff.
[2] Cibber, 2.1.267f.; *Richard III*, 1.2.251f.
[3] Cibber, 2.1.271ff.; *Richard III*, 1.2.255ff.

I'll have my Chambers lin'd with Looking-Glass,
And entertain a Score or Two of Taylors
To study Fashions to adorn my Body.

Richard is not such a Simpleton seriously to intend this: 'tis Laughter all, and Mockery of the Widow's Weakness. Yet I have seen a *Richard*, when he makes his Exit with these Lines,[1]

Shine out fair Sun 'till I salute my Glass,
That I may see my Shadow as I pass.

this Rum-Duke *Richard* has gone halting off, all the Way looking at and admiring his suppos'd Shadow on the Ground.

Is this being the Actor? Is it not Buffoonery? But what shall we think of a *Richard* who, in the last Act, when he is met by *Norfolk* in the Field at the Head of the Army, instead of assuming the Air of Gallantry and Intrepidity which marks the Character of *Richard*, what shall we think of a *Richard* who bounces on like a Madman and bellows out[2]

Well, *Norfolk*, what thinkst thou now?

Might not Master *Norfolk* reply, 'I think you are mad, Sir'? But the mouthing Rant infected the inferior Performer, who in Return roared out[3]

That we shall conquer, Sir.

Nay, to that Extravagance is this Mockery of Spirit carried on that *Richard* reads the few Lines *Norfolk* puts into his Hand in a vociferous angry Tone, as if he knew their Meaning e'er he saw them. Tho' the very Lines that follow shew *Richard* is unmov'd by 'em, and scornfully disregards 'em: 'A weak Invention of the Enemy.'[4] But that cool Scorn I have heard ranted out as if poor *Richard* was quite out of his Wits. What Consistency of Character is here preserv'd, or what Regard paid to Nature? Is it not Mummery all?

The frequent Starts with which our Stage Performances abound at present are not unworthy Notice. They are so common they sometimes tire the Eye, and often so improper they offend the Understanding. Some of this Sort we have seen in *Romeo*. This unhappy Lover, when in the last Act he is inform'd of the Death of his beloved *Juliet*, is at once

1 Cibber, 2.1.278f.; *Richard III*, 1.2.262f.
2 Cibber, 5.7.12 (Vol. 2, p. 126); *Richard III*, 5.3.301.
3 Cibber, 5.7.13 (Vol. 2, p. 126).
4 Cibber, 5.7.17 (Vol. 2, p. 126).

struck with a deep Despair and immediately determines that Night to embrace her, even in Death. He coolly resolves on taking Poison, and sends a Letter to inform his Father of the Cause of his Death. He has but little Time to execute this in, the Night being far spent. Yet the Actor can find Time, it seems, between his quitting the Apothecary and his going to the Tomb to shift his Cloaths that he may die, with the Decency of a Malefactor, in a Suit of Black. This Trick of Stage Drapery puts one in Mind of Miss *Notable*, a young jilting *Coquette* who, when she's informed one of her young Lovers is wounded in a Duel on her Account, amidst her affected violent Exclamations of Grief, says, 'She'll go and see the dear Creature; but it shall be in an Undress. 'Twill be proper, at least, to give her Grief the Appearance of as much Disorder as possible. Yes, I'll change my Dress immediately.' And so she does. But what need for *Romeo* to do this? Has he Leisure, or wou'd he bestow a Thought on such a Trifle?

Well, but he's now going to the Tomb. His first Thought is to dispatch his Servant, from whom he conceals his real Intent and threatens him to presume to watch him at Peril of his Life. Yet on the opening of the Scene the Actor, with folded Arms, advances about three or four Steps, then jumps, and starts into an Attitude of Surprize. —At what?—Why, at the Sight of a Monument he went to look for.— And there he stands 'till a Clap from the Audience relieves him from his Post. Is not this forced? Is it not misplaced? Is it not as improper as ranting loudly those Threats to his Servant which shou'd be delivered in an under Voice, expressive of Terror, but not mouth'd out loud enough to alarm the Watch?

I wou'd also submit it to the Judgment of the Public whether a favourite Attitude into which *Romeo* throws himself on the Appearance of *Paris* is a Beauty or an Absurdity? *Romeo* is a Gentleman, has a Sword by his Side, education is a second Nature. May we not reasonably suppose that, on his being diverted from his Purpose of opening the Tomb when call'd on by *Paris*, that he would immediately drop that unwieldly Instrument, the Iron Crow, and have recourse to his Sword? Would not this be the instinctive Resource of the Gentleman? But then this *Cyclopedian* Attitude wou'd be lost in which *Romeo* now stands long enough to give *Paris* Time to run him thro' the Body, which wou'd be justifiable when a Man saw such a Weapon rais'd by an Enemy to dash out his Brains.

No Wonder the Generality of an Audience clap, as they may well be astonished to see my little *Romeo* wield this massy Instrument with such Dexterity. But their Admiration would cease when let into the Secret that this seeming iron Crow is really but a painted wooden one. Were it not so, it would be as impossible for the fictitious *Romeo* to manage it as it is improbable the real *Romeo* would have made such a Use of it. The Author did not intend he should, since he makes 'em both engage with their Swords, as Gentlemen naturally wou'd. (i, 64–71).

*   *   *

[From the second *Dissertation*]

[In a dream the narrator attends a ceremony at which the worthless plays of recent years are burned.]

*   *   *

Among 'em were the inimitable Comedy of *Gil-Blas*, the incomparable prosaic Tragedy call'd the *Gamester*, and the sublime *Barbarossa*; to these were added that excellent Droll of three Acts called *The Winter's Tale*, the mangled Farce of *Catherine and Petruchio*, that childish Masque called the *Faries*, and that mutilated Play called the *Tempest*, frittered into a mock *English* Opera. All these were immediately, by order of *Minos*, laid on a Pile together and burnt by the Hands of a Printer's Devil. Most of the Spirit and Fire which formerly animated these last mentioned Pieces having been entirely extracted by the present curious hypercritical Editor and malapert Mar-Play, and their poor Remains so damped by the Stuff he had crammed into 'em, no Flame arose from the consuming Leaves, but they evaporated in a thick Smoak.

During this Ceremony News came from Earth that the *English* Opera called the *Tempest* was in no Danger of pestering the Town many Nights, notwithstanding the Puffs and Orders to support it. This Instance of returning Taste, and the proper Contempt the Public shew'd for these Manglers of *Shakespeare* by forbearing to attend these savage Scalpers of this immortal Bard, diffused a general Joy amongst all the Connoisseurs below. A loud Applause re-echoed thro' the Place and wakened me.

Yet waking, I found it was not all a Dream. The Public reassume their Right to judge, they no longer implicitly approve all the Trash this crafty Costard-Monger would impose on 'em, nor, on his *Ipse Dixit*, will accept of a Green-Crab in lieu of a Pine-Apple. Even the last new Tragedy, tho' paraded into the World with the usual Puff of 'its excelling all that went before it!' not, like it's Predecessors, ran rapid on but limpingly endeavour'd to get forward. At length we found (as appeared by the *Public Advertiser*),

> Great *Athelstan* grew sick,—O fatal Stroke!
> Of empty Seats, and Boxes unbespoke!

A fresh Instance of the unbiassed Judgment of the Public has appeared in their candid Reception of Mr *Barry* in the Character of *King Lear*, and the universal Applause they have bestowed on his excellent Performance.

This high-drawn Character has been long the Admiration of the Public. One Actor having the sole Possession of it for these fourteen Years past, and having surprised the Town by his spirited and early Performance of it, most People were so prejudiced in his Behalf that many censured Mr *Barry* for the Undertaking, previous to his appearing therein. Nay, several as rashly as ungenerously (on Notice given of the intended Performance) did not stick to call it an impudent Attempt. So strong is Prepossession that some good-natured Persons had their Doubts concerning him. But to do him Justice his Performance has cleared 'em all. So whimsical were some of these prejudiced Persons in their Objections they even urged he was too tall for the Part; yet I think 'tis generally allowed the Advantage of tall Stature is a Beauty in Nature, it expresses a Kind of natural Dignity. When we read the History of any Monarch or Hero we seldom annex the Idea of a little Man, unless some Passage in the History particularly marks him as such. Nor have I ever heard of any Dramatic Law or Act of Parliament to reduce our Kings to the low Standard in which they are sometimes represented.

I mean no Reflections hereby on any one who may be disqualified, as myself, for a Grenadier, nor do I presume to hint that a great Mind may not inhabit the small Body of a Man, even of but five Foot five Inches. Long since it was remarked 'that daring Souls often dwell in little Men.' Not to give Praise to the little Gentleman [Garrick] for his Performance in some Parts of this Character were doing him Injustice: there is a quick spirited Manner in his Execution that often sets off many Passages therein. But when we consider the chief Characteristicks of *Lear* to be Pride and Impatience—a kingly Pride, hitherto uncontrouled —and an impetuous Temper as soon susceptible of Anger, Rage, and Fury as Flax is ready to catch Fire, and in the Expression of those Passions as quick and rapid as the Lightning's Flash: if this is the Case (and I have often heard it allowed) must we not give the Preference to

Mr *Barry*, not only in majestic Deportment and Gracefulness of Action but also in his Manner of imprecating the Curse this injured Monarch throws out against his unnatural Daughter? Can the Actor be too rapid in the Delivery? Do not long Pauses damp the Fire of it like cold Water dropp'd thereon? 'Tis hasty, rash, and uttered in the Whirlwind of his Passion: too long a Preparation for it seems not consistent with *Lear*'s Character, 'tis here unnatural. Such long Pauses give him Time to reflect, which the hasty *Lear* is not apt to do 'till 'tis too late. This philosophic Manner would become a Man who took Time to recollect; which if *Lear* did, would not the good King, the o'er-kind Father change this dire Curse into a fervent Prayer for his Child's Repentance and Amendment?

To prepare this Curse with an overstrained Look of solemn Address, long dwelt on before the Curse begins, makes what the Author designed to excite Pity and Terror become detestable and horrible. So dire is the Curse, Nature can scarce endure it unless delivered in the rapid Manner the wild Transport of the choleric King, with sudden and unchecked Passion, would surely give it. When it appears premeditated it speaks Rancour, Spleen, and Malice; a cool Revenge; not a Burst of Passion from an o'ercharged Heart. Whether this Remark is just is left to the Determination of the judicious Public.

I have seen both these Gentlemen play *King Lear* within a few Days of one another. I must confess I had Pleasure from the Performance of the lesser Monarch in several Passages. My Expectation had indeed been greatly raised by the many Encomiums lavished on him, but were not answered to my Wish. There was a Petitness attended the Performance which I thought not quite equal to the Character. His Behaviour often liable to Censure, particularly, I thought, at the End of those Scenes where the unnatural Behaviour of his Daughters work him up almost to Frenzy.

Does not the preceding and following Parts point out to us that *Lear* rushes wildly from beneath the Roof where he has been so unhospitably treated? Why then is he to sink into the Arms of his Attendants? Thus helpless, as he there affects to appear, tho' his Daughter turned him out of Doors surely his Attendants would have convey'd him to some Place of Rest. Yet by the Play we find he roams into the Wood, exposing himself unto the Storm. Besides the Error of this fainting Fit let us examine how 'tis executed. His Spirits being quite exhausted, he drops almost lifeless into the Arms of his Attendants. Do they carry him off? Why, no! Relaxed as we may suppose his whole Machine (for his

Head and Body are both thrown extravagantly behind as if his Neck and Back were broke) yet his Knees (which in Nature would most likely falter first) are still so able to support him in that odd-bent Condition that he walks off, with the regular Stiff-Step of a Soldier in his Exercise on the Parade. Is this consistent? Is this natural? Is this Character? Does not this uncouth Appearance, with his bent-back Body and dropping Head, rather resemble the uncomely Distortion of a Posture-Master when he walks the Sea-Crab, as they call it?

By the Introduction of such Extravagancies he seems to have borrowed a Hint from our Brother *Bayes* when he says 'I scorn your dull Fellows, who borrow all they do from Nature, I'm for fetching it out of my own Fancy I.' And a pretty Fancy it is truly! I question if it would have entered into the Imagination of any other Man. But, as *Bayes* again says, 'It serves to elevate and surprise.' Thus the Actor is satisfied if he can gain a Clap from the upper Gallery, while the Pit and Boxes, with a silent Shrug alone, condemn such *outré* Behaviour.

Certainly the Author meant not this fainting Fit, or that *Lear* should stay to be held. He rather meant the King in Hurry of his Rage and Grief, stung to the Heart by those *unnatural Hags*, should fly all Roofs, shun all Attendance, Pomp, and Ceremony, should strive, in his Agony of Soul, to fly himself, if possible.

I have been informed (I know not how true it may be, tho' the Story is not unlikely), that when Mr *Garrick* first undertook the Part of King *Lear* he went to *Bedlam* to learn to act a Madman. It had not been a very improper School, perhaps, had he been to have play'd some of the low ridiculous mad Characters in *The Pilgrim*. But as we do not hear of any mad King being locked up there I do not readily conceive how his Visit to those elder Brothers of the Sky could answer his Purpose. One might imagine his Judgment (if he has any) might have suggested to him a considerable Difference in the Behaviour of a real King, by great Distress drove to distraction, and the Fantasque of a poor mad Taylor who, in a Kind of frolick Delirium, imagines himself a King. Tho' the Mockery of King *Cabbage* might cause a Smile with our Pity, yet sure the deplorable Situation of the real Monarch would rather rive the Heart than excite Risibility.

I am at a Loss to guess what End this Visit to the Palace in *Moor-Fields* could answer. 'Tis probable the most striking Objects he could fix his Eye on, and the most worthy his Attention, are plac'd over the Gate to that Entrance. I imagine no one would think *Shakespeare* would have paid such a Visit, to have learn't from the *Medley Jargon* of those unhappy Maniacs Matter to have furnished out his Scenes of *Lear*'s Madness! No, his amazing Genius, whose extensive Imagination took in all Nature and, with a Judgment adequate arranged his Ideas, giving proper Sentiment, Language, and Spirit to every Character when *Lear*'s Madness struck his raptured Fancy, 'the Poet's Brain, in a fine fiery Fit of Frenzy rowling,' wanted not such mean Resources.

I have heard some Persons objected that Mr *Barry* would want Pleasantry in the mad Scenes of King *Lear*. I must confess I was at a Loss to know what they meant. *Lear*'s Madness claims a serious Attention, sometimes excites our Admiration, often moves our Tears, and ever our Pity and our Terror. If a Spectator of those Scenes should be inclined to laugh might not one suspect such Spectator had no very delicate feeling, or that there was something absurd in the Actor's Performance? It may be observed, tho' *Lear* is turned of Fourscore yet he sinks not into the enervated or decrepid old Man; he no more bends under Age than as Nature (tho' in Spirit and Health) will, at that Time of Day, sometimes give way to Ease. His Deportment will still express the Monarch. We have an Example in a King now living (God grant him long to live) who, from the Blessing of a well preserved Constitution and an elevated Mind, at a very great Age still walks erect and firm as many of his younger Subjects.

I own, I think Mr *Barry* well deserved the uncommon Applause he met with in this Part. It may be a Question whether, in this Character, he has not shewn more of the masterly Actor than in all he has done before. His Voice was well managed, his Looks expressive, his Deportment becoming the Character, his Actions graceful and picturesque. He meant well, and executed that Meaning with a becoming Dignity and Ease. There appeared throughout a well conducted Variety and spirited Propriety. His Attitudes appeared the Result of Nature, and by a happy Transition from one to another, they seemed not study'd. He threw himself into 'em as if his immediate Feeling alone directed him to the Use of 'em. Tho' the whole was pleasing, there is a Passage in the last Act where his Behaviour deserved particular Notice, and wherein he merited that Excess of Applause the roused Admiration of an almost astonished Audience most generously bestowed on him.

When the pious *Cordelia*, as the only Means of escaping the Anguish of a Father's Death, entreats the Ruffians to dispatch her first,[1] which the Villains seem ready to comply with; while *Lear* is with-held from the vain Efforts of a fond Father to preserve his Darling: his Action, Look

[1] Tate's version, 5.6.25ff. (Vol. I, p. 382).

and Voice most exquisitely expressed his distressful Situation. His quick Progression from Surprize to Terror, thence to Rage, 'till all were absorbed in Anguish and Despair, were Master-Strokes. At length his roused Spirits catching the Alarm, endeavouring to snatch her from her Fate, his Recollection of his unhappily being unarmed and unable to preserve her, when he throws himself on his Knees, preserving Majesty in his Distress, his whole Figure and Manner are finely expressive of the reduced Monarch and Heart-torn Father. All these Gradations of well painted Passions would task the Power of one of much superior Talents (much more my small Abilities) to do Justice in the Description. To the Ideas, therefore, of your own lively Imaginations I must leave what I find myself so unequal to paint.

And yet the Subject warms me to take farther Notice of his Behaviour. When he finds himself restored to his Kingdom, the o'ercharged Heart of the Monarch eases itself by joyous Exclamation. At once to his delighted Imagination rush the transporting Ideas of Greatness, Majesty, and Power restored, a Power to revenge and to reward. This latter Thought he immediately indulges by declaring his worthy Child, his dearly beloved Daughter *Cordelia*, shall be a Queen. His distressed Mind thus suddenly relieved by so quick a Transition to Joy, may in that Gust of Rapture drop a Tear, but 'twill be a Tear of Transport that joins those wakeful Expressions of Enthusiasm when he bids 'Winds catch the Sound, and Nature listen to the Change, that *Lear* shall be a King again, and his dear Child a Queen.'—[1]

The Pride of the Monarch and Tenderness of the Father are blended; he herein supports his Dignity amidst his softer Feelings. Can then this be properly expressed by the Whindling of an old fribbling Nykin when reconciled to his naughty Cocky? (ii, 28–41)

[1] Tate, 5.6.105ff. (Vol. 1, p. 384).

158. Joseph Warton on Shakespeare

1756

From *An Essay on the Writings and Genius of Pope* (I: 1756, II: 1782). This text from 'Fifth Edition, Corrected' (1806), 2 vols.

See the headnote to No. 139 above.

[From the *Dedication*]

The sublime and the pathetic are the two chief nerves of all genuine poesy . . .

Our English Poets may, I think, be disposed in four different classes and degrees. In the first class I would place our only three sublime and pathetic poets: SPENSER, SHAKESPEARE, MILTON. In the second class should be ranked such as possessed the true poetical genius in a more moderate degree, but who had noble talents for moral, ethical, and panegyrical poesy. At the head of these are DRYDEN, PRIOR, ADDISON, COWLEY, WALLER, GARTH, FENTON, GAY, DENHAM, PARNELL. In the third class may be placed men of wit, of elegant taste and lively fancy in describing familiar life though not the higher scenes of poetry. Here may be numbered BUTLER, SWIFT, ROCHESTER, DONNE, DORSET, OLDHAM. In the fourth class the mere versifiers, however smooth and mellifluous some of them may be thought, should be disposed. Such as PITT, SANDYS, FAIRFAX, BROOME, BUCKINGHAM, LANSDOWNE. (I, vi–vii)

* * *

[On the rarity of excellence in both comedy and tragedy]

Terence has left us no tragedy; and the *Mourning Bride* of Congreve, notwithstanding the praises bestowed on it by POPE in the *Dunciad*, is certainly a despicable performance: the plot is unnaturally intricate and overcharged with incidents, the sentiments trite, and the language turgid and bombast. Heemskirk and Teniers could not succeed in a serious and sublime subject of history-painting. The latter, it is well known, designed cartoons for tapestry, representing the history of the Turriani of Lombardy. Both the composition and the expression are extremely indifferent, and certain nicer virtuosi have remarked that in the serious pieces of Titian himself, even in one of his Last Suppers, a circumstance of the Ridiculous and the Familiar is introduced which suits not with the dignity of his subject. Hogarth's picture of Richard III is pure and unmixed with any dissimilar and degrading circumstances, and strongly impresses terror and amazement. The modesty and good sense of the ancients is in this particular, as in others, remarkable. The same writer never presumed to undertake more than one kind of dramatic poetry, if we except the *Cyclops* of Euripides. A poet never presumed to plead in public, or to write history, or, indeed, any considerable work in prose. The same actors never recited tragedy and comedy: this was observed long ago by Plato in the third book of his *Republic*. They seem to have held that diversity, nay, universality of excellence, at which the moderns frequently aim, to be a gift unattainable by man. We, therefore, of Great Britain have perhaps more reason to congratulate ourselves on two very singular phenomena; I mean Shakespeare's being able to pourtray characters so very different as FALSTAFF and MACBETH, and Garrick's being able to personate so inimitably a LEAR or an ABEL DRUGGER. Nothing can more fully demonstrate the extent and versatility of these two original geniuses. Corneille, whom the French are so fond of opposing to Shakespeare, produced very contemptible comedies. (I, 118–9)

*   *   *

[On Shakespeare's irregularities]

Correctness is a vague term, frequently used without meaning and precision. It is perpetually the nauseous cant of the French critics, and of their advocates and pupils, that the English writers are generally IN-CORRECT. If CORRECTNESS implies an absence of petty faults this perhaps may be granted. If it means that, because their tragedians have avoided the irregularities of Shakespeare and have observed a juster œconomy in their fables, therefore the *Athalia*, for instance, is preferable to *Lear* the notion is groundless and absurd. Though the *Henriade* should be allowed to be free from any very gross absurdities yet who will dare to rank it with the *Paradise Lost*? Some of their most perfect tragedies abound in faults as contrary to the nature of that species of poetry, and as destructive of its end, as the fools or grave-diggers of Shakespeare. (I, 196–7)

*　　*　　*

With what wildness of imagination, but yet with what propriety, are
the amusements of the fairies pointed out in the *Midsummer Night's
Dream*: amusements proper for none but fairies!

> 'Fore the third part of a minute, hence:
> Some to kill cankers in the musk-rose buds:
> Some war with rear-mice for their leathern wings,
> To make my small elves coats; and some keep back
> The clamorous owl, that nightly hoots, and wonders
> At our queint spirits.   [2.2.2ff.]

Shakespeare only could have thought of the following gratifications for
Titania's lover, and they are fit only to be offered to her lover by a
fairy-queen.

> Be kind and courteous to this gentleman;
> Hop in his walks, and gambol in his eyes;
> Feed him with apricocks and dewberries,
> With purple grapes, green figs, and mulberries.
> The honey-bags steal from the humble bees,
> And for night-tapers crop their waxen thighs,
> And light them at the fiery glow-worm's eyes,
> To have my love to bed, and to arise:
> And pluck the wings from painted butterflies,
> To fan the moon-beams from his sleeping eyes.   [3.1.150ff.]

If it should be thought that Shakespeare has the merit of being the first
who assigned proper employments to imaginary persons in the foregoing lines, yet it must be granted that by the addition of the most
delicate satire to the most lively fancy POPE, in the following passage,
has excelled any thing in Shakespeare or perhaps in any other author.

> Our humbler province is to tend the fair;
> Not a less pleasing, though less glorious care;
> To save the powder from too rough a gale,
> Nor let th' imprison'd essences exhale;
> To draw fresh colours from the vernal flow'rs,
> To steal from rainbows, ere they drop in show'rs,
> A brighter wash; to curl their waving hairs,
> Assist their blushes, and inspire their airs;
> Nay, oft in dreams invention we bestow,
> To change a flounce, or add a furbelow.   (I, 223–4)

* * *

[On the superiority of dramas based on historical events]

If we briefly cast our eyes over the most interesting and affecting stories, ancient or modern, we shall find that they are such as, however adorned and a little diversified, are yet grounded on true history and on real matters of fact. Such, for instance, among the ancients are the stories of Joseph, of Oedipus, the Trojan war and its consequences, of Virginia and the Horatii; such, among the moderns, are the stories of *King Lear*, the *Cid*, *Romeo and Juliet*, and *Oroonoko*. The series of events contained in these stories seem far to surpass the utmost powers of human imagination. In the best-conducted fiction some mark of improbability and incoherence will still appear. (I, 250)

* * *

[On 'a domestic story' as material for drama]

I cannot forbear wishing that our writers would more frequently search for subjects in the annals of England, which afford many striking and pathetic events proper for the stage. We have been too long attached to Grecian and Roman stories. In truth the DOMESTICA FACTA[1] are more interesting, as well as more useful: more interesting because we all think ourselves concerned in the actions and fates of our countrymen: more useful because the characters and manners bid the fairest to be true and natural when they are drawn from models with which we are exactly acquainted. The Turks, the Persians, and Americans of our poets are, in reality, distinguished from Englishmen only by their turbans and feathers, and think and act as if they were born and educated within the bills of mortality. The historical plays of Shakespeare are always particularly grateful to the spectator, who loves to see and hear our own Harrys and Edwards better than all the Achilleses or Cæsars that ever existed. (I, 272–3)

[1] Horace, *A.P.* 287; compare Hurd, Vol. 3, pp. 363f.

159. Tobias Smollett on Shakespeare's imperfections

1756

From a review of Warton's *Essay on the writings and Genius of Pope* in the *Critical Review*, i (1756), pp. 226–40.

This review is assigned to Smollett in the annotated copy of the *Critical Review* in the University of Oregon library; see D. Roper, *RES* n.s. 10 (1959), p. 42.

With respect to *Shakespeare*, though we revere the might of that creative genius we are not so dazzled with his excellencies but that we can perceive a number of imperfections scattered up and down his works. These his warmest admirers will not deny, and there are an hundred characters in his plays that (if we may be allowed the expression) speak out of character. We shall mention a few of those glaring improprieties, even in his most distinguished personages. The famous soliloquy of *Hamlet* is introduced by the head and shoulders. He had some reason to revenge his father's death upon his uncle, but he had none to take away his own life. Nor does it appear from any other part of the play that he had any such intention. On the contrary, when he had a fair opportunity of being put to death in *England* he very wisely retorted the villainy of his conductors on their own heads.

We find *Othello*, in the midst of those jealous conceptions which in a manner desolated his whole soul, breaking out into a puerile lamentation in which he recapitulates a number of idle circumstances as the objects of his regret.

> Farewell the neighing steed, and the shrill trump,
> The spirit stirring drum, th' ear-piercing fife,
> The royal banner, (*which by the bye he could not unfold in the service of Venice*) and all quality,
> Pride, pomp, and *circumstance* of glorious war!

And (*mark the prosopopeia*) oh, you mortal engines whose rude
  throats
Th' immortal Jove's (*he was a Christian too*) dread clamours counterfeit,
Farewell!   [3.3.352ff.]

Let us only ask the candid reader, Whether or not this speech or
exclamation has not all the air of an affected rhapsody; and if he does not
think it would have been more properly assigned to *Iago* when he
attempted to dissuade the simple *Roderigo* from returning to *Venice?*
(234–5)

Macbeth, even after he has almost undertaken to murder his prince
and benefactor, expresses a noble sentiment which would have better
become the virtuous *Macduff*.

> I dare do all that may become a man;
> Who dares do more, is none.   [1.7.46f.]

In the perturbation of his thoughts which succeeded the aggravated
murder he had committed he launches out into conceited similes, which
ill describe the horror of his mind.

> the innocent sleep;
> Sleep that knits up the ravelled sleeve of care,
> The death of each day's life, sore labour's bath,
> Balm of hurt minds, great nature's second course,
> Chief nourisher in life's feast.   [2.2.36ff.]

Are not these rather the quaint productions of an idle invention than
the broken accents and distracted images of horror and remorse?

160. Samuel Johnson, Proposals for an edition of Shakespeare

1756

Proposals For Printing, by Subscription, The Dramatick Works of William Shakespeare, Corrected and Illustrated by Samuel Johnson. London, June 1, 1756.

These *Proposals* aroused much interest (Murphy reprinted them in 1757: No. 161n. below) and show Johnson at his most commanding. But the edition promised for Christmas 1757 did not appear until the autumn of 1765 (see Vol. 5, No. 205).

CONDITIONS.

I. That the Book shall be elegantly printed in Eight Volumes in Octavo.

II. That the Price to Subscribers shall be Two Guineas; one to be paid at Subscribing, the other on the Delivery of the Book in Sheets.

III. That the Work shall be published on or before *Christmas 1757.*

When the works of SHAKESPEARE are, after so many editions, again offered to the publick it will doubtless be enquired why SHAKESPEARE stands in more need of critical assistance than any other of the English writers, and what are the deficiencies of the late attempts which another editor may hope to supply.

The business of him that republishes an ancient book is to correct what is corrupt and to explain what is obscure. To have a text corrupt in many places and in many doubtful is, among the authours that have written since the use of types, almost peculiar to SHAKESPEARE. Most writers, by publishing their own works, prevent all various readings and preclude all conjectural criticism. Books indeed are sometimes published after the death of him who produced them, but they are better secured from corruptions than these unfortunate compositions. They subsist in a single copy, written or revised by the authour, and the faults of the printed volume can be only faults of one descent.

But of the works of SHAKESPEARE the condition has been far different: he sold them not to be printed but to be played. They were immediately copied for the actors and multiplied by transcript after transcript, vitiated by the blunders of the penman, or changed by the affectation of the player; perhaps enlarged to introduce a jest, or mutilated to shorten the representation; and printed at last without the concurrence of the authour, without the consent of the proprietor, from compilations made by chance or by stealth out of the separate parts written for the theatre: and thus thrust into the world surreptitiously and hastily they suffered another depravation from the ignorance and negligence of the printers, as every man who knows the state of the press in that age will readily conceive.

It is not easy for invention to bring together so many causes concurring to vitiate a text. No other authour ever gave up his works to fortune and time with so little care: no books could be left in hands so likely to injure them as plays frequently acted yet continued in manuscript; no other transcribers were likely to be so little qualified for their task as those who copied for the stage at a time when the lower ranks of the people were universally illiterate; no other editions were made from fragments so minutely broken and so fortuitously reunited; and in no other age was the art of printing in such unskilful hands.

With the causes of corruption that make the revisal of SHAKESPEARE's dramatick pieces necessary may be enumerated the causes of obscurity, which may be partly imputed to his age, and partly to himself.

When a writer outlives his contemporaries, and remains almost the only unforgotten name of a distant time, he is necessarily obscure. Every age has its modes of speech and its cast of thought; which, though easily explained when there are many books to be compared with each other, become sometimes unintelligible and always difficult when there are no parallel passages that may conduce to their illustration. SHAKESPEARE is the first considerable authour of sublime or familiar dialogue in our language. Of the books which he read, and from which he formed his stile, some perhaps have perished and the rest are neglected. His imitations are therefore unnoted, his allusions are undiscovered, and many beauties, both of pleasantry and greatness, are lost with the objects to which they were united, as the figures vanish when the canvas has decayed.

It is the great excellence of SHAKESPEARE that he drew his scenes from nature, and from life. He copied the manners of the world then passing before him, and has more allusions than other poets to the traditions and superstition of the vulgar; which must therefore be traced before he can be understood.

He wrote at a time when our poetical language was yet unformed, when the meaning of our phrases was yet in fluctuation, when words were adopted at pleasure from the neighbouring languages, and while the Saxon was still visibly mingled in our diction. The reader is therefore embarrassed at once with dead and with foreign languages, with obsoleteness and innovation. In that age, as in all others, fashion produced phraseology, which succeeding fashion swept away before its meaning was generally known or sufficiently authorised: and in that age above all others experiments were made upon our language which distorted its combinations, and disturbed its uniformity.

If SHAKESPEARE has difficulties above other writers it is to be imputed to the nature of his work, which required the use of the common colloquial language, and consequently admited many phrases allusive, elliptical, and proverbial such as we speak and hear every hour without observing them; and of which, being now familiar we do not suspect that they can ever grow uncouth, or that, being now obvious they can ever seem remote.

These are the principal causes of the obscurity of SHAKESPEARE; to which may be added that fulness of idea which might sometimes load his words with more sentiment than they could conveniently convey, and that rapidity of imagination which might hurry him to a second thought before he had fully explained the first. But my opinion is that very few of his lines were difficult to his audience, and that he used such expressions as were then common, though the paucity of contemporary writers makes them now seem peculiar.

Authours are often praised for improvement or blamed for innovation, with very little justice, by those who read few other books of the same age. Addison himself has been so unsuccessful in enumerating the words with which Milton has enriched our language as perhaps not to have named one of which Milton was the authour: and Bentley has yet more unhappily praised him as the introducer of those elisions into English poetry which had been used from the first essays of versification among us, and which Milton was indeed the last that practised.

Another impediment, not the least vexatious to the commentator, is the exactness with which SHAKESPEARE followed his authours. Instead of dilating his thoughts into generalities, and expressing incidents with poetical latitude, he often combines circumstances unnecessary to his main design only because he happened to find them together. Such passages can be illustrated only by him who has read the same story in the very book which SHAKESPEARE consulted.

He that undertakes an edition of SHAKESPEARE has all these difficulties to encounter and all these obstructions to remove.

The corruptions of the text will be corrected by a careful collation of the oldest copies, by which it is hoped that many restorations may yet be made: at least it will be necessary to collect and note the variations as materials for future cricks, for it very often happens that a wrong reading has affinity to the right.

In this part all the present editions are apparently and intentionally defective. The cricks did not so much as wish to facilitate the labour of those that followed them. The same books are still to be compared; the work that has been done is to be done again, and no single edition will supply the reader with a text on which he can rely as the best copy of the works of SHAKESPEARE.

The edition now proposed will at least have this advantage over others. It will exhibit all the observable varieties of all the copies that can be found, that, if the reader is not satisfied with the editor's determination he may have the means of chusing better for himself.

Where all the books are evidently vitiated, and collation can give no assistance, then begins the task of critical sagacity: and some changes may well be admitted in a text never settled by the authour and so long exposed to caprice and ignorance. But nothing shall be imposed, as in the Oxford edition,[1] without notice of the alteration, nor shall conjecture be wantonly or unnecessarily indulged.

It has been long found that very specious emendations do not equally strike all minds with conviction, nor even the same mind at different times; and therefore though perhaps many alterations may be proposed as eligible very few will be obtruded as certain. In a language so ungrammatical as the English and so licentious as that of SHAKESPEARE emendatory criticism is always hazardous; nor can it be allowed to any man who is not particularly versed in the writings of that age, and particularly studious of his authour's diction. There is danger lest peculiarities should be mistaken for corruptions, and passages rejected as unintelligible which a narrow mind happens not to understand.

[1] Sir Thomas Hanmer's, 1745: see Vol. 3, No. 96, and Johnson's earlier comments on it, Vol. 3, pp. 184–5.

All the former criticks have been so much employed on the correction of the text that they have not sufficiently attended to the elucidation of passages obscured by accident or time. The editor will endeavour to read the books which the authour read, to trace his knowledge to its source and compare his copies with their originals. If in this part of his design he hopes to attain any degree of superiority to his predecessors it must be considered that he has the advantage of their labours; that part of the work being already done, more care is naturally bestowed on the other part; and that, to declare the truth, Mr Rowe and Mr Pope were very ignorant of the ancient English literature; Dr Warburton was detained by more important studies; and Mr Theobald, if fame be just to his memory, considered learning only as an instrument of gain, and made no further enquiry after his authour's meaning when once he had notes sufficient to embellish his page with the expected decorations.

With regard to obsolete or peculiar diction the editor may perhaps claim some degree of confidence, having had more motives to consider the whole extent of our language than any other man from its first formation. He hopes that by comparing the works of SHAKESPEARE with those of writers who lived at the same time, immediately preceded, or immediately followed him he shall be able to ascertain his ambiguities, disentangle his intricacies, and recover the meaning of words now lost in the darkness of antiquity.

When therefore any obscurity arises from an allusion to some other book the passage will be quoted. When the diction is entangled it will be cleared by a paraphrase or interpretation. When the sense is broken by the suppression of part of the sentiment in pleasantry or passion, the connection will be supplied. When any forgotten custom is hinted care will be taken to retrieve and explain it. The meaning assigned to doubtful words will be supported by the authorities of other writers or by parallel passages of SHAKESPEARE himself.

The observation of faults and beauties is one of the duties of an annotator, which some of SHAKESPEARE's editors have attempted and some have neglected. For this part of his task, and for this only, was Mr Pope eminently and indisputably qualified: nor has Dr Warburton followed him with less diligence or less success. But I have never observed that mankind was much delighted or improved by their asterisks, commas, or double commas; of which the only effect is that they preclude the pleasure of judging for ourselves, teach the young and ignorant to decide without principles; defeat curiosity and discernment by leaving them less to discover; and at last shew the opinion of the critick without the reasons on which it was founded, and without affording any light by which it may be examined.

The editor, though he may less delight his own vanity, will probably please his reader more by supposing him equally able with himself to judge of beauties and faults which require no previous acquisition of remote knowledge. A description of the obvious scenes of nature, a representation of general life, a sentiment of reflection or experience, a deduction of conclusive argument, a forcible eruption of effervescent passion, are to be considered as proportionate to common apprehension, unassisted by critical officiousness; since to conceive them nothing more is requisite than acquaintance with the general state of the world, and those faculties which he must always bring with him who would read SHAKESPEARE.

But when the beauty arises from some adaptation of the sentiment to customs worn out of use, to opinions not universally prevalent, or to any accidental or minute particularity, which cannot be supplied by common understanding or common observation, it is the duty of a commentator to lend his assistance.

The notice of beauties and faults thus limited will make no distinct part of the design, being reducible to the explanation of obscure passages.

The editor does not however intend to preclude himself from the comparison of SHAKESPEARE's sentiments or expression with those of ancient or modern authours, or from the display of any beauty not obvious to the students of poetry; for as he hopes to leave his authour better understood he wishes likewise to procure him more rational approbation.

The former editors have affected to slight their predecessors: but in this edition all that is valuable will be adopted from every commentator, that posterity may consider it as including all the rest and exhibiting whatever is hitherto known of the great father of the English drama.

161. Arthur Murphy, Shakespeare in the London theatres

1757

From the *London Chronicle: or Universal Evening Post*, an evening newspaper for which Dr Johnson wrote the 'Introduction' to the first issue and which he read constantly: as Boswell reported, 'it has all along been distinguished for good sense, accuracy, moderation and delicacy' (*Life of Johnson* (1756), *ad. inf.*).

The theatre reviews in this journal appeared under the heading 'The Theatre', numbered separately, and amounting to thirty-seven essays between 22 January and 19 April 1757, and four essays from November to 10 December. For their ascription to Murphy, based on numerous parallels with his signed works, see C. H. Gray, *Theatrical Criticism in London to 1795* (New York, 1931), pp. 136–9; J. P. Emery, *PMLA* 54 (1939), pp. 1099–104 and in his biography *Arthur Murphy* (Philadelphia, 1946), pp. 33–9; H. H. Dunbar, *The Dramatic Career of Arthur Murphy* (New York, 1946), pp. 305–10. C. H. Gray ranked this series with the work of Leigh Hunt and Hazlitt 'as vivid and intelligent writing about the contemporary stage . . . perhaps the best of the century' (*op. cit.*, p. 106).

---

[a] COVENT-GARDEN, Jan. 25, 1757.

Was performed, the first Part of *Henry the Fourth*, written by *Shakespeare*. The Plays of this Author must never be judged by the strict Rules of Dramatic Poetry, with which it is to be imagined he was not acquainted; and therefore to try him by what he did not know would be trying him by a Kind of *ex post facto* Law, Regularity of Design being introduced in this Country since the Decease of that great Genius. Mr *Hume*, in his *History of Great Britain*,[1] has given a pretty just Character of him when he says 'A striking Peculiarity of Sentiment, adapted to a

[1] See above, p. 173.

274

singular Character, he frequently hits as it were by Inspiration; but a reasonable Propriety of Thought he cannot for any Time uphold;' unless the Character of *Falstaff* be an Exception to this very sensible Writer's Opinion. For indeed the Character of Sir *John* no where flags, and he generally upholds a Propriety of Thought if it be considered in regard to the Manners of the Speaker. Bullying, Cowardice, Vaunting, Detection, boasted Activity and bodily Indolence, Profligacy and Pretensions to Decorum, form such a party-coloured Groupe as moves our Laughter irresistibly. His Wit and, on all Occasions, the Pleasantry of his Ideas provoke us to laugh with him, and hinder the Knight's Character from sinking into Contempt; and we love him, in Spight of his degrading Foibles, for his enlivened Humour and his companionable Qualities.

It is somewhat surprizing that the Players have agreed to supersede one of the best Scenes in the Play, which is that between *Falstaff* and the Prince, where Sir *John* personates by Turns the King and his Son with such a Vein of Humour as perhaps would divert an Audience beyond any thing in the Comedy. (96)

[b] COVENT-GARDEN, Jan. 29, 1757.

Was repeated *Richard the Third*, by Mr Barry. The Qualities which constitute Richard's Character are such as require a nice Discernment of Spirits, otherwise the Actor will be likely to fail in the distinguishing Singularities of this very complicated Hero. This, we imagine, is the Case in many Scenes as this Actor performs them. The deep designing Villainy of Richard is generally converted into Rant in the Soliloquies, which are never agitated with the Passions, except where Joy transports him. They are mostly Situations of dark, cool, and deliberate Wickedness, and should be uttered with deep and grave Tones of Voice and a gloomy Countenance. These two Requisites Nature has denied this Performer, tho' she has been very liberal to him in Qualifications for Love, Grief, and enraged Tenderness. Accordingly he does not seem to carry with him that covered Spirit of Enterprize, which is so peculiar a Mark of the Character. He is too turbulent in all the Scenes where he is alone; and the Humour of Richard, which never should take off the Mask, is with him too free and open. Richard's Pleasantry never rises to Mirth; it always proceeds from what the Poet[1] calls the *mala mentis gaudia*, the wicked Pleasures of the Mind, and it should therefore never become totally jocund, but should ever be a mixed Emotion of Joy and

---

[1] Virgil, *Aeneid* 6.278f.: 'the soul's guilty joys.'

Malice. Where he jokes about his Score or two of Taylors, and finds himself a marvellous proper Man, there should be no free Exultation, because his Mirth is ironical and he is still sensible of his own Deformity; and therefore he should smile and smile, and be a Villain. This Rule will hold all through, except in the triumphant Self-Congratulations of Ambition. The Love Scene, we apprehend, he entirely mistakes. Richard has a Tongue that can wheedle with the Devil, but not pour out the melting Harmony of Romeo. Richard indeed says afterwards, He truly loved; but his Love was nothing more than Lust. Were he capable of having any real Regard for a Woman he could never have recourse to Expressions of his Passion suitable to a Varanes; and as he only intended to have her, but not keep her long, however he might smooth his Face in Smiles his Words could not come from him like Flakes of feathered Snow, that melted as they fell.

In the Scenes of Hurry and Bustle Mr Barry rises upon his Audience, but is sometimes apt to set out with his Voice strained to its utmost; by which Means it becomes thin, and therefore does not carry with it sufficient Terror. Upon the whole, we think this Contest lies between Mr Barry and Mr Mossop. If the former could play the three first Acts as well as Mr Mossop he would excel his Antagonist: and if the latter were as quick and animated as Mr. Barry in the two last Acts, he would approach very near to Mr Garrick. (112)

[c] COVENT-GARDEN, Feb. 12, 1757.

Was performed the Tragedy of *Romeo and Juliet*. This Play is founded upon an Italian Novel, by Bandello. There is Reason to think Shakespeare was not Master of the Italian Language, as it appears that the Circumstance of Juliet's awaking before Romeo's Death is omitted in a Translation of the Novel to be seen in the *Court of Pleasure*. Had Shakespeare seen the Original, he would never have omitted such a fine dramatic Incident. Otway perceived this Omission, and in his *Caius Marius* has taken Advantage of so beautiful a Circumstance.[1] But we cannot help agreeing with Mr Garrick in his Preface to the Play[2] as it now stands, that it is surprizing such a Genius as Otway has not struck out a Scene of more Nature, Terror, and Distress. He who generally spoke the Language of the Heart has in this Instance given us nothing but unaffecting Conceits, which can never agitate the Passions; as was proved some Winters ago when Mr Sheridan attempted to restore

[1] See Vol. 1, pp. 316f., and Murphy's earlier essay, Vol. 3, No. 124.
[2] See Vol. 3, No. 117.

Otway's Lines amidst the general Hissing of the whole House.[1] The Scene as it now stands is written by Mr Garrick, and has not an Idea or Expression through the whole which is found ineffectual; so well has he judged of the natural Force of unornamented Dialogue in Distress. It is in Parts of this Sort that Mr Barry should attempt to rival the modern Roscius; because we believe, in this he has divided the Town with him. If we were to decide the Palm between them we should, perhaps, give it to Mr Barry; though the Romeo of Drury-Lane has peculiar Strokes in many Passages where he snatches a Grace, as the Poet has it, beyond the Reach of Imitation. However, in the last Act Mr Barry's Tones of Voice are purely elegiac, and he captivates all Hearts with such a resistless Harmony that perhaps the Distresses of Love were never better impressed upon an Audience, unless the Performance of *Tancred and Sigismunda* may be allowed an Exception. (159–60)

[d] COVENT-GARDEN, Feb. 17, 1757.

The Tragedy of *Hamlet*, written by *Shakespeare*, was performed at this Theatre. This Play is formed upon the Story of Amleth in the *Danish History* of Saxo-Grammaticus. If the Reader has a Mind to see the Use Shakespeare made of it, we refer him to Mrs Lenox's *Shakespeare Illustrated*,[2] where he will find the Passage translated to his Hand by a Friend of that Lady's. The story has a very romantic Air, abounds with Improbabilities, and is such altogether as would scarce have struck any Imagination but Shakespeare's. Amleth, we are told, put on the Guise of Folly, rolled on the Ground, covered his Face with Filth, raked the Embers with his Hands, &c. How finely has Shakespeare taken this Hint! And what a dignified Mind has he presented to us in young Hamlet!

The Ghost is entirely his own Invention, nothing of this Sort being in the History. How nobly is that imaginary Personage introduced! And what a Solemnity of Ideas the Poet has assigned him! The Scene in which young Hamlet first hears of his Father's Spirit is not the most important, but is as finely conducted as any Passage in the Play. The young Prince's disjointed Manner of asking Questions, and the minute Exactness of those Questions—Staid it long?—Armed, say ye?—Pale—or Red—and fixed his Eyes upon you? &c. [1.2.226ff.] All these little Touches are agreeable to the Affections of the Mind, when we talk of a

1 This happened on 20 November and 26 December 1754, Sheridan acting Romeo at Covent Garden.
2 See above, No. 141.

Person we love either absent or dead, and in the present Case they serve to alarm the Imagination, and to raise our Expectation of the Event.

In the original Story the Catastrophe is full of Terror. Amleth, having made the Nobility drunk, set Fire to the Palace, and during the Confusion goes to the Usurper's Apartment and tells him that Amleth was then to revenge his Father's Death; upon which the King jumping out of Bed, he was instantly put to Death, and Amleth was proclaimed King. The Historian concludes with this Remark: 'O brave young Man, who covered more than human Wisdom under the Guise of a Natural, and not only secured his own Safety by that Artifice but obtained the Means of completely revenging his Father; and it is now left to every Body to judge which was greater, his Bravery or Wisdom.' If Shakespeare had not deviated from this Circumstance he would perhaps have given the finest Scenes of Terror in the last Act that ever have been imagined; and then a Subject that opens so nobly would have been grand also in the Close. As the Play now stands the Innocent, contrary to Tradition, falls with the Guilty; like the Personage in *Tom Thumb*, all he boasts is that he falls the last, and the World is left to judge which is worst, the Fencing of the Actors, or the Folly of the Poet in introducing it. (167-8)

*　*　*

[e] DRURY-LANE, Feb. 17, 1757.

Shakespeare's Play, called, *The Life of King Henry the Eighth*, was performed here this Evening. The Author of *Shakespeare Illustrated* observes, very justly, that there is a Misnomer in the Title as the whole Piece only takes in the Transactions of twelve Years of King Henry's Reign. Holinshed, it appears, was our Author's historical Guide, the Characters being copied from him; and in general many of the Sentiments and not seldom whole Speeches are the original Property of the Historian. In treating Facts so well ascertained, and Characters in general so well understood, Shakespeare's Invention was fettered, and he could not make any considerable Departure from authenticated Tradition. However, he seems upon most Occasions, as has been remarked of a celebrated French Poet, to create the Thoughts of others: Every Thing comes from him with an Air of Originality. When we once forgive him the Violation of all the Rules of the Drama we must allow that he greatly compensates for this want of Regularity by very striking Beauties. The Incidents in *Harry the Eighth* are very interesting. The Death of the Duke of Buckingham, the Divorce of Queen Catharine, the Wedding of Anne Bullen, and the Fall of Woolsey are important Events, which cannot fail to attract our Attention. The Character of the King is set off in such a Glow of Colouring that though the Poet has faithfully taken it from Holinshed it seems a Personage of his own Invention.

The haughty Churchman is likewise admirably drawn; and if we should add that Mr Mossop's Performance seems to correspond with the Poet's Idea it would be very far from a Compliment. A well imitated sacerdotal Pride appears in every Cast of his Countenance and in his whole Manner; his subtlety, his unfeeling Stiffness, and a certain mean Kind of Craft are preserved amidst all his Grandeur. The Dejection of Spirits which takes Possession of him afterwards has still a Sort of fallen Dignity, and whoever has a Mind to hear the following Lines, among many others, uttered with all the Graces of Elocution is desired to attend this Actor the next Time he appears in this Character.

> This is the State of Man; To-day he puts forth
> The tender Leaves of Hopes, To morrow blossoms,
> And bears his blushing Honours thick upon him;
> The third Day comes a Frost, a killing Frost,
> And when he thinks, good easy Man, full surely
> His Greatness is a ripening, nips his Root,
> And then he falls, as I do. [3.2.352ff.]   (175)

*   *   *

[f] DRURY-LANE, Feb. 24, 1757.

Shakespeare's Tragedy of *Macbeth* was performed here this Evening. *Holinshed's Chronicles of England, Scotland, and Ireland*, have supplied our great Dramatic Poet with the Materials of many of his Plays, and whoever chuses to compare the Play with the Original will find that the Poet has traced the Historian very closely in this Performance. It has been said by many Critics that the Writing of this Play is the best of our Author's Production. Why this Opinion should be subscribed to we cannot perceive; we think him equally beautiful in *The Tempest*, not to mention *Lear, Othello,* and *Hamlet.* The Stile of *Macbeth* is indeed peculiar, abounding in Words infrequent in their Use, but remarkably strong and picturesque. The Language takes a Tincture from the Subject, which, being dark and gloomy, it thence follows that the Poets Choice of Words, and their Arrangement, are calculated to fill the Mind with Imagery of the most solemn and awful Aspect. In Consequence of this the Writing of *Macbeth* is distinguished from the Poet's general Stile, and has been called the best merely because it is different.

As the supernatural Agency of Witches is very early introduced it may not be amiss to mention, in the Words of so fine a Critic as Mr Johnson that 'in the Time of Shakespeare the Doctrine of Witchcraft was established by Law and the Fashion, and as Prodigies are always seen in proportion as they are expected Witches were every Day discovered, and multiplied so fast in some Places, that Bishop Hall mentions a Village in Lancashire where their Number was greater than that of the Houses. Upon this general Infatuation (continues the same judicious Writer) Shakespeare might be allowed to found a Play, especially since he has followed with great Exactness such Histories as were then thought true; nor can it be doubted that the Scenes of Inchantment were, both by himself and his Audiences, thought awful and affecting.'[1] This Criticism justifies the Poet for introducing a Machinery so whimsical as it may appear in the present Age.

The Use he has made of it is certainly admirable. *Macbeth*'s Mind, in itself not bad, is by these Personages filled with Ideas of Royalty, and very naturally the Account of them kindles a Blaze in the more combustible Temper of his Wife, who omitted nothing that might urge him to perpetrate the Deed. Bœtius says, *Animus etiam Macbethi per se ferox prope quotidianus conviciis conjugis stimulabatur.*[2] Shakespeare has nobly conceived the Character of Lady *Macbeth* from this Hint, and has given her Features the highest Colouring and the strongest Proportions. The gloomy Meditations of *Macbeth* very finely describe the Irresolution of his Mind, and in order to abate the Horror Shakespeare has occasionally softened his Temper. His Wife, however, laid the Daggers ready, and the Deed Must be done. What strong Workings has the Poet given the Imagination on this Occasion! Visions become Realities; the Ideas of the Mind are embodied: 'Is this a Dagger that I see before me?' [2.1.33] nay, they are thrown into Action: 'Thou marshal'st me the Way that I was going.' [2.1.42] So strong is the Painting that with all his Efforts he can hardly recollect his Senses to find out that it was the bloody Business informed thus to his Mind. One would imagine the Horror in this Scene could hardly be carried further; and yet immediately we are told 'It is now the witching Hour of Night, when Murder is alarmed by his Centinel the Wolf,' &c. [2.1.49ff.] The Imagination could not well be filled with more awful Ideas.

The Confusion of conscious Guilt is finely marked in the succeeding

---

1 See Vol. 3, p. 167, and Murphy's earlier essay on *Macbeth*, above, No. 140a.

2 Murphy quotes and translates this sentence above, p. 86, in borrowing from Guthrie.

Scene, and our Author has contradicted what he had told us in the Beginning of his Play, viz. 'Present Feats are less than horrible Imaginings' [1.3.137f.]—'Hark!—Who lies in the Antichamber?—This is a sorry Sight!—How is it with me when ev'ry Noise appalls me?' &c. [2.2.19, 20, 58] After this *Macbeth* never knows a Moment's Peace of Mind, but is full of Scorpions which incessantly goad him; and the more he is goaded by them the more he hardens himself in Villainy.

We cannot but mention this as an amazing Proof of our Author's Insight into Nature, who has, in three different Characters, separated the Workings of Remorse, and shewn its Operation to be productive of remarkable Effects in each, according to their respective Tempers. For this Remark we are not sure to whom we are indebted.[1] But it would lead us beyond the Bounds of these Remarks to insist on this at present, and therefore we shall continue our Observations in a subsequent Paper. (199–200)

*   *   *

[g] *Continuation of Remarks on* MACBETH. DRURY-LANE, Feb. 26, 1757.

We mentioned in our last the different Effects of Remorse in three different Characters of Shakespeare. It would have been expressed with more Accuracy had we said four, as we may trace the Workings of a guilty Conscience in four of his capital Personages. In Richard we perceive it in short transitory Goadings, which, however, the Obstinacy of his Villainy finds the Means of silencing, till at length we find him starting off his Couch in all the Horrors of the wildest Despair; but this only prevails while his scattered Senses are lost in a Confusion between sleeping and waking. In *King John* we see a Mind quite desolated by incessant Corrosions, and he has not the guilty Fortitude to oppose the Assaults of Conscience, but he intirely abandons himself to Melancholy. The Usurper in *Hamlet* seeks Occasion to excite the Feelings of Repentance in his Breast, but Vice has such an Hold of him that he cannot extricate himself and he declares himself incurable. The Species of *Macbeth*'s Remorse differs from them all. His Temper of Mind seems to be naturally superstitious, and thence he is easily overcast with Clouds of Horror, and his creative Fancy, the sure Concomitant of Superstition, fills him with a thousand visionary Fears. It is owing to this that the 'Table's full'; the real Introduction of the Ghost being only to impress the Scene deeper on the Minds of the Audience. He tells us

[1] To William Guthrie: see above, p. 90, and vol. 3, p. 195.

> Stones have been taught to move, and Trees to speak;
> Augurs that understand Relations, have
> By Magpies, and by Choughs, and Rooks, brought forth
> The secret'st Man of Blood.   [3.4.123ff.]

The Consequence of this is that he resolves to indulge his gloomy Turn of Thought by a superstitious Visit to the Witches, and from the very Torture of Mind which his Guilt occasions he hardens himself still more in Villainy.

> I will To-morrow,
> Betimes I will unto the weird Sisters—
> More shall they speak—   [3.4.132ff.]

And a little after,

> I am in Blood,
> Stept in so far, that, should I wade no more,
> Returning were as tedious as go o'er.   [3.4.136ff.]

In this Manner we find he does not, like King John, abandon himself to Despair, like Hamlet's Father-in-law, endeavour at Repentance, nor, like Richard, to subdue his Tendencies to Remorse; but he is at once resolute and timorous, determined to pursue the bloody Tract of Ambition and at the same Time a Prey to all the Vulture-Cares of Wickedness. Thus Intrepidity and Superstition, Remorse and Cruelty, are all blended together and render *Macbeth* a different Villain from any other on the Stage. If the Reader will take this Hint and review the Play it will immediately strike him how masterly the Poet is in the Execution of this complicated Character.

As we have mentioned his Visit to the weird Sisters, it may not be improper to transcribe Mr Johnson's admirable Remarks on the magic Incantation.[1] 'As this is the chief Scene of Inchantment in the Play (says that judicious Writer) it is proper in this Place to observe with how much Judgment Shakespeare has selected all the Circumstances of his infernal Ceremonies, and how exactly he has conformed to common Opinions and Traditions. Thrice the brinded Cat hath mew'd, &c.

> Toad, that under the cold Stone,
> Days and Nights has forty-one,
> Swelter'd Venom sleeping got,
> Boil thou first i' th'charmed Pot.
> Fillet of a fenny Snake,

[1] See Vol. 3, p. 179, and Murphy's earlier essay on *Macbeth*, above, p. 87.

In the Cauldron boil and bake;
Eye of Neut, and Toe of Frog, &c.   [4.1.6ff.]

The Babe whose Finger is used must be strangled in its Birth; the
Grease must be human, but must be dropped from a Gibbet, the Gibbet
of a Murderer; and even the Sow whose Blood is used must have
offended Nature by devouring her own Farrow. These are Touches of
Judgment and Genius.'

There are many more elegant Remarks of this Author, which we are
constrained to suppress as they would exceed the Bounds of our Paper.
But we refer our Readers, if they have a Mind to read a fine Criticism,
to a small Pamphlet called *Miscellaneous Observations on the Tragedy of
Macbeth*, published some time since by Mr Johnson as a Specimen of a
new Edition of Shakespeare which, we have the Pleasure to inform our
Readers, he is now about. From his Erudition and Genius we may
expect to see our great Dramatic Poet restored to us in his Habit as he
lived.

But to return to *Macbeth*:—In the Scene where the Apparitions
appear that Piece of Machinery is also managed in such a Manner as to
be perfectly agreeable to the fantastic Practices of Witches; and at the
same time they are, as Mr Upton[1] observes, symbolical Exhibitions of
what hereafter is to happen to *Macbeth* while (according to the Delight
these extraordinary Personages are supposed to feel in Mischief) they
palter with him in a double Sense, which at length brings on that wild
Confusion which, as Truth dawns upon the Mind, makes this wicked
Hero venture every thing in all the Agonies of Guilt, Horror, Rage,
and Despair. In the last Act, before the Fallacy of the Witches is
discovered, his Spirits sink into a settled Gloom, and occasionally he
gives into a Strain of the finest Moralities that ever were uttered on any
Stage or in any Language. Besides their acknowledged Truth they take
such a Tincture of Melancholy from *Macbeth*'s State of Mind that from
that very Circumstance they have something more peculiarly affecting
than perhaps was ever felt from Sentiment before.

Having said so much of this Play, we shall take another Opportunity
to attend Mr Mossop thro' his Performance, when, we imagine, we
shall find that he has conceived this Character very justly, and that he
has great Merit in the Execution. (207–8)

*   *   *

1 In his *Critical Observations on Shakespeare* (1746, 1748): see Vol. 3, p. 294 and note.

[h] DRURY-LANE; March 1, 1757.

This Evening was presented Shakespeare's Play called *Measure for Measure*. The Story of this Piece is extremely affecting and interesting. It is taken, according to our Author's Custom, from an Italian Narrative in Cinthio's Novels; and is in brief as follows. The Duke of Vienna, in order to have an Opportunity of mending the Laws and gaining a Knowledge of his Subjects, makes a temporary Abdication under Pretext of retiring for some time from his Dominions. But instead of withdrawing he betakes himself to a Convent, and disguises himself in the Habit of a Fryar. It happened that Claudio had seduced a young Lady, for which he is ordered to be executed by the Substitute of the Duke. Upon which Isabella, Sister to Claudio, immediately interests herself in his Cause and endeavours to deprecate his Fate. The Deputy, who proves deaf to her tenderest Importunity, is caught by her Youth and Beauty, and offers to save him if she will gratify his inordinate Desires. Superior to Disgrace, she rejects it with Scorn; and when her Brother intreats her to save his Life with Loss of her Honour she is fired with a noble Indignation. Mean time the Duke, in the Habit of a Fryar, finds a Succedaneum by sending, in Isabella's room, another Lady to whom the Vice-Duke had been formerly contracted. Notwithstanding this Claudio is ordered again for Execution; when the Duke shakes off his Fryar's Dress and enters the City. Isabella seizes the Opportunity to complain of the Administration during his Absence, and after some Incidents, not unentertaining, the whole Secret is cleared up and Angelo the Deputy, is, in his Turn, ordered for Execution. The generous Isabella here again interposes and sollicits his Pardon. The Duke marries Isabella, and thus Virtue is crowned with a bright Reward.

This, if we are not mistaken, is the Sum of Shakespeare's Story. In the Conduct of the Fable the Poet has made some Mistake, and he has unnecessarily overcharged it with supernumerary Incidents which do not much conduce to the main Business, and he has crouded it with episodical Characters. The Reader who has not seen this Play may, however, easily conceive how touching many of the above described Situations must be in so masterly an Hand as Shakespeare's. In Isabella's Character there is a fine Variety of Passions, and a beautiful Struggle between her Virtue and her tender Sentiments for her Brother. The Duke is likewise a very important and interesting Character; and, notwithstanding some farcical Scenes, the Business of the Piece irresistably commands Attention. As there is very fine Writing in many Passages of this Play, and as many of the Characters are admirably acted, a critical Enquiry into the Beauties of these two different Arts shall be offered to our Readers when *Measure for Measure* shall happen to be repeated. (215)

* * *

[i] DRURY-LANE, March 5, 1757.

This Evening was performed *King Richard the Third*, King Richard by Mr Mossop. It was in this character the Actor now before us appeared first on the English Stage, and gave strong Assurances of that theatrical Excellence which he has ever since supported by good Sense and fine Powers of Voice. As we have already given a summary Account of his Merit in Richard, in the Distinction we made between him and Mr Barry, we need not at present follow him through the several Scenes of this Play. We shall therefore content ourselves with saying that he has justly conceived the Character in every Situation; that he seems to know the real Drift of Richard in every Speech of designing Villainy or of artful Hypocrisy; and that the Tone of his Voice is generally justly varied, and never fails to be an Eccho to the Sense. Should Mr Garrick's Constitution remain so tender as to render it not adviseable for him to go through the Fatigue of this laborious Part any more, we think we may safely say to him, *Tu nunc eris alter ab illo*,[1] though equal Spirit and Brilliancy can hardly be expected. (231)

* * *

[j] COVENT-GARDEN, March 7, 1757.

Was acted Shakespeare's *Othello*, by Mr Barry. It was in this Part this excellent Tragedian started on the English Stage; and it is not to be wondered that such a Performance met with such warm and general Approbation. Mr Barry's Powers in general are nobly adapted to this Character. From his first Entrance into Cyprus, in the second Act, we have nothing left but to admire. The Vehemence of his tender Passion for Desdemona seizes every imagination. His Dignity in quelling the Riot is commanding. His first Tendencies to Jealousy are beautifully expressed and are finely smothered, till at length they burst out into an amazing Wildness of Rage. In the Scene where he collars Iago nothing can be more masterly than his whole Performance. The Extravagance

---

[1] Virgil, *Eclogues* 5.49: 'now you will be next after him.'

of all his Ideas, and of the Emotions attendant on them, is perfectly characteristic. When we hear him speak 'I had been happy if the general Camp,' &c. [3.3.349] we cannot help being hurried away with his Enthusiasm; and when he collars Iago it is actually astonishing how his Powers carry him through such a long continued Climax of Terror; and yet he adds further to our Admiration when, a little after, he bursts out with 'If there be Cords, or Knives, Poison, or Fire,' &c. [3.3.392f.] The whole is vented with the impetuous Ferocity natural to one of Othello's Complexion, still improved with the wildest Harmony of Voice. Every ensuing Scene is greatly supported, and his acting through the whole fifth Act, where the most violent Passions rise and fall in the quickest succession, is such that were he never to play any thing else it is sufficient to stamp him an admirable Tragedian. Were it our Business at present to decide which Part this Actor performs best we should not hesitate to pronounce that in Othello he has more Strokes of Genius than in any other Character whatever; and perhaps on some future Occasion we shall endeavour to point out these to the Reader. (231)

* * *

[k] DRURY-LANE, March 19, 1757.

Shakespeare's Comedy, called *Much Ado About Nothing*, was performed this Evening. Benedick is one of Mr Garrick's best Parts in Comedy. All thro' the Part his Pleasantry is inimitable, and if he had no other Merit in it would sufficiently recompence his Auditors in the Speech where he first deliberates whether he shall marry Beatrice. His Manner of coming forth from the Arbour, and the Tone of his Voice when he says 'This is no Trick,' &c. [2.3.201] is diverting in the highest Degree. His Arguments to reason himself out of his former youthful Resolutions against Marriage are exquisitely humourous; and they are quite agreeable to the Practice of Mankind in general, who seldom want delusive Fallacies to urge in Behalf of their Passions when once they are become fond of any Object whatever. Many of the Scenes in this Comedy are both interesting and entertaining, and particularly when Mr Garrick resolves to give the Challenge, his Performance is perhaps equal to any Thing we have seen from this masterly Actor. (279)

* * *

[l] DRURY-LANE, March 24, 1757.

Shakespeare's Play, intitled *The Winter's Tale*, was performed here this

Evening for the Benefit of Mr Woodward. The Plot of this Play is taken from the old Story of *Dorastus and Faunia*. The Poet has introduced a greater Variation of Circumstances in this Piece than is common with him when he builds his Fable upon the Story-Books or Novels that were then in vogue. Notwithstanding many Improbabilities in the Conduct there is something that pleases and attaches the Mind very strongly in the several Incidents. The Jealousy of Leontes is somewhat sudden; but as Shakespeare was thoroughly acquainted with this Passion (as indeed he was with all our Affections) he here gives several masterly Strokes of Nature, though it must be observed that the Colouring is sometimes indelicate and coarse. The Laws of Hospitality are destroyed by this blind Rage, Polixenes, King of Bohemia (or, according to Sir Thomas Hanmer, Bythinia, as the former is an inland Kingdom and the latter a maritime Country, which is necessary from many Incidents in the Play) is obliged to fly to avoid being murdered, and the infant Daughter of Leontes is sent after him for Protection, the jealous Monarch being possessed with a Notion that the Child was not his own.

In Consequence of this Fancy the Queen Hermione is imprisoned, and afterwards, for her Preservation, reported to be dead. The Loves of Florizel and Perdita, the Daughter of Sicilia, commence sixteen Years after. In order to get over this long Space Shakespeare makes Time a Personage of his Drama, and puts the following Apology into his Mouth:

> I that please some, try all, both Joy and Terror
> Of Good and Bad, that mask and unfold Error;
> Now take upon me in the Name of Time
> To use my Wings—Impute it not a Crime
> To me, or my swift Passage, that I slide
> O'er sixteen Years, and leave the Growth untried
> Of that wide Gap— [4.1.1ff.]

In the Days of our great Poet the Unities of the Drama were very little understood: Romances and Books of Chivalry were the Taste of the Times. Hence Regularity of Design was not looked for by an Audience, and it is no Wonder, therefore, if Shakespeare embraced a fashionable Error which gave rise to a Variety of Incidents and well agreed with his unbounded Genius.

The Pastoral Scenes throughout this Play are wrought with a masterly Hand. How naturally is the old Shepherd introduced in the

Storm. 'They have frighted away (says he) two of my Sheep, which I fear the Wolf will sooner find than the Master; if any where I find them, 'tis by the Sea-Side brouzing of Ivy.' [3.3.65ff.]—The Description of the Shipwreck in the Mouth of his Son the Clown, is admirably picturesque. 'I would you did but see how it chafes, how it rages, how it takes up the Shore,—but that's not to the Point—Oh! the most piteous Cry of the poor Souls—Sometimes to see 'em, and not to see 'em—now the Ship boring the Moon with her Mainmast, and anon swallowed with Yest and Froth,' &c. [3.3.86ff.]—The Ship boring the Moon with her Mast is finely natural from an untutor'd Rustic. The Fate of Antigonus, who was charged with the Child of Leontes, is well told by the same Person: 'To see how the Bear tore out his Shoulder-Bone; how he cried to me for Help, and said his Name was Antigonus, a Nobleman.' [3.3.92ff.]

The Loves of Florizel and Perdita form a subordinate Plot, which is productive of many beautiful and entertaining Scenes. By Means of their Affection we are plainly led on to the Discovery of Perdita's being Leontes' Daughter. It were to be wished this had been effected without changing the Scene again into Sicilia. But Space as well as Time are annihilated when Shakespeare pleases, and the Delusion is so pleasing that we are at all Times ready to give into it.

The Relation given to Autolycus of the Manner how the Shepherd found the Bundle artfully prepares us for the Denouement. Circumstance rises upon Circumstance: 'The Mantle of Queen Hermione—Her Jewel about the Neck of it—the Letters of Antigonus found with it', &c. [5.2.32ff.] The subsequent Account of the Meeting of Polixenes and Leontes is exquisitely tender, and we naturally acquiesce in their Conviction: 'Leontes being ready to leap out of himself for Joy of his found Daughter, as if that Joy were now become a Loss, cries—Oh thy Mother! thy Mother!—then asks Bohemia Forgiveness, then embraces his Son-in-Law; then again worries he his Daughter with clasping* her.' [5.2.47ff.] We could wish that the Discovery of Hermione was unfolded by Means as natural and probable. Her having lived sequestered for many Years might be allowed if she did not stand for a Statue at last. This Circumstance is certainly childish, as is likewise the pretended Revival of her by Musick. Had Hermione been discovered to us in a rational Manner the Close would have been pathetic, whereas at present, notwithstanding many Strokes of fine Writing, Reason operates too strongly against the Incident, and our Passions subside

* *Clipping her* is the common reading; we have ventured to change it for a Word that gives a clearer Idea, and may possibly have been altered by an hasty Compositor.

into Calmness and Inactivity. We shall conclude this long Paragraph with two Remarks: First, That Mr Garrick has judiciously altered this Play for Representation, as it is possible that extended into five Acts the Improbabilities and Changes of Place would have tired, whereas at present the whole is more compact, Absurdities are retrenched, and our Attention is alive throughout. Secondly, As the Circumstances of the Infant's being taken up with Jewels about it, of the Person who had Care of the Child being lost, and the subsequent Discovery by Means of those Jewels have a palpable Resemblance to the Incident in the Tragedy of *Douglas*, it may be observed that the Author of that Piece has been happy in a beautiful Coincidence of Thought, or has successfully kept his Eye on Shakespeare's Passage, which he has converted to his own Use, and embellished with many elegant Touches of his own. (295)

*　　*　　*

[m] April 7–9, 1757.

There being a Cessation of theatrical Business this Week, we think we cannot better fill up this Department of the CHRONICLE than by recommending to the Perusal of our Readers Mr Havard's ODE to the Memory of SHAKESPEARE. The ingenious Author of this little poetic Composition has not adopted the Practice of the Generality of his cotemporary Ode-writers. He has not, like them, merely endeavoured to give us a motley Piece of patch-work Versification composed of Shreds and Remnants from Spenser, Milton, and Shakespeare. The modern Way of writing Poetry resembles the Method among Boys at School, where he succeeds best who remembers the greatest Number of choice Phrases and Hemisticks from the Classics, and contrives to weave them altogether in one Piece. This Artifice, with the Help of a little unintelligible Imagery and a few abstract Ideas and Passions personified, will help to furnish out an Ode that shall elevate and surprize and make us gaze and stare, but leave no Kind of Trace of Thought or Sense behind it. This lofty Jargon Mr Havard has not aspired to, but has modestly contented himself with uniting both Sentiment and suitable Diction; at the same time that it is poetical, it is a Critique on Shakespeare and in some Places it rises to the Sublime. We shall not detain our Readers any longer from the Piece itself than just to mention that it cannot fail to be a good Entertainment on the Stage, when it is rendered still more enthusiastic by the musical Graces of such a Genius as Dr Boyce.

An ODE to the Memory of SHAKESPEARE.
Written by Mr. HAVARD.
And set to Music by Dr. BOYCE.
To be sung at Drury-Lane Theatre, Tuesday the 12th inst. by
Messrs. Beard, Champness, &c. &c.

Titles and Ermine, fall behind;
Be this a Tribute to the Mind:
 O for a Muse of Fire,
 Such as did Homer's Soul inspire!
Or such an Inspiration as did swell
The Bosom of the Delphic Oracle!
 Or one *yet more divine,*
 Thine, SHAKESPEARE, thine!
Then should this Song immortal be;
Nor the Verse blush that praises thee.
Taught by yourself alone to sing,
Sublime you soar on Nature's Wing;
How sweet the Strain! how bold the Flight!
 Above the Rules
 Of Critic Schools,
And cool Correctness of the Stagyrite.

When Horror ombers o'er the Scene,
And Terror with distorted Mien,
Erects the Hair, and chills the Blood;
Whose Painting must be understood
To strike such Feelings to the Soul,
What *Master-Genius* works the whole?
 SHAKESPEARE alone.
He, pow'rful Ruler of the Heart,
 With ev'ry Passion plays;
 Now strikes the String, and every Part
 The magic Touch obeys.
 He reigns alone;
 Nor can his Throne
Fear Usurpation, or Decay,
Lasting as Time, and bright as Southern Day.
 SHAKESPEARE! no single Merit's thine:
 How can we sep'rate what's Divine?
 Thy Mind effulgent shoots forth Rays,

Like the bright Sun, ten thousand Ways,
　　Yet is the Body all intire,
One glorious Mass of intellectual Fire.

Now roars the Scene with Humour's Jest;
　　Now plaintive Sorrows flow:
And now, with Pity's Sigh opprest,
　　We feel, we share the Lover's Woe.
　　　When jealous Passions rage,
　　　What Thunder shakes the Stage!
Loud as the Trump th'Arch-Angel bears,
When the last Sound shall rend the Spheres.

　　Others may by unwearied Aim,
　　One Passage only find to Fame;
　　Thro' one unvaried Track pursue,
　　And keep the destin'd Mark in View:
But, SHAKESPEARE, that undaunted Soul,
Leaps into Space, and occupies the Whole.
　　　If e'er thy lofty Wing
　　　Too daringly has flown,
　　　'Twas but, Columbus-like,
　　　To find out Worlds unknown.
　　　CHORUS.
Then, Britain, boast that to thy Sons was giv'n
The greatest Genius ever sent from Heav'n!　　　(343)

*　　　*　　　*

[n] April 12–14, 1757.

To the Admirers of SHAKESPEARE.

Having nothing new to say of theatrical Matters at present, we embrace
the Opportunity of informing all Persons of Taste that an Edition of the
Works of our great dramatic Genius is now preparing for the Public
by one of the best Critics of this Age (to speak of him in the most
moderate Terms) who has approved himself, in various Branches of
Writing, an English Classic of the first Magnitude. It need not be
mentioned that Mr Samuel Johnson is the Gentleman whom we here
intend. His manly Way of Thinking, his extensive Erudition, his
exquisite Taste and sound Judgment, have been sufficiently displayed
in *The Rambler*. In these beautiful Compositions there is not only to be

found a fine Vein of original Sentiment but he hath also enriched the English Language with a copious Variety of Diction beyond any of his Cotemporaries. Add to this that *Monumentum Ære perennius*[1] which he hath erected in Honour of his native Tongue—we mean his Dictionary, in which he hath supplied the Want of an Academy of Belles Lettres, and performed Wonders towards fixing our Grammar and ascertaining the determinate Meaning of Words, which are known to be in their own Nature of a very unstable and fluctuating Quality. To his Labours it may hereafter be owing that our Drydens, our Addisons, and our Popes shall not become as obsolete and unintelligible as Chaucer; and from him we may reasonably expect a more correct Edition of our great Shakespeare than has been hitherto offered to the Public, as he is undoubtedly acquainted with the Rise and Progress of English Literature, and as he is thoroughly possessed of all the requisite Qualifications of a great Critic. By such a Genius the Public may promise themselves that Difficulties will be explained without torturing the Sense; that Errors will be detected, and the true Reading restored, without Licentiousness or obtruding unnatural and unwarranted Alterations; that the Author's Way of thinking will be preserved without an Insertion of childish Conceits; that Beauties will be pointed out, agreeably to that sublime Imagination which he is known to be possessed of; and in short, that we shall have an Edition worthy of Shakespeare and of Mr Johnson. In this we have delivered our own Opinion with Candour and Sincerity, and we now beg the Reader will peruse his own Proposals which, at the same Time that they shew the Modesty of the Author in speaking of himself, will also prove how thoroughly sensible he is of the Difficulties of his Undertaking, and therefore how likely he is to succeed in the Removal of them, since we know him to be possessed of a Genius to which we may apply what was said of Cæsar, 'the Alps and Pyreneans sink before him.' But we shall detain our Readers no longer from Mr Johnson's own Words. (358)

[Reprints Johnson's *Proposals*: above, No. 160.]

★   ★   ★

[o] DRURY-LANE, April 16, 1757.

Shakespeare's historical Tragedy of *Macbeth* was performed here this Evening. As we have, in two former Papers, given an Account of the

---

[1] Horace, *Odes* 3.30.1: 'a monument more lasting than bronze'.

Plan and Writing of this Play we have only to remark at present that Mr Mossop has very great Merit in the Performance of this Character. He seems to have studied the Poet with great Accuracy, and indeed the Part requires great Labour and Application from any Performer who is ambitious of excelling in it. If our Readers will please to recollect our former Criticisms they will perceive, at one View, what a Variety of Situations Macbeth is placed in; and certainly there is nothing in the whole Compass of the Player's imitative Art so difficult as to support a Character through a long Series of different Actions, and to preserve the same original Man through a Vicissitude of Emotions, sometimes exalting, sometimes depressing, now driving to Madness, and now falling into Melancholy and Despair. If Mr Mossop fails in any of the Requisites for this Part it is in his Deportment, which, we think, has not sufficient Freedom and Gallantry.

In the Scene where his guilty Conscience pictures to him a visionary Dagger we are of Opinion that he displays a great Judgment: His Countenance is strongly impressed with Terror, and the deep Tones of his Voice very justly suit the Solemnity and Awfulness of the Occasion. In the Scene is perhaps one of the hardest to be well executed among all Shakespeare's Plays, because the Poet does not here so much help the Actor as in other Passages, but on the contrary he requires great Aid from the Performer to give, as it were, Reality to airy nothing, and terrify an Audience against the Testimony of the faithful Eyes, as Horace calls them. The Effect in this Case must proceed from the strong Tokens the Player gives of his being possessed with the Idea; and the Idea cannot be excited but by a strong and creative Imagination. In the Scene where Banquo's Ghost appears the Apparatus of the ghastly Look and bloody Forehead help the Audience and the Actor, because the Object appears terrible of itself. Therefore, though Mr Mossop performs well in this last Situation, yet we cannot ascribe to him the same Degree of Merit as in the former. In general throughout the Play he speaks the Soliloquies with great Propriety, but now and then is he not somewhat out of Time in his Pauses? That is to say, does he not continue too long in them? In Musick a sudden Cessation of the whole Band has a fine Effect, because it breaks out again very quickly into a full Tumult of Harmony, which would be greatly hurt if the Pause were allowed to be too long.

We observed in a former Paper that a melancholy Gloom overcasts the Mind of Macbeth; but this is by slow and imperceptible Degrees, till at length it settles into a Kind of determined Despondency that makes him *grow a weary of the Sun* [5.5.49], and therefore resolved desperately to hazard every Thing. We think this Performer very just in his Execution of this difficult Part of the Character; in him we perceive the strong Brilliancy of the Colouring fade away by proper Gradations till it finally ends in the darkest Shade. Upon the whole, we are clearly of Opinion that if Mr Mossop will resolve to play this Part more carelessly he will play it better. Because while he is over studious to please, his Deportment becomes constrained, whereas every Attitude of Macbeth requires Boldness and Freedom; and indeed in this last Circumstance consisted the superior Merit of Mr Garrick, who supported this extreme hard Part with such a commanding Air in every Movement and such a graceful Horror, if we may so express it, as has hardly been equalled even by himself in any other Performance. (375)

* * *

[p] DRURY-LANE, Nov. 30, 1757.

On last Monday-night, whilst the Play of *Henry the Eighth*, the Performance whereof has been lightly touched upon in a former Paper, was acted at Drury-Lane without any other Interruption but that of Applause, the other House was very far from enjoying the same Tranquility. Pleasure was not the only Motive that had brought thither all the Spectators then present, great Part of them were possessed with a Spirit quite different from that of Approbation; for as soon as the Play began the hostile Disposition of Part of the Pit manifested itself in a hollow Murmurings, which were soon improved into more articulate Sounds. The whole House rung with the Name of Barry, and Mr Rich was summoned to appear before his Judges and answer for his not having engaged that necessary Performer for the present Season. But the Manager, fearing *lest they might make the Punishment precede the Tryal*, pitched upon Mr Smith to be his Plenipotentiary and harangue the Public. That Gentleman's Speech appeared far from satisfactory, but unluckily for the Barryists it happened to be backed by an Army of Carpenters and Grenadiers, which proved the RATIO ULTIMA, and some Gentlemen being taken Prisoners paid a forced Visit to the next Justice, where we shall leave them.

I hope the Reader does not expect I should enter into a Discussion of the several Rights of the two Parties; it is to me, whatever it may be to the Town, a Matter of absolute Indifference whether on one Hand a Manager, though acknowledgedly a Servant of the Publick, has a

Right as well as every other Subject to dispose of his Property as he lists; and on the other Hand, whether the Right of rejecting and the Right of demanding any particular Performer are one and the same Thing, and consequently whether the Town, who is certainly possessed of the one, may he deemed in Equity invested equally with the other. But far be it from me to engage in such nice Disputes; they are now in far better Hands, those of the Gentlemen of the Law who, I am sure, will make much more of them every way than the whole Tribe of Writers combined. Therefore without dwelling any longer on this dangerous Topic let us hasten to the Comedy of ALL IS WELL THAT ENDS WELL, presented last Night at Drury-Lane. The Subject of this Comedy is taken from *Il Decamerone di Boccaccio*. As for the Characters, some of them are of Shakespeare's own creating, and the rest were mere Names and Words to which he has adapted proper Beings.

There is not one of Shakespeare's Comedies where he has exerted a greater Share of the *Vis comica* than in this, and I do not imagine there is to be found in all that great Master's Works, if you except his Falstaff, a truer, pleasanter, and more striking Character than that of Parolles. Yet one Thing I have observed in it which I never could answer to myself: it is when, after one of his Scenes with Lafeu, the Bragart in a Soliloquy [2.3.230ff.] talks of wiping off the Disgrace put upon him by that old Lord by fighting his Son, and a good Deal more to that Purpose. Every where else Parolles is thoroughly sensible of his Cowardice: why then should he just at that Instant lack that Consciousness and strive, as it were, to cheer himself into a Notion of his being brave? Besides that it answers no Purpose and breaks off the Continuity of the Character, is not this perverting the End of Soliloquies, which are in themselves but too absurd and have only been allowed for Conveniency, that by their Means the Audience may get an Insight into Characters and Designs of a Nature that require a theatrical Secrecy, that is to say, a Secrecy relative only to the Business of the Play and the Parties concerned in the Plot? This only I offer as my Doubt, and rather incline to think it my Mistake than imagine that incomparable Writer defective in that very Point which was always esteemed his particular Excellence. However, that Character, even admitting that Reproach to be well grounded, is one of the greatest on the English Stage; and Mr Woodward's Exhibition of it fell in nothing short of its Beauties and Humour. As to the rest of the Parts, they are rather just than striking, and I think as much may be said of the Performance. (526–7)

*   *   *

[q] DRURY-LANE, December 5, 1757.

This Night was repeated at this Theatre the Play of *The Tempest*, written by Shakespeare. The Manager caused this Performance to be sung a few Winters ago, and now he hath caused it to be said. In both these acts he was perhaps wrong; for to convert Shakespeare into Shakespearelli[1] is a wilder Transformation than ever Mr Rich and Mr Woodward have exhibited in their Pantomimes, and *The Tempest* as written by our great Poet is a Play fitter for the Closet than for Theatrical Representation. Not but we must acknowledge that Miss Pritchard appears in it with an amiable, elegant Simplicity; and Mr Mossop by a clear, distinct and harmonious Delivery shews himself a Master of Elocution. Since we have mentioned this Performer, it is judged expedient to take this Opportunity of doing the earliest Justice in our Power, by way of Atonement for an injurious Criticism which lately found its way into this Paper.

> Pretty in amber to observe the forms
> Of hairs, and straws, and grubs, and dirt, and worms;
> The things, we know, are neither rich nor rare,
> But wonder how the Devil they got there.

These Lines of Mr Pope we have cited on this Occasion as we think they will suggest to our Readers in what light they may consider the Chronicle, when any thing unworthy of a Place in it shall through hurry or inadvertence be conveyed through this Channell to the public Notice. The Fact is, our Theatrical Intelligence must occasionally consist of Contributions from various Hands; and a Pen is sometimes brandished by Hands unequal to the Task. To a Misfortune of this Sort Candour and Justice require that we should entreat our Readers to impute a long laboured Animadversion on Mr Mossop's Performance in the Character of Bevil. It got into the Hands of the Compositor of the Press before it was revised by a proper Judge of these Matters. For the future Care will be taken to render this Part of the Paper as instructive, amusing, and unexceptionable as the Nature of a quick Publication will admit; and in the mean Time the present Writer thinks proper to declare that the abovementioned Criticism on Mr Mossop's *Bevil* was false almost in every Particular. He does not speak by hearsay, but was an Eye-witness to many Excellencies in his acting of that Character. (544)

---

[1] See Garrick's Prologue to *The Fairies*: above, No. 146.

162. Richard Hurd on Shakespeare

1757

[a] From the notes to his edition of Horace, *Epistula ad Pisones* ll. 47f. (1757); this text from Hurd's *Works*, 8 vols (1811).

[b] From *A Letter to Mr. Mason; on the Marks of Imitation* (Cambridge, 1757).

On Hurd (1720–1808) see the headnote to No. 120 in Vol. 3. The first piece furthers the work of identifying Shakespeare's characteristic linguistic practices that had been begun by Theobald and Upton. The second is a development, with examples, and written at the request of his Cambridge friend, William Mason, of Hurd's theories of imitation, first outlined in a dissertation appended to his translation of Horace in 1751 (No. 128 in Vol. 3).

---

[a] [On Shakespeare's creative vocabulary]

DIXERIS EGREGIE, NOTUM SI CALLIDA VERBUM/REDDIDERIT JUNCTURA NOVUM.—][1] This direction about *disposing* of old words in such a manner as that they shall have the grace of *new* ones is among the finest in the whole poem. And because Shakespeare is he, of all our poets, who has most successfully practised this secret it may not be amiss to illustrate the precept before us by examples taken from his writings.

But first it will be proper to explain the *precept* itself as given by Horace. . . . (I, 74)

On the whole, then, *junctura* is a word of large and general import, and the same in *expression* as *order or disposition* in a *subject*. The poet would say 'Instead of framing new words, I recommend to you *any* kind of artful management by which you may be able to give a new air and cast to old ones.'

Having now got at the true meaning of the precept, let us see how well it may be exemplified in the practice of Shakespeare.

[1] 'You will express yourself most happily if a skilful setting makes a familiar word new.'

1. The first example of this *artful management*, if it were only in complaisance to former commentators, shall be that of *compound epithets*; of which sort are,

> High-sighted Tyranny; A barren-spirited fellow [*Julius Caesar*, 2.1.118; 4.1.36]

> An arm-gaunt steed; Flower-soft hands [*Antony and Cleopatra*, 1.5.48; 2.2.214]

> Lazy-pacing clouds [*Romeo and Juliet*, 2.2.31]

and a thousand instances more in this poet. But this is a small part of his *craft*, as may be seen by what follows. For this end is attained

2. *By another form of composition*, by compound *verbs* as well as compound *adjectives*.

To *candy* and *limn* are known words. The poet would express the contrary ideas, and he does it happily by compounding them with our English negative *dis*:

> The hearts
> That pantler'd me at heels, to whom I gave
> Their wishes, do *discandy*, melt their sweets
> On blossoming Cæsar—   [*Antony and Cleopatra*, 4.12.20ff.]

> That which is now a horse, ev'n with a thought
> The rack *dislimns*, and makes it indistinct
> As water is in water—   [*ibid.*, 4.14.9ff.]

Though here we may observe that for the readier acceptation of these compounds he artfully subjoins the explanation.

3. By a liberty he takes of converting *substantives* into *verbs*:
> A glass that *featur'd* them.   [*Cymbeline*, 1.1.49]

> Sinon's weeping
> Did *scandal* many a holy tear—   [*ibid.*, 3.4.57f.]
> Great griefs, I see, *medicine* the less.   [*ibid.*, 4.2.244]

> that kiss
> I carried from thee, Dear; and my true lip
> Hath *virgin'd* it e'er since—   [*Coriolanus*, 5.3.46ff.]

Or *verbs* into *substantives*:
> Then began
> A stop i' th' chaser, a *Retire*—   [*Cymbeline*, 5.3.39f.]

take
No stricter *render* of me— [*ibid.*, 5.4.16f.]

handkerchief
Still waving, as the fits and *stirs* of's mind
Could best express— [*ibid.*, 1.3.10ff.]

Sextus Pompeius
Hath giv'n the *dare* to Cæsar— [*Antony and Cleopatra*, 1.2.177f.]

4. By using *active* verbs neutrally:
He hath fought to-day
As if a god in hate of mankind had
Destroy'd, in such a shape— [*ibid.*, 4.8.24ff.]

It is the bloody business, that *informs*
Thus to mine eyes— [*Macbeth*, 2.1.48ff.]

And *neutral* verbs actively:
never man
Sigh'd truer breath; but that I see thee here,
Thou noble thing! more *dances* my rapt heart
Than when I first my wedded mistress saw
Bestride my threshold— [*Coriolanus*, 4.5.114ff.]

like smiling Cupids,
With divers-colour'd fans, whose wind did seem
To *glow* the delicate cheeks which they did cool—
[*Antony and Cleopatra*, 2.2.206ff.]

5. By converting *Adjectives* into Substantives:
I do not think
So fair an *outward* and such stuff within
Endows a man but him— [*Cymbeline*, 1.1.22ff.]

6. By converting *Participles* into Substantives:
He would have well become this place, and grac'd
The *thankings* of a King— [*Cymbeline*, 5.5.406f.]

The herbs, that have in them cold dew o' th' night,
Are *strewings* fitt'st for Graves— [*ibid.*, 4.2.285f.]

Then was I as a tree
Whose boughs did bend with fruit. But, in one night,
A storm, or robbery, call it what you will,
Shook down my mellow *hangings*— [*ibid.*, 3.3.60ff.]

Comes in my father,
And like the tyrannous *breathing* of the North
Shakes all our Buds from blowing—   [*ibid.*, 1.3.35ff.]

Which last instance I the rather give for the sake of proposing an emendation which I think restores this fine passage to its Integrity. Before the late edition of Shakespeare it stood thus,

And like the tyrannous breathing of the North
Shakes all our Buds from *growing*—

But the sagacious Editor saw that this reading was corrupt, and therefore altered the last word, *growing*, for unanswerable reasons, into *blowing*. See Mr W's note upon the place. This slight change gives propriety and beauty to the passage, which before had no sort of meaning. Yet still all is not quite right. For as the great Critic himself observes, '*Breathing* is not a very proper word to express the rage and bluster of the north wind.' Besides, one does not see how the *shaking* of these Buds is properly assign'd as the cause of their not blowing. The wind might shake off the *blossoms* of a fruit tree, i.e. the Buds when they were *full-blown*, but so long as the blossom lies folded up in the Bud it seems secure from shaking. At least the *shaking* is not the *immediate* cause of the effect spoken of: it is simply the *cold* of the north-wind that closes the Bud and keeps it from *blowing*. I am therefore tempted to propose another alteration of the text, and to read thus:

And like the tyrannous Breathing of the North
Shuts all our Buds from blowing—

If this correction be allowed every thing is perfectly right. It is properly the *breathing*, the cold breath of the North, that shuts up the Buds when they are on the point of blowing. Whence the epithet *tyrannous* will be understood not as implying the idea of *blust'ring* (an idea indeed necessary if we retain the word *shakes*) but simply of *cruel*, the *tyranny* of this wind consisting in imprisoning the flower in its Bud and denying it the liberty of coming out into *Blossom*. The application too of this comparison, which required the change of *growing* into *blowing*, seems also to require the present alteration of *shakes*. For there was no manner of violence in *the father's* coming in upon the lovers. All the effect was that his presence *restrained* them from that interchange of tender words which was going to take place between them.*

---

* [In the 1766 edition, i 57f., Hurd adds the following note] Thus far I had written in the last edition of these notes, and I now see no cause to doubt the *general* truth and propriety

But to return to other Instances of the Poet's artifice in the management of *known* words. An apparent Novelty is sometimes effected

7. By turning *Participles* into Adverbs—

> *tremblingly* she stood
> And on the sudden dropt—   [*Antony and Cleopatra*, 5.2.340f.]

(One remembers the fine use Mr Pope has made of this word in, 'Or touch, if *tremblingly* alive all o'er'—.)

> But his flaw'd heart,
> Alack, too weak the conflict to support,
> 'Twixt two extremes of Passion, joy and grief,
> Burst *smilingly*—   [*King Lear*, 5.3.196ff.]

8. By *figurative terms*, i.e. by such terms as though common in the *plain* are unusual in the figurative application.

> This common Body
> Like to a vagabond flag, upon the stream,
> Goes to, and back, *lacquying* the varying tide.
>   [*Antony and Cleopatra*, 1.4.44ff.]
> When snow the Pasture *sheets*.   [*ibid.*, 1.4.65]

To this head may be referred those innumerable terms in Shakespeare which surprize us by their novelty, and which surprize us generally on account of his preferring the *specific* idea to the *general* in the *subjects* of his Metaphors and the *circumstances* of his Description; an excellence in poetical expression which cannot be sufficiently studied. The examples are too frequent, and the thing itself too well understood, to make it necessary to enlarge on this article.

9. By *plain words*, i.e. such as are common in the figurative, uncommon in the literal acceptation.

> *Disasters* vail'd the Sun—   [*Hamlet*, 1.1.118]

> Th' *extravagant* and erring spirit hies
> To his confine—   [*ibid.*, 1.1.154]

---

of this emendation. Only it occurs to me that instead of SHUTS the poet's own word might perhaps be CHECKS, as not only being more like in *sound* to the word *shakes* but as coming nearer to the *traces* of the Letters. Besides, CHECKS gives the precise idea we should naturally look for, whether we regard the integrity of the *figure* '—tyrannous—checks—,' or the *thing* illustrated by it, viz. the abrupt coming in of the father, which was properly a *check* upon the lovers. Lastly, the expression is mended by this reading, for though we may be allowed to say *shuts from blowing* yet *checks from blowing* is easier and better English.

Can't such things be
And *overcome* us, like a Summer's cloud,
Without our special wonder?   [*Macbeth*, 3.4.110ff.]

10. By *transposition of words, unauthoriz'd use of terms, and ungrammatical construction*. Instances in all his plays, *passim*.

11. By *foreign idioms*. 'Tis true these are not frequent in Shakespeare. Yet some Latinisms and e'en Grecisms we have, as '*Quenched of hope—*' [*Cymbeline*, 5.5.195f.] and the like. But, which is more remarkable and served his purpose just as well, the writers of that time had so *latiniz'd* the English language that the pure *English* Idiom which Shakespeare generally follows has all the air of *novelty* which other writers are used to affect by a foreign phraseology.

The Reader sees it were easy to extend this list of Shakespeare's arts in the *Callida junctura* much farther. But I intended only a specimen of them, so much as might serve to illustrate the rule of Horace.

It is enough that we have now a perfect apprehension of what is meant by CALLIDA JUNCTURA, and that it is in effect but another word for *Licentious Expression*, the use of which is, as Quintilian well expresses it, '*Ut quotidiani et semper eodem modo formati sermonis Fastidium levet, et nos à vulgari dicendi genere defendat.*'[1] In short, the articles here enumerated are but so many ways of departing from the usual and simpler forms of speech without neglecting too much the grace of ease and perspicuity, in which well-tempered licence one of the greatest charms of all poetry, but especially of Shakespeare's poetry, consists. Not that he was always and every where so happy as in the instances given above. His expression sometimes, and by the very means here exemplified, becomes *hard*, *obscure*, and *unnatural*. This is the extreme on the other side. But in general we may say that he hath either followed the direction of Horace very ably, or hath hit upon his Rule very happily. (I, 77-85)

[b] [On Shakespeare and the imitation of the classics]

Yet all this, you say, comes very much short of what you require of me. You want me to specify those peculiar considerations, and even to reduce them into rule, from which one may be authorised in any instance to pronounce of imitations. It is not enough, you pretend, to say of any passage in a celebrated poet that it most probably was taken from

---

1 *Institutes of Oratory*, 9.3.3.: [Figures of speech 'have one special merit,] that they relieve the tedium of everyday stereotyped speech and save us from commonplace language.'

some other. In your extreme jealousy for the credit of your order you call upon me to shew the distinct marks which convict him of his commerce.

In a word, You require me to turn to the poets, to gather a number of those passages I call Imitations and to point to the *circumstances* in each that prove them to be so. I attend you with pleasure, in this amusing search. It is not material, I suppose, that we observe any strict method in our ramblings. And yet we will not wholly neglect it. . . .

Perhaps, then, we shall find undoubted marks of Imitation both in the SENTIMENT and EXPRESSION of great writers.

To begin with such considerations as are most GENERAL.

I. An identity of the *subject-matter* of poetry is no sure evidence of Imitation: and least of all, perhaps, in natural description. Yet where the *local* peculiarities of nature are to be described, there an exact conformity of the matter will evince an imitation.

Descriptive poets have ever been fond of lavishing all the riches of their fancy on the *Spring*. But the appearances of this *prime of the year* are so diversified with the climate that descriptions of it, if taken directly from nature, must needs be very different. The Greek and Latin, and since them the Provençal poets, when they insist, as they always do, on the indulgent softness of this season, its *genial dews* and *fostering breezes*, speak nothing but what is agreeable to their own experience and feeling.[1]

> It ver; et Venus; et Veneris praenuntius antè
> Pinnatus graditur Zephyrus vestigia propter:
> Flora quibus mater praespergens ante viaï
> Cuncta coloribus egregiis et odoribus opplet.

Venus, or the spirit of love, is represented by those poets as brooding o'er this delicious season:[2]

> Rura foecundat voluptas: rura VENEREM sentiunt.
> Ipsa gemmas purpurantem pingit annum floribus:
> Ipsa surgentis papillas de Favonî spiritu
> Urguet in toros tepentes; ipsa roris lucidi, &c

---

[1] Lucretius, 5.736ff.: 'Spring comes, and Venus, and Venus' winged courier Cupid runs in front. And all along the path that they will tread dame Flora carpets the trail of Zephyr with a wealth of blossoms exquisite in hue and fragrance' (tr. R. E. Latham, Penguin).

[2] *Pervigilium Veneris*, stanzas 19, 4: 'The country quickens with love's delight, the country feels Venus' touch.' 'She herself paints the crimsoning year with flowery jewels; herself coaxes swelling buds into warm clusters under the West Wind's breath; herself sprinkles dripping wetness of the glittering dew' (Loeb).

and a great deal more to the same purpose, which every one recollects in the old classic and in the Provençal poets.

But when we hear this language from the more Northern, and particularly our English bards, who perhaps are shivering with the blasts of the North-east at the very time their imagination would warm itself with these notions, one is certain this cannot be the effect of *observation* but of a sportful fancy; enchanted by the native loveliness of these exotic images, and charmed by the secret insensible power of *imitation.*

And to shew the certainty of this conclusion Shakespeare, we may observe, who had none of this classical or Provençal bias on his mind, always describes not a Greek or Italian or Provençal but an English Spring, where we meet with many unamiable characters, and among the rest instead of Zephyr or Favonius we have the bleak North-east, that *nips the blooming infants of the Spring.*

But there are other obvious examples. In Cranmer's prophetic speech at the end of *Henry VIII*, when the poet makes him say of Queen Elizabeth that

> In her days ev'ry man shall eat with safety
> Under his own vine what he plants.   [5.5.33f.]

and of King James that

> He shall flourish,
> And, like a mountain Cedar, reach his branches
> To all the plains about him—   [5.5.52ff.]

it is easy to see that his *Vine* and *Cedar* are not of English growth, but transplanted from Judæa. I do not mention this as an impropriety in the poet, who for the greater solemnity of his prediction and even from a principle of decorum makes his Arch-bishop fetch his imagery from Scripture. I only take notice of it as a certain argument that the imagery was not his own, that is, not suggested by his own observation of nature. (14–17)

*   *   *

[Imitation is shown when the 'genius of one *people* [is] given to another.']
Still another instance comes in my way. How happened it, one may ask, that Sir PHILIP SIDNEY in his *Arcadia*, and afterwards SPENSER in his *Faerie Queene*, observed so unnatural a conduct in those works, in which the Story proceeds as it were by snatches, and with continual interruptions? How was the good sense of those writers, so conversant besides

in the best models of antiquity, seduced into this preposterous method? The answer, no doubt, is that they were copying the design, or disorder rather, of ARIOSTO, the favourite poet of that time.

III. Of near akin to this contrariety *to the genius of a people* is another mark which a careful reader will observe 'in the representation of certain TENETS, different from those which prevail in a writer's country or time.'

1. We seldom are able to fasten an imitation with certainty on such a writer as Shakespeare. Sometimes we are, but never to so much advantage as when he happens to forget himself in this respect. When Claudio in *Measure for Measure* pleads for his life in that famous speech,

> Ay, but to die, and go we know not where;
> To lye in cold obstruction, and to rot;
> This sensible warm motion to become
> A kneaded clod; and the delighted spirit
> To bathe in fiery floods, or to reside
> In thrilling regions of thick-ribbed ice;
> To be imprison'd in the viewless winds,
> And blown with restless violence about
> The pendant world—   [3.1.119ff.]

It is plain that these are not the Sentiments which any man entertained of *Death* in the writer's age or in that of the speaker. We see in this passage a mixture of Christian and Pagan ideas, all of them very susceptible of poetical ornament, and conducive to the argument of the Scene, but such as Shakespeare had never dreamt of but for Virgil's Platonic hell, where, as we read,

> aliae panduntur inanes
> Suspensae ad ventos: aliis sub gurgite vasto,
> Infectum eluitur scelus, aut exuritur igni.

> Virg. l. vi.[1] (19–20)

*   *   *

I observe that even Shakespeare himself abounds in learned Allusions. How he came by them is another question, though not so difficult to be answered, you know, as some have imagined. They who are in such astonishment at the learning of Shakespeare, besides that they certainly carry the notion of his illiteracy too far, forget that the Pagan imagery

---

[1] *Aeneid*, 6.740ff.: 'Some are hung stretched out to the empty winds, from some the stain of guilt is washed away under swirling floods or burned out in fire.' This parallel was first pointed out by Peter Whalley: see Vol. 3, p. 283.

was familiar to all the poets of his time, that abundance of this sort of learning was to be picked up from almost every English book he could take into his hands, that many of the best writers in Greek and Latin had been translated into English, that his conversation lay among the most learned, that is, the most paganized poets of his age, but above all that if he had never looked into books or conversed with bookish men he might have learned almost all the secrets of paganism (so far, I mean, as a poet had any use of them) from the MASQUES of B. Jonson, contrived by that poet with so pedantical an exactness that one is ready to take them for lectures and illustrations on the ancient learning rather than exercises of modern wit. The taste of the age, much devoted to erudition, and still more the taste of the Princes for whom he writ gave a prodigious vogue to these unnatural exhibitions. And the knowledge of antiquity requisite to succeed in them was, I imagine, the reason that Shakespeare was not over-fond to try his hand at these elaborate trifles. Once indeed he *did*, and with such success as to disgrace the very best things of this kind we find in Jonson. The short Masque in *The Tempest* is fitted up with a classical exactness. But its chief merit lies in the beauty of the *Show* and the richness of the *poetry*. Shakespeare was so sensible of his Superiority that he could not help exulting a little upon it where he makes *Ferdinand* say

> This is a most majestic *Vision*, and
> Harmonious charming *Lays*—   [4.1.118f.]

'Tis true, another Poet, who possessed a great part of Shakespeare's genius and all Jonson's learning, has carried this courtly entertainment to its last perfection. But the *Masque at Ludlow Castle* was in some measure owing to the *fairy Scenes* of his Predecessor, who chose this province of *Tradition* not only as most suitable to the wildness of his vast creative imagination but as the *safest* for his unlettered Muse to walk in. For here he had much, you know, to expect from the popular credulity, and nothing to fear from the classic superstition of that time. (24–5)]

*   *   *

You have now, Sir, before you a specimen of those rules which I have fancied might be fairly applied to the discovery of imitations, both in regard to the SENSE and EXPRESSION of great writers. I would not pretend that the same stress is to be laid on *all*, but there may be something at least worth attending to in every one of them. It were easy, perhaps, to enumerate still more and to illustrate these I have given with

more agreeable citations. Yet I have spared you the disgust of considering those vulgar passages which every body recollects and sets down for
acknowledged imitations. And these I have used are taken from the
most celebrated of the ancient and modern writers. You may observe
indeed that I have chiefly drawn from our own poets, which I did not
merely because I know you despise the pedantry of confining one's self
to learned quotations, but because I think we are better able to discern
those circumstances which betray an imitation in our own language
than in any other. Amongst other reasons an *identity* of words and
phrases upon which so much depends, especially in the article of *expression*, is only to be had in the *same* language. And you are not to be
told with how much more certainty we determine of the degree of
evidence which such identity affords for this purpose in a language we
speak than in one which we only lisp or spell.

But you will best understand of what importance this affair of
expression is to the discovery of imitations by considering how seldom
we are able to fix an imitation on Shakespeare. The reason is not that
there are not numberless passages in him very like to others in approved
authors, or that he had not read enough to give us a fair hold of him,
but that his expression is so totally his own that he almost always sets us
at defiance.

You will ask me, perhaps, now I am on this subject, how it happened
that Shakespeare's language is every where so much his own as to
secure his imitations, if they were such, from discovery, when I pronounce with such assurance of those of our other poets. The answer is
given for me in the Preface to Mr Theobald's Shakespeare, though the
observation, I think, is too good to come from that critic.[1] It is that
though his words, agreeably to the state of the English tongue at that
time, be generally Latin, his phraseology is perfectly English:[2] an
advantage he owed to his slender acquaintance with the Latin idiom.
Whereas the other writers of his age, and such others of an older date
as were likely to fall into his hands, had not only the most familiar
acquaintance with the Latin idiom but affected on all occasions to make
use of it. Hence it comes to pass that though he might draw sometimes
from the Latin (Ben Jonson, you know, tells us, *He had less Greek*) and
the learned English writers, he takes nothing but the *sentiment*; the
expression comes of itself, and is purely English.

I might indulge in other reflexions and detain you still further with

[1] See Vol. 2, pp. 17ff., on Theobald's use of material by Warburton in this Preface.
[2] See Vol. 2, pp. 481–2: the passage was indeed claimed by Warburton.

examples taken from his works. But we have *lain*, as the Poet speaks, *on these primrose beds* too long. It is time that you now rise to your own nobler *inventions*; and that I return myself to those less pleasing, perhaps, but more useful studies from which your friendly sollicitations have called me. (73–5).

163. Unsigned essay on Garrick's Romeo

1757

From *Memoirs of Sir Thomas Hughson and Mr. Joseph Williams, with the Remarkable History, Travels, and Distresses of Telemachus Lovet* (1757).

This anonymous picaresque novel is discussed by R. G. Noyes, *The Thespian Mirror*, p. 105. For another example of contemporary displeasure with Garrick's 'attitudes'—stage postures—see T. Cibber's essay, No. 157 above.

This Acquaintance [Telemachus has met a clergyman and his wife] led him first to public diversions. At DRURY LANE *Theatre* was to be presented the Tragedy of *Romeo and Juliet*; Mrs—was distractedly fond of that Play, and the *Doctor* prevail'd on TELEMACHUS to be of their Party. *Mr* LOVET had but one objection; he was afraid the Doctor's character [as a clergyman], would oblige him to retire into the Gallery, which was a confinement he was never able to endure. The Doctor soon set him right in this; he said it was a play so much run after, and *Mr* GARRICK's attitudes[1] so much admir'd, that there was hardly such a thing as getting into the House unless seats were previously procured: which he said he had done early that Morning, and had got a Row in one of the front Boxes that would with pleasure accommodate them

[1] *Attitude*: 'The posture or action in which a person, statue, or painted figure, is placed' [Johnson's *Dictionary*].

all. One Coach held the four; and they proceeded to the Theatre. . . .

Thro' the rest of the Evening, *Mr* LOVET was silent and attentive. The Doctor began to make some observations on the part of MERCUTIO, and turn'd himself to TELEMACHUS; *Mr* LOVET told him he was sorry he could not give attention to what he said; he beg'd to enjoy the Play. When the 1st Act was over Mrs —— wanted to engage him in a little chat. He beg'd her a thousand Pardons; he would listen to her with pleasure 'till midnight, when the Play was over: but he was a lover of Musick; he had not heard a tolerable consort for a long time past, and he hoped she would permit him to give the Musick his Ear. Finding this the case, the Doctor and the Ladies with a great deal of Good Nature, rather indulg'd than interrupted his silent Attention. The End of the Play took them home; the Entertainment was some trifling affair which they had all of them often seen. . . .

The Discourse then turn'd to the Performances at the Theatre. *Mr* LOVET, being ask'd what he thought of *Mr* GARRICK, he said he was a surprising man.

'But I am sorry to see the Public (said he, continuing) give him such immoderate applause in what is not only turning *Tragedy* into *Harlequin* machinery, but what is most unnatural. I mean those attitudes you are all so fond of. I speak to you Doctor, as a Philosopher: and a little attention must convince you my remarks are just. In Surprizes, the Mind, and of consequence the Body, is variously affected.—If any Object or Idea, strange or shocking, enter the Imagination or mind simply, that is, without any connexion with or succession of other Objects or Ideas, to constitute the dread which siezeth the Mind; the Body then may be thrown into a sort of convulsions, which when well imitated in action may justly please. Of this kind we had an instance in the Character of JULIET a little before she drank the Mixture. Her distracted imagination brings her Cousin *Tybalt's* ghost to her view. The Idea, the Object is simple; nothing else at first succeeds in the fancy but the Apparition, and she is justly thrown into a beautiful attitude of horror in these words:

> *O look!*

As Ideas grow upon the fancy she becomes a little milder—

> *Methinks I see my Cousin's Ghost*
> *Seeking out* ROMEO— [4.3.55f.]

Need I ask any thinking person who has studied the subject, what a ridiculous piece of action it would be in the Actress to throw herself into the same attitude of horror when she asks herself if the mixture may not be a poison? For it is evident that tho' in the narration her reasons for so imagining follows the thought, they must have been previous in the Mind. The mind indeed must have had some small reasoning on the matter; and then, instead of an attitude of horror, a Just Actress will calmly after a sort of bewilder'd pause proceed in the Question,

> What if it be a poison, which the Frier
> Subt'ly hath ministred, to have me dead;
> Lest in this marriage he should be dishonoured
> Because he married me before to ROMEO?   [4.3.24ff.]

And yet I do remember me somewhat to have seen an Actress who because, forsooth, those attitudes strike the Galleries, did always throw herself into one of *them* in this passage.'

'I already (said the *Doctor*) begin to find I have been unthinkingly led by the applause of a Mob.'

'You shall be convinc'd of it immediately, (return'd TELEMACHUS). Now Sir, as touching ROMEO—I mean *Mr* GARRICK; for abstracting this error in Philosophy, he is the very character itself. When we see the monument op'ned, 'tis very nobly illuminated. But are we to suppose it was so in reality?' was this the custom in VERONA? or did even SHAKE-SPEARE intend it so? So far to the contrary we find JULIET to *Lady* CAPULET says:

> Delay this Marriage for a Month, a Week;
> Or if you do not, make the bridal bed
> In that DIM Monument where TYBALT lies.   [3.5.200ff.]

Besides this, when JULIET is considering on what her situation in the Tomb is like to be, she describes it in quite another form:

> Shall I not then be stifled in the vault,
> To whose foul mouth no healthsome air breathes in . . .?
>   . . . Is it not very like
> The horrible conceit of death and NIGHT
> Together with the terror of the place—   [4.3.33ff.]

et cætera—

There are in all this no appearances of that lustre which in the representation takes off from the Gloomyness of the Scene. I have quoted these two passages because this is a principal thing to be settled, that tho' a Manager, the better to shew part of the fifth scene to the Audience, finds it proper to have lights behind the Scene the Actor ought to know no more of them than a spectator ought to know of a Prompter. He is to behave himself, in short, as if all were dark and gloomy about him, seeing nothing but through the assistance of that light which the Author has put into the hands of BALTHASAR. Now let us suppose him at the Monument,

> *A vault, an ancient receptacle*
> *Where for these many hundred years, the bones*
> *Of all my buried ancestors are pack'd—* [4.3.39ff.]

Would not one naturally expect a Gate decay'd through age, which, rusty, hanging on its hinges, would not admit a guest but with grumbling—Having then with his wrenching iron enforced its

> *Rotten jaws to open—* [5.3.47]

he with some force folds aside the leaves—with the calmness and resolution of a Hero descends the dark abode; his light serves him to find out where JULIET lies; over whom, in silent agonies—agonies which the mind can only feel—indulging a solemn pause, the tears at last breaking from him forces from his mouth that tender, natural, calm observation:

> *O my love! My Wife!*
> *Death that suckt the honey of thy breath,*
> *Hath had no power yet upon thy beauty:* [5.3.91ff.]

In this speech he continues for some time; 'till, having drank the poison, taking his last embrace, he perceives she breathes and stirs.

When a person awakes from a swoon, a fit, or trance, it is always by slow degrees they come to themselves. 'Tis so with JULIET, her short incoherent speeches, and the great distance of time betwixt them,[1] plainly show that SHAKESPEARE intended his JULIET's first signs of life should be natural; should be faint and small.—Now in a place of darkness and drear conceit the eye may be much deceived; the Mind knows it—and no great Mind, as ROMEO's must be, can possibly be thrown into any extream emotion upon an uncertainty.—In his actions he is at first Doubtfully serene; and as he grows more assured of the thing a surprize also naturally gains upon him:[2]

> *Soft—she breathes, and stirs!*

[1] This is in Garrick's adaptation, where Juliet awakes before Romeo dies: see Vol. 3, pp. 338ff.

[2] This and the following quotation are from Garrick's adaptation: Vol. 3, p. 338.

Still, however, something doubting—she speaks—doubts are all dis-spell'd, and surprize is turn'd into raptures of Joy.

She speaks, she lives: and we shall still be bless'd!

Here is raptures—here is Joy. But thorough the whole cannot I discover the smallest Thought, Idea, or Expression which, by rushing unexpec-tedly and suddenly upon the Mind, can throw the Body into extravagant attitudes.

Instead of which the modern ROMEO, having broke the fastenings of the Door, is thrown into horror and surprize. What possibly can be the cause of such an emotion? Had not CAPULET been painted o'er the door I should have suppos'd the Scene-shifters had been guilty of some mis-take, or, by design to fright the Actor, had brought from below some of *Harlequin's* machinery.—How ridiculous, an old rusty pair of Gates to fly open as by the assistance of Magick! However, I soon saw it was the injudicious glare of light in the Monument, and the appearance of JULIET there. But this is not all: an attitude more of a like kind must surprize or please the Galleries. And when the Lady begins to shew signs of life, instead of a silent, doubtful, and attentive attitude, mix'd with an increasive surprize, following the word *Soft!*, he is instantly thrown into an attitude of extravagant extream, as if the Ghost of a BANQUO or a HAMLET had fill'd him with Horror and Surprize.

After all, Sir, I must confess *Mr* GARRICK has pleas'd me in his alterations on the play: and he is the only Gentleman ever charm'd me as an Actor.'

'As an Actor then (said the *Doctor*, and was back'd by the Ladies) let us consider him; what have Players to do with Philosophy?'

'Pardon me Sir, (answer'd TELEMACHUS) no People have more; is it not their Art to Copy Nature? Nature is always best studied with the assistance of Philosophy.' (IV, 224-33)

164. John Armstrong, Shakespearian jottings

1758

From *Sketches: or Essays on Various Subjects*, vol. 1 (1758); this text from *Miscellanies by John Armstrong* (1770), vol. II.

Dr John Armstrong (1709–79) was a friend of Smollett, and contributed eighteen reviews to his *Critical Review* in 1756 (Roper, *RES* n.s. 10 (1959), p. 40). His most important poem is *Taste: an epistle to a young critic* (1753), and he combined his interests in medicine and poetry in a verse-treatise, *The Art of Preserving Health* (1744). See Louis M. Knapp, 'Dr. John Armstrong, Littérateur . . .', *PMLA* 59 (1944), pp. 1019–58, for a reconstruction of Armstrong's wide literary acquaintanceship.

OF THE VERSIFICATION OF ENGLISH TRAGEDY.

The greatest part of our modern writers of Tragedy seem to think it enough to write mere blank verse, no matter however hard it be, however void of swelling and harmony. Even those of them who write the best numbers study to be solemn and pompous throughout, and affect a monotony of heroic Versification from the first appearance of the heroine with her confidante to her last fatal exit, without the least regard to the variety of passions which express themselves in quick or slow, flowing or interrupted, in languishing or impetuous movements.

The proper Versification of *English* Tragedy is most certainly blank verse, but as different from the solemn and majestic movement of heroic poetry as the Iambic is from the Hexameter. What a monstrous production would a *Greek* or *Latin* tragedy in Hexameter Verse appear! —The ancients found the grave Iambic their proper measure for tragedy, as it is at the same time capable of all the dignity which that kind of poem requires, and descends with the greatest ease to the level of prose and conversation. Such as is the Iambic in *Latin* is blank verse in *English*: but by no means the blank verse of *Paradise Lost*.

The numbers ought to be accommodated to the passion, and though in some parts of tragedy it is proper they should be slow or solemn or languishing they ought for the most part to run somewhat rambling and irregular, and often rapid and subsultory, so as to imitate the natural cadence and quick turns of conversation.

Shakespeare, who I will venture to say had the most musical ear of all the *English* poets, is abundantly irregular in his Versification, but his wildest licences seldom hurt the ear; on the contrary, they give his verse a spirit and variety which prevents its ever cloying. Our modern tragedy-writers, instead of using the advantages of their own language, seem in general to imitate the monotony of the *French* Versification, and the only licence they ever venture upon is that poor tame one the supernumerary syllable at the end of a line which they are apt to manage in such a manner as to give their verse a most ungraceful halt. But it is not want of ear alone which makes our common manufacturers of tragedy so insipidly solemn and so void of harmony: it is want of feeling. For let the ear be what it will, if the passions are warmly felt they will naturally express themselves in their proper tones. (163–5)

* * *

SENTENCES

Mr *Voltaire* observes very justly of some authors that they have done themselves no good by endeavouring to be universal. It is a foolish enough piece of vanity, to be sure, for it requires no great genius to write a spiritless ode, an affected epistle, an insipid satire, a flat comedy, a cold tragedy, and even a flimsy, foppish, uninteresting epic poem. SHAKESPEARE perhaps possessed the greatest compass of genius that ever man did, and could excel in every thing from the noblest sublime down to the burlesque. (198)

* * *

I have been told that some *French Abbé*, whose name I forget, pronounces with a very decisive air that SHAKESPEARE understood all the passions but *love*.—Good God!—SHAKESPEARE not understand *love?* —Who does then?—VOLTAIRE? (199)

* * *

As there have been many *small* observations made upon *great* classics, I must take the liberty to venture one. *Iago* ends his description of a good woman with

> She was a wight, if ever such there were—

Here he stops, and *Desdemona* asks, *To do what?* [*Othello*, 2.1.157ff.] It does not appear what leads her to this question, except you add a little word, which seems to have dropt out of its place here without being missed. Suppose it was to be read thus:

> She was a wight, if ever there were,
> To—

Here the buffoon pauses, to draw the lady into the question which it is now natural for her to make, and to give, what he is ready to add, its full effect of surprising and disappointing archly.

> *Iago.* She that was ever fair, and never proud,
>   Had wit at will, and yet was never loud; &c.
> She was a wight, if ever such there were,
> To—
> *Desd.* To do what?—
> *Iago.* To suckle fools, and chronicle small-beer.   (200–1)

*   *   *

Why do the players, in the part of Richard the Third, always say 'Give me a horse'?[1] It not only sounds much better but the meaning is, in my opinion, more warm and spirited as it stands in Shakespeare:

> Give me another horse—Bind up my wounds—   (201)

*   *   *

As I feel it, there is a kind of tame impropriety, or even absurdity, in that action of HAMLET where he pulls out the two miniatures of his father and uncle. It seems more natural to suppose that HAMLET was struck with the comparison he makes between the two brothers upon casting his eyes on their pictures, as they hang up in the apartment where this conference passes with the queen. There is not only more nature, more elegance, and dignity in supposing it thus, but it gives occasion to more passionate and more graceful action, and is of consequence likelier to be as SHAKESPEARE's imagination had conceived it. (201–2)

[1] Cibber's version, 5.5.60; Vol. 2, p. 124.

165. Joseph Pittard, Garrick's Lear

1758

From *Observations on Mr. Garrick's Acting, in a Letter to the Right Hon. the Earl of Chesterfield* (1758).

This essay is either plagiarised from No. 148 above, or else 'Pittard' (about whom nothing is known) was a pseudonym for Shebbeare.

It has always appeared to me that notwithstanding the Apparent Raptures with which Men pretend to feel those Passages of an Author which place him above Humanity, if their own Performances in a like Nature fall much short of it—that they have never reached in their Conception the true Spirit of the Author whom they have praised.

Whereas a Player, who personates in every Part the living Manners of a superior Character, manifests beyond Contradiction that he has conceived the true Idea of the Author.

A Poet, therefore, in Raptures with the Character of *Lear* as *Shakespeare* has drawn it, who in his Writings should attempt something of a similar Nature, instead of the sovereign of unfixed Temper, choleric and sudden, whose Ideas and Conceptions express Royalty in every Part of his Anger, should draw a Porter in Rage, replete with every Gothic Grossness, will be infinitely inferior in Genius to him that fills up this Character with all that Fire and Majesty which becomes the Personage as *Shakespeare* has compleated it.

This a Player on the *English* Stage perfectly accomplishes: His Name is *GARRICK*.

It may be a Vanity, but you, my Lord, will pardon even that in a private Letter not designed for the public Eye. In the Action of all other Men I have imagined something yet farther than has been expressed by them; in this Player and in this Part this Man has exceeded all my Imagination; and as *Poussin* is considered the Painter of Men of Taste so in like Manner Mr *Garrick* is the Player.

He is the only Man on any Stage where I have been, who speaks

Tragedy truly and natural. The *French* Tragedians mouth it too much, and to appear something more than Men they lose the Resemblance of Humanity. A Hero on that Stage, in Dress and Expression, is a complete Exotic of all Nations, and seems a Creature just arrived from some distant Planet.

It must be allowed, however, that the Passion of Anger is the easiest to be imitated of all those the human Mind is subject to; but to be angry with superior Sovereignty is as difficult to attain as any Part, to be executed with that Dignity which this *English* Actor imparts to it.

In the first Act of the Tragedy of *Lear*, when *Cordelia* has displeased him by that which ought to have had a contrary Effect, his Anger is shewn by very great Expression, very just Tone of Voice, and Propriety of Action; yet still augments, and becomes more energic as the rising Occasions require it, till at length, when *Goneril* refuses him his hundred Followers, and says[1]

> Be then advis'd by her, that else will take
> That which she begs, to lessen your Attendance.

After these Words of Insolence, *Lear* replies[2]

> Darkness and Devils!
> Saddle my Horses, call my Train together.
> Degenerate Viper, I'll not stay with thee:
> I yet have left a Daughter—Serpent, Monster!
> Lessen my Train, and call them riotous!
> All Men approv'd of choice and rarest Parts,
> That each Particular of Duty know—
> How small, *Cordelia*, was thy Fault? Oh *Lear*!
> Beat at that Gate which let thy Folly in,
> And thy dear Judgment out; go, go, my People.

This all other Actors speak with that kind of Rage with which a drunken Mechanic curses his Daughter that has secretly taken his Money from him, and prevented his going to the Ale-house; it is indeed a sheer Scolding. In *Mr Garrick* it is a Prince in Anger, every Accompaniment expresses it through the whole Passage. 'How small, *Cordelia*, &c.' This Reflection, so natural to human Minds, and Parents in particular, to compare what they think a less Fault in one Child whilst they are suffering under the Influence of a greater in another, is as truly expressed

[1] From Nahum Tate's adaptation, 1.2.56f.; corresponding to *King Lear*, 1.4.246f.
[2] Tate, 1.2.60ff.; *King Lear*, 1.4.252ff., 262ff.

by the Actor as imagined by the Poet; and then reverting on himself at the Words which follow, 'O *Lear*,' he absolutely imparts a Power to them which cannot be conceived but with much Difficulty by those who have never beheld him. The whole bitter Tide of Resentment pours back on himself, and is as fully exprest from the Fingers to the Toes, through the flashing Eye and keen Feature, as *Raphael* has exprest the being possest in his Demoniac (in his Picture of the Transfiguration); and in these Words the Soul of every Hearer shivers as he pronounces them;[1]

> Blasts upon thee;
> Th' untainted Woundings of a Father's Curse
> Pierce ev'ry Sense about thee.

Indeed, I could not avoid expecting a paralytic Stroke would wither every Limb of *Goneril*, the Power of Expression seemed as if of Necessity it must prevail over Heaven.

Then follows that which is so natural to the Soul of Man in excessive Anger, when it suffers equally from the Faults of others and itself. Turning back with Threats upon this Weakness which had made him weep, he utters with the utmost internal Sensibility, and yet weeps in Opposition to his own Resolution:[2]

> —Old fond Eyes,
> Lament this Cause again, I'll pluck ye out,
> And cast you with the Waters that ye lose
> To temper Clay.

It is not possible to decide which is superior in the Knowledge of Nature, the Poet who wrote, or the Player who animates these Passages. Afterwards, when he begins 'Hear, Nature,'[3] and passes on to that most beautiful of all Expressions,[4]

> How sharper than a Serpent's Tooth it is,
> To have a thankless Child!

all is so firmly and interestingly exprest, with Attitude and Action so becoming the Occasion, that, forgetting where I am, Astonishment seizes me that *Goneril* has Power to go off the Stage unblasted at this

---

[1] Tate, 1.2.74ff.; *King Lear*, 1.4.299ff.
[2] Tate, 1.2.76ff.; *King Lear*, 1.4.301ff.
[3] Tate, 1.2.82; *King Lear*, 1.4.275.
[4] Tate, 1.2.95f.; *King Lear*, 1.4.288f.

Imprecation: so perfectly the Character is realized by every Part of the Player.

I thought to have instanced nothing of his Powers in the second Act, but it is impossible to omit those Starts of Expression which accompany so perfectly the Ideas of the Poet in answer to the following Words of *Gloster*,[1]

>You know the fiery Quality of the Duke.

Lear replies,[2]

>Vengeance, Death, Plague, Confusion!
>Fiery! What Quality—why *Gloster*, *Gloster*.
>I'd speak with the Duke of *Cornwall*, and his Wife.

These, and many other Passages, are spoken so justly and with so much Emphasis that their Influence on the Hearer is amazing. They appear amidst the Tempest of his Mind like Flashes of Lightning in a stormy Night, making the Horrors more visible.

In the third Act, *Shakespeare*—into whose Hand Nature had given the Clue that leads through all her Labyrinth of Variety, reserving the other End to herself—has placed *Lear* amidst Thunder-Storms, Whirl-wind, Rain, and Fire; in this Part he shews how every Object finds some Connection with those of a Mind in deep Distress. *Lear* says[3]

>Rumble thy fill, fight Whirlwind, Rain, and Fire;
>Not Fire, Wind, Rain or Thunder, are my Daughters.
>I tax not you, ye Elements with Unkindness;
>I never gave you Kingdoms, call'd ye Children,
>Ye owe me no Obedience; then let fall
>Your horrible Pleasure; here I stand your Slave,
>A poor infirm, weak, and despis'd old Man.

Till the last Line he agrees that these Elements owe him no Gratitude or Obedience because unallied to him by Birth or Duty; yet, the last Line recalling his present Condition to his own Imagination, he immediately conceives it a Kind of mean Cruelty to join with two disobedient Daughters, and says[4]

>Yet will I call you servile Ministers,
>That have with two pernicious Daughters join'd

---

[1] Tate, 2.2.181; *King Lear*, 2.4.90.
[2] Tate, 2.2.182ff.; *King Lear*, 2.4.93ff.
[3] Tate, 3.1.10ff. (see Vol. 1, pp. 355f.); *King Lear*, 3.2.14ff.
[4] Tate, 3.1.17ff. (Vol. 1, p. 356); *King Lear*, 3.2.21ff.

Their engender'd Battle, against a Head
So old and white as mine; oh! oh! 'tis foul.

This Speech is spoken at first with Defiance; then, as the Scene[1] changes the Player falls into Acquiescence with this Suffering, till, coming to the last Part, he feels with much Contempt that coward Cruelty of basely joining with the Perpetrators of filial Disobedience. This is performed with such natural and easy Transition, as if his Soul conceived originally every Sensation as they follow one another in the Poet.

As the Madness advances in the Character of *Lear* it increases in the Action and Expression of the Player. You scarce see where he first begins, and yet find he is mad before *Kent* says[2]

I fear'd 'twould come to this; his Wits are gone.

It steals so gradually and imperceptibly, the Difference grows like a Colour which runs on from the highest to the darkest Tint, without perceiving the Shades but by comparing them at different Parts of the Whole. When he enters mad in the fourth Act, with the mock Ensigns of Majesty on him, thro' this whole Scene that which the Poet has marked so strongly the Player has also preserved: that satyric Turn which accompanies Madness arising from Wrongs is inimitable, conceived by the Poet and sustained by the Player, that vague and fugitive Manner of pronouncing, mixt with the sarcastic Touches of Expression, is truly exhibited. And as in the Poet's Writings so in the Player's Behaviour, the King is never one moment forgotten; it is Royalty in Lunacy. To quote every Passage would make a Letter a whole Play.

In that Part of the fourth Act where *Lear* recovers from his Sleep, as the Poet, who knew that sound Intellect must not appear too suddenly in such Instancies of Lunacy, so the Player recovers his Mind as gradually as he lost it; and at length distrusting his being recovered, he says[3]

I will not swear these are my Hands.

Cordelia answers,[4]

O look upon me, Sir.
And hold your Hands in Benediction o'er me.
No, Sir, you must not kneel.

[1] Shebbeare's text reads 'sense'; see above, p. 195.   [2] Tate, 3.3.99.
[3] Tate, 4.5.28 (Vol. I, p. 392); *King Lear*, 4.7.55.
[4] Tate, 4.5.28ff. (Vol. I, p. 372); *King Lear*, 4.7.57ff.

When, *Lear* kneeling, the Player pronounces with such pathetic Simplicity[1]

> Pray do not mock me!
> I am a very foolish, fond old Man,
> Fourscore and upwards; and to deal plainly with you,
> I fear I am not in my perfect Mind.

Whoever, at the uttering of these Words as Mr *Garrick* speaks them, can avoid joining with *Cordelia*, must be more hardened than *Goneril* or *Regan*. She says:[2]

> Then farewell to Patience: witness for me,
> Ye mighty Powers, I ne'er complain'd till now.

With what Knowledge of human Nature was this written! When a Mind exhausted by its former Wildness recovers, nothing is so weak and vacillating: the unornamented Simplicity of *Lear's* Words, therefore, has more Sublimity and Pathos than all the Powers of Figure and Metaphor could impart to them. And as it was imagined by *Shakespeare* it is spoken by Mr *Garrick*: my Tears have ever testified this Approbation.

The remaining Part of this Act is equally inimitable. Pray tell me, my Lord, what Art is this which, running from Anger to Rage to Madness, then softens and sinks into the timid and suppliant, in Poet and Player? What Power of Nature must those possess who are equal to this Variety and Force?

In the fifth Act, where the old King sleeps in the Lap of *Cordelia,* he breaks out:[3]

> Charge, charge upon their Flank, their last Wing halts.
> Push, push the Battle, and the Day's our own;
> Their Ranks are broke: Down with *Albany.*
> Who holds my Hands?

This he pronounces in that imperfect and indistinct Manner which attends those who talk in their Sleep with Expression of Anger, yet different from that of Madness or a sound Mind; then wakes with a gentle Exclamation:[4]

[1] Tate, 4.5.30ff. (Vol. I, p. 372); *King Lear,* 4.7.59ff.
[2] Tate, 4.5.34ff. (Vol. I, p. 372).
[3] Tate, 5.6.15ff. (Vol. I, p. 382).
[4] Tate, 5.6.18ff. (Vol. I, p. 382).

Oh thou deceiving Sleep!
I was this very Minute on the Chace,
And now a Prisoner here.

This Play terminates happily, as it is acted different from the Manner in which *Shakespeare* wrote it. *Cordelia* is made Queen, and *Lear* retires to pass away his Life in Quietness and Devotion. Many of the Passages are transposed from the order they stand in the Original; for that Reason I have sent you the Alteration, that you may see it as it is played. The words which express the Joy at the Thoughts of *Cordelia's* being a Queen are spoke with an Emphasis and Energy which is peculiar to Mr *Garrick* only: and though the Poet is no longer visible in this Place the Player sustains his Character in this also.

Thus in Anger, in Grief, in Madness, in Revenge, in Weakness, in Contempt, in Joy, all is equally natural and amazing. The same Poet fancies all these; the same Player follows him with equal Justice.

Does it not seem probable then, my Lord, that the Genius of a Player is more analogous to the Painter and Musician than to the Poet? He rather knows with what Attitude, Tone of Voice, and Expression, Characters already written should be expressed and acted, than conceives with what Words the Characters in a Story painted by *Dominiquino, Poussin*, or other eminent Artists should be animated. He can better adjust Sounds to poetical Compositions, than invent Poetry for Airs already made. (6-23)

166. William Shirley, Garrick's sins as actor and adapter

1758

From the *Herald, or Patriot-Proclaimer* (1758); this text from the two-volume reprint (1758).

William Shirley (*fl.* 1739–80) wrote several plays between 1739 and 1765, some poems, and *Brief Remarks on the Original and Present State of the Drama* (1758). He conducted his journal, the *Herald* (under the pseudonym of 'Stentor Tell-Truth, Esq.') for thirty numbers, between 17 September 1757 and 6 April 1758. Shirley was a professed enemy of Garrick, who had appeared in his play *Edward the Black Prince* in 1750, but with whom he subsequently quarrelled.

No. 19 (19 January 1758)

*　　*　　*

[On Garrick's acting]

His powers often fail him in the flow of elocution, insomuch that he is forced to make restings in utterance where no stops are to be found in his authors. To a consciousness of this deficiency may be owing his rarely attempting of sublime characters; and which, when he does attempt, it may be observed that he never succeeds in them. He is neither graceful in his treading of the stage or his bodily deportment; he uses abundance of false action, such as moulding the habit on his stomach, catching at, and grasping the side of his robe; is mean in his approaches of love, and often aukwardly embarrassed with his hat. He lays frequent clap-traps in false pauses, stammerings, hesitations and repetitions; and uses pantomime tricks in affected agitations, tremblings and convulsions; he over-agonizes dying, and many ways debases his own excellencies to extort applause from the injudicious by methods that are offensive to the true judges of his art. (II, 58–9)

★   ★   ★

No. 20 (26 January 1758)
[On Garrick's unwillingness to perform new plays]

★   ★   ★

But time, the unraveller of all craft, clearly reveals at length, to the eye of observant candour, the various frauds and impostures practised by this tinsel tyrant of the stage, with wronging of the public and dishonouring of the age, to oppress or discourage able writers. This the weak and wilful conduct of a rival manager has enabled him with the greater ease and security to do, and his motives for such proceedings are too obvious to be mistaken, being no other than the prevention of rivalry in public regard from a display of superior genius, and the monopolizing of all theatrical profits to himself.

If his reception of a piece could not be withstood, generally from the weight of powerful recommendation, the strength of an author's party, or the fear of attacks on him from a writer in his own cause, the common artifices practiced by him to discourage farther attempts by them have been by disgusts from unreasonable procrastinations of exhibition, or by endless objections and required alterations.

When a play then was not safely resistible it has been his invariable practice to promise that it should appear in its turn, which is after half a dozen others have been acted; for the performance whereof more than an equal number of years have been found too scanty portions of time, because the stage must be kept disengaged for revived and altered plays, new pantomimes, dances, playhouse farces, or an added character in *Lethe*.

Shakespeare is in the mean time, from a pious regard for that venerable father of the stage, sacrilegiously frittered and befribbled one season and the next, perhaps, no less conscientiously restored. All the rubbish of old authors is rummaged over, and their most shabby vestments of science new scoured, furbished up, and carefully darned with the abundant packthread of his ample Parnassian storehouse. And to ornament all in his power such botch-work rarities of obsolete wit, often gross obscenity, and engrafted touches on the times, he exercises his self-beloved and town-admired talent in writing a fashionable prologue and epilogue, which the bright judges of both sexes have the immediate inspiration to consider as the utmost efforts of human wit; and while (from errors to be hereafter descanted on) another manager is doing nothing, all people croud, pay, sweat and clap at the theatre, converse, admire and adore at home! *Roscius* becoming every where the great object of regard, the darling, the glory of the age! and who, in the mean time, like the evil angel in Addison's *Campaign*, 'Smiles in the tumult and enjoys the storm;' that is, hugs himself in the success of his own craft, laughs at the public infatuation, and pockets up their pence—Let me not disgrace his gains but say the multiplied thousands upon thousands by them wantonly lavished, and by him assiduously gleaned up as *actor, manager, author* from the *stage* and *alterer* for the *press*, with all the aggregate circumstances of triumphant preheminence and power, such as applause, courtship, adulation and sway! the adequate acquisitions of his superlative genius, and the truest estimators of the *taste, candour, wisdom, justice, generosity and spirit* of the *times*.

There can be no stronger proofs of the degeneracy of a people than the evidence of their affections being engrossed and their reason enslaved by a meer contributor to their pleasures. And sure when phrenzy becomes so catching and prevalent that prepossessions operate with passion, and opinion is seen liable to intoxication, it is high time that remedies should be applied for lowering the fever of folly. To be an eminent actor is henceforth like to become a more lucrative, nay even consequential employment than that of a general, admiral, minister or great officer of state. It is therefore one among the many reigning evils that contribute to level order and thereby wound and weaken society. Little reading is necessary to convince cool and unprejudiced minds that free states can only be vigorous and prosperous while public attention is rivetted to objects that are really important, and worthy of general regard. The ancient glorious states of *Greece* and *Rome*, nay even the constitutions of most modern nations have been overthrown and subverted by the heedless or designed indulgence of fashionable follies, and the immoderate pursuits of enervating pleasures. I readily own theatrical diversions to be as rationally allowable as any that can be enjoyed by a people. Yet ought we to remember how much infatuations therein contributed to the ruin of *Athens* and the enslaving of *Rome*. And to this day in *Spain* the passion for bull-fighting, which one would think of not so bewitching a nature, rages to such an excess among the common people that even despotism, become as absolute as it is in *Algier*, is aided in its oppressions by their indulgence. (II, 68–73)

167. Unsigned essay, Shakespeare weighed and measured

1758

From the *Literary Magazine, or Universal Review* vol. III (January 1758), pp. 6–8; reprinted in the *London Chronicle,* 4–7 February 1758, p. 125.

The *Literary Magazine* was partly edited by Dr Johnson (together with William Faden) during 1756 and the summer of 1757. This piece seems to be an imitation of Akenside's 1746 'Balance of Poets': see No. 106 in Vol. 3.

The POETICAL SCALE.

This scale is supposed to consist of 20 degrees for each column, of which 19 may be attained in any one qualification, but the 20th was never yet attain'd to.

	Genius.	Judgment.	Learning.	Versifications.
Chaucer ——	16	12	10	14
Spenser ——	18	12	14	18
Drayton —— —	10	11	16	13
Shakespeare — —	19	14	14	19
Jonson —	16	18	17	8
Cowley —	17	17	15	17
Waller —	12	12	10	16
Fairfax —	12	12	14	13
Otway ——	17	10	10	17
Milton ——	18	16	17	18
Lee ——	16	10	10	15
Dryden —	18	16	17	18
Congreve —	15	16	14	14
Vanbrugh — —	14	15	14	10
Steele — ——	10	15	13	10
Addison ——	16	18	17	17

Prior —— ——	16	16	15	17
Swift —— ——	18	16	16	16
Pope ——	18	18	15	19
Thomson ——	16	16	14	17
Gay ——	14	16	14	16
Butler ——	17	16	14	16
Beaumont and Fletcher	14	16	16	12
Hill (Aaron)	16	12	13	17
Rowe ——	14	16	15	16
Farquhar ——	15	16	10	10
Garth ——	16	16	12	16
Southerne ——	15	15	11	14
Hughes ——	15	16	13	16

By *Genius* is meant those excellencies that no study or art can communicate: such as elevation, expression, description, wit, humour, passion, &c.

Judgment implies a preserving that probability in conducting or disposing a composition that reconciles it to credibility and the appearance of truth, and such as is best suited to effect the purpose aim'd at.

By *Learning* is not meant learning in an academical or scholastic sense, but that species of it which can best qualify a poet to excel in the subject he attempts.

Versification is not only that harmony of numbers which renders a composition, whether in rhime or blank verse, agreeable to the ear, but a just connection between the expression and the sentiment, resulting entirely from the energy of the latter, and so happily adapted that they seem created for that very purpose, and not to be altered but for the worse.

I have, in the above list, omitted many who are considered as *English* poets, because I think no greater judgment can be formed from short compositions, and that one may write a very pretty copy of verses yet have no title to the appellation of a poet.

The reader, likewise, is not to be surprized if I have omitted some more voluminous writers in which several bright passages appear; for when a man writes a great deal it is next to impossible but he must, even against his will, stumble upon somewhat that is excellent.

Some I know have been celebrated by the greatest wits of the age as very fine poets, and are omitted here; but I have had long experience of the *partiality* and sometimes *weakness* of excellent poets and critics with regard to their *friends* and even *acquaintances*; nay, sometimes vulgar prejudices get the better of commonsense. *Wilmot,* Earl of *Rochester,* for instance, was celebrated by his contemporaries as a wit and a poet. He might have had some title to the former amongst his companions, but I think he has very little to the latter among his readers. His imitations from *Boileau* and *Meursius* (if they are his) are extremely insipid, and the best of the few other compositions he has left can be called no better than *pretty*. His imitation from *Horace*, which does most honour to his wit and judgment, is in fact a mere rhapsody of false criticism and mistaken characters. The dramatic writers he there praises the most have very little title to his encomiums. No man can find out in *Sedley's* work that melting property he assigns him. *Etheridge* can please no reader of taste. The best comedy of *Wycherley's*, his *Plain Dealer*, not to mention the improbability of the plot and the immodesty of the conduct, loses its greatest merit by having in it very little originality, and indeed is no other than a cento of *French* plays. The truth is, every line of *Wycherley* contradicts that character which the noble peer gives him for judgment and application. Mr *Wycherley* was indeed a fine gentleman, and a very worthy man. But he was far from deserving the compliments paid to him by his cotemporaries. The copy of verses under his name, prefixed to Mr *Pope's* Poems, were revised, altered, and improved by the poet to whom they were addressed. The rest of his works give us but a poor idea of his abilities as a poet. As to *Shadwell*, the other favourite of the noble Lord's, he is below all criticism.

The first-rate wits in *England* have been subject to partialities of this kind. Mr *Prior,* Sir *Samuel* Garth, Mr *Addison,* and most of the fine writers their cotemporaries, for very obvious reasons of interest, celebrated *Montague,* Earl of *Halifax,* as a capital genius, though I don't remember above six lines he ever wrote that entitle him to the character of a tolerable poet. Mr *Pope* has celebrated *Sheffield* Duke of *Buckingham,* who was author of two volumes of Miscellanies in prose and verse that deserve neither the name of true poetry nor good writing. That great poet went even so far as to suffer a commendatory copy of verses from his grace to be prefix'd to his poems, where they now stand, and which would disgrace even *Grub street* itself. Mr *Walsh* is another instance of that poet's partiality, and he not only published but corrected, improved, and dedicated the poems of Dean *Parnell,* though the two finest in them are stolen: his *Hermit* is no more than a story from old *Howel* versify'd, and his feast of *Comus* is a translation from a *Latin* Poem of Augureli, an *Italian* poet of the fifteenth century. I could give many other instances of high encomiums paid by our first-rate wits to very indifferent writers both in prose and verse: and nothing is more dangerous in literary matters than to follow the testimony given by one living author to another. With what respect was the name of *Boyle* celebrated all over *England*! During the time of his controversy with Dr *Bentley* about the Epistles of *Phalaris*, what compliments were paid to his genius, his wit, his address, and learning in almost every Poem of note that was published? And with what contempt has the name of *Bentley* been in ever since? But with what injustice! Let an impartial reader, now that the frenzy of adulation is cooled, take into his hand the performances of both on that occasion, and he will acknowledge *Bentley* to be superior to *Boyle* in wit and spirit as much as he is in learning and argument, and—what I am sorry to say—in facts and candour.

I am sensible that in the calculations I have here exhibited I have, in many instances, strong prejudices against me. The friends of *Milton* will not yield to *Shakespeare* the superiority of genius, which I think lies on the side of *Shakespeare*. Both of them have faults. But the faults of *Shakespeare* were those of GENIUS, those of *Milton* of the MAN of GENIUS. The former arises from *imagination* getting the better of *judgment*; the latter from *habit* getting the better of *imagination*. *Shakespeare's* faults were those of a *great poet*. Those of *Milton* of a *little pedant*. When *Shakespeare* is *execrable*, he is so exquisitely so that he is as inimitable in his blemishes as in his beauties. The puns of *Milton* betray a *narrowness of education* and a *degeneracy of habit*. His theological quibbles and perplex'd speculations are daily equall'd and excelled by the most abject enthusiasts: and if we consider him as a prose writer he has neither the learning of a scholar nor the manners of a gentleman. There is no force in his reasoning, no elegance in his style, and no taste in his composition. We are therefore to consider him in one fixed point of light, that of a great poet, with a laudable envy of rivalling, eclipsing, and excelling all who attempted sublimity of sentiment and description. But he has not that amiable variety that *Shakespeare* possess'd; and *Shakespeare* could have wrote like *Milton*, but *Milton* could never have wrote like *Shakespeare*.

Some may think that I have undervalued the character of *Waller*, but in my own judgment I have rather over-rated it; it is true, we find in him two or three pretty turned, short, Copies of Verses, and about a dozen good Couplets, but in the rest of his works he rises very little above the herd of his cotemporaries, who rather wrote rhyme than poetry. For the same reason I have omitted Sir *John Denham, Suckling,* and several other favourite writers, who give us here and there a sparkle that's exquisitely fine amidst a heap of dross and rubbish.

Even Mr *Pope's* celebrated *Granville*, Lord *Landsdown* has found no admission in this calculation, because had he not been a *Lord* he could have had very little pretentions to be a *Poet*. I have excluded the author of *Phædra and Hippolitus,* because that tragedy is in fact translated from the *French* of *Racine*, who with *Corneille*, I think, does not rise above the genius of *Rowe*. For the same reason I have omitted *Ambrose Philips*, and though his names-sake, the author of *Cyder*, undoubtedly had poetical genius yet I cannot admit him because he was a profess'd imitator of *Milton*. Dr *Donne* was a man of wit, but he seems to have been at pains not to pass for a poet. (6–8)

168. Thomas Edwards on Warburton's Shakespeare

1758

From *The Canons of Criticism, and Glossary . . . The Sixth Edition, with Additions* (1758). An expanded version of the exposure of Warburton's editorial practices first published in 1748.

On Edwards see Vol. 3, introduction, pp. 16f. and the headnote to No. 127. Further information about his friendship with Richardson (who printed the fifth edition of the *Canons*, in 1753, and in whose house he was staying when he died), has been given by T. C. Duncan Eaves and Ben Kimpel, *Samuel Richardson. A Biography* (Oxford, 1971), especially pp. 326–32. See also V. M. Gilbert, 'The Warburton-Edwards Controversy', *Notes and Queries* 199 (1954) pp. 257–9, 291–3.

[On *Measure for Measure*, 3.1.32ff.]

> Thou hast not Youth, nor Age:
> But as it were an after-dinner's sleep,
> Dreaming on both: for all thy blessed Youth
> Becomes as aged, and doth beg the Alms
> Of palsied Eld; and when thou'rt old and rich,
> Thou' hast neither Heat, Affection, Limb, nor Beauty:
> To make thy riches pleasant—

'The drift of this period is to prove that neither Youth nor Age can be said to be really enjoyed:—which conclusion he that can deduce has a better knack at logic than I have. I suppose the poet wrote,

> for *pall'd* thy *blazed* youth
> Becomes *assuaged;* and doth beg &c.

i.e. 'When thy youthful appetite becomes palled, as it will be in the very enjoyment, the blaze of youth is at once assuaged' &c. WARBURTON.

Which is as much as to say, When thy youthful appetite becomes palled, why then—it becomes palled. This is Mr W.'s knack at Logic; and this he supports with his usual trick of 'This is to the purpose.'

Now because one may without over much confidence pretend to as good a knack at Logic as this, let us see what may be made of the passage without Mr W's corruptions of it. And it may be thus explaned:
'In your Youth you are in as bad a condition as an old man; for tho' you have Appetites to enjoy the pleasures of life, yet you are unable to enjoy them for want of the Means to purchase them, *viz*. Riches; not being come to your estate, being dependent on your Elders for subsistence. And because you are advanced in years before you come to your Inheritance, therefore by that time you get riches to purchase the pleasures of life your appetites and strength forsake you, and you are incapable of enjoying them, *on that account*. Appetite, in Shakespeare's loose manner, is signified by two words, *viz*. "heat, affection"; and Strength by two others, "limb, beauty". This last Mr W. does not like, and therefore pronounces
'We should read, bounty; which compleats the sense, and is this; Thou hast neither the pleasure of enjoying riches thy-self, for thou wantest vigour; nor of seeing it enjoyed by others, for thou wantest bounty. Where the making the want of bounty as inseparable from old age as the want of health, is extremely *satyrical*; though not altogether *just*.'

WARBURTON

This reason for the alteration is worthy of the critic by profession; who, not finding in his author what to censure, first corrupts under pretence of amending him, and then abuses him for the imputed sentiment. (31–2).

*　　*　　*

CANON III.
These alterations he may make in spite of the exactness of measure.

[On *Henry VIII*, 2.3.65ff.]

> I do not know,
> What kind of my obedience I should tender,
> More than my All is nothing; nor my prayers, &c.

Where the obvious sense is, If my All were more than it is it would be Nothing (of no value): so that I cannot possibly make any fit return to the king for his favour.

There is a like expression in *Macbeth*,

> More is thy due, than more than all can pay. [1.4.21]

But Mr Warburton pronounces, *ex cathedra*, '*More than my all is nothing*: No figure can free this expression from nonsense. *In spite of the exactness of measure* we should read "More than my All, *which* is Nothing": i.e. which All is Nothing.'

Where, instead of correcting Shakespeare, he should have corrected his own understanding; for, if her All might be Nothing, why might not a little more than her All be so?

By the same figure (a very common one) Phædria in the *Phormio* says, his All is less than Nothing—'unde ego nunc tam subito huic argentum inveniam miser, Cui *minus nihilo* est'—Act III. Sc. 3.[1] (32–3)

*   *   *

[On Warburton's estimates of Shakespeare the man]

We may not improperly add, by way of Supplement to the Examples of this Canon, the *Character* of Shakespeare as drawn by Mr Warburton in his Notes, while he is pretending to explane him.

He was, it seems,

	Vol.	Pag.
Selfish and ungenerous ——	1.	398
Envious of others' happiness —	2.	4
Unjustly satyrical on mankind —	1.	400
Very justly so, on his own countrymen	1.	43
A Hobbist in his notion of Allegiance	4.	18
A Flatterer of King James —	4.	323, 6. 396, 408
An Abuser of Him ——	8.	353
An Abuser of first Ministers ——	5.	350
A cunning Shaver, and very dextrous Trimmer between very opposite Parties	1.	113
A Judge of Statuary ——	7.	349
Ignorant of it —— ——	3.	377
Inventer of a fine sort of Solder	7.	157

Let any one read this short summary of Mr W.'s character of our Poet and then judge whether of the two has been retained in the cause

---

[1] 'Where can a poor devil like me raise the money at such short notice, when I have less than nothing?'

of Dulness against Shakespeare, the Gentleman, or the Preacher, of Lincoln's-Inn. Especially, when it is farther considered that in most of the passages here refer'd to the remark is a mere conundrum of the Editor, without any ground or foundation in the Author's either words or sense! (41-2)

★   ★   ★

[On *Julius Caesar*, 1.2.122]

'His *coward* lips did from their *colour* fly.] A plain man would have said the *colour* fled from his lips; not his *lips* from their colour. But the false expression was from as false a piece of Wit: a poor quibble, alluding to a *coward* flying from his *colours*.' WARBURTON.

Shakespeare had no such miserable stuff in his head. The expression is classical, and the figure of speech as common as any poetical ornament whatever: 'In nova fert animus mutatas dicere formas Corpora;'— (Ovid,)[1] and—'Nullum Sæva caput Proserpina fugit.' (Hor.)[2] are amongst a thousand instances of it. Where the sense is—'Corpora mutata in novas formas'—and—'nullum caput fugit Proserpinam.' (128)

★   ★   ★

CANON XVIII.

He may explane his Author, or any former Editor of him by supplying such words or pieces of words, or marks, as he thinks fit for that purpose.

EXAMPLE I. *Measure for Measure.*

In a note on the title of this play Mr Pope had told us that the story of it was taken from Cinthio's Novels, Dec. 8. Nov. 5: by which a plain man would imagine he meant that it was taken from the fifth Novel of the eighth Decade, as indeed it happens to be, in Cinthio. But Mr Warburton puts it in words at length, *December* 8. *November* 5. though, whether he thought the story was so long that it held for two days and, not being finished the first, was resumed again at almost a twelve-month's distance, or whether he designed to hint that Cinthio wrote his Tale on the *eighth of December* and Shakespeare his Play on the *fifth of November* we can only conjecture.[3]

This is the *only* passage in all this book which has been honour'd

---

[1] *Metamorphoses*, 1.1f.: 'My mind is bent to tell of bodies changed into new forms.'

[2] *Odes* 1.28.19f.: 'cruel Proserpine spares no head.'

[3] The first paragraph of this note had appeared in earlier editions, and was ridiculed by Warburton in his annotated edition of Pope (1751 and subsequently).

334

with Mr Warburton's particular notice. In a note on v. 175 of Mr
Pope's *Imitation of Horace*, book ii. epist. 2 the ridiculous blunder here
laugh'd-at is charged on the Printer, and the author of the *Canons* abused
grossly for imputing it to the Editor. Both parts of this answer should
be replied-to. 'The Printer, it seems, *lengthened* Dec. and Nov. into
December and November.' If Mr W. can give a single instance of any
such *lengthening*, or any thing like it, in Printers, except this and two
or three more which might be mention'd as having happen'd to *Himself*
(one is to be found under Canon VIII. Ex. 28) and one *famous* one,
which is said to have happen'd to a Writer lately the subject of much
controversy, the benefit of it shall be allow'd him very readily. As to the
Duncery, or *Knavery*, of imputing to Mr W. himself this pretended
blunder of his Printer we would observe, in the first place, that the
very great number of cancell'd leaves in his edition of Shakespeare led
us to think that it was revised with extraordinary care and exactness,
and consequently that the many blunders in spelling, pointing, and the
like were as certainly *His* as those in reasoning and emending. In the
second place, He must knowingly and wilfully mistake our design if
he supposes it was *anywhere* intended to charge such gross ignorance
upon him, or any thing more *here* than to expose his heedless haste and
very slovenly inattention in a work which came abroad with such vast
expectation. (153–4)

*   *   *

From *An Essay towards a Glossary*.

*   *   *

CRESTLESS, 'one who has no right to Arms,' i.e. Coat of Arms
(Vol. 4, p. 467):

just as headless would signify one who has no legs. (194)

*   *   *

DEROGATE, 'unnatural.' (Vol. 6, p. 37):

> from her *derogate* body never spring
> A Babe, to honour her!   [*King Lear*, 1.4.280]

I imagine Shakespeare meant degenerate.

DESPITED, 'vexatious'. (Vol. 8, p. 282). (194)

*   *   *

FULL, 'beneficial.' (Vol. 1, p. 439):
so interpreted in order to confute a reading of Mr Theobald.
To GAUDE, 'rejoice'. from the Fr. Gaudir, (Vol. 3, p. 272), a word of Mr W.'s coining. (197)

*   *   *

To HEDGE, 'obstruct.' (Vol. 5, p. 401).
Shakespeare uses it for pursuing one's ends obliquely, cunningly. So Falstaff in the *Merry Wives of Windsor* says

I, I, I myself sometimes leaving fear of heaven on the left hand, and hiding mine honour in my necessity, am fain to shuffle, to *hedge* and lurch. [2.2.18ff.]

but here Mr W. had nothing to say to the word. Indeed it was not so proper a passage wherein to introduce or convey his interpretation. (199)

*   *   *

PRESUPPOSED, 'imposed.' (Vol. 3, p. 204):

> forms which there were *presupposed*.
> Upon thee in the letter.   [*Twelfth Night*, 5.1.337f.]

i.e. forms beforehand described in the letter, such as yellow stockings, cross-garters— &c. (205)

*   *   *

RATED, 'sought for, bought with supplication.' (Vol. 4, p. 299).
TO RECONCILE, 'to bear with temper.' (Vol. 6, p. 407).
REFLECTION, 'influence.' (Vol. 7, p. 238).
RESOLUTION, 'confidence in another's words.' (Vol. 6, p. 422). (205)

*   *   *

STRATAGEM, 'vigorous action.' (Vol. 4, p. 206).
STRIFE, 'action, motion.' (Vol. 6, p. 149). (208)

*   *   *

TO VICE a man, 'to draw, persuade him.' (Vol. 3, p. 294):
As he had seen't, or been an instrument to *vice* you to't. (210)

169. Richard Roderick, Remarks on Shakespeare

1758

From *The Canons of Criticism, and Glossary* . . . *The Sixth Edition, with Additions* (1758), pp. 212–38. Thomas Edwards prefixed this note: 'The following REMARKS are copied from Mr *Roderick*'s papers, and inserted here; as containing acute yet sober criticisms on *Shakespeare*'s words, and judicious yet easy explanations of his sense: a circumstance which recommends also many of the foregoing examples, both to the Canons and Glossary, far more than their polemic merit; of which, however, the candid and intelligent reader will by no means esteem them void' (p. 212).

Richard Roderick (died 1756), was admitted to Queens' College, Cambridge in 1728, and in 1743 became a fellow of Magdalene College. He was elected F.R.S. in 1750 and F.S.A. in 1752. Some poems by him are in Dodsley's *Collection of Poetry* (1766 ed., ii. 309–21), and a translation of an ode by Horace (4.13) is in Duncombe's versions of Horace (ii. 248–9).

[On *King John*, 2.1.184ff.]

That he's not only plagued, &c.

A poor passage this, at best! But yet, tho' low and paltry is not (when properly pointed, and only a single letter inserted) utterly unintelligible; which as it stands now it is.

It is not worth many words. The matter in short is this:—She [Constance] had before said that Elinor's sins were visited upon her Grandson, Arthur: in this speech she adds farther that He was not only punished for Her sins but that God had been pleased to make use of Her as the Means, the Instrument, whereby that punishment was inflicted on him. This is all the sentiment of the speech; which (for the sake of a

337

miserable gingling between *Plague* and *Sin*) is thrice repeated, with varied expressions. Read and point thus:

> That He's not only plagued for Her sin,
> But God hath made Her sin and Her the Plague
> On this removed Issue; plague'd for Her,
> And with Her plague'd; Her sin, His Injury,
> Her injury the Beadle to Her Sin

The last line and half may want some little explanation. 'Her sin, his *injury*': i.e., his loss, his damage, his punishment. 'Her *injury* the Beadle to her Sin': Her injury, her injustice, her violence in taking part with K. John in his endeavours to rob him of his right to the crown. (And by the way, this using the same word, *Injury*, in the same sentence in two different senses is not at all disagreeable to Shakespeare's usual manner, numberless instances of which might easily be collected, if it were worth while, from the worst parts of his works.) But to proceed:

> 'Her injury the *Beadle* to her Sin'

The Beadle in a Corporation is the officer whose business it is to execute the sentences pass'd upon any offenders, such as Whipping &c, to which Shakespeare alludes; and because her injustice was the instrument by which the punishment of her sins was inflicted upon Arthur he therefore calls it the *Beadle* to her sins.

This may, perhaps, be thought at first sight to be a hard and unnatural explanation, but the more we are acquainted with Shakespeare's licentious manner the more, I doubt, we shall have occasion to think that this was the meaning designed by this expression. (214–15)

* * *

[On the verse of *Henry VIII*]

It is very observable that the measure throughout this whole Play has something in it peculiar, which will very soon appear to any one who reads aloud, though perhaps he will not at first discover wherein it consists. Whether this particularity has been taken notice of by any of the numerous commentators on Shakespeare, I know not, though I think it can scarcely escape the notice of any attentive pronouncer. If those who have published this author have taken no notice of it to their readers, the reason may be that they have chosen to pass-by in silence a matter which they have not been able to account for. I think, however, 'tis worth a few words.

1. There are in this Play many more verses than in any other which end with a redundant syllable—such as these:

> Healthful| and e|ver since| a fresh| admi|rer.
> Of what|I saw|there an|untime|ly a|gue.
> I was| then pre|sent saw 'em| salute| on horse|back.
> In their| embrace|ment as| they grew| toge|ther— &c.
>
> [1.1.3ff.]

The measure here ends in the syllables '—mi—a—horse—ge', and a good reader will, by a gentle lowering of the voice and quickening of the pronunciation, so contract the pairs of syllables '—mirer—ague—horse-back—gether—' as to make them have only the force of one syllable each to a judicious hearer.

This Fact (whatever Shakespeare's design was in it) is undoubtedly true, and may be demonstrated to Reason and proved to Sense. The first, by comparing any Number of Lines in this Play with an equal number in any other Play, by which it will appear that this Play has very near *two* redundant verses to *one* in any other Play. And to prove it to Sense, Let any one only read aloud an hundred lines in any other Play, and an hundred in This, and if he perceives not the tone and cadence of his own voice to be involuntarily altered in the latter case from what it was in the former I would never advise him to give much credit to the information of his ears.

Only take Cranmer's last prophetic speech about Queen *Elizabeth* [5.5.17ff.], and you will find that in the 49 lines which it consists of 32 are redundant and only 17 regular. It would, I believe, be difficult to find any 50 lines together (out of this Play) where there are even so many as 17 redundant.

2. Nor is this the only peculiarity of measure in this play. The *Cæsuræ*, or Pauses of the verse, are full as remarkable. The common Pauses in English verses are upon the 5th or the 6th syllable (the 6th I think most frequently.) In this Play a great number of verses have the Pause on the 7th syllable, such as (in the aforesaid speech of *Cranmer*) are these:

> Which time shall bring to ripeness—she shall be.
> A pattern to all princes—living with| her.
> More covetous of wisdom—and fair vir|tue.
> Shall still be doubled on her—truth shall nurse| her.
> And hang their heads with sorrow—good goes with| her.
> And claim by those their greatness—not by blood.

Nor shall this peace sleep with her—but as when.
As great in admiration—as herself.
Who from the sacred ashes—of her ho|nour.
Shall be and make new nations—he shall flou|rish.
To all the plains about him—childrens children.   [5.5.20ff.]

3. Lastly, it is very observable in the measure of this Play that the emphasis arising from the sense of the verse very often clashes with the cadence that would naturally result from the metre: i.e., syllables that have an emphasis in the sentence upon the account of the *sense* or *meaning* of it are put in the uneven places of the verse, and are in the scansion made the first syllables of the foot, and consequently short, for the English foot is Iambic.

Take a few instances from the aforesaid speech:

And all that shall succede. Sheba was ne|ver.   [23]

Than this blĕst sōul shall be: ăll prīncely gra|ces.   [25]
Her foes shăke, līke a field of beaten corn.
And hang their heads with sorrow; gŏod grōws with| her.
In hēr dăys, every man shall eat in safe|ty,
Under his ōwn vine what he plants, and sing.   [31ff.]

Nor shall this peāce sleĕp with her; but as when.   [39]

Wherever the brĭght sūn of heav'n shall shine.   [50]

Shall be, and māke nĕw nations. He shall flou|rish.   [53]

Shall seĕ thĭs, ānd blĕss heav'n—   [55]

What Shakespeare intended by all this I fairly own myself ignorant, but that all these pecularities were done by him advertently and not by chance is, I think, as plain to all sense as that Virgil intended to write Metre, and not Prose, in his *Æneid*.

If then Shakespeare appears to have been careful about measure, what becomes of that heap of emendations founded upon the presumption of his being either unknowing or unsollicitous about it? Alterations of this sort ought surely to be made more sparingly than has been done, and never without great harshness indeed seems to require it, or great improvement in the sentiment is obtained by it. (225-8)

*   *   *

[On *King Lear*, 1.4.286]

her mother's pains and benefits.

i.e., the pains of child-birth and benefits both of nursing and instruction. The small difficulty here arises from the word *Pains* being applicable to one person, and *Benefits* to another: the *Mother*'s pain, the *Child*'s benefit.

A most exquisite stroke of Nature here is in danger of being lost only by being couched under one little syllable—HER—

Lear is wishing to her child (if she is to have one) the severest curses that can happen to defeat and then destroy the natural pleasure which parents take in their children: that is, a froward and curst disposition both of mind and body (for the words *thwart*, *disnatured* are so happily chosen as to be applicable to both). And suddenly, without giving the hearer any previous notice, he talks of the supposed Child as a *Daughter*, not a *Son*. For so I think the passage ought to be understood in order to give it it's full force. Not *only* 'Turn her mother's pains and benefits to laughter and contempt', i.e. make them ridiculous and contemptible to others *passively*, by the form and temper both of her body and mind; but also *actively*, by tauntingly and contemptuously undervaluing and setting them at naught.

Nor do I think that this is too much refining on this passage, for tho' the general character of Shakespeare be justly that of an impetuous and incorrect writer, yet He will do him great injury who shall apply this to all parts of his works indiscriminately: and particularly, the passion of Lear in this scene seems to me to be as much laboured and as highly finished as any passage in any writer. Any one that reads it over attentively will, I think, perceive that the Sentiment is nicely and accurately studied, the language full, compleat and nervous, nothing in it superfluous, nothing lax or weak, every word is striking and as exactly placed as it is judiciously chosen. In short this passage seems to me, for true sublimity of spirit and exact fulness and magnificence of stile, to be worthy of the highest and correctest Genius of Antiquity. (230–2)

* * *

[On *King Lear*, 2.4.132f.]

O Regan, she hath tied
Sharp-toothe'd unkindness, like a vulture, here.
(*Points to his heart.*)

There is something very hard and unnatural in this expression of tying unkindness to his heart. I suspect it should be read and pointed thus—

> O Regan, she hath *tired*,
> (Sharp-tooth'd unkindness!) like a vulture—here.

i.e. She hath preyed on my heart—

> An hawke tyryth upon rumpes,
> She fedyth on all manere of fleshe.
> > Jul. Barns, de Re accipitraria.

The word occurs in our author's *3 Henry VI*:

> Like an empty eagle
> *Tire* on the flesh of me and of my son. [1.1.268f.]

Unkindness I conceive here to have the force of *unnaturalness*: Kind and Nature in the old writers are synonymous. (232)

*   *   *

[On the character of King Lear]

There is a vast stretch of invention, and consummate art, in this character of Lear, and a particular and fine knowledge of nature is shown in his last appearance and death in this scene. He is represented as a man of the nicest sensibility of mind; and our compassion for him is raised to its heighth as well by the tender expressions of his great love to his children, which are interspersed in his speeches, as by the representation of his lamentable distresses. Indeed, the very outrageous expressions of his resentment carry with them by implication the tenderness of his affection, in the feeling sense he shows of his disappointment that it was not returned towards him by his daughters.

We have seen him in the course of the play expressing the most furious transports of desperate rage, pouring forth the bitterest curses and imprecations that I think human imagination is capable of conceiving; and at length transported beyond the bearing of man's faculties, and raised from choler to downright madness. And, even in this shattering of his sense and reason, still giving the most exquisite and piercing strokes of his quick and lively feeling of filial ingratitude.

Here, one would imagine, were *a Period:* and far short of this would have been one in any other writer but Shakespeare. But he has still a reserve, another change in Lear, to a yet higher and more deplorable degree of distress than he has yet suffered. The very fulness and perfection of misery, which (to use his own phrase) *tops Extremity* is reserved for the last scene of his appearance.

Till the last and finishing stroke of Cordelia's death Lear had kept-up the spirit and strength of his resentment, but here he is touched in such a point as utterly afflicts and dismays him. From the highest struggles of fury and passion he is here at once dejected and cast down to the lowest and most dispirited pitch of grief and desperation. Nothing now remains of his vigorous passion. All his expressions dwindle now into faintness and languor. His towering rage lowers and sinks into feeble despair, and his impetuous madness flags into sullen and unnerved stupefaction. The faculties of the mind, like the sinews of the body, become by overstraining, weak, relaxed, and motionless. (235–6)

170. Arthur Murphy, Shakespeare in the London theatres

1758

From the *London Chronicle*, 'The Theatre' section.

For the ascription to Murphy see the headnote to No. 161, and the works cited there by Emery and Dunbar (especially the latter, p. 310), also Arthur Sherbo (ed.), *New Essays by Arthur Murphy* (East Lansing, Michigan, 1963), pp. 75–8.

[a] October 3–5, 1758.

At *Drury Lane* on Thursday the 28th of last month was performed the tragedy of *Romeo and Juliet*; the part of Romeo by a young gentleman who never appeared upon any stage before. The humanity and good-nature of the English is in nothing, perhaps, more conspicuously evident than in their reception of a new performer upon the stage: for however the whole audience in a body may be regarded in the light of his Judge, every individual appears to be of his Counsel by the great anxiety they manifest for his success, and the care they take to lay hold of and blazon every little incident that can possibly redound to his advantage. It was amidst the universal acclamations of such an audience as this that the above-mentioned young gentleman made his first entrance; and perhaps there never came any object before the Publick which seemed more eminently to deserve their support, or to stand in greater need of it. Modesty, they say, is the inseparable concomitant of Merit; it is therefore no wonder that Mr *Fleetwood* should possess a very considerable share of it. To say the truth, it for some time seemed totally to subdue all his other faculties: however, as his confusion wore off, it afterwards turn'd to his advantage by giving an irresistible air to every thing he said and did, and by enforcing those letters of recommendation (as Addison calls them) which were written so legibly in his countenance.

As the character of Romeo is in itself one of the most amiable upon

344

the English stage, so the idea which one may be supposed to conceive of his figure from Shakespeare's description of it cannot be more aptly conveyed than by the appearance of our young Roscius. But as the two first acts require more of ease and grace than any other qualities of a good actor so, in my opinion, he shone less in those than in any other parts of the performance. And here I must take the liberty, in a very particular manner, to recommend to him a close application to his Fencing and Dancing Masters. People of a middle stature are sometimes genteel by nature; but persons inclinable to be remarkably tall are almost all born in original aukwardness, and it requires the greatest pains for a player so circumstanced to correct his motions in such a manner as to avoid shocking the spectator. I cannot help observing in this place that there is hardly one performer upon either theatre that knows how to stand still, except Mr Garrick.

In the third act he appeared to great advantage; and not a little so in the first scene where he encounters that brutal ruffian Tybalt. His pronounciation of

> Tybalt, the reason that I have to love thee
> Doth much excuse the appertaining rage
> Of such a greeting, &c.   [3.1.60ff.]

with what he afterward says upon Tybalt's injurious answer, and in which more is meant than meets the ear, was extremely significant. But in the fifth scene with the Fryar [3.3], he was absolutely masterly. I must own he appeared to me to be a strong imitator of Mr Garrick, but then his imitation was so exquisitely satisfactory that it was rather a proof of his great powers and observation to profit by so excellent an Original, than any want of sufficiency in himself.

The limits which I am prescribed will not suffer me to point out several excellencies, which I took notice of in his performance of this scene, as well as in that of the Garden upon his departure from his wife. But I cannot help taking notice that there was something astonishingly wild and passionate, in his performing of that part of the scene in Fryar Lawrence's cell where, starting from the ground upon the old nurse's telling him the distress'd situation of Juliet and with that particular circumstance of her calling upon Romeo, and then flinging herself down upon her bed, he crys

> As if that name
> Shot from the deadly level of a gun

345

Did murder her. Oh tell me, Fryar, tell me,
In what part of this vile anatomy
Doth my name lodge? tell me, that I may sack
The hateful mansion.   [3.3.102ff.]

There was something remarkably pathetick and tender too, in his taking leave of Juliet.

He does not appear again till the fifth act, in the first scene of which he performed with great spirit; nor did he fall short of any actor I ever saw in the surprize and shock which he expressed at the news of his wife's death. But in the celebrated soliloquy beginning with 'I do remember an apothecary' [5.1.37] he fixed his eyes upon the ground and seemed to be utterly at a loss what to do, either with himself or them. It must be owned that so long a declamation is a fiery tryal for a young actor, and of this the judicious manager seemed to be conscious by curtailing the above-mentioned on the present occasion. But if Mr Fleetwood failed in this point to answer the expectations of a critical inquisitor it only looked like a piece of art to heighten that pleasure which he was preparing to give him in the subsequent catastrophe, and I will close this paper with venturing to affirm, without setting apart any particular instances, that the last scene of *Romeo and Juliet* was never performed with more tenderness, energy, and justness in every respect since the first revival of that tragedy, nor more to the satisfaction of all the judicious part of the audience than it was by Mr Fleetwood the first night of his performance. And I am the bolder to make this assertion as I am assured it agrees with the opinion of the best actor, and judge of acting, in the world; whose great good-nature in instructing young performers and encouraging them with his applause can never be sufficiently commended.

It would be injustice to make an end of this essay without mentioning Miss Pritchard: that amiable young actress can never fail to please. And it would be the highest injury to his merit not to own that Mr Palmer performs the part of Mercutio in such a manner as to leave the town no manner of reason to regret Mr Woodward, at least in that character. (335–6)

*   *   *

[b] October 12–14, 1758.

On Tuesday the 10th instant at the Theatre Royal in DRURY-LANE was acted *Measure for Measure*.

This play was written by our celebrated Shakespeare, and the main design of it is evidently copied from a very beautiful and affecting novel of Cinthio; from which, however, one would rather have expected a tragedy, than a comedy. But Shakespeare, by palliating a few of the circumstances, and by introducing one or two characters entirely of his own invention has, in my opinion, by some very nice strokes of art produced a species of the latter.

The part of Lucio in this piece, an impudent, prating coxcomb, is, as far as I can judge, both for humour and nature by many degrees superior to any character of the same stamp introduced upon the stage since. And notwithstanding the audience have seen it so often inimitably performed by Mr Woodward, the unanimous applause they gave to Mr O' Brien, who appeared in it the above night, was a convincing argument that they thought he displayed very great theatrical talents. For my own part I confess he pleased me infinitely, and I think it would be not only the height of cruelty and ill nature but injustice also should the town be cold in their encouragement of a young performer who seems to want nothing but a little countenance and practice to set him very near on an equality with the most eminent in his profession.

To say that Mr Mossop and Mrs Cibber performed excellently in the parts of the Duke and Isabella would, I apprehend, be a needless testimony in their favour: since every body that frequents the theatre upon hearing their names will immediately unite the idea of perfection in acting with them. Mr Havard, too, supports the character of Angelo with great justice, as indeed a man of his good sense must do every thing he takes in hand. But I could not for a few minutes help making some excuses with myself for his frailty when I saw Mrs Cibber before him on her knees: the elegance of her figure, the musical plaintiveness of her voice, and the gentleness of her manners being sufficient to make any one fall in love with her.

There is in the exhibition of this comedy one or two scenes left out, a tribute which Shakespeare was obliged to pay to the tyrannical taste of his times. But I protest, with all due deference to the severer order of critics, I can hardly pardon the omission of them, since they are highly laughable and diverting and— tho' Nature in an homely dress—so true a picture of her as, I think, must procure them a good reception where-ever she is admired.

There are some little intricacies in the plot of *Measure for Measure* too, which at first sight appear trifling and unnecessary, as well as some other errors, the effects of inadvertency or perhaps the want of a uniform judgment. But tho', if we arraign Shakespeare in any of the courts of Aristotle and try him by a jury of scholiasts, I am afraid he would be condemned for them, yet I am apt to imagine that an English audience will acquit him of faults to which they owe the chief pleasure of their entertainment, a pleasure which no art or correctness could give. And while the beauties of this admirable author are so brilliant and so numerous, I should be ashamed to own that I had suffered my attention to be taken off from them long enough to discover any of his defects. For who indeed but the most dull and stupid of wretches would employ his time in a quarry of diamonds with raking after dirt and pebble-stones, because such things might probably be found there?

But there is an instance of fine writing in this play which shews Shakespeare's genius in a new point of light; and as it has been little taken notice of I will here quote the passage at large, at the same time desiring any of the poets of the present age to excel the following song, either in elegance of thought or expression.

> Take, oh! take those lips away
> That so sweetly were foresworn;
> And those eyes the break of day,
> Lights that do mislead the morn.
> But my kisses bring again,
> Seals of love, but seal'd in vain.   [4.1.1ff.]

Critics will have it that the comedy now before us comes under the censure of a false title; since, as the catastrophe is managed, it is not, strictly speaking, *Measure for Measure*.[1] But, I apprehend, this objection will vanish when we consider that Angelo's crimes were only intentional and not actually commited. (367)

*   *   *

[c] November 7–9, 1758.

To the Printer of the CHRONICLE.

SIR,

Your late correspondent on the Theatre, having dropt you all of a sudden, and that in the midst of some novel and very interesting performances, I take it for granted we are not to have the pleasure of hearing from him any more, and as I know this will be a great disappointment to many of your readers, if you think me capable of

---

[1] See Charlotte Lennox, above pp. 116f.

supplying his place I shall follow the two subsequent essays with the like number upon the same subject on each of your days of publication: And as the *King's Theatre in the Hay-Market* will speedily open, I shall endeavour to entertain your readers with some observations on, and account of the several New Operas, as they appear, considering each under the different heads of Poetry, Musick, Decorations, and Performance. I am your's and your readers humble servant,   N.S.[1]

*   *   *

COVENT-GARDEN

On Friday the 3rd instant was presented *Coriolanus*. The two first acts of this play, as it is performed at the above theatre, were written by Shakespeare, the three last for the most part by Thomson. But how a man of Mr Sheridan's knowledge (who first introduced it there about four years ago) could think of pounding into one substance two things so heterogeneous in their natures as the productions of those authors is to me amazing.

Mr Smith enters in the first act, after having (as we are to suppose) just overcome the Volsci, to the tune of violins and hautboys; but I am afraid the grandeur of his triumph is a little misapplied, considering the early times in which Coriolanus lived, before the Roman empire had arrived to any degree of splendor and magnificence, and was great in virtue only. However it makes a fine shew; and Mr Smith, who has an excellent person, by the help of a little burnt cork and a real coat of mail cuts a very martial appearance. I think it was one of the Gracchi who, when he was speaking to the people, always had a servant behind him in the Rostrum with a pitch-pipe, which he touched whenever he found his master's voice rising beyond a certain height; such an instrument as this would, in my opinion, be of service to Mr Smith, for his fault seems to be that of keeping too much at the top of his voice.

Mrs Hamilton in the part of Veturia, especially in the last act, excells herself; and in particular she repeats that line,[2]

He never can be lost who saves his Country,

with the genuine spirit of a free-born Englishwoman.

[1] This letter is not to be taken literally: disclaimed of authorship or disagreements between various fictitious correspondents were part of the stock-in-trade of eighteenth century journalism, and it is most probable that Murphy continued as theatre-critic. See Arthur Sherbo, *op. cit.*, p. 76.

[2] See above, p. 168.

By the unnatural conjunction which is attempted to be made in this tragedy most of the other characters are robbed of their significance. Those two excellent actors, therefore, Ryan and Sparks, only give us just cause to regret that the parts of Tullus and Volusius are not longer. But I may have an opportunity of mentioning the play of *Coriolanus* in another place, when I can speak of it with more satisfaction, for I own I do not love those fantastical mixtures; I am for wine by itself, and water by itself, all Shakespeare or all Thomson. (455)

171. Alexander Gerard, Shakespeare and enlightened taste

1759

From *An Essay on Taste*, 1759; this text from the second edition (1764), which offers minor revisions.

Alexander Gerard, DD (1728-95), professor of philosophy and divinity, published various theological works and *An Essay on Genius* (1774). His *Essay on Taste* was awarded a prize by the Select Society of Edinburgh, and the publication of it was assisted by Hume, who had been one of the judges. It derives its associationist method from Hume, Hutcheson and Baillie, and influenced Alison and others. Gerard belonged to a literary and philosophical society in Aberdeen which included George Campbell, James Beattie, and other leaders of Scottish intellectual life.

But an excessive or false refinement is equally to be avoided. It is like a weakly constitution, which is disordered by the minutest accident, or like a distempered stomach which nauseates every thing. It is a capriciousness of mind which begets an habit of constantly prying into qualities that are remote, of discovering imaginary delicacies or faults which none else can perceive, while one is blind to what lies perfectly open to his view; like the old philosopher who was so intent on the contemplation of the heavens that he could not see the pit that had been dug directly in his way. Or it is a minuteness of taste, which leads one to seek after and approve trifling excellencies or to avoid and condemn inconsiderable negligencies, a scrupulous regard to which is unworthy of true genius. Or it is a fastidiousness of judgment, which will allow *no* merit to what has not the *greatest*, will bear no mediocrity or imperfection, but with a kind of malignity represents every blemish as inexpiable. . . .

False refinement dislikes on grounds equally chimerical and inadequate as those which procure its approbation. The delicacy of Aristarchus was so much shocked with Phœnix's horrible intention of murdering his father in the extravagance of his rage that he cancelled the lines in which it is, with great propriety, related on purpose to represent to Achilles the fatal mischiefs that spring from ungoverned fury and resentment. The nicety of Rymer is disgusted with the cunning and villany of Iago as unnatural and absurd, soldiers being commonly described with openness and honesty of character*. To critics of this class Homer's low similitudes and simple manners, or Shakespeare's irregularities and unharmonious numbers are intolerable faults. (119–23)

* * *

A perfect and faultless performance is not to be expected in any art. Our gratification must in every case be balanced against disgust, beauties against blemishes; before we have compared and measured them we can form no judgment of the work. For want of the quickness and compass of thought requisite for this, or of inclination to employ it, we often err in our decisions. Excellencies and faults are sometimes united in the same part. A member may be so elegantly finished as to gain the applause of the unskilful, but so unsuitable to its place, so prejudicial to the unity and effect of the whole as to deserve the severest censure. But in every performance beauties and blemishes are to be found in different parts. A contracted mind fixes on one or the other. It is related of Apollodorus, an ancient painter, that he destroyed his finest pictures if he could discover in them any, even the minutest, fault. Some critics, as if they were possessed with the same frantic spirit, will condemn a thousand beauties of the highest rank on account of a few intermingled faults, which bear no proportion to them and do not perhaps at all

* See Rymer's *View of Tragedy*, chap. 7 [Vol. 2, p. 30].

affect the whole. On the contrary, the merit of a single part will strike a more candid judge so strongly as to make him overlook multitudes of faults which infinitely overbalance it.

But a person of true taste forms his judgment only from the surplus of merit, after an accurate comparison of the perfections and the faults. And indeed the greatest critics allow the chief merit not to the greater *number* but to the higher *rank* of beauties, not to that *precision* and constant attention to every trifle which produces a cold and languid mediocrity, but to a noble *boldness* of genius, rising to the height of excellence with a kind of supernatural ardor which makes it negligent with regard to numberless *minutiæ*; in fine, not to that *faultless* insipidity which escapes our blame but to that daring *exaltation* which, however shaded by inaccuracies or even debased by the mixture of gross transgressions, forces our admiration. Demosthenes has been justly preferred to Hyperides, Archilochus to Eratosthenes, and Pindar to Bacchylides. A man should justly expose himself to a suspicion of bad taste who approved a faultless, uninteresting tragedy more than *Othello*, or *King Lear*, or who gave Waller greater applause than Dryden. Titian has been blamed for incorrectness of design, but he will ever hold a rank among painters far superior to Andrea del Sarto, who finished all his drawings with the most scrupulous care and diligence. Where eminent merit is found real taste disdains the malignant pleasure of prying into faults. (143–5)

172. Earl of Orrery, Shakespeare's irregularities defended

1759

From Orrery's Preface to *The Greek Theatre of Father Brumoy.*
Translated by Mrs. Charlotte Lennox, 3 vols (1759).

John Boyle (1707–62), 5th Earl of Cork and Orrery, was a friend
of Swift, Pope, and of Dr Johnson (see Boswell's *Life*), with whom
he contributed to the *Adventurer* (see No. 139 above). He also wrote
essays for the *World* and the *Connoisseur, Remarks on the Life and
Writings of Swift* (1752), and translated the *Letters of Pliny the
Younger* (1751).

After having touched upon the qualities of tragedy, our author [Brumoy]
goes on to consider the length of time which tragedy ought to employ.
His opinion, although not so clearly expressed as might be wished, is
the same as has been pursued by all the best dramatic writers, except
Shakespeare. Our immortal Shakespeare has committed the highest
offences against chronology, history, politics, and every shadow of
probability. He has broke through the unities of action, time, and place.
He has confined himself to no dramatic rules, by which unbounded
licence he has not given us—if the blasphemy against him may be
excused—any one complete play. He has indeed done more. He has
exhibited certain strokes of nature that must have been entirely lost, or
miserably lopped and maimed, had he submitted to wear those shackles
with which neither Eschylus himself nor any of his successors thought
it a pain or a disgrace to be loaded.

I forget the name of the French author who says that the English are
Shakespeare mad. There are some grounds for the assertion. We are
methodists in regard to Shakespeare. We carry our enthusiasms so far
that we entirely suspend our senses towards his absurdities and his
blunders. We behold with a calmness proceeding from a boundless

piety *a ghost returning more than once from that undiscovered country from whose bourne no traveller returns:* and we as devoutly view *Desdemona stifled to death, then so perfectly restored to life as to speak two or three sentences, then die again without another oppressive stroke from the pillow.* How great must be the merit of an author who remains, and most assuredly ever will remain, triumphant and supreme *with all his imperfections on his head?* Those merits arise from a strict and constant conformity to nature, whose laws Shakespeare most happily followed, however he may have neglected the regularity of the drama. He is from thence become a strong instance how far superior nature is to art, since our best, our most correct, our most applauded dramatic writers appear stiff, constrained, and void of force when compared with his native fire and exuberance of imagination. (I, ix–x)

*   *   *

The French theatre has more exactly copied these rules. The error of the English has been owing to a more barbarous and more savage taste, which as it has ceased in the nation should *now* disappear from the stage. In the *Orphan,* altho' a private scene of domestic distress is finely represented, *Monimia* and *Polydore* ought to have died, life was no longer to be enjoyed by them with the least degree of happiness. But why must *Castalio* perish? Or why must he be guilty of fratricide? He was sufficiently unfortunate before, and ought to have lived to comfort the old Acasto. Exaggerated distress leaves a melancholy impression upon the mind, and seldom excites those fine transient emotions that spring from compassion and generous humanity.

The authors of tragedy ought to be thoroughly versed in the rules of the theatrical drama, and to be well acquainted with the powers of the actors, especially of such upon whom the principal parts are to devolve. Many of our English authors have been remarkably deficient in this particular. The length of the speeches, and the continual torrent of passion from beginning to the end, have been too great and violent for the power of any actor whatever. Shakespeare has evidently avoided this error. He always gives the actor a resting place. When Hamlet's powers are gradually raised to the highest pitch by seeing his father's ghost the author relieves him, and gives him a time to breathe, by letting fall his voice most properly to ask a few short pathetic questions. *Say, why is this? Wherefore? What should we do?* [1.5.3ff.]

Most of Shakespeare's important periods finely terminate within the compass of the actor's voice. Every high emotion never fails to have

just pauses. When we add to this the beauty and strength of his sentiments it is no surprize to find how few of his representations excel in the
principal parts, and why those parts will always be the test and standard
of the actor's genius, power, and taste.

This incomparable writer, incomparable both in his beauties and in
his faults, never appeared in more true lustre than in the present age.
The Actor, with the same force and enthusiasm of imagination enters
into the sentiments of the author, and expresses what he feels with such
a power, such a strength, and such an original spirit that we sometimes
almost forget the player in the poet. Thus have they mutually augmented each other's fame, and the statue which Mr Garrick has raised
to the poet, though fine in its kind, and an instance of a laudable and
grateful manner of thinking, is but a weak representation of that real life
which he constantly gives to the memory and writings of *his* Shakespeare. (xxvii–xxviii)

173. Thomas Wilkes, Shakespeare on the stage

1759

From *A General View of the Stage* (1759). This book is sometimes still erroneously attributed to Samuel Derrick. But in an article in the *Times Literary Supplement*, 9 August 1923, 'Samuel Derrick and Thomas Wilkes' (p. 533), W. J. Lawrence showed that Wilkes was not 'a pseudonym' of Derrick, (as *DNB* had stated), since they were two separate people. Like Derrick, Wilkes was Irish, and Lawrence discovered an obituary notice in the National Library, Dublin, recording that Wilkes died on 13 June 1786.

[On the moral effect of the theatre]

Warmed by the strength of character we almost possess it, and we are transported beyond ourselves. The calm Brutus furnishes us with fortitude, the faithful Edgar infuses loyalty, the tender Romeo fills with compassion, and Orlando's care of old Adam inspires with generosity. (4)

*　　　*　　　*

[On the enemies of the theatre]

Perhaps, if we examine into the merits and importance of the herd who write against the Theatre, we shall find the best part of them either ignorant bigots, armed with zeal for the destruction of taste, or obscure scribblers who affect the character of writers, and attack a favourite subject for that purpose with false quotation and willing misrepresentation. If Collier and Bedford have inveighed against the stage with great acrimony, have not Zoilus, Rymer, and Lauder attempted to sully the character and injure the reputation of the most celebrated writers? Yet truth has at length prevailed, and the intrinsic worth of Homer, Shakespeare, Milton, and the Stage will outlast ages of brass, while the fame of their invidious enemies shall melt and be forgotten, like tracks in snow or ice in the sunbeam. (18–19)

*   *   *

[On the moral effect of tragedy]

Who can behold, well acted, and not abhor, the ambition and cruelty of Richard the Third, the pride and prodigality of Wolsey, the treachery of Iago, or the villainy and malice of Shylock? Who can see the equal patriot Brutus, the honest abused Othello, the old injured Lear, the gallant and distressed Horatius, without sharing in their different calamities, admiring and wishing to emulate their virtues? There is a certain moral sense of virtue, an innate generosity impressed on the mind of man in a greater or lesser degree, which interests us in the event of the performance and inclines us to the applause of good, to the detestation of evil. (21–2)

*   *   *

To make our pleasures conduce to our profit is a noble and very useful lesson: this is best done on the Stage by blending a variety of passions in forming the various characters, so that they may be real pictures of man as he is, not as he ought to be; for a perfect character is

A faultless monster that the world ne'er saw.

Some people are so delicate as to be offended at introducing such a villainous character on the stage as Lady Macbeth. But if the character be drawn from history we are to suppose it supplied by the world, and those who can read mankind will tell you that they every day meet with people in whom ambition is as strong, and which—had they the same temptations, the same opportunity—would prompt them to run equal if not greater lengths of barbarity. In this case then Shakespeare was right in exhibiting her because she appears detestable, and may affect some minds properly by correcting in them the seeds of a passion so very hateful.

It is one essential duty of an author to be justly acquainted with the age, nation, and character of the personage he introduces in the Drama. This is what forms the manners of the piece, and was a knowledge in which Shakespeare did not always excel: he is guilty of many anachronisms. But in one thing, however, he is always exact, that is in making his Romans speak like Romans, his Englishmen like Englishmen. This art makes his pieces so very strong, they always interest our affections, and command our admiration. Otway is happy in the former, but not so in the latter.

When a Dramatic Piece has a happy conclusion, tho' all the incidents leading to that conclusion are distressful, yet it cannot with propriety be called a Tragedy, because we depart from it with satisfaction; we feel none of that pity or terror wherewith we are impressed when we see virtue sacrificed to nefarious views, or villainy triumphant. For example, in Tate's alteration of *Lear*, the old man and his favourite daughter are both kept alive and made happy, while all the vicious characters of the Play fall the victims of justice. This catastrophe sends away all the spectators exulting with gladness; and when we look back on the exhibition, and examine it from beginning to end, we find nothing that can induce us to alter our sensation. In some things it were injustice not to own that Tate has changed Shakespeare's plot for the better. In Shakespeare we see the king bringing in the body of his Cordelia, whom he supposes to have hanged herself: the picture here, with all its concomitants, raises disgust and rather excites horror than creates pleasure. But Tate, to make amends for his judicious emendations lest too much merit should accrue to him from them, has left out some of the finest speeches in the character of Lear, which Mr Garrick has properly restored; and they are, I believe, retained by other performers. (29-31)

* * *

[On the comic after-piece]

For my own part, I would chuse to leave the theatre impressed by that gloomy pleasure which I feel from the sublimity of Shakespeare or the tenderness of Otway, and not to have it dissipated by Farce. Yet it is perhaps a dissipation necessary in this Kingdom, where the temperature of the air inclines to gloom and melancholy, a disposition to which we also owe the speaking of comic Epilogues after Tragedies. (63)

* * *

[On the passions and their representation in drama]

Take a shorter instance of the like kind from Shakespeare who, to make the transition from peace of mind to despair more striking, introduces Romeo in the last act of *Romeo and Juliet* as in a settled tranquil state, in full expectation of good news from his dear mistress.

> *If I may trust the flattery of sleep,*
> *My dreams presage some joyful news at hand:*
> *My bosom's lord sits lightly on his throne,*
> *And all this day an unaccustomed spirit*
> *Lifts me above the ground with chearful thoughts,* &c.   [5.1.1ff.]

Here a messenger brings him the news of Juliet's death. The account at first deprives him of the power of speaking. The anguish it creates works inward: grief, despair, and astonishment are displayed in his countenance. At length he takes breath with this one line:

> *Is it even so? then I defy you, stars!*   [5.1.24]

In which there is more real anguish implied than in twenty studied pages; and all who have seen that solemn pause of woe which Mr Garrick shews in this particular will allow that he does the poet inimitable justice.

The apprehension of an approaching evil, or of being deprived of our happiness in any shape, creates fear: its symptoms are a pale countenance, a troubled eye, a depression of the spirits approaching to fainting: when it rises to terror or horror, a tremor and universal agony follow, the speech is broken and confused, and the half formed accents die upon the lips.

In the second part of *Henry IV* Northumberland thus addresses the messenger of his son's death:

> *Thou tremblest, and the whiteness in thy cheek*
> *Is apter than thy tongue to tell thy errand.*
> *Even such a Man, so faint, so spiritless,*
> *So dull, so dead in look, so woe-be-gone,*
> *Drew Priam's curtains in the dead of night,*
> *And would have told him half his Troy was burn'd.*
> *But Priam found the fire ere he his tongue.*   [1.1.68ff.]

And when Juliet retires to her chamber to take the potion she anticipates the horrors of the situation she is just entering into with so much force that we think all the dreadful figures her imagination raises visible.

> *Alas! alas! is it not like that I*
> *So early waking, what with loathsome smells,*
> *And shrieks like mandrakes torn out of the earth,*
> *That living mortals hearing them run mad.—*

359

Or if I wake shall I not be distraught,
(Invironed with all these hideous fears)
And madly play with my fore-fathers joints,
And pluck the mangled Tybalt from his shroud?
And in this rage with some great kinsman's bone,
As with a club dash out my desp'rate brains?   [4.3.45ff.]

Hope is the reverse of the last passion; it gives a desirous eager look, with a mixture of fear and assurance. As the latter prevails the countenance becomes more placid and serene, which is the most can be said of this passion, as its motions are chiefly internal and create but small alteration in the countenance.

Jealousy and Envy proceed from various causes: the peace and prosperity of others, the advantages they are possessed of and which we think ourselves intitled to and qualified for, will give rise to Envy, Hatred, Rancor, Malice, and Revenge. These tormenting, detestable passions have much the same appearances. They cover the countenance with a malignant gloom, the eye is inflamed, and shoots cautious side-glances at the object of resentment: thus Milton represents Satan in Paradise viewing our first parents.

Aside the devil turned
For envy, yet with jealous leer malign
Eyed them askance.

There is a great deal of difference between the malice of a slave and the vengeance of a prince justly provoked; and while we abhor Iago, and view his fall with pleasure, we find something in the character of Zanga[1] that commands our pity. Iago prosecutes to destruction a noble unsuspecting officer for having preferred above him *one Michael Cassio.* He has no other real motive for his villainy. He, indeed, in the first scene of the Play mentions to Roderigo that he hates the general on another account, for, says he, 'He has, between my sheets, done me the unlawful office;' [1.3.380ff.] and again he declares he will not be easy 'till he is even with him wife for wife.' [2.1.293.] But from his deportment through the rest of the play he leaves us at liberty to judge that he

---

[1] A character in Edward Young's play, *The Revenge* (1721). The comparison between these two characters was often made, best of all by Arthur Murphy in the *London Chronicle* for 15 February 1757, who showed that Young's play was based not on *Othello* but on a story in the *Spectator*, yet conceded that 'to succeed after such a masterly hand as Shakespeare is a Proof of an uncommon Genius. In the working of the Jealousy there is nothing like Imitation: Zanga is an original Character, and borrows no Aids from Iago' (p. 136).

has invented this story the better to help his designs on Roderigo, without whom it is impossible his schemes can work. He then proceeds to destroy an honest gallant soldier, an innocent beautiful woman, a well-beloved modest man, and a simple outwitted coxcomb. He completes a mean but barbarous revenge, excited by a very trifling disappointment; he levels every thing in his way, and spares neither age, sex, or condition. When his villanies are detected he deports himself with all the gloomy malice of a slave. 'What ye know, says he, ye know; seek no more of me, for from this hour I never will speak more.' [5.2.306f.] In few words, he has neither the spirit to triumph in his vengeance, nor the least spark of refined feeling for having destroyed characters so amiable as Desdemona and Othello. How very different are the motives and deportment of Zanga! how intimately acquainted was the poet who drew the character with the manner both of his rank and country! . . . (124–9).

In considering the two characters of Iago and Zanga, which appear of a similar nature, I would recommend to the Actor to observe that Iago's revenge is the sheer malice of a villain, who has no consequence to support him; that in Zanga he should take care to infuse an air of dignity through the whole. . . . (131)

*　　*　　*

Disappointment is expressed by desponding down-cast looks, a gloomy eye, and the hand striking the breast. Despair needs not a finer description than we find of it in Shakespeare:

> My conscience hath a thousand several tongues,
> And ev'ry tongue brings in a several tale,
> And ev'ry tale condemns me for a villain.
> Perjury, perjury, in highest degree,
> Murther, murther, stern murther, in the dir'st degree,
> Throng to the bar, all crying, guilty, guilty!
> I shall despair: there is no creature loves me;
> And if I die, no soul shall pity me. [Richard III, 5.3.193ff.]

Anger runs through the mind like a devouring flame. It choaks the voice, gives a savage wildness to the eye; the eye-brow in this disposition is let down, it is contracted and pursed into frowns. This passion will sometimes excite a trembling in the whole frame; and when it swells into an extreme rage all these motions will be yet more violent. . . . The voice of passion is strongly marked in Hotspur.

He said, he would not ransom Mortimer,
Forbad my tongue to speak of Mortimer! [*I Henry IV*, 1.3.219f.]

And of extreme rage in Othello.

Villain, be sure thou prove my love a whore;
Be sure of it; give me the ocular proof,
Or by the worth of my eternal soul,
Thou hadst better have been born a dog
Than answer my waked wrath. [3.3.363ff.]

Revenge will best be expressed by a black gloomy satisfaction in the looks, if successful; and with the most violent paroxisms of rage and regret, when disappointed. . . .

Courage and Resolution are known by a confirmed steady aspect, the eye lively and penetrating, the body erect, every motion firm, the voice steady and nervous. Thus Richard prepares for battle [Quotes *Richard III*, 5.3.316ff.] (132-4)

*   *   *

[On the costumes for Shakespeare]

To see Richard, Henry VIII, Falstaff, &c. dressed in the habits of the times they lived in, and the others in modern ones, quite opposite, is an inconsistency which carries its own conviction with it. What should we think if Le Brun had dressed Alexander's soldiers in modern regimentals, and yet preserved the dress of their ancient commanders? Othello too in modern cloaths is a mistake of the same nature, and yet Zanga and Oroonoko still appear in their national habits. Mr Garrick was sensible of this impropriety, and when he performed this character added the propriety of the dress to his excellent performance.

I think it was Mr Macklin who first dressed Iago properly. Formerly he was dressed in such a manner as to be known at first sight, but it is unnatural to suppose that an artful villain like him would chuse a dress which would stigmatize him to every one. I think, as Cassio and he belong to one regiment, they should both retain the same regimentals. . . .

Time and circumstance in some of our theatrical characters is very often overlooked or mistaken. Thus Clodio comes in full dressed though he's supposed to be just returned from his travels, and his first speech is to bid the grooms take care of his horses. . . . I have seen an

Actor who performed Romeo, who, to heighten the character and feed his vanity, spoke the celebrated speech of Mercutio,

O then I see Queen Mab, &c.   [1.4.53ff.]

in the same solemn declamatory manner as a lawyer pleads a cause. Is it not absurd to see Hamlet just come from on board a ship, where he had been robbed and plundered, with a well-powdered wig and every way as nicely dressed as at court, and even face the court in the church-yard without any alteration of garb, when it is plain he is not known till he discovers himself by crying out 'I am Hamlet the Dane.' [5.1.251f.] (158–61)

*   *   *

[From a short history of the English theatre]

Thus the British Stage, like the antient, had almost the same rude beginnings, and it continued in a state of imperfection till the glorious reign of Queen Elizabeth, when Shakespeare and Jonson arose, the glories of their age and nation. The first by the force of heaven-born genius, and the other with the most consummate learning and art, almost all at once raised the Stage to such dignity and perfection as has never since been out-done. (208)

*   *   *

[On Shakespeare and Garrick]

Shakespeare excelled in portraying the passions and their method of acting upon the human mind; when he had explored, he painted them with boldness, he delineated them so exactly, the assimilation was so nice, that the copy was scarcely to be distinguished from the original. Who is there that reads Clarence's dream in *Richard the [third]* that does not see every image that he describes, and feel the effect which he attributes to it? His account of the struggles which he supposed himself to have with the waters before he was suffocated is so striking, the torments that he went thro' after death are so powerfully painted that one would be almost apt to believe that Shakespeare had passed by the channel of drowning to the regions of immortality, from whence, by some strange chance, he escaped back into life—like some of those visionaries whom we find mentioned in the Roman Martyrology and Venerable Bede. The best writers of the Drama who have succeeded this great master, whether in the different provinces of serious or comic, are in comparison of him but twilight to sunshine.

To copy his manners, to catch his spirit and illustrate his text is a task to which scarcely any actor was ever equal; he who is must confessedly be allowed to stand among performers in a light as superior as Shakespeare does among poets, and there is no body who has traced Mr Garrick through all his walks but what will allow him deservedly the situation.

Nature has furnished him with great sensibility and fire, with a lively eye—not quite black, but extremely dark and piercing. His countenance taken altogether is strikingly marking, and no man is better able to suit his natural advantages to the different characters in which he appears. The perfection of his performance is sufficiently acknowledged by the repeated approbation of his audience. It would require more than a folio volume to describe the various excellencies which this gentleman displays in his cast of characters, whether tragic or comic. We shall pass some strictures upon his appearances in a few parts of each, and thence some idea of his merit may be fairly deduced. Perhaps it may be said, with as much justice as truth, that he is the greatest, if not the only actor who has appeared in Lear and Abel Drugger, Macbeth and Benedick, Hamlet and Sir John Brute, Chamont and Archer, Tancred and Ranger, Jaffeir and Bays, Lusignan and Lord Chalkstone. It would be difficult to determine which of the tragic characters we have mentioned require the strongest attributes, which of the comic stand in need of the greatest abilities.

His performance in *Lear* is certainly very capital, nor is it in man's power to vary the passions which actuate that character in a manner more striking. If it was the master-piece of Shakespeare to write, so is it the Chef-d'œuvres of Garrick to act, nor is there a beauty of the Play which he does not wonderfully illustrate; and thro' the whole his genius appears almost as powerfully creative as that of the Divine Author from whose pen it dropped.

Whether we consider him seated upon his throne in fullness of a content, which he shares out with infinite complacency among his *pelican daughters* [3.4.74], raving at the affronts under which they lay him, drenched in the *pitiless storm* [3.3.29], exposed to all the fury of the heavens: or mad as the vexed winds; whether we view him wearied *with vile crosses*[1] or at the last extremity, calling forth all the strength and spirits of an almost exhausted old man to free himself from surrounding

---

[1] Tate's adaptation, 5.6.46 [Vol. 1, p. 383].

peril and save his dear Cordelia, we must pronounce him inimitable. His knowledge of the passions, and their several methods of operating on the mind, are by him through the whole very properly marked. With what emphatic rage does he pronounce

> *Darkness and devils—Saddle my horses;*
> *Call my train together.* [1.4.252ff.]

What heart of sensibility is there that does not swell with horror at the awful solemnity with which he utters the curse of[1]

> *Blasts upon thee,*
> *Th' untented woundings of a father's curse*
> *Pierce every sense.*

How beautifully expressive appears the bitterness of his anger subsiding into a reflection on his own folly! How artfully does he endeavour to suppress the justly provoked tear when he says[2]

> *Old fond eyes,*
> *Lament this cause again, I'll pluck ye out,*
> *And cast ye with the water that ye lose*
> *To temper clay.*

His manner of conveying his feeling here makes every other eye overflow. The alteration of his countenance from sensibility to madness, the foolish laugh, and indeed his whole performance of the mad part must impress every body capable of the smallest tenderness. I never see him coming down from one corner of the Stage with his old grey hair standing, as it were, erect upon his head, his face filled with horror and attention, his hands expanded, and his whole frame actuated by a dreadful solemnity but I am astounded and share in all his distresses. Nay, as Shakespeare in some different place, with elegance, observes upon another subject, *one might interpret from the dumbness of his gesture.* [*Timon*, 1.1.36f.] Methink I share in his calamities, I feel the dark drifting rain and the sharp tempest, with his[3]

> *Blow winds—'till you have burst your cheeks.*

It is here that the power of his eye, corresponding with an attitude peculiar to his own judgment and proper to the situation, is of force

---

[1] Tate's adaptation, 1.2.74ff.; *King Lear*, 1.4.299ff.
[2] Tate, 1.2.76ff.; *King Lear*, 1.4.301ff.
[3] Tate, 3.1.1.; *King Lear*, 3.2.1.

sufficient to thrill through the veins and pierce the hardest bosom. What superlative tenderness does he discover in speaking these words:[1]

> *Pray do not mock me; for as I am a man,*
> *I take that lady to be my child Cordelia.*

His whole performance in the fifth act of this Play is inimitably graceful. The spirit which he exerts, the endeavouring to collect all his strength to preserve his dear daughter from the hand of the assassin, are not to be described. His leaning against the side of the scene panting for want of breath, as if exhausted, and his recollecting the feat and replying to the fellow who observes that the good old King has slain two of them, *Did I not, fellow?*[2] have more force, more strength, and more propriety of character than I ever saw in any other Actor. Nor, in saying this, let it be at all supposed that I have the least design of detracting from the merits of Mr Barry. It must be allowed that he utters the imprecations against his children in a masterly manner, and that he excels in many places where no great hurry of passion agitates the scene: but there is a vivacity, a strain of judgment, and a pleasing power of varying and keeping up the passions in Garrick which Barry never can reach. It has been conjectured by a friend of mine, whose critical judgment I highly respect, that from Garrick's performance of the mad scenes in *Lear* Gray, in his poem on Eaton college, borrowed the idea of

> *Moody madness laughing wild.*

Shakespeare was always particularly careful in his characters, and in none more so than in Richard the Third, whom history has represented as the poet has drawn, deformed, wicked, perfidious, splenetic, and ambitious. All these marks of the character are spiritedly preserved by Garrick in the part. In the first act we see in him all the settled malice of the murderer, and after he kills the King, the unrelenting irony with which he views the blood upon his sword is perfectly preserved. It is something astonishing that when Cibber first brought his alteration of *Richard the Third*, in which he has shewn great abilities as a tragic writer, on the Stage this Act was ordered by the licenser to be left out,[3] lest it should remind people of drawing a comparison between the justly banished James and the unfortunate Henry; which to do, in my opinion, required a large straining of judgment. However, it has been for many years restored.

[1] Tate, 4.5.40f. [Vol. 1, p. 372]; *King Lear*, 4.7.59f., 69f.
[2] Tate, 5.6.43 [Vol. 1, p. 382]; *King Lear*, 5.3.275.   [3] See Vol. 2, pp. 101f.

It is to be observed of this character that wherever he speaks of his own imperfections, he shews himself galled and uneasy; and in one particular passage his drawing a parallel between himself and the rest of human kind, to all whom he finds himself unequal, determines him in villainy: *Then I am like no brother, &c.*[1] Garrick in all these places shews by his acting the cross-grained splenetic turn of Richard the Third; he shews you how the survey hurts him. Whereas I have seen some people here smile upon themselves, as if well pleased with their own appearance, in which that they were wrong the performance of this masterly Actor confirms. In his courtship to Lady Anne the dissimulation is so strong that we are almost induced to think it real, and to wonder how such deformity could succeed with so much beauty. When Mr Barry appeared in this character, for which I am not the only person that imagined him unfit, he was thought happy in this Scene; in which, however, all his abilities could not set him on a level with this darling of nature, whose tone of voice is happily insinuating, his manner perfectly engaging. Perhaps his exquisite judgment is shewn no where to more advantage than in the distinction he makes between the real and affected character of Richard the Third, particularly in that Scene of the Third Act wherein, as has been before concerted, Buckingham with the Mayor and Aldermen persuade him to accept the crown. Let his demeanor be observed in each of these speeches and the truth of this observation will be admitted.

When Buckingham leaves him in a passion, disgusted at his refusing the crown, Richard desires the Mayor to[2]

> *Call him again—*
> *You will enforce me to a world of cares:*
> *I am not made of stone,*
> *But penetrable to your kind entreaties.*

What fire lights up his eye, what satisfaction glows in his countenance when he thus expresses himself![3]

> *Why now my golden dream is out;*
> *Ambition, like an early friend, throws back*
> *My curtains with an eager hand, o'erjoy'd*
> *To tell me what I dreamt is true—a crown, &c.*

[1] Cibber's adaptation, 1.3.78 = *3 Henry VI*, 5.6.80.
[2] Cibber, 3.2.242ff.; *Richard III*, 3.7.221, 223ff.
[3] Cibber, 3.2.270ff.

Amidst all the discouraging tydings which he receives in the latter end of the fourth Act, amidst all the bustle of repeated disappointment he maintains the intrepidity and fire of the character in a manner which none but himself can sustain.

There is a fine contrast in the tent Scene of the last Act, between the calm soliloquy spoken by Richard before he retires to his couch and the horror with which he starts up and comes forward after the ghosts have uttered their predictions and retired,[1] which Garrick never fails to illustrate. I do not recollect any situation in Tragedy in which he appears to more advantage than that in which he rises and grasps his sword before quite awake; nor could any thing afford a finer subject to a masterly painter than his manner of receiving Catesby. (230-9). . . .

There is not any character in Tragedy so seldom hit off by the Actor as Macbeth, perhaps there are few more difficult; and in the hands of Garrick it acquires an inconceivable ease. It is curious to observe in him the progress of guilt from the intention to the act. How his ambition kindles at the distant prospect of a crown when the witches prophecy, and with what reluctance he yields, upon the diabolical persuasions of his wife, to the perpetration of the murder! How finely does he shew his resolution staggered, upon the supposed view of the air-drawn dagger, until he is rouzed to action by the signal, viz. the ringing of the closet bell!

It is impossible for description to convey an adequate idea of the horror of his looks when he returns from having murdered Duncan with the bloody daggers, and hands stained in gore. How does his voice chill the blood when he tells you, 'I've done the deed!' [2.2.14.] and then looking on his hands, 'this is a sorry sight!' [2.2.20] How expressive is his manner and countenance during Lenox's knocking at the door, of the anguish and confusion that possess him; and his answer, ''twas a rough night,' [2.3.59] shews as much self-condemnation, as much fear of discovery, as much endeavour to conquer inquietude and assume ease as ever was infused into, or intended for, the character. What force, what uncontroulable spirit does he discover in his distresses when he cries out

> They have tied me to a stake—I cannot fly;
> But bear-like I must fight my course.   [5.7.1f.]

In short he alone, methinks, performs the character.

As it is usual with Shakespeare particularly in every place to seize the

[1] Cibber, 5.5.24ff., 6off. [Vol. 2, pp. 123f.].

strongest likenesses that nature can furnish, to diversify every passion with exact colouring and propriety, and accurately to mark the different situations and predominant qualities of characters, so is it with Mr Garrick to transfuse them thro' his whole performance. He delineates them so that they are seen by every eye; nor is this virtue any where more plainly shewn than in *Hamlet*. The author has drawn this prince of a reserved cautious turn, arising from a melancholy stamped on him by his father's untimely death and some consequent misfortunes. The passions whereby he is actuated do not, except in a few places, rise to any height, and to distinguish his feigned madness from his real provocation is a master-piece which he hits off admirably. His manner of receiving his father's ghost on its first entrance has a fine mixture of astonishment, deference, and resolution; and the recollection and reverence which Garrick preserves in speaking

> *Go on, I'll follow thee*   [1.4.79]

as well as all thro' the next Scene, are by him better kept up than by any other Actor I have seen in this character. In the Closet Scene with his mother, where Hamlet says, 'he will speak daggers to her, but use none,' [3.2.386] he preserves a proper air of filial affection amidst the most bitter reproaches, until it gives way to the awe and surprize that must naturally arise from the re-appearance of the ghost, who

> *Comes to whet his almost blunted purpose.*   [3.4.111]

His real tenderness for Ophelia, and his ineffectual endeavours to hide it, are distinctions which he is as nice in conveying as the poet was in drawing.

All thro' the character of Romeo I think him at least equal to any one who ever performed; and where other passions besides love are to be displayed he is vastly superior. This is evinced particularly in the last act. His transition from the settled satisfaction of his presages, to silent horror and despondency on receiving the news of Juliet's death, that despair which he ever after maintains thro' the character, are as strong proofs as any I know of his judgment and abilities. The attitude into which he throws himself when disturbed by Paris in the church-yard is very striking, and which was stolen from him by a certain performer who owed to his instruction many, if not most of the strokes on which was founded his great reputation in *Romeo*. In the dying scene of this play he is particularly happy. His manner of expressing this single line,[1]

[1] From Garrick's adaptation: see Vol. 3, p. 340.

Parents have flinty hearts, and children must be wretched,

carries with it so much of that sort of frenzy which is proper to Romeo's melancholy situation, and it is delivered in a tone so affecting, so different from any thing we before heard him express that it makes one's blood run cold; and I dare say there is not a person that hears this line spoken by him, and who can charge himself with any parental neglect, that will not feel remorse, and shudder. (248–52)

*   *   *

[On James Barry as Macbeth]

In the *Humorous Lieutenant* he performs Demetrius, a young prince possessed of many virtues, but actuated by very strong passions. There is a tincture of romance in it, but it is not bad; and in his hands it loses no part of its merit. In all the Scenes with Celia, whether representing tenderness, jealousy, or despondence, he is just and pleasing. Not so much can be said for his Macbeth. There is a character in the same Tragedy to which he is much better adapted. How delightful would the plaintive notes of his voice sound in Macduff's bewailing the loss of his children. There is a stern, murderous savageness in the first that becomes him not near so well as would the tenderness and affection of the last, in which Wilkes was always received with great applause, and is complimented by the *Tatler*, Numb. 68.[1] Garrick exhibits this Play as it was written.[2] Barry performs it with Betterton's alterations, which I cannot think any ornament to the piece. They put us in mind of German money, wherein we find copper and silver intermixed. Perhaps Shakespeare has nowhere left us finer writing than in this Play, the speaking and acting of which is as hard as the writing is great. I cannot say I ever saw the character played all through equal to what I conceive of it. Mr Barry has many beauties in it, on which neither my leisure nor space permit me to descant. I shall, however, delay a little here to remark to him that I think him wrong in his manner of stopping this speech: 'To-morrow, to-morrow, &c.' In this place, Macbeth, among other perplexities, receives the news of his wife's death, and cries out

> *She should have died hereafter—*
> *There had been time for such a word to-morrow—*
> *To-morrow, to-morrow, and to-morrow,*
> *Creep in a slow and stealing pace along, &c.*   [5.5.17ff.]

[1] See Vol. 2, p. 206.   [2] Not quite: see Vol. 3, No. 100.

Macbeth's situation is at this time so very critical that he has not leisure to indulge private grief. Hence he is led to observe that his wife's death had better happened at any other time than now, when his circumstances are so very perplexed, and which have now reached such a point that they must, in the course of things, sustain some considerable change even by *to-morrow*; that this change he is persuaded will be for his advantage through a reliance on the equivocal and delusive promises of the witches. His mentioning the word *Morrow* leads him into a chain of reflections upon its meaning and consequences which are otherwise abruptly, nay, absurdly introduced, and this is the case in Barry's way of replying to the account of his wife's death, which he delivers thus:

> *She should have died hereafter—*
> *There had been time for such a word,*
> *To-morrow, &c.*

But he makes up for this mistake, if it may be called one, in that scene wherein he says.

> *Is that a dagger which I see before me?*   [2.1.33]

in which he is extremely happy, as well as in receiving the ghost of Banquo, and all thro' the last Act. (294–7)

*   *   *

[On Aristotle's rules]

As nature is always the same, though at different times she may wear different aspects, and as the first dramatic Genius drew her as he found her, I see no reason why our Shakespeare may not have as good a right to vary from, or reject the antient model by drawing from something more grand and august than had been before discovered. [Aristotle's rules are not as] perpetual . . . obligation for any future poet to observe. (327)

174. Oliver Goldsmith, Shakespeare's absurdities and theatrical revivals

1759

From chapter xii, '*Of the STAGE*' in *An Enquiry into the Present State of Polite Learning in Europe*, 1759.

Oliver Goldsmith (1730?–74) was educated at Trinity College, Dublin, and pursued his medical studies in Edinburgh and Leyden. Having tried, and failed, to establish himself as a doctor in London between 1756 and 1758, he turned entirely to literature, and this *Enquiry* was his first published work. His criticism of the theatre managers for pandering to public tastes and quick profits was resented by Garrick, who refused both of Goldsmith's plays for Drury Lane and damaged the success of *The Good Natur'd Man* in 1768 by mounting a rival new comedy. Goldsmith's enormous output for the periodicals (see the bibliography by Arthur Friedman, revising the original one by R. S. Crane, in *NCBEL* II, pp. 1191–1210) reveals surprisingly little interest in Shakespeare.

But it is needless to mention the incentives to vice which are found at the theatre, or the immorality of some of the performers. Such impeachments, though true, would be regarded as cant, while their exhibitions continue to amuse. I would only infer from hence that an actor is chiefly useful in introducing new performances upon the stage, since the reader receives more benefit by perusing a well written play in his closet than by seeing it acted. I would also infer that to the poet is to be ascribed all the good that attends seeing plays, and to the actor all the harm.

But how is this rule inverted on our theatres at present! Old pieces are revived and scarce any new ones admitted; the actor is ever in our eye and the poet seldom permitted to appear; the public are again obliged to ruminate those hashes of absurdity which were disgusting to our ancestors, even in an age of ignorance; and the stage, instead of serving the people, is made subservient to the interests of an avaricious few. We must now tamely see the literary honours of our country suppressed, that an actor may dine with elegance; we must tamely sit and see the celestial muse made a slave to the histrionic Dæmon.

We seem to be pretty much in the situation of travellers at a Scotch inn: vile entertainment is served up, complained of and sent down; up comes worse, and that also is changed; and every change makes our wretched cheer more unsavoury. What must be done? only sit down contented, cry up all that comes before us, and admire even the absurdities of Shakespeare.

Let the reader suspend his censure; I admire the beauties of this great father of our stage as much as they deserve but could wish, for the honour of our country, and for his honour too, that many of his scenes were forgotten. A man blind of one eye should always be painted in profile. Let the spectator who assists at any of these new revived pieces only ask himself whether he would approve such a performance if written by a modern poet; if he would not, then his applause proceeds merely from the sound of a name and an empty veneration for antiquity. In fact, the revival of those pieces of forced humour, far-fetch'd conceit, and unnatural hyperbole which have been ascribed to Shakespeare, is rather gibbeting than raising a statue to his memory; it is rather a trick of the actor, who thinks it safest acting in exaggerated characters, and who by out-stepping nature chuses to exhibit the ridiculous outré of an harlequin under the sanction of this venerable name.

What strange vamp'd comedies, farcical tragedies, or what shall I call them, speaking pantomimes,[1] have we not of late seen. No matter what the play may be it is the actor who draws an audience. He throws life into all; all are in spirits and merry, in at one door and out at another; the spectator, in a fool's paradise, knows not what all this means till the last act concludes in matrimony. The piece pleases our critics, because it talks old English, and it pleases the galleries, because it has fun. True taste, or even common sense, are out of the question. (167–70)

---

[1] Compare Goldsmith's opinions in conversation with Boswell and Thomas Davies: 'Goldsmith: "I am afraid we will have no good plays now. The taste of the audience is spoiled by the pantomime of Shakespeare[,] the wonderful changes and shifting." Davies: "Nay, but you will allow that Shakespeare has great merit?" Goldsmith: "No, I know Shakespeare very well." [Boswell:] Here I said nothing, but thought him a most impudent puppy.' Boswell's London Journal, ed. cit., p. 106; entry for 25 December 1762 (Boswell's first meeting with Goldsmith).

175. William Hawkins, from his adaptation of *Cymbeline*

1759

From *Cymbeline. A Tragedy Altered from Shakespeare*, (1759). Performed 15 February 1759.

William Hawkins (1722–1801), clergyman and poet, was Professor of Poetry at Oxford from 1751 to 1756 and a fellow of Pembroke College. He wrote poems, plays, sermons, theological works, and a translation of the first four books of the *Aeneid* (1764). His collected works, *Tracts in Divinity* . . . (3 vols, Oxford, 1758) were unfavourably reviewed by Goldsmith in the *Critical Review* for August 1759.

PREFACE.

The Tragedy of *Cymbeline* is, in the whole oeconomy of it, one of the most irregular productions of *Shakespeare*. Its defects however, or rather its superfluities, are more than equalled by beauties and excellencies of various kinds. There is at the same time something so pleasingly romantic and likewise truly *British* in the subject of it that, I flatter myself, an attempt to reduce it as near as possible to the regular standard of the *drama* will be favourably received by all who are admirers of *novelty* when *propriety* is its foundation. I have accordingly endeavoured to new-construct this Tragedy almost upon the plan of *Aristotle* himself, in respect of the *unity* of *Time*, with so thorough a veneration however for the great *Father* of the *English* stage that even while I have presumed to regulate and modernize his design I have thought it an honour to tread in his steps, and to imitate his Stile with the humility and reverence of a *Son*. With this view I have retained in *many* places the very language of the original author, and in *all* others endeavoured to supply it with a diction similar thereunto, so that, as an unknown friend of mine has observed, the present attempt is intirely

374

new, whether it be considered as an *alteration from* or an *imitation of Shakespeare*.

The *difficulty* of such an attempt, as *rational* as it may be, has a kind of *claim*, I presume, to the *indulgence* of the public, especially as it has been attended likewise with *disadvantages*. For I found myself necessitated by my plan to *drop some* characters, to *contract others*, and to omit *some* scenes and incidents of an interesting nature, or rather to bring the substance and purport of them within the compass of a few short narrations. A loss irreparable, this, but that conveniencies are likewise to be thrown into the opposite scale. For as, I hope, I have not *injured* any characters by *contracting* them but have left them to *all intents* and in point of *importance* the *same*, so I have had an opportunity of *enlarging* and *improving some* of the original parts, (those particularly of *Palador*, and *Philario*—the *Pisanio of Shakespeare*) and, by varying certain incidents and circumstances, of giving a *new cast* to the whole *drama*. After all I am very far from meaning to detract from the merit of *Shakespeare*, or from insinuating that the plays of so exalted a genius *require* such new-modelling as the present in order to the rendering them useful or entertaining. I have ventured publicly to defend this great *dramatic* Poet in the liberties he has taken, but still *Shakespeare* himself needs not be *ashamed* to *wear* a *modern dress*, provided it can be made tolerably to *fit* him.

The only question then will be, whether the present *alteration* be a judicious one?—And this with all due deference is left to the candour and justice of the public.

*　　*　　*

PROLOGUE

Britons, the daring Author of to-night,
Attempts in Shakespeare's manly stile to write;
He strives to copy from that mighty mind
The glowing vein—the spirit unconfin'd—
The figur'd diction that disdain'd controul—
And the full vigour of the poet's soul!
—Happy the varied phrase, if none shall call
This imitation, that original.—

For other points, our new advent'rer tries
The bard's luxuriant plan to modernize;
And, by the rules of antient art, refine
The same eventful, pleasing, bold design.

Our scenes awake not now the am'rous flame,
Nor teach soft swains to woo the tender dame;
Content, for bright example's sake, to shew
A wife distress'd, and innocence in woe.—
For what remains, the poet bids you see,
From an old tale, what Britons ought to be;
And in these restless days of war's alarms,
Not melts the soul to love, but fires the blood to arms.

Your great forefathers scorn'd the foreign chain,
Rome might invade, and Cæsars rage in vain—
Those glorious patterns with bold hearts pursue,
To king, to country, and to honour true!—

Oh! then with candour and good will attend,
Applaud the author in the cordial friend:
Remember, when his failings most appear,
It ill becomes the brave to be severe.—
Look ages back, and think you hear to-night
An antient poet, still your chief delight!
Due to a great attempt compassion take,
And spare the modern bard for Shakespeare's sake.

SCENE, partly a Royal Castle and partly in and near a Forest in WALES

[Act I, Scene i. A Royal Palace]

*   *   *

[*Flourish. Exeunt all but* Cloten.]

Cloten. Thanks to my mother for this joyless crown—
It fills not half my wish: while Leonatus
Reigns in the bosom of fair Imogen,
'Tis I am banish'd, and a sov'reign he:
Wou'd I cou'd pluck their loves up by the roots!
And I am strong in hope—if young Pisanio
(Whom I made mine by making myself Cæsar's
When he was last in Britain) hath been true
To the employ I gave him, long ere now
The jealous exile pines him in belief
His lady's truth is tainted.—Come, Pisanio—
He said, he'd quit the train, and here return
T'unlade his secrets to me.—Oh! sir, welcome!
Enter PISANIO.

What shall I ask thee first?—How fares Augustus?
Is Leonatus mad? Thou might'st have told
A history ere this.
   Pisanio.   I pray you patience—
First, sir, my lord commends him to your highness;
Next, the diseased Leonatus hath
Italian fits of jealousy too strong
For hellebore to cure.
   Cloten.   That's well—his grief
Is medicine to mine; but when, and how?
Give me particulars at large—my ear
Shall catch thy narrative as greedily,
As doth the sick man the kind drops that fall
Upon his fever's flame.
   Pisanio.   My lord, as soon
As I had foot in Italy, I challeng'd
Th' abused Leonatus with some friends
To the appointment of a merry meeting;
Where, as the wine danc'd brainward, I began
To praise the freedom of the British ladies,
Their lib'ral hearts, and am'rous 'complishments;
When Leonatus vow'd I did them wrong,
And was too bold in my persuasion.
   Cloten. So.
   Pisanio.   I fast held me to my sentiment,
And, for his doubt provok'd me, swore myself
Had tasted half the court, and his own princess,
(Whose virtue he had deem'd unparagon'd)
At her own suit in bed.
   Cloten.   Most brave, brave Roman!
   Pisanio. On this the Briton vaults me from his seat,
And bids my ready sword avow th'affront
Done his pure lady's honour—I with looks
Of calm assurance, and arms folded thus,
Wish'd him attend my proofs. This fair proposal
Had sanction from all sides, and liquor'd noddles
Jostled to hear my tale.
   Cloten.   Why so—Proceed.
   Pisanio. First, roundly I describ'd her bed-chamber,
The arras, cieling, pictures; (for of these

I took most faithful inventory, when
I lay concealed there); then I produc'd
The bracelet that I ravish'd from her arm,
As sleep, the ape of death, lay dull upon her;
And last I quoted the cinque-spotted mole
That richly stains her breast, like crimson drops
I'th'bottom of a cowslip.

 Cloten.   There was voucher
Stronger than ever law made.—Well, sir, what
To this the Briton?

 Pisanio.   He was quite besides
The government of patience—He roll'd round
His bloodshot eyes, stamp'd with his foot, and writh'd
His form into all postures; strove to speak,
And chatter'd monkey-like;—at length, his choler
Burst into utt'rance rash—'tis well, he cried,
The fiends of hell divide themselves between you—
And so without more ceremony, left
Our board, to cast conjectures, as they might,
Whereto his fury tended.

 Cloten.   Thanks, Pisanio;
Saw you him since?

 Pisanio.   No; but the rumour was,
Ere I left Rome, that he had turn'd his thought
To bloody purpose of revenge.

 Cloten.   'Tis good—
Pisanio, I did love this lady—lie
I should not, if I said I love her still—
O she is sweeter than the breath of spring
Wooing the maiden violet—'tis past—
And I have lost her.

 Pisanio.   She hath wrong'd you.

 Cloten.   True—
She hath disdain'd me—spurn'd me—once she vow'd,
The meanest garment that e'er clip'd the body
Of Leonatus, was in her respect
Dearer than all the hairs upon my head,
Were they all made such men.—The south-fog rot
Him, her, and Cæsar's foes.

* * *

Philario. [Leonatus] writes me here, (*Pulling out letters*)
In spleenful terms of most confirm'd belief,
That he hath cognizance of her incontinence;
And wills me, by the love and truth I owe him,
To murther her.—Perhaps some false Italian
Hath the infection of foul slander pour'd
In his too ready ear.—Perhaps she's fall'n.—
She's fair,—that's much; she's young,—that's more.—I hold
The virtue of the best attemptable.—
I must proceed with wary steps herein.—
Here's that will 'tice her from her prison-house,
Or for true love, or seeming.—I will steal
This way to her apartment.   [*Exit.*

[Act I, Scene ii]

SCENE *opens, and discovers* Imogen *in her apartment, sitting by a table;
a book on the table.*

Imogen. A father cruel, and a suitor base,
A banish'd husband too—O that's the grief
That gives the deepest wound.—Then am I sure
The shes of Italy will not betray
Mine int'rest, and his honour?—Wicked fear!
Where he abides, falshood is out of fashion,
And truth the law to action.—Hark! the clock!   (*Clock strikes.*)
'Tis the tenth hour of morn—the very time
I bad him think on me, and combat heav'n
With prayers, as I would do.—O bless him Gods,
And sweeten all his cares with drops of comfort.
—Now to my book—Philosophy, best doctor,
Thou wisely dost prescribe to human woe
The lenitive of patience.   (*Reads.*)

Enter PHILARIO
                              There she sits—
Sweet student! with a look as chaste as Dian's.
If she's disloyal, falshood never yet
Hung out so fair a sign—yet *seems*, we know,
Is often read for *is*—I must disturb her—

379

Imogen—lady—

Imogen.   Hah! what now, Philario?

Philario. Dear lady, here are letters from your lord—

Imogen. From whom? from Leonatus?—Let me see—

Oh! learn'd indeed were that astronomer,
That knew the stars as I his characters—
He'd lay the future open—You good Gods,
Let what is here contain'd relish of love;
Of my lord's health; of his content; yet not
That we two are apart—of his content
In all but that—good wax, thy leave—blest bees
That make these locks of counsel—Good news, Gods.

   Philario. Now let me con her visage as she reads—

   Imogen. (Reading) *Justice and your father's wrath, should he take me in his dominions, could not be so cruel to me, but you, oh! the dearest of creatures, would even renew me with your eyes. Take notice that I am at Milford Haven; what your own love will out of this advise you, follow. So he wishes you all happiness, that remains loyal to his vow, and yours increasing in love,*
                                        LEONATUS.

Oh! for a horse with wings—hear'st thou, Philario,
He is at Milford Haven—prithee tell me
How far 'tis thither. If one of mean affairs
May plod it in a day, why may not I
Glide thither in an hour? Then, good Philario,
Who long'st like me to see thy friend; who long'st
(O let me bate) but not like me, yet long'st,
But in a fainter kind—Oh! not like me—
For mine's beyond, beyond—tell me how far
To this same blessed Milford; and by the way
Tell me how Wales was made so happy as
T'inherit such a haven. But first of all,
How may we steal from hence? I prithee speak!
How far to Milford?

   Philario.   Madam, we may reach it,
With horses swift and sure of foot, before
The sun has ended his day's journey.

   Imogen.   Well—
But how to get from hence—

   Philario.   I have a thought—
Lady, a thousand eyes keep centinel

To watch your motions here—yet haply these
Unquestion'd we may pass—suppose you did
Assume another mien, and but disguise
That, which t'appear itself must not now be
But by self-danger—cannot you awhile
Forget to be a woman?
    Imogen.   I'm almost
A man already.
    Philario.   Make yourself but like one,
And ev'ry gate shall kindly open to us,
Tho' Argus' self were porter.
    Imogen.   In my closet
I have a suit of boy's apparel ready,
That was my page's—under which disguise,
And with what imitation I can borrow
From youth of such a season, I will quit
This castle's loathsome hold.
    Philario.   You are resolv'd then
To tie yourself to Leonatus' fortune,
And leave your father and the court behind you?
    Imogen. No court, no father now—(for what's a father
Whose mind my crafty stepdame poison'd, that
Bore all down with her brain) no, nor no more
Of that harsh, sullen, haughty, princeling Cloten,
That Cloten, whose love-suit has been to me
As fearful as a siege.
    Philario.   Hie to your chamber,
And fit you to your manhood—dull delay
Is sin 'gainst resolution.
    Imogen.   I am arm'd
Ev'n for events of peril infinite,
And woman's love is courage.
    Philario.   I will hence,
And able horse and furniture prepare
For this adventure: I'll be with you, lady,
Before you're well equipp'd.
    Imogen.   Do, good Philario:
The gracious Gods direct us!   *[Exeunt severally.*

★   ★   ★

[Act III, Scene i. In and near a Forest in Wales; a cave]

*   *   *

Bellarius. Well—to the field—tis the fourth hour o'th' morn.
Philario, and Fidele will remain
Here in the cave—We'll come to you after hunting;
Or are you for our sport?
    Imogen.   I am not well—
A sudden laziness creeps o'er my senses,
As if fatigue acknowledg'd no repair
By this nights' sleep—
    Philario.   The drug begins to work—   (*Aside*)
    Palador. Go you to hunting—I'll abide with him.
    Imogen. No—to your journal course—the breach of custom
Is breach of all—My uncle will stay here—
Farewel—I wish you sport—I shall be well
By your return—
    All.   We'll not be long away.
                    [*Exeunt* Bellarius, Palador, *and* Cadwal.
    Philario. These are kind creatures, lady.
    Imogen.   On my life
I'd change my sex to be companion with 'em,
Since my dear lord is false.
    Philario.   I would confer
Once more upon that theme.
    Imogen.   I'm sick already;
And would you minister fresh pain, Philario?
    Philario. Come—I'll no more dissemble—you are known
False to your banish'd lord.
    Imogen.   What hear I, Gods!
    Philario. The truth, the killing truth—art not asham'd?
—But shame is masculine—Could I find out
The woman's part in me—for there's no motion
That tends to vice in man, but I affirm
It is the woman's part; be't lying, note it,
The woman's flatt'ring, yours; deceiving, yours;
Lust and rank thoughts, yours, yours; revenges, yours;
Ambition; covetings; change of prides; disdain;
Nice longings; slanders; mutability;

All faults that may be nam'd, nay, that hell knows,
Why yours in part, or all; but rather all—
For ev'n to vice
You are not constant, but are changing still
One vice but of a minute old, for one
Not half so old as that.
    Imogen.   Am I awake?
Or have you senses perfect?
    Philario.   'Tis enough—
I have atchieved more than er'e did Julius,
And will be chronicled 'mongst those wise few
That have out-craftied woman.
    Imogen.   You amaze me.
    Philario. Oh! no more fooling—I have proof that tells
The time, the place, the—fie upon it, lady,
It wounds my modesty to quote the deeds
That cost thee not a blush.
    Imogen.   Blasphemer, hold!
Thou art in league with perjur'd Leonatus,
And dost traduce a lady that despises
Malice and thee like.
    Philario.   Go to—you're naught—
    Imogen. Villain, your proof? Why stand you idle thus?
If thou do'st see a speck upon my honour,
Prick at it with the sword, your just remorse
E'en now let drop.
    Philario.   Mistake not, lady mine,
Remorse was counterfeit, my purpose real;
I found you past all grace, and did commence
Cunning in my revenge; your punishment
Were nothing if not such; you have your death,
Yet never felt his sting.
    Imogen.   What says Philario!
    Philario. O now you tremble like a guilty soul
Beneath the furies lash—now you would pour
A deluge of salt grief to wash your crimes—
It is too late, thou hast out-liv'd repentance—
That draught was tinctured with a mortal juice,
And he that drinks an acron on't, is serv'd,
As I would serve a dog.

Imogen.   Sir, my surprize
Relishes not of fear.—This is a cure
Which you do call a chastisement—I feel
The death thou speak'st of curdling in my veins.
How sweetly do they sleep whom sorrow wakes not!
Farewel—my innocence is sacrifice,
Or to the blindfold rage of jealousy,
Or to estranged love—O Leonatus,
The Gods have pity on thee.

Philario.   Do I speak?
Is this my hand? are these my eyes?—All this
I will to question put, if thou art true—
O Imogen, but that I thought thee foul,
And thy confession a superfluous warrant,
I would have ta'en my sucking infant's throat,
And broach'd it with my martial scymeter,
E're touch'd thy precious life.

Imogen.   I do forgive thee—
Thy judgment (which how warp'd it matters not)
Condemn'd me to this death—Nay, weep not, sir,
Commend me to my lord—alas! Philario,
I grieve myself to think how much hereafter,
When the belief, or false affection, which
Holds pris'ner now his mind, shall leave him free,
His mem'ry will be pang'd by looking back
On my hard case of woe—my brain is heavy—

Philario. The mighty Gods throw stones of sulphur on
All jealous, head-sick fools—He saw it not—
And ev'ry day's experience doth disprove
The strong'st report—O the accursed fate
That damn'd me to this office—

Imogen.   Curb thy rage
Unprofitably loos'd—I'll in, and die—
Follow me not—my soul has that to do
Which is best done in secret—fare thee well—
Present to our good host, and my sweet brothers,
My thanks and choicest blessings.   [*Exit.* Imogen *into the Cave.*

Philario.   It goes well,
Her honour I have fann'd, and found it chaffless—
Friend, thou art fool, or villain—If I prove

Thou would'st betray my love to purposes
Of hell-black colour, tho' our friendship stood
Upon a brazen base, it should dissolve,
And, like the film that dews the morning flower,
Break into unseen air.

*   *   *

[Act IV, Scene ii. A Field of Battle]

Alarum. Enter LEONATUS *in disguise.*

   Leonatus. They go to battle with a jocund spirit—
But ah! how heavy is his heart, who bears
A bosom-war within him? O Philario,
(For I well know thy friendship such, thou'st done
The letter of my will) thou should'st have paus'd—
Anger is indiscreet in his commands—
Too true, the noble Imogen did wrong me;
(And so, I doubt not, did my mother him
I call'd my father, tho' she still was held
The non-pareil of virtue) yet her fault,
The nat'ral failing of her sex, not hers,
Was ill pursu'd with vengeance capital
By me—O Britain, I have kill'd my wife,
Who was thy mistress—therefore thus array'd
Like a poor soldier, neither known, nor guess'd at,
Pitied or hated, to the face of peril
Myself I'll dedicate—Heav'n knows my life
Is ev'ry breath a death.

*   *   *

[Act IV, Scene iv]

*   *   *

Enter LEONATUS.

   Leonatus.   Hermit, our wars are done;
The Romans turn their backs, and victory
To-day is wedded to great Cymbeline.
O that the joy of all should touch not me!
I am not mortal sure; for death I sought,
Yet found him not where I did hear him groan,

385

Nor felt him where he struck. This ugly monster,
'Tis strange he hides him in fresh cups, smooth beds,
Sweet words, and hath more ministers than we
That draw his knives in war.

    Palador.   Art thou a Briton,
And dost not laugh to-day? Sad looks are treason,
And take the part of Rome; the man that feels
His own distress, hates more his pers'nal grief,
Than he doth love his country.

    Leonatus.   O you know not—
Hah! who lies there? Ye Gods, it is Pisanio—
The damn'd Italian fiend that stain'd my honour;
I would have sav'd an hundred lives in fight
To have met his.

    Palador.   If thou art Leonatus,
(As by thy talk thou should'st be) I have matter
For your quick hearing.

    Leonatus.   I am Leonatus,
I would I were aught else!

    Palador.   That villain there
Did much abuse you, Sir.

    Leonatus.   He did abuse me
Beyond the pow'r of all his worthless tribe
To make amends—Who robs me of my wealth,
May one day have ability, or will
To yield me, full repayment—but the villain
That doth invade a husband's right in bed,
Is murd'rer of his peace, and makes a breach
In his life's after-quiet, that the grief
Of penitence itself cannot repair.

    Palador. Thou dost mistake thy woe, good Leonatus,
Which yet (if the great Gods are merciful)
I have a cure for—

    Leonatus.   How! where! which way! when!

    Palador. Sir, your belief in your dear lady's truth
Is falsely wounded, who, be sure (for aught
This arch impostor Roman could disprove)
Has kept her bond of chastity uncrack'd,
And is as cold as Dian.

    Leonatus.   Ay, and colder;

For Dian is alive—If thou not fool'st me,
Thou curest common sickness with the plague,
And killest with relief—I could not find
The virtue of my wife untainted now,
(That once I priz'd to adoration)
For the best carbuncle of Phœbus' wheel,
Nay, all the worth of's car.
    Palador.   Alas! I'm sorry
Your much wrong'd judgment hath proceeded thus.
For free and full confession made this wretch
Of most refined stratagem to change
Your biass of affection: Sir, this note,
Which with his dying hand he did bequeath you,
Will more at large illustrate what my tongue
Faulters in utt'rance of.   *(gives the note.)*
    Leonatus.   Quick, let me see it,
Impatient misery longs to know the worst,
E'en when the worst is fatal.   *(reads)*
    The Lord Cloten *to the* Roman *Knight* Pisanio.
Cloten! the name is ominous—it bodes
More than the raven's sullen flap that scents
Cadaverous infirmity.—But on—
    If thou lov'st me, let me see thee ere night. I have bought the fidelity of the
princess's woman with my gold; she will give thee admittance into her chamber,
when nothing will be awake but anger and policy; where thou may'st make
such note as will be sufficient to the madding of the abhorred Leonatus. Thy
service herein will tie me closer to thyself, and to Augustus thy lord. No more
till thou dost console with thy presence, thine and Cæsar's in affection,
                                      CLOTEN.

    Palador. How fare you, sir? Alack! his grief is dumb.
    Leonatus. Are there no Gods? or are they Gods that sleep,
And leave us to ourselves?—Oh! I have done it—
I've reach'd the point of shame, and villainy
Is less than 'twas.—Twice doubly curst be he
That first did graff the failings of his wife
On a fool's head's suspicion.—I've destroy'd
The temple of fair virtue, yea herself—
Spit, and throw stones, cast mire upon me, set
The dogs o'th' street to bait me; ev'ry fool
Be Leonatus call'd. O! Imogen,

My queen, my love, my wife, oh! Imogen!
  Palador. Mark thou unhappy Briton, how my soul
Catches thy grief—my eyes half drown my tongue.

*   *   *

[Act V, Scene i. The Forest, before the cave]

*   *   *

Enter PHILARIO.

  Philario. Fairest, and best of women, pardon me   (*kneeling*)
The tortures I have put thy virtue to
In trial, not in malice.—O forgive me;
For till thy lips have pass'd remission on me,
Mine must be lock'd in silence.
  Imogen.   Rise, Philario!
Thy stratagem has more complexion in't
Of wisdom, than of guilt—my honour tried,
I'm serv'd, and not offended—That same drug,
Murd'rous awhile to sense, I thank'd thee for
With the first breath I wak'd with—hence of that
Put the remembrance by—My brothers tell me
Of something strange at hand.
  Philario.   My gracious lady,
Since last we parted, the big hours have teem'd
With great, and sad events—pardon me, Gods,   (*aside.*)
One fiction more.
  Imogen.   Hast thou heard aught, Philario,
Of Leonatus? What is in thy mind
That makes thee stare thus? Wherefore breaks that sigh
From th' inward of thee? Speak—where is my husband?
  Philario. Say he were dead—his villainous intent
Should cure thy present sorrow.
  Imogen.   Thy supposing
Confirms his death, and my hereafter woe—
Thou tell'st me he was jealous, false, and cruel—
Grant he had faults, yet they were faults that others
Haply infus'd into his honest nature—
Grant he had faults, yet faults his future life
Might have amended all.—But, oh! this death
Chills mortally, and with the scythe of winter

388

Cuts down my spring of hope—O Leonatus!
   Philario. Nay, lady, mark me—He did leave the world
Without one drop of pity for your fate.
I saw him down in fight, whereto his rage
Had brought him, 'midst the hottest fumes of war
To make a desp'rate end; and first explaining
This hermit's garb, (which I to-day put on
To cheat the wary eye of Cymbeline)
Vow'd in the doing his will my heart
Rebell'd against my hand. ''Tis well, he cry'd,
I go to meet the strumpet, and consign her
To other fires than lust.' He said no more,
But to the last breath'd anger.
   Imogen.   If 'tis so,—
Some dæmon, envious of his peace and mine,
Did witch his sober judgment; nought but magic
In subtle potency of transformation,
Could ruin make of such a noble piece
Of heav'nly workmanship. Gods! what is man
When error outlives honour? Yet, Philario,
I will remember the good thing he was,
Ere fury bent him wrongwards—What he did
Let insolence, that wags his head in scorn
O'er virtue fall'n, proclaim—but never so
Shall his poor wife reproach him—O my lord,
Wise, valiant, gentle, constant, just, and true,
The world did tack to thy all-honour'd name;
Thou wert the mark that Jupiter did point to,
When he prais'd mortal beings.
   Philario.   Noblest princess,
What shall my wonder call thee?—thy great father
Yet knows not half thy worth—hither he's coming;
And I will put into his royal pow'r
The now-disposal of our destinies—
Lo, he is here—Be silent, and attend—
Hail to king Cymbeline.

Enter CYMBELINE, BELLARIUS, LEONATUS, *and* Lords.

   Cymbeline.   We thank you, hermit.
   Bellarius. Good heav'ns! Fidele living!

Philario.   Hist—a word—

(Phil. *whispers* Bell.)

Cymbeline. In troth, this rock hath a most pleasant site
To tempt a king from home—O luxury,
How art thou put to shame, if comfort lives
Where lowliness inhabits—our good hosts,
Where are the valiant boys?
    Philario.   Dread sovereign,
They shall come forth.—Ho! Cadwal! Palador!

Enter CADWAL *and* PALADOR *from the Cave.*

And now, so please your highness, I will ope,
Before you do betake you to repast,
A volume of high marvels to your ear.
    Cymbeline. Pray you begin.
    Philario.   First know then, mighty sir,
He, that addresses here your royal presence,
No hermit is, but your true slave Philario.
Nay, start not, sir, but know all criminals,
And then proceed to justice—here is one   (*pointing to* Leonatus.)
Has travell'd far to meet your fierce displeasure,
Yet once deserv'd your grace—
    Leonatus.   Ay, I am he—
No beggar, king, but yet a wretch more curst
Than ever fortune spurn'd at.—Know'st me not?
Send for ingenious torturers; command
The art of cruelty to practise on me,
For I do all abhorred things amend
By being worse than they.—Know'st me not yet?
The villain that did steal thy princely daughter;
(Yet that was theft for Gods!) the damned villain
That, in a fit of jealous lunacy,
Murder'd all precious qualities that man
Loves woman for—that—
    Imogen. (*running, and laying hold of him.*) Peace, my lord, hear, hear—
    Leonatus. Shall's have a play of this? thou scornful page
Come not athwart my grief—   (*strikes her.*)
    Philario.   Hold, Leonatus,
Or thou wilt murder do, who art so hurt
In a conceit 'tis done—Why gaze you so?

Didst thou not hear her speak? and know'st thou not
The tune of Imogen?
   Cymbeline.   The rock goes round.
   Philario. Nay, wonder is the gen'ral word to all!
You that ne'er lov'd, look on that virtuous pair—
Mark! how he anchors upon Imogen!
See! how she hangs on Leonatus' arm!
While both are mute in sweet extremity
Of truest love, and joy!
   Leonatus (after a pause.) Joy! who names joy?
It is a word too cold—What heav'n shall be
Hereafter, I feel now—Whom had I lost,
But Imogen? —Whom did I hold corrupt,
But Imogen?—Whom did I drive to death,
But Imogen?—Yet Imogen is found—
Yet Imogen is purer than the star
That leads her virgin train to light the morn—
Yet Imogen still lives, and lives to love me!—
—Divide all matter of discourse among you—
What can I say or think but Imogen!
   Imogen. How do the gracious Gods hide kindness, 'neath
The sable veil of sad appearances?
O Leonatus! had we never parted,
Had I ne'er stood the mark of thy revenge,
Ne'er had we known what 'tis to meet again,
What 'tis to meet again in life, and love!   *(Embrace.)*

*   *   *

EPILOGUE, spoken by the actress who played Imogen.

Well, Sirs—the bus'ness of the day is o'er,
And I'm a princess and a wife no more—
This bard of our's, with Shakespeare in his head,
May be well-taught, but surely is ill-bred.
Spouse gone, coast clear, wife handsome, and what not,
We might have had a much genteeler plot.
What madness equals true poetic rage?
Fine stuff! a lady in a hermitage!
A pretty mansion for the blooming fair—

No tea, no scandal,—no intriguing there.

—The gay beau-monde such hideous scenes must damn—
What! nothing modish, but one cordial dram!
—Yet after all, the poet bids me say,
For your own credit's sake approve the play;
You can't for shame condemn old British wit,
(I hope there are no Frenchmen in the pit)
Or slight a timely tale, that well discovers,
The bravest soldiers are the truest lovers.

Such Leonatus was, in our romance,
A gallant courtier, tho' he cou'd not dance;
Say, wou'd you gain, like him, the fair one's charms,
First try your might in hardy deeds of arms;
Your muffs, your coffee, and down-beds fore-go,
Follow the mighty Prussia thro' the snow;
At length bring home the honourable scar,
And love's sweet balm shall heal the wounds of war.

For me, what various thoughts my mind perplex?
Is't better I resume my feeble sex,
Or wear this manly garb? it fits me well—
Gallants instruct me—ladies, can you tell?
The court's divided, and the gentle beaux,
Cry—no disguises—give the girl her cloaths.
The ladies say, to-night's example teaches,
(And I will take their words without more speeches)
That things go best when—women wear the breeches.

176. Charles Marsh, from his adaptation of *Cymbeline*

1759

From *Cymbeline: King of Britain. A Tragedy, Written by Shake-speare. With some Alterations, by Charles Marsh. As it was agreed to be Acted at the Theatre-Royal in Covent-Garden,* 1759.

On Marsh see the headnote to No. 153 above.

PREFACE.

In the Summer of 1752 I waited on Mr *Rich* at *Cowley*, and read to him an Alteration of *Romeo and Juliet* wherein I had separated the Tragedy from the Comedy, and thrown the latter quite away. He approv'd of what I had done, but being undetermin'd as to accepting it, advis'd me to shew it to Mr *Barry* and Mrs *Cibber*. When I came to Mr *Barry* He told me he was sorry he could not assist me, for the House was to be open'd with *Romeo* as the Stage then possess'd it. But in Order to make me Amends, If I wou'd alter *Cymbeline* He wou'd engage for the Performance of it.

Induc'd by this Promise, and struck with the numberless Beauties of the Piece, I thought it a pleasing Task to endeavor to amend the *Conduct* of the *Fable* by confining the Scenes at least to this Island. Soon after I had began it Mr *Barry* carried what I had written to Mrs *Cibber*, who very judiciously pointed out some Passages that might be improv'd. The next Season Mr *Rich* Cast the several Parts of the *Play*, and it went thro' seven *Readings* or *Rehearsals* in the Green-Room. And Mrs *Cibber* was so sanguine in Favor of it that She spoke to me, in these remarkable Words: 'Now, Now, it will do! Mr *Marsh*, it will do! as long as the *Stage* exists, this will be an *Acting Play*, and as long as I know the *Theatre*, I shall choose to appear in the Character of *Imogen*.' Soon after this the Time was mentioned by Mrs *Cibber* in the Presence of Mr *Rich*, when the Play shou'd be brought on the Stage.

393

Her Words were to this Effect: That She thought it wou'd be wrong to oppose the new Play of *Eugenia*, then acting at *Drury-Lane*, till the Author's first Benefit was over; and therefore fix'd on the fourth Night of the Run of that Play for the performing of *Cymbeline*. As Mr *Rich* made no Objection I imagin'd all Difficulties were now surmounted. A few Nights after his Declaration, as I was standing behind the Scenes, Mr *Rich* desired me to speak to Mrs *Cibber* to come to a Rehearsal the next Morning (this was in the Month of *February*). When I address'd myself to her She replied with an exclamatory Voice that, as Mr *Pope* expresses it, yet vibrates on my Ear: 'No, Sir! No! it is too late, I have a long Part to study for myself; several for these People; (pointing to the Actors in the Green-Room) besides, Mr *Rich* never intended it shou'd come on at all.' Thus did my imaginary Poetical Estate, which was to have been *one* Benefit if the Play run *nine* Nights, vanish from me as suddenly as the hopes of making Gold are defeated by the dreadful Explosion in the *Alchymist*.

The next Time I saw Mr *Rich*, which was at the *Bedford Coffee-House*, He began 'Well, Sir, your *Play* is not to be perform'd, I find; did not I tell you *Barry* and *Cibber* never intended it shou'd? What think you now? Will you believe me another Time?' In his Manner was the Cause of my Disappointment attributed alternately by one to the other. As Mr *Barry* was the Person who first engag'd me in this Performance I naturally complain'd to him of the Usage I had receiv'd, and two Seasons ago I met Mr *Rich* and Mr *Barry* in the Dressing-Room of the latter, when Mr *Rich* assur'd me He wou'd play *Cymbeline* early the next Winter, and wou'd *be my Friend* in it. When that Winter came on I wrote two Letters to him reminding him of his Promise (for it was impossible not to be tir'd with dancing Attendance for at least five Years); which, as he never answer'd, I spoke to him for the last Time at the last Feast held for the Celebration of the Memory of *Shakespeare*, when He told me I was a bad Man, for that the Person mention'd in my Letter (meaning Mr *Barry*) had deny'd his having been Witness to any Promise made to me by him. But that Person has since assur'd me he well remembers it.

Having taken up so much of the Reader's Time, and perhaps quite tir'd him, with relating so many Altercations I shall say very little to the Play itself as it now stands; but shall only observe that I have been very *frugal in decorating the Ground of* Shakespeare *with my own Embroidery**. And that I hope the Plot is carried on with Probability.

* See the *Critical Review* for *February* 1756, on the *Winter's Tale* [above, p. 244].

Act 1, Scene i. Cymbeline's *Palace*.

Enter Trebonius *and* Pisanio.

Treb. Methinks, *Pisanio*, wild Disorder reigns
Throughout the Palace: Ev'ry Man I meet
Contracts his Brow, and arms it with a Frown.

Pisan. Our Courtiers wear their Faces to the Bent
Of the King's Looks; they're drest in outward Anger,
And yet, *Trebonius*, cou'd you read the Heart,
'Twou'd plainly there be seen, they scowl at that
Which gives them inward Joy.

Treb.   May one demand
The Reason of these seeming Contradictions?

Pisan. The secret Marriage of the noble *Posthumus*
With *Imogen* the Heiress of our Kingdom,
Has hitherto, as such high Trust deserves,
Within my faithful Breast been safely treasur'd.
But by the Subtlety of our new Queen,
(Whose fond ensnaring Smiles caught *Cymbeline*,
And made him raise her to the Royal Bed)
This Morn it was discover'd;—when, in Rage,
The King pronounc'd a Sentence worse than Death,
The hopeless Doom of Banishment against him.

Treb. In our last Embassy, when I attended here
Our *Roman* Gen'ral, he was th' only Fav'rite.

Pisan. *Cymbeline* lov'd him; bred him from his Birth;
Put him to all the Learning that the Age
Cou'd make him Master of; which he imbib'd,
As we do Air, fast as 'twas minister'd.
He then beheld him with the same Delight
Indulgent Fathers view the promis'd Hopes
Of Virtue, and of Genius, in a Son.
But this vile Step-dame, by insidious Arts,
Has turn'd his noble Nature:—But for her,
With his own Hand he wou'd have giv'n to *Posthumus*
His charming Daughter: What is now a Crime,
Was once design'd him as the greatest Blessing.
O *Imogen*, the loveliest of thy Sex!
How will thy Heart support this fatal Parting?

Treb. She is indeed a Wonder.

Pisan.   All who view
Her radiant Beauty, and her graceful Manners,
Must own perforce she is a Lady such,
As to seek through the Regions of the Earth
For one her like, there would be something failing
In her that should compare. Yet the King's Purpose
Was to bestow her on that half-form'd Wretch,
That moving Piece of Earth, the foolish *Cloten.*

    Treb. I met Lord *Cloten* as I left the Presence,
When with a stupid Gaze, he sudden stop'd;
Ask'd when the General *Lucius* wou'd arrive;
Then cursing *Posthumus*, he hasted from me.

    Pisan. The *Roman Lucius*, what imports his Visit?

    Treb. Our *Emp'ror* has commanded him to urge
The Payment of the Tribute due to *Rome.*
His Ship, 'tis thought, will reach *Lud's* Port to Night.
If *Cymbeline* refuses, all the Legions
We have in *Gaul*, are order'd to embark;
That with our *Roman* Swords we may decide
The bloody Diff'rence.

    Pisan.   And is this a time
To throw away the Shield that shou'd defend us?
How fatal is the Dotage of the Soul
When weak'ning Age impairs its Faculties!
Ere *Cymbeline* became a ductile Slave,
His Judgment, like his Honour, was consummate.
He fill'd his Office with a kingly Grace;
The Virtues of the Monarch, and the Man,
Were kindly mix'd.—
Except one Act, which in unheeding Youth
His Sycophants betray'd him to, no Man
In all his golden Reign e'er felt Oppression,
Thou, only thou, poor good *Bellarius*,
Hast for thy Virtues suffer'd!

    Treb.   You seem mov'd.

    Pisan. I am at the Remembrance.—That great Man
Was such a finish'd Soldier, that ev'n *Rome*,
Albeit she boasts, and with the utmost Justice,
Of mighty *Cæsar*, never bred a braver.
But Slander caught him;—by the vip'rous Breath

Of harden'd Perjury, the Hero fell.
He was accus'd of a Conspiracy
Against his Country; and on trivial Proof,
Condemn'd and sentenc'd to perpetual Exile.
But Heav'n has well aveng'd him; the King's Sons,
Two *Royal Infants*, were soon after stol'n;
Nor cou'd Enquiry, or the strictest Search,
E'er yet discover 'em.—But see, the *Queen*,
With *Posthumus*, and *Imogen*. Let us retire:
My Eyes wou'd overflow to view their Parting.   [*Exeunt*.

*   *   *

Act II, Scene i. Lucius's *House*.

Enter Posthumus *and* Philario.

Posth. Philario, how shall I repay this Kindness! You've bound me
to you by the strongest Ties; by those of Gratitude. To bring me back
to *Britain* under the protecting Power of the noble *Lucius*, so near
that Treasure of my Soul, my *Imogen*, is such an Alleviation to my
Sorrows, that I will awhile forget them.

Phil. The Pleasure of having assisted, when in Distress, the Son of
the brave *Sicillius*, overpays me. It was kind Heav'n that directed the
Meeting of our *Ships*, to frustrate the Designs of the inhuman *Cymbeline*.

Posth. There was a Time, when I was favour'd by him.

Phil. My Heart rejoices when I think on the Accident by which we
were known to each other. Your Father, who was my Fellow-Soldier,
and to whom I have been indebted for no less than my Life, is ever in
my Thoughts. When on your being told our *Ship* was *Roman*, you
cried out, O that *Sicillius* were alive to defend my Country, tho' it
disclaims unhappy me! I thought my Friend again reviv'd, with all the
Bloom of Youth, as when I first beheld him.

Posth. Then did you clasp me, press'd me to your Bosom, call'd me
the young *Sicillius*, kindly ask'd the Reason of that settled Gloom that
overspread my Face; bid me unveil my Grief, and swore by Friendship's holy Laws you'd strive to ease it. When I forget it, may all good
Men despise me, and may my hated Name be rank'd among the
Treacherous and Ungrateful.

Phil. Enough.—To serve a Friend in his Misfortunes, is Recompence
sufficient. *Lucius*, who honours me with his Confidence, has assured me
his House shall prove an *Asylum* to you. I have already told him of your

Sufferings, and he laments the alienated Affections of the King, to whom, when he was last in *Britain*, you appear'd so dear. Here comes the General.

Enter Lucius. [*Speaking to an Attendant at the Door.*]

Luc. Haste to the Court, *Servilius*. Inform *Trebonius* of my Arrival, and that I'm coming to demand an Audience. [*Exit Attendant.*] Come to my Arms, thou noble *Briton!*—Your Injuries touch me nearly; and I should disgrace the glorious Names of *Roman* and of Soldier, cou'd I behold neglected Merit languish, and yet refuse my friendly Hand to raise it.

Posth. This generous Treatment overwhelms me, Sir: No more I'll wonder why the *Roman* Name extends itself to Earth's extremest Limits; Virtue like yours must conquer all the World.—Methinks my Fate begins to soften; to be caress'd thus by the first of Warriours, makes me for a Moment forget my Sorrows, altho' divided from the dearest Wife that ever bound in golden Chains the Heart of Man.

Luc. My Presence is expected at the Palace. I'll leave you with *Philario.*—On my Return depend on such a Welcome as growing Friendship yields, when sensible of another's Worth.　　　　　　[*Exit.*

Phil. Hope all things from the generous *Lucius*. I therefore beg you to assume a chearful Temper, and let me introduce you to two Gentlemen who came over with me from *Rome*, whose Fidelity I will answer for with my Life; and whose Conversation may divert your Melancholy: We will together administer to your Distress, what Consolation we are able.—Here they come.

Enter Iachimo *and a* Frenchman.

I beseech you, Gentlemen, let this young Lord be entertain'd by you as suits with Persons of your knowing to a Stranger of his Quality. I commend him to you as a noble Friend of mine; how worthy he is, I will leave to appear hereafter.

Frenchm. Have we not known each other, Sir, in *Orleans*?

Posth. We have. Since when I have been indebted to you for Courtesies, which I shall be ever yet to pay.

Frenchm. Sir, you over-rate my poor Kindness: I was glad I atton'd my Countryman and you; it had been Pity you had been put together with so mortal a Purpose as then each bore, upon a Matter of so slight and trivial a Nature.

Posth. Your Pardon, Sir; I was then, 'tis true, a young Traveller; but yet upon my mended Judgment (if I offend not to say it is mended) I think my Quarrel was not altogether so slight.

Frenchm. Faith yes, to be put to the Arbitrement of Swords.

Iach. Can we with Manners ask what was the Difference?

Frenchm. Safely I think. 'Twas a Contention in Publick, which may without Contradiction suffer the Report: It was much like an Argument we held last Night, where each of us fell in Praise of our Country Mistresses: This Gentleman at that time vouching (and upon a Warrant of bloody Affirmation) his to be more fair, wise, virtuous, chaste, constant, qualified, and less attemptable, than any of the rarest of our Ladies in *France*.

Iach. That Lady is not now living; or this Gentleman's Opinion, by this, worn out.

Posth. She holds her Virtue still, and I my Mind.

* * *

177. William Kenrick on the adaptations of *Cymbeline*

1759

From the *Monthly Review*, xx (May 1759), pp. 462–3.

William Kenrick (1725?–79), poet, dramatist, satirist, journalist, translator, controversialist, was one of the main contributors to the *Monthly Review* between 1759 and 1765, when he wrote a notorious review of Dr Johnson's edition of Shakespeare (see Vol. 5, No. 207), for which he was apparently dismissed from that journal. Kenrick quarrelled with many of his contemporaries: Dr John Hill, Fielding, Christopher Smart, Goldsmith, Johnson, Boswell, Garrick, Colman, and Thomas Evans. In 1760 he published *Falstaff's Wedding*, a comedy in continuation of *Henry IV*, which was performed once at Drury Lane, 12 April 1766.

Cymbeline. A Tragedy, altered from Shakespeare. As it is performed at the Theatre Royal in Covent-Garden. By William Hawkins, *M.A.*
Among the many alterations of Shakespeare's plays that have been offered to the public we do not know any one more deserving encouragement than this of *Cymbeline*. As it was at first written it is, doubtless, in the whole œconomy of it one of the most irregular productions of that great but excentrick genius. In the present alteration its superfluities are retrenched, its principal defects removed, and out of a parcel of loose incoherent scenes we have the pleasure of seeing composed a beautiful and correct piece of dramatic poesy. The language and images of Shakespeare are throughout the whole admirably preserved, the connecting additions artfully interwoven, and the stile of the original successfully imitated.

Cymbeline: King of Britain. A Tragedy, written by Shakespeare. With some alterations, by Charles Marsh. *As it was agreed to be acted at the Theatre Royal in Covent-Garden.*

As Mr Marsh has not taken equal pains with the author of the preceding alteration, so we think he has not equally succeeded in reducing *Cymbeline* to the regular standard of the drama. He makes the characters, as in the original, speak indifferently either in prose or verse; and has retained the abandoned character of the queen, which Mr Hawkins has judiciously left out. The latter has also omitted several scenes of low prosaic dialogue, which Mr Marsh retains, and is more chaste in his language throughout.

It is to be observed that both these gentlemen complain of the difficulty to which dramatic authors are subjected in getting their works represented on the stage: a circumstance, we presume, that may be given as a reason why so few men of genius and spirit condescend at present to write for the theatre.

178. 'Sir' John Hill on a revival of
Antony and Cleopatra

1759

From *Some Remarks upon the new-revived Play of 'Antony and Cleopatra'*, appended to *A Letter to the Hon. Author of the New Farce, Called 'The Rout'. To which is subjoined An Epistle to Mr. Garrick upon That, and other Theatrical Subjects. With an Appendix.* . . . (1759). The essay is ascribed to 'Sir' John Hill by E. L. Avery in *The New Cambridge Bibliography of English Literature Vol. 2, 1660–1800*, ed. G. G. Watson (Cambridge, 1971), col. 806. On Hill (1716?–75) see Vol. 3, headnote to No. 123. Hill wrote theatre criticisms for the *London Daily Advertiser and Literary Gazette* from 1751 on, under the pseudonym of 'The Inspector', which were published separately (152 numbers). He wrote much for the *Gentleman's Magazine*, the *Monthly Review* (between 1744 and 1752) and also contributed to Smollett's *British Magazine*. He wrote several novels, in imitation of Fielding and Smollett, and in 1755 published a second treatise called *The Actor*.

The edition of *Antony and Cleopatra, Fitted for the stage by abridging only* . . . (1758) was the joint work of Garrick and Edward Capell, future editor of Shakespeare. The omissions include not only speeches but whole scenes, e.g. II, i, iii, iv; III, i, ii, v; IV, i, ii, iii, totalling 647 lines (3 lines were added). See G. W. Stone, 'Garrick's Presentation of *Antony and Cleopatra*', *RES* xiii (1937), pp. 20–38.

Since the penning of the preceding letter the revived tragedy of *Antony and Cleopatra* has been performed and published. With respect to the piece itself we are told in the title page that it is 'fitted for the stage, by abridging only.' As the length of this play was certainly an obstacle to its exhibition we are of opinion its alterations are so much for the better as they have rendered it less tedious, as well for the audience as the actors. I cannot, however, but be of opinion that this piece is inferior to most of Shakespeare's productions, and that it even gives way to Dryden's *All for Love, or the World well lost*, which is founded upon the same historical event. I do not mean by this to give the preference to Dryden as a greater dramatic poet in general than Shakespeare, but must own that his soft flowing numbers are more sympathetic to the tender passion which this story is so particularly animated with than the general language of Shakespeare's *Antony*.

I doubt not but this assertion will be looked upon as blasphemy by the *Garicians* and *Shakespearian-bigots*, who imagine no piece of this great poet can be less than *perfection's-self*, especially when it has received the polish of Roscius's pen. But I could cite several instances in this piece, as well as others that have been altered for the stage, which evince the contrary. Not to enter into a laboured criticism upon this tragedy, for which we have neither time or room, I shall only observe what must be obviously ridiculous to every auditor, Cleopatra *still* talks of playing at *Billiards*, a game utterly unknown at that period, as well as many ages after. This is nearly upon a par with the circumstances of the daggers in *Romeo and Juliet*. This lady, before she takes her soporific draught, lays down one dagger upon her table [4.3.23] which her attendants never find to give any suspicion of her intent of killing herself. When she wakes from the tomb, and Romeo dies, she very opportunely finds another dagger in her bosom, with which she dispatches herself.[1] I suppose it was the Italian fashion in those days to bury the ladies with daggers, in order to provide them with an instrument of death in case they should come to life in their coffins.

This piece Mr G—k informs us in the advertisement to the reader, he altered and adapted to the stage in order to avoid the perpetual jingle that occured, and to give a finer stroke to the catastrophe, by waking Juliet before Romeo's death;[2] however dissonant this chime might be to his ears I can assure him the incidents of these ministers of death are not less incompatible with common sense. It must, however, be owned that the catastrophe is greatly altered for the better, and there is nothing wanting but the *probable* to render it perfect.

The only addition I can perceive made to *Antony and Cleopatra* is a kind of poetical dedication (or whatever else the author chuses to call it)

---

[1] At 5.3.168f. Juliet stabs herself: neither the Quarto nor Folio texts indicate whose dagger she uses, and it was Steevens who added the stage direction found in most modern editions, '*Snatching Romeo's dagger*.'

[2] See Vol. 3, p. 333.

to a countess worthy of all titles, though anonymous. As I acknowledge myself utterly ignorant of the meaning or import of these verses I can say nothing more upon them but what will impeach my understanding and ill compliment my comprehension, for I believe they must be very fine, as they supply the place of a prologue (Mr G—k's *forte* in writing) or complimentary verses to the editor by a friend, &c. &c. . . .

In this form has the new-revived tragedy (so much talked of and so long expected) of *Antony and Cleopatra* appeared. To give the editor his due, the punctuation is very regular; in this, I think, his principal merit consists. That of the printer is much greater: the neatness of the type, the disposition of the parts, and the accuracy of the composing, are very striking, and these considerations apart we can see no reason for imposing an additional tax of sixpence upon the purchasers of this play, containing less in quantity than the original, which may be had for half its price.

However, this piece has already been twice performed and to crowded houses. We shall not attempt to depreciate Mr G—k in quality of an actor, or pretend to assert Mr F— surpasses, or equals him. The town is already very well acquainted with both their merit, and it were almost needless to say they both appear to advantage in their parts. Mrs Y—s's person is well suited to the character, and though she is an inferior Cleopatra to Mrs Woffington she is not without sufficient powers to procure her applause. Upon the whole we think this play is now better suited for the stage than the closet, as scenery, dresses, and parade strike the eye and divert one's attention from the poet. (35–79)

179. Edward Young, Shakespeare's genius

1759

From *Conjectures on Original Composition, in a letter to the author of 'Sir Charles Grandison'* (1759).

Edward Young (1683–1765) had a long career as a writer. Educated at Winchester and Oxford (where he was a Fellow of All Souls), he published his first poem in 1713 and became known in London as a dramatist and as a satirist on a par with Pope. He moved to Welwyn in 1730, where he became rector and wrote *The Complaint, or Night Thoughts* (1742–5), which brought him a European reputation. His *Conjectures on Original Composition* belongs to the debate on originality versus imitation which is also discussed in other essays in this collection, by Richard Hurd (No. 128 in Vol. 3 and No. 163 above), and by Joseph Warton (No. 158). Young's opinions were already widely accepted by the time he wrote this pamphlet.

If I might speak farther of Learning and Genius, I would compare Genius to Virtue, and Learning to Riches. As Riches are most wanted where there is least Virtue, so Learning where there is least Genius. As Virtue without much Riches can give Happiness so Genius without much Learning can give Renown. As it is said in *Terence, Pecuniam negligere interdum maximum est lucrum*[1]; so to neglect of Learning Genius sometimes owes its greater glory. Genius, therefore, leaves but the second place among men of letters to the Learned. It is their Merit and Ambition to fling light on the works of Genius and point out its Charms. We most justly reverence their informing Radius for that favour, but we must much more admire the radiant Stars pointed out by them.

A Star of the first magnitude among the Moderns was *Shakespeare*; among the Antients *Pindar*, who (as *Vossius* tells us) boasted of his No-learning, calling himself the Eagle for his Flight above it. And such

---

[1] *Adelphi*, 216: 'Slighting money at the right moment is sometimes the way to make it.'

Genii as these may indeed have much reliance on their own native powers. For Genius may be compared to the Body's natural strength, Learning to the Superinduced Accoutrements of Arms; if the First is equal to the proposed exploit the Latter rather encumbers than assists, rather retards than promotes the Victory. *Sacer nobis inest Deus*, says *Seneca*.[1] With regard to the Moral world *Conscience*, with regard to the Intellectual *Genius* is that God within. Genius can set us right in Composition without the Rules of the Learned, as Conscience sets us right in Life without the Laws of the Land. *This*, singly, can make us Good as Men: *That*, singly, as Writers can sometimes make us Great.

I say sometimes because there is a Genius which stands in need of Learning to make it shine. Of Genius there are two species, an Earlier and a Later, or call them *Infantine* and Adult. An Adult Genius comes out of Nature's hand, as *Pallas* out of *Jove*'s head, at full growth and mature: *Shakespeare*'s Genius was of this kind. . . . (29–31)

★   ★   ★

Shakespeare mingled no water with his wine, lower'd his Genius by no vapid imitation. *Shakespeare* gave us a *Shakespeare*, nor could the first in antient fame have given us more. *Shakespeare* is not their Son but Brother, their Equal; and that in spite of all his faults. Think you this too bold? Consider, in those antients, what is it the world admires? Not the fewness of their Faults but the number and brightness of their Beauties, and if *Shakespeare* is their equal (as he doubtless is) in that which in them is admired, then is *Shakespeare* as great as they; and not impotence but some other cause must be charged with his defects. When we are setting these great men in competition what but the comparative size of their Genius is the subject of our inquiry? And a giant loses nothing of his size tho' he should chance to trip in his race. But it is a compliment to those heroes of antiquity to suppose *Shakespeare* their equal only in dramatic powers; therefore, tho' his faults had been greater, the scale would still turn in his favour. There is at least as much genius on the *British* as on the *Grecian* stage, tho' the former is not swept so clean—so clean from violations not only of the *dramatic* but *moral* rule, for an honest heathen, on reading some of our celebrated scenes, might be seriously concerned to see that our obligations to the religion of nature were cancel'd by Christianity.

---

[1] A reminiscence of *Epistulae Morales* 41.2: *sacer intra nos spiritus sedet*, 'a holy spirit indwells within us,' perhaps conflated with Ovid, *Fasti* 6.5, *est deus in nobis*; 'there is a god within us.'

Jonson, in the serious drama, is as much an Imitator as *Shakespeare* is an Original. He was very learned, as *Sampson* was very strong, to his own hurt. Blind to the nature of Tragedy, he pulled down all antiquity on his head and buried himself under it: we see nothing of *Jonson*, nor indeed of his admired (but also murdered) antients. For what shone in the Historian is a cloud on the Poet, and *Catiline* might have been a good play if *Sallust* had never writ.

Who knows if *Shakespeare* might not have thought less if he had read more? Who knows if he might not have laboured under the load of *Jonson's* learning, as *Enceladus* under *Ætna?* His mighty Genius, indeed, thro' the most mountainous oppression would have breathed out some of his inextinguishable fire, yet possibly he might not have risen up into that giant, that much more than common man, at which we now gaze with amazement and delight. Perhaps he was as learned as his dramatic province required, for whatever other learning he wanted he was master of two books unknown to many of the profoundly read, tho' books which the last conflagration alone can destroy: the book of Nature, and that of Man. These he had by heart, and has transcribed many admirable pages of them into his immortal works. These are the fountain-head whence the *Castalian* streams of *original* composition flow, and these are often mudded by other waters, tho' waters in their distinct channel most wholesome and pure: as two chymical liquors separately clear as crystal grow foul by mixture, and offend the sight. So that he had not only as much learning as his dramatic province required but, perhaps, as it could safely bear. (78–82)

180. Thomas Francklin, Shakespeare's tragedies supreme

1760

From *A Dissertation on Antient Tragedy*, added to Francklin's *The Tragedies of Sophocles Translated* (1759, 1st edition).

Thomas Francklin (1721–84) was Professor of Greek at Cambridge from 1750 to 1759, and subsequently became a clergyman and popular preacher. His friends included Smollett, for whom he wrote sixty-four reviews in the *Critical Review* in 1756 (Roper, *RES* n.s. 10 (1959), p. 40), and with whom he collaborated in translating the plays of Voltaire, Dr Johnson, and Reynolds, through whose offices he became professor of ancient history at the Royal Academy in 1774. His translations of Sophocles and Lucian brought him most fame, but he wrote several successful plays and numerous miscellaneous works.

It must be confess'd that antient tragedy hath it's share with every thing else of human imperfection. . . . (56)

But because their taste was more correct and severe it doth by no means follow that it was less true and perfect than our own: the moderns heap incident on incident, sentiment on sentiment, and character on character, a change which is perhaps rather to be attributed to the corruption of our taste than to the improvement of it. It is always a mark of a vitiated stomach when wholesome and natural food is rejected with disgust, and provocatives used to raise the appetite. In the same manner I cannot but be of opinion that our impatient thirst after what critics affect to call business is nothing but the result of false taste and depraved judgment. Because antient tragedy is not crowded with a heap of unnatural episodes, stuff'd with similes, metaphors, imagery and poetical flowers the moderns treat it with contempt, and find nothing in it but a poverty of sentiment, a want of order and connection in the

scenes, a flatness and insipidity in the dialogue, a coarseness and in-
delicacy in the expression. But even if we should grant the truth of
every objection there would still remain, to compensate for all these
real or seeming imperfections, a variety of true and striking beauties. In
antient tragedy, and there only, we shall find a most exact and faithful
picture of the manners of Greece, its religious and civil policy; sublimity
both of sentiment and diction; regularity, symmetry and proportion;
excellent moral aphorisms and reflections, together with a most elegant
and amiable simplicity diffused through every page.

In a word, to affirm, as many who have more learning than judgment
sometimes will, that there are no good tragedies but the antient, is the
affectation of scholastic pedantry. To deny them their deserved applause,
and treat them with ridicule and contempt is, on the other hand, the
effect of modern pride, ignorance, and petulancy. Upon the whole,
French, Italian, Spanish, and German critics may perhaps find some
excuse for their severe animadversions on the antient Greek tragedy. It
may exercise their envy, and find employment for their spleen and ill-
nature, as they have nothing of their own to put in competition with it.
But Englishmen should be above such envy and such malevolence,
because they can boast a dramatic writer superior to all that antiquity
ever produced. We may safely join with the most sanguine partisans of
Aeschylus, Sophocles, and Euripides in the sincerest admiration of their
several excellencies, and rejoice within ourselves to see them all united
and surpass'd in the immortal and inimitable Shakespeare. (57–9)

181. Lord Lyttelton, an imaginary conversation on Shakespeare

1760

From the thirteenth of the *Dialogues of the Dead* (1760); this text from the enlarged *Fourth Edition, Corrected. To which are added Four New Dialogues* (1765).

George Lyttelton, 1st Baron Lyttelton (1709–73), was educated at Eton and Christ Church. For a while he had an energetic career in Parliament, becoming privy councillor in 1754, and Chancellor of the Exchequer in 1755. As a poet he was at first an imitator of Pope, but turned to the irregular ode and had much success with his *Monody* on the death of his wife (1747). Most of his verse appeared in Robert Dodsley's *Collection of Poems, by Several Hands* (Volume ii, 1748, eleven editions by 1782). Lyttelton, at one time secretary to Frederick, Prince of Wales, was a friend of Thomson, Joseph Warton, and Fielding, but was disliked by Horace Walpole, Dr Johnson, and Smollett. His *Dialogues of the Dead* (three of which were by Elizabeth Montagu) enjoyed great success, going through three editions in 1760 alone.

BOILEAU [attacking Pope for wasting his poetic energies as a translator and editor]. I cannot but regret that your talents were thus employed. A great poet so tied down to a tedious translation is *a Columbus chained to an oar*. What new regions of fancy, full of treasures yet untouched, might you have explored if you had been at liberty boldly to expand your sails and steer your own course under the conduct and direction of your own genius!—But I am still more angry with you for your edition of Shakespeare. The office of an *editor* was below you, and your mind was unfit for the drudgery it requires. Would any body think of employing a Raphael to clean an old picture?
POPE. The principal cause of my undertaking that task was zeal for the honour of Shakespeare: and if you knew all his beauties as well as I you

410

would not wonder at this zeal. No other author had ever so copious, so bold, so *creative* an imagination, with so perfect a knowledge of the passions, the humours, and sentiments of mankind. He painted all characters, from kings down to peasants, with equal truth and equal force. If human nature were destroyed, and no monument were left of it except his works, other beings might know *what man was* from those writings.

BOILEAU. You say he painted all characters, from kings down to peasants, with equal truth and equal force. I cannot deny that he did so: but I wish he had not jumbled those characters together in the composition of his pictures, as he has frequently done.

POPE. The strange mixture of tragedy, comedy, and farce in the same play, nay sometimes in the same scene, I acknowledge to be quite inexcusable. But this was the taste of the times when Shakespeare wrote.

BOILEAU. A great genius ought to guide, not servilely follow, the taste of his contemporaries.

POPE. Consider from how thick a darkness of barbarism the genius of Shakespeare broke forth! What were the English, and what (let me ask you) were the French dramatic performances in the age when he flourished? The advances he made towards the highest perfection both of tragedy and comedy are amazing! In the principal points, in the power of exciting terror and pity, or raising laughter in an audience none yet has excelled him, and very few have equalled.

BOILEAU. Do you think that he was equal in comedy to Molière?

POPE. In *comick force* I do: but in the fine and delicate strokes of satire, and what is called *genteel comedy*, he was greatly inferior to that admirable writer. There is nothing in him to compare with the *Misanthrope*, the *Ecole des Femmes*, or *Tartuffe*.

BOILEAU. This, Mr Pope, is a great deal for an Englishman to acknowledge. A veneration for Shakespeare seems to be a part of your national religion, and the only part in which even your men of sense are fanaticks.

POPE. He who can read Shakespeare and be cool enough for all the accuracy of sober criticism has more of reason than taste.

BOILEAU. I join with you in admiring him as a prodigy of genius, though I find the most shocking absurdities in his plays; absurdities which no critick of my nation can pardon.

POPE. We will be satisfied with your feeling the excellence of his beauties. But you would admire him still more if you could see the chief characters in all his best tragedies represented by an actor who appeared on the stage a little before I left the world. He has shewn the English nation more excellences in Shakespeare than the quickest wits could discern, and has imprinted them on the heart with a livelier feeling than the most sensible natures had ever experienced without his help.

BOILEAU. The variety, spirit, and force, of Mr Garrick's action have been much praised to me by many of his countrymen whose shades I converse with, and who agree in speaking of him as we do of *Baron*, our most natural and most admired actor. I have also heard of another who has now quitted the stage, but who had filled with great dignity, force, and elevation, some tragick parts; and excelled so much in the comick that none ever has deserved a higher applause.

POPE. Mr Quin was indeed a most perfect comedian. In the part of *Falstaff* particularly, wherein the utmost force of Shakespeare's *humour* appears, he attained to such perfection that he was not an actor, he was the man described by Shakespeare, he was *Falstaff* himself! When I saw him do it the pleasantry of *the fat knight* appeared to me so bewitching, all his vices were so mirthful that I could not much wonder at his having seduced a young prince even to *rob* in his company.

BOILEAU. That character is not well understood by the French. They suppose it belongs not to comedy but to farce: whereas the English see in it the finest and highest strokes of wit and humour. Perhaps these different judgements may be accounted for in some measure by the diversity of manners in different countries. But don't you allow, Mr Pope, that our writers, both of tragedy and comedy, are upon the whole more perfect masters of their art than yours? If you deny it I will appeal to the Athenians, the only judges qualified to decide the dispute. I will refer it to Euripides, Sophocles, and Menander.

POPE. I am afraid of those judges: for I see them continually walking hand in hand and engaged in the most friendly conversation with Corneille, Racine, and Molière. Our dramatick writers seem in general not so fond of their company: they sometimes shove rudely by them, and give themselves airs of superiority. They slight their reprimands and laugh at their precepts. In short, they will be tried by *their country* alone; and that judicature is partial.

BOILEAU. I will press this question no further. (190-4)

182. Unsigned essay 'On the Merits of *Shakespeare* and *Corneille*'

1760

From the *British Magazine*, Volume 1 (June 1760).

Although the journal was edited by Smollett, this piece differs
completely from his estimates of Shakespeare. Some elements
resemble the work of Arthur Murphy: the interest in 'the gloomy
way' of poetry, especially ghost-scenes (compare above Nos 143,
161d), the analysis of different plays' treatment of the same
passion (compare the discussion of remorse in Nos 140a, 161f, g),
and the contrast of the states of mind of Richard III and Macbeth
(Nos 161b, g). Presumably the author of this piece also contributed
the subsequent comparisons printed in this journal, between
Otway and Racine, Milton and Tasso, and Shakespeare and
Milton (below, No. 197).

Nothing can be more conducive to form the taste than to draw a
parallel between the genius's of such as have distinguished themselves
in any branch of literature, and, by weighing their merits in the ballance
of criticism, enable ourselves to ascertain with exactitude at which side
the scale of excellence preponderates. Such a comparison seems much
better calculated to give us a perfect idea of the meaning of the word
Genius, a word made use of by every body but understood by very
few, than a pedantic definition which strives in vain to explain an
abstract term by other terms equally abstracted. Many critics have been
sensible of this, and we find the admirers of classical learning frequently
employed in drawing parallels between Homer and Virgil, Horace and
Juvenal, Plautus and Terence, &c. They have discussed their several
claims to preheminence with an exactness as scrupulous as pleni-
potentiaries adjust the rights of kingdoms, or heralds the punctilios of
ceremony. It therefore appears surprizing that the same attention has

not been given to the moderns, as a comparison of the merits of such as have excelled in living languages must be much more useful and instructive than those of authors who have wrote in languages which we cannot pronounce, and of whose beauties we cannot at this distance of time have a perfect relish.

These considerations will, 'tis apprehended, sufficiently evince the utility of a parallel between the characters of the two great dramatic genius's of France and England. Every body must easily guess that these can mean no other than Shakespeare and Corneille, between whom there is a striking resemblance in many particulars which, to lay before the reader and at the same time trace out the circumstances that characterise both, may contribute in some measure to promote the knowledge of the theatre. It will be found a just observation, tho' it has not hitherto occurred to any of the critics, that an author's peculiar character is stampt upon his works, and may be discovered under the disguise of different forms in all his compositions, at least in all his compositions of the same kind. Whatever may have been asserted to the contrary, it is no more possible for an author totally to vary his manner than for an actor to assume a face entirely new in every character he plays: this cannot be said even of Garrick himself, tho' he understands the art of disguising his face and person so well that he may justly be called the theatrical Proteus. But to return to the subject in question.

Corneille was the father of dramatic poetry in France, as Shakespeare was in England; like him excelled both in tragedy and comedy, and wrote a great number of pieces in both ways. The sublime, however, seems to characterise the genius of Corneille, but that of Shakespeare is so various and fertile that 'tis hardly possible to point out what he excels most in, or shew the predominant beauty of his works. If we may venture to give the preference to his execution in any particular part of poetical composition he seems to have surpassed himself in what Longinus calls the Terrible Graces. How weak is Milton's description of the infernal regions compared with that scene of *Hamlet* in which the ghost makes its appearance! a scene which is undoubtedly the master-piece of poetical painting in the gloomy way. It exhibits a variety of objects and varies appearances a thousand ways, all equally calculated to excite awe and terror in the minds of the spectators. There is not a single change in this scene that would not furnish matter for a picture, and require the pencil of a Raphael in the execution.

To cite all its beauties would make it necessary to transcribe the whole. The reader, 'tis apprehended, will not be displeased with the

following quotation, as it contains a description almost equal to the
admired one of Dover-cliff:

> What if it tempt you to the flood, my lord,
> Or to the dreadful summit of the cliff,
> That beetles o'er its base into the sea,
> And there assume some other horrible form
> That might deprive your sovereignty of reason,
> And draw you into madness? think of it:
> The very place puts toys of desperation
> Into each head that looks so many fathoms to the sea,
> And hears it roar beneath.   [*Hamlet*, 1.4.69ff.]

The dagger-scene in *Macbeth*, and the scene in which King John
excites Hubert to the murder of Arthur, as well as those in which he
upbraids him for it, are farther instances of what has been above
asserted.

The genius of Corneille is entirely of a different kind. An uniform,
sublime, and manly eloquence is what he most excels in, and as these
were the characteristics of Roman eloquence he has taken most of his
subjects from the Roman history. The account which Cinna gives to
Æmilia of his harrangue to the conspirators is a masterpiece in this way;
and his description of the cruelties of the Triumvirs a picture replete
with horror. The reader, by comparing them, will be enabled to form
a judgment of the different talents of these two great masters for
descriptive poetry.

> Je les peins en meurtre a l'envie triumphans;
> Rome entiere noyeé au sang de ses enfans,
> Les un assassinez dans les places publiques,
> Les autres dans le sein de leur Dieux domestiques:
> Les mechans par le prix au meurtre engagez,
> Le mari par sa femme dans son lit egorgé,
> Le fils tout degoutant du meurtre de son pere,
> Et sa tête a la main demandant son salaire.

But tho' Corneille abounds with elevation and manly eloquence, and
with profound and sententious maxims, in which he is not inferior to
Tacitus himself, it will be in vain to search in him for that unexhausted
imagination equally fruitful in the sublime and the pathetic, the fanciful
and picturesque, the gloomy and the gay; or for that variety of
characters, all so strongly marked and well contrasted that there is not a

single speech which could with propriety be transferred from one character to another. In this respect Shakespeare surpasses all other poets, and may be justly looked upon as the mirrour of nature, in which the features of the mind are as exactly reflected as those of the face are by a glass.

In the plans of Corneille's tragedies a striking resemblance is often discoverable in the main plot and characters of different pieces. Thus the struggle between filial piety and the passion of love is the foundation of the distress of the *Cid*, and the struggle between love of country and private affection that of the tragedy of the *Horatii*, represented upon the English theatre under the title of the *Roman Father*. Ximena in the *Cid* sollicits vengeance from the king for the murder of her father, who had been slain in a duel by Roderigo, whom she passionately loved. In the *Horatii* a brother stabs his sister for lamenting the enemy of her country, and her father excuses the action. But all Shakespeare's tragedies turn upon subjects different from each other: 'tis impossible to shew any resemblance between the plans of *Lear, Hamlet, Othello, Julius Cæsar,* and *Romeo*. The distress in the first is founded upon the sufferings of a parent; of the second upon those of a son; of the third upon those of a jealous husband; of the fourth upon those of unfortunate patriots; and of the last upon those of an unhappy lover.

It must be owned, indeed, that Shakespeare has twice treated upon the same subject: ambition is the ground work both of *Macbeth* and *Richard III*. But our admiration of the poet must increase when we consider that he has found the secret to represent two ambitious men in such opposite lights. The ambition of Richard is resolute and determinate, that of Macbeth wavering and distracted.

Corneille, indeed, tho' greatly inferior to Shakespeare in the main, excels him in two respects, namely in the artful and judicious arrangement of incidents, and the correctness and regularity of his pieces; which articles, however, are not peculiar to the province of a poet.

In fine, Shakespeare seems to have been too great a genius to be methodical, Corneille too methodical to be looked upon as a great genius; but it is apprehended that none will dispute that the former was a great poetical genius, and the latter an excellent dramatic poet. (362-5)

183. Unsigned review, an Ode to Shakespeare

1760

From the *Critical Review*, x (September 1760), pp. 246–8

Ode to the Muses. 4to. Pr. 1s.

Had this author chosen any other species of poetry he would probably have deserved warmer praises than we now have it in our power to bestow. There is elegance in his expression, warmth in his colouring, harmony in his numbers, and propriety in his allusions, but the true creative genius and powers of imagination essential to the ode-writer are wanting. . . .

The reader will be pleased with the following character of our immortal Shakespeare, whose vast powers as a tragic writer remain unrivalled.

> If Aristophanes with comick pen,
>> Describ'd the vain pursuits of men;
>> Or Terence knew the gentler part
>> To captivate the willing heart.
>> To the bold numbers of the tragick lore
>> If Sophocles could raise his buskin'd song;
> Bid pity drop the sympathizing tear,
>> Bid the bosom freeze with fear,
>> With unrelenting anger burn,
> Or to despair the hidden frenzy turn:
>> And with heroick tales of yore
>> Arouse the gazing throng;
>> Displaying thus with grateful praise
> The deeds of warlike chiefs in ancient days;
> How o'er the checker'd stage of life they trod,
> What made Ulysses great, or Hercules a god.

417

Let us of Albion's happier shore,
Low at your fane our thankful homage pay,
Exulting hail th' auspicious day
Which to our favor'd isle immortal Shakespeare bore.
Of bloom unfading round his honor'd head
Your variegated wreaths are spread:
Now with unaffected wit
Through Fancy's airy realms he strays,
And now in vulgar life's ignobler ways
Draws the rude clown, or mercenary cit.

Now his sad scenes expand the source of woe,
And teach our streaming griefs to flow:
Now tell how* civil strife and factious rage,
Distain'd chaste record's whiter page;
Or how great Henry's vengeful lance
Humbled the crested pride of France,
With arms triumphant shook the haughty state,
And rear'd his banners in their vanquish'd land;
Or how (O strange reverse of fickle fate!)
Our blasted trophies shrunk beneath a† woman's hand.

* Wars between the houses of York and Lancaster.
† The Maid of Orleans. See Shakespeare's *First Part of Henry the Sixth*.

184. Robert Lloyd, Shakespeare greater than the rules

1760

Shakespeare: An Epistle to Mr. Garrick, (1760); this text from *The Poetical Works of Robert Lloyd,* ed. W. Kenrick, 2 vols, 1774.

Robert Lloyd (1733–64), was educated at Westminster School, where his friends included William Cowper, Bonnell Thornton and George Colman, who subsequently formed the Nonsense Club, which issued a journal, the *Connoisseur.* Lloyd, who was also friendly with Charles Churchill (see No. 86) and Garrick, conducted the *St James's Magazine* (with John Seally and William Kenrick) from 1762 to 1764 and contributed essays and poems to a number of periodicals, including the *Monthly Review,* the *Library: or Moral & Critical Magazine,* and the *North Briton.* Lloyd's attack on the classical critic was said to be directed chiefly against Thomas Francklin, but it is certainly not justified by the excerpt from Francklin's *Sophocles* printed above (No. 180).

> Thanks to much industry and pains,
> Much twisting of the wit and brains,
> Translation has unlock'd the store,
> And spread abroad the Grecian lore,
> While Sophocles his scenes are grown
> E'en as familiar as our own.
>
> No more shall taste presume to speak
> From its enclosures in the Greek;
> But, all its fences broken down,
> Lie at the mercy of the town.
>
> Critic, I hear thy torrent rage,
> ' 'Tis blasphemy against that stage,
> Which Æschylus his warmth design'd,

Euripides his taste refin'd,
And Sophocles his last direction,
Stamp'd with the signet of perfection.'

  Perfection! 'tis a word ideal,
That bears about it nothing real:
For excellence was never hit
In the first essays of man's wit.
Shall *ancient* worth, or *ancient* fame
Preclude the Moderns from their claim?
Must they be blockheads, dolts, and fools,
Who write not up to Grecian rules?
Who tread in buskins or in socks.
Must they be damn'd as Heterodox,
Nor merit of good works prevail,
Except within the classic pale?
'Tis stuff that bears the name of knowledge,
Not current half a mile from college;
Where half their lectures yield no more
(Be sure I speak of times of yore)
Than just a niggard light, to mark
How much we all are in the dark.
As rushlights in a spacious room,
Just burn enough to form a gloom.

When Shakespeare leads the mind a dance,
From France to England, hence to France,
Talk not to me of time and place;
I own I'm happy in the chace.
Whether the drama's here or there,
'Tis nature, Shakespeare, every where.
The poet's fancy can create,
Contract, enlarge, annihilate,
Bring past and present close together,
In spite of distance, seas, or weather;
And shut up in a single action,
What cost whole years in its transaction.
So, ladies at a play, or rout,
Can flirt the universe about,
Whose geographical account

Is drawn and pictured on the mount.
Yet, when they please, contract the plan,
And shut the world up in a fan.

True Genius, like Armida's wand,
Can raise the spring from barren land.
While all the art of Imitation,
Is pilf'ring from the first creation;
Transplanting flowers, with useless toil,
Which wither in a foreign soil.
As conscience often sets us right
By its interior active light,
Without th' assistance of the laws
To combat in the moral cause
So Genius, of itself discerning,
Without the mystic rules of learning,
Can, from its present intuition,
Strike at the truth of composition.

Yet those who breathe the classic vein,
Enlisted in the mimic train,
Who ride their steed with double bit,
Ne'er run away with by their wit,
Delighted with the pomp of rules,
The specious pedantry of schools,
(Which rules, like crutches, ne'er became
Of any use but to the lame)
Pursue the method set before 'em;
Talk much of order, and decorum,
Of probability of fiction,
Of manners, ornament, and diction,
And with a jargon of hard names,
(A privilege which dulness claims,
And merely us'd by way of fence,
To keep out plain and common sense)
Extol the wit of antient days,
The simple fabric of their plays;
Then from the fable, all so chaste,
Trick'd up in ancient-modern taste,
So mighty gentle all the while,
In such a sweet descriptive stile,

While Chorus marks the servile mode
With fine reflection, in an ode,
Present you with a perfect piece,
Form'd on the model of old Greece:

Come, pr'ythee Critic, set before us,
The use and office of a chorus.
What! silent! why then, I'll produce
Its services from antient use.

'Tis to be ever on the stage,
Attendants upon grief or rage,
To be an arrant go-between,
Chief-mourner at each dismal scene;
Shewing its sorrow, or delight,
By shifting dances, left and right,
Not much unlike our modern notions,
Adagio or *Allegro* motions;
To watch upon the deep distress,
And plaints of royal wretchedness;
And when, with tears, and execration,
They've pour'd out all their lamentation,
And wept whole cataracts from their eyes,
To call on rivers for supplies,
And with their *Hais*, and *Hees*, and *Hoes*,
To make a symphony of woes.

Doubtless the Antients want the art
To strike at once upon the heart:
Or why their prologues of a mile
In simple—call it—humble stile,
In unimpassion'd phrase to say
' 'Fore the beginning of this play,
I, hapless Polydore, was found
By fishermen, or others drown'd!'
Or, 'I, a gentleman, did wed,
The lady I wou'd never bed,
Great Agamemnon's royal daughter,
Who's coming hither to draw water.'[1]

---

[1] A parody of the opening verses of Euripides' *Hecuba* and *Electra*.

Or need the Chorus to reveal
Reflexions, which the audience feel;
And jog them, lest attention sink,
To tell them how and what to think?

Oh, where's the Bard, who at one view
Cou'd look the whole creation through,
Who travers'd all the human heart,
Without recourse to Grecian art?
He scorn'd the modes of imitation,
Of altering, pilfering, and translation,
Nor painted horror, grief, or rage,
From models of a former age;
The bright original he took,
And tore the leaf from nature's book.
'Tis Shakespeare, thus, who stands alone—
—But why repeat what *You* have shown?
How true, how perfect, and how well,
The feelings of our hearts must tell.   (I, 77–83)

185. Thady Fitzpatrick, Garrick's speaking of Shakespeare

1760

From *An Enquiry into the Real Merit of a certain Popular Performer, in a Series of Letters, First published in the Craftsman or Gray's-Inn Journal, With an Introduction to D——d G———k, Esq.* (1760).

Thomas (or Thady) Fitzpatrick had been friendly with Garrick, but after a quarrel Garrick gave him the nickname 'Fribble' (i.e. trifler) and satirised him in his farce *Miss in her Teens* (1747). Criticised here for his affected speaking of Shakespeare, Garrick retaliated with a satirical poem *The Fribbleriad*, 1761, in which Fitzpatrick is said to be of neutral sex or hermaphrodite, and is abused under the names Fribble, Fritzgig, Whiffle, Diddle, and so on. Garrick's friends applauded the performance. On 25 January 1763 Fitzpatrick played a leading part in the demands by a group of young men known as 'The Town' to be allowed admittance at the end of the third act of a play for half-price: when Garrick refused they created a riot.

To the CRAFTSMAN,

SIR,

I am appointed by several gentlemen who frequent this coffee-house to return thanks to your correspondents *Theatricus* and *X. Y. Z.*[1] for dissipating an absurd delusion that we have laboured under for several years. The great popularity of a favourite performer so far misled us that, inconsiderately, we acquiesced in all the fulsome incense that adulation has offered up to this theatrical idol. Every character he assumed, we accustomed ourselves to think, appeared with all the advantages of genius and judgment. To persons under this state of deception the appeals to common sense and common grammatical

[1] Despite the different pseudonyms all these letters were written by Fitzpatrick himself.

knowledge lately made in your paper gave, as you may imagine, no small alarm. A consultation was held, at which each member appeared extremely staggered that he should have been so egregiously imposed upon (supposing the criticisms of those writers to be sufficiently authorized), but as our memories did not serve us to clear up the point it was agreed that we should go to the tragedy of *Hamlet* this evening and each man, furnished with a printed play and a pencil, mark such improprieties in respect of speaking as Mr G—— might possibly fall into. We are just returned from the theatre, and after comparing our observations seize this first opportunity of acknowledging (not without some emotions of shame) the ridiculous error we have so long adopted, and profess ourselves converts to the good sense and judicious observations which display themselves so eminently in the letters written by the gentlemen who have lately honoured your paper with their animadversions. That we may not appear proselytes upon insufficient motives it will be proper to communicate a few of the numberless inaccuracies which stand in array before us upon drawing out a list of each person's remarks. It would, we apprehend, prove tiresome should we transcribe a third part of those mutilated lines of unhappy Shakespeare, and as it would give us great concern to encroach on the time and patience of your readers I am directed to present them at present with only TWENTY, which are as follows, viz:

1. Oh that this too too solid—flesh would melt. [1.2.129.]

2. Or that the everlasting had not *fixt*—
His canon 'gainst self-slaughter. [1.2.131f.]

3. As if increase of appetite had *grown*—
By what it fed on. [1.2.144f.]

4. I think it was to see—my mother's wedding. [1.2.178.]

5. Their eyes purging—thick amber and plumb-tree gum. [2.2.197.]

6. He would drown—the stage with tears. [2.2.555.]

7.   Or e're this,
I should have fatted—all the region kites
With this slave's offal. [2.2.573ff.]

8.   that presently
They have proclaimed—their malefactions. [2.2.587f.]

9.   I'll have these players
Play something like—the murther of my father.   [2.2.590f.]

10.   The play's the thing,
Wherein I'll catch—the conscience of the king.   [2.2.600f.]

11. Whether it is nobler in the mind, to *suffer*—
The slings and arrows, &c.   [3.1.57f.]

12. And makes us rather bear—those ills we have.   [3.1.81.]

13.   Let not ever
The soul of Nero enter—this firm bosom.   [3.2.383ff.]

14. When church-yards yawn, and hell itself breaths out—contagion
to the world.   [3.2.378ff.]

15.   O such a deed,
As from the body of contraction plucks—   [3.4.45f.]

16. The very soul, and sweet religion *makes*—
A rhapsody of words.   [3.4.47f.]

17.   Proclaim no shame,
When the *compulsive*—ardour gives the charge.   [3.4.85f.]

18.   Mother, for love of grace,
Lay not that flattering—unction to your soul.   [3.4.144f.]

19. It will but skin and film—the ulcerous place.   [3.4.147.]

20. Why may not imagination trace—the noble
Blood of Alexander, &c.   [5.1.197f.]

At the same time that we thus yield to conviction, let us hope that
your correspondents will continue their endeavours to remove the films
of inattention and prejudice; more especially as they have every encouragement to persist in that liberal design by the impression already
made on the public, and the disposition to be undeceived which all
ranks of people now universally manifest.

   I am, SIR, Your constant reader, and much obliged humble servant,
                                                CANDIDUS.
George's Coffee-house, Temple-bar, Saturday May 10, 11 *o'clock at night.*

To the CRAFTSMAN,

SIR,

Praise undeserved, is scandal in disguise.

In reading a work lately publish'd by an eminent hand, entitled *Dialogues of the Dead*, I find Mr Pope introduced expressing himself, in a conversation with Boileau, upon the subject of Shakespeare,[1] in the following manner, viz: 'You would admire him still more if you could have the pleasure to see the chief characters in all his best plays represented by an actor who appeared on the stage a little before I left the world. He has shewn the English nation more excellencies in Shakespeare, than ever the quickest wits could discern, and has imprinted them on the heart with a livelier sense than the most sensible natures could feel without his help.' I must own that my astonishment was very great in finding our British Homer made use of to convey an encomium of that nature. What! would the elegant Mr Pope, whose admirable versification and peculiar harmony of numbers manifest a most chaste and correct ear, have set up as the elucidator of Shakespeare one who is so far from ever throwing the least light on any difficult passage of that wonderful writer that he has obscured the clear and obvious meaning of the most simple lines in his works by such an unnatural disjointing of the correspondent members as frequently renders the whole an unintelligible jargon.* The illiterate reader will probably be startled at this assertion, but I aver the truth of it, and appeal to real judges of elocution who have attended the performances of this actor. I propose to illustrate the point at large next winter, in a series of letters comprehending the several characters undertaken by this gentleman in the order that they occur, and have not the least doubt that I shall be able to demonstrate beyond all possibility of controversy 'That he never did, nor ever could, speak ten successive lines of Shakespeare with grammatical propriety.' I suppose, therefore, that the respectable author of the dialogue has, upon this occasion, been influenced rather by a disposition of good-will toward the object of his eulogium than that accuracy of taste and penetrating discernment which shine so conspicuously throughout the writings of this noble author. I am the rather inclined to presume this, as the just sense he is pleased to express of Mr Q——'s† merit, and the friendship he honoured him with, seem to make it impossible that he should not most forcibly feel

1 See above, pp. 410ff.

* Vide the letter signed *Candidus.*

† 'BOILEAU. I have also heard of another, who has now left the stage, but who filled with great dignity, force, and elevation some tragic parts, and excelled so much in the comic that none ever has gained a higher applause' [above, p. 412].

the striking contrast between the *dignity, force and elevation* with which *he* delivered the sentiments of his author and the *unconsequential frittering enervate* manner that characterizes his opponent.

I am, SIR, Your humble servant,

X. Y. Z.

Bedford Coffee-house, May 20, 1760.

To the CRAFTSMAN.

SIR,

In my letter of the 20th instant I asserted that Mr G——k never did, nor ever could speak ten successive lines of Shakespeare with grammatical, and I should have added, oratorial propriety; and gave notice of my designing next winter to illustrate this assertion in a series of letters, calculated to amuse the public and restore theatrical taste. At the time of my writing that letter I did not foresee that so fair and so immediate an opportunity would offer for the producing of matters of fact to corroborate what I had so affirmed in opposition to the almost irresistible current of prejudice and prepossession; but his late appearance in the character of Richard the Third invites me so strongly to try his merit in an examination of that part that I will submit to the public whether I can or cannot justify my assertion. The suffrage of applause, which has ever been so lavishly bestowed on his performance of that character by the public, and the very uncommon pains he took that night to exert himself, leave me no reason to doubt of his readily consenting to such a scrutiny, and the staking the whole of his tragical merit on that exhibition; and yet, if I mistake not, I shall be able to shew that the errors he committed were too numerous to have escaped the observation of the judicious, and that they are yet too recent not to be recollected upon a fair recapitulation of them. As I have no private view in this contest, no interested scheme to serve nor envious one to gratify in depreciating his merit, as I am neither a discarded player nor a rejected poet, I have nothing at heart but the rectifying the corrupt taste of the public. To effect this I desire no more than a candid hearing; and when obtained I am persuaded I must receive from every unprejudiced person a determination in my favour. That I have fairly stated his manner of speaking is a fact I most confidently affirm. Each word was marked by different persons equal to the task, and those only in which we all agreed are here observed on. I therefore challenge him, and the warmest of his friends, to exculpate him from the charge of false and absurd speaking or to convict me of misrepresenting him.

428

To facilitate the reading and understanding the following mistaken passages, I must premise that the words printed in Italics are those he thought fit to lay the emphasis on; that such as are in Small Capitals I apprehend he ought to have spoken emphatically; and that where there is a break between words not to be found in the original, he there either paused injudiciously or stopped ungrammatically; and lastly, that where no observation is made the reader will be pleased to imagine that he spoke with propriety.

Richard's first soliloquy opens with an observation on the change of court amusements then induced by peace; and confessing that the deformity of his person made him an improper sharer in these soft, enervating pleasures he resolves on seizing his brother's diadem, as command and power seemed to him to be the only possible means of making him respectable. I shall transcribe the whole of this speech and mark it agreeable to the recited plan, that I may avoid the suspicion of breaking the context with a design of rendering the manner absurd.[1]

1. Now *are* our brows bound with VICTORIOUS wreaths,
   Our STERN alarms are *changed* to MERRY meetings;
   Our DREADFUL *marches* to DELIGHTFUL measures:
   Grim visaged war has smooth'd his wrinkled front,
   And NOW, *instead* of mounting BARBED *steeds*,
   To fright the souls of fearful adversaries,
   He capers nimbly in a lady's chamber
   To the lascivious pleasing of a lute:
   But I that *am* not SHAP'D for SPORTIVE tricks,
   I, that *am* CURTAIL'D of man's FAIR proportion,
   Deform'd, unfinish'd, *sent* BEFORE my time—
   Into this breathing world, *scarce* HALF made up,
   And that so lamely and unfashionable,
   That dogs BARK *at* me as I HALT by 'em,
   Why I, in this WEAK PIPING time of *peace*,
   Have no delight to pass away my hours,
   Unless to *see*—my SHADOW in the Sun,
   And descant on my own deformity.
   THEN *since* this earth *affords* no JOY to me,
   But to command, to check, and o'erbear such—
   As are of HAPPIER *person* than myself:
   Why then to me—this restless world's but hell.

1 Cibber's adaptation, 1.2.1ff. (Vol. 1, p. 109); *Richard III*, 1.1.5ff.

Till this mishapen trunk's—aspiring head—
Be circled in a glorious diadem.
But THEN 'tis fix'd on SUCH a *height:* oh! I
Must stretch the utmost reaching of my soul.
    I'll climb betimes, *without* REMORSE or DREAD,
    And my first step—shall be on Henry's head.

It is needless, I presume, to comment this speech, as I flatter myself that the marks sufficiently evince the impropriety with which it was spoke. I cannot, however, omit observing that the pause in the last line is, in my opinion, very injudiciously placed. Richard, after mature deliberation, concludes that the death of his brother is the first necessary step by which he must ascend the throne. Had the pause been made between the words *be* and *on* it must have had a more pleasing effect on the hearers, evidently pointing out the variety of obstacles that stood in his way, and strongly marking the necessity of Henry's being the first, the preferred victim to his ambition. This, however, is more a matter of fancy than judgment, and I offer it not as a censure but rather as advice.

    2. Suspicion always *haunts* the guilty mind.[1]

The great impropriety of emphasizing the word *haunts* is obvious to every one that attends to the moral of the line, and feels it. Had the words *always* and *guilty* been omitted then the speaking of it would have been just, but the forcible meaning destroyed.

    3. That I should snarl, and bite, and *play* the dog.[2]

In this line the verbs *snarl* and *bite* are strongly characteristic, and with propriety admit of an emphasis; but pray, Mr G——k, inform me why the word *play*, that has nothing peculiarly marking in it, should be forcibly spoke, and *dog*, to which the whole line is appropriated, be neglected?

    4. *Then* since the heav'ns have shap'd my body so,
        Let hell make crook'd my mind to *answer* it.[3]

Here Richard, impiously charging heaven with bestowing on him a mishapen body, seems to wish that hell may form his mind correspondent to it. Why the words *heaven* and *hell, body* and *mind*, which are of great import, were not attended to in the speaking of these lines, and

[1] Cibber, 1.3.16; *3 Henry VI*, 5.6.11.
[2] Cibber, 1.3.75; *3 Henry VI*, 5.6.77.
[3] Cibber, 1.3.76f.; *3 Henry VI*, 5.6.78f.

why the words *then* and *answer*, of but small value, were spoke emphatically is a matter I am not able to account for; Mṛ G——k alone can solve
the difficulty.

> 5. Clarence still breathes, Edward still lives and reigns,
>   When they are *gone*, then I must count *my* gains.[1]

His manner of speaking these lines cannot be sufficiently explained by
marks. Here is a double time, and different persons referred to. Had he
accented *when* and *then*, as marking two periods very opposite to each
other and very interesting to Richard, the emphasis might have been
defensible. But the indisputable way of speaking them is in the opposing
of *they* to *I* —*they* stand between *him* and the crown, and *their* removal is
requisite to give birth to *his* happiness—and therefore the pronouns *they*
and *I* should have been strongly marked in speaking. Why he preferred
accenting the word *gone* I can assign no reason for, except its being a
verb, which he is fond of speaking forcibly. Many reasons might be
assigned for his laying a stress on the word *my* preceding gains, but I
shall omit inserting them as they might appear, perhaps, too particular.

> 6. I'll *take* her passion in its WAIN, and *turn*—
>   This storm of grief to gentle drops of pity—
>   For his REPENTANT *murder*.[2]

In these not quite three lines are two false pointings and three absurd
emphasises. Richard, well knowing that the storm of a woman's passion
cannot last long, wisely determines to take it in its decline, persuaded
that he may then convert her anger into pity for a murderer now grown
penitent. From this motive alone he expects her forgiveness, and yet the
word *repentant* was spoke as if its introduction was barely to fill up the
measure, while *murderer* was strongly marked.

> 7. Poor girl, what pains she takes to *curse* herself.[3]

By this way of speaking it seems as if the simple act of *cursing* was the
sole cause of Richard's ironical pity; to me it appears that he gibes at her
as unknowingly cursing *herself*. But I may be mistaken.

> 8. Sweet Saint, *be* not so hard for CHARITY.[4]

[1] Cibber, 1.3.88f.
[2] Cibber, 2.1.64ff. (Vol. 2, p. 111).
[3] Cibber, 2.1.80 (Vol. 2, p. 112).
[4] Cibber, 2.1.100; *Richard III*, 1.2.49.

9. Whence is it thou, fair excellence, *art* GUILTY.[1]

10. ——————————*but* to ACQUIT myself.[2]

11. ——————————But gentle Lady Anne
    To leave this—keen encounter of our tongues.[3]

Why stop after this? it is not so marked even in the most faulty editions.

12. Nay do not pause, for I did *kill* King Henry,
    But 'twas THY wondrous *beauty* did provoke me:
    Or now dispatch—'twas I that *stabb'd* young Edward,
    But 'twas THY heavenly *face* did set me on.[4]

The acts of stabbing and killing required no forcible speaking towards making an impression on Lady Anne. But the acknowleding that these cruel deeds were committed by him, and through affection for her, makes it requisite that the pronouns *I* and *thy* should be strongly marked, as he seems to expect her forgiveness partly from his confession and partly from his flattery, as her beauty had been the incentive that tempted him to the murderous crimes he had been guilty of.

13. Then bid me *kill* MYSELF, and I will do it.[5]

By his former conduct and confession it appears that he was sufficiently ready to kill, and therefore the verb might have escaped the emphasis; but as he seemed willing to change the object if she ordered him he should have marked *himself.*

14. Oh! if thy poor devoted servant might
    But beg—one favour at thy gracious hand.[6]

This pause after *beg* was certainly very judicious, as Richard was in doubt, and deliberated whether he should ask for one or two favours at her hand, but concluding that she might think him forward, he prudently confined his request.

15. That it may please thee, leave these sad designs—
    To him that has most cause to be a mourner,
    And presently repair to Crosby house;

[1] Cibber, 2.1.107.
[2] Cibber, 2.1.111; *Richard III*, 1.2.77.
[3] Cibber, 2.1.128ff.; *Richard III*, 1.2.114f.
[4] Cibber, 2.1.181ff.; *Richard III*, 1.2.179ff.
[5] Cibber, 2.1.193; *Richard III*, 1.2.186.
[6] Cibber, 2.1.232ff.; *Richard III*, 1.2.206ff.

Where after I have solemnly interr'd—
At Chertsey monastery this injur'd King.[1]

In these few lines the reader may observe that he has twice erred against the sense of the author and the nature of punctuation, and the player must be made to observe that although it is unbecoming me to criticize his provincial pronunciation yet it is advisable in him, for the sake of decency, to be more careful in speaking the word *interr'd*.

16. Whose all not equals—Edward's moiety?[2]

17. That I may *see*—my SHADOW as I pass.[3]

18. The massy WEIGHT *on't* GALLS my laden brow.[4]

19. Poverty, the reward of honest fools,
O'ERTAKE him *for't*.[5]

20. Thus far we *run* BEFORE the wind,
My fortune smiles, and gives me ALL that I DARE *ask*.
The conquered Lady Anne is bound in vows,
Fast as the PRIEST can *make* us, we are one.
The King my *brother* SLEEPS without his pillow,
And I am *left* the guardian of his INFANT heir.[6]

I must beg to know from this supposed unerring performer if he apprehends the word *run* to be expressive of the success at which Richard exults in the opening of this soliloquy? To me it appears to be implied in the metaphor of going *before* the wind, and therefore the emphasis should not be laid on the word *run*. If Lady Anne be bound to him in vows that make them one is this, pray, comprised in the word *make*? or rather, is not the *Priest* the word that should be forcibly expressed as the only possible author of such a tie? If towards compleating the happiness of Richard it were necessary that the life of his brother should be sacrificed to give an open for his obtaining the possession of the infant heir by whose subsequent murder he might seize the diadem for himself, how injudicious was it to mark strongly the degree of consanguinity by laying the emphasis on brother (as he claimed not by descent), and slur

[1] Cibber, 2.1.236ff.; *Richard III*, 1.2.210ff.
[2] Cibber, 2.1.265; *Richard III*, 1.2.249.
[3] Cibber, 2.1.279; *Richard III*, 1.2.263.
[4] Cibber, 2.2.110 (Vol. 2, p. 112).
[5] Cibber, 2.2.116f. (Vol. 2, p. 113).
[6] Cibber, 2.2.128ff. (Vol. 2, p. 113).

over inattentively the jesting manner in which he recites his death, and in consequence of that *his* being left the *guardian* of the *infant* heir? Here the verb seems to be exceedingly undeserving of an emphasis, as Richard's joy arose from *his* being the *guardian* to the heir, then in an *infantile* stile.

It would be endless to observe on every false emphasis. The reader will, I hope, see the strength of my objections to several lines as marked without a special observation on each; and be convinced, I flatter myself, that I have proved my assertion by these few quotations, for few indeed they are when compared with the infinite number that might be taken from the two first acts of Richard. The remaining three shall be commented on when a vacant hour will permit, unless the publisher of this should think it right to inform me that he would prefer giving a new edition of the play, marked agreeable to the specimen of the first soliloquy. In which case I will indulge him with the whole, prefaced with some observations on Mr G——k's present method of playing this character, and contrasted with his former, as well as Mr Q——'s manner. In which I shall be able to shew that the *now* performer has totally changed his manner and consequently lost his merit, as the alteration is not owing to matured reason but impaired execution; that his spirit is evaporated, his fire almost extinct; that his remaining marking countenance and gesticulation may continue for some short time, claptraps for boys and girls; but that he and they must become the objects of contempt to every literary mind.

I am, SIR, Your humble servant,

X. Y. Z.

Bedford Coffee-house, May 28, 1760.

186. Charles Churchill, Shakespeare and Garrick supreme

1761

From *The Rosciad* (1761); this text from the enlarged version in *Poems. By C. Churchill* (1763), pp. 9–14, 49–52. For a modern edition with valuable commentary see D. Grant (ed.), *The Poetical Works of Charles Churchill* (Oxford, 1956).

Charles Churchill (1731–64), poet and parson (albeit a dissipated one), had an enormous success with *The Rosciad*, which went through five editions in 1761 and four more by 1765. The poem received an unfavourable notice in the *Critical Review* (xi. pp. 209ff.), and in retaliation Churchill attacked Smollett in a poem called *Apology to the Critical Reviewers* (1761). Subsequently he contributed to the *North Briton* in 1762–3, and corresponded with John Wilkes, whose political and personal campaigns Churchill supported in his later poetry.

Cold-blooded critics, by enervate sires
Scarce hammer'd out, when nature's feeble fires
Glimmer'd their last; whose sluggish blood, half froze,
Creeps lab'ring thro' the veins; whose heart ne'er glows
With fancy-kindled heat:—A servile race,
Who, in mere want of fault, all merit place;
Who blind obedience pay to ancient schools,
Bigots to Greece, and slaves to musty rules;
With solemn consequence declar'd that none
Could judge that cause but SOPHOCLES alone.[1]
Dupes to their fancied excellence, the crowd,
Obsequious to the sacred dictate, bow'd.

[1] Churchill, like Lloyd (No. 184 above), attacks Francklin, but unjustly, on the evidence of the work reprinted here (above, No. 180).

When, from amidst the throng, a Youth stood forth,
Unknown his person, not unknown his worth;
His looks bespoke applause; alone he stood,
Alone he stemm'd the mighty critic flood.
He talk'd of ancients, as the man became
Who priz'd our own, but envied not their fame;
With noble rev'rence spoke of Greece and Rome,
And scorn'd to tear the laurel from the tomb.

'But more than just to other countries grown,
Must we turn base apostates to our own?
Where do these words of Greece and Rome excel,
That England may not please the ear as well?
What mighty magic's in the place or air,
That all perfection needs must center there?
In states, let strangers blindly be preferr'd;
In state of letters, Merit should be heard.
Genius is of no country, her pure ray
Spreads all abroad, as gen'ral as the day:
Foe to restraint, from place to place she flies,
And may hereafter e'en in Holland rise.
May not, to give a pleasing fancy scope,
And chear a patriot heart with patriot hope;
May not some great extensive genius raise
The name of Britain 'bove Athenian praise;
And, whilst brave thirst of fame his bosom warms,
Make England great in Letters as in Arms?
There may—there hath—and SHAKESPEARE's muse aspires
Beyond the reach of Greece; with native fires
Mounting aloft, he wings his daring flight,
Whilst SOPHOCLES below stands trembling at his height.
Why should we then abroad for judges roam,
When abler judges we may find at home?
Happy in tragic and in comic pow'rs,
Have we not SHAKESPEARE?—Is not JONSON ours?
For them, your nat'ral judges, Britons, vote;
They'll judge like Britons, who like Britons wrote.'

He said, and conquer'd.—Sense resum'd her sway,
And disappointed pedants stalk'd away.

SHAKESPEARE and JONSON, with deserv'd applause,
Joint-judges were ordain'd to try the cause.
Mean-time the stranger ev'ry voice employ'd,
To ask or tell his name.—'Who is it?'—LLOYD.[1] (lines 179–232)

*   *   *

[The court assembles]

In the first seat, in robe of various dyes,
A noble wildness flashing from his eyes,
Sat SHAKESPEARE.—In one hand a wand he bore,
For mighty wonders fam'd in days of yore;
The other held a globe, which to his will
Obedient turn'd, and own'd the master's skill:
Things of the noblest kind his genius drew,
And look'd through Nature at a single view:
A loose he gave to his unbounded soul,
And taught new lands to rise, new seas to roll;
Call'd into being scenes unknown before,
And, passing Nature's bounds, was something more.

Next JONSON sat, in antient learning train'd,
His rigid judgment Fancy's flights restrain'd,
Correctly prun'd each wild luxuriant thought,
Mark'd out her course, nor spar'd a glorious fault.
The book of man he read with nicest art,
And ransack'd all the secrets of the heart;
Exerted Penetration's utmost force,
And trac'd each passion to its proper source,
Then, strongly mark'd, in liveliest colours drew,
And brought each foible forth to public view.
The coxcomb felt a lash in ev'ry word,
And fools hung out, their brother fools deterr'd.
His comic humour kept the world in awe,
And Laughter frighten'd Folly more than Law.

(lines 259–84)

*   *   *

[The notable actors appear one by one]

Last GARRICK came.—Behind him throng a train

[1] Robert Lloyd, a lifelong friend of Churchill: see his *Shakespeare: An Epistle to Mr. Garrick*, above, pp. 419ff., which Churchill paraphrases.

Of snarling critics, ignorant as vain.

One finds out,—'He's of stature somewhat low,—
Your Hero always should be tall you know.—
True nat'ral greatness all consists in height.'
Produce your voucher, Critic—'Sergeant KYTE.'[1]

Another can't forgive the paltry arts,
By which he makes his way to shallow hearts;
Mere pieces of finesse, traps for applause.—
'Avaunt, unnat'ral start, affected pause.'

For me, by Nature form'd to judge with phlegm,
I can't acquit by wholesale, nor condemn.
The best things carried to excess are wrong:
The start may be too frequent, pause too long;
But, only us'd in proper time and place,
Severest judgment must allow them Grace.

If Bunglers, form'd on Imitation's plan,
Just in the way that monkies mimic man,
Their copied scene with mangled arts disgrace,
And pause and start with the same vacant face;
We join the critic laugh; those tricks we scorn,
Which spoil the scenes they mean them to adorn.

But when, from Nature's pure and genuine source,
These strokes of Acting flow with gen'rous force;
When in the features all the soul's portray'd,
And passions, such as GARRICK's, are display'd;
To me they seem from quickest feelings caught:
Each start is Nature; and each pause is Thought.

When Reason yields to Passion's wild alarms,
And the whole state of man is up in arms;
What, but a Critic, could condemn the Play'r,
For pausing here, when Cool Sense pauses there?
Whilst, working from the Heart, the fire I trace,
And mark it strongly flaming to the Face;

---

[1] A character in Farquhar's *The Recruiting Officer* (1706) who preferred his soldiers to be six feet tall.

Whilst, in each sound, I hear the very man;
I can't catch words, and pity those who can.

    Let wits, like spiders, from the tortur'd brain
Fine-draw the critic-web with curious pain;
The gods,—a kindness I with thanks must pay,—
Have form'd me of a coarser kind of clay;
Nor stung with Envy, nor with Spleen diseas'd,
A poor dull creature, still with Nature pleas'd;
Hence to thy praises, GARRICK, I agree,
And, pleas'd with Nature, must be pleas'd with Thee.

    Now might I tell, how silence reign'd throughout,
And deep attention hush'd the rabble rout:
How ev'ry claimant, tortur'd with desire,
Was pale as ashes, or as red as fire:
But, loose to Fame, the muse more simply acts,
Rejects all flourish, and relates mere facts.

    The judges, as the sev'ral parties came,
With temper heard, with Judgment weigh'd each Claim,
And in their sentence happily agreed,
In name of both, Great SHAKESPEARE thus decreed:

'If manly Sense; if Nature link'd with Art;
If thorough knowledge of the Human Heart;
If Pow'rs of acting vast and unconfin'd;
If fewest Faults, with greatest Beauties join'd;
If strong Expression, and strange Pow'rs, which lie
Within the magic circle of the Eye;
If feelings which few hearts, like his, can know,
And which no face so well as His can show;
Deserve the Pref'rence;—GARRICK take the Chair;
Nor quit it—'till Thou place an Equal there.'

(lines 1027–90)

187. George Colman on Shakespeare and the Elizabethan dramatists

1761

From *Critical Reflections on the old English dramatick writers*, prefixed to *The Plays of Massinger* (1761); this text from Colman's *Prose on Several Occasions*, 3 vols (1787).

These 'reflections' were 'thrown together', Colman recorded, 'at the instance of Mr Garrick, to serve his old subject Davies; who, converted from an actor into a Bookseller, had purchased the remaining copies of Coxeter's Edition of the Works of Massinger, to which he added the Critical Reflections as a Preface' (I, x). On Colman see the headnote to No. 138 above.

There is perhaps no country in the world more subordinate to the power of fashion than our own. Every Whim, every Word, every Vice, every Virtue, in its turn becomes the mode and is followed with a certain rage of approbation for a time. The favourite style in all the polite Arts, and the reigning taste in Letters, are as notoriously objects of caprice as Architecture and Dress. A new Poem, or Novel, or Farce are as inconsiderately extolled or decried as a Ruff or a Chinese Rail, a Hoop or a Bow Window. Hence it happens that the publick taste is often vitiated: or if by chance it has made a proper choice becomes partially attached to one Species of Excellence, and remains dead to the Sense of all other Merit, however equal or superior.

I think I may venture to assert with a confidence that on reflection it will appear to be true that the eminent Class of Writers who flourished at the beginning of this century have almost entirely superseded their illustrious Predecessors. The Works of Congreve, Vanbrugh, Steele, Addison, Pope, Swift, Gay, &c. &c. are the chief study of the Million. I say of the Million, for as to those few who are not only familiar with all our own Authors but are also conversant with the Ancients, they are not to be circumscribed by the narrow limits of the Fashion. Shakespeare and Milton seem to stand alone, like first-rate Authors, amid the general wreck of Old English Literature. Milton perhaps owes much of his present fame to the generous Labours and good Taste of Addison. Shakespeare has been transmitted down to us with successive Glories, and you,[1] Sir, have continued or rather increased his Reputation. You have, in no fulsome strain of compliment, been stiled the Best Commentator on his Works: but have you not, like other Commentators, contracted a narrow, exclusive Veneration of your Author? Has not the Contemplation of Shakespeare's Excellencies almost dazzled and extinguished your Judgement when directed to other objects, and made you blind to the Merit of his Contemporaries? Under your dominion have not Beaumont and Fletcher, nay even Jonson suffered a kind of Theatrical Disgrace? And has not poor Massinger, whose cause I have now undertaken, been permitted to languish in Obscurity and remained almost entirely unknown?

To this perhaps it may be plausibly answered, not indeed without some foundation, that many of our Old Plays, though they abound with Beauties and are raised much above the humble level of later Writers, are yet on several accounts unfit to be exhibited on the modern Stage; that the Fable, instead of being raised on probable incidents in real Life, is generally built on some foreign Novel and attended with Romantick Circumstances; that the Conduct of these Extravagant Stories is frequently uncouth, and infinitely offensive to that Dramatick correctness prescribed by late Criticks and practised (as they pretend) by the French Writers; and that the Characters exhibited in our Old Plays can have no pleasing effect on a modern Audience, as they are so totally different from the manners of the present age.

These, and such as these, might once have appeared reasonable objections: but You, Sir, of all persons can urge them with the least grace since your Practice has so fully proved their insufficiency. Your Experience must have taught you that when a Piece has any striking Beauties they will cover a multitude of Inaccuracies, and that a Play need not be written on the severest plan to please in the representation. The mind is soon familiarized to Irregularities which do not sin against the Truth of Nature, but are merely Violations of that strict Decorum of late so earnestly insisted on. What patient Spectators are we of the Inconsistencies that confessedly prevail in our darling Shakespeare! What critical Catcall ever proclaimed the indecency of introducing the

[1] David Garrick.

Stocks in the Tragedy of *Lear*? How quietly do we see Gloster take his imaginary Leap from Dover Cliff! Or to give a stronger instance of Patience, with what a Philosophical Calmness do the audience doze over the tedious and uninteresting Love-Scenes with which the bungling hand of Tate has coarsely pieced and patched that rich Work of Shakespeare!—To instance further from Shakespeare himself, the Grave-diggers in *Hamlet* (not to mention Polonius) are not only endured but applauded; the very Nurse in *Romeo and Juliet* is allowed to be Nature; the Transactions of a whole History are, without offence, begun and completed in less than three hours; and we are agreeably wafted by the *Chorus*, or oftener without so much ceremony, from one end of the world to another.

It is very true that it was the general Practice of our old Writers to found their Pieces on some foreign Novel; and it seemed to be their chief aim to take the story as it stood, with all its appendant incidents of every complection, and throw it into Scenes. This method was, to be sure, rather inartificial as it at once overloaded and embarrassed the Fable, leaving it destitute of that beautiful Dramatick Connection which enables the mind to take in all its Circumstances with Facility and Delight. But I am still in doubt whether many Writers who come nearer to our own times have much mended the matter. What with their Plots, and Double-Plots, and Counter-Plots, and Under-Plots, the Mind is as much perplexed to piece out the story as to put together the disjointed Parts of our Ancient Drama. The Comedies of Congreve have in my mind as little to boast of accuracy in their construction as the Plays of Shakespeare; nay, perhaps, it might be proved that amidst the most open violation of the lesser critical Unities, one Point is more steadily pursued, one Character more uniformly shewn, and one grand Purpose of the Fable more evidently accomplished in the productions of Shakespeare than of Congreve.

These Fables (it may be further objected) founded on romantick Novels are unpardonably wild and extravagant in their Circumstances, and exhibit too little even of the Manners of the Age in which they were written. The Plays too are in themselves a kind of heterogeneous composition; scarce any of them being, strictly speaking, a Tragedy, Comedy, or even Tragi-Comedy but rather an indigested jumble of every species thrown together.

This charge must be confessed to be true: but upon examination it will perhaps be found of less consequence than is generally imagined. These Dramatick Tales, for so we may best stile such Plays, have often occasioned much pleasure to the Reader and Spectator, which could not possibly have been conveyed to them by any other vehicle. Many an interesting Story which, from the diversity of its circumstances, cannot be regularly reduced either to Tragedy or Comedy, yet abounds with Character, and contains several affecting situations: and why such a Story should lose its force dramatically related and assisted by representation, when it pleases under the colder form of a Novel, is difficult to conceive. Experience has proved the effect of such fictions on our minds; and convinced us that the Theatre is not that barren ground wherein the Plants of Imagination will not flourish. *The Tempest, The Midsummer Night's Dream, The Merchant of Venice, As you like it, Twelfth Night, The Faithful Shepherdess* of Fletcher, (with a much longer list that might be added from Shakespeare, Beaumont and Fletcher, and their cotemporaries, or immediate successors) have most of them within all our memories been ranked among the most popular Entertainments of the Stage. Yet none of these can be denominated Tragedy, Comedy, or Tragi-Comedy. The Play Bills, I have observed, cautiously stile them Plays: and Plays indeed they are, truly such if it be the end of Plays to delight and instruct, to captivate at once the Ear, the Eye, and the Mind, by Situations forcibly conceived and Characters truly delineated.

There is one circumstance in Dramatick Poetry which I think the chastised notions of our modern Criticks do not permit them sufficiently to consider. Dramatick Nature is of a more large and liberal quality than they are willing to allow. It does not consist merely in the representation of real Characters, Characters acknowledged to abound in common life, but may be extended also to the exhibition of imaginary Beings. To create is to be a Poet indeed; to draw down Beings from another sphere and endue them with suitable Passions, Affections, Dispositions, allotting them at the same time proper employment, 'to body forth, by the Powers of Imagination, the forms of things unknown, and to give to airy Nothing a local Habitation and a Name' surely requires a Genius for the Drama equal, if not superior, to the delineation of personages in the ordinary course of Nature. Shakespeare, in particular, is universally acknowledged never to have soared so far above the reach of all other writers as in those instances where he seems purposely to have transgressed the Laws of Criticism. 'He appears to have disdained to put his Free Soul into circumscription and confine,' which denied his extraordinary talents their full play nor gave scope to the Boundlesness of his Imagination. His Witches, Ghosts, Fairies, and other Imaginary Beings scattered through his plays are so many glaring violations of the common table of Dramatick Laws. What then shall we say? Shall we confess their Force and Power over the Soul, shall we allow them to be Beauties of the most exquisite kind and yet insist on their being expunged? And why? except it be to reduce the Flights of an exalted Genius by fixing the Standard of Excellence on the practice of Inferior Writers, who wanted parts to execute such great designs, or to accommodate them to the narrow ideas of small Criticks, who want souls large enough to comprehend them?

Our Old Writers thought no personage whatever unworthy a place in the Drama to which they could annex what may be called a *Seity*, that is, to which they could allot Manners and Employment peculiar to itself. The severest of the Antients cannot be more eminent for the constant Preservation of Uniformity of Character than Shakespeare; and Shakespeare in no instance supports his Characters with more exactness than in the conduct of his Ideal Beings. The Ghost in *Hamlet* is a shining proof of this excellence.

But in consequence of the custom of tracing the Events of a Play minutely from a Novel the authors were sometimes led to represent a mere human creature in circumstances not quite consonant to Nature, of a disposition rather wild and extravagant, and in both cases more especially repugnant to modern ideas. This indeed required particular indulgence from the spectator, but it was an indulgence which seldom missed of being amply repaid. Let the writer but once be allowed, as a necessary *Datum*, the possibility of any Character's being placed in such a situation or possest of so peculiar a turn of mind, the behaviour of the Character is perfectly natural. Shakespeare, though the Child of Fancy, seldom or never drest up a common mortal in any other than the modest dress of Nature. But many shining Characters in the Plays of Beaumont and Fletcher are not so well grounded on the Principles of the human Heart, and yet, as they were supported by Spirit they were received with Applause. *Shylock's* Contract, with the Penalty of the Pound of Flesh, though not Shakespeare's own fiction is perhaps rather improbable—at least it would not be regarded as a happy Dramatick Incident in a modern Play; and yet, having once taken it for granted, how beautifully, nay, how naturally is the Character sustained!—Even this objection therefore of a deviation from Nature, great as it may seem, will be found a plea insufficient to excuse the total exclusion of our antient Dramatists from the Theatre. Shakespeare, you will readily allow, possest Beauties more than necessary to redeem his Faults; Beauties that excite our admiration and obliterate his errors. True, but did no portion of that Divine Spirit fall to the share of our other old Writers? (II, 110–19)

*   *   *

If then it must be confessed, both from reason and experience, that we cannot only endure but attend with pleasure to Plays which are almost merely Dramatick Representations of romantick Novels; it will surely be a further inducement to recur to the works of our Old Writers when we find among them many pieces written on a severer plan, a plan more accommodated to real life, and approaching more nearly to the modern usage. *The Merry Wives of Windsor*, of Shakespeare; the *Fox, the Alchymist, The Silent Woman, Every Man in his Humour*, of Jonson; the *New Way to pay Old Debts, The City Madman*, of Massinger, &c. &c. all urge their claim for a rank in the ordinary course of our Winter-Evening Entertainments, not only clear of every objection made to the above-mentioned species of Dramatick Composition but adhering more strictly to ancient rules than most of our later comedies.

In point of character (perhaps the most essential part of the Drama) our Old Writers far transcend the Moderns. It is surely needless, in support of this opinion, to recite a long list of names when the memory of every reader must suggest them to himself. The manners of many of them, it is true, do not prevail at present. What then? Is it displeasing or uninstructive to see the manners of a former age pass in review before us? Or is the mind undelighted at recalling the Characters of our Ancestors while the eye is confessedly gratified at the sight of the Actors drest in their Antique Habits? Moreover, Fashion and Custom are so perpetually fluctuating that it must be a very accurate piece indeed, and one quite new and warm from the anvil, that catches the Damon or Cynthia of this minute. Some Plays of our latest and most fashionable Authors are grown as obsolete in this particular as those of the first Writers, and it may with safety be affirmed that Bobadil is not more remote from modern Character than the ever-admired and every-where-to-be-met-with Lord Foppington. It may also be further considered that most of the best Characters in our old Plays are not merely fugitive and temporary. They are not the sudden growth of yesterday or to-day, sure of fading or withering to-morrow, but they were the delight of past ages, still continue the admiration of the present and (to use the language of true Poetry)

> —To ages yet unborn appeal,
> And latest time th' ETERNAL NATURE feel.

LLOYD's *Actor*.

There is one circumstance peculiar to the Dramatick Tales, and to many of the more regular Comedies of our Old Writers, of which it is too little to say that it demands no apology. It deserves the highest commendation, since it hath been the means of introducing the most capital beauties into their compositions while the same species of excellence could not possibly enter into those of a later period. I mean the poetical stile of their dialogue. Most nations except our own have imagined mere prose—which, with Molière's *Bourgeois Gentilhomme*, the meanest of us have talked from our cradle—too little elevated for the language of the Theatre. Our neighbours the French at this day write most of their Plays, Comedies as well as Tragedies, in rhyme, a Gothick practice which our own stage once admitted but long ago wisely rejected. The Grecian Iambick was more happily conceived in the true spirit of that elegant and magnificent simplicity which characterized the taste of that nation. Such a measure was well accommodated to the expressions of the mind, and though it refined indeed on nature it did not contradict it. In this, as well as in all other matters of literature, the usage of Greece was religiously observed at Rome. Plautus, in his richest vein of humour, is numerous and poetical. The Comedies of Terence, though we cannot agree to read them after Bishop Hare, were evidently not written without regard to measure, which is the invincible reason why all attempts to render them into downright prose have always proved, and ever must prove, unsuccessful; and if a faint effort now under contemplation[1] to give a version of them in familiar blank verse (after the manner of our Old Writers but without a servile imitation of them) should fail it must, I am confident, be owing to the lameness of the execution. The English heroick measure—or as it is commonly called blank verse—is perhaps of a more happy construction than even the Grecian Iambick, elevated equally but approaching nearer to the language of nature, and as well adapted to the expression of Comick Humour as to the Pathos of Tragedy.

The mere modern Critick, whose idea of blank verse is perhaps attached to that empty swell of phraseology so frequent in our late Tragedies, may consider these notions as the effect of bigotry to our old authors rather than the result of impartial criticism. Let such an one carefully read over the works of those writers for whom I am an advocate. There he will seldom or ever find that tumour of blank verse to which he has been so much accustomed. He will be surprised with a familiar dignity which, though it rises somewhat above ordinary

[1] By Colman himself: *The comedies translated into familiar blank verse* appeared in 1765.

conversation, is rather an improvement than perversion of it. He will soon be convinced that blank verse is by no means appropriated solely to the buskin, but that the hand of a master may mould it to whatever purposes he pleases, and that in comedy it will not only admit humour but heighten and embellish it. Instances might be produced without number. It must however be lamented that the modern Tragick Stile, free indeed from the mad flights of Dryden and his cotemporaries, yet departs equally from nature. I am apt to think it is in great measure owing to the almost total exclusion of blank verse from all modern compositions, Tragedy excepted. The common use of an elevated diction in comedy, where the writer was often of necessity put upon expressing the most ordinary matters, and where the subject demanded him to paint the most ridiculous emotions of the mind, was perhaps one of the chief causes of that *easy vigour* so conspicuous in the style of the old tragedies. Habituated to poetical dialogue in those compositions, wherein they were obliged to adhere more strictly to the simplicity of the language of nature, the Poets learnt in those of a more raised species not to depart from it too wantonly. They were well acquainted also with the force as well as elegance of their mother-tongue, and chose to use such words as may be called natives of the language rather than to harmonise their verses and agonise the audience with Latin terminations. Whether the refined style of Addison's *Cato* and the flowing versification of Rowe first occasioned this departure from ancient simplicity, it is difficult to determine. But it is too true that Southerne was the last of our Dramatick Writers who was in any degree possest of that magnificent plainness which is the genuine dress of nature, though indeed the plays even of Rowe are more simple in their style than those which have been produced by his successors.

It must not, however, be dissembled in this place that the style of our Old Writers is not without faults, that they were apt to give too much into conceits, that they often pursued an allegorical train of thought too far, and were sometimes betrayed into forced, unnatural, quaint, or gigantick expressions. In the works of Shakespeare himself every one of these errors may be found; yet it may be safely asserted that no other Author, antient or modern, has expressed himself on such a variety of subjects with more ease and in a vein more truly poetical, unless perhaps we should except Homer (of which, by the bye, the deepest Critick, most conversant with idioms and dialects, is not quite a competent judge).

I would not be understood by what I have here said of Poetical

Dialogue to object to the use of Prose, or to insinuate that our modern Comedies are the worse for being written in that style. It is enough for me to have vindicated the use of a more elevated manner among our Old Writers. I am well aware that most parts of Falstaff, Ford, Benedick, Malvolio, &c. are written in prose, nor indeed would I counsel a modern Writer to attempt the use of Poetical Dialogue in a mere Comedy. A Dramatick Tale, indeed, chequered like life itself with various incidents ludicrous and affecting, if written by a masterly hand and somewhat more severely than those abovementioned, would, I doubt not, still be received with candour and applause. The Publick would be agreeably surprised with the revival of Poetry on the Theatre, and the opportunity of employing all the best performers, serious as well as comick, in one piece would render it still more likely to make a favourable impression on the audience. There is a gentleman not unequal to such a task who was once tempted to begin a piece of this sort, but I fear he has too much love of ease and indolence and too little ambition of literary fame ever to complete it.

But to conclude:

Have I, Sir, been wasting all this ink and time in vain? Or may it be hoped that you will extend some of that care to the rest of our Old Authors which you have so long bestowed on Shakespeare, and which you have so often lavished on many a worse Writer than the most inferior of those here recommended to you? It is certainly your interest to give variety to the Publick Taste, and to diversify the colour of our Dramatick Entertainments. Encourage new attempts; but do justice to the old! The Theatre is a wide field. Let not one or two walks of it alone be beaten, but lay open the whole to the Excursions of Genius! This, perhaps, might kindle a spirit of originality in our modern Writers for the Stage, who might be tempted to aim at more novelty in their compositions when the liberality of the popular taste rendered it less hazardous. That the narrowness of Theatrical Criticism might be enlarged I have no doubt. Reflect for a moment on the uncommon success of *Romeo and Juliet* and *Every Man in his Humour*! and then tell me whether there are not many other Pieces of as antient a date which, with the like proper curtailments and alterations, would produce the same effect? Has an industrious hand been at the pains to scratch up the dunghill of Dryden's *Amphitryon* for the few pearls that are buried in it, and shall the rich treasures of Beaumont and Fletcher, Jonson and Massinger lie (as it were) in the ore, untouched and disregarded? Reform your List of Plays! In the name of Burbage, Taylor, and

Betterton, I conjure you to it! Let the veteran Criticks once more have the satisfaction of seeing *The Maid's Tragedy, Philaster, King and no King, &c.* on the Stage! Restore Fletcher's *Elder Brother* to the rank unjustly usurped by Cibber's *Love Makes a Man*! and since you have wisely desisted from giving an annual affront to the City by acting *The London Cuckolds* on Lord-Mayor's Day, why will you not pay them a compliment by exhibiting *The City Madam* of Massinger on the same occasion?

If after all, sir, these remonstrances should prove without effect, and the merit of these great Authors should plead with you in vain, I will here fairly turn my back upon you and address myself to the Lovers of Dramatick Compositions in general. They, I am sure, will peruse those Works with pleasure in the closet though they lose the satisfaction of seeing them represented on the stage. Nay, should they, together with you, concur in determining that such Pieces are unfit to be acted, you as well as they will, I am confident, agree that such Pieces are at least very worthy to be read. There are many modern Compositions seen with delight at the Theatre which sicken on the taste in the perusal, and the honest Country Gentleman who has not been present at the representation wonders with what his London friends have been so highly entertained, and is as much perplexed at the Town-manner of writing as Mr Smith in *The Rehearsal*. The Excellencies of our Old Writers are, on the contrary, not confined to Time and Place but always bear about them the Evidences of true Genius. (II, 132–41)

188. Benjamin Victor, Shakespeare acted and adapted

1761

From *The History of the Theatres of London and Dublin,* 2 vols (1761).

Benjamin Victor (*d.* 1778), was introduced to Steele by Aaron Hill in 1722, and defended Steele's *The Conscious Lovers* against the attacks of John Dennis. In 1728 he met Booth, the actor, and in 1733 published *Memoirs of the Life of Barton Booth.* From 1746 to 1759 he was treasurer of Drury Lane Theatre. In this *History* (to which he added a third volume in 1771), and in other works, Victor collected much useful information about the theatres of his times.

[On Barton Booth's Othello]

I will not enlarge on the various Characters in which he excelled, and therefore shall only observe that in *Othello* he has left the strongest Impression on me. Mr *Cibber* (who has been sparing of his Praise) admits it to be his best Part. He says in Page 477,[1] 'The Master-piece of *Booth* was *Othello*; there he was most in Character, and seemed not more to animate himself in it than his Spectators.' Let us consider this Character as inimitably drawn by the Author, where all the various Passions of the Soul are called forth.

Othello's Love is excessive, even to the Degree of Dotage, his *Rage* tempestuous and his *Grief* agonizing. In the first capital Scene *Iago* works *Othello* into Jealousy, and takes his Leave as follows.

[Quotes 3.3.256–83]

I look upon this Soliloquy to be the Touchstone for every New Actor. When *Iago* has left him, after a long Pause, the Eye kept looking after him, *Booth* spoke the following Remark in a low Tone of Voice:

[1] Colley Cibber, *An apology for the life of Mr Colley Cibber, comedian* (1740).

This Fellow's of exceeding Honesty,
And knows all Qualities with a learn'd Spirit
Of human Dealings.   [3.3.262ff.]

Then a Pause; the Look starting into Anger.

                        If I do find her Haggard,
Though that her Jesses were my dear Heart-strings,
I'd whistle her off, and let her down the Wind
To prey on Fortune!   [264ff.]

A long Pause, as to ruminate.

                        Haply, for I am black,
And have not those soft Parts of Conversation
That Chamberers have—Or, for I am declin'd
Into the Vale of Years—Yet that's not much—   [267ff.]

After a Pause the following Start of violent Passion.

She's gone! I am abused! and my Relief
Must be to loath her! O Curse of Marriage!
That we can call those delicate Creatures ours,
And not their Appetites!   [271ff.]

What follows in a quicker, contemptuous Tone.

                        I'd rather be a Toad,
And live upon the Vapour of a Dungeon,
Than keep a Corner in the Thing I love
For other's Uses!   [274ff.]

A Look of Amazement, seeing *Desdemona* coming.

                        Look where she comes!   [281]

A short Pause, the Countenance and Voice softened.

If she be false, O then Heav'n mocks itself!
I'll not believe it.   [282f.]

In this Soliloquy the Transitions are frequent and require such
judicious Pauses, such Alteration of Tones and Attitudes, such corresponding Looks that no Actor since *Booth* has been quite compleat in it.

In the distressful Passages, at the heart-breaking Anguish of his
Jealousy, I have seen all the Men susceptible of the tender Passions, in

Tears. Now the Inference to be drawn is that this Man, who had all the Requisites and Powers to excel in that important Character, must be acknowledged a *great Actor*. (II, 9–13)

* * *

[On Colley Cibber's *Papal Tyranny*[1], an adaptation of *King John*]

Mr *Cibber* (as I have before observed), sold his Share of the Patent in the Year 1732, when he quitted the Stage. In the Year 1738 having, as he said, Health and Strength enough to be as useful as ever, he came to Terms with Mr *Fleetwood* for his performing *Richard, Fondlewife,* Sir *John Brute,* &c. All his Comedy Parts he was right in, but in *Richard* he found his Mistake; his usual Strength and Spirit failed him most unhappily. I went behind the Scenes in the third Act, and asking him how he fared? He whispered me in the Ear, *'That he wou'd give fifty Guineas to be then sitting in his easy Chair by his own Fire-side'*. This Secret which the Difficulties of that Night let him into, gave him a Quietus. He retired for some Years, till the almost dying Embers of the Author began to rekindle. His Alteration of *Shakespeare's King John*, which had been forbid by the *Lord Chamberlain* and laid by for thirty Years, was in the Year 1744 got up at *Covent-Garden* Theatre, in which he appeared, for the last Time, in the Character of the *Cardinal*—it might very justly be called an Appearance when his Attitudes and Conduct were all that could distinguish the Master. This Play was opposed by the Revival of *Shakespeare's King John* at *Drury-Lane*, which had the Powers of *Garrick* and Mrs *Cibber* in the Characters of *King* and *Constance*. Mr *Cibber's* Exhibition therefore ended in the Profits of 400 *l.*; after which he retired to his easy Chair and his Chariot, to waste the Remains of Life with a chearful, contented Mind, without the least bodily Complaint but that of a slow, unavoidable Decay. (II, 48–50)

* * *

[From the calendar of stage-performances]

1744. PAPAL TYRANNY, a Tragedy, by Mr *Cibber*.

Mr *Cibber* had been so successful in his Comedies and so very unsuccessful in his Tragedies that one would have thought, if his riper Years had not convinced him that best Monitor, *Experience*, would have opposed his running the Hazard, like poor *Southerne*, of being dismissed at the Close of Life with Disgrace. But as the Failings of human Nature are

[1] See Vol. 3, pp. 9f., and Nos 89, 102, 103.

obvious to a Degree in those blest with Genius, so in *Cibber* we find through his Life and Writings a very strong Propensity both to *act* and *write* Tragedy. *Congreve* could not bear to be celebrated only for his Comedies; and therefore, to shew his Powers for the *Buskin* as well as the *Sock*, he wrote the *Mourning Bride*.

But this *Papal Tyranny* (taken from *Shakespeare's King John*) was wrote by *Cibber* above thirty Years before it was acted, having been objected to and actually forbid.

He acted the Part of Cardinal *Pandolph* himself; led to it, I presume, by his long Performance of Cardinal *Wolsey*, which he had acted many Years with Success. But in 1744, besides his having just lost all his Teeth, he was attempting to speak in a Theatre much larger than that he had been so long used to; therefore my Readers will conclude, his Auditors could only be entertained with his Attitudes and Conduct, which were truly graceful.

Thus the Audience shewed all the Indulgence imaginable to the Merits of this great Actor; but his Son *Theophilus* felt some Part of their Displeasure in the Character of the *Dauphin*. It was then reported that the Father had taught the Son, and all the rest of the Persons in that Play, the *good old Manner of singing and quavering out their tragic Notes*; and though they spared that Fault in the old Man they could not excuse the Son.

But alas! I can remember being of the merry Party in the Pit the first Night of *Cibber's* CÆSAR IN EGYPT, in which he performed the Part of *Achoreus*; and we *then* laught at his *quavering Tragedy Tones* as much as we did at his Pasteboard Swans which the Carpenters pulled along the *Nile*. (II, 161–4)

*   *   *

[On the adaptations of Shakespeare]

1748.

CORIOLANUS, a Tragedy, by Mr *Thomson*.[1]

Though I had the Pleasure of a long Intimacy with this Author in the early Part of our Lives, some Years before this Period (occasioned by our distant Employments) we were separated, and remained so till his Death; I am therefore at a Loss to know the Motives that led him to write on this Subject. That learned Critic, Mr *Dennis*, altered *Shakespeare's Coriolanus*,[2] and had it acted about the Year 1720 with very

1 See above, No. 144.
2 See Vol. 2, No. 64.

little Success. In his angry Dedication to the Duke of *Newcastle*, then Lord Chamberlain, he made heavy Complaints against the Managers. One of them conveys so just an Idea of the Author's ridiculous Humour that I am tempted to relate it. He tells the Duke, the Managers had fixed his Benefit on a *Friday*: 'Now, (said he) *Friday* is not only the worst Night in the Week, but this, my Lord, was the worst *Friday* in the Year.'

But to return to my Question. What could induce Mr *Thomson* (an Author of undoubted Genius) to chuse *Coriolanus* for a Subject when, by turning to his *Shakespeare*, he could read a Play written on that Story by that inimitable Hand, and which is at this Day very justly preferred? Besides, Mr *Thomson* had many Examples before him; *Dennis*, whom he knew, altered *Coriolanus* without Success; his Friend Mr *Hill* new wrote *Henry V*; Mr *Cibber* tamper'd with *King John*; but the immortal *Shakespeare*'s three Plays on those Subjects, written above one hundred and sixty Years ago, are at this Day the Stock Plays in our Theatres, and apparently superior in Merit. (II, 165-7)

189. Hugh Kelly, Garrick's Shakespeare

1761–2

From the *Court Magazine; or, Royal Chronicle*, December 1761, pp. 170–3; November 1762, p. 703; December 1762, pp. 746–8. These theatre criticisms appeared under the title 'The Green Room'.

Hugh Kelly (1739–77), an Irish poet and dramatist, earned a living from 1760 to 1767 by contributing to journals; he edited the *Court Magazine* from 1761 to 1765, wrote for the *Lady's Museum* and the *Public Ledger*, and published a poem commenting on the actors and actresses at Drury Lane under the title *Thespis* (1766, 1767). With his comedy *False Delicacy* (1768), produced by Garrick in opposition to Goldsmith's *The Good Natur'd Man*, Kelly had a tremendous success, which his subsequent plays never repeated. In 1774 he abandoned the theatre for a legal career.

[a] [Garrick's *Lear* and *Cymbeline*]

The death of Mr Rich, late manager of Covent-Garden, has occasioned a variety of opinions among our theatrical politicians, but has as yet produced no alteration in the system of his government. The same ridiculous spectacle which we took some notice of in our paper of last month still continues a satyr upon the taste of the public; and his successors seem resolutely inclined to pursue the same despicable plan of operation which the deceased imaginary monarch chalked out at the beginning of the campaign. But a proceeding of this nature is, as we have before observed, in some measure excusable when the present patentees find it so much their interest to continue it that every evening presents them with a crouded audience, while the universal favourite Mr Garrick is mortified with the appearance of a very slender house.

This circumstance confirms me in the opinion I always entertained of that gentleman's not being the faultless performer in every character

455

he plays which his friends would induce us to believe, and which the generality of the town are too ready to imagine. But when we have once talked a man into reputation it is not only unfashionable to entertain a doubt of his excellence, but we even lessen an opinion of our own understanding by discovering the smallest imperfection.—From this I would by no means have it inferred that Mr Garrick is not possessed of very great merit; but at the same time I have every reason to imagine that no inconsiderable share of his infallibility exists in the good-nature or ignorance of his auditors. His most sanguine admirers must confess, notwithstanding his action may be extremely easy it is very frequently unnatural; that his powers are often unequal to his parts; and that his pauses at the conclusion of his lines are so improper and injudicious that nothing but the high opinion of the town could possibly excuse such an error in *his* performance as they must absolutely condemn in any body else. But as we are more willing to look upon the favourable side of the question, we must confess our great approbation of a number of his parts in which it is but justice to say he has not an equal: such as his *Kitely*, his *Richard*, and his *Lear*, particularly the last, where the circumstances of age and infirmity are more happily suited to the weakness of his powers than in the general run of his characters. Instead of reviving old plays in which he has cut no very capital figure, it would, in our opinion, have been better if he had confined himself to those in which his excellence was established; for which reason we cannot help thinking his Lear would have been more agreeable to the public and consequently more advantageous to himself than the getting up of *Cymbeline*, where the part of Leonatus was by no means an addition to his reputation.—That we may not be accused on this occasion of any prejudice against Mr Garrick, we have obliged our readers with a print of Lear in the storm scene, which in our opinion is one of his principal characters.[1]

In the tragedy of *Cymbeline* there is a great deal of Shakespeare's irregularity, but at the same time no inconsiderable share of his sweetness; and amidst the general hurry and confusion at the catastrophe something so inexpressibly pathetic that, in the words of the poet,

> *Whoe'er could from a scene like this depart,*
> *Nor find a gush of pity round his heart;*
> *Must own that at humanity's expence*
> *He's dead to nature, and quite lost to sense.*

[1] The journal reprinted Benjamin Wilson's famous painting of 'David Garrick in the Character of King Lear', reproduced in Odell, i.378, and Noyes, p. 172.

... In the decorations of *Cymbeline* Mr Garrick indeed has spared no expence. The scenes are painted in a very judicious and masterly manner; and perhaps Imogen's bed-chamber in the second act can scarcely be exceeded. The whole are really executed in a taste that does no little honour to the abilities of the artist, and the judgment of the manager. (172–3)

* * *

[b] [Garrick as King Henry the Fourth]

The little gentleman of Drury-lane theatre begins to be very apprehensive about the issue of the present campaign, and exerts his utmost strength to stem the torrent of victory which seems ready to pour upon his fortunate antagonists at the other house. In order to effect so material an end the strongest plays are getting up with all possible expedition, and the manager finds it a necessary piece of condescension to trouble himself with the study of a new character.

The second part of Shakespeare's *Henry the fourth* has been played at Drury-lane with no little success.—Mr Garrick, in the character of the king, received much applause and we think not wholly without justice; for though in declamation he is by no manner of means equal to Mr Sheridan, yet he has a weight and dignity about his expression not to be found in the heavier parts of tragedy about many actors of the present anno domini. Indeed, this gentleman's excellence rather consists in a violent agitation of the passions than the cooler representations of wisdom or morality.—Thus his execration in the second act of *Lear* may be considered one of the most masterly strokes in the extensive circle of his parts; whereas, when he comes to a soliloquy in *Hamlet*, he flags below himself and maintains no comparative share of either reputation or applause. (703)

* * *

[c] [Garrick as King Richard the Third]

In the theatrical exhibitions of this month at Drury-lane theatre we have met with little more than a repetition of the most general stock plays, of which we have taken notice in several of our preceding numbers. . . .

On Saturday the 18th *Richard the Third* was represented, Mr Garrick appearing in the character of the hero; yet excellent as he undoubtedly is in some scenes, yet in others his recitation is frequently turgid and his gesture unnatural. Unhappy as Mr Sheridan is in his voice he is by much a greater master of this part, nor does he ever run into erroneous expressions through any deficiency in power; which is not the case with Mr Garrick. For the latter has been remarkable for pronouncing the following line just before the beginning of the battle in this manner:

> Draw archers draw; your arrows to the head;[1]

Instead of placing a comma at the word archers, as the proper reading requires, he puts a semicolon after the verb draw, where there should be no stop at all; by which means he recovers his voice to roar out the remaining part of the line, and receives a thunderer from the good-natured citizens in the pit and the critical apprentices in the upper gallery. (747-8)

190. Tobias Smollett on Garrick's adaptation of *The Winter's Tale*

1762

From the *Critical Review*, xiii (February, 1762), pp. 157-8.

For the attribution see Introduction, p. 18.

Florizel *and* Perdita; *or, The Winter's Tale. A Dramatick Pastoral, in Three Acts. Altered from* Shakespeare. *By* David Garrick, *Esq.*

The critics have long regretted the irregularity of Shakespeare's *Winter's Tale*, and the violence offered to probability both in the plan and execution of a performance which contains, in other respects, so many beauties in point of character, invention, recognition, the most interesting situations and the most pathetic touches of nature. The scene is shifted from one kingdom to another, Bohemia is represented as a maritime country, the action is protracted sixteen years, and the author

[1] Cibber's adaptation, 5.7.36 (Vol. 2, p. 126); *Richard III*, 5.3.339.

has been guilty of some other absurdities. All these objections Mr Garrick has removed, except the circumstance of Bohemia (which he probably thought would admit of no remedy), without making too free with his revered author. It must be owned, for the honour of this gentleman's taste, that the jewels which Shakespeare had scattered in disorder he has collected and arranged so judiciously that they produce a very agreeable effect, in the form of a regular, connected and consistent entertainment. The little unavoidable chasms of the original he has supplied and filled with a careful hand, with such caution as became a man treading in the footsteps of Shakespeare and with such success as might be expected from one so intimately acquainted with the manner of that great master. It now appears as a beautiful dramatic pastoral, raised and ennobled by passions, discoveries, and events which influence the fate of princes.

We that live at a distance from the theatre, however, have cause to complain that here is neither prologue, epilogue, nor specification of the *personae dramatis*.

191. Unsigned notices, Garrick's Shakespeare

1762

From the *Universal Museum*, I (1762). These notices appeared in the section called 'The Theatre'.

This journal was edited in 1762 by Arthur Young (1741–1820). At this stage in his career Young had written four novels and was hoping to make a name in London literary society. Disappointed, he took up farming and subsequently became 'the greatest of English writers on Agriculture' (*DNB*). The journal was then edited by John Seally, who also wrote for the *Freeholder's Magazine* and collaborated in the *St James's Magazine* with Robert Lloyd.

[a] *January* 9th. MACBETH.

This tragedy is certainly one of the finest pieces of Shakespeare, contains some of the finest flights of the most poetic fancy, and has several characters that are marked and supported in the strongest manner. In Macbeth we see the traits of ambition opening in his mind by degrees, and forming some transitions in which Mr Garrick was peculiarly natural and great. Macbeth was originally a man of virtue, till his ambition rous'd his villany.

> Why do I yield to that suggestion,
> Whose horrid image doth unfix my hair,
> And make my seated heart knock at my ribs,
> Against the use of nature?   [1.3.134ff.]

The workings of his frighten'd soul were distinctly mark'd in the actor's face. In the fine soliloquy in his own castle we find his fell purpose staggered by the dictates of his conscience; nothing could be finer spoke than this. Lady Macbeth comes in—he tells her

> We will proceed no further in this business.   [1.7.31]

Mrs Pritchard in that horrible part had all the merit so well-drawn a character could confer. When she answered her husband's change of opinion her whole ambitious soul came forth in fury to her face, and sat in terror there; her disdain at her husband's want of resolution was distinctly imaged in her features. When he says,

> Pr'ythee, peace;
> I dare do all that may become a man;
> Who dares do more, is none.　　　　　　[1.7.45ff.]

The audience saluted him with a clap; which I could not help being much pleased with, as it not only showed a good judgment to applaud so fine a sentiment but at the same time a refin'd humanity. The transitions in the remainder of the first act were finely represented by Mr Garrick. Nothing could possibly be greater than Macbeth's seeing the daggers in the air; those terrible phantoms of his guilty imagination were sublime thoughts of the poet, and most naturally acted by this great man. When Macbeth enters after the murder follows one of the finest scenes in all Shakespeare.

> *Lady.*—Had he not resembled
> My father as he slept, I had don't—My husband!
> 　*Mac.* I've done the deed—Didst thou not hear a noise?
> 　*Lady.* I heard the owls scream, and the crickets cry.
> Did not you speak?
> 　*Mac.* When?
> 　*Lady.* Now.
> 　*Mac.* As I descended?
> 　*Lady.* Ay.
> 　*Mac.* Hark!—Who lies i'th' second chamber?
> 　*Lady.* Donalbain.
> 　*Mac.* This is a sorry sight.　　　　　[*Looks on his hands.*
> 　*Lady.* A foolish thought, to say a sorry sight.　　[2.2.12ff.]

This short scene consists of nothing but the pure strokes of nature; and contains a finer and bolder image of the confusion of their guilty minds than if it had been drawn in the most pompous phrases and flowing periods. It is in such strokes as these that the genius of Shakespeare most frequently appears; and in which a great actor has the finest opportunity of displaying his abilities.

Macbeth is overwhelmed with fear and horror when he has murdered

Duncan, and Mr Garrick's looks, motions, and every attitude were those of Macbeth: when he looked on his bloody hands we saw the sad condition of his soul in his eyes. Mrs Pritchard was also very great in this part, and entered into the true spirit of the character and circumstance. Nothing could possibly be greater than Mr Garrick's crying out upon the knocking,

> Wake, Duncan, with this knocking:
> would thou couldst! [2.2.74]

In short, it would be endless to particularize all the fine strokes in Mr Garrick's acting this part. At the entertainment when he sees the ghost of Banquo he is great beyond expression; and in the last act, when his soul is hurried from one violent passion to another, when all is horror and transitions, he still preserves the character of the villain, full of terror, passion and remorse. In a word, Mr Garrick does justice to the sublime genius of Shakespeare throughout this noble tragedy. (45–6)

* * *

[b] *February*. WINTER'S TALE.

This piece is very far from being one of the finest of Shakespeare's. It is such a mixture, such a motley piece of kings and clowns, and the plot so indifferently contrived that it is not an entertaining acting piece; and nothing would make it go down but three such players as those who perform it. Garrick makes every thing of the part that it will admit, and is certainly very great in it. Mrs Cibber acts Perdita very well, but Mrs Pritchard in the part of Hermione is inimitable. Though it is so very short, though she hardly speaks ten words, yet she acts (if I may use the expression) the statue in such a striking manner that every body must allow is truly great. While she descends from the temple her face is a perfect picture, and her countenance so serene and composed, so expressive of that part that perhaps the whole theatre cannot produce so remarkable an instance. Mr Pine chose that moment to show this great actress in; the likeness is striking and the picture has great merit, but yet it sinks far beneath the original. The prologue which Mr Garrick spoke to this play has little of composition to recommend it, but it has humour, and was spoke inimitably; his compliment to Mr Quin was just, and introduced with great propriety. (106)

* * *

[c] *March*. CYMBELINE.

It is very strange that so admirable a piece as this play should have remained so long unacted; but at last Mr Garrick, to whose taste we owe so many excellent revived pieces, has brought it on the stage. In Shakespeare's plays we are not to look for an observance of the unities, his genius soared above restraint. But in the piece before us are many beauties of an higher nature, beauties that are peculiar to this great man, and which far eclipse the faults that are here and there to be espied. In *Cymbeline* are several inconsistencies. The plot itself is founded on an improbability, the wager, on which all turns. Imogen's journey to Milford-haven, and her conduct when she discovers her supposed dead husband, are all unnatural strokes; but it is a disagreeable task to look at spots in the sun.

Mr Garrick's Posthumus was admirable: he entered into the spirit of that fine-drawn character and displayed great power of acting. It is a character that gives the actor a fine opportunity to express the feelings of his soul; the transitions of the passions were exquisitely represented by him. When Iachimo returns from his voyage he asks him, 'Sparkles this stone as it was wont, or is't not too dull for your good wearing?' [2.4.40f.] Nothing could be spoke better than this sneering question; his contempt at Iachimo's confidence was strongly expressed in his *manner* and his features. When Iachimo pulls out the bracelet Posthumus is struck with terror: then ensues two of those pauses which give such an admirable natural expression to this great man's acting. He cries out

> Jove!*
> Once more let me behold it*: Is it that
> Which I left with her?   [2.4.98ff.]

Nothing could be finer than the expression of the passions at the pauses marked in this speech with asterisks.

> *Post.* May be she pluck'd it off
> To send it me.
> *Iach.* She writes so to you? doth she?
> *Post.* O no, no, 'tis true. Here, take this too.
> It is a basilisk unto mine eye,
> Kills me to look on't.   [2.4.104ff.]

Never was distraction of soul more strongly marked on the countenance than on Mr Garrick's in this admirable passage. The ensuing soliloquy, which describes such a rotation of passions, in which he is all sorrow and detestation against women, was most inimitably spoke. When he pursues Iachimo after the fight with what commanding superiority he speaks these few words,

> No, take thy life, and mend it.

While Iachimo is relating his villanous conduct to the King, Posthumus discovered the emotions of his soul at a recital that so nearly concerned him in his expressive face. When he comes forward and cries out 'Ay, so thou do'st, Italian fiend!' [5.5.209f.] he speaks it in such an admirable manner that the souls of the audience are all suspence and attention. His last speech to Iachimo is spoke in the same inimitable manner with all the rest:

> Kneel not to me:
> The power that I have on you, is to spare you.
> The malice towards you, to forgive you. Live,
> And deal with others better.—   [5.5.417ff.]

Miss Bride's Imogen was performed with spirit and great propriety of action, but her voice took off greatly from the appearance of her merit. Mrs Cibber would have done the part incomparably, and it is pity she did not act it. Mr Holland in Iachimo performed extremely well, and spoke many of those noble speeches in that part with great propriety; but I could not help regretting that Mr Packer should speak that sublime description of slander,

>   No, 'tis slander,
> Whose edge is sharper than the sword, whose tongue
> Outvenoms all the worms of Nile, whose breath
> Rides on the posting winds, and doth belye
> All corners of the world, kings, queens, and states,
> Maids, matrons, nay, the secrets of the grave
> This viperous slander enters.   [3.4.31ff.]

Neither the description of Discord in Homer, nor that of Fame in Virgil, are superior to this of Slander; but it was spoke in a tame pitiful manner that must raise indignation in the breast of every spectator. But on the whole, *Cymbeline* is a noble play, and its revival does honour to Mr Garrick's taste. (172–3)

★   ★   ★

[d] *April.* KING LEAR.

Of all the parts in tragedy which Mr Garrick acts in this, I think, we may pronounce him greatest. From the very appearance of Lear he has strong passions to express—nothing indifferent—no insipid dialogue; but all is a whirlwind of transitions from one violent passion to another. Never was character drawn by poet in a more admirable manner, never actor that could do justice to such a master-piece but Mr Garrick. The mind of man cannot form an idea of perfection in the art of acting, and particularly of this part, that is not exceeded by this great man's performance of it. In the first act he flies into a passion with Kent, and expresses the choler of Lear's disposition admirably. When Goneril first throws off her disguise, and talks of taking fifty of his knights away, he is struck with astonishment—never was expression greater:[1]

> O Lear!
> Beat at this gate that let thy folly in,
> And thy dear judgment out.

His passion encreases, 'till he falls on his knees and offers up to heaven the prayer, which he speaks with the greatest propriety imaginable. Every syllable displays the torment of his mind—I mean in the manner of his speaking it; when he concludes 'Away, Away!'[2] nothing could be more expressive. Finding Kent in the stocks, and hearing his account of his offence, he says to himself[3]

> Down climbing rage,
> Thy element's below

Gloster brings his daughter Regan's and Cornwall's excuses for not seeing him; then he flies into a violent passion:[4]

> Fiery! the fiery duke! tell the hot duke—
> No, but not yet; may be he is not well,

Here the transition is admirable. He suddenly recollects himself; but turning round and seeing Kent he takes fire again:[5]

> Or at their chamber door I'll beat the drum,
> Till it cry sleep to death

[1] Tate's adaptation, 1.2.67ff.; *King Lear*, 1.4.270ff.
[2] Tate, 1.2.96; *King Lear*, 1.4.289.
[3] Tate, 2.2.174f.; *King Lear*, 2.4.56f.
[4] Tate, 2.2.190f.; *King Lear*, 2.4.102f.
[5] Tate, 2.2.202ff.; *King Lear*, 2.4.116ff.

Enter Cornwall *and* Regan.
Oh! are you come?

The anger, contempt, and variety of passions that are expressed by this inimitable actor in these last four words are almost inconceivable, so truly does he enter into the spirit of the character in every speech. When his two daughters are together, and he applies from one to the other but finds 'em both such unnatural hags, he is ready to choak with passion. The variety of his emotions were wonderfully expressed in his speaking face; never stroke was greater than the conclusion of that scene,[1]

> You think I'll weep!
> This heart shall break into a thousand pieces,
> Before I'll weep—O Gods, I shall go mad!

There was something so moving and terrible in his speaking 'Oh Gods! I shall go mad', that without hearing him no idea can be formed of it. When he is shut out in the storm his soul is all agony, torment, and despair, the transitions of his passion are amazing★.[2]

> No, I will no more: in such a night
> To shut me out—Pour on, I will endure—
> In such a night as this: O Regan, Goneril!
> Your old kind father, whose frank heart gave all;
> O that way madness lies: let me shun it.
> No more of that.

Finely spoke! How amazingly great he is in the mad scene, when he enters with a coronet of straw: he affects the audience by the natural manner in which he performs it. When he is seized he cries, '*Let me have surgeons. Oh! I am cut to th' brains.*'[3] In the couch scene he is also very great when Cordelia is with him without his knowing her; but looking more earnestly he starts, and says[4]

> Pray do not mock me;
> For as I am a man, I think that lady
> To be my child Cordelia.

★ The reader should observe that I only attempt a criticism on the acting, not on the play: the instances I mention are merely of the former, tho' in this play the poet's part is admirable in many I quote.

[1] Tate, 2.2.327ff.; *King Lear*, 2.4.281ff.
[2] Tate, 3.3.14ff.; *King Lear*, 3.4.17ff.
[3] Tate, 4.4.161f.; *King Lear*, 4.6.193f.
[4] Tate, 4.5.30ff. (Vol. 1, p. 372); *King Lear*, 4.7.59f.

The affecting expressive manner in which he speaks this is extremely moving. Where he and Cordelia with Kent are prisoners ensue a most affecting scene, especially in that stroke where he laments the loss of his trusty Caius, and Kent telling him he was that Caius Lear cries[1]

> My Caius too! wer't thou my trusty Caius?
> Enough, enough

Here he faints. He is carried to prison, and in the next scene we see him asleep in Cordelia's lap; and the officers seizing him to dispatch 'em Cordelia begs to be kill'd first. And they beginning to bind her he snatches out one of their swords and kills two of the men with it, crying out[2]

> Off hell hounds! by the gods I charge you spare her;
> 'Tis my Cordelia, my true pious daughter:
> No pity?—Nay, then take an old man's vengeance.

He is tired with the fray, and leans against the wall. How admirably is it done! His manner of performing this well deserves that thunder of applause it receives. Edgar and Albany, &c. coming in,[3]

> *Gent.* Look here, my Lord; see where the generous
> king has slain two of 'em.
> *Lear.* Did I not, fellow?
> I've seen the day, with my good biting falchion
> I could have made them skip: I am old now,
> And these vile crosses spoil me: out of breath;
> Fie oh! quite out of breath, and spent.

This speech I cannot but regard as the very master-piece of Mr. Garrick—I mean, '*Did I not fellow?*' His soul kindles, he is in that moment animated at the thought, and speaks those words with such generous pride, in short, in that inexpressible manner which makes a way at once to the souls of the audience and overpowers them with sudden amaze. Albany tells the good news to him, in answer to which he cries out in a rapture.[4]

> *Is't possible!*
> Let the spheres stop their course, sun make halt,

[1] Tate, 5.4.65f. (Vol. I, p. 377).
[2] Tate, 5.6.31ff. (Vol. I, p. 382).
[3] Tate, 5.6.42ff. (Vol. I, pp. 382–3).
[4] Tate, 5.6.98ff. (Vol. I, p. 384).

The winds be hush'd, the seas and fountains rest;
All nature pause, and listen to the change.
Where is my Kent, my Caius?
    Kent. Here, my liege.
    Lear. Why I have news that will recall thy youth:
Ha! didst thou hear't, or did th' inspiring gods
Whisper to me alone? *Old Lear shall be*
A King again.

    It is impossible to form an idea of any thing greater than this passage; but the two parts in Italics were inimitable—never was any thing more expressive. In short, the whole last scene is certainly the greatest performance in the world: no mortal can behold it without the strongest emotions. Mrs Cibber in Cordelia was very great, as was Mr Havard in Edgar; but Mr Garrick in Lear is like the sun, which eclipses every other planet. (224-6)

192. David Garrick, the coronation procession in *Henry VIII*

1762

From *King Henry the Eighth, With the Coronation of Anne Bullen. Written by Shakespeare. With Alterations* (1762).

Act IV, Scene i.

The Order of the Coronation.

1. The Queen's Herb-woman, strewing Flowers.
2. Her six Maids, two and two, *ditto*.
3. The Beadle of *Westminster*.
   The High Constable.
4. One playing on the Fife.

5. Four Drums, two and two.
6. The Drum-Major.
7. Four Trumpets, two and two.
8. Kettle Drums.
9. Four Trumpets, two and two.
10. Serjeant Trumpet.
11. Two Civilians.
12. Four King's Chaplains, two and two.
13. Two Masters in Chancery.
14. Two Tipstaves.
15. Two Judges.
16. Two Aldermen.
17. Lord Mayor.
18. Two Esquires of the Houshold.
19. Four Boys of the Choir.
20. Serjeant of the Vestry.
    Serjeant Porter of the Palace.
21. Four Choristers, two and two.
22. Five Boys of the Choir of the King's Chapel.
23. Two Bishops.
24. Master of the Jewel House.
25. Six Privy Counsellors, not Peers.
26. The Vice Chamberlain.
27. Two Heralds.
28. Bath King at Arms.
29. Four Knights of the Bath, two and two.
30. Two Knights of the Garter.
31. Two Heralds.
32. Two Baronesses.
33. Two Barons.
34. Two Viscountesses.
35. Two Viscounts.
36. Two Countesses.
37. Two Earls.
38. Two Dutchesses.
39. Two Dukes.
40. The Lord Chancellor.
41. Dukes of *Aquitain* and *Normandy*.
42. Two Officers of the Household.
43. The Lord High Chamberlain.

44. Two Gentlemen Ushers.
45. The Archbishop of *Canterbury*.
46. The Bishops of *London* and *Lincoln*.
47. Four Gentlemen Pensioners.
48. The Queen, the Canopy supported by four Barons of the *Cinque-ports*.
49. Five Ladies as Trainbearers.
50. A Dutchess as Mistress of the Wardrobe.
51. Eight Ladies of the Bed-chamber, two and two.
52. Captain of the Guards.
53. Lieutenant and Ensign of the Guards.
54. Six Beef-eaters.

The Champion's Procession in the Hall.

1. Two Trumpets.
2. Serjeant Trumpeter.
3. Two Heralds.
4. The Champions, two Esquires.
5. The Herald at Arms.
6. Earl Marshal. Lord High Constable.
7. The Champion on Horseback.
8. Four Pages.

193. Lord Kames, Shakespeare's beauties and faults

1762

From *Elements of Criticism* (1762); this text from *The Sixth Edition. With the Author's Last Corrections and Additions*. 2 vols (Edinburgh, 1785).

Henry Home, Lord Kames (1696–1782), trained as a lawyer and was a judge in Edinburgh for more than thirty years. In addition to over a dozen legal works he wrote books on natural religion, the history of man, flax-husbandry, farming, and the culture of the heart. His *Elements of Criticism* was one of the most popular works of criticism of its period: praised by Boswell and Dugald Stewart (but criticised by Johnson and Goldsmith), it had seven editions between 1762 and 1788, and was translated into German between 1763–6. At least twenty-five editions and abridgments appeared in England and America between 1716 and 1883, while many chapters gained enormous currency through being reprinted in the *Encyclopaedia Britannica* from 1771 on. Kames's theories were influenced by the associationist principles of Locke, Hartley, and Hume.

[On Shakespeare's depiction of self-deception; from Chapter 2, 'Of Emotions and Passions.']

Shakespeare exhibits beautiful examples of the irregular influence of passion in making us believe things to be otherwise than they are. King Lear in his distress personifies the rain, wind, and thunder, and in order to justify his resentment believes them to be taking part with his daughters:

> *Lear.* Rumble thy belly-full, spit fire, spout rain!
> Nor rain, wind, thunder, fire, are my daughters.
> I tax not you, you elements, with unkindness;

I never gave you kingdoms, call'd you children;
You owe me no subscription. Then let fall
Your horrible pleasure.—Here I stand, your brave,
A poor, infirm, weak, and despis'd old man!
But yet I call you servile ministers,
That have with two pernicious daughters join'd
Your high-engender'd battles, 'gainst a head
So old and white as this. Oh! oh! 'tis foul!   [3.2.14ff.]

King Richard, full of indignation against his favourite horse for carrying
Bolingbroke, is led into the conviction of his being rational:

> *K. Rich.* Rode he on Barbary? tell me, gentle friend,
> How went he under him.
> *Groom.* So proudly as he had disdain'd the ground.
> *K. Rich.* So proud that Bolingbroke was on his back!
> That jade had eat bread from my royal hand.
> This hand hath made him proud with clapping him.
> Would he not stumble? would he not fall down,
> (Since pride must have a fall), and break the neck
> Of that proud man that did usurp his back? [*Richard* II, 5.5.81ff.]

Hamlet, swelled with indignation at his mother's second marriage, was
strongly inclined to lessen the time of her widowhood, the shortness of
the time being a violent circumstance against her; and he deludes himself by degrees into the opinion of an interval shorter than the real one:

> *Hamlet.*   That it should come to this!
> But two months dead! nay, not so much; not two;—
> So excellent a king, that was, to this,
> Hyperion to a satyr: so loving to my mother,
> That he permitted not the winds of heav'n
> Visit her face too roughly. Heav'n and earth!
> Must I remember—why, she would hang on him,
> As if increase of appetite had grown
> By what it fed on; yet, within a month—
> Let me not think—Frailty, thy name is *Woman!*
> A little month! or ere those shoes were old,
> With which she follow'd my poor father's body,
> Like Niobe, all tears— Why she, ev'n she—
> (O heav'n! a beast that wants discourse of reason,
> Would have mourn'd longer—) married with mine uncle,

My father's brother; but no more like my father,
Than I to Hercules. Within a month!—
Ere yet the salt of most unrighteous tears
Had left the flushing in her gauled eyes,
She married—Oh, most wicked speed, to post
With such dexterity to incestuous sheets!
It is not, nor it cannot come to good.
But break, my heart, for I must hold my tongue.   [1.2.137ff.]

The power of passion to falsify the computation of time is remarkable in this instance; because time, which hath an accurate measure, is less obsequious to our desires and wishes than objects which have no precise standard of less or more.

Good news are greedily swallowed upon very slender evidence: our wishes magnify the probability of the event as well as the veracity of the relater, and we believe as certain what at best is doubtful. . . .

For the same reason bad news gain also credit upon the slightest evidence. Fear, if once alarmed, has the same effect with hope, to magnify every circumstance that tends to conviction. Shakespeare, who shows more knowledge of human nature than any of our philosophers, hath in his *Cymbeline* [2.4.106ff.] represented this bias of the mind; for he makes the person who alone was affected with the bad news yield to evidence that did not convince any of his companions. And Othello is convinced of his wife's infidelity from circumstances [3.3] too slight to move any person less interested. (I, 160–3)

*　*　*

[On Shakespeare's word-play; from chapter 13, 'Of Wit']

Having discussed wit in the thought we proceed to what is verbal only, commonly called *a play of words*. This sort of wit depends for the most part upon chusing a word that hath different significations: by that artifice hocus-pocus tricks are play'd in language, and thoughts plain and simple take on a very different appearance. Play is necessary for man, in order to refresh him after labour; and accordingly man loves play even so much as to relish a play of words, and it is happy for us that words can be employ'd not only for useful purposes but also for our amusement. This amusement, tho' humble and low, unbends the mind, and is relished by some at all times and by all at some times.

It is remarkable that this low species of wit has among all nations been a favourite entertainment in a certain stage of their progress toward refinement of taste and manners, and has gradually gone into disrepute. As soon as a language is formed into a system and the meaning of words is ascertained with tolerable accuracy, opportunity is afforded for expressions that, by the double meaning of some words, give a familiar thought the appearance of being new; and the penetration of the reader or hearer is gratified in detecting the true sense disguised under the double meaning. That this sort of wit was in England deemed a reputable amusement during the reigns of Elizabeth and James I is vouched by the works of Shakespeare, and even by the writings of grave divines. But it cannot have any long endurance: for as language ripens and the meaning of words is more and more ascertained words held to be synonymous diminish daily, and when those that remain have been more than once employ'd the pleasure vanisheth with the novelty.

I proceed to examples which, as in the former case, shall be distributed into different classes.

A seeming resemblance from the double meaning of a word:

> Beneath this stone my wife doth lie;
> She's now at rest, and so am I.

A seeming contrast from the same cause, termed *a verbal antithesis*, which hath no despicable effect in ludicrous subjects. (I, 391-3)

Falstaff. My honest lads, I will tell you what I am about.
Pistol. Two yards and more.
Falstaff. No quips now, Pistol: indeed, I am in the waste two yards about; but I am now about no waste; I am about thrift.
> [*Merry Wives of Windsor*, 1.3.36ff.]

An assertion that bears a double meaning, one right one wrong, but so introduced as to direct us to the wrong meaning is a species of bastard wit, which is distinguished from all others by the name *pun*. For example:

> *Paris.*   Sweet Helen, I must woo you,
> To help unarm our Hector: his stubborn buckles,
> With these your white enchanting fingers touch'd,
> Shall more obey, than to the edge of steel,
> Or force of Greekish sinews; you shall do more
> Than all the island kings, disarm great Hector.
> [*Troilus and Cressida*, 3.1.142ff.]

The pun is in the close. The word *disarm* has a double meaning: it signifies to take off a man's armour and also to subdue him in fight. We are directed to the latter sense by the context, but with regard to Helen the word holds only true in the former sense. . . .

> *Chief Justice.* Well, the truth is, Sir John, you live in great infamy.
> *Falstaff.* He that buckles him in my belt cannot live in less.
> *Chief Justice.* Your means are very slender, and your waste is great.
> *Falstaff.* I would it were otherwise: I would my means were greater, and my waste slenderer.   [*2 Henry IV*, 1.2.129ff.]

Though playing with words is a mark of a mind at ease and disposed to any sort of amusement, we must not thence conclude that playing with words is always ludicrous. Words are so intimately connected with thought that if the subject be really grave it will not appear ludicrous even in that fantastic dress. I am, however, far from recommending it in any serious performance. On the contrary, the discordance between the thought and expression must be disagreeable: witness the following specimen.

> He hath abandoned his physicians, Madam, under whose practices he hath persecuted time with hope: and finds no other advantage in the process, but only the losing of hope by time.
>   [*All's Well that Ends Well*, 1.1.12ff.]

> *K. Henry.* O my poor kingdom, sick with civil blows!
> When that my care could not with-hold thy riots,
> What wilt thou do when riot is thy care?
>   [*2 K. Henry IV*, 4.5.134ff.]

If any one shall observe that there is a third species of wit different from those mentioned, consisting in sounds merely, I am willing to give it place. And indeed it must be admitted that many of *Hudibras*'s double rhymes come under the definition of wit given in the beginning of this chapter: they are ludicrous, and their singularity occasions some degree of surprise. Swift is no less successful than Butler in this sort of wit; witness the following instances: *Goddess—Boddice, Pliny—Nicolini, Iscariots—Chariots, Mitre—Nitre, Dragon—Suffragan.*

A repartee may happen to be witty, but it cannot be considered as a species of wit: because there are many repartees extremely smart and yet extremely serious. (I, 396–9)

*   *   *

[On the unnaturalness of Lady Macbeth;
from chapter 16, 'Of Sentiments']

Immoral sentiments exposed in their native colours, instead of being
concealed or disguised, compose the fifth class.

The Lady Macbeth, projecting the death of the King, has the following soliloquy.

> The raven himself's not hoarse
> That croaks the fatal entrance of Duncan
> Under my battlements. Come all you spirits
> That tend on mortal thoughts, unsex me here,
> And fill me from the crown to the toe, top-full
> Of direct cruelty; make thick my blood,
> Stop up th' access and passage to remorse,
> That no compunctious visitings of nature
> Shake my fell purpose. [*Macbeth*, 1.5.35ff.]

This speech is not natural. A treacherous murder was never perpetrated,
even by the most hardened miscreant, without compunction: and that
the lady here must have been in horrible agitation appears from her in-
voking the infernal spirits to fill her with cruelty and to stop up all
avenues to remorse. But in that state of mind it is a never-failing artifice
of self-deceit to draw the thickest veil over the wicked action, and to
extenuate it by all the circumstances that imagination can suggest: and
if the crime cannot bear disguise the next attempt is to thrust it out of
mind altogether, and to rush on to action without thought. This last was
the husband's method:

> Strange things I have in head, that will to hand;
> Which must be acted ere they must be scann'd. [3.4.139f.]

The lady follows neither of these courses, but in a deliberate manner
endeavours to fortify her heart in the commission of an execrable crime
without even attempting to colour it. This I think is not natural; I hope
there is no such wretch to be found as is here represented. (I, 483-4)

* * *

[From chapter 17, 'Of the language of passion']

Shakespeare is superior to all other writers in delineating passion. It is
difficult to say in what part he most excels, whether in moulding every

passion to peculiarity of character, in discovering the sentiments that proceed from various tones of passion, or in expressing properly every different sentiment. He disgusts not his reader with general declamation and unmeaning words, too common in other writers: his sentiments are adjusted to the peculiar character and circumstances of the speaker, and the propriety is no less perfect between his sentiments and his diction. That this is no exaggeration will be evident to every one of taste upon comparing Shakespeare with other writers in similar passages. If upon any occasion he fall below himself it is in those scenes where passion enters not: by endeavouring in that case to raise his dialogue above the style of ordinary conversation he sometimes deviates into intricate thought and obscure expression.* Sometimes, to throw his language out of the familiar, he employs rhyme. But may it not in some measure excuse Shakespeare (I shall not say his works) that he had no pattern in his own or in any living language of dialogue fitted for the theatre? At the same time it ought not to escape observation that the stream clears in its progress, and that in his later plays he has attained the purity and perfection of dialogue; an observation that, with greater certainty than tradition, will direct us to arrange his plays in the order of time. This ought to be considered by those who rigidly exaggerate every blemish of the finest genius for the drama ever the world enjoy'd. They ought also for their own sake to consider that it is easier to discover his blemishes, which lie generally at the surface, than his beauties, which cannot be truly relished but by those who dive deep into human nature.

---

* Of this take the following specimen:

> They clepe us drunkards, and with swinish phrase
> Soil our addition; and, indeed it takes
> From our atchievements, though perform'd at height,
> The pith and marrow of our attribute.
> So, oft it chances in particular men,
> That for some vicious mole of nature in them,
> As, in their birth, (wherein they are not guilty,
> Since Nature cannot chuse his origin),
> By the o'ergrowth of some complexion
> Oft breaking down the pales and forts of reason;
> Or by some habit, that too much o'er-leavens
> The form of plausive manners; that these men
> Carrying, I say, the stamp of one defect,
> (Being Nature's livery, or Fortune's fear),
> Their virtues else, be they as pure as grace,
> As infinite as man may undergo,
> Shall in the general censure take corruption
> From that particular fault.

[*Hamlet*, 1.3.19ff.]

One thing must be evident to the meanest capacity, that where-ever passion is to be display'd Nature shows itself mighty in him, and is conspicuous by the most delicate propriety of sentiment and expression.*

I return to my subject from a digression I cannot repent of. (I, 500-3)

* * *

[On Shakespeare's soliloquies]

If in general the language of violent passion ought to be broken and interrupted, soliloquies ought to be so in a peculiar manner. Language is intended by nature for society, and a man when alone, tho' he always clothes his thoughts in words, seldom gives his words utterance unless when prompted by some strong emotion, and even then by starts and intervals only. Shakespeare's soliloquies may be justly established as a model, for it is not easy to conceive any model more perfect. Of his many incomparable soliloquies I confine myself to the two following, being different in their manner.

> *Hamlet.* Oh, that this too too solid flesh would melt,
> Thaw, and resolve itself into a dew!
> Or that the Everlasting had not fix'd
> His canon 'gainst self-slaughter! O God! O God!
> How weary, stale, flat, and unprofitable
> Seem to me all the uses of this world!
> Fie on't! O fie! 'tis an unweeded garden,
> That grows to seed: things rank and gross in nature
> Possess it merely.—That it should come to this! . . .
> It is not, nor it cannot come to good.
> But break, my heart, for I must hold my tongue. [1.2.129-59]

Ford. Hum! ha! is this a vision? is this a dream? do I sleep? Mr Ford, awake; awake, Mr Ford; there's a hole made in your best coat, Mr Ford! this 'tis to be married! this 'tis to have linen and buck baskets! Well, I will proclaim myself what I am; I will now take the leacher; he is at my house; he cannot 'scape me; 'tis impossible he should; he cannot

---

* The critics seem not perfectly to comprehend the genius of Shakespeare. His plays are defective in the mechanical part, which is less the work of genius than of experience, and is not otherwise brought to perfection but by diligently observing the errors of former compositions. Shakespeare excels all the ancients and moderns in knowledge of human nature, and in unfolding even the most obscure and refined emotions. This is a rare faculty, and of the greatest importance in a dramatic author, and it is that faculty which makes him surpass all other writers in the comic as well as tragic vein.

creep into a half-penny purse, nor into a pepper-box. But lest the devil that guides him should aid him, I will search impossible places; tho' what I am I cannot avoid, yet to be what I would not, shall not make me tame.   [*Merry Wives of Windsor*, 3.5.123ff.]

These soliloquies are accurate and bold copies of nature. In a passionate soliloquy one begins with thinking aloud, and the strongest feelings only are expressed; as the speaker warms he begins to imagine one listening, and gradually slides into a connected discourse.

How far distant are soliloquies generally from these models! So far indeed as to give disgust instead of pleasure. . . . (I, 506–8)

Soliloquies upon lively or interesting subjects, but without any turbulence of passion, may be carried on in a continued chain of thought. If, for example, the nature and sprightliness of the subject prompt a man to speak his thoughts in the form of a dialogue the expression must be carried on without break or interruption, as in a dialogue between two persons; which justifies Falstaff's soliloquy upon honour:

What need I be so forward with Death, that calls not on me? Well, 'tis no matter, Honour pricks me on. But how if Honour prick me off, when I come on? how then? Can Honour set a leg? No: or an arm? No: or take away the grief of a wound? No. Honour hath no skill in surgery then? No. What is Honour? A word.—What is that word *honour*? Air; a trim reckoning.—Who hath it? He that dy'd a Wednesday. Doth he feel it? No. Doth he hear it? No. Is it insensible then? Yea, to the dead. But will it not live with the living? No. Why? Detraction will not suffer it. Therefore I'll none of it; honour is a mere scutcheon; and so ends my catechism.   [*1 Henry IV*, 5.1.128ff.]

And even without dialogue a continued discourse may be justified where a man reasons in a soliloquy upon an important subject; for if in such a case it be at all excusable to think aloud it is necessary that the reasoning be carried on in a chain, which justifies that admirable soliloquy in *Hamlet* upon life and immortality, being a serene meditation upon the most interesting of all subjects. (I, 509–10)

*   *   *

[On Shakespeare's use of language inappropriate to feeling]

In a fourth class shall be given specimens of language too light or airy for a severe passion.

Imagery and figurative expression are discordant, in the highest degree, with the agony of a mother who is deprived of two hopeful sons

479

by a brutal murder. Therefore the following passage is undoubtedly in a bad taste:

> *Queen.* Ah, my poor princes! ah, my tender babes!
> My unblown flow'rs, new appearing sweets!
> If yet your gentle souls fly in the air,
> And be not fixt in doom perpetual,
> Hover about me with your airy wings,
> And hear your mother's lamentation.   [*Richard III*, 4.4.9ff.]

Again,

> *K. Philip.* You are as fond of grief as of your child.
> *Constance.* Grief fills the room up of my absent child,
> Lies in his bed, walks up and down with me,
> Puts on his pretty looks, repeats his words,
> Remembers me of all his gracious parts,
> Stuffs out his vacant garment with his form;
> Then have I reason to be fond of grief.   [*King John*, 3.4.93ff.]

A thought that turns upon the expression instead of the subject (commonly called *a play of words*), being low and childish, is unworthy of any composition, whether gay or serious, that pretends to any degree of elevation. Thoughts of this kind make a fifth class.

> *K. Henry.* O my poor kingdom, sick with civil blows!
> When that my care could not with-hold thy riots,
> What wilt thou do when riot is thy care?
> O, thou wilt be a wilderness again,
> Peopled with wolves, thy old inhabitants.   [*2 Henry IV*, 4.5.134ff.]

Antony, speaking of Julius Cæsar:

> O world! thou wast the forest of this hart:
> And this, indeed, O world, the heart of thee.
> How like a deer, striken by many princes.
> Dost thou here lie!   [*Julius Cæsar*, 3.1.208ff.]

Playing thus with the sound of words, which is still worse than a pun, is the meanest of all conceits. But Shakespeare, when he descends to a play of words, is not always in the wrong, for it is done sometimes to denote a peculiar character, as in the following passage:

> *K. Philip.* What say'st thou, boy? look in the lady's face.
> *Lewis.* I do, my Lord, and in her eye I find

A wonder, or a wond'rous miracle;
The shadow of myself form'd in her eye;
Which being but the shadow of your son,
Becomes a sun, and makes your son a shadow.
I do protest, I never lov'd myself
Till now infixed I beheld myself
Drawn in the flatt'ring table of her eye.
    Faulconbridge Drawn in the flatt'ring table of her eye!
Hang'd in the frowning wrinkle of her brow!
And quarter'd in her heart! he doth espy
Himself Love's traitor: this is pity now,
That hang'd, and drawn, and quarter'd, there should be,
In such a love so vile a lout as he.   [*King John*, 2.1.495ff.]

A jingle of words in the lowest species of that low wit, which is scarce sufferable in any case, and least of all in an heroic poem: and yet Milton in some instances has descended to that puerility. (I, 513–16)

*   *   *

[On Shakespeare's word-play; from chapter 18, 'Of Beauty of language']

Next as to examples of disjunction and opposition in the parts of the thought imitated in the expression, an imitation that is distinguished by the name of *antithesis*.

Speaking of Coriolanus soliciting the people to be made consul:

With a proud heart he wore his humble weeds.
    [*Coriolanus*, 2.3.149f.]

Had you rather Cæsar were living, and die all slaves, than that Cæsar were dead, to live all free men?   [*Julius Cæsar*, 3.2.20ff.]

He hath cool'd my friends and heated mine enemies.
    [*Merchant of Venice*, 3.1.48]

An artificial connection among the words is undoubtedly a beauty when it represents any peculiar connection among the constituent parts of the thought; but where there is no such connection it is a positive deformity, as above observed, because it makes a discordance between the thought and expression. For the same reason we ought also to avoid every artificial opposition of words where there is none in the thought. This last, termed *verbal antithesis*, is studied by low writers because of a certain degree of liveliness in it. They do not consider how incongruous

481

it is in a grave composition to cheat the reader, and to make him expect a contrast in the thought which upon examination is not found there.

> A *light* wife doth make a *heavy* husband.
> [*Merchant of Venice*, 5.1.130.]

Here is a studied opposition in the words not only without any opposition in the sense but even where there is a very intimate connection, that of cause and effect, for it is the levity of the wife that torments the husband.

> Will maintain
> Upon his *bad* life to make all this *good*.
> [*Richard II*, 1.1.98f.]

> *Lucetta*. What, shall these papers lie like tell-tales here?
> *Julia*. If thou respect them, best to take them up.
> *Lucetta*. Nay, I was *taken up* for *laying them down*.
> [*Two Gentlemen of Verona*, 1.2.133ff.]

A fault directly opposite to that last mentioned is to conjoin artificially words that express ideas opposed to each other. . . .

It is unpleasant to find even a negative and affirmative proposition connected by a copulative:

> If it appear not plain, and prove untrue,
> Deadly divorce step between me and you.
> [*All's Well that Ends Well*, 5.3.311f.]

(II, 29–31)

* * *

[On Shakespeare's 'impropriety' in similes; from chapter 19, 'Of comparisons']

But it will be a better illustration of the present head to give examples where comparisons are improperly introduced. I have had already occasion to observe that similes are not the language of a man in his ordinary state of mind, dispatching his daily and usual work. For that reason the following speech of a gardener to his servant is extremely improper:

> Go, bind thou up yon dangling apricots,
> Which, like unruly children, make their sire
> Stoop with oppression of their prodigal weight:
> Give some supportance to the bending twigs.

Go thou; and, like an executioner,
Cut off the heads of too fast-growing sprays,
That look too lofty in our commonwealth;
All must be even in our government.

[*Richard II*, 3.4.29ff.]

The fertility of Shakespeare's vein betrays him frequently into this error.
There is the same impropriety in another simile of his:

Hero. Good Margaret, run thee into the parlour;
There shalt thou find my cousin Beatrice;
Whisper her ear, and tell her, I and Ursula
Walk in the orchard, and our whole discourse
Is all of her; say, that thou overheard'st us:
And bid her steal into the pleached bower,
Where honeysuckles, ripen'd by the sun,
Forbid the sun to enter; like to favourites,
Made proud by princes, that advance their pride
Against that power that bred it.

[*Much Ado about Nothing*, 3.1.1ff.]

Rooted grief, deep anguish, terror, remorse, despair, and all the severe
dispiriting passions are declared enemies, perhaps not to figurative
language in general, but undoubtedly to the pomp and solemnity of
comparison. Upon that account the simile pronounced by young
Rutland, under terror of death from an inveterate enemy and praying
mercy, is unnatural:

So looks the pent-up lion o'er the wretch
That trembles under his devouring paws;
And so he walks insulting o'er his prey,
And so he comes to rend his limbs asunder.
Ah, gentle Clifford, kill me with thy sword,
And not with such a cruel threat'ning look.

[*3 Henry VI*, 1.3.12ff.]

A man spent and dispirited after losing a battle is not disposed to
heighten or illustrate his discourse by similes:

York. With this we charg'd again; but out, alas!
We bodg'd again; as I have seen a swan
With bootless labour swim against the tide,
And spend her strength with over-matching waves.

483

Ah! hark, the fatal followers do pursue;
And I am faint and cannot fly their fury.
The sands are number'd that make up my life;
Here must I stay, and here my life must end.
[*3 Henry VI*, 1.4.18ff.]

Far less is a man disposed to similes who is not only defeated in a pitch'd battle but lies at the point of death mortally wounded:

Warwick.   My mingled body shows,
My blood, my want of strength, my sick heart shows,
That I must yield my body to the earth,
And, by my fall, the conquest to my foe.
Thus yields the cedar to the ax's edge,
Whose arms gave shelter to the princely eagle;
Under whose shade the ramping lion slept,
Whose top-branch overpeer'd Jove's spreading tree,
And kept low shrubs from winter's pow'rful wind.
[*3 Henry VI*, 5.2.7ff.]

Queen Katharine, deserted by the King, and in the deepest affliction on her divorce, could not be disposed to any sallies of imagination; and for that reason the following simile, however beautiful in the mouth of a spectator, is scarce proper in her own:

I am the most unhappy woman living,
Shipwreck'd upon a kingdom, where no pity,
No friends, no hope! no kindred weep for me!
Almost no grave allow'd me! like the lily,
That once was mistress of the field, and flourish'd,
I'll hang my head, and perish.   [*Henry VIII*, 3.1.147ff.]

Similes thus unseasonably introduced, are finely ridiculed in the *Rehearsal*.

Bayes. Now here she must make a simile.
Smith. Where's the necessity of that, Mr Bayes?
Bayes. Because she's surprised; that's a general rule; you must ever make a simile when you are surprised; 'tis a new way of writing.

A comparison is not always faultless even where it is properly introduced. I have endeavoured above to give a general view of the different ends to which a comparison may contribute. A comparison, like other human productions, may fall short of its aim, of which defect instances are not rare even among good writers; and to complete the present subject it will be necessary to make some observations upon such faulty comparisons. I begin with observing that nothing can be more erroneous than to institute a comparison too faint. A distant resemblance or contrast fatigues the mind with its obscurity instead of amusing it, and tends not to fulfil any one end of a comparison. The following similes seem to labour under this defect.

> *K. Rich.* Give me the crown.—Here, Cousin, seize the crown,
> Here, on this side, my hand; on that side, thine.
> Now is this golden crown like a deep well,
> That owes two buckets, filling one another;
> The emptier ever dancing in the air,
> The other down, unseen and full of water:
> That bucket down, and full of tears, am I,
> Drinking my griefs, whilst you mount up on high.
>
> [Richard II, 4.1.181ff.]

> *King John.* Oh! Cousin, thou art come to set mine eye;
> The tackle of my heart is crack'd and burnt;
> And all the shrowds wherewith my life should sail,
> Are turned to one thread, one little hair:
> My heart hath one poor string to stay it by,
> Which holds but till thy news be uttered.   [*King John,* 5.7.51ff.]

> *York.* My uncles both are slain in rescuing me:
> And all my followers, to the eager foe
> Turn back, and fly like ships before the wind,
> Or lambs pursu'd by hunger-starved wolves.
>
> [3 Henry VI, 1.4.2ff.]

The latter of the two similes is good: the former, by its faintness of resemblance, has no effect but to load the narration with an useless image. . . . (II, 206–12)

A writer of delicacy will avoid drawing his comparisons from any image that is nauseous, ugly, or remarkably disagreeable: for however strong the resemblance may be, more will be lost than gained by such comparison. Therefore I cannot help condemning, though with some reluctance, the following simile, or rather metaphor:

> O thou fond many! with what loud applause
> Did'st thou beat heav'n with blessing Bolingbroke
> Before he was what thou wou'dst have him be?
> And now being trimm'd up in thine own desires,

485

Thou, beastly feeder, art so full of him,
That thou provok'st thyself to cast him up.
And so, thou common dog, didst thou disgorge
Thy glutton bosom of the royal Richard,
And now thou woud'st eat thy dead vomit up,
And howl'st to find it.　　　　[2 *Henry IV*, 1.3.91ff.]

The strongest objection that can lie against a comparison is that it consists in words only, not in sense. Such false coin, or bastard wit, does extremely well in burlesque but is far below the dignity of the epic, or of any serious composition:

The noble sister of Poplicola,
The moon of Rome; chaste as the isicle
That's curled by the frost from purest snow,
And hangs on Dian's temple.　　[*Coriolanus*, 5.3.64ff.]

There is evidently no resemblance between an isicle and a woman, chaste or unchaste. But chastity is cold in a metaphorical sense, and an isicle is cold in a proper sense: and this verbal resemblance, in the hurry and glow of composing, has been thought a sufficient foundation for the simile. Such phantom similes are mere witticisms, which ought to have no quarter except where purposely introduced to provoke laughter. . . .

But for their spirits and sou*l*s
This word *rebellion* had froze them up
As fish are in a pond.　　　　[2 *Henry IV*, 1.1.198ff.]

Queen. The pretty vaulting sea refus'd to drown me;
Knowing, that thou wou'dst have me drown'd on shore,
With tears as salt as sea, through thy unkindness.

[2 *Henry VI*, 3.2.94ff.]

Here there is no manner of resemblance but in the word *drown*, for there is no real resemblance between being drown'd at sea and dying of grief at land. But perhaps this sort of tinsel wit may have a propriety in it when used to express an affected, not a real passion, which was the Queen's case. (II, 217–21)

*　　　*　　　*

[On Shakespeare's use of personification; from chapter 20, 'Of figures']

Even Shakespeare is not always careful to prepare the mind for this bold figure. Take the following instance:

Upon these taxations,
The clothiers all, not able to maintain
The many to them 'longing, have put off
The spinsters, carders, fullers, weavers; who,
Unfit for other life, compell'd by hunger,
And lack of other means, in desp'rate manner
Daring th' event to th' teeth, are all in uproar,
And *Danger* serves among them.   [*Henry VIII*, 1.2.30ff.]

Fourthly, Descriptive personification, still more than what is passionate, ought to be kept within the bounds of moderation. A reader warmed with a beautiful subject can imagine, even without passion, the winds, for example, to be animated. But still the winds are the subject, and any action ascribed to them beyond or contrary to their usual operation, appearing unnatural, seldom fails to banish the illusion altogether. The reader's imagination, too far strained, refuses its aid, and the description becomes obscure instead of being more lively and striking. In this view the following passage describing Cleopatra on shipboard appears to me exceptionable:

The barge she sat in, like a burnished throne,
Burnt on the water: the poop was beaten gold,
Purple the sails, and so perfumed, that
The winds were love-sick with 'em.
[*Antony and Cleopatra*, 2.2.195ff.]

The winds in their impetuous course have so much the appearance of fury that it is easy to figure them wreaking their resentment against their enemies by destroying houses, ships, &c; but to figure them love-sick has no resemblance to them in any circumstance. In another passage where Cleopatra is also the subject the personification of the air is carried beyond all bounds:

The city cast
Its people out upon her; and Antony
Inthron'd i'th'market-place, did sit alone,
Whistling to th' air, which but for vacancy,
Had gone to gaze on Cleopatra too,
And made a gap in nature.
[*Antony and Cleopatra*, 2.2.217ff.]

The following personification of the earth or soil is not less wild:

> She shall be dignify'd with this high honour,
> To bear my Lady's train; lest the base earth
> Should from her vesture chance to steal a kiss;
> And of so great a favour growing proud,
> Disdain to root the summer-swelling flower,
> And make rough winter everlastingly.
>
> [*Two Gentlemen of Verona*, 2.5.154ff.]

Shakespeare, far from approving such intemperance of imagination, puts this speech in the mouth of a ranting lover. (II, 248–50)

*   *   *

[On Shakespeare's use of hyperbole]

Having examined the nature of this figure, and the principle on which it is erected I proceed, as in the first section, to the rules by which it ought to be governed. And in the first place it is a capital fault to introduce an hyperbole in the description of any thing ordinary or familiar; for in such a case it is altogether unnatural, being destitute of surprise, its only foundation. Take the following instance, where the subject is extremely familiar, *viz.* swimming to gain the shore after a shipwreck:

> I saw him beat the surges under him,
> And ride upon their backs; he trode the water;
> Whose enmity he flung aside, and breasted
> The surge most swoln that met him: his bold head
> 'Bove the contentious waves he kept, and oar'd
> Himself with his good arms, in lusty strokes
> To th'*shore*, that o'er his wave-borne basis bow'd,
> As stooping to relieve him.   [*The Tempest*, 2.1.107ff.]

In the next place, it may be gathered from what is said that an hyperbole can never suit the tone of any dispiriting passion. Sorrow in particular will never prompt such a figure, for which reason the following hyperboles must be condemned as unnatural.

> *K.Rich.* Aumerle, thou weep'st, my tender-hearted cousin!
> We'll make foul weather with despised tears;
> Our sighs, and they, shall lodge the summer-corn,
> And make a dearth in this revolting land. [*Richard II,* 3.3.160ff.]

Draw them to Tyber's bank, and weep your tears
Into the channel, till the lowest stream
Do kiss the most exalted shores of all.   [*Julius Cæsar*, 1.1.59ff.]

Thirdly, A writer, if he wish to succeed, ought always to have the
reader in his eye. He ought in particular never to venture a bold
thought or expression till the reader be warmed and prepared. For that
reason an hyperbole in the beginning of a work can never be in its
place. Example:[1]

> *Iam pauca aratro iugera regiæ*
> *Moles relinquent.*   Horat. Carm.lib. 2. ode 15.

The nicest point of all is to ascertain the natural limits of an hyperbole beyond which, being overstrained, it hath a bad effect. Longinus,
in the above-cited chapter, with great propriety of thought enters a
caveat against an hyperbole of this kind. He compares it to a bow-string,
which relaxes by overstraining, and produceth an effect directly opposite
to what is intended. To ascertain any precise boundary would be difficult,
if not impracticable. Mine shall be an humbler task, which is to give a
specimen of what I reckon overstrained hyperboles; and I shall be brief
upon them because examples are to be found every where. No fault is
more common among writers of inferior rank, and instances are found
even among classical writers; witness the following hyperbole, too bold
even for an Hotspur. Hotspur, talking of Mortimer:

> In single opposition hand to hand,
> He did confound the best part of an hour
> In changing hardiment with great Glendower.
> Three times they breath'd, and three times did they drink,
> Upon agreement, of swift Severn's flood;
> Who then affrighted with their bloody looks,
> Ran fearfully among the trembling reeds,
> And hid his crisp'd head in the hollow bank,
> Blood-stained with these valiant combatants.
> [*1 Henry IV*, 1.3.99ff.]

Speaking of Henry V:

> England ne'er had a king until his time:
> Virtue he had, deserving to command:
> His brandish'd sword did blind men with its beams:
> His arms spread wider than a dragon's wings:

1 'A short time and our princely piles will leave but few acres to the plough.'

His sparkling eyes, replete with awful fire,
More dazzled, and drove back his enemies,
Than mid-day sun fierce bent against their faces.
What should I say? his deeds exceed all speech:
He never lifted up his hands, but conquer'd.

[*1 Henry VI*, 1.1.8ff.] (II, 262–5)

* * *

[On Shakespeare's 'impropriety' in metaphor]

The rules that govern metaphors and allegories, are of two kinds: the construction of these figures comes under the first kind, the propriety or impropriety of introduction comes under the other. I begin with rules of the first kind, some of which coincide with those already given for similes, some are peculiar to metaphors and allegories.

And in the first place it has been observed that a simile cannot be agreeable where the resemblance is either too strong or too faint. This holds equally in metaphor and allegory, and the reason is the same in all. In the following instances the resemblance is too faint to be agreeable.

> *Malcolm.* But there's no bottom, none,
> In my voluptuousness: your wives, your daughters,
> Your matrons, and your maids, could not fill up
> The cistern of my lust.   [*Macbeth*, 4.3.60ff.]

The best way to judge of this metaphor is to convert it into a simile, which would be bad because there is scarce any resemblance between lust and a cistern, or betwixt enormous lust and a large cistern. Again:

> He cannot buckle his distemper'd cause
> Within the belt of rule.   [*Macbeth*, 5.2.15.f]

There is no resemblance between a distempered cause and any body that can be confined within a belt. Again:

> Steep me in poverty to the very lips. [*Othello*, 4.2.51]

Poverty here must be conceived a fluid, which it resembles not in any manner.

Speaking to Bolingbroke banished for six years:

> The sullen passage of thy weary steps
> Esteem a soil, wherein thou art to set
> The precious jewel of thy home-return. [*Richard II*, 1.3.265ff.]

Again:

> Here is a letter, lady,
> And every word in it a gaping wound
> Issuing life-blood.   [*Merchant of Venice,* 3.2.265ff.]
>   (II, 282–3)

We proceed to the next head, which is to examine in what circumstance these figures are proper, in what improper. This inquiry is not altogether superseded by what is said upon the same subject in the chapter of Comparisons. Because upon trial it will be found that a short metaphor or allegory may be proper, where a simile drawn out to a greater length, and in its nature more solemn, would scarce be relished.

And first a metaphor, like a simile, is excluded from common conversation and from the description of ordinary incidents.

Second, in expressing any severe passion that wholly occupies the mind metaphor is improper. For which reason the following speech of Macbeth is faulty.

> Methought I heard a voice cry, Sleep no more!
> Macbeth doth murder sleep; the innocent sleep;
> Sleep that knits up the ravell'd sleeve of Care,
> The birth of each day's life, sore Labour's bath,
> Balm of hurt minds, great Nature's second course,
> Chief nourisher in Life's feast.   [2.2.35ff.]

... There is an enchanting picture of deep distress in *Macbeth* [4.3.204ff.] where Macduff is represented lamenting his wife and children inhumanly murdered by the tyrant. Stung to the heart with the news he questions the messenger over and over: not that he doubted the fact, but that his heart revolted against so cruel a misfortune. After struggling some time with his grief he turns from his wife and children to their savage butcher; and then gives vent to his resentment, but still with manliness and dignity:

> O, I could play the woman with mine eyes,
> And braggart with my tongue. But, gentle Heav'n!
> Cut short all intermission; front to front
> Bring thou this fiend of Scotland and myself;
> Within my sword's length set him.—If he 'scape,
> Then Heav'n forgive him too.   [4.3.230ff.]

The whole scene is a delicious picture of human nature. One expression only seems doubtful: in examining the messenger Macduff expresses himself thus:

> He hath no children—all my pretty ones!
> Did you say, all? what, all? Oh, hell-kite! all?
> What! all my pretty little chickens and their dam,
> At one fell swoop!   [4.3.216ff.]

Metaphorical expression, I am sensible, may sometimes be used with grace where a regular simile would be intolerable: but there are situations so severe and dispiriting as not to admit even the slightest metaphor. It requires great delicacy of taste to determine with firmness whether the present case be of that kind. I incline to think it is; and yet I would not willingly alter a single word of this admirable scene.

But metaphorical language is proper when a man struggles to bear with dignity or decency a misfortune however great. The struggle agitates and animates the mind:

> *Wolsey*. Farewell, a long farewell, to all my greatness!
> This is the state of man; to-day he puts forth
> The tender leaves of hope; to-morrow blossoms,
> And bears his blushing honours thick upon him;
> The third day comes a frost, a killing frost,
> And when he thinks, good easy man, full surely
> His greatness is a ripening, nips his root,
> And then he falls as I do.   [*Henry VIII*, 3.2.351ff.]
>   (II, 295–8)

★   ★   ★

[On Shakespeare's 'confusing' of literal and figurative senses
in metaphor]

Thirdly, In a figure of speech every circumstance ought to be avoided that agrees with the proper sense only, not the figurative sense; for it is the latter that expresses the thought, and the former serves for no other purpose but to make harmony.

> Write, my Queen,
> And with mine eyes I'll drink the words you send,
> Though ink be made of gall.   [*Cymbeline*, 1.1.99ff.]

The disgust one has to drink ink in reality is not to the purpose where the subject is drinking ink figuratively.

492

In the fourth place, To draw consequences from a figure of speech, as if the word were to be understood literally, is a gross absurdity, for it is confounding truth with fiction:

> Be Moubray's sins so heavy in his bosom,
> That they may break his foaming courser's back,
> And throw the rider headlong in the lists,
> A caitiff recreant to my cousin Hereford. [*Richard II*, 1.2.50ff.]

Sin may be imagined heavy in a figurative sense, but weight in a proper sense belongs to the accessory only, and therefore to describe the effects of weight is to desert the principal subject and to convert the accessory into a principal:

> *Cromwell.* How does your Grace?
> *Wolsey.* Why, well;
> Never so truly happy, my good Cromwell.
> I know myself now, and I feel within me
> A peace above all earthly dignities,
> A still and quiet conscience. The King has cur'd me,
> I humbly thank his Grace; and from these shoulders,
> These ruin'd pillars, out of pity, taken
> A load would sink a navy, too much honour.
>
> [*Henry VIII*, 3.2.376ff.]

Ulysses speaking of Hector:

> I wonder now how yonder city stands,
> When we have here the base and pillar by us.
> [*Troilus and Cressida*, 4.5.211f.]
> (II, 316–17)

*   *   *

[On Shakespeare's avoidance of general terms; from chapter 21,
'Of Narration and Description']

Abstract or general terms have no good effect in any composition for amusement; because it is only of particular objects that images can be formed. Shakespeare's style in that respect is excellent: every article in his descriptions is particular, as in nature, and if accidentally a vague expression slip in, the blemish is discernible by the bluntness of its impression. Take the following example. Falstaff, excusing himself for running away at a robbery, says

493

By the Lord, I knew ye, as well as he that made ye. Why, hear ye, my masters; was it for me to kill the heir-apparent? should I turn upon the true prince? Why, thou knowest, I am as valiant as Hercules; but beware instinct, the lion will not touch the true prince: *instinct is a great matter.* I was a coward on instinct: I shall think the better of myself, and thee, during my life; I for a valiant lion, and thou for a true prince. But, by the Lord, lads, I am glad you have the money. Hostess, clap to the doors, watch tonight, pray to-morrow. Gallants, lads, boys, hearts of gold, all the titles of good fellowship come to you! What, shall we be merry? shall we have a play *extempore?*   [*1 Henry IV*, 2.4.258ff.]

The sentence I object to is, *instinct is a great matter*, which makes but a poor figure compared with the liveliness of the rest of the speech. It was one of Homer's advantages that he wrote before general terms were multiplied: the superior genius of Shakespeare displays itself in avoiding them after they were multiplied. (II, 352-3)

*   *   *

[On suffering and responsibility in Shakespearian tragedy; from chapter 22, 'Of Epic and Dramatic Compositions']

Thus Aristotle's four propositions above mentioned relate solely to tragedies of the moral kind. Those of the pathetic kind are not confined within so narrow limits. Subjects fitted for the theatre are not in such plenty as to make us reject innocent misfortunes which rouse our sympathy, tho' they inculcate no moral. With respect indeed to subjects of that kind, it may be doubted whether the conclusion ought not always to be fortunate. Where a person of integrity is represented as suffering to the end under misfortunes purely accidental we depart discontented, and with some obscure sense of injustice. For seldom is man so submissive to Providence as not to revolt against the tyranny and vexations of blind chance: he will be tempted to say 'This ought not to be.' Chance, giving an impression of anarchy and misrule, produces always a damp upon the mind. I give for an example the *Romeo and Juliet* of Shakespeare, where the fatal catastrophe is occasioned by Friar Laurence's coming to the monument a minute too late. We are vexed at the unlucky chance, and go away dissatisfied. Such impressions, which ought not to be cherished, are a sufficient reason for excluding stories of that kind from the theatre. The misfortunes of a virtuous person, arising from necessary causes or from a chain of unavoidable circumstances, are considered in a different light. A regular chain of causes and effects directed by the general laws of nature never fails to suggest the hand of Providence, to which we submit without resentment, being conscious that submission is our duty. For that reason we are not disgusted with the distresses of Voltaire's *Mariamne*, though redoubled on her till her death without the least fault or failing on her part: her misfortunes are owing to a cause extremely natural, and not unfrequent, the jealousy of a barbarous husband. The fate of Desdemona in the *Moor of Venice* affects us in the same manner. We are not so easily reconciled to the fate of Cordelia in *King Lear*: the causes of her misfortune are by no means so evident as to exclude the gloomy notion of chance. In short, a perfect character suffering under misfortunes is qualified for being the subject of a pathetic tragedy, provided chance be excluded. (II, 380–1)

* * *

[On Shakespeare's intermingling of prose and verse]

Rhyme, being unnatural and disgustful in dialogue, is happily banished from our theatre: the only wonder is that it ever found admittance, especially among a people accustomed to the more manly freedom of Shakespeare's dialogue. By banishing rhyme we have gained so much as never once to dream of any further improvement. And yet however suitable blank verse may be to elevated characters and warm passions, it must appear improper and affected in the mouths of the lower sort. Why then should it be a rule that every scene in tragedy must be in blank verse? Shakespeare, with great judgement, has followed a different rule, which is to intermix prose with verse and only to employ the latter where it is required by the importance or dignity of the subject. Familiar thoughts and ordinary facts ought to be expressed in plain language: to hear, for example, a footman deliver a simple message in blank verse must appear ridiculous to every one who is not biassed by custom. In short, that variety of characters and of situations which is the life of a play requires not only a suitable variety in the sentiments but also in the diction. (II, 403)

* * *

[From chapter 23, 'Of the Three Unities']

Modern critics, who for our drama pretend to establish rules founded on the practice of the Greeks, are guilty of an egregious blunder. The unities of place and of time were in Greece, as we see, a matter of necessity not of choice; and I am now ready to show that if we submit to such fetters it must be from choice, not necessity. This will be evident upon taking a view of the constitution of our drama, which differs widely from that of Greece; whether more or less perfect is a different point, to be handled afterward. By dropping the chorus, opportunity is afforded to divide the representation by intervals of time, during which the stage is evacuated and the spectacle suspended. This qualifies our drama for subjects spread through a wide space both of time and of place. The time supposed to pass during the suspension of the representation is not measured by the time of the suspension, and any place may be supposed when the representation is renewed, with as much facility as when it commenced. By which means many subjects can be justly represented in our theatres that were excluded from those of ancient Greece. This doctrine may be illustrated by comparing a modern play to a set of historical pictures; let us suppose them five in number, and the resemblance will be complete. Each of the pictures resembles an act in one of our plays. There must necessarily be the strictest unity of place and of time in each picture, and the same necessity requires these two unities during each act of a play, because during an act there is no interruption in the spectacle. Now when we view in succession a number of such historical pictures—let it be, for example, the history of Alexander by Le Brun—we have no difficulty to conceive that months or years have passed between the events exhibited in two different pictures, though the interruption is imperceptible in passing our eye from the one to the other; and we have as little difficulty to conceive a change of place, however great. In which view there is truly no difference between five acts of a modern play and five such pictures. Where the representation is suspended we can with the greatest facility suppose any length of time or any change of place. The spectator, it is true, may be conscious that the real time and place are not the same with what are employed in the representation: but this is a work of reflection; and by the same reflection he may also be conscious that Garrick is not King Lear, that the playhouse is not Dover cliffs, nor the noise he hears thunder and lightning. In a word, after an interruption of the representation it is no more difficult for a spectator to imagine a new place or a different time than at the commencement of the play to imagine himself at Rome, or in a period of time two thousand years back. And indeed it is abundantly ridiculous that a critic who is willing to hold candle-light for sun-shine, and some painted canvasses for a palace or a prison, should be so scrupulous about admitting any latitude of place or of time in the fable beyond what is necessary in the representation.

There are, I acknowledge, some effects of great latitude in time that ought never to be indulged in a composition for the theatre. Nothing can be more absurd than at the close to exhibit a full-grown person who appears a child at the beginning. The mind rejects, as contrary to all probability, such latitude of time as is requisite for a change so remarkable. The greatest change from place to place hath not altogether the same bad effect. In the bulk of human affairs place is not material; and the mind, when occupied with an interesting event, is little regardful of minute circumstances. These may be varied at will because they scarce make any impression.

But though I have taken arms to rescue modern poets from the despotism of modern critics I would not be understood to justify liberty without any reserve. An unbounded licence with relation to place and time is faulty for a reason that seems to have been overlooked, which is that it seldom fails to break the unity of action. In the ordinary course of human affairs single events, such as are fit to be represented on the stage, are confined to a narrow spot, and commonly employ no great extent of time. We accordingly seldom find strict unity of action in a dramatic composition where any remarkable latitude is indulged in these particulars. I say further, that a composition which employs but one place, and requires not a greater length of time than is necessary for the representation is so much the more perfect: because the confining an event within so narrow bounds contributes to the unity of action and also prevents that labour, however slight, which the mind must undergo in imagining frequent changes of place and many intervals of time. But still I must insist that such limitation of place and time as was necessary in the Grecian drama is no rule to us; and therefore, that though such limitation adds one beauty more to the composition it is at best but a refinement which may justly give place to a thousand beauties more substantial. And I may add that it is extremely difficult, I was about to say impracticable, to contract within the Grecian limits any fable so fruitful of incidents in number and variety as to give full scope to the fluctuation of passion.

It may now appear that critics who put the unities of place and of time upon the same footing with the unity of action, making them all equally essential, have not attended to the nature and constitution of the modern drama. (II, 414–17)

194. Tobias Smollett, Shakespeare's faulty style

1762

From the *British Magazine* III (April, May, June, and November 1762), pp. 186–7, 262–4, 317–19, 595–7.

This series of articles appeared under the title *An Introduction to the Study of the* Belles Lettres; the attack on Hamlet's soliloquy is from the section headed *Upon Taste*. For the ascription to Smollett see above, p. 7, and Caroline F. Tupper, 'Essays Erroneously Attributed to Goldsmith', *PMLA* 39 (1924), pp. 338–41.

Over and above an excess of figures, a young author is apt to run into a confusion of mixed metaphors, which leave the sense disjointed, and distract the imagination: Shakespeare himself is often guilty of these irregularities. The soliloquy in *Hamlet*, which we have so often heard extolled in terms of admiration, is, in our opinion, a heap of absurdities, whether we consider the situation, the sentiment, the argumentation, or the poetry. Hamlet is informed by the ghost, that his father was murdered, and therefore he is tempted to murder himself, even after he had promised to take vengeance on the usurper, and expressed the utmost eagerness to atchieve this enterprize.

It does not appear that he had the least reason to wish for death; but every motive which may be supposed to influence the mind of a young prince, concurred to render life desirable. Revenge towards the usurper; love for the fair Ophelia; and the ambition of reigning. Besides, when he had an opportunity of dying without being accessory to his own death; when he had nothing to do, but, in obedience to his uncle's command, to allow himself to be conveyed quietly to England, where he was sure of suffering death; instead of amusing himself with meditations on mortality, he very wisely consulted the means of self-preservation, turned the tables upon his attendants, and returned to Denmark.

But granting him to have been reduced to the lowest state of despondence, surrounded with nothing but horror and despair, sick of this life, and eager to tempt futurity, we shall see how far he argues like a philosopher. (186–7)

In order to support this general charge against an author so universally held in veneration, whose very errors have helped to sanctify his character among the multitude, we will descend to particulars, and analyse this famous soliloquy. Hamlet having assumed the disguise of madness, as a cloak under which he might the more effectually revenge his father's death upon the murderer and usurper, appears alone upon the stage in a pensive and melancholy attitude, and communes with himself in these words:

> To be, or not to be? That is the question. [*Hamlet*, 3.1.56ff.]

We have already observed that there is not any apparent circumstance in the fate or situation of Hamlet, that should prompt him to harbour one thought of self-murder; and therefore these expressions of despair imply an impropriety in point of character. But supposing his condition was truly desperate, and he saw no possibility of repose, but in the uncertain harbour of death, let us see in what manner he argues on the subject. The question is, 'To be, or not to be'; to die by my own hand, or live and suffer the miseries of life. He proceeds to explain the alternative in these terms, 'Whether 'tis nobler in the mind to suffer, or endure the frowns of fortune, or to take arms, and by opposing, end them.' Here he deviates from his first proposition, and death is no longer the question. The only doubt is, whether he will stoop to misfortune, or exert his faculties in order to surmount it. This surely is the obvious meaning, and indeed the only meaning that can be implied in these words,

> Whether 'tis nobler in the mind to suffer
> The slings and arrows of outrageous fortune;
> Or to take arms against a sea of troubles,
> And by opposing, end them.   [57ff.]

He now drops this idea, and reverts to his reasoning on death, in the course of which he owns himself deterred from suicide, by the thoughts of what may follow death;

> the dread of something after death,
> (That undiscovered country, from whose bourne
> No traveller returns)   [78ff.]

This might be a good argument in a Heathen or Pagan, and such indeed Hamlet really was; but Shakespeare has already represented him as a good catholic, who must have been acquainted with the truths of revealed religion, and says expressly in this very play,

> had not the Everlasting fix'd
> His canon 'gainst self-murder. [1.2.131f.]

Moreover, he had just been conversing with his father's spirit, piping hot from purgatory, which we presume is not within the *bourne* of this world.—The dread of what may happen after death, (says he)

> Makes us rather bear those *ills* we have,
> Than fly to *others* that we know not of. [3.1.81f.]

This declaration, at least, implies some knowledge of the other world, and expressly asserts, that there must be *ills* in that world, though what kind of *ills* they are, we do not know. The argument, therefore, may be reduced to this lemma.—'This world abounds with *ills* which I feel: the other world abounds with *ills*, the nature of which I do not know: therefore, I will rather bear those *ills* I have, than fly to *others* which I know not of.' A delusion amounting to a certainty, with respect to the only circumstance that could create a doubt, namely, whether in death he should rest from his misery; and if he was certain there were evils in the next world, as well as in this, he had no room to reason at all about the matter. What alone could justify his thinking on this subject, would have been the hope of flying from the ills of this world, without encountering any *others* in the next. Nor is Hamlet more accurate in the following reflection.

> Thus conscience does make cowards of us all. [3.1.83]

A bad conscience will make us cowards; but a good conscience will make us brave. It does not appear that anything lay heavy on his conscience; and from the premises we cannot help inferring that conscience in this case was entirely out of the question. Hamlet was deterred from suicide, by a full conviction that in flying from one sea of troubles which he did know, he should fall into *another* which he did not know.

His whole chain of reasoning, therefore, seems inconsistent and incongruous.—'I am doubtful whether I should live, or do violence upon my own life: for I know not whether it is more honourable to bear misfortune patiently, than to exert myself in opposing misfortune, and by opposing, end it.' Let us throw it into the form of a syllogism, it will stand thus: 'I am oppressed with ills: I know not whether it is more honourable to bear those ills patiently, or to end them by taking arms against them; *ergo*, I am doubtful whether I should slay myself or live.— To die, is no more than to sleep; and to *say* that by a sleep we end the heartach, &c. 'tis a consummation devoutly to be wish'd.' Now, to *say it*, was of no consequence unless it had been true. 'I am afraid of the dreams that may happen in that sleep of death; and I choose rather to bear those ills I have in this life, than fly to *other ills* in that undiscovered country from whose bourne no traveller returns. I have ills that are almost insupportable in this life. I know not what is in the next, because it is an undiscovered country: *ergo*, I'd rather bear those ills I have, than fly to others which I know not of.' Here the conclusion is by no means warranted by the premises. 'I am sore afflicted in this life: but, I will rather bear the afflictions of this life, than plunge myself in the afflictions of another life: *ergo*, conscience makes cowards of us all.' But, this conclusion would justify the logician in saying *negator consequens*; for it is entirely detached both from the major and minor proposition.

This soliloquy is not less unexceptionable in the propriety of expression, than in the chain of argumentation.—'To die,—to sleep—no more', contains an ambiguity which all the art of punctuation cannot remove; for it may signify that 'to die, is to sleep no more'; or the expression 'no more', may be considered as an abrupt apostrophe in thinking, as if he meant to say 'no more of that reflection'.

'Ay, there's the rub' is a vulgarism beneath the dignity of Hamlet's character, and the words that follow leave the sense imperfect;

> For in that sleep of death, what dreams may come,
> When we have shuffled off this mortal coil,
> Must give us pause. [3.1.65ff.]

Not the dreams that might come, but, the fear of what dreams might come, occasioned the pause or hesitation. *Respect* in the same line, may be allowed to pass for consideration: but,

> Th' oppressor's wrong, the proud man's contumely, [71]

according to the invariable acceptation of the words *wrong* and *contumely*, can signify nothing but the wrongs sustained by the oppressor, and the contumely or abuse thrown upon the proud man; though it is plain, that Shakespeare used them in a different sense; neither is the word *spurn* a substantive; yet as such he has inserted it in these lines:

The insolence of office, and the spurns
That patient merit of th' unworthy takes.   [73f.]

If we consider the metaphors of this soliloquy, we shall find them
jumbled together in strange confusion. (262-4)

If the metaphors were reduced to painting, we should find it a very
difficult task, if not altogether impracticable, to represent with any
propriety, outrageous Fortune using her slings and arrows, between
which indeed, there is no sort of analogy in nature. Neither can any
figure be more ridiculously absurd than that of a man taking arms
against a sea, exclusive of the incongruous medley of slings, arrows, and
seas, justled within the compass of one reflection. What follows is a
strange rhapsody of broken images, of sleeping, dreaming, and shifting
off a *coil*, which last conveys no idea that can be represented on canvas.
A man may be exhibited shuffling off his garments or his chains: but
how he should shuffle off a *coil*, which is another term for noise and
tumult, we cannot comprehend. Then we have long-lived calamity,
and time armed with whips and scorns; and patient merit spurned at by
unworthiness; and misery with a bare bodkin going to make his own
quietus, which at best, is but a mean metaphor. These are followed by
figures sweating under fardles of burthens, puzzled with doubts, shaking
with fears, and flying from evils. Finally, we see resolution sicklied o'er
with pale thought, a conception like that of representing health by
sickness, and a current of pith turned away so as to lose the name of
action, which is both an error in fancy, and a solecism in sense. In a
word, this soliloquy may be compared to the *Ægri somnia*, and the
Tabula, cujus vanæ fingentur species.[1]

But while we censure the chaos of broken, incongruous metaphors,
we ought also to caution the young poet against the opposite extreme
of pursuing a metaphor until the spirit of it is quite exhausted in a
succession of cold conceits. . . .

Homer, Horace, and even the chaste Virgil, is not free from conceits.
The latter, speaking of a man's hand cut off in battle, says,[2]

> *Te decisa suum, Laride, dextera quærit:*
> *Semianimesque micant digiti; ferrumque retractant.*

[1] Horace, *A.P.* 6ff.: 'a book, whose idle fancies shall be shaped like a sick man's
dreams.'

[2] *Aeneid*, 10.395f.: 'while thy severed hand, Larides, seeks its master, and the dying
fingers twitch and clutch again at the sword.'

Thus enduing the amputated hand with sense and volition. This, to be sure, is a violent figure, and hath been justly condemned by some accurate critics; but, we think they are too severe in extending the same censure to some other passages in the most admired authors. . . .

Shakespeare says

I've seen
Th' ambitious ocean swell, and rage, and foam,
To be exalted with the threat'ning clouds,

[*Julius Cæsar*, 1.3.6ff.]

And indeed more correct writers, both ancient and modern, abound with the same kind of figure, which is reconciled to propriety, and even invested with beauty by the efficacy of the prosopopœia which personifies the object. . . .

Thus in the regions of poetry, all nature, even the passions and affections of the mind, may be personified into picturesque figures for the entertainment of the reader. Ocean smiles or frowns, as the sea is calm or tempestuous. A Triton rules on every angry billow; every mountain has it's nymph; every stream it's naiad; every tree it's hamydryad; and every art it's genius. We cannot therefore, assent to those who censure Thomson as licentious for using the following figure:

O vale of bless! O softly swelling hills!
On which the power of cultivation lies.
And joys to see the wonders of his toil.

. . . Neither can we join issue against Shakespeare for this comparison, which hath likewise incurred the censure of the critics:[1]

The noble sister of Poplicola,
The moon of Rome; chaste as the isicle
That's curdled by the frost from purest snow,
And hangs on Dian's temple   [*Coriolanus*, 5.3.64ff.]

This is no more than illustrating a quality of the mind, by comparing it with a sensible object. If there is no impropriety in saying such a man is true as steel, firm as a rock, inflexible as an oak, unsteady as the ocean, or in describing a disposition cold as ice, or fickle as the wind: and these expressions are justified by constant practice, we shall hazard an assertion, that the comparison of a chaste woman to an isicle, is proper and picturesque, as it obtains only in the circumstances of cold and purity;

[1] See Kames, above p. 486.

but that the addition of its being curdled from the purest snow, and hanging on the temple of Diana, the patroness of virginity, heightens the whole into a most beautiful simile, that gives a very respectable and amiable idea of the character in question. (317-19)

*   *   *

[On hyperbole]

The hyperbole is an exaggeration with which the muse is indulged for the better illustration of her subject, when she is warmed into enthusiasm. . . . [Discusses hyperbole in Homer and Virgil] There is not in any of Homer's works now subsisting such an example of the false sublime as Virgil's description of the thunder-bolts forging under the Hammers of the Cyclops:[1]

> *Tres imbris torti radios, tres nubis aquosae*
> *Addiderant, rutili tres ignis, et alitis Austri.*

> 'Three rays of writhen rain, of fire three more,
> Of winged southern winds, and cloudy store,
> As many parts the dreadful mixture frame.' *Dryden.*

This is altogether a fantastic piece of affectation, of which we can form no sensible image, and serves to chill the fancy rather than warm the admiration of a judging reader.

Extravagant hyperbole is a weed that grows in great plenty through the works of our admired Shakespeare. In the following description, which hath been much admired, one sees he had an eye to Virgil's thunderbolts:

> O then I see Queen Mab hath been with you. . . .
> The collars, of *the moonshine's watry beams*, &c.
> > [*Romeo and Juliet*, 1.4.53ff.]

Even in describing fantastic beings there is a propriety to be observed. But surely nothing can be more revolting to common sense than this numbering of the *moon beams* among the other implements of Queen Mab's harness, which, tho' extremely slender and diminutive, are nevertheless objects of the touch, and may be conceived capable of use. (595-7)

[1] *Aeneid*, 8.429f.

195. Daniel Webb, Shakespeare's poetry

1762

From *Remarks on the Beauties of Poetry* (1762): this text from Webb's *Miscellanies* (1802).

Daniel Webb (1719?–98) was educated at New College, Oxford, and spent most of his life in Bath. His works include *An Inquiry into the Beauties of Painting* (1760; four editions by 1777, an Italian translation in 1791), and *Observations on the Correspondence between Poetry and Music* (1769; German translation in 1771). He was one of the most adventurous English writers on aesthetics in this period.

[On Shakespeare's versification]

[*Eugenio.*] In treating the second part of my subject you will no doubt expect that I should borrow, as I have already done, my examples from Milton. But here I am tempted to change my author; principally, as it gives me an opportunity of doing justice in this particular to the most extraordinary genius that our country, or perhaps any other, has produced. It seems then to me that Shakespeare, when he attends to it, is not only excellent in the mechanism of his verse but in the sentimental harmony equal, if not superior, to any of our English poets. The first example I shall give you of his merit in this kind is in the celebrated speech of King John to Hubert when he first opens to him his designs on the life of Arthur.

> *K. John.* I had a thing to say—but let it go:
> The sun is in the heaven, and the proud day,
> Attended with the pleasures of the world,
> Is all too wanton, and too full of gawds,
> To give me audience. *If the midnight bell*
> *Did, with his iron tongue and brazen mouth,*
> *Sound on unto the drowsie race of night;*

If this same were a church-yard where we stand,
And thou possessed with a thousand wrongs;
Or, if that surly spirit, Melancholy,
Had bak'd thy blood and made it heavy-thick,
Which else runs tickling up and down the veins. &c.   [3.3.33ff.]

Hortensio. I allow you that in these lines there is a general agreement between the sound, or rather, between the movement of the verse and the idea which it conveys, but it will not so readily be allowed you that this was designed: and the generality of readers will, I dare say, esteem it rather casual than artificial.

Eugenio. When a man strongly affected by any passion expresses himself in words, the natural tones of which correspond with his ideas, it may possibly be by accident. But when we observe the same coincidence in a Poet it is most reasonable to suppose that it is the effect of design. For as he has time to select his images and sentiments so he has likewise to accommodate the movement of his numbers to the nature of those ideas he means to express.

Aspasia. I have heard that there have been Philosophers who supposed that all the beauties in nature were produced by chance: I fancy they would not have been well pleased to have had the beauties in their writings included in the jumble.

Eugenio. Were we to follow the common notions concerning Shakespeare we should be induced to think that he struck out his pictures by dashing his pencil against the canvas; or that, like the Sibyl in Virgil, he was only a temporary instrument to convey the dictates of a superior agent.

Hortensio. Mr Pope has given some encouragement to this notion where he says—'The poetry of Shakespeare is inspiration indeed: he is not so much an imitator as an instrument of nature; and 'tis not so just to say that he speaks from her, as that she speaks thro' him.'[1]

Aspasia. These distinctions are too subtle for me. I shall never be brought to consider the beauties of a Poet in the same light that I do the colours in a Tulip.

Eugenio. The beauties of Shakespeare's versification appear accidental when they are most artificial: for the mechanism of his verse, however carefully formed to have this effect, is so fashioned to the temper of the speaker and nature of the subject that we overlook the artifice, and it passes along unheeded as the casual flow of an unstudied eloquence. Thus the bold and resolute Petruchio:

[1] See Vol. 2, p. 404.

Have I not in my time heard lions roar?
Have I not heard the sea, puffed up with winds,
Rage like an angry boar chafed with sweat?
Have I not heard great ord'nance in the field?
And Heaven's artillery thunder in the skies?
Have I not in a pitch'd battle heard
Loud 'larums, neighing steeds, and trumpets clangue?
[*Taming of the Shrew*, 1.2.197ff.]

In support of the sentimental harmony in these lines you may observe
how, by changing the pauses and varying the movement, the poet has
at once guarded against a monotony and enforced his ideas. Would
you see his artifice in its full light, let us follow him through a succession
of varied movements. Is there not something mournful in the cadence
of these lines?

Constance. What dost thou mean by shaking of thy head?
Why dost thou look so sadly on my son?
What means that hand upon that breast of thine?
Why holds thine eye that lamentable rheum? [*King John*, 3.1.19ff.]

How different are the accents of unhappy Constance in this solemn and
earnest address to Heaven!

Arm, arm, ye Heavens, against these perjur'd kings!
A widow cries, Be husband to me, Heaven!
Let not the hours of this ungodly day
Wear out the day in peace; but ere sun-set,
Set armed discord twixt these perjured kings.
Hear me, oh hear me! [3.1.107ff.]
(115–19)

* * *

In agreement with the ideas the poet has drawn out these lines into
a languid monotony.

Othello. Farewell the plumed troops, and the big war,
That make ambition virtue! Oh, farewell;
Farewell the neighing steed, and the shrill trump,
The spirit stirring drum, th'ear piercing fife,
The royal banner, and all quality,
Pride, Pomp, and circumstance of glorious war;

And, oh, you mortal engines, whose rude throats
Th' immortal Jove's dread clamours counterfeit,
Farewell!—*Othello's occupation's gone.*   [3.3.352ff.]

Aspasia. That close, Eugenio, was happy. Or is it that the change in your voice has given that effect to the verse?

Eugenio. The voice of a Garrick cannot lend beauties to Shakespeare: it is no small praise that he can do him justice. When such contrasts as these which I have brought together are made to succeed each other suddenly and in the same breath, so that we immediately feel the transitions, then the several parts have not only the intrinsic beauties of musical imitation but likewise a relative advantage from their comparison one with another; and this may, with some allowance, be called the clear-obscure of harmony. The following passage in *Cymbeline* is a proof and illustration of what I have advanced.

> *Bellarius.*   O! thou Goddess,
> Thou divine nature! how thyself thou blazon'st
> In these two princely boys! they are as gentle
> As Zephyrs blowing below the violet,
> Not wagging his sweet head; and yet as rough
> (Their royal blood enchaf'd) as the rud'st wind,
> That by the top doth take the mountain pine,
> And make it stoop to th' vale.   [4.2.170ff.]

With what dignity do the numbers move in the opening of this address! In the close they spring into a storm and sweep all before them.

Hortensio. I recollect, in *Lear,* a beautiful example of a most affecting transition in the sound, corresponding with a sudden and pathetic change in the idea.

> *Lear.* I tax not you, you elements, with unkindness;
> I never gave you kingdoms, called you children;
> You owe me no subscription. Then let fall
> Your horrible pleasure;—here I stand your brave;
> *A poor, infirm, weak, and despis'd old man.*   [3.2.16ff.]

Again, when Hamlet prevents Horatio from drinking the poison:

> *Hamlet.* If thou didst ever hold me in thy heart,
> Absent thee from felicity a while,
> *And in this harsh world draw thy breath in pain.*   [5.2.338ff.]

The breast actually labours to get through this last line.

Eugenio. And yet these arts pass unnoticed in Shakespeare, while they are celebrated in Poets of inferior merit. The cause of this may be that we more readily observe any artifice in the management of the sounds when we are not much affected by the ideas. It is in excellent poetry, as in capital painting, the fine and delicate touches of art are lost in the general effect. It requires some degree of temper to trace the minute and auxiliary beauties of poetic harmony thro' such a passage as this:

> *Othello.* Do you go back dismay'd? 'tis a lost fear:
> Man but a rush against Othello's breast,
> And he retires. Where should Othello go?
> Now—How dost thou look now? Oh ill-starr'd wench,
> Pale as thy smock! when we shall meet at compt,
> This look of thine will hurl my soul from Heav'n,
> And fiends will snatch at it. Cold, cold, my Girl,
> Ev'n like thy chastity. O cursed slave!
> Whip me, ye Devils,
> From possession of this heav'nly sight,
> Blow me about in winds, roast me in sulphur,
> Plunge me in steep-down gulphs of liquid fire.   [5.2.272ff.]

Before we quit Shakespeare's versification, I must observe to you that he intended it to be nothing more than a measured* or musical prose, except when he meant to rise in his subject or give a distinction to a thought, and then we shall always trace in his numbers the influence of his feelings and find that they assume a regularity and harmony in proportion as he was interested in the effects. Nothing could be more opposite to the genius and character of this Poet than a constant equality of versification; nay, it is easy to see that he has often been careful to avoid it. The same is observable in Milton, who sometimes descends into a prosaic negligence merely to interrupt the monotony, and has frequently chosen to disgrace his measures rather than to fatigue the ear.

---

* In general, Shakespeare's verse has the easy prosaic flow of the Iambic: on extraordinary occasions it rises into the dignity and harmony of the Hexameter. Thus he has greatly the advantage of the Greek Tragedians, who were confined to the Iambic, and of the French, who from the regularity of the Couplet cannot loosen their verse into a prosaic movement. That Shakespeare's versification is agreeable to nature may be proved from the authority of Aristotle, who having observed that the Iambic measure was best adapted to the genius of tragedy because it came the nearest to common discourse, proceeds thus [quotes *Poetics*, ch. 4.]

Hortensio. Some Critics do not understand this so when they tax his verse with being often weak and unequal.

Eugenio. The error then must have been in his judgment, for these inequalities were most certainly designed.

Having in this place supported an observation on Shakespeare by a proof drawn from the practice of Milton, it may not be improper to shew that the versification of these two poets had other points of resemblance.

> Full many a Lady
> I've ey'd with best regard, and many a time,
> Th' harmony of their tongues hath into bondage
> Brought my too diligent ear; for several virtues,
> Have I lik'd several Women, never any
> *With so full soul, but some defect in her*
> *Did quarrel with the noblest grace she ow'd,*
> *And put it to the foil. But you, O you!*
> *So perfect, and so peerless are created*
> *Of every creature's best.* [*The Tempest*, 3.1.39ff.]

In this passage the rising from the feeble and prosaic movement of the first lines to the even tenor of harmony in the last is entirely Miltonic. Or, to speak more justly, it is one of those fine gradations in poetic harmony which give a kind of growing energy to a thought, and form a principal beauty in the versification of Shakespeare and Milton. (121–5)

*   *   *

[On Shakespeare's imagery]

I observed just now that the distinctive property of genius is to surprize, either by original beauty or greatness in the idea.

The principal beauties in poetry spring from the force or elegance of its images. Of these we will first examine such as are peculiar to Poetry; after which we will pass to those which are in common to Poetry and Painting. Of the former class are all images founded on comparisons, either direct or implied. The merit of these consists in a striking similitude between two objects which to common observation have no apparent or necessary connexion: hence we may judge of the merit of a comparison by the degree of our surprize, which arises from a combined admiration of its justness, its novelty, and beauty. A comparison is direct in the following instance—

On her left breast
A mole cinque-spotted, like the crimson drops
I' th' bottom of a cowslip   [*Cymbeline*, 2.2.37ff.]

An implied comparison—or, in the language of the critics, a metaphor
—consists in conveying an idea intirely by the substitution of an image:
this will be best understood by an example.

Angelo in *Measure for Measure*, observing that his guilty passion for
Isabella was inflamed by his knowledge of her innocence, is shocked at
the wickedness of his nature, which he aggravates by the force of a
metaphor:

Can it be,
That modesty may more betray our sense
Than woman's lightness! *having waste ground enough,*
Shall we desire to raise the Sanctuary,
And pitch our evils there? Oh, fie, fie, fie!   [2.2.168ff.]

Sometimes a poet has the happiness to blend these two kinds of
beauty in the same image. He sets out with illustrating his object by a
direct comparison and continues to support it by a metaphor. This is a
high degree of beauty, for it can only happen when the comparison is
so exquisitely just that the qualities essential to the borrowed object are,
with the utmost propriety, transferred to the original one. Thus Bellarius,
describing to his pupils the ruin of his fortunes at court:

Cymbeline lov'd me,
And when a soldier was the theme, my name
Was not far off: then was I as a tree,
Whose boughs did bend with fruit. But in one night
A storm, or robbery, call it what you will,
Shook down my mellow hangings, nay, my leaves;
And left me bare to weather.   [*Cymbeline*, 3.3.58ff.]

Of this species of beauty the following is perhaps a still more elegant
example—

She never told her love,
But let concealment, like a worm i' th' bud,
Feed on her *damask* cheek.   [*Twelfth Night*, 2.4.109ff.]

Shakespeare's images are not mere addresses to the fancy; they do not
play about the surface of an object, they carry us into its essence. As,
where the mother of Hamlet endeavours to excuse his extravagance:

> This is mere madness;
> And thus a while the fit will work on him:
> Anon, as patient as the female dove,
> Ere that her golden couplets are disclos'd,
> His silence will *sit drooping*.   [5.1.278ff.]

Had the Poet commanded at one view the whole circle of Nature he could not have selected such another contrast to madness. It is the most perfect image of a patient, innocent, and modest silence that ever sprung from human invention. It is by the frequency and degree of these beauties, principally, that an original Genius is distinguished. Metaphors are to him what the Eagle was to Jupiter, or the Doves to Venus, symbols of his Divinity, the sure indications of Majesty and Beauty.

Hortensio. It has been a matter of wonder to many that an imagination at times so wild and ungovernable as that of Shakespeare should, in the finer imitations of Nature, be distinguished by an unequalled elegance and propriety.

Eugenio. If we consider the nature and progress of the imagination we need not wonder that superior spirits should be the most subject to these excesses. The extremities of poetic boldness, like those of personal courage, will often have a tincture of extravagance. But this will not be the case in men of subordinate talents. Trusting more to imitation than their own feelings they move in one even tenor. With them judgment is but an observance of rules, a security to their weakness:

> And often, to their comfort shall they find
> The sharded Beetle in a safer hold
> Than is the full-wing'd Eagle. [*Cymbeline*, 3.3.19ff.]

The last species of beauty in comparative imagery which I shall speak of here consists in reducing a metaphor to a point. When a picture is given us in a single word, to make out which in our own imagination we must go through a succession of ideas, then are we surprized in the most agreeable manner and the beauty, of course, is consummate. . . .

It is by the force or elegance of its allusions and images that a poetic diction is distinguished from simple versification. The Muses, according to Jonson, have their anvil, and a verse may be laboured into precision and harmony. But the sallies of the imagination are prompt and decisive; they spring at once into being, and are beauties at their first conception. Thus in the language of a Poet the sun is the *eye* of heaven [Sonnet 18]; the heaven itself—a starry *pavement*; a canopy *fretted* with *golden fire*. [*Hamlet*, 2.2.297ff.]

Does the mind exult in its fullest freedom? It is

> As *broad*, as *general* as the *casing* air. [*Macbeth*, 3.4.23]

What are the repeated calamities of life?

> The *slings* and *arrows* of outrageous fortune? [*Hamlet*, 3.1.58]

The properties of sleep?

> The *birth* of each day's *life*; sore labour's *bath*;
> *Balm* of *hurt* minds. [*Macbeth*, 2.2.38f.]

Are our tender years exposed to the infection of vice?

> The canker *galls* the *Infants of the Spring*. [*Hamlet*, 1.3.39]

Is the night invoked to countenance deeds of horror and cruelty?

> Come, thick night!
> And *pall* thee in the dunnest smoke of hell. [*Macbeth*, 1.5.47f.]

Hortensio. How miserably naked of these beauties are the works of our ordinary songsters! Their metaphors are like the scattered trees in a desert, starved and solitary: in Shakespeare they are vigorous, luxuriant, thickly spread over every part of his poetry.

Eugenio. This comparison will hold with respect to images in general. As to these which we have been just describing they seem to me to bear some resemblance to those drawings of the capital Painters in which, though the parts are rather *hinted* than made out, yet the ideas are complete: they both give a delightful exercise to our minds in continuing and enlarging the design. Thus, when the queen would persuade Hamlet to lay aside his mourning:—

> Good Hamlet, cast thy *nighted* colour off. [1.2.68]

This metaphor seems at first to reach no farther than the gloominess of Hamlet's dress, but if our ideas go along with the poet's we shall extend it to the melancholy of his mind.*

Hortensio. The manner in which you have expressed yourself in this place gives me some reason to imagine that, joined to the pleasure which you have here remarked, we have a kind of selfish enjoyment on these occasions. For while we enter into the views and obey the direction of

---

* This is plain by Hamlet's answer.
> 'Tis not alone my inky cloak, good mother,
> No, nor the fruitful river in the eye,
> That can denote me truly.—[1.2.77ff.]

the Poet we fancy that we co-operate with him: we grow proud of the connexion, and plume ourselves in his beauties.—But let me not interrupt you.

Eugenio. The purpose of Imagery is either to illustrate or aggrandize our ideas: of the former enough has been said. (133-8)

*   *   *

Eugenio. As a great effect was produced in the last instance by a gradation in a single image, so may it equally proceed from the arrangement or succession of different ideas of: this the following description of a storm is a singular example

> *Prospero.*   Hast thou, Spirit,
> Perform'd to point the tempest that I bad thee?
> *Ariel.*   To every article:
> I boarded the King's ship: now on the beak,
> Now in the waste, the deck, in every cabin
> I flam'd amazement. Sometimes I'd divide
> And burn in many places: on the top-mast,
> The yards, and boltsprit, would I flame distinctly,
> Then meet and join. Jove's lightnings, the precursors
> Of dreadful thunder-claps, more momentary
> And sight out running were not; the fire and cracks
> Of sulphurous roaring, the most mighty Neptune
> Seem'd to besiege, and make his bold waves tremble;
> Yea, his dread trident shake.   [*Tempest*, 1.2.193ff.]

The circumstances in this description are brought together in a manner so unexpected, they crowd on each other with such force and rapidity, that our spirits are in one continued hurry of surprise. You may observe that this impetuosity gives way by degrees to a more regular climax: we set out with surprise, we end in wonder.

Hortensio. I must add one remark to those which you have made on this passage. The substituting the divinity of the sea to the thing itself was a masterly stroke of conduct. How it sublimes the object!

Eugenio. You have seen in the last instance that the sublime is produced partly by the choice of great circumstances, partly by the rapid succession of those circumstances; on the other hand the Beautiful, which tends to delight, not to transport us, may receive an equal advantage from the succession of the ideas, and this on a principle quite opposite to the former—

From camp to camp, through the foul womb of night,
The hum of either army stilly sounds:
That the fixt sentinels almost receive
The secret whispers of each other's watch.
Fire answers fire, and through their paly flames
Each battle sees the other's umber'd face,
Steed threatens steed, in high and boastful neighs,
Piercing the Night's dull ear; and from the tents
The armourers accomplishing the knights,
With busy hammers closing rivets up,
Give dreadful note of preparation.   [*Henry V*, 4.Prol. 4ff.]

We may observe in the progression of sounds a perfect correspondence with what has been here remarked concerning our ideas. For in
music we are *transported* by sudden transitions, by an impetuous reiteration of impressions: on the contrary, we are *delighted* by a placid
succession of lengthened tones, which dwell on the sense and insinuate
themselves into our inmost feelings. The analogy between Poetry and
Music is not confined to these two effects. We know that in both these
arts a well supported climax is a constant source of the sublime. Again,
as in musical composition harmony is the result of a well-chosen union
and succession of sounds, so in Poetry there is a harmony or beauty
which springs from the most natural and pleasing arrangement of our
ideas.

Aspasia. I readily comprehend that a gradual rise from smaller
circumstances to a greater should be productive of the sublime, because
a contrary process has always a mean effect. Of a beauty of order distinct
from this I have not so clear a conception.

Eugenio. The beauty of order may be proved by the following
experiment. Were you in the above description of a night scene to
change the order of the circumstances, you would find that each particular idea would lose a part of its force, and that the general effect
would be considerably weakened. What can be the reason of this but
that the arrangement of the ideas is at present such as to give the greatest
truth and evidence to the thing represented; so that the imagination, not
being delayed or embarrassed by the necessity of studying its object,
receives every impression as it offers, with facility and promptness? It
is on this principle that in the general plan or the disposition of a subject we are so well pleased with that perspicuity of order, that clearness
of connexion by which the several parts seem to grow out of each

other, and the satisfaction of the understanding every where keeps pace with the pleasures of the imagination. From these observations we may draw the following conclusions: first, that fine writing depends as much on a happiness in the arrangement as in the choice of our ideas; in the next place that all such progressive energy or beauty as has been here described must, equally with those images which are founded on comparison, be entirely foreign to painting.—

Hortensio. We cannot, it is true, paint a comparison or a metaphor, but we may represent the various affections and passions of the mind by cloathing them in images, and as it were drawing forth the soul into feature and action. Here it should seem that the Painter and Poet go hand in hand, and it may be with some advantage to the former, as his imitations come nearer to a reality.

Eugenio. You have opened upon us a new scene of imagery. As to your remark on the Painter's advantage, I must observe to you that the merit of these *simple Images,* or Pictures, whether it be in poetry or painting, cannot consist merely in their justness, for this is no more than we *expect*: it must therefore spring either from an exquisiteness in the degree of beauty or from a happiness in the circumstances. Of the former we have a fine example in the description given by Bellarius of his princely pupil—

> This Paladour,
> (The heir of Cymbeline and Britain) Jove!
> When on my three-foot stool I sit, and tell
> The warlike feats I've done, his spirits fly out
> Into my story; say, Thus mine enemy fell,
> And thus I set my foot on's neck;—even then,
> The princely blood flows in his cheek, he sweats,
> Strains his young nerves, and puts himself in posture
> That acts my words.   [*Cymbeline*, 3.3.86ff.]

Of equal beauty, though in a different kind, is the following picture of Love and Sorrow.—Imogen, on her husband's going into banishment, had sent her servant Pisanio to attend him to the ship; on his return she questions him as to the particulars of her husband's departure—

> *Imogen.* Thou should'st have made him ev'n
> As little as a Crow, or less, ere left
> To after-eye him—
> *Pisan.* Madam, so I did.

Im. I would have broke mine eye-strings, crack'd 'em but
To look upon him—
Nay, follow'd him, till he had melted from
The smallness of a gnat, to air, and then
Have turn'd mine eye, and wept.   [*Cymbeline*, 1.3.14ff.]

The difference between poetic and real Painting may be clearly seen
in this last example. The circumstances in this description which tend
to heighten the beauty of the image in the last line cannot be expressed
by the Painter; he can have no advantage from a succession of ideas. If
in subjects that are in common to the Poet and Painter the latter be
limited, so again there are many from which he is totally excluded.
In this view I shall continue, as I began, to mark the advantages peculiar
to poetry. In each of these two last examples the image surprises by the
degree of its beauty. But there are others which owe their effect, as I
have said, to a happiness in the circumstances. Of this we have, I think,
an example in that beautiful scene in *The Tempest* between Ferdinand
and Miranda.

Mir. Do you love me?
Ferd. O heav'n, O earth, bear witness to this sound,
And crown what I profess with kind event,
If I speak true; if hollowly, invert
What best is boaded me, to mischief! I
Beyond all limit of what else in the world,
Do love, prize, honour you.
Mir.   I am a fool
To weep at what I'm glad of.   [*The Tempest*, 3.1.68ff.]

Tears of gladness are not uncommon; but Miranda, from her particular education, could have no knowledge of the passions in their extremes. She is therefore surprised at this apparent confusion in their
symptoms: her surprise is a spring to ours.

This leads us, you see, to an essential point in the pathetic, namely
when a sentiment speaks with a peculiar happiness from the character
and the occasion. . . .

The uniformity in our feelings on similar motives, though it be the
ground-work of the pathetic, yet at the same time it naturally produces
in us an indifference to all such indications of passions as are obvious
and general.

The business therefore of the Poet is to give some unexpected advantage to these general feelings; either by a happiness in the incidents from which they spring, or some peculiarity in the situation and character of the person affected. Of this we have a complete example when the Daughters of Lear press hard upon him to reduce the number of his Knights—

> *Regan.* If you come to me,
> (For now I spy a danger) I intreat you
> To bring but five and twenty; to no more
> Will I give place or notice.—
> *Lear. I gave you all.* [*King Lear*, 2.4.245ff.]

The ingratitude of a daughter, who owed every thing to a father's generosity, might naturally produce such a reproach as this, but it receives an additional tenderness from the violent character of Lear, and the aggravating circumstances of his children's conduct.

If the Pathetic, as should seem from these proofs, must owe its effect to the occasion which produced it, the same may be affirmed in part of the sublime. I say in part, because though great sentiments, when produced in the Drama must, in common with the pathetic, derive a particular and specific beauty from a happiness in their application, yet there will be this difference between them, that if a pathetic sentiment be considered independent of the occasion which produced it, it loses its pathetic force. On the other hand, if a sublime sentiment be considered in the same light, it loses the advantage it received from a happiness in its application but retains its intrinsic greatness. This, I think, will appear by comparing the answers of Aspasia and Lear, in the two last examples, with the following reply of Guiderius to the rash and foolish Cloten, who had threatened to kill him.

> *Cloten.* Art not afraid?
> *Guid.* Those that I rev'rence, those I fear, the wise;
> At fools I laugh, not fear them. [*Cymbeline*, 4.2.95ff.]

This sentiment had been noble on any occasion; on this, it is happy as well as great.

From these observations it is evident that the variety and force of our sentiments, particularly in the pathetic, must depend on the variety and nature of their motives. In this the Painter is extremely confined, for among the infinite turns and workings of the mind which may be expressed by words and become the springs of sentiment, there are so few to which he can give a shape or being; and his indications of peculiar and characteristic feelings are so vague and undecisive that his expressions, like their motives, must be obvious and general.

It is observable that the same Critics who condemn so much in Shakespeare a neglect of the unities are equally forward in acknowledging the singular energy and beauty of his sentiments. Now it seems to me that the fault which they censure is the principal source of the beauties which they admire. For as the Poet was not confined to an unity and simplicity of action* he created incidents in proportion to the promptness and vivacity of his genius. Hence his sentiments spring from motives exquisitely fitted to produce them: to this they owe that original spirit, that commanding energy which overcome the improbabilities of the scene and transport the heart in defiance of the understanding. I do not mean by this to justify our Poet in all his excesses. It must be confessed that he has often carried the indulgence of his genius much too far, but it is equally certain that a rigid observance of the dramatic unities is not free from objections. For as no one simple and confined action can furnish many incidents, and those, such as they are, must tend to one common point, it necessarily follows that there must be a sameness and uniformity in the sentiments. What must be the result of this? Why, narration is substituted in the place of the action, the weakness in the manners supplied by elaborate descriptions, and the quick and lively turns of passion are lost in the detail and pomp of declamation.

Hortensio. May we not add to these an objection which has often struck me, and which extends to the conduct of the fable itself? When the action is confined to the time of the representation the Poet must often bring events together within the space of four hours which, in the natural course of things, would have taken up as many days. Thus by a strange kind of management he commits a violence on nature in order to come nearer to truth.

---

* Aristotle, in his *Poetics*, chap. vi. observes that the first Dramatic Poets were irregular in the conduct of the Fable, but excelled in the Manners and in the Diction; that the Poets of his time, on the contrary, excelled in the conduct of the Fable but were weak in the Manners, and declamatory in the diction. By the Manners are to be understood all those sentiments which become indications of Character. The advantage of these in Tragedy, according to Aristotle, consists in this, that they give us a rule by which we may judge what the resolutions and actions of the persons in the Drama will be. After this he censures the Poets of his time for being weak in the Manners. Dacier, his Commentator, has passed the same censure on the French Drama—'Aujourdhui, dans la plus part des pièces de nos Poetes, on ne connoit les mœurs des personnages qu'en les voiant agir.' As both the Greek and French Poets here spoken of were rigid observers of the dramatic Unities, these facts must strongly confirm what has been advanced on this subject.

Eugenio. It is to soften in some measure this impropriety, as well as to conform to the unities, that these events instead of being brought into action are so often thrown into narration. But this is a subject which cannot be properly examined in a morning's conversation; beside, we have other objects which demand our attention.

It is a point that has not yet been determined how far Imagery may take place in the Pathetic. Were the imagination to have no share in our designs upon the heart the Poet's task would be indeed a hard one. The difficulty then can only be to set bounds to this indulgence. It must be allowed that in the extremities of passion all studied and ambitious ornaments are to be avoided. Hence I should judge that those images which are founded on comparison can have little agreement with the simplicity of the Pathos, and this disagreement will always be found to increase in proportion as the points of similitude are specified and enlarged. But this objection will not extend to simple images. These are often happily employed in the Pathetic; in these Poetry co-operates with Painting, and even borrows her ideas from her sister Art.

Thus in anger

> *Romeo.* Alive, in Triumph, and Mercutio slain?
> Away to heav'n respective lenity,
> And fire-ey'd★ Fury be my conduct now!   [3.1.119ff.]

In grief—

> *Juliet.* Is there no pity sitting in the clouds,
> That sees into the bottom of my grief?   [3.5.197f.]

Of all our passions that of Love should seem to have the greatest connexion with the fancy. If, therefore, the distinction here made between simple and comparative imagery should hold good in this passion it will hardly be disputed in others. I shall rest the truth of my observation, as I have hitherto done, on examples.

> *Juliet.*   Sweet, good night;
> This bud of love, by summer's ripening breath,
> May prove a beauteous flower when next we meet.
>   [*Romeo and Juliet*, 2.2.120ff.]

This is not the language of nature; true passion is impatient of studied embellishments. Let us now see how far the operations of the fancy may

★ Should this compound Epithet 'fire-ey'd' be thought inconsistent with the true Pathos it will be the strongest proof that can be given of the necessity of a strict simplicity on all such occasions.

be brought to correspond with the movements of the heart:

> *Ferdinand.*   Wherefore weep you?
> *Miranda.* At mine unworthiness, that dare not offer
> What I desire to give; and much less take
> What I shall die to want: but this is trifling;
> And all the more it seeks to hide itself,
> The bigger bulk it shews. Hence *bashful Cunning,*
> *And prompt me, plain and holy Innocence.*
> I am your wife, if you will marry me;
> If not I'll die your maid: to be your fellow
> You may deny me; but I'll be your servant,
> Whether you will or no.
> *Ferdinand.* My mistress, dearest,
> And I thus humble ever.
> *Miranda.* My husband then.
> *Ferdinand.* Ay, with a heart as willing
> As *Bondage* e'er of freedom; here's my hand.
> *Miranda.* And mine, with my heart in't. [*The Tempest*, 3.1.76ff.]

In the images here employed there is no artifice, no design: they are as simple as Truth herself.

Thus far, Aspasia, I have endeavoured to give you some general ideas of the principal beauties in Poetry. I shall now proceed to those which I call the subordinate Beauties; not that they are always inferior in their effects but because those effects are produced by means less obvious, and spring more from the manner than from the idea itself. This is a distinction which in some cases will be preserved with ease, in others with difficulty. However, if the nature of the beauty, whatever it is, be well understood I cannot think it of any great consequence in what class it is to be ranked.

It is the peculiar province of Poetry to raise us above the level of our ordinary ideas. But we are not to expect that this can be done by a continued succession of beautiful images or affecting sentiments. Here, then, Art comes in aid of Nature; and our ideas must derive an importance from the manner in which they are conducted.—With what a singular delicacy does Ophelia, when she solicits Hamlet to take back his presents, reproach him with the change in his affections!

> *Hamlet.* No, I never gave you aught.
> *Oph.* O my good Lord, you know right well you did,

And with them, words of so sweet breath compos'd,
As made the things more rich; *that perfume lost*,
Take these again.   [3.1.96ff.]

The manner is somewhat varied in the following instance. Camillo, in *The Winter's Tale*, endeavours to dissuade the young Lovers from exposing themselves to the crosses of fortune.

> You know,
> Prosperity's the very bond of Love,
> Whose fresh complexion, and whose heart together,
> Affliction alters.
>   *Perdita.*   One of these is true;
> I think affliction may subdue the cheek,
> But not take in the mind.   [4.4.564ff.]

From an elegance in the turn of the thought, we naturally pass to a Felicity in the expression. Thus Posthumus, reflecting on his Wife's infidelity:

> Me of my lawful pleasures she restrain'd,
> And pray'd me oft forbearance; did it with
> *A pudency so rosie*, the sweet view on't
> Might well have warm'd old Saturn; that I thought her
> As chaste as *unsunn'd snow*.   [*Cymbeline*, 2.5.9ff.]

Hortensio. UNSUNN'D Snow.—The expression is beautiful: but is not the image likewise new, and wholly Shakespeare's?

Eugenio. You're in the right, Hortensius: but I was so intent on the force of the Expression that I quite overlooked the novelty in the idea. The completion of Beauty is in their Union: of this we have an exquisite example where Iachimo steals upon Imogen as she slept.

> The crickets sing, and man's o'erlabour'd sense
> Repairs itself by rest: our Tarquin thus
> Did softly press the rushes, *ere he waken'd*
> *The Chastity he wounded.*   [*Cymbeline*, 2.2.11ff.]

To represent Lucretia by personifying her virtue was a beauty in the Thought; the elegant precision with which the action is described is a beauty in the Manner. In this analysis we discover the limits between Nature and Art. For if by Nature we mean the intrinsic Merit in the Thought, by Art must be understood, 1. Every advantage given to that thought to the improvement of its original beauty; 2. Every such happiness in the manner as supplies the want of Novelty in the Idea.

Aspasia. The first part of your description of Art has been fully explained by the examples you have given: but I do not as yet clearly comprehend how a happiness in the manner can supply the want of Novelty in the Thought.

Eugenio. We can bestow a Novelty on a known object either by discovering in it some new circumstance or quality, or by varying and improving its usual impression. We have an example of the former in the reflexion made by Helena on the vanity of her love for Bertram.

> Indian like,
> Religious in mine error, I adore
> The sun that *looks upon his worshipper*,
> *But knows of him no more.*
>
> [*All's Well that Ends Well*, 1.3.195ff.]

Again, when the Shepherd in *The Winter's Tale* is questioned by Polyxenes concerning the love of Florizel for Perdita—

> *Shepherd.* Never did the *Moon*
> So *gaze upon the waters*, as he'll stand
> And read my Daughter's eyes. [4.4.172ff.]

I now come, Aspasia, to the explanation you desire. When a known object presents itself to us through a new and unpractised medium we consider the novelty as inherent in the object. It is much the same with respect to our ideas: whatever is original in the Representation is transferred to the Thing represented. For instance:—the consideration that all men have sprung from the same origin and are destined to the same dissolution has been often employed as a check on human pride, and an incitement to a social affection. How is this urged by the Poet!

> *Arviragus.* Brother, stay here;
> Are we not Brothers?
> *Imo.* So man and man should be;
> But clay and clay differs in dignity,
> Whose dust is both alike. [*Cymbeline*, 4.2.2ff.]

Is not the energy with which this Idea is conveyed equivalent to a novelty in the Idea itself? The same effect may be produced by a happiness in the use and application of a known image, as in the advice given by Lady Macbeth to her Husband.

> *Look* like the innocent flower,
> But *be* the serpent under't. [1.5.62f.]

Hortensio. From the light which you have thrown on this subject we may account for the opposition in our judgments when we bestow on Writers the reputation of being Original. For a Poet may be original in the manner and not at all so in his ideas.

Eugenio. True genius, Hortensio, will be original in both: of this we shall have a further proof in the use that Shakespeare has made of the qualities and attributes of the Heathen Divinities. And here I cannot but wonder that a Poet whose classical images are composed of the finest parts, and breathe the very spirit of the antient Mythology, should pass for being illiterate.

> See what a grace was seated on his brow!
> Hyperion's curls; the front of Jove himself;
> An eye like Mars, to threaten or command;
> A station, like the herald Mercury
> New-lighted on a heav'n-kissing hill.   [*Hamlet*, 3.4.55ff.]

In this portrait the features are borrowed from the antique, but they are united into a character by creative fancy. This power of giving an advantage to the most familiar objects by some unexpected happiness in their use and application is particularly distinguished in our Poet when he touches on the Fables of Antiquity. Thus Perdita, at a loss for a variety of flowers to bestow on her guests:

> O Proserpina,
> *For the flow'rs now, that frighted thou let'st fall*
> *From Dis's waggon!* Daffadils
> That come before the Swallow dares, and take
> The winds of March with beauty; Violets dim,
> But sweeter than the lids of Juno's eyes,
> Or Cytherea's breath.   [*The Winter's Tale*, 4.4.116ff.]

Exclusive of the purpose for which I have produced these lines, you must have observed the uncommon art of the Poet in characterizing his flowers: 'They at her coming sprung.' A fine imagination, like the presence of Eve, gives a second vegetation to the beauties of nature. In these principles, and in the examples by which they have been supported we see clearly the reason why every enlightened age has had, and must continue to have, its original Writers. We have no right, therefore, to complain that Nature is always the same, or that the sources of Novelty have been exhausted. It is in Poetry as in Philosophy, new relations are struck out, new influences discovered, and every superior genius moves in a world of his own. (140–57)

196. Benjamin Victor, from his adaptation of *The Two Gentlemen of Verona*

1762

Performed at Drury Lane on 22 December 1762.

For Victor see the headnote to No. 188 above.

ADVERTISEMENT.

It is the general opinion that this comedy abounds with weeds, and there is no one, I think, will deny, who peruses it with attention, that it is adorned with several poetical flowers such as the hand of a Shakespeare alone could raise. The rankest of those weeds I have endeavoured to remove; but was not a little solicitous lest I should go too far and, while I fancy'd myself grubbing up a weed, should heedlessly cut the threads of a flower.

The other part of my design, which was to give a greater uniformity to the scenery and a connection and consistency to the fable (which in many places is visibly wanted), will be deemed of more importance if it should be found to be executed with success.

As to the two additional scenes of Launce and Speed in the last act, I shall leave them to the candid judges of dramatic composition whether they contribute any thing to the representation, or afford any amusement to the reader.

*   *   *

Act V, Scene i. The Outlaws' *part of the forest.*

Enter Valentine.

Val. How use doth breed a habit in a man!
This shadowy desart! unfrequented woods!
I better brook than flourishing peopled towns.
Here I can sit alone, unseen of any,

525

And to the nightingale's complaining notes,
Tune my distresses, and record my woes!
O thou, that dost inhabit in my breast,
Leave not the mansion so long tenantless,
Lest growing ruinous, the building fall,
And leave no memory of what it was.
Repair me with thy presence, Silvia!
Thou gentle nymph, cherish thy forlorn swain!

[*Hallowing heard at a distance.*]

What hollo'ing, and what stir is this to-day?
These are my mates, that make their will their law,
Have some unhappy passenger in chase:
They love me well, yet I have much to do
To keep them from uncivil outrages.
Withdraw thee, Valentine—they come this way.   *Exit.* Val.

[Act V, Scene ii] *a Part of the Forest.*

Enter Launce, *in a fright, follow'd by* Crab.

   Launce.   We are lost and undone! what will become of us? what could my master mean by sending me into this frightful forest, and saying he would follow? and then flew away out of my sight like lightning! a man that follows a young fellow in the pursuit of his mistress, might as safely ride after the devil upon a broomstick.—I have seen two or three horrid, ill looking fellows at a distance!—and heard cries of distress! [*looking about frighted.*] Have mercy on us!—ay—it is even so.—This is the place I have often heard of at Milan—They say this forest is inhabited by outlaws—cruel villains that eat men up alive! —What will become of me and my poor fellow traveller? [*cries*] They will roast poor Crab, and eat him for a tit bit! See—the harden'd wretch—he discovers no fears!—but he has more prudence than I have —and perhaps more courage too—however, I'll imitate his prudence— and appear valiant at least. [*Launce sings.*]

> And when that he lost both his legs,
> He fought upon his stumps.

I'm afraid that's more than I could do—or my friend Crab either, [*starting*] have mercy on us! I thought it was a gun levell'd at us—and 'tis only the wither'd branch of an old tree! Ay—these are the dangers my poor mother (with tears in her eyes) said her dear, sweet, boy would be expos'd to.

Enter three Outlaws, *who present their guns at* Launce.

4 Out. Stand there!

Launce. [*trembling.*] Ay, dear, good gentlemen come and hold me quickly, or I shan't be able to stand long.

4. Out. Why do you tremble, friend?

Launce. Ay, sir, it is a disease I am troubled with—it will end with the falling-sickness—but I hope it won't cost me my life.

4. Out. That's as you behave—you must go before our captain, and be search'd and examin'd—bring him along.

Launce. Pray, good gentlemen—however you treat me,—pray use my poor Crab with a little humanity.

4. Out. What, does the rascal insult us?—drag him along.   [*Exeunt.*

[Act V, Scene iii]

Enter three Outlaws, *bringing in* Silvia.

1. Out. Come, come, madam, be patient; we must bring you to our captain.

Sil. A thousand more mischances than this one, have learned me how to brook this patiently. Consider my sex and breeding—you shall have noble ransom!

2. Out. Come, bring her away.

1. Out. Where's the gentleman that was with her?

2. Out. Being nimble footed, he hath outrun us;
But Moyses and Valerius follow him,
The thicket is beset, he cannot 'scape—
Conduct the lady.—We'll follow him that fled—

Two of them run off, and leave the first Outlaw *with* Silvia.

1. Out. Come, I must bring you to our captain's cave,
Fear not—he bears an honourable mind.

Sil. O Valentine! this I endure for thee!
                    [*The* Outlaw *is leading* Silvia *off.*

Protheus *rushes on, follow'd by* Julia, *their swords drawn.*

Pro. Villain! unhand the lady, or thou dy'st
                    [*The* Outlaw *runs off.*]

Madam—this service I have done for you
(Though you respect not ought your servant doth)
To hazard life, and rescue you from those
That would have forc'd your life and honour from you—
Vouchsafe me for my meed but one kind look;

A smaller boon than this I cannot beg,
And less than this, I'm sure you cannot give.

    Sil. O miserable! unhappy that I am!

[*Here the* Outlaw *that was driven off returns with* Valentine.]

    Pro. Unhappy were you, madam, ere I came;
But by my coming I have made you happy.

    Val. [*Aside.*] Silvia! love lend me patience to forbear awhile!

    Sil. By thy approach, thou mak'st me most unhappy—
I'd rather be the hungry lion's prey,
Than have false, perjur'd Protheus rescue me!
Oh! heav'n be judge, how I love Valentine!
Whose life's as tender to me as my soul!
And full as much, for more there cannot be,
Do I detest false, perjur'd Protheus!
Therefore begone, solicit me no more.

    Pro. What dangerous action, stood it next to death,
Would I not undergo for one calm look?
Oh! 'tis the curse in love, and still approv'd,
When women cannot love, where they're belov'd!

    Sil. When Protheus cannot love where he's belov'd!
Read over Julia's heart, thy first, best, love!
For whose dear sake thou then didst rend thy faith
Into a thousand oaths! and all those oaths
Descended into perjury! false man!
Thou counterfeit to thy true friend, Valentine!

    Pro. In love who respects friends?

    Sil. All men but Protheus.

    Pro. Nay, if the gentle spirit of moving words
Can no way change you to a milder form,
I'll move you like a soldier, at arms end,
And force you.   [*He seizes her.*]

    Sil. O Heavens!

    Val. [*comes forward*] Ruffian! let go that rude, uncivil touch!
Thou friend of an ill fashion! Seize him.

    Pro. [*starting.*] Valentine!

[*Protheus retires to the side of the scene, guarded by the* Outlaws *and attended
by* Julia.]

    Val. My dearest Silvia,   [*runs and catches her in his arms.*]
Kind heav'n has heard my fervent prayer!

And brought my faithful Silvia to my arms!
There is no rhetorick can express my joy!

   Sil. It is delusion all! alas! we dream!
And must awake to wretchedness again!
O Valentine! we are beset with dangers!

   Val. Dismiss those fears, my love;—here, I command!
No power on earth shall ever part us more. [*Turning to* Proth.]
Thou common friend! that's without faith or love!
For such a friend is now! thou treach'rous man!
Thou hast beguil'd my hopes; nought but mine eye
Could have persuaded me: now, I dare not say
I have one friend alive! thou would'st disprove me.
Who should be trusted now, when the right hand
Is perjur'd to the bosom? Protheus,
I'm sorry I must never trust thee more,
But count the world a stranger for thy sake.
The private wound is deepest: O time accurst!
When, among foes, a friend shou'd be the worst!
Prepare for death.

   Pro. My shame and guilt confound me—
If to repent—if hearty sorrow
Be a sufficient ransom for offence,
I tender't here: I do as freely suffer,
As e'er I did commit—I merit death.

   Jul. Ah me, unhappy—   [*swoons.*]
   Silvia. Look to the youth.

   Val. Why boy! how now? what's the matter? look up—speak.

   Julia. [*on the ground.*] O good sir, my master charg'd me to deliver a ring to madam Silvia, which out of my neglect, was never done.

   Pro. Where is that ring, boy?

   Julia. Here 'tis.   [*gives the ring.*]

   Pro. How? let me see!
This is the ring I gave to Julia!

   Julia. Oh, cry you mercy, sir, I have mistook;
This is the ring you sent to Silvia.

   Pro. How cam'st thou by this ring? at my depart I gave this unto Julia!

   Julia. And Julia herself did give it me,
And Julia herself hath brought it hither.   [*rising from the ground.*]

   Pro. How! Julia!

Julia. Behold her that gave aim to all thy oaths;
And entertain'd them deeply in her heart:
How oft hast thou with perjury cleft the root?
—Oh, Protheus, let this habit make thee blush!
Be thou asham'd, that I have took upon me
Such an immodest rayment! If shame live
In a disguised love—
It is the lesser blot modesty finds,
Women to change their shapes, than men their minds.

    Pro. Than men their minds? 'tis true: oh heav'n! were man
But constant, he were perfect; that one error
Fills him with faults; makes him run through all sins:
Inconstancy falls off ere it begins.
What is in Silvia's face, but I may spy
More fresh in Julia's with a constant eye?

    Sil. Come, come, a hand from either—

[*She joins the hands of* Protheus *and* Julia; *and then takes the hand of* Valentine *to give to* Protheus.]

Let me be blest to make this happy close:
Nor must such friends as you be longer foes.

    Pro. If the poor penitent can be forgiven?

    Val. Forgiven, say'st thou? Ay—thus I am paid   [*embracing him.*]
And once again I do receive thee honest:
Who by repentance is not satisfy'd,
Is not of heav'n, nor earth; for these are pleas'd:
By penitence th' Eternal's wrath's appeas'd!
Thy Valentine, and Julia, both are thine.

    Pro. Bear witness, heav'n! I have my wish for ever.

    Jul. And I mine.   [*A noise is heard without, 'A prize! a prize!'*]

Enter Outlaws *with the* Duke *and* Thurio.

    Val. Forbear, forbear—It is my lord the duke.
Your grace is welcome to a man disgrac'd,
The banish'd Valentine!

    Duke. Sir Valentine!

    Thurio. Yonder is Silvia! and Silvia is mine.   [*Advancing.*]

    Val. [*draws.*] Thurio, give back; or else embrace thy death!
Come not within the measure of my wrath.
Do not name Silvia thine! if once again,
Milan shall not behold thee! here she stands;

Take but possession of her with a touch!
I dare thee but to breathe upon my love—
   Thu. Not I! sir Valentine, I care not for her—
I hold him but a fool that will endanger
His body for a girl that loves him not,
I claim her not; and therefore she is thine.
   Duke. O thou poor, thou base, degenerate lord!
I see my error now—and not too late, thank heav'n.
—Now by the honour of my ancestry.
I do applaud thy spirit, Valentine!
And think thee worthy of an empress' love!
Know then, I here forget all former griefs;
Cancel all grudge, repeal thee home again,
Plead a new state in thy unrivall'd merit,
To which I thus subscribe: sir Valentine,
Thou art a gentleman, and well deriv'd;
Take thou thy Silvia, for thou hast deserv'd her.
                             [presenting Silvia *to* Valentine.]
   Val. I thank your grace; the gift hath made me happy.

Enter Speed, *with a disguise on his arm.*
   Speed. Well—since his grace hath made my good master happy, I beg I may have leave to make him and this good company merry; I only pray you to conceal your faces a little, and I'll introduce two of the most comical prisoners that ever were yet taken in this forest—
                                 [He claps on his disguise.]
Here my brethren—Bring them along—

[The Outlaws *drag in* Launce, *and his dog* Crab, Launce *crying.]*
   Speed. Why, you crying, whoreson knave, what's the matter with you? Are you afraid of dying?
   Launce. Yes, dear sir—because the poor family of the Launces we left behind us in Verona, will break their hearts when they hear of our untimely end—poor Crab and I—ay—this comes of travelling into foreign parts for improvement.
   1. Out. Come, come, you whining rascal, no more complaining, prepare to die like a man.
   Speed. Why, your companion, Crab, here, behaves better than you—he don't take on so—he don't shed one tear.
   Launce. No—no—he has no bowels—he is hard-hearted—I knew that before—He won't shed one tear if you were to execute me (his best

friend) before his face—when I should drown myself in tears, if you were to put him to the least torture—but we are not all made alike—and yet, we are sometimes doom'd to suffer alike—

Speed. Come, let us be contented with one of their lives—let them draw lots which shall suffer.

1. Out. Agreed.

Speed. Come—draw—the longest straw lives.

Launce. Ah, dear sir,—I cannot die—nor can I live, if you kill my poor Crab.

    [*The company burst into a laughter;* Launce *seems amaz'd.*]

Speed. [*uncovers.*] Why, Launce! why, the fright you are in about dying takes away your eye-sight! why, you can't see your best friends! Permit me, my dear Launce, to welcome you to the forest.

           [*Takes his hand.*]

Launce. What do I see? I shall lose my breath! I shall now certainly die with joy! what! my master? Sir Valentine, the duke, and the whole court!—I am disgrac'd! I am undone. Who the devil would have thought of such a masquerade trick as this?   [*All come forward.*]

Val. 'Tis well—all here are friends—my noble lord,
I now beseech you, for your daughter's sake,
To grant one boon that I shall ask of you.

Duke. I grant it for thine own, whate'er it be.

Val. These banish'd men that I have kept withal,
Are men endu'd with worthy qualities:
Forgive them what they have committed here,
And let them be recall'd from their exile.
They are reform'd, civil, full of good,
And fit for many useful employments—

Duke. Thou hast prevail'd: I pardon them and thee;
Dispose of them, as thou know'st their deserts.
Come—let us go—we will include all jars
With triumphs, mirth, and rare solemnity.

Val. And as we walk along, I dare be bold,
With our discourse, to make your grace to smile.
What think you of this page, my worthy lord?

Duke. I think the boy hath grace in him;—he blushes.

Val. I warrant you, my lord, more grace than boy.

Duke. What mean you by that saying?

Val. Please you, I'll tell you as you pass along,
That you will wonder what hath fortun'd.

Come, Protheus, 'tis your penance but to hear
The story of your loves discover'd:
That done, our day of marriage shall be yours,
One feast, one house, one mutual happiness,
   Pro. A convert to this truth *I* stand confess'd,
That lovers must be faithful, to be bless'd.

                                        [*Exeunt omnes.*

197. K.L., 'Shakespeare and Milton Compared'

1763

From the *British Magazine*, IV (July 1763), pp. 333–6.

See the headnote to No. 182 above, with its similar method, and similar interests in the ghost-scene in *Hamlet* and in Shakespeare's arousal of 'terror'.

I have always considered it as a very pleasing task to compare the different talents of celebrated writers, at the head of which Shakespeare and Milton may be justly placed: the former excelled in rising terror, the latter in grand and sublime images. The second act of *Macbeth*, where the king is murdered, and indeed the whole play, as well as great part of many others, cannot be read without our feeling all the force of the passions, and giving us the strongest emotions. Milton no where so strongly excites this passion; even the fall of the infernal spirits and his description of hell itself, though painted in the most masterly manner, cannot raise such powerful emotions. But this may in a great measure proceed from two causes: first, we are not so capable of feeling the distresses of the apostate spirits as we are of the abandoned part of our own species; and secondly, we are more affected when the terror is felt by the person who rises it, as in Shakespeare, than when excited by a third person, as is generally the case of Milton. And indeed, he who is supposed to feel what he suffers may make use of expressions that could not be used by a third person with propriety. This will more plainly appear from a comparison between that justly admired passage where Milton describes the situation of the fallen angels,[1] and the account of purgatory given by the ghost in *Hamlet*.

> Nine times the space that measures day and night
> To mortal man, he with his horrid crew
> Lay vanquish'd, rolling in the fiery gulph
> Confounded, tho' immortal—
> Round he throws his baleful eyes,
> That witness'd huge affliction and dismay,
> Mix'd with obdurate pride and stedfast hate.
> At once as far as angels ken, he views
> The dismal situation waste and wild;
> A dungeon horrible, on all sides round
> As one great furnace flam'd; yet from those flames
> No light, but rather darkness visible,
> Serv'd only to discover sights of woe,
> Regions of sorrow, doleful shades, where peace
> And rest can never dwell, hope never comes,
> That comes to all; but torture without end
> Still urges, and a fiery deluge, fed
> With ever burning sulphur unconsum'd:
> O! how unlike the place from whence they fell!

This description cannot be sufficiently admired; but Shakespeare, instead of describing purgatory, raises even greater terror by mentioning what would be the effects of his revealing what he is obliged to conceal.

> But that I am forbid
> To tell the secrets of my prison-house,
> I could a tale unfold, whose lightest word
> Would harrow up thy soul, freeze thy young blood,
> Make thy two eyes like stars start from their spheres,
> Thy knotty and combin'd locks to part,

[1] *Paradise Lost*, 1.50ff.

And each particular hair to stand on end,
Like quills upon the fretful porcupine:
But this eternal blazon must not be
To ears of flesh and blood; list, list, Oh list!
If thou did'st ever thy dear father love.   [1.5.13ff.]

Nothing can be imagined more proper to fill the mind with terror
than this speech; nothing could more fully express the anguish of the
speaker, nor the horrors of what he calls his Prison-house. But such
language would be altogether improper in Milton, though it were
applied to hell, since he has not a character that could utter it with
propriety. Milton's description is exactly suited to an epic poem, which
ought to be grand and wonderful, and Shakespeare's to a tragedy
designed to excite terror. The poet, as a Protestant, was, however,
guilty of an absurdity in making a ghost talk of purgatory. It is evident
that while he was attentive to the idea of making his living characters
of the religion of the country in which they were placed he did not
consider that an unembodied spirit was not bound by the same law, or
that when the soul leaves the body the distinctions of religion vanish,
truth strikes upon the mind and, in a case like this, error must be
banished by the force of experience. Milton has no fault of this kind,
except it be his unnecessarily introducing heathen fables, which he
sometimes mentions as facts.

Shakespeare had a greater power over the human passions than was
ever possessed by any other man. He could excite rage and pity, could
melt into tears and raise laughter at his pleasure. The most opposite
passions were equally under his controul, and 'his characters, says Mr
Pope, are so much nature, that 'tis a sort of injury to call them by so
distant a name as copies of her. Every single character in Shakespeare is
as much an individual as those in life itself.'[1] Milton's genius here seems
to fall short of Shakespeare's, and to be confined within narrower
limits. At least he has not left us such an infinite variety of different
tempers and humours; nor does he seem to have been capable, like
him, of entering into the ridiculous and idle sensations of human nature.
He has, however, sufficiently distinguished the character of every being
he has represented. Every angel and every devil has something peculiar
to itself and by which they may be distinguished. His characters, tho'
not the same are, in their own nature, as different as those of Shakespeare, as just in themselves, and as well preserved.

[1] See Vol. 2, p. 404.

Shakespeare's muse was not always confined within the bounds of decency; he sometimes sinks into the obscene. Milton expresses himself on the nicest circumstances with the extremest delicacy, and never offers the least offence (as he expresses it in his *Comus*) to the sun-clad power of chastity.

Shakespeare has been censured for the low puns with which he has debased most of his plays; but it must be remembered that he not only copied nature but the folly and ridicule of every character. Milton has sometimes fallen into the same fault, though this is a licence he has seldom taken even in his lightest pieces. We have, however, a remarkable instance of his playing upon words in *Paradise Lost*, where the evil spirits, elated with the success of their new invented artillery, ridicule the confusion it causes in the heavenly host by the following strings of puns uttered by Belial.

> Leader, the terms we sent were terms of *weight*,
> Of *hard contents*, and full of force urg'd home,
> Such as we might perceive amus'd them all,
> And *stumbled* many; who receives them right,
> Had need, from head to foot, well *understand*;
> Not *understood*, this gift they have besides,
> They show us when our foes *walk not* . . . upright. (6.621ff.)

This passage Mr Addison very justly thinks the most exceptionable in the whole book: and indeed, though put in the mouth of an evil spirit whose mirth Milton would render as ridiculous as it was foolish, it is much too low for the dignity of an epic poem. But some allowance ought to be made on account of the prevailing taste of the age in which Shakespeare and Milton lived, when the gravest divines had such an extreme fondness for these low conceits that their sermons consisted of little else. A right reverend prelate, preaching against the views of the age, says '*All houses* are *ale-houses.*—The holy state of *matrimony* is become a *matter of money.*—Some men's *paradise* is a *pair of dice*; was it so in the days of *No-ah?*—*ah-no.*'

It would take up too much room to examine the noble sentiments of those poets and the strength and variety of language in which they frequently clothe their ideas, how Shakespeare wins upon us by surprize and the boldness of his images, and Milton by the dignity of his thoughts.

Shakespeare's admirable incursions into the ideal world, the land of fiction, are justly admired. His madmen, his monsters, his fairies, his witches, and his magic have something so astonishing, so agreeable, and at the same time so extravagant that they can never be read or heard without amazement at the fruitfulness of an invention that was confined within no bounds. Here he has been generally thought to stand alone, and yet perhaps there is nothing in which Milton resembles him more. His characters, his thoughts, and language in his masque of *Comus*, though different from those of Shakespeare, have the same spirit and partake of the same sportive mildness of fancy.

Mr Addison, after enumerating the principal faults of Milton's *Paradise Lost*, very genteely adds: 'I have seen in the works of a modern philosopher a map of the spots in the sun; my paper on the faults and blemishes in Milton's *Paradise Lost* may be considered as a piece of the same nature.'[1] The like may also be said of Shakespeare, whose blemishes serve as foils to set off the striking beauties that every where start forth to our views.

All nature was too small a boundary for the genius of a Shakespeare. 'Our language', says the above admired critic, 'sinks under the genius of a Milton, and was unequal to that greatness of soul which furnished him with such glorious conceptions.'[2] Shakespeare sinks lower than Milton, but rises in sudden flashes; and before we are aware he is all flames, the thunder roars, and his thoughts have all the fire and force of lightening. Milton is also uneven, though in a less degree. But his fire resembles the milder glory of the sun-beams, which gild and enliven all nature, and what he wants of this piercing heat is made up by the more constant glow of his poetic fire, by a superior dignity, propriety, and harmony.

July 8,
1763.

Your's, &c.
K. L.

[1] *Spectator*, 303.
[2] *Spectator*, 297.

198. Unsigned essay, 'An Account of the Novel and Play of *Romeo and Juliet*'

1764

From the *Universal Museum*, III (1764), pp. 509–10.

Account of the Novel and Play of *Romeo and Juliet*.

The novel on which this play is formed was originally written in Italian by Bandello. This was translated, or rather paraphrased into French, and the French again into English, but the author's sense is frequently mistaken and many circumstances are injudiciously altered, added, and omitted. If Shakespeare had understood Italian it is probable that he would not have copied the translation; and that he did copy the translation appears from his having adopted all the alterations which his judgment could not but condemn upon a comparison with the original, and which therefore he would certainly have rejected.

In Bandello, when Romeo is informed of Juliet's death, astonishment and grief for some moments deprive him of speech; recovering a little, he breaks into complaints and self-reproaches; then, wild with despair, he flies to his sword and endeavours to kill himself. But, being prevented by his servant, he sinks into an excess of silent sorrow and, while he weeps, calmly deliberates on the means he should use to die in the monument with Juliet.

The translator makes Romeo upon receiving the news resolve immediately to poison himself, dissemble his affliction, and walk about the streets upon pretence of amusement but indeed to procure poison, which at length he buys of an apothecary.

The original makes no mention of the apothecary but supposes Romeo to have had poisonous drugs long in his possession, the gift of a Spoleto mountebank. Shakespeare, on the contrary, makes him in the midst of his affliction for the death of his wife, and while the horrible design of killing himself was forming in his mind, give a ludicrous detail of the miserable furniture of a poor apothecary's shop; a description which, however beautiful, is here ill-timed and totally inconsistent with the condition and circumstance of the speaker.

In the play Romeo dies before Juliet awakes. The Fryar, fearing to be discovered by the watch, presses her to leave the monument; she refuses, he runs away, and she stabs herself with Romeo's dagger.

In Bandello, while the dying husband is holding, as he supposes, the lifeless body of his wife in his arms and shedding the last tears for her death, she awakes, opens her eyes, gazes on him and entreats him to carry her out of the monument.

Romeo is for some moments lost in a transport of surprize and joy but, reflecting that he is poisoned and must shortly die and leave her, his agonies return with double force, and the mutual distress of the lovers as they discover their situation is in the highest degree tender and affecting.

Just as Romeo is expiring the Fryar enters the monument. Juliet, hearing his voice, passionately upbraids him with not sending to Romeo. He justifies himself by an account of the delay of his messenger, descends into the monument, and seeing Romeo stretched almost lifeless on the earth breaks into an exclamation of surprize and grief. Romeo then opening his eyes for the last time, recommends Juliet to his care and, imploring pardon of heaven for his offence, expires.

The Fryar tenderly expostulates with Juliet after Romeo's death, but she continues in a gloomy silence and fixed despair, and at length dies by the violence of her stifled grief.

These incidents are truly tragical, and their beauty is so striking, that the best apology for Shakespeare's having omitted them is that he never saw them. He has supplied no incident by his invention but the death of Paris by Romeo, which seems to be of no use but to divert our compassion from the two principal persons whose deaths were to make up the catastrophe of the play.

Mr Pope, in his preface to his edition of Shakespeare tells us 'that Shakespeare's characters are Nature herself, and that it is a sort of injury to call them by so distant a name as copies of her.'[1] It is, however, certain that all the characters in *Romeo*, except that of Mercutio, are exact copies of those in the novelist, and since he copied them from the translator and not the original, in this instance Mr Pope's observation of other authors may be applied to Shakespeare that 'his picture, like a mock rainbow, is but a reflexion of a reflexion'.[2]

[1] See Vol. 2, p. 404.
[2] *Ibid.*

199. Edward Watkinson on Shakespeare

1764-5

From *An Enquiry into the Nature and Tendency of Criticism, with regard to the Progress of Literature. Part V. Including a concise View of the Progress of the Arts and Sciences from 1485 to 1603*; in the *Critical Review* xviii (1764) and xix (1765).

Edward Watkinson, M.D., was rector of Little Chart in Kent (see the *Critical Review* vii, 470, of May 1759, where the editors thank him for his advice; in 1764, however, his essays in the journal are sent from Ackworth, near Ferrybridge, Yorks). His *Enquiry*, which appeared in several instalments over a number of years, reveals the vaguest notion of literary history.

[During the Reformation] the contests ran high between the papists and the Lutherans, and the *rage* of controversy took place of calm reasoning, candid enquiry, and cool disquisitions. But though the virulence of these disputants retarded for a time the progress of the arts, sciences, and belles-lettres yet *some* extraordinary geniuses adorned the 16th century, whose enlightened understanding surmounted all obstacles. Amongst these *Shakespeare* merits attention in the first place. His amazing talents must excite the admiration of every person endued with taste and sensibility. *He* entered as deeply into the feelings of the human heart as can possibly be conceived. 'Nullius tantum est *flumen* ingenii—tantavis —tantaque copia.'[1] He spoke the language of nature, he knew the several workings of the passions, and tho' his unrestrained genius betrayed him into slight inaccuracies, yet so many animated and striking beauties are interspersed that candour is naturally prompted to cast a veil over the errors of such an extraordinary genius, and whilst we admire the strength of his imagination, the elegance of his imagery, the height of his colourings, the admirable pathos of his natural descriptions,

[1] Cicero, *Pro Marcello* 4.ii: 'There is no genius so overflowing, no power of tongue or pen so lofty or so exuberant. . . .'

540

and the force of his talents we are apt to forget his blemishes whilst we are struck with his beauties. His peculiar excellence is certainly in the pathetic; he *commands* all the emotions of the soul, excites all the mental faculties, and, in the emphatical expression of the prince of poets, 'He bids *alternate* passions *fall* and *rise*.' (Pope.) But what is still more an object of admiration in this self-taught genius is that the force and fire of his imagination is regulated and tempered with a *solid judgment* (faculties that seldom unite in one and the same person!). This is remarkably conspicuous from the exact *propriety* with which he sustains his characters (undoubtedly a great perfection in dramatic composition) and at the close of each scene (to wind up the whole) he brings into a full point of view a series of incidents, and by thus freeing the mind from *recollection* he gives full force to the influence of the passions and leaves the reader at liberty to attend to the catastrophe. To exemplify only in that justly admired tragedy *Othello*, with what energy doth he awake the passions, excite every tender emotion, and kindle resentment in every breast. Even jealousy (a passion that requires peculiar descriptive skill) is wrought up with the most admirable address, with all the force of nature, beauty of description, and power of imagination! (xviii, 8–9)

★   ★   ★

Shakespeare (touched on in my last) was one of those self-taught genius's which nature rarely produces, or at most but once in an age. His poetry was *inspiration* indeed, and he was, as Pope observes, truly an *original*. He seems to have discerned mankind by intuition—to have seen through human nature at one glance—*master* of every passion. I cannot convey a *juster* idea of his amazing genius than is contained in the couplet of a modern poet.

> *Nature* list'ning stood, whilst Shakespeare play'd,
> And wonder'd at the work herself had made.   CHURCHILL.

Shakespeare is compared by a certain acute critic to the *English Homer*[1] —both extraordinary genius's, but each marked by those peculiar characteristics which distinguish productions of nature. As our language sunk under Milton (unequal to convey a just idea of the force and fire of his genius, the sublimity of his flights, and the strength of his imagination) so nature was too confined a theatre for the fertile invention and

[1] See above, No. 154a: the critic was Smollett. For the formula 'our *British Homer*' see Dodd, Vol. 3, p. 475.

luxuriant fancy of Shakespeare. In a word, whilst we view the *latter* every passion is awakened; and whilst we admire the *former* we are 'caught up into the third heavens'. (xix. 5)

200. Richard Hurd, Shakespeare and Gothic romance

1765

From *Letters on Chivalry and Romance* (first edition 1762).

These passages (from Letters VI and VII) were added in the revised version, *Moral and Political Dialogues; with Letters on Chivalry and Romance*, 3 vols (1765).

[The mythology of the writers of Romance] was not so properly a single system as the aggregate

—of all that nature breeds
Perverse; all monstrous, all prodigious things,
Which fables yet had feign'd or fear conceiv'd.

For to the frightful forms of antient necromancy (which easily travelled down to us when the fairer offspring of pagan invention lost its way, or was swallowed up in the general darkness of the barbarous ages) were now joined the hideous phantasms which had terrified the Northern nations; and to complete the horrid group, with these were incorporated the still more tremendous spectres of Christian superstition.

In this state of things, as I said, the Romancers went to work; and with these multiplied images of terror on their minds, you will conclude, without being at the pains to form particular comparisons, that they must manage ill indeed not to surpass in this walk of magical incantation the original classic fablers.

But if you require a comparison I can tell you where it is to be made with much ease and to great advantage: I mean, in SHAKESPEARE's *Macbeth*, where you will find (as his best critic[1] observes) 'the *Danish* or *Northern*, intermixed with the *Greek* or *Roman* enchantments; and all these worked up together with a sufficient quantity of our own country superstitions. So that SHAKESPEARE's *Witch-Scenes* (as the same writer adds) are like the *charm* they prepare in one of them. where the ingredients are gathered from every thing shocking in the *natural* world; as here, from every thing absurd in the *moral*.'

Or if you suspect this instance as deriving somewhat of its force and plausibility from the *magic* hand of this critic, you may turn to another in a great poet of that time, who has been at the pains to make the comparison himself and whose word, as he gives it in honest prose, may surely be taken.

In a work of B. JONSON which he calls THE MASQUE OF QUEENS there are some Witch-scenes written with singular care and in emulation, as it may seem, of SHAKESPEARE's; but certainly with the view (for so he tells us himself) *of reconciling the practice of antiquity to the neoteric, and making it familiar with our popular witchcraft.* (iii, 254–7) Thus much, then, may serve for a cast of SHAKESPEARE's and JONSON's magic: abundantly sufficient, I must think, to convince you of the superiority of the *Gothic* charms and incantations, to the classic. (iii, 258–9)

*   *   *

[On the Gothic influence in Spenser and Milton]

The conduct then of these two poets may incline us to think with more respect than is commonly done of the *Gothic manners*, I mean as adapted to the uses of the greater poetry.

I shall add nothing to what I before observed of SHAKESPEARE because the sublimity (the divinity, let it be, if nothing else will serve) of his genius kept no certain route, but rambled at hazard into all the regions of human life and manners. So that we can hardly say what he preferred or what he rejected, on full deliberation. Yet one thing is clear, that even he is greater when he uses *Gothic* manners and machinery than when he employs classical: which brings us again to the same point, that the former have by their nature and genius the advantage of the latter in producing the *sublime*. (iii, 265–6)

1 William Warburton, in his edition of Shakespeare Vol. VI, p. 338.

201. Thomas Percy, Shakespeare and the History Play

1765

From *Reliques of English Poetry*, 3 vols (1765).

Thomas Percy (1729–1811), was an antiquarian and scholar who collected, translated (and sometimes 'improved') 'ancient poetry', whether English, Runic (from the Icelandic), or 'Moorish' (Spanish). He also edited Surrey's poetry in 1763, and wrote theological works; in 1782 he became Bishop of Dromore. His *Reliques*, (an edition of a seventeenth-century manuscript collection of older poems of various dates, which he had found 'lying dirty on the floor in a bureau in the parlour' of a friend's house, 'being used by the maids to light the fire') did much to popularise the early English ballad.

As for the old Mysteries, which ceased to be acted after the Reformation, they seem to have given rise to a third species of stage exhibition which, though now confounded with Tragedy or Comedy, were by our first dramatic writers considered as quite distinct from them both. These were Historical Plays or HISTORIES, a species of dramatic writing which resembled the old Mysteries in representing a series of historical events simply in the order of time in which they happened, without any regard to the three great unities. Those pieces seem to differ from Tragedy just as much as Historical poems do from Epic: as the *Pharsalia* does from the *Æneid*. What might contribute to make dramatic poetry take this turn was that soon after the Mysteries ceased to be exhibited there was published a large collection of poetical narratives called *The Mirrour for Magistrates**, wherein a great number of the most eminent characters in English history are drawn relating their own misfortunes. This book was popular and of a dramatic cast, and

* The first part of which was printed in 1559.

therefore, as an elegant writer* has well observed, might have its influence in producing Historic Plays. These narratives probably furnished the subjects, and the ancient Mysteries suggested the plan.

That our old writers considered Historical Plays as somewhat distinct from Tragedy and Comedy appears from numberless passages of their works. 'Of late days,' says Stow, 'instead of those stage-plays† have been used Comedies, Tragedies, Enterludes, and HISTORIES both true and fained.' *Survey of London‡.*—Beaumont and Fletcher, in the prologue to *The Captain,* say

This is nor Comedy, nor Tragedy,
Nor HISTORY.

Polonius in *Hamlet* commends the actors as the best in the world 'either for Tragedie, Comedie, HISTORIE, Pastorall,' &c. And Shakespeare's friends Heminge and Condell, in the first folio edit. of his plays in 1623, have not only intitled their book 'Mr. William Shakespeare's Comedies, HISTORIES, and Tragedies', but in their Table of Contents have arranged them under those three several heads: placing in the class of HISTORIES *K. John; Richard II; Henry IV,* 2 pts; *Henry V; Henry VI,* 3 pts; *Richard III,* and *Henry VIII.*

This distinction deserves the attention of the critics. For if it be the first canon of sound criticism to examine any work by those rules the author prescribed for his observance, then we ought not to try Shakespeare's HISTORIES by the general laws of Tragedy or Comedy. Whether the rule itself be vicious or not is another inquiry, but certainly we ought to examine a work only by those principles according to which it was composed. This would save a deal of impertinent criticism. (I, 126–7)

* *Catalogue of Royal and Noble authors* [by Horace Walpole, 1758], Vol. 1, p. 166, 7.
† *The Creation of the world,* acted at Skinners-well in 1409.
‡ See *Mr. Warton's Observations* [on the Faerie Queene, 1754, 1762], Vol. 2, p. 109.

202. Horace Walpole on Shakespeare and French rules

1765

From *The Castle of Otranto, A Gothic Story. The Second Edition* (1765).

Horace Walpole (1717–97), 4th Earl of Orford, son of Sir Robert Walpole, was educated at Eton and King's College, Cambridge, where he continued his schooltime friendship with Thomas Gray, whom he took with him on the Grand Tour to France and Italy from 1739 to 1741. In 1749 he bought Strawberry Hill, Twickenham, and remodelled it in the Gothic style; there, in 1757, he set up a private printing press from which he published some of his own works. *The Castle of Otranto* (published 24 December 1764) was the first of the 'Gothic' novels, and was remarkably successful. Walpole is chiefly celebrated for his enormous correspondence, which includes many (mostly slight) references to Shakespeare.

Preface.

The favourable manner in which this little piece has been received by the public calls upon the author to explain the grounds on which he composed it. But before he opens those motives it is fit that he should ask pardon of his readers for having offered his work to them under the borrowed personage of a translator. As diffidence of his own abilities and the novelty of the attempt were his sole inducements to assume that disguise, he flatters himself he shall appear excuseable. He resigned his performance to the impartial judgment of the public, determined to let it perish in obscurity, if disapproved, nor meaning to avow such a trifle unless better judges should pronounce that he might own it without a blush.

It was an attempt to blend the two kinds of Romance, the ancient and the modern. In the former all was imagination and improbability: in the latter nature is always intended to be, and sometimes has been, copied with success. Invention has not been wanting, but the great resources of fancy have been dammed up by a strict adherence to common life. But if in the latter species Nature has cramped imagination, she did but take her revenge, having been totally excluded from old Romances. The actions, sentiments, conversations, of the heroes and heroines of ancient days were as unnatural as the machines employed to put them in motion.

The author of the following pages thought it possible to reconcile the two kinds. Desirous of leaving the powers of fancy at liberty to expatiate through the boundless realms of invention, and thence of creating more interesting situations, he wished to conduct the mortal agents in his drama according to the rules of probability: in short, to make them think, speak and act as it might be supposed mere men and women would do in extraordinary positions. He had observed that in all inspired writings the personages under the dispensation of miracles and witnesses to the most stupendous phenomena never lose sight of their human character: whereas in the productions of romantic story an improbable event never fails to be attended by an absurd dialogue. The actors seem to lose their senses the moment the laws of Nature have lost their tone. As the public have applauded the attempt, the author must not say he was entirely unequal to the task he had undertaken: yet if the new route he has struck out shall have paved a road for men of brighter talents, he shall own with pleasure and modesty that he was sensible the plan was capable of receiving greater embellishments than his imagination or conduct of the passions could bestow on it.

With regard to the deportment of the domestics, on which I have touched in the former preface, I will beg leave to add a few words. The simplicity of their behaviour, almost tending to excite smiles, which at first seem not consonant to the serious cast of the work, appeared to me not only not improper but was marked designedly in that manner. My rule was Nature. However grave, important, or even melancholy the sensations of Princes and heroes may be, they do not stamp the same affections on their domestics: at least the latter do not, or should not be made to express their passions in the same dignified tone. In my humble opinion the contrast between the sublime of the one and the *naiveté* of the others sets the pathetic of the former in a stronger light. The very impatience which a reader feels, while delayed by the coarse pleasantries of vulgar actors from arriving at the knowledge of the important catastrophe he expects, perhaps heightens, certainly proves that he has been artfully interested in the depending event. But I had higher authority than my own opinion for this conduct. That great master of nature, *Shakespeare*, was the model I copied. Let me ask if his tragedies of *Hamlet* and *Julius Cæsar* would not lose a considerable share of their spirit and wonderful beauties if the humour of the grave-diggers, the fooleries of *Polonius*, and the clumsy jests of the *Roman* citizens were omitted, or vested in heroics? Is not the eloquence of *Antony*, the nobler and affectedly-unaffected oration of *Brutus*, artificially exalted by the rude bursts of nature from the mouths of their auditors? These touches remind one of the *Grecian* sculptor who, to convey the idea of a Colossus within the dimensions of a seal, inserted a little boy measuring his thumb.

No, says *Voltaire* in his edition of *Corneille*, this mixture of buffoonery and solemnity is intolerable. *Voltaire* is a genius, but not of *Shakespeare*'s magnitude. Without recurring to disputable authority I appeal from *Voltaire* to himself. I shall not avail myself of his former encomiums on our mighty poet, though the *French* critic has twice translated the same speech in *Hamlet*, some years ago in admiration, latterly in derision; and I am sorry to find that his judgment grows weaker when it ought to be farther matured. But I shall make use of his own words, delivered on the general topic of the theatre when he was neither thinking to recommend or decry *Shakespeare*'s practice, consequently at a moment when *Voltaire* was impartial. In the preface to his *Enfant Prodigue*, that exquisite piece of which I declare my admiration and which, should I live twenty years longer, I trust I shall never attempt to ridicule, he has these words, speaking of Comedy—but equally applicable to Tragedy if Tragedy is, as surely it ought to be, a picture of human life; nor can I conceive why occasional pleasantry ought more to be banished from the tragic scene than pathetic serious-ness from the comic—'On y voit un mélange de serieux et de plaisan-terie, de comique et de touchant; souvent même une seule avanture produit tous ces contrastes. Rien n'est si commun qu'une maison dans laquelle un père gronde, une fille occupée de sa passion pleure; le fils se moque des deux, et quelques parens prennent part differemment à la scene, &c. Nous n'inferons pas de là que toute Comédie doive avoir des scenes de bouffonerie et des scènes attendrissantes: il y a beaucoup de tres bonnes pieces où il ne regne que de la gayeté; d'autres toutes serieuses; d'autres melangées: d'autres où l'attendrissement va jusques aux larmes: il ne faut donner l'exclusion à aucun genre: et si l'on me demandoit quel genre est le meilleur, je repondrois,* *celui qui est le mieux traité.*'[1] Surely if a Comedy may be *toute serieuse* Tragedy may now and then, soberly, be indulged in a smile. Who shall proscribe it? Shall the critic who in self-defence declares that *no kind* ought to be excluded from Comedy give laws to *Shakespeare*? (v–xii)

*   *   *

I will not enter into a discussion of the *espece de simplicité* which the *Parterre* of *Paris* demands, nor of the shackles with which *the thirty thousand judges* have cramped their poetry, the chief merit of which, as I gather from repeated passages in *The New Commentary on* Corneille, consists in vaulting in spite of those fetters (a merit which, if true, would reduce poetry from the lofty effort of imagination to a puerile and most contemptible labour—*difficiles nugæ*[2] with a witness!). I cannot however help mentioning a couplet which, to my *English* ears, always sounded as the flattest and most trifling instance of circumstantial propriety, but which *Voltaire*, who has dealt so severely with nine parts in ten of *Corneille*'s works, has singled out to defend in *Racine*:

> *De son appartement cette porte est prochaine,*
> *Et cette autre conduit dans celui de la* Reine.
> In *English*.
> *To Cæsar's closet through this door you come,*
> *And t'other leads to the Queen's drawing-room.*

Unhappy *Shakespeare!* Hadst thou made *Rosencrantz* inform his compeer *Guildenstern* of the ichnography[3] of the palace of *Copenhagen*, instead of presenting us with a moral dialogue between the Prince of *Denmark* and the grave-digger, the illuminated pit of *Paris* would have been instructed *a second time* to adore thy talents.

The result of all I have said is to shelter my own daring under the canon of the brightest genius this country, at least, has produced. I

---

1 'We find there a mixture of seriousness and jesting, of the comic and the pathetic; often even a single incident produces all these contrasts. Nothing is more common than a house in which a father is scolding, a daughter—absorbed in her emotions—weeping; the son makes fun of both of them, some relatives take different sides in the scene, and so on. We do not infer from this that every comedy ought to have scenes of buffoonery and scenes of touching emotion: there are many excellent plays in which gaiety alone reigns; others completely serious; others of mixed mood; others where the feeling of pity is so strong that it produces tears: one cannot afford to exclude any genre. If someone were to ask me which genre is the best, I would reply, that which is best handled.'

2 Martial, *Epigrams*, 2.86.l. 9: 'difficult trifles.'

3 'Ichnographie: A ground plot' (Johnson, *Dictionary*); that is, the ground-plan of a building.

might have pleaded that having created a new species of romance I was at liberty to lay down what rules I thought fit for the conduct of it. But I should be more proud of having imitated, however faintly, weakly, and at a distance, so masterly a pattern than to enjoy the entire merit of invention, unless I could have marked my work with genius as well as with originality. Such as it is the Public have honoured it sufficiently, whatever rank their suffrages allot to it. (xiv–xvi)

203. Benjamin Heath on restoring Shakespeare's text

1765

From *A Revisal of Shakespeare's Text, Wherein The ALTERA-TIONS introduced into it by the more modern Editors and Critics, are particularly considered* (1765).

Benjamin Heath (1704–66) inherited £30,000 from his father, and spent the rest of his life collecting books and writing scholarly notes on classical literature, including textual criticism of Aeschylus, Sophocles, Euripides, Hesiod, Virgil, Catullus and Tibullus. His notes on the text of Beaumont and Fletcher are preserved in manuscript in the British Library.

[On *The Tempest*, 1.2.28ff.]

> *I have, with such provision in mine art,*
> *So safely order'd, that there's no soul lost,*
> *No, not so much perdition as an hair,*
> *Betid to any creature in the vessel.*

The second of these lines, in all the editions preceding that of Mr Rowe, stood thus:

So safely order'd, that there is no soul—

Mr Rowe, offended at the irregularity of the construction, altered it to the present reading in which he is followed by Mr Pope and Mr Warburton, but in my opinion without necessity. The construction is of that kind which the grammarians call the ἀνακόλουθον, and instances of it occur not rarely in the works of the best writers. In the present case the construction is broken off and left imperfect at the end of the second line, and it takes a new form in what follows; so that to compleat it the participle *lost* must be supplied from the word *perdition* in the third line. The import is exactly the same as if the poet had written 'I have so safely ordered, that there is no soul.—Why do I say soul? No, there is not so much perdition as an hair betid to any creature in the vessel.' The ancient reading corresponds with the impetuosity of the poet's genius, the present with the timid regularity of the critical corrector. Mr Theobald substitutes his own conjecture:

So safely order'd that there is no foyle;

interpreting the word *foyle* to signify damage, loss, detriment, in order to accommodate it to the context. But in truth this is a sense that it will by no means bear. Its true meaning is that of defeat or disappointment, a meaning utterly inconsistent with the scope of the poet, since it is certain the king and his attendants were foyled and disappointed in the purpose of their voyage, their intended return to Naples. (4–5)

*   *   *

[On Caliban's language]

When Lord Falkland, Lord C. J. Vaughan, and Mr Selden concurred in observing that Shakespeare had not only found out a new character in his Caliban but had also devised and adapted a new manner of language for that character,[1] I suppose they must be understood to mean that the poet had given him a language adapted to the brutality of his manners and the coarseness of his sentiments, and accordingly we commonly find him expressing himself in terms which betray his diabolical origin and the baseness of his slavish nature. Among people who speak the same tongue the language is extremely different, and in particular persons in great measure determined by the natural disposition, the degree of understanding, the education, the conversation they have been accustomed to, and other circumstances of a similar nature. I do

[1] See Rowe's preface, Vol. 2, p. 197.

not well understand Mr Warburton's explanation, that Shakespeare gave his language a certain grotesque air of the savage and antique which, he adds, it certainly has.[1] The epithet 'antique' must refer to the terms and expressions, and he fancies he hath discovered one antique word in this page, to wit, *wicked dew* [1.2.321], which perhaps may be so, though he doth not seem to have hit upon its true meaning in the place where it stands when he says it is used for *unwholsome*. This latter epithet immediately follows, applied to the fen from whence the dew was brushed, and the immediate repetition of the same idea is certainly not very elegant. I should rather think the poet, in giving this qualification to the dew, intended to express the wickedness of the purposes for which it was gathered, that is the pernicious and destructive use the witch designed to make of it. But be this as it may, it would perhaps be difficult to find another instance of antique expression in the whole part assigned to Caliban, whose language, in point of antiquity, seems to be just of the same date with that of his master Prospero, of whom indeed he learned it. As to the epithet savage, if that too be understood of the terms and expressions, independently of the sentiments, as we may presume is intended from its being coupled with that other we have just considered, I must own myself at a loss to comprehend what idea it is designed to convey, since I know of no savage terms or expressions in the part of Caliban, nor indeed where they are to be found in the whole English language. (9–10)

*　　*　　*

[On *The Tempest*, 1.2.355ff.]

> *when thou couldst not, savage,*
> *Shew thine own meaning, but wouldst gabble like*
> *A thing most brutish, I endow'd thy purposes*
> *With words that made them known.*

The ancient and authentick reading was

> *when thou* didst *not, savage,*
> Know *thy own meaning.*

The present reading is a mere conjecture of Mr Warburton's, and in order to introduce and recommend it he has endeavoured to cast a mist before the reader's eyes, which at first view indeed hath something of a philosophical appearance, but when examined to the bottom the learned dust is soon dissipated, and we presently discover that it was not raised

[1] See Vol. 3, p. 227.

from any ground which nature will acknowledge, but owes its origin solely to the critick's own cloudy imagination.

Though brute creatures sometimes express their wants, their passions, or, if you please, their purposes by certain sounds, yet who doth not know that in general they utter the sounds peculiar to their kind without any particular design or certain purpose whatsoever. They are no more than the natural customary expression of their actual feeling. At least this is the common received opinion, which is sufficient to justify the poet in adopting it. So in the case under consideration, when Prospero first met with Caliban this latter would gabble out certain uncouth noises like the jabbering of an ape, destitute of any determinate meaning; and though he had indeed purposes yet he had never adapted any of those noises to a particular expression of them, nor perhaps could signify them twice successively by the same precise sound. So that though he had purposes, and knew the purposes he had, yet it may very properly and truly be said that he did not know his own meaning, that is, the meaning of that gabble he was perpetually uttering without any certain design or determinate signification. (10–11)

*   *   *

[On *A Midsummer Night's Dream*, 1.1.6]

Long wintering on a young man's revenue.

Wintering on is a conjecture of Mr Warburton's.[1] The common reading was

Long withering out *a young man's revenue:*

an expression which he confidently assures us is not good English, though he hath not condescended to give us his reasons. Notwithstanding which unsupported assertion, it may however be Shakespeare's English, the energy of whose language not unfrequently soars, as we have already seen, beyond the comprehension of the verbal critick. I must own the metaphor appears to me extremely apposite to denote the lingering consumption and decay of an estate, the owner of which is impairing it by continual drains in consequence of his youthful prodigality, at the same time that the clearest part of its income is intercepted before it comes to his hands. (41)

*   *   *

1 See Vol. 3, p. 230.

[On *A Midsummer Night's Dream*, 1.1.168ff.]

Her. *My good Lysander,*
Lys. *I swear to thee by Cupid's strongest bow, &c.*

Mr. Warburton seems so little acquainted with the genuine undisguised workings of nature and the human passions that he is unable to recognize them when fairly exhibited to his view. This very passage affords the strongest proof of his inability in this respect, since in his attempt to correct it he hath, under the pretext of following nature, distorted and mangled the fine drawing our poet had given from her by putting the greatest part of Hermia's answer to the proposal of Lysander into the mouth of the latter. Let us consider his objections: 'Lysander does but just propose her running away from her father at midnight, and straight she is at her oaths that she will meet him at the place of rendezvous.' No doubt such a conduct is not to be justified according to the strict rules of prudence. But when it is considered that she is deeply in love, and a just allowance is made for the necessity of her situation—being but just sentenced either to death, a vow of perpetual virginity, or a marriage she detested—every equitable reader, and I am sure the fair sex in general, will be more inclined to pity than blame her. 'Not one doubt or hesitation, not one condition of assurance for Lysander's constancy.' The intimacy of their love, and their perfect confidence in each others fidelity, surely rendered such distrustful precautions unnecessary. The ladies, I believe, will generally agree that if she could not rely on her servant's love her security would be very little bettered by his professions and verbal assurances, however solemnly given. 'Either she was nauseously coming';—the poet supposes her not only coming but actually come, and that each of the lovers had been long in the full and conscious possession of the other's heart, and in this situation the same behaviour would be extremely proper which might reasonably disgust a stranger or slight acquaintance. 'Or she had before jilted him; and he could not believe her without a thousand oaths.' He asks no oaths of her. They are the superfluous but tender effusion of her own heart-felt passion. On the other hand how manifest is the impropriety of the following lines in the mouth of Lysander?

> *And by that fire which burn'd the Carthage queen,*
> *When the false Trojan under sail was seen;*
> *By all the vows that ever men have broke,*
> *In number more than ever women spoke.* [1.1.173ff.]

Would any man in his senses, when he is giving the strongest assurances of his fidelity to his mistress, endeavour at the same time to defeat the purpose and destroy the effect of them by expressly reminding her how often her sex had been deceived and ruined by trusting to such security? Whereas in her mouth these expressions have the greatest beauty. She finely insinuates to her lover that she is not insensible of the hazard she runs from the entire confidence she reposes in him; but at the same time she lets him see that she loves him with a passion above being restrained by this or any other consideration. This excess of tenderness, expressed with so much delicacy, must very strongly affect every mind that is susceptible of a sympathy with those generous sentiments. It is plain that Mr Warburton hath so little sensibility of them that he doth not even understand their language; a most unhappy symptom of his incapacity for the part of a commentator on such a poet as Shakespeare, whose soul was full of them, and felt them in their utmost force and delicacy. (42–3)

*　　*　　*

[On Shakespeare's versification]

The observation our critick makes on this occasion, 'that Shakespeare entirely neglected the metre of his verse,' is so injurious to the character of the prince of our dramatick poets that it ought not to be passed over in silence. He hath not indeed confined himself, like our modern tragick poets, to metre of one kind only. His is very various, and of very different kinds, but it is in general regular with very few exceptions, unless where it is interrupted by the alternative interposition of the several speakers in the dialogue, in which case the incompleat verses ought to be regarded with the same indulgence as the hemistichs of Virgil; and in this liberty he hath been followed both by Otway and Dryden. (98–9)

*　　*　　*

[On *All's Well That Ends Well*, 1.1.153ff.]

Not my virginity yet.
There shall your master have a thousand loves,
A mother, and a mistress, and a friend, &c.

The meaning of the hemistich which begins this speech is, My virginity is not yet that old virginity, which in your description is a mere withered pear. In order to ascertain the sense of the two next lines, on which depends that of the eight following ones, may I have leave to ask where

Bertram was to find all these thousand loves, with a mother, a mistress, and a friend into the bargain? Not surely in Helena's virginity. That were as errant nonsense as any Mr Warburton hath rejected. But at court undoubtedly, whither he was then going. It is evident, therefore, that something hath by some accident been omitted in which his going to court was mentioned. There indeed he might soon have amours enough on his hands, and find fair ones enough who would supply the place of, and whom his passion for them would induce him to treat with all the duty, tenderness and confidence due to a mother, a mistress, and a friend; whom he would address with the fantastick appellations of a phœnix, an enemy, a guide, a goddess, and a world more

> *Of pretty fond adoptious christendoms,*
> *That blinking Cupid gossips.* [1.1.162f.]

For all the other intermediate whimsical titles are in truth the offspring of a poetick lover's imagination, which he hath at some time or other bestowed on his mistress; and I believe it would not be difficult, if it were worth the search, to find in the love poetry of those times an authority for most if not every one of them. At least I can affirm it from knowledge that far the greater part of them are to be found in the Italian Lyrick poetry, which was the model from which our poets chiefly copied. Upon the supposition, then, of this omission, which perhaps was only of these five words, 'You're going to court', the following eight lines lose all that absurdity which induced Mr Warburton to reject them as being 'such finished nonsense as is never heard out of Bedlam', and we perceive them to be a not inelegant satire on the extravagance of love-poetry. As they stand at present they are much too absurd to have proceeded from the most 'foolish conceited player' that ever lived. But indeed these players are of great convenience to the criticks on Shakespeare. When these do not readily apprehend his meaning the nonsensical player is ever ready at hand to bear the whole blame and relieve them from any further trouble or concern about it. (164–5)

*   *   *

[On *2 Henry IV*, 4.2.93ff.]

> *And, good my Lord, so please you, let our trains*
> *March by us, that we may peruse the men*
> *We should have cop'd withal.*

This speech is addressed to the archbishop, for the Earl of Westmorland had just before quitted the stage. It is evident therefore that we should read *your trains*. The design of the Prince in making this request appears very clearly, from the event, to have been to draw in the rebels, under the specious pretext of taking a view of the men he was to have coped with, to disband their army in his presence while he preserved his own entire; that he might seize the opportunity of arresting the chiefs when abandoned by their followers, and of falling upon these when they were scattered and unable to make resistance. This whole proceeding, as it is represented by the poet, is founded in strict historical truth, and therefore, in an historical play like this, he is undoubtedly justifiable in giving it us as he found it. It hath however a very unhappy and disagreeable effect on the reader or spectator, as instead of acquiescence at least in the punishment of the rebels it cannot fail of exciting in him compassion towards them when so treacherously ensnared, as well as a very high degree of indignation against Prince John, who is on all other occasions represented as a Prince of great gallantry and magnanimity, for prostituting his character by so deliberate and odious a piece of perfidy. I believe there are few readers who do not wish Shakespeare's plan had permitted him to follow Horace's rule,[1]

et quæ
Desperat tractata nitescere posse, relinquat. (260–1)

* * *

[On *Henry VIII*, 3.2.435]

Say, Wolsey, that once trod the ways of glory.

Mr Warburton, out of regard to the uniformity of the metaphor, is inclined to think Shakespeare wrote *the waves of glory*. But what an unmeaning expression is 'treading the waves of glory?' What image doth it represent to the imagination? When a thought is illustrated by a metaphor the object from which the metaphor is drawn ought to be more clearly apprehended, and better known to the reader, than the thing illustrated, else this last would be obscured by it instead of being represented in a clearer and more striking light; and thus the intention of the writer would be disappointed. If the poet's design therefore had been to pursue the same metaphor throughout he would have chosen some expression which had a reference to shipping and navigation. But in truth, our critick is mistaken in the very nature and purport of that rule concerning the use of the metaphor which he is inculcating on every

[1] *A.P.*, 149f.: 'and what he fears he cannot make attractive with his touch he abandons.'

occasion, and frequently misapplying. The integrity of the metaphor doth not denote its uniformity but its consistency. It is not meant by it that metaphors may not be accumulated when they are consistent with each other—as in the present case the same person may very consistently tread the ways of glory and sound the depths and shoals of honour—but only that the propriety of the metaphor is to be preserved as far as it goes. Thus it would have been wrong to have said, sounded the ways of glory, and trod the depths and shoals of honour. (311)

*   *   *

[On *King Lear*, 1.2.128]

Pat!—he comes like the catastrophe of the old comedy.

That is, just as the circumstance which decides the catastrophe of a play intervenes in the very nick of time, when the action is wound up to its crisis and the audience are impatiently expecting it. As to all that critical parade concerning the dramatick unities, the hackneyed topick of every Italian, French, and English critick for above a century last past, and which the bountiful fecundity of Mr Warburton's imagination makes a present of to Shakespeare on the occasion of this passage, there is not the least reason to believe it ever entered into his thoughts at the time he wrote it, nor indeed that he was ever initiated in this doctrine, much less that he was convinced of the necessity and advantages of conforming to it. The trite argument drawn from the observation of these unities in *The Tempest* hath very little force in it: this circumstance appears to have been owing not to choice and design but to a necessity arising from the very nature of his subject. The constitution of the fable was such, by the whole transaction being confined within a little desolate island, as not to admit of a violation of the unities of time and place; and as to that of action he hath actually violated it to a very great degree by the introduction of those episodick scenes of Trinculo, Stephano and Caliban, which may be all struck out without the least injury or inconvenience to the main action. And after all, what doth the poet get by this illjudged liberality towards him? Only the imputation of a sneaking submission to the ignorance and unimproved taste of the age he lived in, when he himself had it in his power by the superior knowledge we would attribute to him to have instructed, and by the unrivalled ascendency of his genius, which is indisputable, to have reformed it. (323-4)

*   *   *

[On *King Lear*, 1.4.227f.]

Either his notion weakens, his discernings
Are lethargied—Ha! waking—'tis not so.

I think the true and natural sense of this passage may be thus expressed: 'Either his apprehension is decayed, his faculty of discernment whereby he is enabled to distinguish persons and things, and know one thing from another is buried under a lethargick sleep.' Here Lear was proceeding to mention the other alternative, 'or he is in his sober senses, and broad awake'; but the sudden and rapid whirl of passion, bursting in upon him from all quarters on the bare imagination that what had passed was real, overwhelms him to that degree that he cannot bear the thought of it for a moment, and obliges him to break off and reject that supposition instantaneously. 'Ha! what? that it should be possible that I am now awake? It cannot be, 'tis impossible.' No language in the world could express so strongly and feelingly those violent convulsions of passion which agitated the breast of Lear, or the dreadful shock which his whole frame, both of mind and body, must have received from this unexpected discovery of his daughter's undutiful and ungrateful behaviour. All the flattering hopes and promises of happiness for the remainder of his life, which he had so fondly indulged and with the most entire confidence relied on, under the full assurance of his daughters love and duty, vanish in an instant; and his own folly in depending on their continuance stares him at the same time in the face. But this is a view he is not able to sustain; he therefore starts from it at once, and with the utmost eagerness takes refuge in the only tolerable supposition which remained to him, that he is either disordered in his senses or asleep and in a dream.

Mr Roderick's interpretation (in the *Canons of Criticism*, pp. 228–30) in which these lines, with the two preceding and the subsequent one, are considered as a mere irony and a taunt, as also the several emendations he proposes in consequence of it, are in my poor opinion not only mistaken but unnatural to a person in Lear's situation, just then transported to the highest pitch of astonishment and not yet sufficiently familiarized to his misfortunes, nor cool enough, to treat the author of them ironically. By understanding too the passage in this light all that struggle of the passions, which is affecting to the highest degree and painted with all the force and energy which words can possibly give it, is quite lost and obliterated by being degraded into a bare ironical expression of anger and resentment. (325–7)

★   ★   ★

[On *Titus Andronicus*]

Mr Upton (in his *Critical Observations*, pp. 273, 274), gives us a calculation of Mr Theobald's, founded on a passage in Ben Jonson's Induction to his *Bartholomew Fair*,[1] by which it appears that this play made its first appearance on the stage not later at least than the year 1589, and this he affirms (upon what grounds I know not) was before Shakespeare left Warwickshire to come and reside at London. From these premises Mr Upton concludes that this play is spurious, and could not possibly be Shakespeare's. But his conclusion is a little too hasty. That year was the twenty-fifth of Shakespeare's age, and it is scarce conceivable that so strong a propensity of genius towards the drama could have lain so long dormant without exerting itself in some production. This production might have been sent to town and brought on the stage before he himself quitted Warwickshire, and might have been the very circumstance that introduced him to his acquaintance with the players upon his first arrival. The internal evidence against the play is much stronger. The fable is at the same time shocking and puerile, without the least appearance of art or conduct. The characters are unnatural and undistinguishable, or rather absolutely none, whereas those of Shakespeare are always strongly marked beyond those of any other poet that ever lived. The sentiments are poor and trivial, the stile flat and uniform, utterly destitute of that strength and variety of expression which, with a certain obscurity sometimes attending it, are the distinguishing characters of Shakespeare. There are however, scattered here and there, many strokes something resembling his peculiar manner, though not his best manner, which, as they could not be imitated from him would incline one to believe this might possibly be his most juvenile performance, written and acted before his poetical genius had had time to unfold and form itself. (370–1)

★   ★   ★

[On *Macbeth*, 2.1.52ff.]

> *and wither'd murder, . . .*
> *thus with his stealthy pace,*
> *With Tarquin's ravishing strides, tow'rds his design*
> *Moves like a ghost.*

---

[1] For Upton's discussion see Vol. 3, p. 307. Ben Jonson's reference is to the out-of-date playgoer who swears that '*Jeronimo* [i.e., *The Spanish Tragedy*] or *Andronicus* are the best plays yet', so revealing that his judgment 'hath stood still these five and twenty or thirty years', thus reckoning back (if he can be taken literally) from 1614 to 1584 or 1589.

Mr Johnson[1] informs us that the reading of all the editions before Mr Pope's was *sides* and not *strides*, and further objects that a ravishing stride is an action of violence, impetuosity, and tumult, very unlike the stealthy pace of a ravisher or an assassin; and from these premises concludes the true reading to be

> *With* Tarquin *ravishing*, slides *tow'rd his design:*

adding that Tarquin is in this place the general name of a ravisher. To all which I have this to say, that I understand the poet very well when he mentions Tarquin's ravishing strides, that they are no other than those strides which conducted him to the intended rape. But to tack Tarquin or the ravisher, and that too in the very act of ravishment, as a companion to the murderer stalking towards the perpetration of his crime is so absurd a circumstance that all the respect I justly have for Mr Johnson's great abilities ought not to restrain me from calling it by its true name, nonsense. But in truth the objection to the common reading is founded wholly in a mistake. Whoever hath experienced walking in the dark must have observed that a man under this disadvantage always feels out his way by strides, by advancing one foot, as far as he finds it safe, before the other, and that if he were to slide or glide along, as ghosts are represented to do, the infallible consequence would be his tumbling on his nose. (386–7)

* * *

[On *Macbeth*, 2.2.37]

Sleep that knits up the ravell'd sleeve of care.

Mr Seward[2] (in his notes on Fletcher's *Two Noble Kinsmen*, vol. x. p. 60) very ingeniously conjectures that the genuine word was *sleave*, which it seems signifies the ravelled knotty gouty parts of the silk, which give great trouble and embarrassment to the knitter or weaver. So that sleep is said, by a very expressive metaphor, to knit up and reduce to order all that confusion and vexation in which our cares and solicitudes had involved our waking thoughts. (387)

* * *

[On Shakespeare's 'obscurity' and Warburton's editing]
Whoever hath but dipped into Shakespeare must have observed a

---

[1] See Vol. 3, pp. 174f., and Dodd's comments, *ibid.*, pp. 475f.
[2] Thomas Seward: see Vol. 3, No. 126.

certain obscurity, which may be considered as one of the characteristick peculiarities of his style, arising in great measure from the grandeur, the strength, and the exactness of his conceptions, which he could not equal by the force of his expression, though his powers even of this kind were perhaps never excelled by any other writer. It is the business of a critick to illustrate these obscurities, but he would be justly laughed at and exploded if he should set about multiplying their number under the pretext that he was strictly adhering to Shakespeare's manner. But our critick, not trusting wholly to his reasoning, appeals to fact and experiment; and for this purpose lays before the reader another emendation of his own, which we must therefore look upon as his palmary emendation of this kind, carrying with it such clear evidence of its truth as at once to command an universal assent and fully justify every other similar liberty which he hath taken. The experiment is made on a line in our poet's *Tarquin and Lucrece* where, enumerating the various performances of Time, he mentions among many others the following one:

> *To dry the old oak's sap, and cherish springs.*
>
> [*The Rape of Lucrece*, 950]

It must be admitted that the latter part of the line, being mere nonsense, is certainly corrupt; to remedy which, and restore sense to the text, Mr Warburton positively assures us that the poet wrote

> *To dry the old oak's sap, and* tarish *springs.*

'That is, To dry up springs, from the French word, *tarir*.'

But notwithstanding this gentleman's confidence in the certainty of his correction, and the authoritative air with which he obtrudes it, I will venture to affirm that this favourite specimen of his French coinage is of as bad an alloy, and will as little bear the touchstone as any the most exceptionable of those which in the course of these notes I have already been obliged to reject. All the achievements of Time which the poet here enumerates are the regular effects of the power of that personated agent, and never fail to take place within certain periods. They are the natural and necessary consequences of his influence constantly and uniformly operating. Thus there is no oak now in the world whose sap will not be dried up within a certain revolution of time; and the same regular uniformity of operation holds in every one of the other instances mentioned by the poet. But is this the case with springs? Are all the springs which existed at the recovery of the earth from the deluge now dried up? Or have we any reason to imagine that all those now subsisting

will, by the natural course of events, be dried up till the general conflagration, at however great a distance we suppose it? Is the drying up
of springs one of those regular changes in nature which we naturally
expect will, and which from the constitution of things necessarily must
happen within certain periods? The answer to these questions will undeniably evince that Mr Warburton's emendation must be wrong. . . .
(430–1)

$$\star \qquad \star \qquad \star$$

[On *Antony and Cleopatra*, 4.12.20f.]

> *the hearts,*
> *That pantler'd me at heels.*

That is, as Mr Warburton interprets it, that 'run after me like footmen,
or *pantlers*'.[1] But a *pantler* is a very different employment from a footman, and signifies that servant in great families who hath the particular
care of providing the bread and sending it to table, as is evident from
Act III, Scene 2 of Fletcher's *Bloody Brother*. Mr Warburton indeed
would persuade us that this appellation is used for 'a menial servant in
general'; but he hath not been able to produce a single instance where
it is so used. The two instances he hath produced are quite beside the
purpose, and in one of them the word itself is not even so much as
found. Mr Upton (in his *Critic. Observ.* p. 203)[2] conjectures that
Shakespeare wrote

> *That* paged *me at the* heels.

But there is no necessity of departing so far from the ancient reading,
which was

> *That* pannell'd *me at heels:*

from which I think it is natural to conclude that the poet wrote

> *That* spaniel'd *me at heels:*

that is, That followed me at the heels like spaniels.[3] (462–3)

$$\star \qquad \star \qquad \star$$

[On *Othello*, 4.1.41]

Nature would not invest herself in such shadowing without some induction.[4]

1 See Vol. 3, pp. 245f.
2 See Vol. 3, p. 302.
3 This emendation had already been made by Sir Thomas Hanmer in his edition of
1744, apparently unknown to Heath.
4 This is Warburton's emendation.

In my opinion the common reading, *without some instruction*, gives us a sense more apposite and better expressed. Othello feels all his faculties failing him on the sudden, and a cloudy or misty darkness creeping on very fast upon him. This circumstance suggests to him the thought that his very nature, which sympathizes with him in his present agony, must have received some secret mysterious instruction, intimation, or instinctive knowledge of the reality of that calamity which so deeply oppresses him, otherwise she would never have spontaneously invested herself in that horrid darkness which he now felt overwhelming him. I will not dispute that 'vast sublimity of thought' which Mr Warburton discovers in his comparison of Othello falling into a trance to the sun in eclipse by the induction of the moon between it and the earth; but of this I think I may be pretty certain, that if Shakespeare had intended such comparison he would have taken care to express it at least so intelligibly as to have been visible to some one of his readers besides Mr Warburton. The only two words which give us the least glimpse of it are *shadowing* and *induction*, and unfortunately the latter of them is his own interpolation. (569)

204. George Steevens on restoring Shakespeare's text

1765

From the *Critical Review* xix (March, 1765); a review of Benjamin Heath, *A Revisal of Shakespeare's text*.

The 'Castrated Sheet' referred to is a work by Philip Nichols, *The Castrated Letter of Sir Thomas Hanmer* . . . (1761) which revealed that in the *Biographia Britannica* Nichols had printed a letter from Sir Thomas Hanmer alleging that Warburton had tried to plagiarise from his Shakespeare edition. Warburton prevailed on the publishers to cancel the page containing this letter (hence the 'castrated sheet'), since he had in fact lent notes to Hanmer who had refused to return them and attempted to traffic in his Shakespeare notes 'without consent or knowledge'. Warburton was in the right here: see A. W. Evans, *Warburton and the Warburtonians* (Oxford, 1932), pp. 149ff. I ascribe this review to George Steevens, who was well known as a writer for the *Critical Review*. For numerous echoes and self-quotations see further reviews in Vol. 5.

We have often bewailed among the literati a pruriency of criticism, which seems to spring rather from envy than emulation, because it is generally attended with abuse. The force of Shakespeare's genius was often felt and admired before many passages of his works were understood; and when Mr Rowe published his edition of our great poet it was bought up with avidity, because he appeared in what we may call a decent habit, and was more legible than before, not to mention that the editor's name gave great sanction to the publication.

As critical knowledge gained ground many imperfections were discovered in Mr Rowe's edition; and Mr Pope, who chiefly delighted in those districts of Parnassus that are watered with the golden streams of Pactolus, undertook to give the world a new edition, though he was qualified for such an undertaking neither by study nor inclination. His conjectures, however, are sometimes just and often pretty, nay ingenious. The rage of emendation at this period seized several other learned gentlemen, Mr Theobald in particular, Mr W. now bishop of G., Dr Thirlby, Sir Thomas Hanmer, and many other minor critics, among whom Mr Theobald carried round a literary begging-box and made such collections as enabled him to give a better edition of Shakespeare than that published by Mr Pope. Had he done this in a modest genteel manner, without any illiberal reflections on that great poet's performance, we are persuaded he never would have become the hero of *The Dunciad*. Mr W. could not resist the impulse. He called in his own critical property, augmented it with a fresh stock and then bundled it up into a new edition, in which he was not more complaisant to some of his contemporaries than Mr Theobald was to Mr Pope. His dictatorial manner, however, gave great offence to one Mr Edwards, author of *The Canons of Criticism*. This gentleman's animadversions upon Mr W.'s corrections of Shakespeare are without doubt in many places fortunate enough, but unluckily he falls into the very train of abuse which had disgraced the labours of his predecessors in the same walk of criticism.

As to the learned knight above-mentioned, his critical rage seems to have carried him not only beyond the bounds of decency but of morality, as our readers may find in the account we have given of the Castrated Sheet in the sixth Volume of the *Biographia Britannica*.* His l——p of G. certainly acquitted himself with great honour in that infamous attack made upon his moral character; and whatever failings may be imputed to his literary functions yet his rank, reputation, and the services he has done religion as a divine ought to cancel the memory of those unimportant slips which he may have committed as a critic. The author of this work [Heath] seems to be of a different opinion. A double portion of the spirit of *The Canons of Criticism* has fallen upon him, and he treats the bishop in a manner, to speak in the softest terms, in which he would not wish to be treated himself.

As we are peculiarly concerned for the dignity of criticism we beg leave to observe that acrimony, either literary or personal, ought to be expelled from that province. A critic who has real address and genius will never debase the merit of his adversary, because it renders his own victory easy and despicable; and if Mr W. (for so our critic affects to call the bishop) was so contemptible a writer as he represents him, a schoolboy ought to be ashamed of the trophies which the publication

* See *Critical Review*, vol. xvi. [1763] p. 306 [–9].

before us has erected. Before we dismiss this introduction we beg leave to mention an obvious, but we believe a most certain fact, the reflection upon which ought to be mortifying to every editor of Shakespeare; we mean that his greatest merit must arise not from acquired but from that accidental knowledge, of which the greatest dunce in England may be possessed. There are now places in Great Britain where the language of Shakespeare is spoken, and the terms he made use of are understood in his sense. We will venture to say, and before we finish this article hope to produce some proofs of what we advance, that it is through an ignorance of this accidental knowledge that the most material assassinations upon Shakespeare's meaning have been committed; nor in that respect does this reviser of Mr Edwards seem to be better qualified than the bishop of G—.

In the preface prefixed to this performance the author follows the old hackneyed custom of bewailing the mangled condition of Shakespeare, and treats his modern editors very cavalierly. (161–3)
[Quotes Heath's statements that he only knows of Hanmer's edition from Warburton's account of it, and that he has relied on the editions of Pope and Theobald for his knowledge of the Shakespeare quartos and folios.]

This is a frank and generous acknowledgment, but we cannot think that the reviser of Shakespeare's text ought to have taken even Sir Thomas Hanmer's edition upon the credit of a declared enemy; and we must be of opinion that he would have discharged the task he has imposed upon himself much more to the satisfaction of the public if, instead of the eyes of others, he had employed his own in collating the old editions of his author, which are undoubtedly the standards that ought to have regulated his criticisms. With regard to his censure of Mr W. we cannot admit it to be either fair or liberal. If we are truly informed, that right reverend personage has been so far from pertinaciously insisting upon his mistakes that he has taken all possible means to prevent their spreading, a sacrifice to candor to which few authors of his complexion and eminence would have submitted! Our reviser should have considered that when the poet advises *debellare superbos*, he premises *parcere subjectis* . . .[1] (164)

We perceive the author follows the common order in which Shakespeare's plays are printed, and consequently begins with *The Tempest*. We cannot say we are greatly edified by his revisal of this play. His observations upon it seldom, if ever, exceed unwarranted conjecture,

[1] *Aeneid* 6.853: 'to spare the humbled, and to tame in war the proud!'

for had the old readings continued Shakespeare's meaning could not have suffered. We think it would be a kind of insult upon our readers to specify one of his corrections or remarks on this play with any degree of approbation. The author's triumph over Mr W., who says that Shakespeare gave Caliban's language a certain grotesque air of the savage and antique, is unjust and ill-judged; and we believe every man who has the least knowledge of Shakespeare will subscribe to Mr W.'s opinion.

When our reviser comes to the address of Ferdinand to Miranda, he makes the following observation: 'If this is not the original reading of the first folio edition, as I am inclined to believe it is, but an alteration of Mr Pope's, I think, however, it is sufficiently warranted by the former part of this speech.'

A true critic, instead of making this trite remark, would have taken notice of the striking similarity between Ferdinand and Eneas, in the like circumstances, when the latter discovers his mother on the coast of Afric.—'Most sure the goddess,' says Ferdinand [1.2.421]. *O Dea certé*, says Eneas, who is in doubt whether Venus is a created (made) being or not—*O quam te memorem Virgo*.[1] The pun with which the lady answers is silly enough, but it is Shakespearean; it comes in his way, and he cannot avoid stumbling on it.

The sagacity of our author in the following emendation gives but too great a handle for Mr W.'s friends to recriminate upon him. Says Miranda,

> Make not too rash a trial of him; for
> He's gentle, and not fearful.   [*The Tempest*, 1.2.467f.]

Says our reviser: 'I cannot help thinking that Shakespeare wrote,

> Make not too *harsh* a trial of him; for
> He's gentle, and not fearful.

That is, Do not treat him with too much severity, for he is gentle, and by no means one for whom you can justly entertain any apprehensions.' But a reviser of Shakespeare's text ought to have been so well acquainted with the English language, as to have known that the word *fearful* does not here signify *timorous*, but is used in the sense it has in our translation of the Scriptures and the compilers of our Liturgy. We have a striking example of this in the following pathetic sentence of the priest's address

---

[1] *Aeneid* 1.327f.: 'but by what name should I call thee, O maiden? . . . O goddess surely!'

to the people in the Commination office: 'It is a FEARFUL thing to fall into the hands of the living God.' Of like import is the expression 'I am *fearfully* and wonderfully made', an expression which is retained in both our translations of the Psalms. Perhaps, setting authorities apart, the genius of our language vindicates the sense of the word by applying it to the object where the cause of *fear* exists, and therefore becomes *fearful*. Many examples of the same kind, had we room, might be adduced. The reader who has any knowledge of Shakespeare will easily perceive the propriety of the contrast: 'He's gentle, and not *fearful*,' that is, *terrible*. . . .

This author, in his stale explanation of 'the putters out on five for one,' [3.3.48] ought to have observed that in Gonzalo's description of the men 'whose throats had hanging at them wallets of flesh,' and 'whose heads stood in their breasts,' [3.3.45ff.] he ridicules Sir Walter Raleigh's description of the inhabitants of Guiana.

In the fourth act, when Prospero, in the old edition, says 'I have given a third of my own life,' [4.1.3] we are somewhat suspicious that Shakespeare had an eye to the antient partition of lands called *thirdings*, corruptly *ridings*: but this we only offer as a conjecture. Our reviser, in imitation of Mr W. and Mr Theobald, puts a note of reprobation upon the word *twilled* [4.1.64] as applied to banks of rivers, or their brims. The former prefer *tulip'd*, the other *lilied*, and very gravely tells us, on Milton's authority, that lilies grow on the banks of rivers. Mean while we can almost venture to pronounce that the old reading ought to stand, and that it is a Shakespeareanism in his best manner. It is by the operation of *twilling* or tweeling (tho' the former is the true word) that the beautiful borders, the *ouvrages figurées*, are raised on the damask and fine linen made use of at the tables of the great, and it is here peculiarly picturesque and beautiful; tho' this author pronounces the word to be *evidently corrupt* (meaning, we suppose, *corrupted*).

Our reviser, though severe upon Mr W., takes no notice that the old reading '*pole-clipt* vineyard,' [4.1.68] ought to stand as being the most poetical, and signifying the vineyard whose poles are embraced by vines. We cannot think the rest of his criticisms upon the remaining part of this play merit any notice.

This author introduces the *Midsummer-Night's Dream* with the like uninteresting string of criticisms. Admitting that Mr W. is wrong, can that excuse our reviser when he consumes pages in exposing and explaining errors which must at the first glance be obvious to the merest tyro of learning? We can by no means agree to our author's substituting, in one of Hermia's speeches, the word *sweet* for *swelled*. . . . Neither can we agree to Mr Theobald's restoring those four lines[1] to rhime, for two very plain but substantial reasons: first, because they are unrithmetized in the old editions; secondly, because they make better sense without the rhimes. . . . (165-7)

The reader may observe that we are not, in our review of this performance, defending Mr Warburton's alterations but examining those of our reviser. In *The Two Gentlemen of Verona* he has made no animadversion on the word *lac'd mutton* [1.1.93] tho' he had there a very fair opportunity of displaying at a very moderate expence of attention his knowledge of Shakespeare's idiom, and of outshining Mr Warburton, Mr Theobald, and all the emendators who have gone before him.

[HEATH:] '*Oh that she could speak now like a wode woman!*' [2.3.26]

The first folios agree, it seems, in the same reading, *would woman*, for which Mr Pope substituted, by a very natural conjecture, *ould woman*. Launce supposes one of his shoes to stand for his mother and, to make the representation more lively, wishes it 'could speak like an old woman'. It is uncertain to whom the honour of the present reading is due, whether to Mr Theobald or to Mr Warburton, since both in their several editions have admitted and recommended it without mention of the other. But this is a claim not worth the determining since the conjecture, whosesoever it be, is certainly wrong. In this passage it is not the mother who is spoken of but the shoe which represents her, as is evident from what immediately follows. 'Well, I kiss her; why there 'tis; here's my mother's breath up and down.' [2.3.27] It is plain therefore that the expression *like a wode* or mad *woman* can have no propriety here.'

Such is our sagacious reviser's commentary upon this passage; and we cannot refuse doing him the justice to own that we are somewhat inclined to believe that Launce means the *shoe*, notwithstanding the aukwardness of giving it a feminine gender. . . .

It is with regret we find ourselves obliged to divide our review of this work, which we think is not without merit; but we shall in our subsequent review of it endeavour to establish our observation that a knowledge of Shakespeare's idiom is necessary for revising his text, and without that the greatest critical abilities must be ineffectual. (168-9)

[Part II]

In the course of our observations on this work we apprehend that we

---

[1] *A Midsummer-Night's Dream*, 1.1.216ff.: Theobald's note is reprinted in Vol. 2, p. 492.

have undeniably proved this reviser, as well as his antagonists, to have been deficient as to the fundamentals of what ought to constitute true criticism, we mean the knowledge of Shakespeare's language so far as relates to individual words or the ideas annexed to them when that great poet lived. What a figure must a critic upon Virgil or any of the Roman classics make, should he pronounce *olli* to be a word *evidently* CORRUPT because the dative of *ille* is *illi*, or that *quiris* is no Latin word, because none of the etymologists have accounted for its derivation.

Had we room to spare we could carry this observation much farther, and prove that even a syntax prevailed in Shakespeare's time different from what is now commonly received; and we might perhaps carry the like observations through all the other parts of grammar. This theatrical vernacularity seems for very obvious reasons to have been lost between the years 1638 and 1665, when a species of another but a more depraved kind took place, and which we have the pleasure to observe is now discouraged by the improving taste and morals of the public. Terence had no vernacularities; the plays of Shakespeare could not, when exhibited, have been received without them. (250–1)

Our reviser thus comments upon Ford's soliloquy, in which is the following line, *And stand so firmly on his wife's frailty.* [2.1.209]

'. . . I therefore readily agree with Mr Theobald and Sir Thomas Hanmer in substituting *fealty*, or rather, to avoid ambiguity, though the alteration be somewhat greater, *fidelity*.'

Thou sacred rage of correcting! to what absurdities dost thou not impel human brains, *quid non mortalia pectora cogis!*[1] Never, surely, did words carry a more evident meaning than those do. *On his wife's frailty:* to every one but a critic the obvious meaning of Ford is that Page is very obstinate on *the subject of* his wife's frailty, and that he stands upon it like a secure fool who thinks himself firm. . . . We must in general observe that this author is seldom mistaken when he supports the ancient readings; and when he ventures to amend he is far more tolerable than any of the editors he condemns.

We now proceed to *The Merchant of Venice*: 'Mr Pope was mistaken in imagining the word, *argosie* [1.1.9] to signify "a ship from *Argo*." This last is an inland town of the Morea, and consequently could have no shipping. In the primary signification of the word it denoted a ship of Ragusa; and as that city was in the middle ages famous for its trade and extensive navigation, and particularly for building merchant ships

---

1 Virgil, *Aeneid* 4.412: '[O tyrant Love,] to what dost thou not drive the hearts of men!'

of the largest size, every very large merchant vessel came to be called an *Argosie*. Hence too *Ragozine*, for *Ragusain*, the name of the pirate in *Measure for Measure.*'

Indeed Mr Reviser you are as far mistaken as Mr Pope, and you here give us a fresh instance of the necessity a critic upon Shakespeare is under to understand Shakespeare's language. An *Argosie* in its etymology has a relation to the ship *Argos*, in which the Argonauts sailed; and in Shakespeare's time every large ship, especially a trading one, was called an *Argosie*, without the smallest allusion to Ragusa. . . .[1]

In *The Winter's Tale* we find an observation of equal sagacity with the preceding:

> 'To let him there a month, beyond the gest
> Prefix'd for's parting. [1.2.41f.]

Mr Warburton defends this reading, and informs us that *gest* signifies a stage or journey. Be it so. Let us therefore substitute either of those two words in the place of *gest*, and we shall still find the passage will be nonsense. I am inclined to believe our poet wrote,

> *beyond the* list,

that is, beyond the limit; in which sense Shakespeare hath several times used that word.'

The ignorance of the meaning of the word *gests* among all the commentators of Shakespeare is very surprizing; but it must be owned that Mr W. has in the passage before us come nearest its meaning. Before a king of England undertook a progress the lord-chamberlain or proper officer presented him with a paper containing the *gests* (which we suppose to have come from the French word *gist*), and it regulated not only the places where the king was to lie every night but the time of his continuing at each. The word is very common in old writers, and may be yet seen in the sense we have explained it in the hand of a royal author, Edward VI, in his journal published by bishop Burnet. In this signification we hope Shakespeare's original stands unimpeached, and if we may be allowed a pun, will remain master of the *lists*. We have been the more full in explaining this term because it occurs more than once in Shakespeare, and has occasioned his text receiving many a dreadful stab from the pens of his editors and revisers.

The bounds we are obliged to prescribe to ourselves in reviewing a work of the bulk before us do not suffer us to give farther particulars of

---

1 Here Heath, however, would seem to be right.

the author's verbal mistakes, especially as we are in hopes of soon reviewing an edition of Shakespeare which will be final and decisive of that great poet's text. We cannot, however, take leave of the work before us without again doing the author the justice to own that Shakespeare's text is greatly obliged to his labours in establishing the authority of its original printing. In intricate passages, where there is no disputes about printing, punctuation, or words he has been very happy in his explanations; and a reader who is not a professed critic may study Shakespeare in his closet with far more ease and advantage than he did before. We are, however, of opinion that this author takes too much pains in confuting readings and emendations that confute themselves, and sometimes in establishing meanings that are clear to the lowest capacity. He does not write in the liberal manner that should prevail among gentlemen and scholars; and he has taken more pains to understand Shakespeare's meaning than his words, two studies which have so mutual a relation that they ought to be inseparable. (252–5)

A Select Bibliography of Shakespeare Criticism

1753–65

Note: Items which cover a wide range, including this period, which were listed in Vol. I are not repeated here.

(A) LITERARY CRITICISM

GREEN, C. C., *The Neo-Classic Theory of Tragedy in England During the Eighteenth Century* (New York, 1934, 1966).

BABCOCK, R. W., *The Genesis of Shakespeare Idolatry, 1766–1799* (Chapel Hill, North Carolina, 1931): includes some material from the period immediately preceding. *N.B.* Babcock's bibliography (an earlier version of which appeared in *Studies in Philology* extra series 1, 1929) is to be used with caution: it includes works which have the most peripheral connection with Shakespeare, and contains numerous errors.

RAYSOR, T. M., 'The Downfall of the Three Unities', *Modern Language Notes* 42 (1927), pp. 1–9; 'The Study of Shakespeare's Characters in the Eighteenth Century', *ibid.*, pp. 495–500.

LOVETT, D., 'Shakespeare as a Poet of Realism in the Eighteenth Century', *ELH* 2 (1935), pp. 267–89.

GRIFFITH, P. M., 'Joseph Warton's Criticism of Shakespeare', *Tulane Studies in English* 14 (1965), pp. 17–27.

SHERBO, A. (ed.), *New Essays by Arthur Murphy* (East Lansing, Michigan, 1963).

(B) THEATRICAL HISTORY, ADAPTATIONS

STONE, G. W. Jr (ed.), *The London Stage, 1747–1776*, 3 vols (Carbondale, Ill., 1962).

HOGAN, C. B., *Shakespeare in the Theatre, 1701–1840*, 2 vols (Oxford, 1952, 1957).

NOYES, R. G., *The Thespian Mirror. Shakespeare in the Eighteenth-Century Novel* (Providence, Rhode Island, 1953). Studies allusions to Shakespeare in 750 novels published between 1740 and 1780.

GRAY, C. H., *Theatrical Criticisms in London to 1795* (New York, 1931, 1964).

SPRAGUE, A. C., *Shakespeare and the Actors* (Cambridge, Mass., 1944).

SPRAGUE, A. C., *Shakespearian Players and Performances* (Cambridge, Mass., 1953).

STRAUSS, L., *The Drama's Patrons. A Study of the Eighteenth Century London Audience* (Austin, Texas, 1971).

PRICE, C., *Theatre in the Age of Garrick* (Oxford, 1973).

See also the works by Odell and Branam listed in Vols 1, 2.

(c) TEXTUAL CRITICISM

SHERBO, A., *Samuel Johnson on Shakespeare* (Urbana, Ill., 1956). Discusses Johnson's criticism before the 1765 edition, also many of his predecessors.

ISAACS, J., 'Shakespearian Scholarship', in *A Companion to Shakespeare Studies,* ed. H. Granville-Barker and G. B. Harrison (Cambridge, 1934).

Index

The Index is arranged in three parts: I. Shakespeare's works; II. Shakespearian characters; III. General index. Adaptations are indexed under the adapter's name, in III below. References to individual characters are not repeated under the relevant plays.

II SHAKESPEARIAN CHARACTERS

III GENERAL INDEX

THE CRITICAL HERITAGE SERIES

GENERAL EDITOR: B. C. SOUTHAM